HD 1531 .D6 T87 2003
Turits, Richard Lee.
Foundations of despotism

D0207894

Foundations of Despotism

D A T E   D U E

COSUMNES RIVER COLLEGE LIBRARY

Overdue rates are **$.50** per day with maximum fine of
$20.00 per item. Fines **Will** be charged for days the
library is closed.

NOV 1 2 2008	
NOV 1 8 2008 ()✓	

COSUMNES RIVER COLLEGE
LEARNING RESOURCE CENTER
8401 Center Parkway
Sacramento, California 95823

LIBRARY

Foundations of Despotism

PEASANTS,

THE TRUJILLO REGIME,

AND MODERNITY

IN DOMINICAN HISTORY

Richard Lee Turits

STANFORD UNIVERSITY PRESS

STANFORD, CALIFORNIA

Stanford University Press
Stanford, California
© 2003 by the Board of Trustees of the
Leland Stanford Junior University
Printed in the United States of America

Library of Congress Cataloging-in-Publication Data

Turits, Richard Lee.
    Foundations of despotism : peasants, the Trujillo regime, and modernity in
Dominican history / Richard Lee Turits.
        p.   cm.
    Includes bibliographical references and index.
    ISBN 0-8047-4353-3 (alk. paper)   ISBN 0-8047-5105-6 (pbk.: alk. paper)
    1. Peasantry—Dominican Republic—Political activity.   2. Dominican
Republic—History—1930–1961.   3. Trujillo Molina, Rafael Leonidas,
1891–1961.   4. Agriculture and state—Dominican Republic—History—
20th century.   I. Title.

HD1531.D6 T87   2003
972.9305'3'092—dc21   2002010778
                                                                            CIP

This book is printed on acid-free, archival quality paper.

Original printing 2003
Last figure below indicates year of this printing:
12   11   10   09   08   07   06   05   04

Designed and typeset at Stanford University Press in 10/12.5 Minion

For Hannah

Acknowledgments

Over the years working on this book, many persons and institutions have generously assisted me. I would like to thank the following bodies for supporting my research and writing: the MacArthur Foundation; the Fulbright-Hays Program; the Joint Committee on Latin American and Caribbean Studies of the Social Science Research Council and the American Council of Learned Societies with funds from the Andrew Mellon Foundation; the National Endowment for the Humanities; the Harvard Academy for International and Area Studies; Princeton University's Program in Latin American Studies and University Committee on Research in the Humanities and Social Sciences; and the Latin American and Caribbean Studies Program of the University of Michigan. I am also grateful for an IIE Fulbright Grant for Collaborative Research. In addition, I thank Duke University Press for permission to reprint here, in modified form, portions of my essay "The Foundations of Despotism: Agrarian Reform, Rural Transformation, and Peasant-State Compromise in Trujillo's Dominican Republic, 1930–1944," which appeared in *Identity and Struggle at the Margins of the Nation-State: The Laboring Peoples of Central America and the Hispanic Caribbean*, edited by Aviva Chomsky and Aldo Lauria-Santiago (Durham, 1998).

I am indebted as well to the staffs of the institutions in the Dominican Republic and the United States that have preserved and made available the documents used in this study. Above all, I would like to thank Edward Jáquez Díaz of the Archivo General de la Nación (AGN) in Santo Domingo. His expertise in Dominican primary sources and extensive assistance over many years made a critical contribution to this project. I would also like to thank Manuel de Jesús Trinidad Domínguez and the entire staff of the AGN for their help. I am grateful as well to Eduardo Payamps, Manuel Morales, and María Cuesta at the Biblioteca Central of the Universidad Autónoma de Santo Domingo; Eddy Pereyra Ariza at the Biblioteca del Congreso Nacional; Luis Rosa at the Biblioteca Nacional; and the staff of the Tribunal Superior de Tierras, all in Santo Domingo. I also thank the staffs of the National Archives and Records Administration in Washington, D.C., and in College Park, Maryland, for much skillful assistance.

This study would not have been possible without the generous contributions of the 130 persons I interviewed between 1992 and 1994, as well as those interviewed in collaboration with Lauren Derby in 1987 and 1988. To all, I express my appreciation for what they have taught me and for their willingness and ability to recall often difficult and delicate histories. Not only does their testimony appear in specific ways throughout the text, but overall they shaped my work by providing context, perspective, and insights essential for writing this history.

I would like to express my gratitude also to Jeremy Adelman, Michiel Baud, Alejandro de la Fuente, Sheldon Garon, and Lowell Gudmundson for reading and commenting on drafts of this work. Their suggestions played an important role in shaping the ultimate contours of the book. I express my appreciation as well to the many who commented on drafts of chapters and related works, including Kate Bjork, Roberto Cassá, Sueann Caulfield, Miguel Centeno, Aviva Chomsky, Emiliano Corral, Lauren Derby, Jorge Domínguez, Michael Ducey, Ada Ferrer, Michel Gobat, Matthew Hill, Thomas Holt, William Chester Jordan, Aldo Lauria-Santiago, Juan Linz, Claudio Lomnitz, Yolanda Martínez-San Miguel, Mark Mazower, Lucía Melgar Palacios, Kenneth Mills, Michelle Molina, David Myhre, Susan Naquin, Philip Nord, James Scott, Rebecca Scott, Stephanie Smallwood, Christine Stansell, Stanley Stein, Mark Wasserman, Neici Zeller, and especially Bruce Calder, Fernando Coronil, Rosario Espinal, Julie Franks, Catherine LeGrand, and Julie Skurski. I also thank the participants in Harvard University's Tuesday Latin America Seminar, Princeton University's Latin American History Workshop and Shelby Cullom Davis Center for Historical Studies, the University of Michigan's Evening Seminar Series on Ethnicity and Migration in the Caribbean and New Series in Politics, History, and Culture, and the New York Latin American History Workshop for their comments. I am grateful as well to Edward Jean Baptiste, Ramonina Brea, Walter Cordero, Francisco Cueto, Jorge de la Cruz, Ramón Delgado Bogaert, Orlando Inoa, Antonio Lluberes, Frank Moya Pons, Altagracia Pou, Filomena Pujols, Pedro San Miguel, Rubén Silié, Cyrus Veeser, and Bernardo Vega for assistance, guidance, and insights. Thanks go as well to Raquel Castillo, Rosemery Fanfán, Jean Ghasmann Bissainthe, Angela Gutiérrez, Zenaida Lemos, Enemencia Matos, Domingo Mota, and Michael Werner for help with research, transcription, and editing. My most recent debts are to Norris Pope, Editorial Director of Stanford University Press, John Feneron, the book's editor at Stanford, and Martin Hanft, who copyedited the work, for their astute suggestions and generous assistance in the process of turning the manuscript into a book. And finally, I express my profound debt to several historians of rural Santo Domingo from whose published work I have benefited immensely, above all Michiel Baud, Raymundo González, and Pedro San Miguel.

Certain intellectual contributions transcend the rubric of "acknowledgments," though written works offer no other place to recognize them. I would like to thank several scholars for playing important roles in the production of this book, starting with the members of the doctoral committee at the University of Chicago who oversaw this project in its first incarnation as a dissertation. George Steinmetz helped me move beyond the limits of the historiography on the Trujillo regime and the conventional models used to interpret it. He has since helped push the project in innovative and important directions. Friedrich Katz forcefully encouraged me to pursue my at-first tentative hypothesis that even a regime as horrific as Trujillo's must have had a strong social base to have survived for as long as it did. His advice was critical in my continuing to pursue this topic despite the contrary thrust of the existing literature and my own reactions to state terror under the Trujillo dictatorship. And John Coatsworth played the central role in guiding the dissertation and making suggestions on the book manuscript. He has continually intervened with sharp insight, lapidary criticism, and wise historical and comparative perspective.

Several other scholars played equally vital roles in the production of this book. Raymundo González has spent myriad hours during the last fifteen years conversing with me about Dominican history, responding to my queries, and inspiring me with his interpretations of and commitment to exploring the rural Dominican past. Our discussions energized my work and are reflected throughout the book. Ciprián Soler also influenced the contours of this work through his invaluable collaboration in conducting interviews and through our discussions of this fieldwork and Dominican history over many years. I also conducted fieldwork with Lauren Derby in 1987–88 as part of a collaborative project on Dominican-Haitian relations, anti-Haitianism, and histories and representations of the 1937 Haitian massacre. Many ideas in Chapter 5 were thus first developed in collaboration with her. Finally, Hannah Rosen made a profound contribution to the writing of this book. She devoted endless hours to reading, discussing, and commenting on many drafts, offering suggestions that in so many vital ways strengthened the final product. Our intellectual partnership shaped the evolution of this book in critical fashion.

I would like to express my appreciation to several persons not only for their scholarly collaboration but also for the gifts they have given me on a personal level. I am grateful to John Coatsworth for his unflagging support and friendship, for his kindness as well as his intelligence. And my *compadre* Ciprián Soler and close friend Raymundo González have greatly enriched my life throughout the process of writing this book and beyond. I am also very grateful to my mother, Nancy Morse, and to Andrew Freund, a lifelong friend, both of whom have been extremely supportive during the completion of this project. Finally, while writing this book, as in every other endeavor, Hannah Rosen has filled my life with fascination and bliss.

Contents

Foundations of Despotism

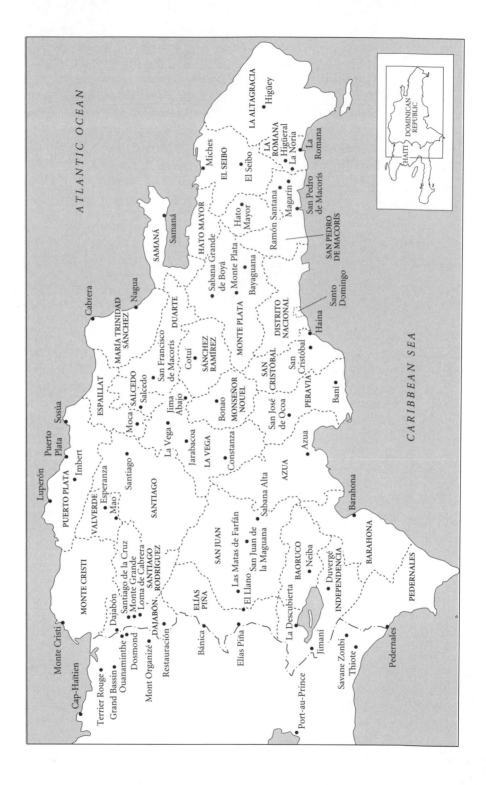

Introduction

The Paradoxes of Despotism

"My best friends are the men of work." With these words, the dictatorial president of the Dominican Republic, Rafael Leonidas Trujillo Molina, began a series of speeches in November of 1932 during an extensive tour of the Dominican countryside. Trujillo, who had seized power two years earlier, spoke before thousands of rural residents unaccustomed to being addressed by presidential leaders. He called upon these rural denizens to be active participants in the national state through devotion to agriculture as well as loyalty to his regime. In doing so, he highlighted the phrase—"my best friends are the men of work"—that peasants would associate with Trujillo even decades after the dictator's demise: "My best friends are the men of work because nations rise up from poverty through labor. . . . My visiting you signifies a guarantee for your labor and new encouragement, through both my words and my assistance, for expanding agricultural work. Now and forever, those who cultivate the land will be the best friends of my government. . . . In [my government] all men who live by the sweat of their brow will have a place."[1] In light of Trujillo's record as one of the most ruthless and long-reigning dictators in the history of the Americas, his populist rhetoric comes across today as empty propaganda. Yet for Dominican peasants in 1932, it was indeed noteworthy to hear the president of the country celebrate them at mass rallies and to call those who labored in the field his "best friends."[2] For centuries most national state leaders and members of the urban elite had scorned the peasantry, which had lived largely removed from the market and out of reach of the national state, as being constitutionally resistant to all things imagined to represent progress. Yet in these and future speeches, Trujillo envisaged a critical place for the peasantry, then the overwhelming majority of the population, in the nation's identity and modernity.[3] This vision and the policies it generated would help integrate peasants into commercial markets, the national state, and a common national community to a far greater degree than ever before in the Dominican Republic. And it would establish the foundations for Trujillo's hegemony over the nation.

Trujillo came to power in 1930 in the wake of a small civil rebellion that overthrew a democratically elected president, Horacio Vásquez. This so-called Civic Movement found widespread support, particularly among a group of liberal nationalist leaders and intellectuals who decried the growing corruption and disorder of Vásquez's government and blamed it for perpetuating the nation's long history of political instability, economic stagnation, and compromised national sovereignty. For the Civic Movement to succeed, however, it required the support of the Dominican military. The movement's leader, the charismatic young lawyer and former secretary of foreign affairs, Rafael Estrella Ureña, therefore entered into a secret alliance with Trujillo, then commander of the National Army. The leaders of the movement had not expected that Trujillo would, in turn, seize control from Estrella once Vásquez was overthrown. Yet, notwithstanding his lack of an independent political base and the vigorous opposition of many elite Dominicans, as well as the U.S. legation in Santo Domingo, Trujillo indeed forced Estrella (at first the acting president after the coup) into the vice presidential slot and stole the presidency through intimidation and violence in an election held later that same year.[4] Amid this rapid and confusing turn of events, many members of the Civic Movement continued to support the Trujillo-Estrella government. Indeed, numerous political figures and intellectuals were reportedly "easy prey" for tempting state positions and Trujillo's coercive efforts to bring them into his government.[5] Many others, however, openly opposed the dictator's seizure of power. Ultimately, Trujillo consolidated power only by ordering the assassination of hundreds of his opponents during his first year in office.[6]

Despite the initially shaky foundations of his rule and his reliance essentially on violence to install his regime, Trujillo would subsequently govern this second largest Caribbean nation and face little open resistance for the following three decades. This extraordinary political control and longevity finds explanation partly in the support Trujillo cultivated among the peasantry. The remarkable degree of peasant backing for this tyrannical regime was perceived by many contemporaneous observers, including Juan Bosch, a left-wing leader of the Dominican exile community during most of Trujillo's rule, later president of the Dominican Republic (1962–63), and an important Dominican intellectual. In 1991, Bosch recalled warning other revolutionary exiles embarking on an invasion of the Dominican Republic in the late 1950s that "they were mistaken if they believed that they were going to confront Trujillo's army and nobody else, because in addition to the soldiers, they were going to have to combat the peasants. . . . 'Don't think,' I told them, 'that Dominican peasants are going to support you. In thirty years, Trujillo has done many things. . . .' And that's what happened. The peasants confronted the patriots that went to combat the *trujillato*, and in many cases it was they, those peasants, who turned in the guerrillas."[7] The legacy of peasant loyalty to

Trujillo, an adherence that impelled peasants to defend the regime against revolutionary exiles, would endure even for decades after Trujillo's assassination. It remained salient in testimony I collected between 1992 and 1994 in the Dominican Republic.[8] When I expressed surprise at Jorge Castillo's strong support for Trujillo, this elderly peasant cautioned against interpreting the Trujillo regime without incorporating peasants' perspectives:

You never knew Trujillo. . . . For example, you say Trujillo was a dictator, a wretch, you know, a son of a bitch. But you are saying that because you are looking at a map that a man created who wanted nothing to do with [Trujillo], not because you actually saw Trujillo and what he did. . . . You are only children compared to me. . . . You only know a history made by the powerful who no longer wanted anything to do with Trujillo, and they tell you, "No, Trujillo was a wretch. . . ." No *señor*, to speak truly, we the downtrodden were not going to say that Trujillo was [a wretch]. The bad ones were those who came after him.[9]

What histories can explain Castillo's impassioned defense of Trujillo? How did a ruthless tyrant achieve this level of popular support for his rule? This book treats the history of the Dominican Republic, as it evolved from the first European colony in the New World in the 1490s into a modern nation under Trujillo's rule, in order to investigate the social foundations of Trujillo's enduring regime and, more broadly, how power sustains itself in such nondemocratic systems. In addition to illuminating the processes by which Trujillo secured support among the peasantry, this book explores the ambivalent nature of that support. And it argues that this ambivalence reflected not only the repressive dimensions of the regime but also contradictory sentiments regarding the Trujillo state's intervention into long-standing contests over modernity in the Dominican Republic.

This approach, along with the perspectives offered by peasants like Castillo who lived through the *trujillato*, is at odds with most of the existing literature on the regime. This literature focuses on coercion and terror as the overwhelming explanation for Trujillo's long rule. Statements such as Castillo's have typically been dismissed in the historiography as simply the products of Trujillo's self-aggrandizing and nationalist propaganda, coupled with a putative authoritarian political culture and the supposed "ignorance" or "false consciousness" of the popular rural classes.[10] Similarly, comparative social-scientific work that treats the Trujillo regime generally portrays the dictatorship as being almost all-powerful, penetrating in virtually totalitarian fashion every corner of society, while, paradoxically, having no social base, popular policies, bureaucratic institutions, or public perception of order and relative prosperity that would help explain Trujillo's exceptional political control and longevity.[11] Indeed, Trujillo's dictatorship was the original inspiration for so-

cial scientist Juan Linz's model of a "sultanistic" regime, an exceptional political system supposedly able to thrive without any form of consent, legitimation, authority, desirable policies, or credible ideology. Linz has characterized sultanistic systems as lacking the institutional development, constraints, and order of most nondemocratic regimes. They are supposedly
dominated by a single leader who exercises virtually unlimited discretion,
displays fantastic cruelty and hedonism, acquires vast riches through corruption, and sustains power only by means of material rewards and harsh punishments meted out to a circle of cronies—who are themselves terrorized by
the dictator—and typically through support from foreign interests and powers.[12]

At the same time, scholars (Linz prominent among them) have demonstrated how other enduring twentieth-century dictatorships, including the
most violent, garnered substantial social acceptance and, in some cases, even
popular enthusiasm by promoting or opposing socioeconomic change, mediating class and social conflict, or imposing forms of order.[13] And numerous
political philosophers from Niccolò Machiavelli to Antonio Gramsci have affirmed the need for forms of consent in all political systems, even among
subject peoples, to foster enduring and effective government.[14] Yet many social scientists concerned with nondemocratic rule nonetheless contend that
an exceptional regime type, given various labels in addition to sultanism,
such as mafiacracy, kleptocracy, or predatory state, wherein the political concerns and opinions of the population have been uniquely inconsequential,
has abounded throughout the less-developed nations of the twentieth century. Included in the wide range of rulers imagined to embody this ideal type
are the Somozas in Nicaragua, Ferdinand Marcos in the Philippines, Fulgencio Batista in Cuba, the Pahlavi Shahs in Iran, Mobutu Sese Seko in Zaire, and
the Duvaliers in Haiti—rulers all characterized by an unexplained longevity
as well as an ostensible lawlessness. The Trujillo dictatorship has generally
been considered one of the most extreme versions of this regime type.[15]

Such depictions, however, suspiciously reproduce a long European tradition of projecting the most extreme forms of political despotism and otherness onto non-Western societies and imagining beyond the edges of the
European universe oddly passive or irrational peoples who mysteriously accept intolerable regimes. The term "despotism" was first deployed in the
eighteenth century for what literary critic Alain Grosrichard calls "European
fantasies" of Asiatic regimes, above all the sultans who ruled the Ottoman
Empire, as being utterly lawless, unpredictable, and unrestrained personalistic systems ruling solely through fear. Many other European thinkers have
discounted such portrayals of despotism as dystopian political caricatures,

and have dismissed the very possibility of a lawless polity ruled by one person to whose exploitation and abuse virtually all others inexplicably submit. Already in the eighteenth century, Voltaire contended, for instance: "It is a great untruth that a government of this kind exists and it seems to me a great untruth that a government of this kind can exist."[16] Indeed, despotism, in the sense of absolute personalistic power or an autonomous state, did not exist even under Trujillo in the Dominican Republic. Given that his regime inspired Linz's sultanistic model, we have further reason to doubt all such representations of enduring absolute rule.

It is nonetheless true that many of Trujillo's baneful and at times absurd extremes appear to correspond even to the most exoticist images of despotism. Certainly Trujillo corruptly used state power and intimidation to establish monopolies for his own, his relatives', and his associates' businesses. These allowed his family to amass a spectacular fortune. By the close of the regime, the Trujillos' holdings were estimated at $500 million, a sum close to the Dominican national income.[17] At that time, Trujillo is said to have effectively controlled three-quarters of the nation's industrial production and employed almost 60 percent of the country's wage laborers (though a still relatively small class), either as part of the large public sector or of Trujillo's personal enterprises.[18] Although not of the same proportions as their industrial control, the Trujillo family and their associates also accumulated massive properties, especially during the 1950s. After the regime fell, their confiscated estates constituted approximately 9 percent of the nation's occupied land.[19]

In some realms, moreover, Trujillo was indeed capable of exercising seemingly unconstrained power and discretion. This included glorifying himself and his family in extreme and even surreal fashion. For instance, Trujillo's son Ramfis was publicly afforded military honors as a full colonel from the young age of four and as a brigadier general as soon as he turned nine. Evincing both Trujillo's unbridled vanity and the unprecedented power he had already consolidated, in 1936 he rechristened the Americas' oldest colonial city, named Santo Domingo de Guzmán in 1497, after himself, Ciudad Trujillo (Trujillo City). Streets, bridges, parks, buildings, provinces, monuments, and the country's—and the Caribbean's—highest mountain peak were also named or renamed after Trujillo and his family. A new calendar would supplement the standard one, counting years in what was officially deemed "the Era of Trujillo," beginning with Trujillo's presidency in 1930. Approximately eighteen hundred sculptures of the dictator dotted the nation's public spaces, some of enormous proportions.[20] The press heaped seemingly limitless praise on Trujillo that bordered on apotheosis, more effusive even than the Soviet press's glorification of its leaders, according to one

U.S. State Department official.[21] And signs were erected throughout the country glorifying the dictator, one of the most droll being "We Owe It All to Trujillo," posted on the front door of a mental hospital near the capital.[22] Another infamous sign, "God and Trujillo," greeted ships entering the port of Ciudad Trujillo, as well as Dominicans in other locations.[23]

Trujillo's tyranny was marked by extraordinary violence and abuse. For instance, Trujillo was notorious until his death for his incessant sexual exploitation of women, demanding lovers without regard to their wishes, whether from families of modest means in small towns or from those of important Dominican officials. Women who acquiesced to Trujillo's wishes, along with their relatives, were variously rewarded with houses, jobs, money, government positions, even husbands.[24] The alternative to acquiescence to Trujillo was perilous in this regard, as in all others. Trujillo tolerated no opposition. At his orders and through indirect official pressure, his opponents and, in many cases, their relatives and associates were dismissed from jobs in both the public and private sector, expelled from private high schools and the University of Santo Domingo, and arrested on false charges. And although the regime generally deployed means of domination other than assassination, hundreds were killed by agents of the Trujillo regime simply for expressing criticism of the dictatorship, for purported links to opposition efforts, or for being closely connected by friendship or family to a putative enemy of the state (and not sufficiently disavowing those relations).[25] This apparatus of terror extended outside Dominican borders, with various assassinations carried out in the United States, Cuba, Puerto Rico, and Mexico. Among Trujillo's most notorious crimes was the abduction from a New York City subway station and subsequent murder in the Dominican Republic of Spanish exile, former Santo Domingo resident, and Columbia University graduate student and instructor Jesús de Galíndez, who had just completed a dissertation on Trujillo that was far from laudatory.[26] Galíndez was assassinated at the beginning of the end of the regime, when, in particular, Trujillo flailed out against all perceived opponents, arresting and torturing hundreds of mostly middle-class Dominicans in the major towns and cities and executing more than one hundred expeditionaries captured in an invasion led by anti-Trujillo exiles in 1959.[27] But by far Trujillo's most extensive act of state terror occurred earlier in the regime. In 1937 the Dominican military massacred some fifteen thousand ethnic Haitians whose families had been living peacefully for generations in the northern frontier region near the border that the Dominican Republic shares with Haiti. The following year Trujillo ordered the deportation to Haiti of thousands of ethnic Haitians from the southern frontier zones, many of whom were killed in this military action.

Terror also existed in varying degrees within the state itself. Many of Trujillo's highest-ranking officials and advisers were subject to harsh punishments and personal abuse by the dictator for alleged errors. They were browbeaten, publicly humiliated, denounced, and in a few cases killed when they fell into disfavor.[28] And Trujillo continually shuffled cabinet members and other important officials in and out of government posts to prevent their developing an independent power base. He exerted still tighter control over the Dominican legislature. Upon assumption of office, members of the National Congress were obliged to sign their own resignations, a document that on Trujillo's order could be handed to them at any moment, signifying the immediate end of their term. In certain cases, these resignations were reportedly delivered to legislators in the middle of their speeches before the assembly. In the 1942 to 1947 period, for instance, there were 32 resignations in a Senate with 19 members, and 139 resignations in a House composed of 42 deputies.[29] Yet the state maintained strict constitutional and democratic form even while the reality was highly dictatorial. The wide gap between form and substance was perhaps most obvious to the population with regard to Trujillo's placement of figurehead presidents in office between 1938 and 1942 and between 1952 and 1961, while Trujillo's actual power remained undiminished, and perhaps was even amplified, by demonstrating his capacity to rule without corresponding legal authority. Jacinto Peynado, the first puppet president, placed a large neon sign on the roof of his house celebrating "God and Trujillo" in order to clearly acknowledge his subordination.[30]

Histories of terror and extreme personalistic rule are salient dimensions of the Trujillo years. Nonetheless, they cannot by themselves elucidate the Trujillo state's capacity to sustain power and authority for decades, nor fully illuminate the experiences of most of society during the regime. State violence and repression can mobilize as well as immobilize opposition and are in and of themselves not an adequate explanation for a regime's capacity to endure. Jorge Castillo's admonition against relying solely on prevailing "maps"—by definition selective and reductive representations—suggests the need for deeper historical research into how the regime actually affected everyday life and was perceived by various sectors of society. The currently canonical view of the Trujillo regime as a paradigm of sultanism or personalistic despotism is, in fact, based on a problematic methodology that is transfixed by the dictator himself, his inner circle, and the most widely known operations of the regime at the expense of comprehending the vast plexus of the Trujillo state and the range of experiences of the population as a whole. Indeed, the most cited treatment of the regime is still Robert Crassweller's 1966 biography of Trujillo, which concentrates almost exclusively on the dictator and his sub-

ordinates within a framework of high politics, and which gives special attention to the personalistic, the sinister, and the seemingly bizarre.[31] But focusing
solely on the corruption, brutality, and eccentricity of dictators, even long
after their evils are in any serious dispute, leaves largely unexplored the realities of everyday life and the sinews of political power, including a regime's
often difficult-to-face appeal for certain groups as well as its hidden vulnerabilities. These can be investigated only through archival sources showing the
local and daily operations of the state, research into public policies and their
implementation, and, if possible, testimony from pertinent social groups.[32]
Foundations of Despotism focuses on this more quotidian level, relying on
thousands of daily intrastate documents, letters written to the state by peasants, and interviews with elderly peasants from across the country. This approach reveals far more complex and paradoxical foundations to Trujillo's
rule than traditional perspectives on despotism would suggest. First, it throws
into relief the critical historical conjuncture that the Trujillo years represented within the larger frame of Dominican history. It elucidates both material and symbolic exchanges between the state and the peasantry at this critical juncture that gave rise to the latter's at least ambivalent consent to the regime. And it affirms that however violent, personalistic, and seemingly
autonomous from societal constraints, all enduring systems of rule must—
and do—foster forms of social acceptance, political constituencies, and effective state institutions in order to extend, deepen, and sustain their control
over society.

In the case of Trujillo, there is ample evidence that his regime generated
surprisingly widespread support in the countryside by implementing popular
agrarian policies and by variously responding to and transforming peasants'
needs, cultures, and identities so as to promote their acceptance of and identification with the state. As a result, the Trujillo dictatorship carved out broad
spheres of hegemony among a large population of landholding peasants.[33]
Historians have tended to discount the degree of popular support for Trujillo's policies in light of the inhumane and repressive character of his rule.
Yet Trujillo's efforts to achieve a type of rural populism and foster paternalistic policies were far more substantial than previously imagined.[34] They were
backed by concrete government actions and material benefits, at least for
those ready to offer both productivity and outward loyalty in return. Specifically, the regime distributed and maintained peasant access to large amounts
of the nation's territory, while calling upon peasants to become active citizens
through a variety of civic obligations and rituals linking them to the national
state.[35] The regime was able, moreover, to effectively frame its rural policies in
a discourse that not only celebrated the peasantry's role in the nation as never

before but also echoed peasants' own pre-existing norms, above all a moral economy deeply rooted in rights to the land.[36]

In addition to revealing how the regime secured peasant support, the history of Trujillo's rural policies also illuminates processes of state formation, how the state expanded its political and economic control over the nation and increasingly integrated city and countryside following three centuries of relatively deep separation. During his thirty-one-year reign, Trujillo oversaw virtually every key aspect of modern state formation. For the first time the Dominican state effectively established direct taxes, a national currency, and full customs operations, the last returning to Dominican control in 1940 after more than three decades of U.S. receivership. The Trujillo regime also extinguished the extant control of local *caudillos*, strongmen known in the Dominican Republic as *generales,* who were able to mobilize small informal armies against the government.[37] It established and policed a clear and continuous international border with Haiti and diffused an official monoethnic nationalism. And it rapidly expanded the nation's infrastructure, public health care system and schools, and government ministries and state bodies.[38]

In this process of state formation, the greatest sea change was evident in the state's expanding reach into the Dominican countryside. The dictatorship penetrated and permeated rural life through new state policies and institutions. Trujillo's agrarian reforms served to modernize and incorporate into the national state a peasantry that had been able to elude state control, taxation, and monitoring for hundreds of years—ever since runaway and manumitted slaves, along with marginal colonists, first gave rise to its relatively autonomous and autarkic existence in the 1600s. State formation was predicated on the sedentarization and concentration of a still generally dispersed and footloose Dominican peasantry, much of it accustomed to slash-and-burn farming and collective use of forests, wildlife, and animals on the open range (open-access, unenclosed lands). By distributing fixed plots of land and by providing aid, irrigation, and infrastructure upon which sedentary agriculturalists came to depend, the state brought the peasantry within its range of vision and effective control.[39]

Peasants' support for the regime's agrarian policies and acceptance of an expanding and interventionist national state were, in part, a reaction to a wave of economic and political modernization that had already begun to shake and transfigure parts of the Dominican countryside in the early 1900s. These developments followed three centuries of what could be called aborted modernity and peasant vitality in the Dominican Republic. In the late 1500s, a massive but inchoate slave plantation society producing large quantities of sugar for European markets collapsed as quickly as it had grown. Some three hundred years of commercial stagnation followed. This opened up the space for the emergence of a large, independent peasantry—mostly former slaves and their descendants—who lived for generations primarily from slash-and-burn farming and collective exploitation of forests and wildlife across the nation's vast, untamed lands. In the early twentieth century, however, peasants began to face ominous changes in property relations and land tenure arrangements that threatened to eliminate their free access to land. From 1900 to 1930, prior to Trujillo's seizure of power, growing enclaves of commercial farming and rising land values in several areas had led to increasing efforts to enclose, survey, and claim lands throughout the countryside. Moreover, new forms of private property were established through laws promulgated by the U.S. military government during the U.S. occupation between 1916 and 1924. By 1930 thousands of peasants had been displaced by U.S. sugar companies that had secured title to vast tracts of land in the Eastern region of the country, between Santo Domingo and the town of La Romana. And throughout the country, the establishment of property claims, fences, and other enclosures expanded at a fever pitch, thus impeding peasants' access to lands that they had formerly exploited without titles.

Confronting this critical juncture, the Trujillo regime engaged in a massive campaign of land distribution and property reform in an effort both to garner political loyalty among the peasantry and to increase agricultural production in order to help feed the towns and develop export crops. The state sought to integrate the peasantry into its modernization project by offering land and eventually property rights to peasants, almost none of whom had previously had title to the land they used. The distribution campaign commenced in 1934 and was most active during the following decade. Although this campaign continued throughout the regime, in the late 1940s the state began granting more plots in what were called "colonies" (state-organized agricultural settlements, many in remote areas) than directly to peasants in the areas in which they already lived. By 1958 these agrarian reforms, both colonization and the land distribution campaign, reportedly comprised almost 500,000 hectares, or 22 percent of the nation's farm land. The number of recipients, 140,717, was equivalent to 31 percent of landholders.[40] And many other peasants obtained legal property simply on the basis of squatters' rights ("prescription"), as the state surveyed land occupations and awarded land titles across the country.

But the state secured and provided land for peasants only on the condition that they farm as productively as the government demanded. Laws that classified any peasant cultivating less than ten *tareas* (0.63 hectare) of land as "vagrant" were vigorously enforced throughout the country. The state engaged in a constant campaign to ensure that plots were carefully maintained, to supply basic tools and agricultural inputs, to build infrastructure and improve market access, and to eliminate peasants' pastoral practices.

This process of turning the popular rural classes into sedentary and surplus-producing farmers rather than peasants exploiting open access woodlands, pasture, and wildlife required many to forsake aspects of their way of life that in most areas of the country they had been unwilling in the past to renounce. For generations most peasants had maintained their high level of autonomy, geographic mobility, and exploitation of the open range, despite legislation and public policies variously seeking to further their sedentarization, agrarianization, or proletarianization. But in the wake of the widening land enclosures and evictions beginning in the early 1900s, peasants were obliged to exploit smaller amounts of land more efficiently and indeed were threatened with complete landlessness unless they forged an effective alliance with the state. Government-protected land access combined with assistance for agriculture and new infrastructure and markets made sedentary, intensive farming attractive and feasible for most peasants for the first time in Dominican history.

Thus, in the 1930s and 1940s, the state acted primarily as a source and protector of land access for the rural poor. Yet peasant-state relations changed in the 1950s. Early in the decade the regime shifted course and began emphasizing a political economy oriented around large-scale export agriculture, in which the regime appropriated the central role that foreign capital had previously played in this sector. Specifically, the Dominican state and Trujillo personally entered the sugar industry, not only taking over most foreign sugar interests but also doubling sugar production by developing new plantations—primarily in the province of Monte Plata—and, in the process, becoming an agent of peasant dispossession. The consequences of this transformation were devastating for peasants in the newly developed sugar areas, thousands of whom were displaced. They were also damaging to the regime. Trujillo stretched the state's finances beyond its limits in pursuit of his sugar empire, actions contrasting sharply with the regime's previously conservative fiscal policies. As the economy floundered in the late 1950s, middle- and upper-class opposition grew, as did misery and discontent among the popular classes in the new sugar areas. At the same time, Trujillo responded with increasingly widespread and arbitrary repression that would prove counterproductive for the regime. Trujillo seemed to many, including many peasants, to be descending into madness, especially when he viciously attacked a once staunch and important ally, the Catholic Church. Thus in the 1950s, the regime undermined its own forms of legitimation, ruled with perceived irrationality, and eventually approached the fantastic degree of despotism that social scientists have attributed to the dictatorship as a whole. But rather than being the foundations of Trujillo's power, this style of rule led to his downfall. By 1960, Trujillo had lost much of the social acceptance he had once enjoyed, including among a portion of the peasantry, and the regime quickly spun out of control.

To illuminate these transformations in peasant-state relations, *Foundations of Despotism* constructs two dialectically linked narratives that offer new portraits of the rural Dominican past. The first narrative commences in the late sixteenth century with the demise of early sugar plantations. It recounts how runaway and manumitted slaves and their descendants turned themselves into independent peasants and over several generations consolidated a highly autonomous mode of existence.[41] To these former slaves and their progeny, as well as to marginal colonists with whom they mixed, exploitation of the island's immense, untamed *monte* (woodlands)—ideal for hunting, shifting *conucos* (small agricultural plots), and raising free-ranging animals— came to symbolize freedom and security. At the end of the nineteenth century, however, new commercial interests gave force to longstanding state efforts to restrict peasants' land access and eliminate their largely autarkic way of life. At that time peasants' political and economic freedoms gradually but inexorably began to wane. The second narrative takes place in the narrower time frame of the Trujillo regime. This history tells of a modernizing but economically reformist dictator who sought to expand the state and promote economic development, while simultaneously promising the nation's peasantry *protección*, or support, against the threats of land and agricultural commercialization. In essence, the Trujillo state promised an alternative, controlled modernization.[42] And in so doing, the dictator secured the foundations for widespread acceptance and rural stability, at least until he shifted course in the 1950s and began undermining the policies, alliances, and economic success that had previously served to legitimate his rule.

These two histories converge, first, because the Trujillo state provided land and agricultural support only at the cost of peasants' high level of political and economic autonomy, which for centuries had been seen by state and intellectual leaders as one of the primary impediments to all that was imagined to represent civilization and progress. Peasants were now compelled to farm more intensively and to cease clearing new plots and raising animals on the open range; to demonstrate loyalty to the regime in mass political demonstrations and to attend local meetings called by state officials where they were instructed on vagrancy and other laws; and to pay a poll tax in the form of an annual renewal fee for the *cédula personal de identidad*, or national identity card, and to serve as corvée laborers, known as *prestatarios*, building and maintaining area roads and irrigation in lieu of cash payments for a road tax. Also, many peasants would have to continue to depend on the state for their land, given that full property rights were adjudicated slowly and, in agricultural colonies, were often never granted at all. Furthermore, sedentary agricultural practices made peasants increasingly reliant on roads, irrigation, fertilizer, credit, and other inputs, as well as on public order, to sustain and expand their production, and thus they increasingly depended on state assistance for their livelihood. Under these conditions, the contours of peasant politics shifted. Rather than simply eluding and resisting the state, peasants now appealed to state officials for support. Trujillo's rural populist policies and discourse thus found a more amenable social base.[43] From a state perspective, the peasantry was, at last, integrated and disciplined during the Trujillo dictatorship. It was rendered into an active citizenry in the sense of participating in the overall political and economic projects of the national state, its civic obligations, and rituals of rule.

On the other hand, these histories also converge because the Trujillo regime's populist discourse affirmed an important aspect of peasants' culture and independence—access to one's own conuco, and therein subsistence security and a measure of socioeconomic autonomy. It was by pursuing an alternative modernity sustaining this land access and independent production, and by framing state policies within—and having state policies substantiate—a political discourse appealing to and including the popular rural classes, that the regime secured widespread peasant acceptance. This book will thus illuminate not only the paradoxes of popular consent to despotic rule, but also how, in the Dominican case, peasants' ambivalent consent reflected a contradictory relationship to modernity. Peasants recalled the policies of development and state intervention under the Trujillo regime as eviscerating certain traditional freedoms, but also as offering desirable benefits—such as land and infrastructure, as well as health care and overall state responsiveness. It was in the context of both the agonies and opportunities for the peasantry of an expanding national state that Trujillo successfully negotiated the material and cultural conditions for hegemony in the Dominican Republic.

This book thus treats Trujillo's personalistic despotism, but it also explores its paradoxical social base and the key role of government figures other than the despot. It treats the intervention of the state into rural society to tax, regulate, and control the population as never before, but it also reveals how peasants sought and benefited from certain aspects of state intervention. And this book treats the processes by which the popular rural classes were disciplined, rendered into modern subjects—"orderly," "productive," part of a larger na-

tional community, and participants in the political and economic projects of
the central state—but argues that this transformation was feasible and fruitful
only because the Trujillo regime approached peasants to some extent on their
own terms, casting state policies within their vision and moral economy as
well as subjecting the peasantry to urban norms and state exigencies.[44]

The historical transformations explored in this book can be framed in
terms of the Trujillo regime bridging the centuries-long divide in the Dominican Republic between city and countryside, and between the central state and
the rural majority. Chapter 1 treats the emergence of this divide after the collapse in early colonial Santo Domingo of the New World's first plantation society. Colonial neglect and commercial stagnation for the next three hundred
years, phenomena which are typically described as producing only widespread
misery, in fact opened up the space for a transition from plantation slavery to
a peasant economy constituted mostly by free people of color, who were able
to forge an essentially autonomous existence and live largely outside the reach
of the colonial state. To a large extent, two separate worlds emerged with a
weak state and urban society unable to impose their norms, in particular racial
hierarchy and slavery, on most of the countryside. Chapter 1 also explores how
rural dwellers' independence from the central state was facilitated by the peculiar land tenure and property arrangements known as *terrenos comuneros*
that predominated in Santo Domingo. Over time, this system of jointly owned
lands belonging to particular co-owners evolved in peasants' eyes into a type
of "nobody's lands," wherein all of the montes could be freely exploited for
hunting, raising animals, and (shifting) agriculture. This loose form of joint
property in land and, above all, its customary use as open-access areas by the
entire population—use that owners generally tolerated or were obliged to accept—allowed former slaves, their descendants, and other peasants to exploit
the country's then seemingly endless woodlands, wildlife, and natural pasture
largely removed from the colonial state and its metropolitan norms. When
slavery was formally abolished in 1822 at the onset of the Haitian occupation of
the Dominican Republic (1822–44), emancipation occurred under conditions
of widespread land availability, and this completed the colonial transition
from slaves to independent peasants.

Peasants' independent mode of existence persisted throughout the nineteenth century following independence from Haiti in 1844, despite the state's
continued efforts to impose its rural projects, essentially commercial farming,
through property and vagrancy laws. The popular rural classes found ample
means to resist the central state, given widespread land availability, entrenched customary property rights, and their participation as soldiers in a
steady stream of independence wars and caudillo rebellions against govern-

ments without effective standing militaries. Yet, as we will see in Chapter 2, new economic developments began to threaten peasant autonomy at the close of the nineteenth century. Cuban, Dominican, and, above all, U.S. corporations developed large sugar plantations in sparsely settled Eastern areas of the country, provoking unprecedented accumulation and commercialization of land in that region. At the same time, small-scale commercial farming began to expand in the fertile north-central Cibao region, which also led to new land pressures and the growth of private property. Although limited at first predominantly to those two areas, this process would soon begin spreading to other regions in the following decades.

Dominican leaders had long advocated the expansion of commercial agriculture. But in the period from 1900 to 1930, a number of them grew disillusioned with developments in those areas of the country being engulfed by foreign sugar plantations. New forms of rural unemployment and food shortages in the cities threatened the country's social and economic stability, as mostly U.S.-owned corporations evicted thousands of peasants, displaced Dominican landowners, and imported tens of thousands of immigrant laborers from other parts of the West Indies to expand the sugar industry. Some of the country's leading thinkers and political figures began to question whether giant plantations and mills, dominated by both foreign owners and workers, constituted genuine progress and could move the country toward the utopia of modernity that they envisioned. These misgivings occurred, moreover, in the context of growing overall nationalist ferment and anxiety. In the early twentieth century, some even expressed doubts that the Dominican Republic was a nation at all, given its lack of stable government, its deep regionalism and constant civil wars, its subordination to foreign powers and capital, and the autarkic and rebellious character of the popular rural classes.[45] Nationalist concerns and frustration were further provoked when the United States gained control of Dominican customs in 1904 as part of an arrangement to pay down the country's massive foreign debt (as ratified in a 1907 accord between the two nations) and, above all, when the United States occupied the Dominican Republic between 1916 and 1924. Under the full weight of both U.S. imperialism and U.S. sugar companies' rapid monopolization of land, a number of leading Dominicans began to oppose the expansion of foreign agribusiness and to call instead for economic development via small farmers, as already characterized a substantial part of the Cibao. In the press and political circles, there emerged a new nationalist and populist project for economic growth and political autonomy, wherein the nation's still largely pastoral peasants would be transformed into sedentary, surplus-producing farmers, rather than proletarians, unemployed workers, and urban migrants.[46]

At this time, despite the expansion of large-scale sugar production in the East and small-scale coffee, tobacco, and cacao farming in the Cibao, the Dominican economy overall remained rudimentary by almost any standard. The majority of the population were peasants engaged primarily in subsistence exploitation.[47] Besides foreign interests, there was no wealthy agricultural elite, in contrast to the majority of Latin America at that time. And manufacturing scarcely existed outside the U.S.-dominated sugar industry. In 1920 the country's only university, though founded in the early sixteenth century, claimed a mere 169 students.[48] There were only approximately one hundred doctors in the country, roughly one for every eighty-five hundred persons, and most of them were concentrated in the urban centers.[49] The capital, Santo Domingo, had a population of just thirty thousand, one-fifth the size of Havana a century earlier.[50] Most of the government's main form of revenue, customs taxes, was appropriated by U.S. officials.[51] And regional caudillos and bandits, although suppressed and weakened during the U.S. occupation, continued to threaten public order and the state into the early Trujillo years.[52]

Hence it is not surprising that at the time Trujillo came to power the political imagination of the country's leaders and small lettered class was fixed on becoming what they considered a modern nation, one characterized by economic growth, public order, and national autonomy. And for those who envisioned a small-farmer mode of modernity far from what had taken place in the Eastern sugar areas, incorporating the peasantry and realizing its economic potential were critical. They believed, as historian Eugen Weber said of late-nineteenth-century France, that "the peasant had to be integrated into the national society, economy, and culture: the culture of the city."[53] Yet the integration of the popular rural classes remained a formidable challenge.

After Trujillo seized the presidency, several proponents of a small-farmer project of modernity joined his cabinets and would attempt to harness the unprecedented power of his regime to realize their reformist vision. We will see in Chapter 3 how those cabinet members gave concrete form to Trujillo's early populist rhetoric by designing and implementing policies of land distribution, agricultural assistance, and property reform both to promote rural development and to integrate rather than decimate the peasantry in the early processes of modernization. It was these policies that would end peasants' pastoral practices, foment sedentary agriculture, draw peasants into the projects and vision of the national state, and identify them as "men of work" whose production, habits, and values were central to the nation and its progress.

This is not to say that the Trujillo state was truly committed to or fully successful at either assisting peasant agriculturalists or remaking the rural economy in the image envisaged by reformist intellectuals and members of the state. At the end of the regime, some peasants continued to live in the hills and woodlands practicing slash-and-burn farming. And most still lived largely from their own subsistence production.[54] The regime's willingness and capacity to produce an alternative modernity based on small-scale agriculture were uneven and constrained not only by market forces and limited resources, but also by the resistance of foreign landowners and a few better-off Dominicans, the maintenance of pre-existing legal norms, and Trujillo's own financial self-aggrandizement. As we will see in Chapter 4, these constraints were especially severe in the Eastern sugar zone, the region where peasants faced the most dire conditions when Trujillo seized power. There the regime was unable or unwilling to overcome resistance to its agrarian policies by mostly foreign interests, whose properties, in contrast to most of the country's landholdings, had already undergone the process of adjudicating definitive titles in accordance with laws promulgated under the U.S. military government. As a result, in the heart of the Eastern sugar zone, thousands of squatters were ultimately evicted. Yet rather than reflecting the unrestrained power of the Trujillo state, as might appear to be the case, these evictions demonstrate more the limits of the regime's autonomy and discretion.

In addition to long-standing concerns about a foreign sugar enclave and the effacement of national autonomy and interests in the East, many political figures and intellectuals who participated in the regime and helped shape its trajectory condemned what they termed the "denationalization" of the Dominican "frontier," a vast region (or combination of regions) bordering with Haiti. Chapter 5 explores how, until the late 1930s, a frontier population composed largely of ethnic Haitians—perhaps the majority Dominican-born—who were integrated with ethnic Dominicans in a fluidly bicultural and transnational world, both sustained and was sustained by a highly porous Haitian-Dominican border. Condemnations of the ethnic composition, Haitian-Dominican integration, and borderlessness of the frontier world by Dominican intellectuals and political leaders stemmed not only from their monoethnic construction of the nation, as was gaining hegemony around the globe at the time. They also stemmed from pervasive racist myths in the Dominican Republic (and throughout Europe and the Americas) that cast the influence of popular Haitian religion and culture as an obstacle to modernity.[55] Elite Dominicans had clamored for decades for a definitive and well-controlled border with Haiti, for nationalist cultural policies in the frontier, and for European immigration to help implant putatively superior cultural and agricultural practices and to develop a region they perceived to be imperiled by Haitian territorial claims and cultural influences. Many—but not all—of these nationalist and racist objectives would be realized by the Trujillo state. It established for the first time a firm territorial border and, after an early period of exceptional official solidarity with Haiti, diffused long-standing urban and elite constructs of a Dominican nation necessarily exclusive of Haitians and Haitian-ness. Yet elite constructs of Dominican nationality, of a monoethnic nation, rigid borders, and anti-Haitianism would be effectively promoted by the national state and adopted by ethnic Dominicans in the frontier only following the 1937 Haitian massacre. This region farthest from the reach of the central state would thus be brought into dominant constructs of the nation only through genocidal violence.

At times, the Trujillo regime also voiced much support for the racist fantasy of ushering in European immigrants and establishing European colonies in the frontier. And some immigrants were indeed welcomed by the regime, at least if they were ready to farm idle lands. Yet, as explored in Chapter 6, rural development and land distribution to Dominicans, not European immigration, generally structured colonization policies under Trujillo. Although first promoted as part of a racist and nationalist project to bring European immigrants to the borderlands, colonization was transformed during the Trujillo years primarily into an instrument of agrarian reform. This was particularly the case during the second half of the dictatorship, when the land distribution campaign faced shortages of nearby and desirable lands as the population exploded and commercial agriculture expanded. Trujillo's colonization program provided thousands of landless Dominican peasants with individual plots and government assistance and opened up new farm areas, frequently through expanding infrastructure. The spread of agricultural colonies also served to increase state control over the rural population, especially in formerly isolated areas. Whereas traditional pastoral practices and rural dispersion had rendered state regulation problematic, colonists were granted fixed agricultural plots in officially recorded locations within nucleated communities that were close to roads, tied to population centers, and within reach of state assistance and control as well as commercial markets. The central state thus gained greater knowledge of, access to, and power over the rural population. Although many prior residents in the remote or marginal locations where numerous colonies were established resented their forced inclusion and nucleation within state-supervised agricultural villages, colonization served overall, like the land distribution campaign, to give credence to the Trujillo state's populist rhetoric and to lend legitimacy to the regime in the eyes of peasants.

Peasants' own perspectives on the Trujillo years suggest, though, that it was not simply the state's land policies but also broader social and cultural measures that, for many, legitimated Trujillo's rule. Elderly peasants' present-day depictions of everyday life during the Trujillo years, which are explored in Chapter 7, recall multiple and profound forms of oppression, above all ubiquitous surveillance and harsh repression of even civil offenses. Yet overall Trujillo has been remembered nostalgically for land distribution and agricultural assistance as well as for ensuring social and political order, and even for many aspects of the national state's novel presence in rural life. The regime was able, it seems, to frame the state's interventions and rural modernization project within peasants' own discourse, norms, and concerns. Peasants remember the state upholding their moral economy of free access to land, as well as traditional patriarchal values in the countryside. A culture of "decency," deference, and mutual respectfulness in interpersonal relations and across social hierarchies, encapsulated in the term *respeto*, was loosely but powerfully associated with Trujillo's rule in peasants' memories. Furthering Trujillo's association with a culture of respeto was his regime's extensive financial support of the Catholic Church, a formerly weak institution that expanded momentously in this mostly Catholic nation during his rule. And the church's constant, often effusive praise of Trujillo and the progress of his era in speeches and masses throughout the country similarly contributed to the regime's legitimacy in peasants' eyes. Ruling during the early stages of modernization, Trujillo was able to cast himself, in short, as a leader impelling the nation's progress while simultaneously perpetuating traditional values.

Yet by the end of the regime, in certain areas of the country Trujillo ceased to be associated with the maintenance of rural values. And, as a result, the extent of his hegemony diminished. Chapter 8 takes us through the final years of Trujillo's rule to explore how, as a result of the regime's sugar expansion, peasant dispossession, and dramatic conflict with the Catholic Church in the 1950s, it undid the instruments of legitimation that it had so painstakingly cultivated among the popular rural classes. These shifts in policy produced profound peasant disillusionment with Trujillo's rule in some areas and, in one instance, open resistance to the dictatorship. In the late 1950s, the regime was also faced with a potent underground resistance movement in the towns and cities, which gained strength among a small, new middle class with the first real economic decline under Trujillo—a crisis provoked largely by the dictator's expansive sugar policies. Confronting this opposition, Trujillo would seek to revive his peasant social base. This effort, though, would be too little and too late to reconsolidate Trujillo's rule. The timing of the regime's collapse in 1961 suggests that its endurance for decades was predicated on the appeal of earlier state policies and that Trujillo might have been deposed far sooner had he ruled in the 1930s and 1940s as he did in the 1950s.

Yet until the 1950s—and even then in much of the country—there remained a significant degree of coherence in the Trujillo state's rural policies. Their aims were to secure popular acceptance of the regime, to boost agricultural production and national self-sufficiency, and to incorporate peasants into what was considered modernity and thus to subject them to the control of the national state. If we accept peasants' own recollections as well as state records, it is clear that the Trujillo regime fostered an effective peasant-state compromise. Policies to secure land for peasants and increase their production helped make Trujillo's Dominican Republic a virtually self-sufficient country in agricultural terms (save wheat), in contrast to the rest of the twentieth-century Caribbean and much of Latin America. Export agriculture expanded, grown largely by small farmers with the exception of sugar. The gross national product grew markedly throughout the dictatorship.[56] And despite the perils of becoming dependent on sedentary, small-scale agriculture and upon the state—then a brutal dictatorship, moreover—elderly peasants generally remember Trujillo as having carried out policies that were relatively beneficial to them.

Certainly, memories are far from a transparent index of past experiences and perceptions. People fashion the past to speak to the present. Or, as Ronald Grele has put it, "All histories, whether written or spoken, are discussions (texts) of both past and present. They tell of then, and of the now of their creation as well."[57] Recollections are shaped by both implicit and explicit comparisons with other periods of time, before as well as after recorded events. And in order to critique the present, nostalgia highlights the positive dimensions of the past and obscures the negative. In the Dominican case, the problematic character of political liberalism in the post-Trujillo era—the weakness of civil rights, the prevalence of corruption, the extralegal discretion of the armed forces, and the lack of public services and state accountability to the popular classes—coupled with economic hardship, nationalist wounds, and intensifying social inequality amid increasingly neoliberal economic policies all have helped produce selective nostalgia about the Trujillo era among elderly Dominicans. In other words, peasants' testimony about the dictatorial past not only suggests much about the Trujillo regime but also represents an unsettling critique of the limitations and illiberal aspects of democracy in the Dominican Republic today.[58] Finally, oral testimony, unlike written documents, is inevitably a "'social act' . . . in which the investigator and the informant continually influence one another," collaborating in a sense to produce texts.[59] However much one seeks to pose neutral questions, the form of one's inquiries as well as one's social identity—in my case as an academic from the

United States living in Santo Domingo—inevitably influences oral histories, though in ways that are not necessarily transparent or consistent.

Such methodological constraints must be taken into account, and testimony must be analyzed critically, as is the case with all historical evidence. That being said, it is nonetheless clear that peasants' recollections of the Trujillo years represent rich and otherwise unavailable sources for reconstructing rural life and peasant-state relations during the dictatorship and for exploring peasants' political culture and subjectivity. When analyzed (and challenged) in conjunction with documentary sources, these testimonies add needed voices, corroboration, and perspective to that evidence. While doubtless overly nostalgic at times in light of present concerns, the testimony that I collected from elderly peasants in the Dominican Republic gains power and credence by its generally complex articulation of both perceived benefits and hardships during the Trujillo years. Indeed, peasants' recollections of the multiple and often contradictory effects of state power under Trujillo embody a nostalgia shot through with dread, a dread of the repression, surveillance, and general lack of liberty that accompanied a regime now remembered mostly for its paradoxical protección and culture of respeto. These testimonies provided a unique window into the complexity of peasants' relationship to the regime and the ambivalence complicating their seemingly strong support for it.

In accounting for the Trujillo state's substantial degree of rural populism, it should be emphasized that in contrast to many other countries in the region, for example El Salvador, the economic elite had been exceptionally weak in the Dominican Republic, given peasant autonomy and the country's poverty.[60] Furthermore, the Dominican military, having been created by the U.S. military government, was relatively independent of, and unrestrained by, domestic elites. They had, in fact, shunned this constabulary formed by foreign interlopers, which had nonetheless emerged as one of the most cohesive forces in Dominican politics by 1930. These structural conditions opened up the possibilities for an enduring and powerful dictatorship that was relatively autonomous from the existing upper classes and that could carry out major reforms and take forceful actions that were contrary to their interests. The relative ease with which the Trujillo state was able to implement its agrarian reforms was also due to the absence of clear and definitive land titles in most of the country, the abundance of undeveloped public and private lands, and the limited scope of commercial agriculture in the 1930s. Trujillo's reforms thus did not require an attack on an existing rural elite but instead functioned by impeding its development, eviscerating unrealized property claims, and forestalling its opportunities for expansion.

Diminished prospects for export agriculture during the world depression and the relative decline of U.S. domination in the Caribbean and Central America during the 1930s also opened up the prospects for reformist projects in the region.[61] But this reformism was far from inevitable. In El Salvador, for instance, state policy was heavily influenced by interests of the nation's coffee elite following the world economic crisis.[62] The Trujillo regime differed sharply from other depression-era dictatorships such as that of General Maximiliano Hernández Martínez in El Salvador (1931–44), as well as from later regimes such as that of Carlos Castillo Armas in Guatemala (1954–57) or of Augusto Pinochet in Chile (1973–90), all of which supported the interests of pre-existing elites in stopping popular mobilization and halting social and economic reforms. Trujillo, by contrast, implemented agrarian reforms before any major social movement emerged from below.

When Trujillo came to power, the vast majority of peasants had been squatters. Central to his hegemony in the Dominican countryside was the state's capacity to secure their access to land during a menacing period of land and agricultural commercialization. To the contrary, in prerevolutionary Cuba and Nicaragua, large numbers of embattled squatters were ultimately abandoned by the state, and the regions where their struggles were salient became, not coincidentally, the main centers of revolution. In Cuba, a war was already raging between squatters and landowners upon the arrival of Fidel Castro's minuscule band of eighteen insurgents in Oriente province. There, a substantial population of peasant landholders had been battling for decades with sugar companies seeking to evict them by both legal and violent means.[63] Although some officials and intellectuals advocated transforming rural squatters into productive small farmers, as in the Dominican Republic, and certain agrarian reform measures were legislated in the period from 1936 to 1952, these measures remained limited and the state increasingly sided with the sugar companies.[64] Thus, when Castro's band arrived in 1956, they offered squatters the means of finally tipping the balance against the sugar companies and the state supporting their eviction. Their support of Castro was a critical factor explaining the otherwise miraculous-seeming success of his rural forces.[65]

In Nicaragua, members of the military and the state who had once mediated tensions between landowners and peasants over land access increasingly accumulated land themselves during the latter half of the long Somoza dynasty. And important elements of the national state that had been supportive of peasant interests abandoned them in the 1960s.[66] At the same time, the agroexport economy boomed to the detriment of the nation's squatters and previously large independent peasantry.[67] In some areas, certain agrarian reform efforts partially offset these developments through land colonization programs and, above all, squatter entitlements. But in many other areas, the Somoza state increasingly lost its measure of credibility as a mediator of rural interests. As a result, many peasants began to support the opposition, and space was opened for revolution in a way that never occurred in the Dominican Republic.[68] With the notable exception of those dispossessed in the 1950s by the new state sugar industry, Trujillo remained for the majority of Dominican peasants a politically effective mediator of land distribution and modernity, promising continuity in rural norms amid changes toward which they were inevitably ambivalent. Thus, when armed exiles landed in the Dominican Republic, they were unable to enlist rural support for an uprising. The regime successfully maintained a large class of small landholding peasants who, relative to the perceived alternatives, felt they had a stake in, and identified with, Trujillo's rule.[69]

To argue that the Trujillo state's agrarian reforms, however problematic, were relatively appealing to the bulk of the peasantry is not to disavow the substantial, contradictory policies and actions of the regime that contributed to latifundia, particularly its massive land appropriations and sugar expansion in the Monte Plata region during the 1950s. Indeed in 1960, large estates of more than 3,000 tareas (189 hectares, or 466 acres) constituted 30 percent of the nation's landholdings, and immense properties of over 25,000 tareas (1,572 hectares) 14 percent. At the same time, though, holdings of less than five hundred tareas (30 hectares, or 77 acres) still made up half of the country's occupied land.[70] There are multiple histories to be told about the Dominican Republic, and the story of latifundia and sugar interests should not blind us to the breadth and vitality, as well as the political imagination, of a large independent peasantry prevailing into the post-Trujillo period. However extensive latifundia became in certain areas and however grim a number of conflicts were between peasants and the state during the Trujillo years, neither represented the experience, nor determined the consciousness, of most peasants over the course of the regime, and should not be the sole focus of scholarly work. No matter how undemocratic or despotic a state is, it may nonetheless develop important public policies and political discourses that shape and transform society in critical ways. Hence, rather than retelling the history of the dictator's already infamous and well-documented corruption and machinery of terror, this book brings to the center the undisclosed and unexpected material and cultural dimensions of the Trujillo state's rural policies, and thus the paradoxical foundations of despotism.

1

Freedom in *el Monte*

From Slaves to Independent Peasants in Colonial Santo Domingo

At the dawn of European colonialism, the island of Santo Domingo, or Hispaniola, became the cradle of modernity in what Spanish colonists deemed to be the New World.[1] Santo Domingo was the initial venue for modern, transoceanic colonialism, the site for the earliest sugar mill complexes in the Americas, and the New World's first plantation society.[2] Its sugar industry boomed dramatically between 1520 and 1600 via the systematic exploitation of enslaved Africans. But at the end of the sixteenth century, the sugar industry collapsed as quickly as it had developed. The Spanish colony of Santo Domingo, or Española, became a land with few plantations, making it contrast sharply with the subsequent development of lucrative plantation economies in most of the Caribbean, including the French colony of Saint Domingue that took over the western third of Hispaniola in the late seventeenth century. Thus while the non-Hispanic Caribbean followed what anthropologist Sidney Mintz has called a "rocket-like trajectory toward modernity" and developed spectacular export-agriculture systems, Santo Domingo, and the Spanish Caribbean in general, became a colonial backwater with largely pastoral and subsistence-based economies.[3] The Spanish Crown and Spanish settlers increasingly neglected the Caribbean colonies following the discovery of gold on the mainland and, above all, the development of lucrative silver mines in Mexico and Peru.

Spanish neglect had not developed rapidly enough, though, to prevent the elimination of pre-Columbian societies caused by Spanish violence, the introduction of fatal diseases, and socioeconomic disruption. The large indigenous population of Hispaniola—some 500,000 to 750,000 persons—appears to have been virtually exterminated within some fifty years of Columbus's arrival.[4] This destruction of the aboriginal population, together with the early, massive importation of enslaved Africans and the subsequent colonial neglect and absence of commercial development, would have a profound impact on Dominican history, particularly on the creation and character of the Dominican peasantry.

The Dominican peasantry was aptly described as the "offspring of slavery" by a leading nineteenth-century Dominican intellectual, Pedro Francisco

Bonó.[5] After the decline of the sixteenth-century plantation society, large numbers of slaves were able to escape bondage and withdraw into remote areas of the relatively vast and sparsely populated Caribbean colony, where they subsequently mixed with poor colonists and forged a more or less autonomous existence. The society that gradually emerged in this context consisted of a modest cattle economy in combination with a large and essentially self-sufficient peasantry. Exploiting abundant woods and natural pasture, this dispersed and somewhat footloose population would live for centuries a relatively independent existence of open-range hunting and animal grazing (*crianza libre*) coupled with shifting, slash-and-burn farming on tiny subsistence plots (conucos). Just as neighboring French Saint Domingue would become the colonial plantation economy par excellence in the 1700s, Spanish Santo Domingo gave birth early on to an exceptional and enduring Caribbean peasantry, one constituted largely by former slaves and their descendants together with some settlers of European origin.[6]

Generally residing in dispersed, isolated, and informal communities, Santo Domingo's rural population was far from the typical image of Spanish American peasants: extensive indigenous populations drawing on pre-Columbian traditions and identities and living in cohesive village communities with strong political institutions and communal property forms.[7] The "traditional" rural economy and mode of existence that prevailed in colonial Santo Domingo was not a legacy of a precapitalist world, but rather was born, ironically, of modernity. It had no precolonial past and followed rather than preceded the penetration of world market forces. As anthropologist Michel-Rolph Trouillot has written about the Caribbean in general, "The 'peasant way of life' fully blossomed only upon the ruins of plantations."[8] And even as modern plantations declined and receded in collective memory, the peasantry would always bear their traces, existing in tacit opposition to them and efforts at their re-establishment.

In the interest of expanding colonial Santo Domingo's wealth and revenues, over time Spanish and creole elites became preoccupied with re-establishing plantation agriculture (based on slavery while it continued to be legal) or, in some other fashion, extending their control over and extracting a surplus from a peasantry accustomed to living more or less independently of commercial forces, constructs of property in land, and the vision and authority of the central state. But efforts commencing in the late eighteenth century toward this objective remained in vain, given the weakness of the state and colonial elites, and given the evident preference of the majority of the population for their existing way of life. Indeed, most peasants would continue to live a largely pastoral and subsistence-oriented existence into the twentieth

century, despite persistent state efforts to agrarianize, sedentarize, or prole-
tarianize them. And the rural majority in Santo Domingo would never again
be incorporated into large-scale export agriculture; when plantations re-
emerged in the late nineteenth century, they would depend on immigrant labor. And the contest over peasant autarky would not be resolved until the
authoritarian regime of Rafael Trujillo forged an effective peasant-state compromise in the twentieth century.

The history and culture of peasant independence in the Dominican Republic originated in the transition from slavery to a free peasantry in colonial
Santo Domingo. This transition occurred over centuries. It commenced long
before slavery was officially abolished in 1822, when Santo Domingo came
under Haitian rule. Indeed, it had taken on major proportions reshaping the
Dominican countryside already by the end of the seventeenth century. An independent peasantry of color was thus consolidated and comprised most of
the population at the same time that legal systems of slavery and racial hierarchy prevailed. The autonomy of this peasantry was sustained through casual
land tenure arrangements and customary forms of property together with the
then seemingly endless expanses of uncleared land, or el monte, across this
large island. This chapter explores the history of slavery, the development of
an independent peasantry, and the contours of land tenure in colonial Santo
Domingo in order to illuminate rural life and norms and their enduring impact on the Dominican Republic. Deeply rooted in peasants' moral economy
was a right to the land. Especially in the historical context of slavery, an independent means of subsistence became associated with freedom—autonomy
from economic subordination to and control by others as well as from the
vagaries of market and central state forces. The valorization of economic independence and land access would continue to shape peasant politics even
after the abolition of slavery and the achievement of national independence
during the nineteenth century. The construction of rights and freedom in
terms of free access to land also sheds light on the peasantry's paradoxical acceptance of the Trujillo dictatorship in the twentieth century, as that regime's
policies and reforms would sustain peasant land access and a sense of rural
independence notwithstanding its harsh and repressive system of rule.

From Slaves to Peasants

The origins of Santo Domingo's independent peasantry date back to the
precipitous rise and equally sudden fall of the colony's putative golden age in
the sixteenth century. An initial gold-mining bonanza was quickly exhausted
between 1510 and 1520, precipitated by the destruction of the large indigenous
population upon whose exploitation this industry had depended.[9] The sugar

plantation economy that developed in its wake expanded quickly and dramatically. Spanish records indicate that in the 1530s, there were between thirty
and forty sugar mills in operation in any given year.[10] By 1544, according to
one plantation owner, the colony exported 1,375 tons of sugar.[11] And annual
sugar production reportedly reached several thousand tons during the mid–
sixteenth century.[12] In 1568, *Oidor* (Justice) Juan de Echagoian reported to the
king of Spain that among the more than thirty mills then in service in Española, two belonging to Melchor de Torres were together worked by nine
hundred slaves, an astonishing number for the time. "The rest [of the mills
have] 200, and some 300, and there are ones with 100 and 150 *negros*." Altogether, he believed, there were some twenty thousand slaves working at the
sugar mills, on other rural estates and ranches, as servants, and as laborers in
the city, at the same time that there were reportedly only six thousand Spaniards and five hundred indigenous Caribbeans.[13] This estimate of the number
of slaves is consistent with the fact that up to two thousand enslaved Africans
disembarked each year at Santo Domingo during this era.[14] The colony's massive slave population produced great wealth that fostered a relatively developed society for the period. At midcentury the Spanish chronicler Gonzalo
Fernández de Oviedo reported that Santo Domingo was dotted with "many
fine houses belonging to prominent men, in which any lord or grandee could
lodge." Save Barcelona, he wrote, "there is no town in Spain better constructed" than Santo Domingo.[15]

But the sugar plantations fell into almost complete decline by the close of
the sixteenth century, and with it went Santo Domingo's precocious integration in the early modern Atlantic world. This sudden collapse appears to have
been caused not primarily by local conditions but rather by the constraints
imposed by Spain's evolving commercial policies toward the New World:
limitations on trade with ports other than Seville, high prices demanded by
Spanish merchants for imports, licensing restrictions hindering the expansion
of the slave trade (thus raising slave prices), and, most decisively, a dramatic
decline in the number of vessels docking on Santo Domingo's shores and
hence the colony's inability to market its sugar. This scarcity of shipping from
Spain was largely a product of the fleet system, by which Spain sought to
protect its trade from pirates and privateers by requiring transatlantic ships to
sail in a convoy with an armed escort. By 1570 only two fleets traveled per year
to the Americas. And within this limited shipping regime, Spain gave priority
on their ships to bullion, which demanded less cargo space in relationship to
its value than did sugar (or hides, Santo Domingo's second great export at the
time). Thus, as Spanish merchants and the Crown concentrated their efforts
on precious metals from Peru and New Spain rather than the products of

Caribbean plantations, Santo Domingo's market access collapsed.[16] Yet given the fantastic economic potential of its Caribbean possessions, why Spain would not overcome these early constraints for centuries and why it so cavalierly abandoned the slave plantation model its colonists inaugurated in the New World begs further analysis.

These commercial policies of the Spanish Crown along with heavy taxes and high slave prices would render plantations relatively unprofitable in the Spanish Caribbean for the next two hundred years. That remained the case even while other European empires developed spectacular sugar-plantation economies in the region and transformed it into a center of world trade in the eighteenth century, above all in neighboring Saint Domingue and Jamaica.[17] Spain's restrictive and neglectful policies not only left the Spanish Caribbean essentially devoid of plantations and economically unproductive but also gave rise to extremely weak state apparatus in the region. A minuscule bureaucracy in Santo Domingo exercised scant power and authority over the countryside, unable to subject it to the metropolitan norms and aspirations central to Spanish colonial ideology.[18]

Española's economic and political underdevelopment in the seventeenth century have led many historians to label it the "century of misery," a time of unqualified "historical regression" from its former "splendor" in the 1500s.[19] Twentieth-century Dominican intellectual Juan Bosch described the period as the "very image of backwardness," a time when "the country languished in almost complete wretchedness."[20] Natural disasters, epidemics, droughts, and war (conflicts with buccaneers), and the resultant extinction of most remaining plantations, did indeed foster misery among all classes during the 1600s. Yet from another perspective, underdevelopment and colonial neglect provided certain advantages for the majority of the population.[21] The end of the plantation economy in the seventeenth century was a boon for freed people and runaway slaves (*cimarrones*), who swelled the ranks of a growing independent peasantry.

Although much of the history of slavery and manumission in Santo Domingo has yet to be uncovered, it is evident that Española's overall poverty undermined the possibility of large-scale slavery. As sugar production became unfeasible and ground to a halt, ginger and subsequently cacao plantations expanded. But they too fell into almost complete ruin by the second half of the seventeenth century in the wake of crop diseases, natural disasters, and the scarcity and costliness of slaves. This left cattle ranches, or *hatos*, as the only real commercial endeavor on the island. Some slaves did work on these large cattle estates, but they had minimal labor needs.[22] Over time, many slaveholders rented out slaves for whom they no longer had any use.[23]

These conditions of underdevelopment in a modest cattle economy opened up substantial opportunities for many slaves to purchase, be granted, or escape to their freedom. At the same time, Spanish monopolies, high slave prices, and the elite's lack of capital limited new slave imports.[24] Thus, the slave population would steadily decline from more than three-fourths of the total in the sixteenth century to an estimated 15 percent of the colony at the twilight of Spanish rule in Santo Domingo at the end of the eighteenth century, with even the absolute number of slaves decreasing over time.[25] And already in 1681, nearly three-fourths of Santo Domingo's non-white population (the majority of the colony) were legally free.[26]

Also contributing to declining slave numbers was the relatively liberal character of manumission laws and practices in Santo Domingo. As in most of Spanish and Portuguese America, and unlike slave systems in the rest of the New World, no spate of legislation developed to impede manumission through prohibition, taxation, or other official hurdles and economic disincentives.[27] To the contrary, customs developed, eventually with the force of law, that permitted slaves (or their parents or godparents) to purchase their freedom as soon as they paid their masters their market value.[28] In the case of conflict with their owners over the price of liberty, slaves could—and at times did, as historian Raymundo González has found—take the matter to court, where their value was appraised and freedom granted after that sum was paid.[29] Yet given the poverty of the colony and the limited market and need for slaves, many owners appear to have been ready to sell freedom to slaves for less than the requisite amount in order to obtain scarce income or to be freed from the responsibility of supporting children or the elderly. Slaves often accumulated the necessary funds for securing their liberty by saving their portion of the wages they received when contracted out as laborers.[30] Also, a substantial number of slaveholders freed their slaves at no cost reportedly in return for "loyalty" and good service and for not "abandoning" them during difficult times (illness, poverty, old age).[31] Not infrequently, though, those manumissions were conditioned on slaves continuing to serve their elderly masters until their owners' death.[32] In other cases, masters freed without payment children they had fathered with slaves—especially, no doubt, if they were the owners' sole offspring and heirs, a tendency seen elsewhere in the Americas.[33]

Notwithstanding the relative ease of manumission in the eighteenth century, the comparatively high level of independence (as ranch hands and as slaves hired out for wages), and the overall lesser degree of surveillance and regimentation than prevailed in plantation slavery, slaves in Santo Domingo, not surprisingly, were subjected to violence, terror, abuse, dishonor, and the lack of full legal personhood defining chattel slavery.[34] And these conditions heightened slaves' drive to be free. In addition to self-purchase and other means of manumission, the slave population declined as thousands fled into the colony's dense wilderness (el monte). Santo Domingo's vast unpopulated landscape, teeming wildlife, rugged terrain, and minimal infrastructure provided optimal conditions for runaway slaves both to hide and to secure subsistence. In the sixteenth century, when the state was financing efforts to recapture runaway slaves, most were obliged to live in highly militarized, concentrated communities for protection. A dozen or so important maroon communities (*manieles*) were founded in Santo Domingo during the sixteenth and early seventeenth centuries. By the 1540s, thousands of cimarrones inhabited these villages.[35] But in the mid-seventeenth century, when plantations virtually disappeared and the state stopped sponsoring military expeditions against maroons, runaway slaves were no longer compelled to organize themselves in defensive communities.[36] Although slave owners continued to pay private *buscadores* (maroon hunters), the scale and frequency of their operations was minimal given owners' declining labor needs and financial resources.[37] Under these conditions, former slaves chose to live dispersed throughout the countryside, where they and their descendants provided for themselves by hunting pigs in the woods, grazing cattle on the open range, foraging for natural fruits, fishing where possible, and cultivating shifting subsistence plots.[38] Peasants who lived near cattle ranches occasionally worked as ranch hands, but this was not the norm. Former slaves thus found freedom in los montes and constituted a new peasant class. They would frustrate colonial visions of the subjection of the countryside to the city and remain relatively autonomous from urban elites under Spanish rule.[39]

Large numbers of runaway slaves from Saint Domingue also swelled the Spanish colony's independent peasantry as the former's plantation economy boomed in the eighteenth century. Santo Domingo's bountiful natural resources and freely available land offered an attractive refuge to successful runaways. Despite constant petitions by the French state, few maroons were ever returned to Saint Domingue, even during those moments when the Crown agreed to do so. When runaway slaves were caught by authorities in Santo Domingo, some were sold to Spanish slaveholders. Others were allowed to settle in San Lorenzo de los Negros Minas, a village outside the capital (today a *barrio* of Santo Domingo known as Los Minas) that was founded in the late seventeenth century by maroons from Saint Domingue. But most who fled from Saint Domingue escaped into the country's sparsely populated montes and scattered villages and formed part of the expanding Dominican peasantry.[40] Finally, there were numerous creoles of European de-

scent who headed to the montes during the eighteenth century, preferring rural autonomy and subsistence security to the poverty and constraints they
faced in the towns. Exploitation of woods, wildlife, and shifting conucos thus
became the predominant mode of existence in the eighteenth-century Dominican countryside.[41]

Official racism and racial categories figured prominently in Spanish colonial ideology. And some 325 years of racial slavery and racist colonial discourse would give rise to various racist representations (and underrepresen-
tations), constructions of "beauty," popular aphorisms, and forms of privi-
lege and stigma that would persist after independence from Haiti in the 1840s,
albeit in often paradoxical fashion.[42] But how race and racism evolved under
conditions of freedom in el monte of Santo Domingo during the colonial period and after remains far from clear. The vast majority of the colony's rural
inhabitants were always nonwhite, as was true also among urban denizens.
Various European observers and officials had classified the largest portion of
the population as mulatto or *pardo* (brown) by the eighteenth century.[43] This
demographic makeup along with the peasantry's distance from metropolitan
institutions, the small white presence in rural areas, and the relatively low degree of economic segmentation by race or color (shade) in peasant society
may have minimized the everyday significance of racial categories among the
popular rural classes.[44]

At the same time, the state maintained, in principle at least, a clear racial
hierarchy similar to that in other parts of the Spanish empire. Free people of
color were barred from the *cabildos* (municipal councils) by local laws (approved by the king) and were considered inappropriate for positions within
the clergy, the bureaucracy, the armed forces, and the university. In practice,
however, racial restrictions were eased during the eighteenth century, for instance in order to secure sufficient troops to defend Santo Domingo's territory from Spain's European rivals. Moreover, some persons of color were
able to enter upper echelons of the army, the church, the state, and the
teaching professions, though this may have been feasible only for elite and
lighter-skinned mulattos.[45] Despite some liberalization, prejudice and discrimination continued to weigh heavily on the urban free population of
color, who were largely confined to jobs such as saddlers, cobblers, and car-
penters, and who had to compete for these jobs with slaves. Also it appears
that in the colony's towns the small population of those considered white
tended toward racial endogamy—whiteness being one of few means of
marking social distinction given the limited wealth and education of all but a
narrow elite. Overall, although research remains to be done on this subject, it
seems that racial distinctions were more rigid, and racial hierarchy more sig-

nificant, in the towns and cities than in the countryside. Small wonder then that most freed slaves and their descendants chose to withdraw into the relative freedom and equality offered by life in el monte.[46]

Two Dominican worlds thus coexisted in the post-plantation colonial era. Slavery, legal racial hierarchy, and ties to the colonial metropole characterized urban areas (primarily Santo Domingo and Santiago) and the relatively few large rural estates.[47] Meanwhile, most peasants lived beyond these spaces, essentially apart from the cities and out of the reach of the colonial state and its racial distinctions. This is not to say, though, that people of color in the countryside faced no threats or influences from metropolitan forces. Urban society's norms of racial exclusion and prejudice may have radiated out, in certain senses, into the rural areas. And peasants may have faced them directly if they ventured too close to metropolitan zones or ended up confronting the arm of the state. Indeed, one reason that many peasants relied heavily on hunting and foraging in the woods rather than sedentary agriculture may have been the geographic mobility this form of subsistence afforded, useful if eluding colonial officials and buscadores became necessary. A peasantry on the move could more easily escape the state's gaze and resist its dictates.

Yet economic developments over the course of the eighteenth century generated new state and elite interests in closing the gap between the peasantry in the Dominican interior and the small elite world in the cities and on large rural estates. In the latter 1700s, various efforts would be made both to redevelop plantation slavery and to capture the colony's Afro-Dominican peasantry to provide sorely needed inexpensive labor. Early in the century, neighboring Saint Domingue's plantation economy had taken off in spectacular fashion. As a result, Santo Domingo experienced some commercial revival through intra-island trade. The French colony's escalating demand for cattle to feed its skyrocketing population, drive its mills, transport merchandise, and supply leather provided a giant market for Dominican ranchers. Furthermore, in 1765, Spain's Bourbon king, Charles III, partially liberalized external trade in an effort to promote agricultural development and to capture the revenues that were being lost to contraband (constituting at the time a major portion of Santo Domingo's commerce). These reforms permitted the Spanish Antilles to trade directly with nine Spanish ports rather than having to channel all commerce through Cádiz (which in 1717 acquired the trade monopoly formerly controlled by Seville). Together with the growing market in Saint Domingue for primary goods, this "free trade" stimulated agricultural development. Peasant tobacco production developed in the Santiago area of the north-central Cibao region in combination with continued subsistence exploitation. Lumber exports to Spain also grew substantially after the Crown authorized woodcutting in 1786. And the country's small number of extant sugar plantations expanded.[48]

As the prospects for commercial agriculture expanded, upper-class Dominicans clamored for royal aid to supply slaves to the colony on easy terms. The governor of Española made several requests in the 1760s and 1770s that the Crown exempt slaves from import taxes and extend credit to planters for slave purchases. But the governor must have realized that assistance from Spain would not be sufficient for any rapid or massive introduction of slaves to Santo Domingo, and that its elite remained too poor to exploit expeditiously any royal concessions that were offered. Hence, in 1767 he also proposed "that the Monteros, that is the men who relying on Hunting are always dispersing and moving about as vagrants, be relocated into Villages at the cost of [the] Royal Treasury" and be obliged to work as agriculturalists.[49] Thus local elites and colonial officials set their sights not only on slave imports but also on the colony's large unexploited peasantry. Former slaves and their descendants living in the montes now represented a potential source of labor and agricultural production. The governor envisaged the settlement of scattered monteros and so-called vagrants into villages close to roads, haciendas, markets, and the eyes of the state, where, as the Spanish king stated, "they may live in subjection to rational existence, and dedication to work."[50] Further reflecting elite disdain for the colony's mostly nonwhite peasantry, a 1772 state development commission recommended that other villages (or "colonies") be founded with whites—namely, immigrants from the Canary Islands—who could "offer an example of sociable customs and agricultural diligence to those born and raised in barbarism and indolence."[51]

Even though these proposals reproduced traditional racist conceptions of civilization and barbarism, some were also profoundly innovative within Spanish colonial as well as white creole discourse, and European colonial discourse more broadly. Their novelty rested on representing free people of color not as constitutional vagrants whose only industry and contribution to society could be as laborers working for—and obliged to work for—others, but rather as potential agriculturalists.[52] In other words, some new proposals sought to transform much of the peasantry—albeit repressively—into small sedentary farmers. This innovation implicitly recognized the unlikely success of any effort to oblige peasants to work as (wage) laborers, given land availability, underpopulation, police and overall state weakness, and the traditional liberties already consolidated by free persons of color.

It was because these proposals represented a profound shift from traditional racist understandings of the Dominican peasantry that many officials and members of the elite quickly rejected them. For instance, the *fiscal* of the

Consejo de Indias, Pablo Agüero, dismissed the feasibility of the plan to agrarianize and concentrate the rural population and framed his anti-peasant discourse in racist terms:

It would be reasonably doubted that it is opportune to form villages or towns of blacks . . . the reason being that because of their dim-wittedness, they do not consider themselves free unless they live in perfect idleness. . . . Even when they live in slavery, and under the whip, no punishment is enough to overcome the bad habits that at some point were acquired. . . . [Moreover] there are not so many white subjects that can be removed from the cities, towns, and other locations as would be necessary to govern [*sugetar*] the dispersed blacks that live spread across the island.[53]

If it could be shorn of its intense racism, Agüero's skepticism would seem well founded. Peasants were, in fact, not ready to abandon their exceptionally autonomous, self-sufficient existence in el monte either to work for others for meager wages or to cultivate cash crops in a context of low commodity prices or still inaccessible markets. Moreover, they were not willing to subject themselves to colonial officials and to the racist ideology of those like Agüero.

As the impetus to capture and transform the rural population collided with the inclinations of most peasants, officials increasingly demonized peasants' way of life. In 1788 the chief justice of the Royal Audiencia (High Court) of Santo Domingo and governor of the colony, Pedro Catani, bemoaned the conditions that gave rise to a free peasantry and blamed this peasantry for the colony's economic stagnation:

The ease with which the masses obtain their subsistence, especially those that live in the countryside on root vegetables . . . and by hunting wild animals abounding in the woods, which here they call runaways, makes them forget the labor of cultivation, and live in a perpetual state of idleness. The excessive number of such freed persons living in the countryside, is one of the radical vices [leading to] the backwardness of agriculture. This [situation] originates in the ease with which slaves obtain their freedom.[54]

In a similar vein, another report by Catani—one concerned with rural criminality—divided the countryside into three popular classes: slaves working on their owner's estate; slaves working for wages and paying their masters a portion of their earnings; and "free blacks, who live wherever it occurs to them, working for themselves or for others as they wish." Of the three, he wrote, "the free blacks are the worst . . . those without any subjection [to others]. Generally residing in los montes, they live as they please with every liberty and completely independent. They walk about virtually naked and are the cause and origin of all the harm that is commented upon and may occur on this Island."[55]

It is not a coincidence that during this same period of Bourbon reforms, emerging agricultural interests, and racist representations of the peasantry, local elites and subsequently the Crown made various efforts to draw up a slave code, much like France's 1685 Code Noir, intended to transform legal norms and customary practices regarding race, manumission, and slavery in Santo Domingo (and other Spanish colonies). Hoping to emulate the lucrative plantation economy of neighboring Saint Domingue, the municipal council of Santo Domingo drew up the first Spanish Black Code in 1768. It was divided into sections: slave control, prevention of maroonage, and punishment of disobedience. At first, the Crown was not receptive to this emulation of "inferior" French jurisprudence, and the code was not approved. Yet in 1783, the Crown reversed its stance and ordered the governor of Santo Domingo to draw up "regulations for the economic, political, and moral government of blacks on that Island like those that the French have designated the Black Code." The new legislation was envisaged as "the first step" toward the "prosperity that, with reason, we admire among the French of that island." Less than a year later, with the assistance of a commission of local political and ecclesiastical authorities and large landowners, the Audiencia's *oidor decano* (chief justice), the Basque jurist Agustín Emparán, had already completed the Carolino Black Code (named in honor of King Charles III).[56]

What, in fact, most stands out in reports made to Emparán by the appointed commission are not concerns with slavery per se nor with maroonage, but rather with the growing independent peasantry. The commission denounced the frequency of manumission and the resultant massive free population of color living in imagined idleness in the countryside. Colonel Joaquín García, a member of the local elite who soon became governor, protested that manumission upon an owner's death had become almost a standard practice, and that each new freed slave meant "one more that one has to count among the black vagrants." He complained: "There are an infinite number of blacks and mulattos who live in dispersed huts throughout the countryside, without any more patrimony than that which they or their ancestors brought from Guinea. And they are happy and at ease simply because they are free. They never work, except when they are hungry—a hunger which they alleviate at the expense of their nearest neighbor with provisions or animals they can poach." García voiced concerns not only about underproduction but also the limited significance of race in rural society. Free persons of color, he objected, travel across the colony with "absolute confidence and impertinence" and confuse their identity with that of their white neighbors "as if there were no more classes [dividing society] than free or slave." Desiring greater racial stratification within free society, which would have limited the autonomy of most peasants, he argued that it was a necessity that the code "encompass all the classes constituted by blacks. . . . If it only treats the slaves, all the existing difficulties will persist."[57]

When Emparán actually wrote the code, he responded to these elite concerns about the free population of color. The code put forth measures both to sedentarize peasants and to compel them to work for a daily wage, such as harsh vagrancy laws and ordinances requiring that the "free blacks and even slaves" living "wild" (*alzados*) in los montes be resettled into population centers, namely Los Minas. Without such resettlement, the code stated, vagrancy laws would not be enforceable. Emparán's code responded as well to elite concerns over the lack of racial stratification among the free population. Hence, in addition to seeking "the useful and assiduous occupation of free blacks and slaves in the cultivation of the products needed by the Metropolis," the preamble to the code also demanded "their appropriate division into classes and races." García had expressed concerns primarily about the lack of respect for racial hierarchy in the countryside. Some of the code's stipulations suggest that Emparán himself was deeply concerned, in addition, about a lack of respect for racial hierarchy even in the towns and cities. The code sought to establish racial difference and hierarchy through strict codes of public deference—"complete subordination and respect . . . toward all white people" by all persons of color; through racially distinct punishments, including public whipping of free blacks and mulattos; through restrictions on employment and geographic mobility for blacks, mulattos, and *tercerones* (thirds); through sumptuary regulations prohibiting blacks and mulattos from wearing fine attire; and through bans on education for blacks and mulattos ("who must all dedicate themselves to agriculture" but not "mix with whites"), and the segregation of tercerones and quadroons from whites in schools, where previously "confusion and mixture" had supposedly created a "sinister sense of equality and familiarity." The code also legislated an end to the occupation "of blacks, freedpeople, and even some slaves . . . [in] all the artisan and mechanical professions and jobs, stealing jobs from the white and light-colored [*color medio*] population."[58]

The Carolino Black Code was approved, but, for reasons that remain uncertain, it was never actually promulgated by the Crown. It would serve as the basis for a subsequent 1789 royal edict "Concerning the Education, Treatment, and Occupation of Slaves throughout the Dominion of the Indies and the Philippine Islands," but this too was never implemented. It was abandoned following protests by slaveholders in various colonies against the rights, however minimal, that it afforded to slaves (for instance, guaranteed holidays, religious instruction, and limitations on permissible punishments).

Moreover, after the Haitian Revolution commenced in 1791 and sparked fears of rebellions elsewhere, colonial officials opposed any dramatic change in policy.[59] In any case, the Black Code embodied a Spanish fantasy of elaborate racial distinctions that could never have been realized in Santo Domingo without a massive expansion of police forces, genealogical records, government expenditures, and the colonial state apparatus in general.

In 1793, Justice Catani again proposed that peasants be prohibited from living in los montes. They would be required instead to live near the main routes and to farm at least 10 tareas (0.63 hectare) of land, which was viewed then as the area "one man can cultivate through moderate effort."[60] But plans for peasant sedentarization and agrarianization in the colony were, most likely, no longer being contemplated by the Crown. Since the Bourbon reforms had been initiated in 1765, the development of Santo Domingo had been modest, in striking contrast with neighboring Cuba to the west of Hispaniola. The elite did not possess the capital necessary to import slaves. And the state was not strong enough to capture and control the labor of an autarkic peasantry.[61] Given these conditions, the Bourbon reforms had liberalized trade with Santo Domingo in too limited and inconsistent a fashion to give any great impetus to agriculture.[62] When Spain did finally implement more effective reforms in the late 1780s—namely, the liberalization of the slave trade and elimination of slave taxes—Santo Domingo's slave population quickly increased by several thousand, thus paralleling developments throughout the greater Spanish Caribbean at the time.[63] These reforms, though, occurred too late to have an impact in Santo Domingo, as they came on the eve of the Haitian Revolution (1791–1803), which curtailed the prospects for plantations on both sides of the island.

Following the Haitian Revolution, political commotions and economic difficulties ushered in a long period of instability and emigration from Santo Domingo that destroyed the traditional elite and terminated the nascent economic prospects originating in the mid–eighteenth century. Most important, the revolution initiated a destructive cycle of war and shifting sovereignty engulfing both sides of the island. This sustained turbulence destroyed the main market for Dominican cattle, led to a series of Haitian invasions and occupations, and propelled many elite Dominicans to migrate to Cuba and other Spanish colonies. In 1795, Spain ceded Santo Domingo to France in return for French recognition of Spanish territory in Europe by virtue of the Treaty of Basle. France sought to use its acquisition as a base from which to quash the revolt in Saint Domingue, thus drawing Santo Domingo deeply into the battles of the Haitian Revolution. Haitian, French, Spanish, and even English forces would invade Santo Domingo in the early nineteenth century, and a series of successful liberation wars would be fought until the Dominican Republic finally achieved permanent independence in 1865.[64]

In 1908, the Dominican secretary of agriculture, Emiliano Tejera, recounted this history: "The sad occurrences at the end of the eighteenth century and a good part of the first half of the nineteenth century again brought about the ruin of rural property. The haciendas were abandoned [and] agriculture was reduced to subsistence plots."[65] Yet analogous to the "century of misery," the history of nineteenth-century economic stagnation represented a critical moment when commercial decline thwarted the development of a plantation economy and helped consolidate instead an independent peasantry. This decline may, in fact, have negatively affected only a narrow group. Although economic revival in the mid–eighteenth century had fomented incipient commercial activity among large cattle herders, tobacco producers in the Cibao, and some sugar, cacao, and coffee planters, most of the population still consisted of isolated, self-sufficient, and autonomous peasants. And the crises faced by large cattle ranchers, who lost their main market after the Haitian Revolution, were a boon for this peasantry. The abandonment of these estates opened up new areas to be used as public lands for hunting, herding, foraging, and shifting agriculture. And in the case of the fertile Cibao region, the ranching crisis helped expand small tobacco farming.[66] In these ways commercial decline and political commotion contributed to peasant autonomy and empowerment.

Rights in el Monte: Terrenos Comuneros and Customary Forms of Land Use

The transition from slavery to a free peasantry was furthered by colonial Santo Domingo's flexible system of land use in areas known as *terrenos comuneros*. This system of property expanded over the course of the eighteenth century and came to comprise the largest part of the nation's territory until the Trujillo regime in the twentieth century. It originated as a form of joint ownership of large estates among heirs and other co-owners—similar to arrangements within Cuba's *haciendas comuneras* and to many Puerto Rican hatos in the eighteenth century[67]—but soon degenerated in Santo Domingo into a lack of enforceable property altogether. The ambiguous character of land ownership in terrenos comuneros along with the vast expanses of uncleared lands throughout the country provided former slaves, marginal colonists, and their descendants with the material foundations for an essentially autarkic existence; that is, free access to woodlands and natural pasture for hunting and grazing animals, slash-and-burn farming, and collecting wild fruits.

Despite how most peasants may have understood these areas, terrenos comuneros were neither legally nor universally viewed as common lands in the sense of an "open-access land regime."[68] Technically, terrenos comuneros were a type of group or jointly owned property claimed by an exclusive association of co-owners who possessed rights (or *acciones*) to the property proportional to the number of "land pesos" (*pesos de tierra*) to which they held title. These titles did not refer to any specific plot or quantity of land. Instead they supported rights to utilize any unused area within a comunero site's vaguely defined parameters. It was, however, the effective breakdown of this quasi-legal system of terrenos comuneros and the pervasive free use of the nation's uncleared lands, including these sites, by those without title that undergirded peasant independence.

The precise origins of terrenos comuneros remain obscure. The conventional explanation for their emergence is that landowners holding Crown grants and colonial titles of various kinds, rather than breaking up their estates among their heirs, bequeathed to each heir a proportion of an estate's total value. According to this theory, the value of an estate was estimated at a certain number of pesos, and then that number was divided up in land pesos among the various heirs. This did occur in many cases in the nineteenth century.[69] However, the evidence suggests that all terrenos comuneros did not derive from such a neat subdivision of a property's value. Many of the earliest recorded landholdings apportioned in land pesos were for small quantities— typically less than fifty—too small, it seems, to indicate simply subdivisions among heirs to a large estate. These amounts represented a small percentage of the total value of comunero "sites," many of which, according to later records, comprised thousands of hectares and thousands or even tens of thousands of land pesos.[70] Thus it appears instead in these cases that as the economy improved in the eighteenth century, large landholders controlling the colony's desirable lands began selling access to—or rights to nonspecific parts of—their estates to third parties. At first these sales were simply for "a piece" or "some land," but by the mid–eighteenth century, sales of a set number of "pesos of land in [a particular] hato or site" were common (presumably with the number of land pesos in the original sale equal to the number of pesos the purchaser paid for rights to the estate).[71] One hypothesis is that some of these early land peso transfers were actually concessions from cash-short owners in return for labor performed by ranch workers and administrators.[72] Some peso titles might also have been records of payments to estate owners for permission to use uncultivated parts of their properties. The many plausible but inconclusive theories for the origins of terrenos comuneros reflect not only the vacuum of historical information on the subject but also the probably multiple paths to this form of property. Since there were no laws promulgated regarding terrenos comuneros, no written "grammar" to stabilize its use, owners may have readily interpreted and reinvented the system for their own purposes. We do know that by the late eighteenth century properties held in land pesos by joint owners were already referred to as terrenos comuneros.[73] And by the mid–nineteenth century, most property claims in Santo Domingo were represented in terms of land pesos to terrenos comuneros. Few other land titles remained extant.[74]

More important than the origins of terrenos comuneros were its functions and uses. Some observers have assumed that Santo Domingo's property was demarcated in land pesos because it was too expensive and cumbersome to survey each person's holdings. It seems more likely, however, that the system evolved to serve a needed function in Santo Domingo's cattle economy. As the colony's plantations declined in the sixteenth and seventeenth centuries, many landowners emigrated, abandoned their estates, and left their livestock to roam freely. Hunting and herding the expanding numbers of wild cattle, pigs, goats, and other animals became central to the rural economy. When the rural population grew and commercial interests resurfaced during the eighteenth century, desirable lands became less abundant, and estates, or zones to which one had ranching or property rights, were increasingly subdivided among multiple owners. Yet multiple and successive land divisions were problematic and cumbersome for those living off free-ranging cattle. Livestock could not thrive if restricted to one particular, relatively small portion of property. And an estate's resources, such as bodies of water needed to sustain livestock, could not be conveniently or equitably divided among numerous individuals.

In this context, a system was to some extent formalized by the mid–eighteenth century for jointly owned lands—comprising pasture, woods, streams, palm groves, and fertile terrain—to be collectively utilized rather than subdivided among heirs and other co-owners.[75] As titles were delineated not by land quantities but rather by land pesos representing owners' relative rights or property share, they permitted the allocation of individual rights without having to physically divide the land. Thus livestock could be raised with little property and expense by all classes of co-owners. Sales of land pesos or divisions among heirs meant not diminished access to the estate, but rather only that growing numbers of co-owners enjoyed usufruct rights to the entire site. Cattle grazed freely, while individuals enclosed generally small areas for farming. Any unoccupied or abandoned areas were fair game for co-owners to cultivate and fence off to protect their plots from free-ranging animals.

Yet however much terrenos comuneros derived from this functional system of joint property among entitled co-owners, they were generally also used by large numbers of squatters who emptied the term "terrenos comuneros" of its meaning as a quasi-legal form of exclusively owned property. The degeneration of this property form in practice into virtual common lands was evident already in the mid–eighteenth century when terrenos comuneros first became prevalent. In 1746 the co-owners of Baiguá complained to local officials that those with "almost nothing in the lands," meaning few if any land pesos, were exploiting the estate as if they had full rights to it.[76] And in 1785, Antonio Sánchez Valverde, then a prominent Dominican intellectual, reported on one area of the Cibao:

In these terrenos comuneros . . . there are a very considerable number of poor who have only their hovels in the fields and their pigpens, in which they raise animals or grow tobacco. In addition there are an equal or greater number of persons who are engaged in these same activities who have been fostered by the original owners of the large estates. To these persons we can give the name *Accionistas*, as they have, what they call an *acción* [right or share] of lands varying from twenty *reales* (two and half pesos *fuertes*) to twenty-five or thirty.[77]

This description indicates that from early on these areas were utilized not only by the co-owners or accionistas but also by squatters or usufructuaries who increasingly served to efface, at least at the popular level, the effective distinction between jointly owned property and common (open-access) lands.

At the same time, however, no system of laws or clear traditional rights protected peasant squatters exploiting comunero lands. In this sense it is important to distinguish between "common lands" and "terrenos comuneros." Peasants without peso titles were able to use land freely only because land had little value given the country's still scarce population, minimal farming, and overall commercial poverty. These conditions were furthered when many owners neglected and abandoned their lands during the political upheavals and economic crises of the period from 1789 to 1822. And given the constancy of war, shifting sovereignty, and caudillo rebellions during the nineteenth century, the weak Dominican state was hardly capable of excluding the rural majority from lands formally owned by accionistas. Yet peasant occupants remained highly vulnerable if political and economic conditions changed. They had no clear legal claims or rights to the areas they used, while co-owners holding peso titles maintained the view that they were simply tolerating squatters for the time being.[78]

Squatters' exploitation of lands that were in theory limited in ownership and use rights to associations of peso title holders was tolerated because their small plots, few grazing animals, and subsistence hunting presented few problems for the country's ranchers. This would not have been the case for an agricultural elite engaged in intensive land use. In addition, peasants' leverage would grow during the nineteenth century as they provided the soldiers needed for the nation's multiple independence revolutions against France, Spain, and Haiti, as well as its seemingly constant caudillo-led insurrections.[79] This balance of power hardly encouraged title owners to attempt to evict the country's nearly ubiquitous, armed, and battle-ready peasant squatters. Also, given that the associations of joint owners in terrenos comuneros were generally large, unenumerated, and did not meet as a group, owners could not always distinguish squatters from other owners. Finally, the fact that the overall boundaries of comunero sites were only vaguely defined added to the difficulty of preventing their use by those without titles.

More important still, what was seen by owners as tolerance, or an ephemeral concession, was seen by squatters as natural rights to areas that they themselves had cleared and cultivated and to wildlife that they had hunted, branded, and raised in the country's woodlands and pasture. For them, in other words, "comunero" came to mean common, or "nobody's lands." Los montes belonged to former slaves, their descendants, and the rest of the rural population that had forged Santo Domingo's peasantry and had lived in and exploited these untamed areas for centuries. Even to the extent that peasants recognized ownership in these areas by peso title holders, those property rights were not imagined as including the right to bar others from lands that the owners were not using. It appears that, at least by the twentieth century, the popular rural classes in general referred to these areas not as terrenos comuneros but rather as *tierras comuneras*, a term that included all unoccupied lands. The fact that peasants employed a slightly different term than that found in most written sources suggests perhaps that they were implicitly drawing a distinction between their own understanding of property and a competing view held by peso title holders and the state.[80]

Dominican poet Pedro Mir portrayed popular understandings of property and tierras comuneras when he wrote of the early twentieth century as a time when land "belonged to no one like the wind like the rain like the nights like life and death."[81] Indeed, as late as the 1990s, many elderly Dominican peasants recalled land rights based on possession rather than property "in the old days." These recollections suggest the perpetuation into the twentieth century of the same rural practices and constructs that had once facilitated the transition from slavery to an independent peasantry: forms of customary property conditioned on cultivation, informal land tenure arrangements, and collective exploitation of the woods and open range by the population at large. Given the minor and shifting character of agriculture in an economy based largely on open-range grazing and hunting, landed property had been, from peasants' perspective, almost nonexistent until the early twentieth century. As one peasant, Francisco Salazar, explained: "In the old days, no one owned anything, because the land belonged to everyone. You made your conuco in one place and when it was no longer suitable, you abandoned it and made one somewhere else."[82] "In that era," another elderly peasant told me, "there was no need to look for land. You simply worked wherever and that was your land, your property, your conuco to farm."[83]

The Haitian Occupation (1822–44): The Abolition of Slavery and the Consolidation of an Independent Peasantry in Santo Domingo

In the early nineteenth century, world revolutionary currents, notably the Haitian Revolution, the liberal 1812 Spanish constitution, and independence movements throughout Spanish America, contributed to political ferment among Dominicans.[84] At the same time, with Santo Domingo again subject to Spanish rule (since 1809), some ranchers who sought free trade with the other side of the island began advocating unification with Haiti. Unification also found widespread support among slaves and the nonwhite Dominican majority in general, who anticipated that it would lead to the formal abolition of slavery and greater equality overall. Commencing on November 15, 1821, the leaders of several Dominican frontier towns adopted the Haitian flag. This propelled other Dominican forces who opposed unification with Haiti and the abolition of slavery, and who perceived the Crown as incapable of reviving the economy and establishing order, to declare independence from Spain on November 30. This latter group quickly ousted the Spanish governor, captured the capital, and founded the Independent State of Spanish Haiti. However, this independence movement's support for slavery and its extant dreams of plantation development precluded popular support for the new state. Thus in 1822, just seven weeks after Santo Domingo gained independence from Spain, when Haitian president Jean-Pierre Boyer ordered the occupation and annexation of Spanish Haiti, his troops met virtually no resistance. After Haiti annexed Santo Domingo, slavery was immediately abolished, land was promised to freed slaves, and equality decreed for all men— policies that garnered much support for the Haitian regime among Santo Domingo's nonwhite population.[85]

As historian Pedro San Miguel has argued, Haitian rule marked a critical juncture in Dominican history that consolidated "the secular development of the peasantry."[86] Haitian annexation and the abolition of slavery permanently foreclosed the possibilities of a plantation economy in Santo Domingo precisely when new market forces and colonial policies were finally driving the rest of the Spanish Caribbean toward it. Spain's liberalization of its onerous trade policies during the 1780s, along with its partial liberalization of colonial trade in general, had created the conditions under which slave plantations in the Spanish colonies could compete with other parts of the Americas for the first time. Furthermore, after the Haitian Revolution, Cuba, and to some extent Puerto Rico as well as Spanish Louisiana, began capturing the sugar markets formerly supplied by Saint Domingue and emulated the French colony's lucrative plantation model.[87] A plantation economy soon engulfed western and central Cuba, while sugar estates expanded dramatically along Puerto Rico's coasts, developments that were underwritten by massive imports of enslaved Africans.

Yet, as we have seen, the Haitian Revolution had almost the opposite effect on Santo Domingo, an effect furthered by twenty-two years of Haitian rule. The occupation crushed what was left of a small Dominican elite of slaveholders, some of whom fled the country taking with them much of their wealth. And once freed, the slave population (still perhaps 15 percent of the total at this time[88]) chose not to continue laboring on others' estates for meager wages, but rather pursued a relatively autonomous life of independent production in Santo Domingo's seemingly endless montes.[89] The trend since the sixteenth century in Santo Domingo of former slaves and their descendants constituting an ever larger independent peasantry was thus furthered by the Haitian occupation and the abolition of slavery.

But an autarkic peasantry living independently of market forces was far from Boyer's goal. The Haitian regime confiscated extensive church lands as well as the properties of exiles and other political enemies. These lands were then distributed to former slaves as well as to soldiers, civil servants, and other clients of the regime.[90] Certainly, these policies impeded plantation agriculture and latifundia and thwarted commercial production in parts of the rural economy.[91] At the same time, however, the Haitian regime's ideology of economic growth and its enormous fiscal needs (especially after having agreed in 1825 to compensate France for property confiscated during the Haitian Revolution) inspired state efforts to promote cash crop production and peasants' integration into the market.[92] State land was ceded to freed slaves and peasants on the condition that it be fully cultivated, at least in part with export crops. For similar reasons, Boyer enacted strong measures favoring agriculture over cattle, such as the law permitting agriculturalists to kill any stray animal that had damaged their crops.[93] Finally, the Haitian ruler promulgated radical legislation aimed at consolidating private property, eliminat-

ing terrenos comuneros, and therein acquiring further property for distribution. For this purpose, he ordered a national cadastral survey to delineate the
individual property each person was entitled to by law. In 1834 all claimants
were required to submit titles for verification by a certain date or sacrifice
their property rights to the state.[94]

These demands for property reform and commercial agriculture were effectively resisted by both the old cattle elite and much of the peasantry, and
would help secure the demise of Haiti's rule over Santo Domingo. In 1843,
under Boyer's successor, General Charles Hérard, protests forced the regime
to repeal its land legislation.[95] The grievances these laws produced would be
made clear in the 1844 manifesto declaring Dominican independence. In
listing its "causes for separation" from Haiti, the independence leaders excoriated the Haitian regime for having "prohibited for the state's own benefit
the community of terrenos comuneros . . . [thus] resulting in the destruction
of animal husbandry and the impoverishment of a multitude of families."
Interestingly, nationalist and culturalist justifications were scarcely emphasized in the manifesto, suggesting that it was threats to traditional rural practices more than national or ethnic identity that mobilized popular support for
the movement.[96] Dominican forces achieved independence with surprising
ease in 1844.

Boyer was doubtless perplexed that not only elite Dominicans but many
peasants had refused to cooperate with his land policies.[97] Certainly, the
church and Dominican exiles who had lost their property would oppose the
Haitian regime, as would those claiming great quantities of land without clear
or sufficient title. In addition, many co-owners of terrenos comuneros might
not be receptive, especially if they had been able to leverage a minimum of
land pesos into unrestricted access to large estates. Yet why had titleless peasants not been supporters of policies in which land was supposed to be freely
distributed to squatters, the landless, and former slaves? The answer to this
question was not simply that land reform served only as a pretext for state
appropriation and distribution to cronies of the regime, nor that the Haitian
regime did not understand the significance and utility of terrenos comuneros.
These issues, along with rural vagrancy laws and new taxes, did contribute to
widespread frustration with Haitian rule and aid the Dominican independence movement.[98] But, above all, the Haitian leaders never grasped that peso
title owners' "tolerance" of squatters meant that there was minimal popular
interest in agrarian reform. Given the scarce population and cattle ranchers'
unintensive forms of land use, peasants had access to the land they needed
without legal titles.[99]

The Haitian project of fostering small property owners obliged to cultivate cash crops remained relatively unattractive to the peasantry in most of the country, compared with exploiting the country's vast open range, immense woods, and multiplying pigs, cattle, goats, and other animals. The appeal of this way of life included its autonomy, the relatively small amount of labor time it required, and, in most instances, the comparatively high degree of subsistence security it provided.[100] As descendants of slaves, moreover, peasants may have taken particular solace in their freedom from the orders of superiors, control over their own production and time, and unconstrained geographic mobility. But the preference for subsistence exploitation rather than the development of commercial farming was also shaped by economic constraints. This is made clear by the fact that in those areas where agriculture could thrive because of soil fertility and profitable markets, Dominicans did welcome the Haitian project. In the highly fertile areas of the north central Cibao where peasant tobacco production had already been expanding and fixed property spontaneously developing, Haitian rural policies reportedly fostered substantial support.[101] As a result of state interventions—such as an 1830 agreement to purchase at "a fair price" all the tobacco that farmers produced—and two decades of political stability under Haitian rule, tobacco production climbed approximately sixfold, from around 300,000 pounds in 1822 to some 2 million pounds in 1842. Historian Michiel Baud has suggested that this was why the Cibao—by far the nation's most agriculturally advanced region at the time—made little contribution to the 1844 struggle for independence from Haiti.[102]

Overall, peasants in the nineteenth-century Dominican Republic pursued a way of life oriented around subsistence exploitation and the open range, except in the relatively few circumstances in which commercial agriculture offered inducements sufficient to secure their interest.[103] Initially, popular desires for freedom, land, and autonomy fostered support for Haitian annexation among slaves and peasants of color. But those same desires ultimately mobilized popular opposition to the Haitian occupation, when Boyer attempted to impose a new mode of existence upon those exploiting los montes.

Despite the rapid defeat of the Haitian regime, the annexation to Haiti left an important legacy in the Dominican Republic. For one, the Haitian occupation had quickly eliminated white racial privileges and legal discrimination in Santo Domingo precisely at the time that they became more salient in Cuba in the context of its staggering expansion of plantation slavery.[104] After independence from Haiti in 1844, whites would not again dominate state power in the Dominican Republic during the nineteenth century.[105] In order for the 1844 independence movement to succeed (in contrast to the stillborn

1821 struggle), and to quell internal rebellions, it was obliged to explicitly reject any return of slavery and publicly affirm racial unity. The independence movement's military forces and leadership consisted largely of persons of color, such as General José Joaquín Puello and Francisco del Rosario Sánchez.[106] And when in 1861 the Dominican government voluntarily reannexed the country to Spain, the War of Restoration erupted with massive popular support, and by 1865 the Spaniards were ejected. This war began as a peasant rebellion, but, according to historian Frank Moya Pons, soon took on the appearance of a "racial war," in light of the extensive mobilization of the non-white majority against the Spanish.[107] For the remaining decades of the century, the Dominican presidency would be occupied mostly by persons of African descent, including Buenaventura Báez, the child of a slave mother, and Ulises Heureaux, the son of a Haitian father and Saint Thomasian mother.

These political leaders would be variously stigmatized by opponents for their lineage, physical appearance, and supposedly dubious Dominican nationality.[108] And European culture and appearance would continue to be privileged by elite Dominicans. In the early 1870s, one New England traveler to the Dominican Republic was struck by how an intense sensitivity to color or shade distinctions among the upper class coexisted with a high level of legal and political racial equality:

Although the Dominicans are a mixed race . . . there is some species of gradation, according to the "amount of coffee," as the phrase is here. This was explained to me by a lady of the city of Santiago de los Caballeros. . . . One might philosophize upon the peculiar system of calculation . . . but . . . the government here knows no such arithmetic, and counts in its service all "points of coffee" indiscriminately, many of the most able being quite black. Still, it is impossible to avoid notice of this feeling, because it exists very strongly in Santo Domingo.[109]

Contradictions abounded between the relative absence of racial discrimination in political and legal realms and both an unabashed aesthetic racism, or more precisely colorism, and culturalist prejudices valorizing practices associated with Europe and disparaging those associated with Africa. These contradictions would continue to prevail as the nation's peasantry and population of color consolidated and expanded their power and status in the nineteenth century—the consequence, in part, of their crucial role in staffing numerous independence and caudillo rebellions—even while they suffered ideological attacks by urban, elite, and lighter-skinned Dominicans. Only at the onset of the twentieth century, with economic growth, the emergence of a national bourgeoisie, and the diffusion of scientific racism throughout Europe and the Americas, did whites reassert political dominance, for instance occupying the presidency until Rafael Trujillo seized power in 1930.[110]

The Haitian occupation of the Dominican Republic completed a three-century-long transition from slavery to a free peasantry. Haitian rule thus put the Dominican Republic on a course different from that being followed by Cuba and Puerto Rico during the nineteenth century, wherein plantation slavery expanded, racial hierarchy hardened, and the peasantry declined under Spanish control. Juan Bosch blamed the Haitian Revolution (and previous Spanish neglect) for the Dominican Republic's "historical arrhythmia." The Haitian Revolution had thwarted a critical opportunity for the Dominican Republic to redeem itself from the "fatal consequences" of the decline of the sixteenth-century plantation economy and to re-enter "the great current of capitalist development," therein "synchronizing its history with America's rhythms."[111] Yet, despite this common positivist wail in Dominican historiography, the story of the Dominican peasantry presented in this chapter illuminates another perspective. The spectacular failure of Santo Domingo's sixteenth-century plantation society, the long history of Spanish neglect, the dearth of commercial agriculture, the irrelevance of legal property forms, and the transformations provoked by the Haitian Revolution and the Haitian occupation all provided the conditions under which successive generations of Dominicans were able to liberate themselves from slavery and constitute a vital, independent peasantry. Analogous processes occurred throughout the Caribbean in varying degrees.[112] Some peasants had thrived even in the interstices and marginal spaces of slave plantation systems and in the internal frontiers of these colonies to the extent that they existed.[113] But the dimensions of the transition from slavery to a free peasantry in Santo Domingo were comparable probably only to postrevolutionary Haiti; both Haiti and the Dominican Republic became peasant nations in the nineteenth century. Moreover, while the Haitian and other non-Hispanic peasantries in the Caribbean expanded primarily after the abolition of slavery during the 1800s, Santo Domingo's large independent peasantry extended back to the 1600s, long before emancipation, and would continue into the late twentieth century.

This enduring and important peasant population would condition the contours of Dominican history and the Dominican nation. The peasantry forged an essentially agro-pastoral and autarkic economy across this relatively large Caribbean colony. And it secured and valorized land access and subsistence production within an ethos of freedom, self-determination, and opposition to slavery and, subsequently, to dependence on the uncertainties of wage labor and commercial production. Also, the peasantry's relative autonomy from Spanish and urban control and its own minimal racial segmentation impeded, it seems, the establishment of metropolitan racial groups, identities, and, to some extent, hierarchy and furthered the possibilities for a common, protonational sense of local or creole culture in the Dominican countryside. On the other hand, the perpetuation of racial slavery and Spanish racial ideology simultaneously sustained and, to a degree, diffused European forms of racism. This contradictory set of conditions gave rise to notions of race and modes of racism in the Dominican Republic wherein physical differences have marked individuals along a racist color continuum but have generally not constituted social groups or communities. Thus, despite the prevalence of this colorist mode of racism, those considered Dominican have not been divided by "race" in the sense of collective ascriptions of otherness.[114] The seeming absence of a black identity, and indeed any collective identities or notions of community based on color among nonwhites, in the Dominican Republic—to this day puzzling to outsiders—doubtless stemmed originally from the lack of plantation slavery since the early 1600s along with the existence of a majority population that was free and of color hundreds of years before formal emancipation.[115]

Finally, the Dominican peasantry would both condition and help consolidate an independent Dominican nation. It would play a critical role both in overthrowing colonial rule and in resisting urban domination of the nation's politics and culture through a series of successful independence wars and rural uprisings mobilized by regional caudillos during the country's long nineteenth century. Although Spanish colonists had settled permanently in significant—though still relatively small—numbers, imposed the dominant urban and official discourses, and monopolized political power, they never truly controlled Santo Domingo's rural population. At the same time, among that rural population, the history of limited slavery and plantations and the cross-racial popular mobilization in numerous independence wars and caudillo rebellions shaped a less class-divided and more racially fluid creole society than in the non-Hispanic, early modern Caribbean.

The periods of Spanish and Haitian rule in Santo Domingo thus established a contradictory legacy of domination and freedom. Exploiting the opportunities opened up by Spanish neglect and economic underdevelopment and by Haitian policies of emancipation and agrarian reform, an independent peasantry grew steadily out of the horrors of colonization, Indian genocide, and the New World's first but unsuccessful experiment with a plantation economy based on the labor of enslaved Africans. On the one hand, during the Spanish colonial period peasants' lives remained economically harsh and marginal ones, and were constrained by a racist and oppressive slave-based colonial order that to a large extent continued to prevail at least in and around the cities. On the other hand, slaves-turned-peasants, their descendants, and marginal colonists constituted an agro-pastoral class with a substantial measure of autonomy and subsistence security. Their geographic dispersion, mobility, and land access impeded colonial efforts to capture their labor and to impose on them the laws and ideologies of metropolitan elites.[116]

Not only were commercial and state forces glaring by their absence in much of the Dominican countryside in the colonial period but, as we will see in the following chapter, they remained scarce in the nineteenth century, only modestly affecting most of the nation's largely autarkic peasantry. When commercial forces did develop and begin to threaten peasants' way of life in the early twentieth century, peasants' long history of autonomy would mold both their politics and those of the Trujillo regime, which promised to preserve and accommodate, but also profoundly compromise, that autonomy. In this way, the nation's independent peasantry would continue to shape the Dominican Republic, even as that peasantry would, in turn, be reconfigured under Trujillo. As we will see, Trujillo's particular brand of rural populism would thus finally bridge the centuries-long divide between the city and countryside.

2 Imagining Modernity

Peasants, Property, and the State in the Century after Independence

The nineteenth century was in many ways the century of the peasantry in the Dominican Republic. In most Latin American nations during this period, regions of peasant autarky became increasingly isolated in the face of commercial development. But in the bulk of the Dominican Republic, subsistence exploitation prevailed into the twentieth century, and the country remained relatively closed off from Atlantic markets. Given limited commercial opportunities, Dominicans had few incentives to accumulate land and forcibly modernize land tenure arrangements and property laws. In much of the country, better-off Dominicans continued to rely on unenclosed ranching. And peasants' pastoral traditions of collective and temporary land use provided few impediments to this economy. The nineteenth-century Dominican state did seek to eliminate peasants' autarkic practices, promulgating vagrancy, private property, and stock fencing laws, as occurred throughout the Americas and Europe at this time. In practice, however, these remained bootless efforts by governments backed only by a weak economic elite and paralyzed by a seemingly endless series of independence wars and caudillo uprisings to topple the president in power. Thus the nation's relative poverty, isolation, and political instability permitted the perpetuation of customary practices serving peasant interests—namely, the free use of unfenced and uncultivated lands, which remained abundant in most of the country.

In the latter nineteenth and early twentieth centuries, incentives for land accumulation and private property began to develop in some areas. Specifically, commercial agriculture expanded in parts of the Cibao and, more dramatically, around the Eastern coastal towns of San Pedro de Macorís and subsequently La Romana, where primarily foreign interests established large sugar plantations. This land accumulation spurred new processes of land commercialization, enclosure, and dispossession that would gradually spread to other parts of the country. In the early twentieth century, peasants were thus facing for the first time formidable threats to their way of life and customary rights to the land.

The sudden spread of foreign sugar plantations across large swaths of the

East and the beginnings of peasant dispossession had undesirable effects also from the perspective of some members of a small but growing lettered class. A number of intellectual and political figures were disillusioned with this first real brush with modernity and global forces since the 1500s. These men perceived the monocultural enclave economy that developed in the Eastern sugar areas to be detrimental to the nation, rural stability, and urban food markets. They started to reconsider the prevailing orthodox liberal support for foreign capital and the free flow of market forces and to envisage instead a small-farmer mode of development that would require increased state intervention vis-à-vis both foreign capital and the peasantry. This group of Dominican intellectuals in no way rejected the pursuit of modernity and still demanded that peasants abandon their autarkic lives of subsistence exploitation. But they espoused an alternative project of state-controlled modernity that would integrate the peasantry as farmers—that is, sedentary, surplus-producing agriculturalists—who would contribute to a model of economic growth and social transformation considered more suitable and beneficial to the nation.

Support for this alternative project also gained impetus from strong nationalist currents that developed in response to the sudden expansion of U.S. imperialism in the Caribbean and Central America in the period from 1898 to 1934; that is, to the spate of U.S. military interventions in the region stimulated by efforts to secure propitious environments for expanding U.S. capital, political influence, and military power abroad. In particular, the U.S. occupation of the Dominican Republic between 1916 and 1924 generated fierce and widespread nationalist resentment. This gave rise to the Nationalist Party, which formed part of the burgeoning intellectual and political movement embracing an alternative model of modernity based on Dominican small farmers.[1] This movement would ultimately help shape the culture of the early Trujillo state and its agrarian policies.

The threats posed to peasants by ongoing processes of land accumulation and commercialization were compounded by the U.S. military government in the Dominican Republic, when it promulgated the country's first clear system for adjudicating private property. This system would serve the interests of the largest land claimants in the country, U.S.-owned sugar companies, by legally consolidating their property claims to areas formerly exploited and still squatted on by thousands of peasants. And yet because the U.S. military dictatorship made the initial adjudication of property rights flow primarily from possession rather than titles, this system would have contradictory effects across time and space, including potentially positive ones for the peasantry. It opened up the possibility of awarding land to peasant squatters where sugar and latifundia had not yet invaded. Peasant squatters would, in fact, secure much of the nation's lands during the Trujillo regime on the basis of possession alone. This chapter will examine the shifting balance of power between the Dominican peasantry and the state in the century after independence, the complex and confused process by which clear property rights were claimed and defined, and the emergence of a nationalist-populist project of modernity among Dominican intellectuals and state officials. This history will set the stage for understanding the rural policies and legitimation project of the Trujillo state and an otherwise unreadable alliance that developed between Trujillo and the peasantry.

Peasant Vitality and State Weakness in the Early National Period

When the Dominican Republic achieved independence from Haiti in 1844, the nation was not an agricultural but rather a pastoral one. To the extent that an economic elite existed, it was composed mainly of *hateros* (large cattle ranchers) who had recently stepped into the vacuum created when most of the colonial upper classes left the country in the tumultuous era commencing with the Haitian Revolution.[2] One Cuban observer remarked in 1860 that, with the exception of a few pockets of tobacco farming near Santiago in the central Cibao and of small- and medium-scale sugar production in certain Southern locations (the meager remains of the sixteenth-century sugar industry), "no agriculture exists" in the Dominican Republic.[3] The colonial legacy bequeathed an economy in which not only commercial but also subsistence agriculture played a limited role. In a few areas, namely parts of the fertile Cibao region, peasants had begun to produce a significant agricultural surplus for the market. And peasant woodcutting together with large-scale timber operations had developed in parts of the country after the Crown made logging legal at the end of the eighteenth century. Overall, though, peasants were mostly subsistence-oriented and depended as much on open-range stock breeding, hunting, foraging, and fishing as on farming individual plots. The nation itself was also largely autarkic, having relatively few imports and exports tying its small and dispersed population (only 10.4 persons per square mile in 1860) to the Atlantic world.[4]

Yet furthering commercial agriculture was seen as crucial by political and intellectual leaders, as well as a new stratum of Dominican merchants and farmers in the Cibao who would challenge the political dominance of large cattle ranchers over the course of the nineteenth century.[5] These leaders sought to promote commercial agriculture to augment the nation's wealth, expand the state's tax base, and inexpensively feed urban denizens. Over the next century the Dominican state would seek to further surplus production through various policies intended to compel peasants to renounce their subsistence economy. State leaders and many intellectuals would justify these efforts by lauding commercial agriculture as a requisite to what they imagined to constitute progress and an advanced civilization and by condemning the peasant economy as nothing more than rural idleness. This ideology reproduced the discourse of the former Spanish Bourbon, French, and Haitian rulers.[6] Both colonial regimes and the independent Dominican state essentially defined any noncommercial, noncapitalist existence as vagrancy.

The post-Haitian-occupation Dominican government acted quickly to restrict the freedom that peasants enjoyed and to compel them to produce a surplus. Local regulations and national police laws in 1848 and 1855 ambitiously sought to extend the fledgling state's arm far into rural life. The 1855 law established for the first time a system of alcaldes *pedáneos* in which a local authority was named for each "section" into which the country's communes, or municipalities, were divided—a small, often isolated community of perhaps a few hundred people, or else a neighborhood within a town.[7] These officials constituted the lowest rung of the nation's judicial police. They were responsible for ensuring order and enforcing new prohibitions on cultural and leisure activities seen as obstacles to production—such as gambling, drinking, and late-night festivities—and even on abandoning the career dictated by one's father (thus reinforcing patriarchal control over family labor). The new laws also restricted peasant mobility. Relocating required official confirmation that one had an "honest means of subsistence" or a "useful profession" at one's destination. And the laws required all inhabitants to donate their labor for the upkeep of local roads.[8]

Above all, new legislation sought to promote agricultural production and eliminate rural "vagrancy," which these laws deemed "the origin of all vices" and was vaguely defined as the failure to produce "in proportion to one's ability"—that is, the availability of family labor.[9] Unlike vagrancy laws in much of the Americas, Dominican laws were not aimed at ensuring a supply of wage laborers for a growing agro-export sector.[10] Given the still bleak prospects for commercial agriculture in the Dominican Republic and the limited power the state had to coerce peasants, it sought instead to expand peasant production and thereby create a marketable surplus to feed the towns, supply external markets, and build state revenues through taxes on trade. Thus the laws stipulated that alcaldes pedáneos periodically verify that peasants were farming an adequately sized area (generally understood, as in the colonial era, to be at least 10 tareas per adult male), and had properly fenced their plots to prevent animal intrusions.[11] "Vagrants" without adequate-sized plots were subject to arrest and compulsory community labor unless they immediately cultivated sufficient land.[12] Peasants were also legally obligated to devote part of their plots to export crops.[13]

Furthermore, the 1848 and 1855 Police Laws sought to systematize and enforce terrenos comuneros as a system of exclusive property rights by prohibiting those without legal title or authorization by a co-owner from entering or hunting animals in any comunero areas. To help enforce this prohibition, the laws required hunters to present the ears (or hide) of all kills to local authorities to demonstrate either that they were unmarked or that the insignia on them was that corresponding to the hunter. Similar rules obtained for restricting wood cutting to the proprietors of comunero wood rights. These laws were aimed at curbing squatters and poachers in terrenos comuneros but stopped short of abolishing the comunero system itself in favor of absolute, individualized property.[14] Although many state and intellectual leaders believed that this form of joint land ownership based on use rights, collective exploitation, and overlapping titles impeded market forces and economic development, the state dared not eliminate it.[15] It was only recently that the Haitian occupation government had tried to do so, only to meet stiff resistance from ranchers, peso title holders, and peasants.

These new laws represented the ideals and goals of government leaders, rather than what could actually be implemented at the time. The central state was far too weak to intervene in and retool rural society to such an extent. In 1860 the state drew on a mere $200,000 in revenues.[16] During most of the period from 1844 to 1916, there was no real national army but instead, as sociologist Harry Hoetink wrote, "small [armed] groups that, competing, offered their services in the political marketplace," in exchange for state jobs and favors. Thus the government was periodically overthrown by armies composed only of several hundred troops.[17] And to build these armies, regional caudillos competed for the adherence of peasants by offering benefits or protection that in turn limited the national state's ability to dominate the countryside.[18] The dearth of roads and infrastructure across the country also contributed to regionalism, limited central state officials' access to rural areas, and helped "put the capital further from its provinces [and left] it more isolated, weaker, and even impotent to exercise its mandate," as Pedro Bonó stated in 1881.[19]

Under these conditions, state measures to reorganize and regulate the countryside could hardly be carried out. Peasants' customary practices and constructs of property continued to prevail. Throughout the nineteenth century terrenos comuneros were used in practice almost equally by those without titles as by those with them.[20] Sometimes whole towns formed within terrenos comuneros, as Boca Chica did in the site of Hato Viejo and San Pedro de Macorís within Yeguada del Sur.[21] And peasants remained dispersed and mobile, frequently shifting plots and, to some extent, residence. Without sedentary practices, concentrated communities, national infrastructure, or even tractable local leaders, the nineteenth-century Dominican countryside remained largely impenetrable and illegible to the central state, as it had been in the colonial era.[22] As a result, the government could hardly force peasants' integration into the market. Rather, until at least the end of the nineteenth century, that integration would be largely on peasants' own terms or not at all.

One aspect of peasant life that the Police Laws and other state measures did not attempt to change at this time was crianza libre. Given the influence of large ranchers on the state, national stock fencing laws, even for isolated areas, were delayed until the last years of the century. Before then, municipal governments had sometimes declared "agricultural zones" within their jurisdiction, thus requiring stock fencing. But, by default, all other areas permitted the free-ranging of animals.[23] This practice was ardently opposed by the nation's lettered class. In 1894, later secretary of agriculture Emiliano Tejera contended that the open range of unenclosed livestock was the "true cause" of the country's agricultural stagnation. Instead of ranchers having to corral their animals, it was agriculturalists who had to erect fences, in order to protect their crops from roving livestock—a formidable disincentive to expanding cultivation. Under these conditions, Tejera wrote wryly, "What is astonishing is not that there are so few agriculturalists, but rather that there is even one." Tejera also argued that crianza libre contributed to political upheaval, writing, "With a decrease in freely roaming pigs [to hunt], the number of revolutionaries would decline, because rarely will a man of work with resources to lose become a revolutionary, and when free-ranging animals are no longer permitted there will be many men of work."[24] The expatriate Spanish agronomist José Ramón Abad equally condemned crianza libre as a "pernicious, no good, fatal system . . . that maintained the countryside in laziness, bad faith and deceit, in order to foster a limited number of scrawny and pathetic animals for our consumption."[25]

Although this portrayal of crianza libre as the ruin of rural life was nearly universal among Dominican intellectuals and state officials at this time, this perspective was not shared by most peasants themselves. As long as free lands remained available, crianza libre was closer to an "original affluent society" than to what Abad referred to as an "absolute evil."[26] Despite the rigors of hunting and foraging, and the limitations that this subsistence exploitation placed on overall economic growth, crianza libre permitted even the poorest peasants to live off of livestock and wild animals. Just as these conditions had facilitated the transition from slavery to an independent peasantry, the immense, extant open range continued to underwrite that independence generations later.

Still in the late twentieth century, many elderly Dominican peasants recalled the ease of raising animals on the open range. In numerous interviews, peasants described how pigs, cattle, and goats had roamed freely and how those not yet claimed with a distinctive earmark or brand (engraved with a heated machete) could be hunted and eaten or marked and released back into the wild to graze and breed. The main labor involved in crianza libre was caring for new-born animals. Baby calves had to be overseen until their navels healed and were no longer prone to infections. They were then marked with the owner's insignia and let loose to roam at will. Juan Justo, an elderly peasant living in the far Eastern town of Higüey romanticized this past as being as distinct from the present "as heaven from earth."[27] Antonio Amparo from a northeastern area near Miches believed: "That life was bountiful. One only needed to look for what one needed and there it was for the taking."[28] And Negro Castillo, also from Higüey, explained that though cultivating even half a hectare (6 tareas) was difficult in the old days, because one had to fence one's farm to protect it from roaming animals, overall "one lived better [then] because there was so much meat."[29]

Contrary to intellectuals' critiques of crianza libre, even agriculture was recalled as easier in certain ways in this pastoral economy. Fencing one's small conuco was burdensome, but not overly so because wood was readily available in el monte. When a fence around one's plot rotted after a couple of years, one cleared land for farming elsewhere and used the newly fallen wood to build a fence there.[30] Shifting plots every couple of years meant not only that fences did not have to be repaired, but also that little if any weeding was necessary, soil was always at its most fertile, and farming could be done without plows or fertilizer. José Mota Rivera explained that his family in Mata de Palma del Seibo would clear a new plot every few years as soon as the old conuco became overgrown with weeds and lost its "virginity" and "power."[31] And Mariano d'Oleo Mesa explained that the "flower" of slashing and burning fertilized the soil and maximized yields.[32]

This erstwhile rural economy was remembered for its cultural practices as well as its material conditions. Elderly peasants portrayed a culture of mutual aid and trust associated with the open range. As animals roamed at will, peasants depended on each other to keep track of where their animals were and even to care for them to a certain degree. Indeed, despite peasants' dispersed residences, crianza libre fostered an imagined community of interdependence, as animals traveled sometimes dozens of kilometers away, requiring that people whom one had never met cooperate actively in the system.[33] By all accounts, stealing occurred less frequently than one might expect. At times, one peasant family would take in another's pregnant cow and then care for the newborn calf until its owner arrived.[34] Other forms of collective behavior also marked the "old days," such as the often-described custom of sharing meat with neighbors whenever an animal was slaughtered.[35] When asked about how the old days were, Francisco Soriano, an elderly peasant from Ramón Santana, stressed the pastoral economy's reliance on mutual aid: "One lived by marking [animals]. You had your brand and your earmark. You released a mother pig here, and it went over there, far away, fifteen or twenty kilometers. And there [someone said], 'Oh, this brand isn't [from here]. This is the brand of a person from Ramón Santana,' or 'This is their earmark.' "[36]

The first legislation prohibiting crianza libre was passed in 1895, but it would not be widely implemented until decades later. Entitled "Concerning the Raising of Domestic Animals in Pasture," this new law reversed the 1855 Police Law's requirement that crops rather than animals be fenced by their owners. (Years later, after being appointed secretary of agriculture, Tejera would quip: "Strange that those legislators [of the Police Laws] did not also decree that . . . all the honorable inhabitants be locked up with their belongings while all the thieves remain in complete freedom.")[37] The new law was designed to facilitate a slow but steady retrenchment of crianza libre by unilaterally declaring all densely populated or cultivated areas to be agricultural zones.[38]

Even though it was enacted during a period of unprecedented political control and economic growth under the Ulises (Lilís) Heureaux dictatorship (1882–84; 1887–99), the law against crianza libre met immediate opposition and galvanized efforts to overthrow the government. Less than five months after the law was passed the state was forced to repeal it under pressure from the large ranchers, who had long been the peasantry's powerful allies in the fight to preserve the open range. A provisional, weaker law was passed in 1900, and new areas continued to be declared agricultural zones, reportedly increasing agricultural production substantially in the central Cibao province of Santiago.[39] But overall these reforms were effectively resisted and had minimal impact. The general inspector of Santo Domingo complained in 1908 that "the age-old, pernicious practices of crianza libre remain deeply entrenched in the spirit of our rural population."[40] Only in 1911 was relatively forceful fencing legislation again passed in favor of farming.[41] Yet, even then change would remain slow and problematic. In 1912 the secretary of the interior stated that crianza libre continued to represent the "greatest obstacle and worst enemy" for the country's development and prosperity.[42]

Although ineffective at the time, the 1895 legislation marked the end of an era and adumbrated the direction in which powerful new agricultural interests and ideologies would take the country. Large cattle ranchers were losing political influence to new agricultural interests, notably merchants and intermediaries primarily in the Cibao and gigantic sugar corporations as well as sugar *colonos* mainly in the East, all of which opposed crianza libre.[43] Also, many of the old hateros were, of their own volition, beginning to corral their animals and fence their ranches in order to supervise their animals more closely and breed more valuable livestock. And some turned to agricultural pursuits as they became more profitable with the beginnings of infrastructural development and new markets in the early twentieth century.[44] Thus the open range began to vanish and crianza libre became increasingly problematic for peasants. This transformation occurred first in parts of the Cibao and the East and continued to spread only slowly elsewhere. But the dissipation of the open range heralded a sea change for the country and a new world for the Dominican peasantry.

Rural Transformation and Competing Visions of Modernity in the Late Nineteenth Century: The East and the Cibao

At the end of the 1800s, commercial agriculture began to expand and pastoral practices declined in the Cibao region and the lands near the Eastern coastal town of San Pedro, but they did so in strikingly different fashions. These transformations were warmly welcomed by government leaders frustrated by peasant autarky and impatient for wealth and revenues via commercial agriculture. But economic development also provoked unanticipated consequences in the Eastern sugar zones, producing misgivings among members of a new lettered class emerging in tandem with the expansion of commerce.[45] For some of the nation's prominent observers, the changes occurring in the two regions came to represent polar models of economic growth: small Dominican farmers producing a marketable surplus in the Cibao versus foreign plantations, monoculture, and proletarianization in the East. While developments in the East soon occasioned sharp criticism and disillusionment, the Cibao was valorized as the ideal paradigm for growth and progress.

In the last quarter of the nineteenth century, cacao and, to a lesser degree, coffee production grew dramatically in the Cibao, while tobacco continued to expand and remained the region's principal export. Several major railroads were also constructed in the region, which facilitated the movement of crops, especially cacao, to nearby ports.[46] Agricultural development was stimulated in part by the arrival of a number of better-off European immigrants in this period, who became merchants and farmers. But production in the Cibao remained primarily in the hands of Dominican peasant families. And while their cultivation of cash crops was substantial, they never became highly dependent on the market. As historian Michiel Baud has shown, peasants in the Cibao maintained and even privileged subsistence production. They thus perpetuated and expanded their autonomy through a partial allocation of land and resources to cash crops.[47]

On the other hand, the sugar zones, primarily in the East, witnessed seismic economic transformations that destroyed the pre-existing way of life. Beginning in the 1870s, numerous sugar plantations and mills were established near Santo Domingo and, above all, in the contiguous province of San Pedro de Macorís (part of El Seibo until 1882), where monteros and better-off ranchers had formerly reigned supreme. The area enticed sugar companies with its vast, untamed landscape and proximity to the coast, permitting easy transport of sugar. The revival of the Dominican sugar industry was triggered by the exodus of several thousand Cubans to the Dominican Republic during the unsuccessful Ten Years War (1868–78) for Cuban independence. Many arrived prepared to organize sugar operations and eager to profit from the high sugar prices during the war. In the wake of the sugar crisis beginning in the early 1880s, when the development of European beet sugar led to a glut in the world market and prices plummeted, a large number of the country's mills went out of business. Subsequently, U.S. investors began displacing Cuban and Dominican interests and soon dominated the industry. In the early twentieth century, U.S. capital spread widely into El Seibo, and sugar production expanded dramatically. Canefields engulfed the lands near the coastal town of La Romana where also a pastoral economy had previously prevailed, along with small cacao farms and banana plantations in recent decades. With a few notable exceptions, the state welcomed foreign investors, who seemed to promise an instant modernity via expanding sugar exports, new technology, and fresh capital.[48]

These two modes of commercial agriculture produced divergent consequences for the populations of the Eastern sugar zones and the Cibao. In the latter, most of the peasantry continued to exploit their own land, produce their own subsistence, and maintain substantial autonomy while at the same time taking advantage of expanding markets and somewhat improved infrastructure to boost cultivation of cash crops.[49] The development of commercial agriculture in the Dominican Cibao contributed to peasant prosperity for a relatively long period of time, even compared with other Latin American countries characterized by an initial abundance of land.[50] In much of the East, on the other hand, the growth of sugar, which quickly became the

country's most important export, relied on a massive number of wage laborers and steadily exhausted the open range upon which the regional economy
and society had been based.

The transformation of the Cibao is evidence that Dominican peasants had
no inherent aversion to commercial agriculture. To the contrary, when offered adequate incentives—accessible markets, remunerative prices, and the
requisite infrastructure—peasants actively sought new lands and opportunities to expand their cultivation of cash crops without any pressure to do so
from taxation or any other compulsion.[51] An analogous readiness to participate in labor markets, without being obliged to do so by dispossession, was
demonstrated among peasants in the Eastern sugar region. Initially, wages
offered by the sugar corporations were high and attracted many peasants.
Cutting cane often complemented subsistence production performed by laborers' families, or by laborers themselves during the long dead season in
sugar production.[52] In 1884 there were six thousand sugar workers in the
country, only five hundred of whom were immigrant laborers.[53] After the
1884 crisis, though, when sugar prices dropped, the Dominican industry
faced a major decline that lasted until 1902. Consequently, wages for cane-
cutters fell to a level that, given peasants' continued access to land, no longer
attracted sufficient native labor. Sugar companies responded by shifting to
immigrant workers, at first primarily British West Indians, who were themselves driven from other areas of the Caribbean thrown into depression following the 1884 crisis.[54] But even with lower wages, semiproletarianization
remained attractive to some Dominican peasants, given that most expected
to be employed for a limited period and then return to their conucos after
accumulating a small measure of capital. This was the experience, for example, of Tavares Blanc, who was a young man living in the northern frontier
region in the 1920s, where there had been ample food and land but little
means of securing money. When available at all, wage labor offered only a
fraction of sugar wages. So, eager to earn money and seeking adventure,
Tavares left for San Pedro to cut cane. He returned home a few years later
with exciting stories to tell, new shoes, and enough money to acquire a pregnant cow.[55]

Peasants living in the Eastern sugar region also offered little initial resistance to sugar companies' accumulation of immense properties. Oral histories I completed in the region suggest that many peasants willingly sold their
land, or technically their improvements (that is, their crops), to sugar companies, and left the area they were exploiting. One elderly peasant I spoke
with believed that the landowners and sugar corporations "did not force
anyone." Those who sold their land were "people who had certain needs and

obligations. And they believed that selling their little pieces of land, they would be able to resolve their needs."[56] Given that at first lands in contiguous areas remained plentiful and accessible, a small but novel sum of money was sufficient to convince many to leave land that until recently had been considered to have virtually no monetary value. Peasants hardly suspected that the land frontier in this region would be exhausted within a generation. And yet that is exactly what occurred. In stark contrast to the Cibao, almost all those who lived in the Eastern sugar areas were eventually cut off from their means of production.

While the state profited from the rising revenues ushered in by agro-industry, the perspective of some of the nation's leading thinkers began to shift. Despite his liberal world-view, Pedro Bonó was the first major Dominican writer to critique the prevailing ideology of progress. In 1884 he condemned the antinational and antipopular dimensions of the country's new sugar industry: "I have seen the transformation of the East; property transferred almost free of charge to new occupants concealing themselves under the guise of Progress. Progress it would be if what was occurring was progress for Dominicans, if the old peasantry . . . were in part the owners of the sugar mills and plantations. . . . But instead of that, while before they were poor and rough, at least they were owners, now they are coarser and poorer proletarians. What form of progress is that?"[57] Bonó rejected what he perceived as the hollow and invidious modernity in the Eastern sugar zone. Technology and foreign capital had only turned poor but autonomous peasants into poorer and less autonomous proletarians. The "guise of Progress" was, in other words, obscuring and rationalizing growing inequity. Bonó fractured the presumed linkage of technology and large-scale commercial agriculture with improving general living standards and the advancement of the nation, and argued that there were multiple paths to, or forms of, modernity. Bonó's perspective would gain adherents over the next two generations among Dominican writers and policy-makers, as they began to discern contradictory effects of the country's incipient modernization and to envisage divergent forms of economic development.

Those like Bonó who criticized the particular mode of modernity unfolding in San Pedro de Macorís reacted against an array of unanticipated and unprecedented social and economic consequences arising from the sugar industry. Even in the best of times, sugar's long "dead period" meant high levels of seasonal unemployment. The sugar industry thus ushered in a new type of vagrancy. Whereas the charge of vagrancy previously had been leveled against peasants living a noncapitalist existence and yielding no surplus to help sustain an expanding state and nonagricultural population, now the term "vagrant" was being applied to unemployed workers who, ironically, represented a consequence of rather than an absence of commercial and capitalist development.[58] Lamenting "the impoverished state" of both agriculture and the peasants who had become proletarians, the Santo Domingo newspaper *El Eco de la Opinión* wrote in 1892: "The poor laborer who until recently faithfully brought home each day the fruits of his labor and satisfied the needs of his family, today wanders the streets without finding anywhere to honorably earn a tiny bit of bread. . . . Lack of labor dissipates his energies, until, as a last desperate resort in his misery, he goes to the corrupt gambling houses that are opened just about everywhere, sacrificing the self-respect he once possessed as someone exerting his will and muscles in an honorable effort to earn a livelihood."[59] Members of the urban, lettered class were beginning to view the rural poor with sympathy rather than simply disdain.

In addition to fueling unemployment, the sugar industry was also criticized for exacerbating rather than ameliorating the problem of feeding the towns. In both Santo Domingo and San Pedro, food became scarce and expensive. In 1884 the Puerto Rican sociologist Eugenio María de Hostos, who lived in the Dominican Republic between 1879 and 1888, joined Bonó in condemning the country's "misguided progress": "Paradoxical as it may seem, the country became poorer [with the rise of sugar plantations], as the State grew wealthier. We have all felt here the daily consequences of that contradiction. We have all been dying of hunger . . . hunger for the crops that spontaneously grow in tropical lands, but which are becoming scarcer every day and therefore more expensive. . . . Of what value is it to a country to have its capital increase if it does not benefit the general good?"[60]

Several writers in the Dominican Republic contrasted the impact of sugar plantations in San Pedro with the perceived salutary expansion of small farming in the Cibao.[61] And this critique took on more explicitly nationalist terms in the post-1898 period as the United States emerged as an imperial power, and particularly after it took control of Dominican customs in progressive steps between 1904 and 1907. For the next almost four decades, the United States would govern this main source of Dominican state revenue, retaining 55 percent of Dominican customs receipts to service the country's foreign debt. (These obligations had been taken over by U.S. bankers from European creditors after their governments sent warships to the Dominican Republic in 1904 to press their claims.)[62] In this context, in 1906 the writer Rafael Abreu Licairac condemned foreign sugar plantations as a "pacific invasion" (*penetración pacífica*) of "progress." He argued that the sugar industry would compromise Dominican sovereignty and dignity if it were not constrained by domestic legislation and international agreements. On the other hand, he romanticized the Cibao's small farmers as an alternative model of modernity, counterposed to both foreign sugar enclaves and the supposedly backward and nomadic pastoral practices of the peasantry still prevailing in most of the country. Abreu portrayed the Cibao as the model the rest of the country needed to adopt so as to end rural stagnation while consolidating the nation and benefiting the peasantry:

There is the true rural life with all its attractions and advantages, characterized by re-munerative work, . . . relative wealth . . . [and] the independence of the producer . . . [who] is more or less ensured that he will not fall into poverty. . . . Every family has its own area of land, which is well cultivated. . . . The greater the distribution of property and the greater diversification of crops, the more wealth is available for the advance of progress and general well-being.[63]

In light of the negative effects of the sugar invasion, an imagined small-farmer mode of development was gaining adherents. Rather than dismissing Dominican peasants as primitive and indolent by nature or trying to tear them completely away from their land and autonomous existence, a new stripe of liberal intellectuals slowly emerged who sought to integrate the peasantry into a modernizing nation.

Numerous political figures and intellectuals, though, still did not adhere to this project. In 1907, for instance, José Ramón López extolled the virtues of the sugar industry while discounting the possibility of a small farmer path to modernity. "Error, gross error," he wrote disdainfully. For peasant agri-culture to succeed, he explained, "it is necessary [that peasants] weed and repair fences. . . . That is beyond the patience and foresight of the average Dominican peasant."[64] And despite mounting demands for new development projects to foster incentives for small farmers, such as roads, public irriga-tion, credit, and the provision of seeds, tools, and technical advice,[65] the early twentieth-century state continued to promote large-scale foreign investment through liberal concessions of state lands and tax exemptions.[66] Peasants could not compete with the sugar companies for government attention, given the capital the latter were pumping into the economy. That capital was desperately sought in the period from 1899 to 1916 in between the Lilís and U.S. military dictatorships. Political leaders then faced an extraordinary fiscal crisis and constant threats from caudillo rebellions that resulted in fifteen different governments in eighteen years.[67] Thus the sugar companies contin ued to expand their control, turning a large portion of the East (and by 1920 a slice of the southern frontier region around the town of Barahona) into a foreign-dominated, monocultural economy relying mostly on immigrant labor and destroying the pre-existing mode of life in the region. Nationalist condemnation of these developments also continued to grow. Even the erstwhile defender of the sugar industry, now Senator José Ramón López, protested in 1911 that growing land monopolization threatened to turn the majority of Dominicans into "servants" and "exploited renters" and thus to undermine public order.[68] Yet many nationalist intellectuals still could not envisage Dominican economic and national redemption flowing from the rural popular classes. These figures turned instead to *arielismo*—an early-twentieth-century Spanish American discourse celebrating the region's putative "Latin" or Spanish culture and idealism (versus Anglo-American materialism)—as a bulwark against escalating U.S. domination and influence.[69]

Nonetheless, the impetus, and the common ground, for an alliance between the peasantry and the state was emerging. In light of the perceived negative consequences of foreign-owned, large-scale agribusiness for various social groups and for national sovereignty, a number of leading Dominicans were moving away from unconditional and undifferentiated support for expanding commercial agriculture. By the 1920s, under the full weight of the U.S. occupations in Haiti and the Dominican Republic, as well as a steep decline in world sugar prices, more and more nationalist thinkers looked to the small Dominican farmer as an alternative for a growing economy.[70] At the same time, peasants were in an increasingly weak position, unable to maintain their pastoral life as the open range began to close down. Indeed, not only their agro-pastoral existence but also their entire identity as independent peasants was threatened by dispossession of even their small conucos and therein compulsory proletarianization. In other words, as the state and intellectuals were increasingly impelled to incorporate the peasantry into their project of modernity, evolving material conditions were simultaneously driving the peasantry to accept some form of modernization—that is, agrarianization—and, gradually, commercial farming. This convergence opened up the possibility for a type of peasant-state compromise after a century of conflict: state maintenance of peasant land access in return for sedentarization, an agricultural surplus, and political loyalty.

However, both the threats to the peasantry and the reformist impetus among intellectuals were developing only gradually. And the state remained too weak and too conditioned by other interests and ideologies to realize the increasing potential for a peasant-state pact. In fact, that would have to wait until Trujillo seized the presidency and forged a powerful state, comparatively autonomous from pre-existing elite interests. But before turning to Trujillo's paradoxically reformist—and even populist—brutal dictatorship, we need to examine major transformations in property laws that, in conjunction with land and agricultural commercialization, began to threaten peasants' subsistence, land access, and way of life in the period from 1900 to 1930.

The Division of Terrenos Comuneros and the Rise of Private Property

The contradictions inherent in the system of terrenos comuneros had been largely tolerated or ignored until the late 1800s in the Dominican Republic; lands long utilized by peasants without any legal title as if they were communal or public lands were, in fact, owned by an association of joint proprietors with ambiguous, overlapping claims. In most areas, this system functioned more or less smoothly as long as most residents wished to use the land for hunting, foraging, and grazing without fences, and for farming small, shifting plots.[71] However, the expansion of commercial agriculture beginning at the end of the nineteenth century would shatter the ostensible harmony among squatters and comunero owners in the Dominican Republic.

Customary forms of land use and popular understandings of property came under attack first and foremost in the sugar region to the east of the capital. Despite the absence of clear and definitive land titles, or any means of adjudicating them, the rapid development of sugar began to push up land values. Efforts to grab uncultivated areas and speculate in peso titles developed first in this region, but then gradually in the rest of the country. Not only sugar companies but also individual Dominicans began to claim exclusive ownership and use of vast holdings, as never before. A few of those accumulating land were descendants of the small number of elite families from the colonial era that remained in the Dominican Republic and were inheritors of peso titles to colonial estates that were bequeathed and sold as terrenos comuneros.[72] And some were likely the heirs of small farmers who purchased titles from the Crown at the end of the eighteenth century (in part to protect their lands from elite creoles who might otherwise claim them simply through power and prestige).[73] But most were individuals who had gained means in the 1800s and, foreseeing how quickly land was gaining value, took risks staking out vast property claims. This process of land accumulation occurred prior to any legal clarification of property rights and titles. For instance, Juan (Juancito) Rodríguez García and Ramón (Mamón) Henríquez, who became the Cibao's two largest ranchers during the early twentieth century, acquired their vast holdings before modern private property titles for individual and exclusive ownership had been instituted in the lands that became their estates.[74]

Those accumulating land, those whom elderly peasants referred to as "the powerful" and "the clever," cleared huge expanses of woods and then marked their claims with fences or *trochas* (paths) cleared around the area's perimeter and sometimes with land surveys. They also paid, pressured, and when necessary coerced squatters to abandon what were technically almost all comunero or state lands.[75] Many land claimants also purchased peso titles to support their (expanding) occupations and property claims with the expectation that these sites would eventually be divided up among co-owners in proportion to the number of land pesos that each held. Indeed, numerous speculators simply bought up land pesos without ever staking out or utilizing particular lands in comunero sites. Others, though, concentrated on establishing material claims to ownership and showed little concern for the number of land pesos they had to support those claims. At the turn of the twentieth century, then, the ambiguities of terrenos comuneros facilitated land accumulation. The prescient and the powerful took advantage of a liminal legal moment when the basis for determining property had not yet been established to claim and enclose large landholdings in terrenos comuneros as well as state lands.

Yet because the existing system provided no clear or irrefutable property titles, landholders and claimants soon began to seek a new system of property that issued definitive individual titles for specific tracts of land. In essence, after exploiting this moment of confusion and transition, many landholders, like the sugar companies in much of the East, sought to consolidate their gains and stabilize the system. A preliminary step in this direction was taken in the final decades of the nineteenth century, when co-owners began proceedings to survey and divide up comunero sites on the basis of each person's proportion of total land pesos. This occurred without any new legislation. At the behest either of co-owners or the state, commissions were formed, generally under the aegis of a public notary, for the purposes of collecting titles and conducting a survey of the outside boundaries of a site (known as a *mensura general*). Then by simple division of the site's area by the total number of land pesos, the commission determined the amount of land each peso was worth and to which each accionista (peso title-holder) was entitled. Afterward, accionistas were free to hire a surveyor and mark off the quantity of land assigned to them in accordance with their land pesos, the exact location of the plot, it seems, being simply a matter of first come, first served.[76]

The initiation of land divisions spawned a new growth industry, the fabrication of fraudulent peso titles. Fraud was, in fact, virtually unstoppable given the vague and obscure character of property held as terrenos comuneros. Numerous writers from the period described the many ways that peso titles were fabricated on a large scale.[77] False titles harmed those holding valid ones by diminishing these legitimate claimants' proportional share. But for most rural denizens the more pressing question was what would happen upon land divisions to those without any title who for generations had enjoyed free access to unoccupied lands, woods, and pasture.[78] The rural majority, which lacked titles of any type, were threatened with dispossession equally by those with valid as well as forged titles.

In addition to the perils for peasants that were occasioned by the surveying and division of comunero sites among co-owners, threats were also posed at the turn of the century by individuals who independently commissioned private surveys (*mensuras particulares*) of lands they claimed through enclosures and improvements.[79] Surveying laws did require that property titles first be examined by surveyors to ensure they were "sufficient" and "in order."[80] However, the surveyors were paid by land claimants and they charged by the hectare; they thus had an interest in surveying as large an area as possible in favor of the person who commissioned their work. Surveys, moreover, were not subject to any judicial regulation or oversight to ensure that they were legitimately conducted. Without a numerical division of all peso titles to a given site, it would have been impossible in any case to determine if a claimant had sufficient land pesos for the area being claimed. And private surveyors almost always ignored peasant squatters (they were not paying the surveyor, after all), who were perhaps unaware of or, at first, unconcerned with such procedures. Like fences and other enclosures, the investment required for surveying was, in a sense, the only constraint on these property claims. At times, the same lands were even surveyed to different persons.[81] Property was thus being claimed wildly, illegally, and extrajudicially, with the ultimate basis on which competing claims and modes of possession and ownership would be adjudicated remaining a matter of speculation. It was also almost always occurring at the expense of the peasantry, few of whom had any titles, surveys, or enclosures with which to claim land.

In the early twentieth century, the state did step in to assert some control over the chaotic and nebulous world of emerging private property, and, in particular, to impede fraud. Most important, new legislation in 1911 regulated and simplified the division of terrenos comuneros among accionistas. The streamlined process delineated in the Law for the Partition of Terrenos Comuneros evidently responded to forceful interests, as it was immediately utilized by many individuals, primarily in the Eastern sugar areas and the Cibao, and dozens of comunero sites underwent the process of division in the period from 1912 to 1919.[82] Conspicuous by its absence in this law, though, was any discussion of the world of squatters. The law voiced no rec-

ognition of or concern for whether squatters were already occupying and exploiting an area claimed by peso title owners. In other words, it granted no
rights on the basis simply of individual possession, let alone collective exploitation of forest and pasture. As the subsequently established Land Court
(Tribunal de Tierras) would explain, the 1911 law was not concerned with al-
locating rights based on possession, but only with "the distribution of the
lands of the site, in proportion to the rights of each accionista."[83]

In 1912 the state issued a second law requiring the registration of all land
titles within one year in a useless effort to curb fraud.[84] This law was innovative mainly in that it did not completely ignore the country's titleless occupants. It permitted registration of what were known as "prescription" claims
to property on the basis of long-term possession, whether in terrenos comuneros or state lands. Following Roman Law, prescription was a legal mode of
property acquisition predicated on uninterrupted, peaceful, visible, and unequivocal possession of land as if one were the owner (that is, without paying
rent or being placed on the land under another's authority). Although colonial jurisprudence is scarce on the subject, the period of possession required
for prescription in lands belonging to the Spanish Crown generally ranged
between ten and forty years.[85] Rights to prescription had not been specified
in any Dominican legislation after independence. But they were outlined in
the country's Civil Code, adopted from France in 1825 during the Haitian occupation.[86]

Although the 1912 law made only a cursory reference to prescription, this
was the first time that such rights were outlined for terrenos comuneros as
well as state lands (the Civil Code did not discuss terrenos comuneros).[87] Yet,
despite the potential benefits created for peasant squatters by this innovation, in practice poor occupants without titles continued to play little if any
role in land divisions made in accordance with the 1911 legislation. Peasants
were not likely to be well-informed regarding the subtle implications of prescription in the 1912 law. And they were mistrustful of the government and
had little means to press their claims before the authorities. Furthermore, the
meaning of the 1912 law's allusion to prescription rights was far from clear, as
what constituted "possession" was not specified. Would possession be defined by cultivation or by the use of fences or other enclosures? What would
be considered legitimate forms of enclosure? And, as important, for how
long would possession be required until a landholding could become property? Typically, peasants farmed the same area for only two or three years,
which had never been considered sufficient time for prescription rights. Nor
was prescription possible for the woods and pasture that peasants exploited
in common. In order to promote peasant land ownership and small farming

in the process of dividing terrenos comuneros, the state would have had to help peasants legalize their plots, regardless of how long they had occupied them—in other words, to have recognized peasant property norms of short-term possession as a future basis for a system of permanent and absolute property. And yet, despite the misgivings of a growing number of intellectual and state figures, the government continued to offer no effective support for small farmers.

Indeed, on the eve of the first U.S. military occupation, squatters on ter-renos comuneros were already being criminalized and evicted in certain ar-eas of the country, as these sites began to be divided up among accionistas. In a few cases, squatters responded with armed resistance. For instance, Miguel Garrido repeatedly attempted to survey the site of Pizarrete, near a sugar plantation in the Baní area, but each time he was attacked by "title-less occupants," who opposed a local court order to divide up and adjudicate property in that site.[88] Also, some of those recently dispossessed in the East joined the growing number of bandits, political gangs, and informal leaders (known as *gavilleros*) concentrated in that region since the turn of the cen-tury. These forces stole or demanded protection money from the sugar com-panies and others (including peasants), and would, along with other armed groups mobilized in reaction to the U.S. occupation itself, engage in guerrilla warfare against U.S. troops when they tried to impose central state authority in the region.[89] But even prior to the U.S. occupation, private property was emerging in the Dominican countryside. The U.S. military dictatorship would institutionalize this nascent process of property formation but also dramatically reconfigure it in ways that would have profound but contra-dictory effects on the peasantry.

The Institutionalization of Private Property under the U.S. Military Dictatorship

From 1916 to 1924, the U.S. military occupied and governed the Domini-can Republic, actually replacing its executive branch until 1922. U.S. officials did not see their imperialist adventures and overseas dictatorships as simply self-interested, but rather imagined them to be paternalistic, even noble, ef-forts to impose order and progress on nations portrayed as unruly children in need of discipline and instruction.[90] In this light, it is not surprising that the U.S. military government often acted in contradictory and circuitous ways, meshing the interests of U.S. business interests with paternalistic dis-course. These contradictions were exemplified by important new property laws imposed during the occupation.

From its onset, the U.S. military dictatorship sought to solidify a system of private property and clear land titles.[91] But it approached the issue in a manner contrary to prior Dominican legislation. The U.S. dictatorship established what one surveyor described in 1926 as the "empire of possession," which he praised for "eliminating in one fell swoop the [problem] of fraudulent land titles based on peso rights." New legislation under the U.S. occupation, he argued, was "more rational and just" than the prior 1911 Law for the Partition of Terrenos Comuneros, which had awarded property rights "without hearing witnesses, without having to examine signs [of possession] and on the basis of a title that might have been forged two months before and at the expense of real interests created through years of effort and supported by our laws [that is, prescription stipulations from the Civil Code]."[92]

The emphasis on possession in laws promulgated by the U.S. military government had the potential to further the interests of peasant squatters. Yet the definition of "possession" in these laws could also be highly destructive to peasants, because it recognized almost any type of existing enclosure or land survey as a form of possession. There would be a clear geography to the laws' paradoxical effects. Their negative potential was realized primarily in the sugar areas of the East, where symbolic forms of possession (surveys and enclosures) were most common and, in general, belonged to major sugar companies. But the new laws that rendered secure the holdings of the sugar companies by privileging possession also potentially favored squatters in other regions of the country, where peso title owners, not those with symbolic possessions, represented the main threat to peasant land access.

The U.S. military regime did not imagine itself as, nor was it, simply the executive committee of foreign sugar interests. Its tax policies heavily burdened the sugar companies.[93] And its internal records testify to the fact that antagonism as well as complicity existed between these two sites of U.S. power.[94] Policy makers influential in the U.S. regime envisaged the development of capitalism in the Dominican Republic as a popular as well as elite phenomenon.[95] Military governor Harry Knapp, for instance, reported to the secretary of the navy in 1917:

I am far from convinced that the large business corporations that are in Santo Domingo are of very great value to the Dominican people. . . . I would greatly prefer to see the Dominican people, and especially the poorer classes, brought to the point where they can work a small plot of land on their own account and leaving the fruits of their labors in Santo Domingo, than to see great companies come here . . . and exploit the country, taking out of it immense sums in the form of their profits.[96]

The professed ideal, at least, of various representatives of the military government was to promote a capitalist nation of productive farmers via a liberal homestead law, not to assist sugar companies monopolizing lands that small agriculturalists might otherwise use.[97]

On the surface, these ideals seemed to be embodied in the overall outlines of land legislation promulgated by the U.S. dictatorship. Yet biases toward certain definitions of property and misunderstandings of the agro pastoral practices of Dominican peasants, as well as fine print that favored the sugar companies, undermined the equitable potential of the legislation.[98] First, in 1919, the military government suspended the 1911 Law for the Partition of Terrenos Comuneros with Executive Order no. 363. This order prohibited all surveys of or within terrenos comuneros, with the exception of areas that had been occupied prior to the 1919 law.[99] It thus simultaneously condoned such claims from the past while placing restrictions on them in the future. Probably most of the sugar corporations' lands were already occupied in some form at this time, and thus, if they had not already, they could complete surveys of the areas they wished to claim. But the U.S. sought to ensure that this method of land accumulation exploited by the sugar companies would not remain available to others at the expense of small farmers.

Then, in 1920, a new executive order, no. 511, dramatically reversed the prevailing bias in favor of title owners over occupants in property adjudications and clearly affirmed and expanded prescription rights.[100] The important procedural transformations ushered in by this new executive order dramatically altered property laws and even the structure of the Dominican state. The law established the Torrens system of land registration and the Superior Land Court (Tribunal Superior de Tierras), which together provided the mechanisms for issuing the first clear, precise, and irrevocable land titles in Dominican history.[101] This system of property registration, and judicial control was relatively uncontroversial and common in countries throughout the world. The new legislation's profound innovations lay elsewhere, specifically in 511's mechanisms for resolving the problems presented by terrenos comuneros and age-old questions in the country about the nature of property.

The 1920 executive order effectively reversed many of the rules and implications of the 1911 Law for the Partition of Terrenos Comuneros. In contrast to the earlier law's stipulation that one or more co-owners could simply demand that their site be divided, under the new legislation a long, state-supervised, and compulsory procedure referred to as a *mensura catastral* (cadastral survey) had to be initiated by the Superior Land Court. The court could initiate the process whenever it determined that the "public interest" would be served by having an area surveyed, its titles judged, and property awarded.[102] The first and most important step in a mensura catastral was the survey of the comunero site—henceforth given a "cadastral district" number—in which not only the outside limits were surveyed (as in a mensura general) but also all occupations and improvements within the area were mapped and described. Each such occupation was given a "lot" or *parcela* number within the district. Subsequently, these plans were submitted to a local Land Court judge who would often travel to the areas in question to verify or augment the information provided by the surveyor. The court then listened to testimony concerning the nature and length of occupations and thereby determined which parcels would be prescribed to their occupants and awarded irrevocable titles, and which would—along with any idle areas—remain comunero.

If any land was declared comunero, a separate procedure could then be ordered to have an examiner verify or reject peso titles to the area, in order ultimately to divide the comunero portion among those holding acceptable titles. Finally, a surveyor divided the areas that had been declared comunero into specific plots matching each owner's share of peso titles (*partición en naturaleza*). The Superior Land Court then rendered the final decision, known as a *saneamiento*, in which the court either awarded clear and irrevocable titles, or ordered a new local hearing and investigation because of inadequate information or evidence.

For the first time in Dominican history, the 1920 law clearly established prescription rights within terrenos comuneros and provided effective mechanisms for guaranteeing the acquisition of such rights. In addition, the maximum period for prescription (applying to those without any type of title acquired in good faith) was reduced from thirty to ten years for all occupants whose possession included the six months following the promulgation of 511. The claims of peso title holders were now valid only in the absence of squatters' rights. Ironically, though, the law simultaneously eliminated the role of possession in determining property rights in the future; once a title was registered in the mensura catastral, land was no longer subject to prescription.

The U.S. military dictatorship thus conditioned the acquisition of property rights at this time essentially on possession rather than (peso) titles. Prior to 511, the military government issued a proclamation intended to clarify this and thereby, it hoped, to quiet growing fears and opposition to U.S. policies. The proclamation read: "Every honorable owner who cultivates the land and by the sweat of his brow wins his daily bread will have to be pleased with the security that the new Law will guarantee for his property, since by means of this Law, he will find himself freed from the malicious efforts against his right to enjoy the land. . . . [S]uch owners will be favored both to foment cultivation of the soil and because it is believed that, in the absence of other evidence of property, occupation and use of land constitutes in and of itself authentic proof of the true right of property." Although privileging possession might have been a potentially important step toward aiding a vulnerable peasantry, the proclamation also suggested the military government's ignorance or disregard of peasant practices and their relationship to the land. The occupation government proclaimed: "It is the desire of the Government that the benefits [of the land laws] . . . should not accrue to those, without scruples, who speculate in land, but rather to the true owners; and above all to those small-scale independent possessors who are dedicated to productive labor, and strongly tied to their native soil."[103] Yet peasants were traditionally not tied to any one plot of land over time, and thus would not be recognized as "true owners" by the U.S. regime.

The 1920 legislation could not provide in itself the social equity it promised, because most peasants still practiced shifting agriculture. And while peasants rarely had held the same plot long enough to claim property via prescription as outlined in 511, the sugar companies generally could claim such "squatters" rights. Perhaps that is why the proclamation was not successful in thwarting opposition to U.S.-imposed land laws. The U.S. legation later wrote regarding 511: "The first reaction was a storm of criticism on the part of the press and the public. The American Military Occupation was of course unpopular, and it was believed that this was merely a Yankee trick to despoil the small landholders for the benefit of the sugar estates and other American interests."[104]

Peasants were also greatly harmed by the 1920 law's delineation of the forms of possession from which property could flow. The law established three methods of demonstrating possession: "cultivation . . . or other beneficial use"; "fences, walls, hedges, ditches, trochas, or similar means of indicating boundaries"; and a properly documented individual land survey (mensura particular). However, fulfilling U.S. policy-makers' professed commitment to promoting small farmers would have required, among other things, limiting the meaning of "possession" to "cultivation . . . or other beneficial use" rather than placing on ostensibly equal terms merely symbolic possessions. That, though, would have run contrary to a legal tradition in the United States reaching back to the Colonial era rooted in English law. British colonists, unlike the Spanish, had based their right to property in the New World solely on possession defined by surveys, enclosures, and other "improvements." (Among other things, this legal tradition served to rationalize English ownership of land formerly used by native Americans, who, like Dominican peasants, neither fenced off property nor enclosed animals.)[105] This tradition was not entirely foreign in the Dominican Republic. Large land-

holders had claimed property by carving insignias into trees and clearing trochas around the perimeter of their holdings. But the legal status of such
claims remained problematic. And they had not been respected by peasants
as establishing a right to restrict their access to idle terrain and unmarked
animals within those claimed areas.[106]

The 1920 law's ratification of symbolic possessions may also have
stemmed from the role of the sugar interests in its conception. The U.S.
military government consulted lawyers for the sugar companies to assist in
writing the law. And they appear to have successfully conditioned the equitable aspects of this legislation so as to meet the interests of their clients.[107]
This might explain, for instance, why the law would recognize possession on
the basis of traditional surveys when, paradoxically, the thrust of the new
legislation was mistrust and rejection of such surveying because of its well-
known history of abuse and exploitation by those with means and power.[108]
Indeed the heart of 511 was the imposition of strong judicial control upon
surveyors and the novel obligation that they survey every occupation regardless of title, or lack thereof. Both of these features had been altogether
lacking in the many prior surveys commissioned by land claimants that were
nonetheless recognized as evidence of possession under the new legislation.
Also, the law's recognition of fences and trochas as legitimate forms of possession served to reward particularly the sugar companies concentrated in
the East that had thus far been the largest accumulators and enclosers of
land, often land which they were not cultivating and which large numbers of
peasants and others had been and were, in fact, still using. Timing was critical to the building of the territorial empires of these corporations, which
before the question "What is property?" had been answered had utilized
fences, trochas, and surveys to stake claims to areas far beyond their actual
use for sugarcane or even pasture. That the 1920 legislation recognized these
physical markers as a type of possession by which one could secure property
via prescription greatly facilitated the acquisition of much of the Dominican
East by U.S. sugar interests.[109]

Ultimately, Executive Order no. 511 reads as a contradictory text reflecting
a modus vivendi between the opposed forces shaping it—namely, the sugar
companies and the advocates of small agriculture within the military government. On the one hand, the spirit of the law seems to have clearly favored
material possession and granting ownership to titleless peasants of the land
they occupied. Yet the law was overdetermined by a powerful mixture of ignorance, cultural bias, and self-interest that made it favorable to the large
sugar companies and perilous for the peasantry.

The detrimental effects of the 1920 law in practice were most evident in the triangular sugar area formed by the towns of San Pedro, La Romana, and Ramón Santana. In this region, sugar companies used the law to consolidate ownership over gigantic areas, leading to much displacement and land scarcity as well as escalating class conflict. Indeed, after 1920, sugar companies increasingly resorted to terror to eject squatters from lands the companies had claimed and, more and more, now owned. In several infamous incidents, corporations set fire to entire villages in order to evict residents. In 1921 the village of Higüeral along with the small hamlet of Caimoní near La Romana was burned to the ground after a twenty-four-hour eviction notice was given to the nearly 150 families residing there. An official from the Central Romana (a subsidiary of the U.S.-owned South Porto Rico Sugar Company), R. L. Waddell, was arrested for ordering the fires. Nonetheless, the occupants were never allowed to return, even though the site, Chavón Abajo, was still undergoing a mensura catastral and titles for the area had not yet been adjudicated. Similarly, in Távila the houses of reportedly four hundred residents were burned in order to push occupants off the land. Tense eviction struggles continued throughout the decade in the region.[110]

Finally, without the prospects of prescription for itinerant farmers under the 1920 legislation, peasants faced the threat of losing their land not only in those still relatively few areas that had been surveyed and enclosed but also throughout the nation's vast terrenos comuneros, now legally belonging to entitled co-owners in the absence of long-term squatters' rights. If possession were really to reign supreme, as the U.S. regime's discourse surrounding 511 promised, then the executive order had not gone nearly far enough. Peso titles would have had to be rejected altogether. Thus, as the president of the Land Court commented in 1986, all of the land laws, even paradoxically Executive Order no. 511, had given

an importance to peso title rights that, in truth, they did not have or deserve, thus diverging from the spirit of the Law for the Registration of Lands [511] to give preference to possession. . . . It is unjust that by virtue of such titles, whose origins cannot be discerned to determine their validity and good faith, land may be awarded to persons who have never even been to the comunero site in question, at the expense of those who work these lands, simply because the latter have not completed sufficient time for prescription.[111]

The Emergence of a Nationalist-Populist Project

However baleful land monopolization and destruction of peasant traditions were in much of the East, land tenure and rural existence had still changed only modestly in most of the country upon the conclusion of the U.S. military dictatorship. Although the export sector relied heavily on sugar, the Dominican Republic overall had not become a monocultural or plantation economy. Certainly the expansion of sugar was dramatic. Between 1905 and 1925, sugar production increased sixfold from 48,169 to 331,270 tons.[112] But even in 1940, sugar was grown on less than one-tenth of the country's cultivated land.[113] Nor had many Dominican peasants been proletarianized, though tens of thousands of immigrant laborers were being imported to cut cane. Unlike neighboring Cuba, cane fields had not engulfed the bulk of the country but had remained relatively isolated to particular areas, mostly in the East and around Barahona. Beyond these zones, the journalist Rafael Vidal contended in 1926, "there are [generally speaking] no latifundia. . . . Our most fertile valley, the Cibao, is parceled out with such equity that it seems almost to have been inspired by ancient wisdom." Although the scramble for property had already spread outside the sugar areas, by 1929 only an estimated sixth of the country's area had been surveyed by the state, and less still had completed the process of title adjudication. The process of determining property rights had hardly begun outside the sugar zones.[114]

Yet Vidal and others were aware that latifundia and agribusiness could quickly expand to other areas and that extant conditions for securing landed property via peso titles as well as by symbolic possession pointed in that direction. Thus, two years after the end of the U.S. occupation, during Horacio Vásquez's presidency, Secretary of Agriculture Rafael Espaillat, a middle-class Cibaeño, recommended that the state "colonize" and distribute as much untitled land as possible in order to prevent it from being accumulated by the sugar companies and to foment instead an economy "free of the economic slavery endured by [wage laborers]."[115] Vidal lauded Espaillat's efforts to promote small farmers so that "the octopus of conquest cannot penetrate [our nation] in the guise of foreign capital."[116]

The U.S. occupation and foreign sugar expansion had mobilized powerful nationalist sentiments among Dominican intellectuals, who were now highly critical of traditional liberal visions of modernity, laissez-faire economics, and growth via foreign investment and agribusiness.[117] Editors, journalists, and state officials under Vásquez almost unanimously called for new laws to impede the growth of foreign ownership, latifundia, and monoculture in the name of social equity, nationalism, and far-sighted economic policy. The Dominican lettered class was keenly aware of the collapse suffered by Cuban farmers after the precipitous rise and fall of world sugar prices in 1921, which had compelled them to sell their properties to large U.S. sugar corporations and which threw the island into what would be decades of stagnation.[118] Witnessing this process, Cuban intellectual Ramiro Guerra y Sánchez wrote that "within a quarter of a century either the *latifundium* or the republic will no longer exist. The Cuban people will have land and independence, or they will have lost them both."[119] In 1927 a representative Dominican editorial exhorted the country to eschew the path that Cuba had followed and "to defend [the Dominican nation] from the traps set by the glitter of foreign gold—only the glitter . . . [and] not fall for false illusions and mirages . . . believing that the bustle of cities indicates economic progress."[120] The U.S. legation reported that same year:

There are students of the economy of the country who for some time have looked with some apprehension upon the gradual expansion by the sugar interests. They have cited Cuba as presenting an example of economic evils which result from the lack of diversified industry and which should be guarded against here. . . . They have favored the small farmer as against great sugar plantations. The Secretary of State for Agriculture, Mr. Espaillat, has been conspicuously in that group.[121]

Espaillat and other members of the new generation of reformist thinkers, the inheritors of an intellectual movement that had been gradually gaining momentum since the early 1880s when "progress" first alighted on the Dominican Republic, would become key figures in the early Trujillo state. Under the dictatorship, their visions for agrarian reform and of an alternative modernity would be paired with a state apparatus that promised the means necessary to realize them.

One of these reformist thinkers who joined the Trujillo regime was Rafael César Tolentino. Tolentino was also a member of Santiago's small middle class and an important nationalist leader, who had been persecuted during the U.S. military dictatorship for his opposition to the occupation. He was also a notable journalist in the late 1920s and the owner and director of Santiago's daily newspaper, *La Información*. Playing on the traditional phrase of local revolutionaries, "We have to take to el monte," a 1927 editorial in Tolentino's paper declared: "We have to take to el monte with plows and machetes as our weapons. Our state of poverty is the product of our mistaken orientation, of not seeing the salvation of our Country in the only place it can be found: in the countryside."[122] The leaders of the early Trujillo state would heed Tolentino's call to turn to the countryside for the salvation of the nation. And they would envisage a nation of sedentary, surplus-producing farmers, rather than of foreign agribusiness and landless peasants, or of pig hunters and rebels. What is most remarkable is that this vision would shape not only the rhetoric but also the actual public policies and course of the early Trujillo regime, and indeed the making of the modern Dominican Republic.

3 Peasant-State Compromise and Rural Transformation under the Trujillo Dictatorship

The most dramatic and enduring consequence of the U.S. occupation was the creation of the Guardia Nacional Dominicana. This was the country's first truly centralized standing army, and it would allow the state to consolidate an effective monopoly on the means of political violence.[1] In order to facilitate the Guardia's control, the U.S. military government had also taken measures to disarm the civilian population, subjugate rebels and gavilleros, and undermine the power of regional caudillos. In 1919, Rafael Leonidas Trujillo Molina, a literate but poorly educated, lower-middle-class man from the town of San Cristóbal, entered the Guardia as a second lieutenant. Trujillo's relentless drive, unscrupulous machinations, and skills as a leader quickly carried him up the military ranks, as did the reluctance of better educated members of the middle and upper classes to join the Guardia out of opposition to the U.S. occupation. Eight years after joining the force, Trujillo was named commander-in-chief of the Guardia during the postoccupation government of President Horacio Vásquez.[2]

At the same time that Trujillo was handed control of the military, Vásquez confronted growing opposition and instability. Although generally supportive of civil liberties and economic development, Vásquez's government had become increasingly characterized by corruption, personalist rivalries, and perceived anti-democratic measures in its final years, including reforms extending Vásquez's presidency from four to six years and permitting his re-election. The country was also suffering from economic decline and a fiscal crisis exacerbated by the 1929 world depression. In addition, Washington sent a commission to Santo Domingo headed by vice president Charles Dawes to formulate a plan for paying the Dominican foreign debt, as a result of which, according to the U.S. embassy, Vásquez's "prestige suffered perceptibly."[3] As opposition grew, Vásquez faced threats of assassination and even armed rebellion. Ominous signs of civilian rearmament had appeared even before the U.S. military withdrawal. And the Vásquez government itself contributed to this process by granting arms to members of its own party, arms which inevitably ended up in the hands of enemies as well. This in turn added to discontent as Dominicans began to fear that the country was re-

turning to the violent and unstable personalistic politics of the preoccupa-
tion years. In this context, Rafael Estrella Ureña, who had been a nationalist
opponent of the U.S. occupation and once served as Vásquez's secretary of
foreign affairs, secretly joined forces with General Trujillo. Knowing that the
army would support him, in February 1930, Estrella staged a small, successful
rebellion against the government that found broad support.[4]

Trujillo's control over the National Army was critical to his ability to help
overthrow Vásquez and subsequently to seize political control from Estrella
(at first the acting president). Not only did the National Army exercise power that was unprecedented in Dominican history. Having been forged in the
fires of the U.S. occupation, the military also remained exceptionally autonomous from the interests and influence of national elites. Three months after
the February 1930 "revolution," Trujillo deployed the military against his opponents and stole the presidential election. He did so in the face of virulent
elite opposition and despite the fact that he had mobilized no popular base.[5]
Trujillo also thwarted vigorous diplomatic efforts by U.S. foreign minister
Charles Curtis to prevent him from becoming president. Curtis's objections
to Trujillo, though, were never openly supported by the U.S. State Department in light of Washington's newly proclaimed policy of nonintervention
in Latin American affairs.[6]

Trujillo quickly established political control. He incorporated into his
cabinet numerous nationalist and populist figures who had supported Estrella. These men now joined Trujillo both in response to intimidation and
with hopes—and rationalizations—that, while sacrificing recent advances in
liberal rights, the dictatorship would nonetheless achieve many national
goals that they espoused.[7] Trujillo also soon co-opted or eliminated his political rivals and the country's extant caudillos. Several opposition groups
mobilized by regional leaders did at first take to the hills, where they accumulated some heavy weaponry both from abroad and from stolen government munitions. But these forces, led mostly by caudillos from the Cibao
and the frontier regions, were unable to unify in a timely manner, acquire
adequate arms, and garner broad support. Hence they disbanded or were
easily defeated by Trujillo's army.[8]

After coming to power through military force and an alliance, via Estrella,
with a group of nationalist intellectuals, Trujillo would soon seek to consolidate his regime by securing popular acceptance in the countryside. He would
also promote economic development and national autonomy through new
rural policies aimed at increasing peasant agricultural production. This chapter will explore how the Trujillo state simultaneously gained acceptance
among the peasantry and transformed the rural popular classes and economy

along the lines of the small farmer model of modernization long espoused by many of Trujillo's early advisers. These developments would in turn be critical to the regime's success in penetrating, administering, and controlling Dominican society over the next three decades.

Popular acceptance of Trujillo, despite the harshness of his rule, should be seen in light of the critical juncture during which he seized power—namely, the growing threats that the Dominican peasantry faced in 1930 to the economic autonomy and subsistence security it had enjoyed for centuries. Peasants had been largely disarmed by the U.S. military dictatorship, and there were no longer strong local caudillos competing for their loyalty and able to provide protection and assistance in return. Above all, peasants were threatened by the ominous changes in property relations and land tenure prompted by the development of commercial agriculture that were beginning to jeopardize their access to land. With land in much of the country being accumulated and enclosed for the first time and stock fencing being legally required in widening areas, peasants' economic practices and way of life were rapidly becoming untenable. They were in danger of being lost altogether if peasants failed to forge an effective alliance with a national state capable of mediating rural transformations and representing their interests.

It was in this context that the Trujillo state orchestrated several large-scale campaigns to distribute, legalize, or at least temporarily cede to peasants lands they sought or were already cultivating without title. The relative ease with which the Trujillo regime was able to implement this agrarian reform was due to the abundance of uncleared public and private lands and to the lack of clear and absolute land titles in most of the country. These conditions meant that few expropriations of utilized land or definitive property were required for this reform. The Trujillo state also vastly expanded the nation's infrastructure of roads, bridges, and irrigation, rendering peasant production marketable and profitable for the first time in many areas. These rural reforms would become the basis for claims by Trujillo to be the patron, or *protector*, of the peasantry. The combination of decreasing land availability with state-protected land use, new market access, and various forms of agricultural support made intensive farming attractive to the peasantry for the first time in Dominican history. A peasant-state compromise thus became possible, given the alternative prospect of landlessness.

Yet in exchange for land access and state assistance, peasants were compelled to farm in a more sedentary, intensive, and land-efficient manner than had generally been practiced or desired in the past. The dual nature of the Trujillo state's *protección*, or support, of the peasantry was evident in the severe methods it used to augment peasant production. The state distributed rewards to those it deemed "men of work" by variously providing them with land, irrigation, tools, seeds, credit, and technical assistance, while it harshly punished with vagrancy penalties (jail and forced labor) and withdrawal of usufruct rights those it considered to be idle—namely, any unemployed adult man not cultivating at least 10 tareas of land. Also, the regime's land distributions included woods and pasture that previously had been used in common for grazing, hunting, and foraging, as well as for itinerant farming. On the one hand, land distribution insulated these areas from the widening enclosures and property claims being established by peso title owners and others. On the other, it facilitated the demise of open-range animal raising, increasingly forced peasants to expand agricultural production to secure subsistence, and impelled the transition from a largely pastoral to a more agricultural and sedentary mode of existence.

This project of rural modernization through land reform, vagrancy laws, and the valorization of small farmers also served to pry open the countryside to state power. The expansion and effectiveness of the national state in rural areas was predicated on the sedentarization and concentration of a peasantry that was still highly dispersed and relatively footloose.[9] In its campaign to transform the countryside, the state distributed fixed plots, surveyed the nation's landholdings, and established permanent property rights. It relocated thousands of peasants, developed an impressive network of roads and infrastructure, and provided much aid and irrigation upon which sedentarized agriculturalists would increasingly depend. Fixed addresses, nucleation of the population, and the linkage of settlements to nationwide systems of transportation and communication in turn rendered the rural population accessible, observable, taxable, and, in general, within reach of both state assistance and repression.[10] These rural policies thus brought the countryside under the vigilant gaze of the central state for the first time, allowing it to mediate transformations in rural society in unprecedented fashion. In short, the Trujillo regime effectively incorporated and subjected to the national state a peasantry that for hundreds of years had remained largely invisible to it, eluding its control, surveillance, and taxation. Peasants' integration was facilitated by a wide array of new state institutions that extended throughout the country: inter alia, an official mass party called the Dominican Party; the expanded national military and police; agricultural boards, or juntas; a strengthened system of alcaldes pedáneos; a bureau to issue and renew the cédulas personales de identidad; and a growing body of government statisticians and census-takers.

Thus the early Trujillo years represented a portentous and contradictory time for the Dominican peasantry. On the one hand, the emerging threats of landlessness and the perils of land commercialization rendered peasants increasingly open to the state's offers of protección to maintain their land access and independent production. For centuries peasants' conucos were the emblem and guarantor of a measure of freedom and autonomy. Peasants were doubtless determined to preserve them and ready to accept a state that allowed them to do so. Yet, at the same time, state protection of peasant land access was coupled with the demand for new rural practices that would increasingly compromise peasants' centuries-old autonomy vis-à-vis the national state and market forces. The contradictory impact of state intervention in the countryside under Trujillo produced diverse perspectives on the transformations that occurred during those years. Most elderly peasants nostalgically recalled the regime's agrarian policies as distribution and assistance. But those living in marginal areas that still had ample forest and pasture for collective exploitation and shifting agriculture instead generally remembered with bitterness the compulsory sedentarization and agrarianization pursued by the regime.

Yet the regime was successful overall in its use of agrarian reform as a means of shoring up political stability and transforming peasant practices. The country's agricultural production and self-sufficiency grew substantially during the dictatorship.[11] And peasants skillfully negotiated the constraints and opportunities of new state and market forces under Trujillo's rule.[12] Furthermore, notwithstanding the formidable losses, griefs, and perils of becoming dependent on an authoritarian state, most elderly peasants recall Trujillo as having been a leader who generally respected their concerns and carried out key rural policies from which they benefited.[13] There were certainly deep contradictions for peasants in this transitional period, as they were finally domesticated, in a sense, by the Trujillo state. But, as a result of land distribution, agricultural assistance, and Trujillo's own political skills, the regime was able to represent itself as both a sponsor of modernity and the protector of peasants' customary rights and ways of life—namely, free land access and a measure of social and economic independence.

The Evolution of Trujillo's Peasant Politics and Agrarian Reform

After seizing the presidency, Trujillo turned his attention to extending political control, securing popular acquiescence, and developing the country's economy. In pursuit of each of these goals, he looked to the rural popular classes. They remained a major untapped resource for agricultural production and taxes as well as a source of potential political instability if they again supported regional caudillos or joined gavilleros in opposition to the national state. Successfully enlisting peasants' cooperation would, however, entail a sea change in Dominican history, one bridging the centuries-old distance and antagonism between the capital and the countryside. Although it would be several years before Trujillo's actual policies to incorporate the peasantry took shape, Trujillo wasted no time in commencing this project rhetorically.

During his first several years as president, Trujillo conducted extended tours of the countryside on horseback. He held town meetings and visited homes, listening to hundreds of people voice their concerns. He attended dances and parties in his honor.[14] And he organized large rallies, known as *revistas cívicas* (civic parades), often in areas where no presidential leader or candidate had spoken before.[15] The revistas served as a platform for Trujillo to outline the terms of a political contract. The dictator represented himself as the "best friend of the man of work" and "the staunchest supporter of the Dominican agriculturalist."[16] He promised state support and accountability through his personal intervention. All *campesinos* (rural dwellers), he announced, "who feel that they or their interests have been harmed by local officials can communicate directly with me with the confidence that they will be attended to." (Thousands of letters from Trujillo were also distributed among the rural population affirming that any complaint would be brought directly to his attention.)[17] In exchange, Trujillo demanded that peasants cooperate with his plans for transforming the nation and augmenting its wealth. This required, he said, opposing armed rebellions against the national state, which had not only caused political instability in the past but also been a disincentive to agricultural production. Above all, it depended upon peasants' participation in a project of national development by becoming more productive, sedentary farmers. "To cultivate the land . . . is the obligation of every citizen and . . . of all my friends," Trujillo told a large audience in 1932.[18]

Echoing official discourse, an editorial in *La Opinión* praised the revistas as an efficient means of bringing Trujillo "in contact with the rural masses" and giving peasants "the encouragement of his presence, [demonstrating] to the man of the countryside that the nation has a government that knows that the greatness and prosperity of the country depend more than anything else on . . . [those] who work with their hands and irrigate the fields . . . by the sweat of their brow."[19] While explicitly affirming peasants' importance to the nation and representing himself as a leader offering support, Trujillo, in his tours of the countryside, was also implicitly threatening potential opponents. In 1932, Trujillo gave a speech in Gurabo in the Cibao, not far from what had been the stronghold of one of the most powerful of the country's regional caudillos, Desiderio Arias, who had been killed the year before by Trujillo's forces. Here, by rhetorical means, Trujillo presented the audience with a stark choice between being honored and protected as "men of work" or being hunted down like Arias: "I have not come to inspire fear, because only the trouble-makers fear me. . . . For you, honorable and hard-working people . . . my presence signifies the profound solidarity that I feel with those who contribute through their labor to the greatness of my people."[20] Trujillo's warning that "trouble-makers" should fear him was backed by the unprecedented military power he displayed in parades around the country.[21]

In addition to the large revistas in the pueblos where Trujillo spoke, both local officials and government functionaries touring the countryside held small community meetings in the sections. Reports by the latter stressed that these represented the first time that outside government figures had arrived in these rural areas.[22] At these meetings, residents were apprised of national laws; instructed in agricultural techniques (how far apart coffee trees should be planted, for instance); granted free seeds, tools, and farm and breeding animals; and told of Trujillo's support for the "hard-working men," his efforts for improving social welfare, and his faith in their labor as the avenue to the nation's progress. They were also warned against continuing the practice of slash-and-burn agriculture and living from subsistence exploitation of the woods and open range. "It is the wish of the honorable President Trujillo that all Dominicans throw themselves into farming because that is where our national wealth is," an agricultural instructor explained to participants at one of these local gatherings.[23]

This flurry of state activity in the countryside and efforts at popular mobilization were celebrated by the press as both uniting the country's scattered rural population and integrating it with the pueblos and cities into a larger national community. "In the revista, the countryside and the city embrace each other," a 1933 editorial in *La Opinión* put it simply and approvingly.[24] An article two months later marveled at how these demonstrations assembled "men of all colors, from all walks of life, from the humble cultivator of a small plot to the wealthy and powerful, including all classes. And women, women who have never come together before in our country." This article reported how because of Trujillo's support for extending citizenship to women, he was being praised by "feminists" as "the only Dominican President who has believed that women . . . should have rights."[25] (The state would recognize women's equal civil rights in 1940, require them to carry a cédula that same year, and implement universal suffrage in the 1942 "election." Rural women, though, were reportedly not obliged to attend political demonstrations to the same extent that men were.)[26] The symbolism of incorporation generated by the Trujillo state's political rituals appears to have had some impact on the peasantry. Although Leonardo Núñez, an elderly peasant, resented being obliged by local authorities to attend a rally for Trujillo in Santiago, he was nonetheless struck by its novelty: "For us, [the revistas] were something interesting, because here . . . we have never belonged. . . . But for Trujillo, we belonged."[27]

Another means by which the early Trujillo state incorporated the peasantry was the national identity card, the cédula, established in 1932. The cédula served many purposes. It was eventually a major revenue generator. All adults were required to pay a yearly fee to renew their cédula, save the few who were exempted on the grounds of destitution. For the peasantry and the poor, this fee, until the 1950s, was 1 peso. Beginning with changes in the law in 1940, the cédula turned, in practice, into the country's first graduated income and property tax. It would be scaled ultimately to thirty-five different categories of wealth, the highest of which required an enormous annual payment for the time of 3,000 pesos, while the poor paid 1 to 3 pesos.[28] Although a relatively modest fee, the tax was nonetheless onerous for subsistence-oriented peasants with little or no available cash. And it obliged them to engage with the market at least to a small degree in order to gain the necessary funds, either selling surplus crops or working several days as a wage laborer.

The cédula was also an instrument for enforcing the obligation to vote; after one "voted," one's cédula was stamped to that effect and would be periodically checked by military officials. Although Trujillo would scrupulously uphold the formal structure of a liberal, constitutional government, in practice he tolerated no opposition and generally the official Dominican Party offered the only candidates in elections. The entire adult population could vote for the first time during the dictatorship, but only for Trujillo or a figurehead candidate running at Trujillo's behest. Elections and other practices of citizenship during the Trujillo regime were scarcely veiled authoritarian rituals rather than exercises of liberal political rights. Yet they signaled a turning point in the Dominican Republic when the rural popular classes were encompassed by ceremonies of national political community and took part in performances that legitimated the national state. By carrying a cédula, sharing in the obligation to pay taxes, "voting," and attending mass rallies, peasants participated—and did not participate—as citizens in the same fashion as urban dwellers, rather than, as in the past, chiefly by manning rebellions of regional caudillos and leading independence wars.

The inclusive and populist discourse of the early Trujillo state opened up space for local authorities, Trujillo's advisers, and even peasants themselves to begin proposing concrete measures to benefit peasants. This is first evident during the early and mid-1930s, when rural authorities began reporting to Trujillo on impediments to peasant production and, in some instances, possibilities of public disorder in the countryside. Officials described the mounting constraints on peasants' land access, as vast areas were being cordoned off by would-be owners. These officials condemned the fact that most of the enclosed lands remained uncultivated by their "owners" while large numbers of peasants wishing to farm or raise animals no longer had access to them. One rural authority in the Cibao complained to Trujillo in March 1934 that "it is well known that a large portion of those who claim to be landowners neither work their land nor let others do so." In response to this situation, he explained, he had, with the approval of the Santiago governor, provided many landless peasants with uncultivated lands in nearby Maimón, Esperanza. Around the same time, the governor of San Pedro de Macorís commanded the army to stop peasant evictions by large landowners near Juandolio and Guayacanes. He asked the central state to assist those who had already been dispossessed, including more than 150 families, as they represented a problem for "public order."[29]

Individual members of Trujillo's cabinet began to shape a national policy to address these conditions. Drawing on and giving substance to Trujillo's propeasant rhetoric, they pushed state policies in novel directions in terms of both land distribution and property rights. The populist nationalist writer Rafael César Tolentino, whom Trujillo had appointed as secretary of agriculture, was one of the main forces behind emerging policies to ensure peasant land access. Tolentino was one of the prominent intellectuals who had supported the February 1930 revolt against Vásquez.[30] Under Trujillo, Tolentino quickly became an advocate for popular sectors. In December 1933, he made several public speeches in which he reportedly encouraged "the movement of squatters" onto private lands, including those of the U.S.-owned Central Romana sugar company. The U.S. State Department received complaints that "under recent presidential decree Dominican citizens were permitted to enter and occupy unused lands in the Republic." The U.S. legation in Santo Domingo stated that its sources were "hopeful that when this matter comes to the attention of President Trujillo, Señor Tolentino's enthusiasm for the interests of squatters and the poor classes generally, would take a more rational form." However, the powerful Italian-Dominican Vicini family, the owners of the largest sugar conglomerate after those belonging to U.S. corporations, had already protested to Tolentino only to receive a firm defense of "his speeches and the action of the squatters in pursuance of the speeches."[31]

Nonetheless, the state eventually retreated. Pressure from the Central

Romana forced a reluctant Tolentino to issue a circular to local officials in the Eastern sugar areas disavowing "misinterpretations" of his comments concerning

the plan for the distribution of state lands, [and] . . . the interest of the Dominican Government in improving the present condition of the peasants [and] being able to make a landowner of each man of work and good will. . . . Often complaints are communicated to this Department from agriculturalists who occupy lands that have been adjudicated in favor of sugar companies. . . . In this regard, it must be borne in mind that the agrarian policy which this Department has put into practice cannot be interpreted in a way that hinders the operation of justice.[32]

And yet, though ostensibly bowing to powerful foreign sugar interests, the government would later that year inaugurate a new land distribution policy—sponsored by Tolentino—that would essentially legalize throughout the country what Tolentino had earlier adumbrated. Distributing land and legalizing squatter occupations would become the heart of subsequent rural policy, especially during the next few years.

It is likely that the actions of peasants themselves also helped shape Trujillo's rural policies. While Trujillo's early propeasant rhetoric remained short on specifics and focused primarily on promoting production, peasants were already petitioning directly to Trujillo for help in securing land access. In myriad letters to the state, peasants invoked Trujillo's proclamation that the laboring men were his "best friends," as a rhetorical strategy to demand assistance from the state, above all land distribution and protection from eviction.[33] For example, in 1934, Fidelio Trinidad, a peasant from La Romana, explained that he had been farming for four years on uncultivated lands belonging to the *Ingenio* (sugar mill) Santa Fé, when he was suddenly prevented from working there. He recounted his plight to Trujillo, addressing him as the peasantry's *palanca* (patron or friend with pull):

Where there is an immense amount of [unused] land . . . we, the residents of these parts, eager for work, decided to cultivate certain farms in this land. But we have been stopped by employees of this company [the Santa Fé].

Knowing . . . that you are the true patron of the agriculturalist obliges me to write to you . . . to see if by your efforts we could obtain from this company permission to farm these lands, even if it were under a Contract, one that may be favorable to us, since we are not unaware that the land belongs to said company.

There are more than two hundred of us, seeming like vagrants. Even though we are genuinely men of work, we cannot find any place to earn a living and provide for our families.[34]

At the time that the letter was received, the state had just retreated from encouraging squatters on sugar company property and the land distribution

campaign had not yet been initiated. The secretary of agriculture informed
the secretary of the presidency that the former could not force the Ingenio
Santa Fé to cede its lands.[35] Nonetheless, the regime's emerging land distribution policies would subsequently assist agriculturalists in exactly the manner that Trinidad had requested. And peasants would shrewdly deploy Trujillo's rural populist and paternalist discourse as a means of soliciting state
support: "Knowing that you are the true patron of the agriculturalist," our
benefactor and best friend, we know that you will help us in this hour of
need.[36] Although deference to this discourse was strategic and somewhat disingenuous, it would also contribute to the regime's authority, to a political
culture of dependence on the state, and to Trujillo's hegemony in the countryside.

The Trujillo regime's land distribution campaign commenced in 1934. It
was then that Trujillo commissioned Major Rafael Carretero to travel to the
southwestern area around Barahona to investigate and to try to resolve land
tenure problems in that region. Little is known about the background of this
relatively bold figure in the early Trujillo state. But like Tolentino, Carretero
appears to have been an effective force in shaping the regime's rural policies
and impelling agrarian reform, notwithstanding the ostensibly personalistic
character of Trujillo's rule. After several weeks in the southwest, Carretero
wrote to Tolentino that he had appropriated and distributed 912 hectares in
nearby Neiba, despite the trochas that had been established around them by
would-be owners "who could never have cultivated them even in fifty
years."[37] He distributed these lands to agriculturalists "ready to work them
immediately," some of whom had come from as far as El Cercado to obtain
them.

During the next month, Carretero distributed 6,975 hectares to 2,217 persons (with plots varying substantially in size but averaging 3 hectares each) in
this same area of Neiba and Barahona. As large parts of these lands had previously been marked off and claimed by landowners, Carretero wrote to Secretary Tolentino: "I would like you to know that many persons in this area
had possessed huge extensions of land marked off with trochas that they
would never have been able to cultivate, and I have given out contracts for
some of that land. Some unfounded complaints may therefore reach this
Secretary of State, as these *trochadores* have always lived by exploiting the
poor." Comparable circumstances existed in neighboring Enriquillo, from
where Carretero filed a similar report in early February. He wrote that many
who claimed to be landowners had opened trochas around montes in terrenos comuneros, carving out vast "extensions of land that they could never

cultivate in their lives . . . [and which] are requested by peasants who wish to work them but have been restricted from doing so."[38]

Throughout most of the country, land grabbing had become a major obstacle to the early Trujillo regime's goal of boosting agricultural production while consolidating a small-farming peasantry. The forest ranger for the Southern commune of San José de Ocoa, Francisco Paulino, protested to Major Carretero that "the people cannot open up new farms in accordance with the desires of the Honorable President Trujillo because they do not have access to lands. The local bosses have all the lands marked off with trochas, seemingly for the purpose of making the poor unable to live." The ranger of the Northwest commune of Monte Cristi wrote of a similar situation, in which "the lust for woods among some owners [had led them to] cordon off immense areas with two cords of wire and wood fences. . . . These are places where there has never been a land survey. The small agriculturalists are complaining, saying why are these montes being cordoned off if they are producing no crops, and the result is that there is less area for raising animals."[39]

To confront these and other land problems, Tolentino recommended to Trujillo that Carretero's "highly beneficial plan for the distribution of lands among the rural poor" be extended throughout the country, "with the assistance of an Agricultural Instructor, a work team, seeds and the necessary [farming] techniques."[40] The bureaucratic structure responsible for the campaign would be the recently created *juntas protectoras de la agricultura* (agricultural support boards) now put under Carretero's supervision with branches in each section. These juntas would seek to provide free access to idle terrain on the basis of contracts whose conditions depended on whether the lands in question were terrenos comuneros, state lands, or privately owned.

The campaign to distribute land would be one of the Trujillo state's most important policies. It reflected the regime's fundamental objectives, the first of which was to expand agricultural production and further national self-sufficiency through increased concentration on farming. Note, for example, the exhortation by the governor of Monseñor de Marino "to increase by ALL MEANS POSSIBLE agricultural production, especially articles for subsistence needs. . . . THE COUNTRY MUST HARVEST ENOUGH TO SUSTAIN ITSELF, AND EVEN TO SELL ABROAD AND OBTAIN ECONOMIC BENEFITS."[41] To do so, the government sought to free up the forces of production and maximize output in a situation of supposedly idle labor, excess land, and capital shortage. "To move men to work and make idle soil productive in our fun-

damentally agricultural country" was the essence of the new campaign, one
journalist argued. With this "socialization of the land . . . the Republic [will
attain] the maximum development of its economic potential!" A bald example of the regime's fixation on production was Carretero's instruction to one
junta leader: "Double the agricultural work of each inhabitant and put in
good condition all the abandoned plots" left by swidden cultivation.[42]

Echoing reformist thinkers from the turn of the century, the perennial
elite critique of rural "vagrancy" was not cast as the consequence of an inexorable peasant laziness, but rather as the result of material constraints on
the popular rural classes—namely, a lack of secure land access as well as inadequate infrastructure, irrigation, farming techniques, and markets. In 1935
an editorial in the nation's most prominent newspaper, Listín Diario, exemplified this view: "The new southern usufructuaries having been provided
for, the Commissioner of President Trujillo [Carretero] is at present in the
Communes of the East, carrying out the same program and winning for our
incomparable Chief the grateful applause of the legion of country people
who had been leading an idle life for lack of four clumps of soil to cultivate
in order to meet the needs of themselves and their families."[43] Notions of
peasant vagrancy, moreover, were subtly redefined to signify agricultural
production below that perceived to be necessary for self-sufficiency (10 tareas) rather than a broader lambasting of peasants' supposed proclivity for
mere subsistence exploitation. Indeed, by emphasizing peasants' need to
cultivate land "to meet the needs of themselves and their families," the state
echoed peasants' own norms of independence, while fostering a discourse of
self-sufficiency for the nation as well. Rather than decrying the ways in which
rural and national autarky could, in fact, be at odds, the regime celebrated
self-sufficiency at both levels, and therein valorized peasant farming as never
before.

At the same time, those who did not readily accept the regime's modus
vivendi—state support in return for production (and allegiance)—were arrested as vagrants, and either sentenced to three months in jail or alterna-
tively granted 10 tareas to cultivate immediately, and then carefully scruti-
nized.[44] The 10-tarea vagrancy law was first promulgated at a national level
under the U.S. military government in 1920, but it was strictly enforced for
the first time by the Trujillo state.[45] Addressing peasants at local meetings,
the governor of Samaná made the regime's harsh antivagrancy policy and
ideology crystal clear: "To the lazy, to the work renegades, to those who are
but parasites living off of other people's labor, I want to warn you . . . [have]
your ten tareas cultivated as soon as possible. Because if you do not, you will
be pursued and brought to justice for vagrancy, a stigmatizing crime that

carries a stiff penalty."[46] Although neither official discourse nor the law specified the sex of those who could be considered "vagrant," the law does not appear to have applied to women. Instead, it seems that female vagrancy remained legally defined as women who did not live "in accordance with their sex," or who led an "idle, loose, and scandalous life," in the language of the 1855 national police statute.[47]

In addition to the drive simply to further production, state efforts at land distribution embodied an ideology of development based on Dominican farmers rather than foreign agribusiness. The debate that had raged between these two imagined paths to progress since the second half of the nineteenth century tilted further in favor of small farming during the early Trujillo regime. The land distribution campaign was perceived as a check on the sugar industry, rural dispossession, and migration to the cities. In 1935 the editors of *Listín Diario* wrote:

On many occasions we have discussed the important problem of the peasant exodus, an uncontrollable hemorrhage which is significantly weakening the social body, ... increasing poverty and decreasing public and private wealth. ... Within a few months [in the city], the misguided peasants are besieged with the most complete failure ... often ending up in prison. ...

With the current distribution of lands that is being systematically carried out in the twelve Provinces, the afflictions that we suffered before will disappear. ... Having land to cultivate as their own, assured of good, productive crops, the attraction disappears of a modest wage offered by the nearest estate, as does the asphyxiating atmosphere created by *latifundistas* monopolizing all the land, which forces landholders to become humble farm workers or to migrate [to the city] and be crushed by failure.[48]

An analogous mixture of conservatism and populism was evinced in an authoritative missive from Tolentino and his colleagues, in which they advised Trujillo that "the return to the countryside of the agricultural worker is what is needed for our Country so as to foster the small independent producer who loves the land that is cultivated with one's own hands. ... The small landowners are the pillars of the social order and the basis for the Nation's wealth."[49]

It was already a long-standing argument among certain Dominican writers that political stability required a nation of sedentary farmers rather than of pastoral or "nomadic" peasants or landless, underemployed workers. Men without ties to property were viewed as ready recruits for the armed rebels who had perpetuated the nation's long history of political upheavals.[50] In support of the land distribution campaign, the editors of the country's important national newspaper, *La Opinión*, wrote: "The Government has as its highest ideal the hope that the day will soon arrive when every Dominican family has its own farm and its own home. . . . [Then] there will be no more revolutionary upheavals."[51]

Listín Diario extolled the land distribution campaign in even broader terms as an antidote to "degenerate capitalism":

The Generalissimo . . . is carrying out with unflagging energy . . . the socialization of Dominican lands. Without violent outbursts, without pedantic speeches, without noise, President Trujillo is bringing about the success of one of the most vital measures of a true, modern statesman: reforming the land to meet collective and private needs. Possession will come to correspond with those who cultivate [the land], awakening it from the heavy sleep of inertia and unproductiveness. That infliction of degenerate capitalism which has cost humanity so many rivers of blood and so many tears, the latifundium, is being fought and steadily overcome.[52]

Trujillo's agrarian reforms were represented here as an effort to mediate capitalist modernization and to shift it in a direction more salutary than that based, as the prominent figure Francisco Peynado had written of the East in 1919, on "latifundia and a miserable proletariat . . . , ephemeral foundations . . . out of which quickly grow class hatred, discontent and desperation."[53] As one official proclaimed, these reforms preempted the need for peasant revolution by countering the otherwise relentless expansion of latifundia.[54]

The regime's idealization of the small farmer and its efforts at agrarian reform dovetailed with nationalist concerns. In his 1936 annual report, the new secretary of agriculture, Rafael Espaillat, praised the land distribution campaign as a "model of prudent, nationalist politics with imponderable benefits for the well-being, unity, and independence of the Republic. . . . Peoples divested of dominion over their land are enslaved peoples." As we saw in the last chapter, Espaillat had been an impassioned advocate of peasant agricultural production and restrictions on the sugar industry since the 1920s, when he had been secretary of agriculture under Vásquez. He came from Santiago, as did Tolentino. This perhaps influenced both men's vision of the nation following a model of small-farming approximating what had already developed in much of the Cibao. Interestingly, Espaillat had also been a staunch opponent of General Trujillo when he was in Vásquez's cabinet. At the start of 1930, he had led a failed effort to persuade President Vásquez to remove Trujillo from his position as head of the army.[55] Yet this history did not prevent President Trujillo from integrating Espaillat into the regime (and conceivably it may have inspired Trujillo to do so). Along with Tolentino and Carretero, Espaillat moved the Trujillo regime in reformist directions. Indeed, he even compared the land distribution campaign to the Mexican

Revolution's policies in favor of the "most abandoned members of the Mexican citizenry: the country's Indians and poor agriculturalists."[56]

The aim of Trujillo's land reform was not only to promote nationalist ideals and create political stability but also to wrap the regime in a type of rural populism. In fact, the aforementioned letter from Tolentino and his colleagues counseling Trujillo appears to have been written in response to the dictator's expressed interest in gaining support among the popular classes. Apparently, Trujillo had been considering pursuing this also in an urban context through new housing for workers. Tolentino et al. continued their letter to Trujillo with this forceful recommendation:

Our country is not industrial and at present there does not exist a class of industrial laborers that need the immediate assistance of the State to improve their living conditions. The construction of housing for workers is justified . . . in the big cities that live on industrial factories. Our country, on the contrary, is essentially agricultural. . . . Therefore we believe that whatever investment . . . is made by the State in terms of helping the working people should be used for fostering agriculturalists, creating small property owners, [and] stimulating and furthering production from the land. . . . The industrial workers will not be excluded from agricultural distributions. Any worker can acquire a farm.[57]

Trujillo's desire to project a populist image is also evinced in Carretero's frequent correspondence with the generalissimo regarding the progress of the land distribution campaign. Carretero's accounts of popular acclaim for Trujillo are sufficiently consistent and effusive as to stand out from most intrastate missives and suggest that Trujillo was eager to hear of popular support in this regard. In December 1934, at the outset of the campaign, Carretero telegrammed Trujillo: "The future small proprietors [of Azua] are overtaken with gratitude . . . [and] deliriously acclaim your name." Other examples abound, such as: "The inhabitants of these areas regard you with love and admiration, repeatedly cheering your name"; "I can assure you that the peasants genuinely thank you for this help"; and "I have spoken at length [to them] about the protection and aid you offer men of work, and . . . [have told them that] I came at your behest to resolve their problems and offer them help." Often, when Carretero gave out plots, he also distributed photographs and portraits of Trujillo to his "peasant friends," reflecting Trujillo's wish to be associated personally with the land grants and thus to be "loved" as well as feared. The distribution of lands under Trujillo was represented as a gift more than a right and thus served to dramatize the dictator's personal power.[58]

The land distribution campaign quickly brought dramatic results in virtually every province of the country. By June 30, 1936, the state had reportedly distributed 107,202 hectares of land to 54,494 agriculturalists (heads of household), representing 6 percent of occupied land and an impressive 29 percent of the nation's farms. Plot size varied. Although they averaged around 2.1 hectares (34 tareas), in land-scarce areas the government ceded plots of generally around 10 to 20 tareas; in other areas peasants each received between 60 and 100 tareas of land.[59] The precipitous operation also soon realized much of its potential, even though its significance would continue, to some extent, throughout the regime. Half of all distributions occurred between December 1934 and June 1936 while Carretero was spearheading the campaign and while Tolentino and subsequently Rafael Espaillat were secretaries of agriculture. By 1945 a total of 178,793 hectares had reportedly been given out to 85,554 agriculturalists.[60] And by 1955, 222,016 hectares had been distributed to 104,707 persons, representing 10 percent of occupied land and the equivalent of 31 percent of rural producers.[61] These amounts do not include the permanent distribution of lands provided by the regime's agricultural colonization program, founded by Espaillat under President Horacio Vásquez in the late 1920s. (Colonization and irrigation efforts to some extent supplanted the land distribution campaign in the latter half of the regime as fertile, nearby areas became unavailable.) These figures also do not represent all forms of land distribution, given that property reforms under Trujillo served, as we will see, to legalize squatter holdings throughout the country, only a portion of which were included in land distribution statistics. Finally, these figures do not include the areas given out during the final years of the regime, when it made renewed efforts to acquire and distribute territory to a growing landless population.

Yet what exactly was this land distribution campaign, which involved the allocation of millions of tareas within only a few years to tens of thousands of peasants? What land was distributed and under what conditions? The answers are as complex as were the various forms of property in the country and the contradictory power relations within the Trujillo regime. In fact, the land distribution was neither a straightforward agrarian reform nor an illusory manipulation designed simply to enhance the regime's image. The campaign was far from a uniform policy simply imposed from the top down. Squatters, peasants, landowners, peso title holders, foreign corporations, local officials, and members of the central state all competed to shape the meaning and significance of the campaign. It was flexible, experimental, and varied widely in its scope and meaning across the diverse regions of the country and in response to a multiplicity of distinct land tenure problems and power relations. In addition, the campaign was sometimes blurred with the colonization program, which also provided land to peasants. Essentially, however, there were three types of property distributed: comunero, state, and private, each of which had its own dynamics and conditions. Technically, almost all of these distributions were made via a contract between the owner and the beneficiary in which the latter agreed to return the land to the owner after a certain number of years. However, the evidence suggest that in the majority of cases, land never had to be returned—indeed there was no one to return to it—and property rights were consolidated by the tenant.

During the height of the campaign, 1935 to 1940, cropland increased by a dramatic 47 percent, as woods were cleared and cultivated.[62] Peasants had secured free access to land that "owners" were claiming but not using; and, in return, the state was able to effectively accelerate the transition from a pastoral economy to one based on sedentary agriculture and intensive land use. This would mean that many peasants would ultimately have to eke out a subsistence on tiny plots. At the same time, though, it also meant that the vast majority of rural denizens, who owed no land tribute or rent and rarely had to work as wage laborers, had maintained a substantial measure of economic independence.[63]

Distribution of Terrenos Comuneros

When Trujillo came to power, terrenos comuneros were the most common form of property.[64] Much of the Eastern sugar region had already had private property titles allocated, generally awarded to the sugar companies via prescription rights based on surveys and enclosures from the turn of the century that the companies (or their assignors) used as evidence of occupation. But in most places where enclosures existed outside of the sugar areas, they had been established too recently to secure prescription rights. In addition, private surveys had been prohibited since 1920. Thus the main extant threat to peasant land access was that of peso title owners proceeding with land divisions in unoccupied areas or, worse still, where existing occupants had not yet consolidated prescription rights.

Yet, during the 1930s and 1940s, the Trujillo regime significantly reduced the threat of peasant eviction by peso title holders. It did so first by distributing idle lands and woods in comunero sites to landless peasants and by providing existing squatters with long-term contracts guaranteeing their possession of the plots they were already cultivating. In effect, the state was slowly dismantling the comunero system of property by assigning fixed plots of land to specific individuals or families, many of whom would eventually obtain property rights to them via prescription (at the expense of absentee accionistas and other title holders not fully utilizing the land). Unless co-owners had already completed the legal steps necessary for the division and saneamiento of a particular comunero site, local officials treated the area as if it were simply state owned for the purposes of land distribution. The state thus effectively nullified potential peso title claims and secured the rights of existing squatters to the land they cultivated. Given the predominance of ter-renos comuneros and the only recent emergence of clearly defined private property, it is probable that the greatest amount of land distributed by the Trujillo state was terrenos comuneros.[65]

The regime's policy of viewing comunero areas that had not yet been le-gally divided as if they were state lands can be seen as a reflection by the Tru-jillo state of traditional peasant norms. As we have seen, peasants had treated all unoccupied lands—whether technically comunero or state lands—as "no-body's lands," accessible to all on a first-come, first-served basis. State func-tionaries now cemented this popular conflation of state and comunero land through its land distribution practices. For instance, when the *juez alcalde* (justice of the peace) reported in 1936 a cumulative distribution of 1,542 hec-tares in Enriquillo, he stated without differentiation that these lands were all "comunero or state land." In this context, "comunero" referred to any land without clear private ownership, whether historically state land or not, all of which was now subject to unilateral distribution by the government. Carret-ero was once questioned by a local resident—perhaps an accionista—about Carretero's ignoring land rights based on existing titles. Jesús Ramírez, who would subsequently be appointed head of the junta of La Descubierta (a sec-tion of Neiba in the southern frontier region), recalled Carretero's arrival there in 1935 and a meeting he called for all the "men of the section":

Major Carretero told us that . . . vagrancy would be punished with public work and to show that you were not a vagrant, we who lived in the countryside had to have at least ten tareas [cultivated]. He also told us that he was going to organize a junta protectora de la agricultura to distribute the neglected lands that were not being worked by their owners. We were all absolutely silent and only Major Carretero was speaking. . . . Then all of a sudden we heard old Bartolo Tá ask: "So, chief, all the ti-tles of [Queen] Isabel *la Católica* are no longer worth anything?"

Carretero "didn't know how to answer the old man," and simply did not re-spond to the rhetorical question posed by don Bartolo.[66] And Carretero would continue to treat property as if it were either private land or state land, with the latter including, and indeed at times being called, "comunera." This was clear a year later when he asked the San Cristóbal junta president for a report of all lands either "offered [by private owners] or comuneras" so that they could be distributed by him.[67]

Despite the ways in which the regime discounted peso titles, they were not, in fact, legally annulled. And this left space for divergent interpretations among state officials in charge of the juntas. Some junta officials, who may themselves have owned land pesos, subscribed more to the view intrepidly suggested by don Bartolo than that of Carretero. For instance, José Pichardo, the local junta leader in San José de Ocoa, protested to his superiors that, in this area, "most of the lands . . . are being exploited by those who are not landowners, who do not have one centavo of [peso] titles that would permit them to exploit these lands, to the detriment and violation of those who have sacrificed their money to be owners." Pichardo's denunciation continued, suggesting that many peasants were being equally vocal about their own perspective on what constituted a legitimate claim to property: "[Occupants are] always alleging their imaginary right [to the land] based, they say, on possession, without realizing, whether out of ignorance or bad faith that their possession . . . is squatting, never a just entitlement." And Pichardo revealed the embrace of such popular notions by other officials, complaining: "Worst of all, there are authorities supporting and condoning the unjust claims, creating confusion, as never can one be an owner according to our legislation without having bought, been given, or inherited a proper title." The new supervisor of the agricultural juntas, Bayoán de Hostos, who replaced Carretero in 1936,[68] responded in a curt manner to Pichardo's complaint, including his misrepresentation of the nation's property laws: "In terms of abuses of terrenos comuneros you can denounce them to the president of the Tribunal de Tierras." But Hostos did not suggest that Pichardo intervene in the matter, nor was any investigation commissioned, nor did the state pressure squatters to leave. Instead, Hostos objected to the only limited land distribution that had so far been carried out in Pichardo's area.[69]

Pichardo's position was rarely expressed in official correspondence. Overall, the record indicates that most comunero sites were distributed as if they were state lands. And peso title owners were not recognized as having any rights to lands that they were not already using. In a few cases, the state legitimated its distribution of terrenos comuneros by itself acquiring peso titles to a site and then declaring it all state land. But generally on the bureaucratic forms and contracts documenting distributed plots, the "owners" of comunero sites were listed either as "comunero" or, paradoxically, as the recipients themselves. In Villa Tenares, for instance, of the thousand hectares given out by November 1936, 301 had been listed with the owner as "comunero."[70] In another commune, four hundred peasants were listed simultaneously as the recipients and the "owners" of some 465 hectares that were distributed in April and May of 1936.[71] Ownership was also frequently ascribed to "the junta" that organized the distributions or simply left blank.[72]

These contracts were typically for ten to twenty years; but presumably, as there were no recognized owners other than the state or the recipients themselves, the lands never had to be returned and ultimately became the property of the beneficiaries through prescription.

In the years prior to Trujillo's rule, those claiming land with peso titles or enclosures had in certain instances required occupants to sharecrop or, less frequently, to pay rent. Although formal tenancy arrangements never dominated Dominican agriculture, they became more common in the early twentieth century as land was being valorized. Land "distribution" often served to eliminate these practices.[73] The regime's early ideology of establishing a nation of small, independent agriculturalists clashed with the practice of sharecropping, which was represented as inequitable and a disincentive to expanding production beyond subsistence needs. State officials cast sharecropping as "exploitation" and a "noxious practice" at odds with peasant independence. In 1935, for example, Carretero complained to Trujillo of the "landlords who exploit the humble charging them 25 percent and 50 percent of the crops harvested."[74] With few exceptions at this time—namely, especially fertile and developed areas such as La Vega in the Cibao—the agricultural juntas distributed private as well as comunero and state lands without any sharecropping or monetary obligations.

When Dulce Echevarría of Azua demanded a fourth of the crop from occupants of the land that she claimed by virtue of peso titles, Carretero responded that her claim was validated only by a private land survey, which was insufficient for claiming property in terrenos comuneros. Carretero rejected other demands for various forms of tribute from peasants by those without absolute titles issued through a saneamiento; and he excoriated the "abuses that certain powerful individuals committed . . . [against] poor agriculturalists because . . . the powerful . . . had some documents to a piece of land that had never been surveyed [and saneado]." As other peasants heard about the land distribution campaign, they demanded the same rent-free conditions for themselves and appealed to the state for assistance in this regard. Such appeals were forwarded from the secretary of agriculture to Carretero, who asserted that "these situations will be resolved and the peasants will be pleased with the elimination of those obstacles that are being placed before them and hindering their labor."[75]

The second dimension to the Trujillo regime's agrarian reform was the revision and manipulation of the reigning system of property adjudication. Above all, new state policies greatly delayed the already slow process of submitting national territory to official surveying and entitling while peasants—now obliged to be sedentary for the first time—could extend their period of possession long enough to consolidate prescription rights. The regime thereby facilitated peasants' acquisition of property via prescription both on the lands that the state granted them and on plots they were already farming without title. In 1934 the Trujillo-controlled congress passed Law no. 670, prohibiting privately initiated and funded mensuras catastrales. (These had been allowed since 1923, because state revenues for underwriting surveys had been depleted.) This new legislation effectively curtailed the power of peso title owners to have comunero sites surveyed and divided before occupants (squatters or land recipients) had consolidated property rights via prescription.[76] It was now solely the responsibility of the state where and when surveying and title adjudication would take place. And in the 1930s, the Trujillo state underwrote few such efforts. In most cases, it had neither the funds nor evident interest to underwrite surveys and determine titles, when doing so would generally have meant awarding land to peso title holders over squatters and land recipients. While an estimated 17 percent of the nation's land had been surveyed between 1920 and 1929, only approximately 7 percent more was surveyed by 1940. Thus, after the first decade of Trujillo's rule still only a fourth of the country's land had been submitted to a mensura catastral.[77] The state had effectively stymied the process of land division and title adjudication among peso title holders while peasants became sedentary farmers and accumulated time toward prescription.[78]

After fostering fixed landholdings among peasants through policies of land distribution and sedentarization during the 1930s, the state sponsored a massive, nationwide land survey during the 1940s and 1950s. An additional 40 percent of land would be surveyed between 1941 and 1955.[79] This surveying produced cadastral maps throughout the country documenting all land occupations in a given area, and thus assisted peasants in obtaining prescription rights during the subsequent process of determining titles. The possibilities for peasants to acquire property via prescription were furthered, moreover, by both the snail's pace at which titles were actually adjudicated and new laws that reduced the necessary period of possession. In 1941, Law no. 585 reduced the longest period of prescription from thirty to twenty years.[80] By the time property was ultimately adjudicated, often many years after an area had been surveyed, records from the Tribunal de Tierra indicate that most occupants were able to claim permanent property rights by means of prescription. Doing so required producing witnesses who would testify that the land had been occupied by the claimants for sufficient time. As one peasant from near Azua explained to me, after a survey had been ordered by Trujillo, "you took two or three witnesses [to the Tribunal de Tierras] and verified that this land had been under your control for so many years. . . .

COSUMNES RIVER COLLEGE
LEARNING RESOURCE CENTER
8401 Center Parkway
Sacramento, California 95823

And then it was awarded [to you]. . . . The order was for land to be awarded to those who occupied it. . . . And that is how we obtained our title."[81]

Certainly, some occupants, unable to consolidate prescription rights, lost in property adjudications to accionistas. But it is doubtless because the mensura catastral granted property rights to peasant occupants in most instances that I heard only a few complaints about it in my interviews with elderly peasants across the country. Most peasants stated that the mensura was, in fact, a positive measure because it secured their property.[82] Also few mentioned any difficulty with regard to the cost of surveying. Technically, those awarded land by the Tribunal de Tierras were obliged to repay the state for surveying costs either in cash or with 20 percent of their land. However, the law also stipulated that the owners' economic condition should be considered for forgiving or reducing their obligations to the state. And, in practice, peasants generally did not have to pay the surveying fees for many years if at all. They were obliged to do so only when requesting a copy of their title. Even then a title might be issued without payment, with a lien inscribed on the back of it for the amount the state had paid the surveyor.[83]

Surveying and allocation of property to peasants contributed to the sedentarization of agriculture and a new discourse of private land ownership. Some elderly peasants explained to me that they had continued to practice shifting agriculture until the mensura catastral came to their area.[84] After the mensura, though, they remained on the specific plots that had been documented in surveys as the sites they occupied in order to ensure that these properties would ultimately be awarded to them via prescription. This sedentarization was at times accompanied by official efforts to solidify a new set of private property norms for peasant landholdings. One person recounted how under Trujillo a state functionary accompanying the surveyor explained to her that this was now her property and that no one else could enter it or take fruits from her tree the way people had customarily done in the past.[85]

The essence of Trujillo's agrarian reform was that through the regime's complementary land policies and judicial measures with regard to property, most cultivators—both distribution recipients and squatters—were eventually able to consolidate property rights in terrenos comuneros (as well as in state lands, as will be discussed below). At the same time, accionistas were generally prevented from gaining property rights simply on the basis of their titles, while the shrewd and economically powerful were restricted in their efforts to enclose, accumulate, and speculate with the nation's formerly unoccupied areas. Angel Luciano Novoa, an elderly peasant from Sabana Alta, explained: "If I was a landowner . . . saying that because I fenced off this land . . . and because I had money . . . it was mine . . . Trujillo took on the landowner and told him, 'I need this amount of that land to carry out land distribution.' If the señor did not come to an agreement with [Trujillo], well he had only two choices, either he had to go to prison or catch a plane [out of the country].'[86] If lands were not being worked, they were considered "nobody's lands" by the regime. And, as such, they were available for distribution and the early regime's program of development based on increased peasant production and national self-sufficiency.

In 1933, Trujillo publicly considered eliminating the Tribunal de Tierras altogether on the grounds that surveying under existing conditions was "contrary to the supreme economic interest of the country whose goal is the maximum distribution of lands."[87] Despite the boldness of this unrealized proposal, the Trujillo dictatorship appears to have been wary of openly repudiating existing notions of legal property, even while it undermined them in practice. Shrewdly, it attacked elite interests indirectly, preferring to manipulate laws and operate on a case-by-case basis rather than transparently striking group interests and eviscerating fundamental legal constructs. Similarly, the regime did not simply turn the Tribunal de Tierras into a sham but rather sought to create the material and legal conditions permitting rulings in squatters' and recipients' favor without recourse to any blatant miscarriage of justice and destruction of the court's overall independence. Trujillo waited until 1961 to promulgate bold legislation expropriating all peso titles. At that point, terrenos comuneros became legally equivalent to state lands, as had been the practice and ideology of the Trujillo regime throughout its rule.[88]

Distribution of State Lands

State lands in the Dominican Republic were essentially a residual category consisting of all land that had been neither ceded by the Crown in the colonial era (through varying concessions that had evolved over time into terrenos comuneros in almost every case) nor occupied for sufficient duration for settlers to claim private property via prescription. During the Trujillo regime, local juntas oversaw the distribution of state lands to peasants who were either immediately given property rights or who were granted permission to occupy the land free of charge for periods generally lasting, in principle, ten to twenty years.[89] The contracts granting this permission listed as "owners" of the distributed lands either the state or—again paradoxically—the recipients themselves. In most instances, occupants would be able to maintain possession for a period of time sufficient to consolidate property rights via prescription.

When Carretero commenced his campaign around Barahona, the lands he first assigned to peasants were mostly in areas assumed to be state property. Distributions in the region during 1936 continued to be listed as taken from predominantly state lands. In Duvergé, for instance, one monthly report documented a distribution of 768 hectares of state land compared with only 12 hectares of private land. Throughout the country, varying amounts of state land were made available. Near Jima Abajo in the Cibao, for instance, 262 hectares of state lands were given to 110 individuals in one two-month period, with the plots ranging from 1 to 6 hectares. Although the contracts were for ten years, a recipient from this distribution informed me that the land never had to be returned, but rather became the property of recipients. The varying plot sizes in Jima Abajo reportedly reflected the beneficiaries' different resources, family size above all.[90]

In other instances, a wide variance in the size of distributed plots may indicate that the grants were a legalization of pre-existing occupations by squatters. Legalization protected occupants from the possibility of eviction and permitted the eventual consolidation of property rights by those cultivating the land. For instance, at the end of 1934, the state planned to "distribute" its lands in Pedro García near Santiago by demarcating the cultivated areas of some two hundred persons already occupying plots there. Free tenancy contracts would be given to occupants for the area of actual cultivation, and the remaining territory would be distributed to others, regardless of whether or not it was already enclosed by various land claimants.[91] For the many people already utilizing the area, this was thus more a legalization than a distribution of land, as squatters became secure occupants and potential owners of private property.

The state acted similarly in Enjuagador in the commune of Guerra. Saturno Pagán, a Puerto Rican immigrant, claimed nearly 188 hectares, which he had begun clearing around 1912 mainly for cattle grazing. Over time, squatters increasingly entered "his" land. In 1934, some inhabitants complained to the state that Pagán had threatened to let his animals ravage their crops if they did not leave. Tolentino defended the squatters, informing Pagán rhetorically that he knew this "rumor could not be true" and that the Department of Agriculture was rethinking "the situation of these state lands and how they can be better utilized." Subsequently, the department made plans to "distribute" the lands to existing occupants as part of an agricultural colony.[92]

In many areas, land distribution was thus as much about securing possession and establishing property rights as it was about providing land. Peasants had traditionally had access to most state, as well as comunero, lands, but now they were acquiring the basis for private property. Antonio Taveras from Jima Abajo, near La Vega, was one of thousands of recipients listed in the Department of Agriculture records for land distribution.[93] When I spoke to him in 1994, he explained that for years he had used what he thought were state lands before he was given his plot by Trujillo in the same area. He told me that he was grateful for the 50 tareas (3 hectares) he received because having his own property was "more appealing and had more value" than using other lands. He said that in the past he never knew if the land he used actually belonged to someone else and might be taken from him.[94]

In addition to distributing uncleared state lands and legalizing areas already held by squatters, the secretary of agriculture acquired substantial new lands to distribute from areas appropriated from private owners in return for public irrigation. These represented the most valuable lands distributed. Whenever the government built a new irrigation project, private landowners were obligated to cede one-fourth of all cultivated lands and one-half of idle areas that were reached by the canal. This was required regardless of whether the owners wished to use irrigation, which large ranchers often did not. According to the law establishing this policy, Law no. 961 of 1928, the lands acquired were supposed to be distributed to "poor agriculturalists, with preference given to Dominican residents in the area of the canal." In return, recipients were required to farm the area they received within two months of its acquisition.[95]

This "fourth-part" policy dated back to before Trujillo's seizure of power and had antecedents as well in legislation under the U.S. military dictatorship (Executive Order no. 318). However, the pre-Trujillo state built few aqueducts, and defiant landowners generally refused to cede what lands they did owe.[96] Thus the policy's impact was felt primarily during Trujillo's rule. Furthermore, Trujillo substantially modified the original legislation, which had permitted state appropriations of irrigated private lands only "after sixteen years of uninterrupted irrigation." From the onset of the regime, this stipulation was ignored—as Vásquez had tried unsuccessfully to do—and it was suppressed in a 1942 legal reform. This reform also abolished the original law's stipulation that in idle areas comprising less than 1,000 tareas (63 hectares), only one-fourth of the area had to be ceded; instead the new legislation required that one-half of all idle lands be relinquished to the state.[97]

Public irrigation was a dramatic feature of the Trujillo state's efforts to expand agriculture and crop yields. Whereas in 1935 only 3,000 hectares of Dominican land was irrigated, by 1955 "constructed or almost complete" canals reportedly reached 165,000 hectares of land as a result of more than $20 million in state investment. This gave the Dominican Republic one of the highest proportions of irrigated land in Latin America.[98] And under Trujillo's revamping of the fourth-part policy, the state acquired somewhere between 40,000 and 80,000 hectares of highly desirable, irrigated lands to redistribute.[99]

It should be emphasized that many of those who received irrigated land had themselves been obliged to help build the canals as prestatarios. Formalized into law in 1907, but with antecedents dating back to the police laws of the mid–nineteenth century, *prestación del servicio* referred to public labor required in lieu of paying a road tax. It was used primarily, but not exclusively, for work developing and maintaining country roads in the area in which the prestatarios lived. However, until Trujillo's rule, the level of resistance to this onerous obligation prevented it from running successfully on a large scale.[100] Not only was it effectively implemented under Trujillo, but it was utilized to a far greater degree than ever imagined before in terms of number of days of labor demanded by the state. And it was a critical factor in the development of an impressive network of roads and a system of public irrigation during the regime.

For public irrigation canals built by the regime, in some cases the mobilization of prestatarios from surrounding areas was truly vast. At the height of their operation, several thousand prestatarios might be at work in a single month and occasionally even on a single day.[101] There was certainly some peasant resistance to this labor. And some were arrested when they did not appear for public work duty and then faced all the brutality that being imprisoned under Trujillo often entailed.[102] Yet overall, the state managed to secure peasants' cooperation in this onerous labor, which, in retrospect at least, elderly peasants rarely condemned. Peasant attitudes varied, though, depending on the type of work required—namely, whether it was seen as addressing a local need and whether there was land granted in return, as there was with most irrigation work. (Similarly, prior to Trujillo's rule, popular opposition was expressed mostly toward labor for public works outside the community and on the main highways, such as those that the U.S. military government developed.)[103] But overall, work as prestatarios under Trujillo actually appears to have been accepted as necessary to produce public works considered highly desirable by the rural popular classes: good local roads and irrigation canals. In this sense, the system of prestatarios was a type of microcosm of the regime's rural policies: harsh and repressive but appearing to serve ends desired by much or most of the country. And this led to a relatively efficient modernization project and popular acquiescence to it and to Trujillo's dictatorial rule.

The most powerful incentive to cooperate willingly with the prestatario system was the prospect that one might receive one's own irrigated plot from the state. It appears that state officials generally gave priority in the distribution of irrigated lands obtained by the fourth-part law to the prestatarios who had helped build the canal.[104] Newly irrigated lands were valuable and widely coveted, including by powerful individuals who in some cases attempted to obtain them through connections with members of the regime. As president of a local junta, Santiago Rodríguez of Las Matas de Farfán was responsible for the selection and approval of land recipients in his area. In one instance, he was obliged to defend himself to Bayoán de Hostos regarding his failure to respond to a request by "JY," presumably a man of influence. "JY" had asked for a sizable amount of land in the newly irrigated El Llano area. Rodríguez explained:

Everyone wants some of the lands in El Llano. Requests are coming in all the time . . . but no one can be promised or given anything since the Junta must attend to the over two thousand prestatarios who are the ones who labored in the removal of the land to build the canal, and who did so without even any sustenance provided to them. . . . It seems to this Junta that when it succeeds in obtaining the 50 percent of the lands owed [to it], it should be distributed to the poor agriculturalists who fertilized these lands with the sweat of their brow, and thus it will fulfill the desires of the Generalissimo. . . . If, for example, 400 tareas [25 hectares] were conceded to him ["JY"], that would deprive forty needy prestatarios of the urgent government assistance they are requesting.[105]

Although the outcome of this case is not known, Rodríguez's insistence on the official discourse of assisting the poor suggests the commitment of certain individual state actors to popular ends and the space they felt they had to shape the local consequences of distribution. At the same time, Rodríguez's need to defend his actions in favor of "poor agriculturalists" implies that it was not unheard of for the well-connected to obtain valuable lands.[106]

A few applicants seeking irrigated land from the state justified their requests on the basis of previous service to Trujillo—such as having supplied, in one case, fifty voters for him in the 1930 "election."[107] Similarly, a few letters were accompanied by recommendations from influential persons writing on their behalf. Connection to those with political or military power was doubtless a factor in some cases.[108] Nonetheless, most land appears to have been given to peasants. The many distributions of areas appropriated in return for the provision of public irrigation documented in Department of Agriculture records show that the vast majority of grants were for small plots. In the Baní region, for example, a large number of squatters and sharecroppers requested and received irrigated plots ranging from 10 to 50 tareas.[109] Similarly in Valverde, some 440 hectares were appropriated from six landowners and redistributed in amounts of only 10 tareas each to hundreds of recipients. In this case, the distributions involved legalizing the possessions of 412 squatters. And the government planned to place almost 300 additional peasants on the land.[110] Also, not infrequently, the "fourth part" was taken from small and medium landholdings (even 2- to 3-hectare plots, yielding even smaller plots for redistribution). Such small plots of land were of interest only to the poor, not the regime's powerful clients.[111] I asked Francisco Salazar, a ninety-year-old resident of Nizao, where irrigation had been developed under Trujillo's rule and who had once been a low-level civil servant in the area, if one had needed a connection to receive irrigated land. "In those days, you didn't," he answered. "During the Trujillo years, land was given to those who had none. And you really had to show you had none. Land wasn't given to the rich, but instead to the humble [la gente infeliz]."[112] Although there were certainly exceptions, as a rule the regime's control over the countryside depended more on securing many humble clients than cultivating an elite few.[113]

On the other hand, there were limits to official policy to assist the poor, for reasons of production as well as politics, particularly in regard to valuable, irrigated lands. Uladislao Mejía, for instance, was recommended as a worthy land recipient by the head of his agricultural district because Mejía was "in good economic condition . . . [and] a good agriculturalist." The state's production concerns prevailed here over commitment to distribute plots to those in greatest need. Generally, the state sought to further production by distributing land only in amounts commensurate with what, given skills, family size, or other economic resources, an individual was perceived to be capable of cultivating. When the director of a musical band requested 50 tareas (3.14 hectares) near the Mijo Canal in San Juan de la Maguana, he was given only 25. Despite his "enthusiasm," he had to prove himself apt for agricultural labor. Meanwhile others, such as Domingo Sánchez and his brothers, were given 50 tareas each.[114]

In addition, errors sometimes interfered with distribution policies. In one case, the fourth-part law initially worked against an existing squatter, Francisco Valenzuela. Apparently unaware of his presence, the officials had not considered him when they appropriated the land he was utilizing from its owner following state irrigation; they therefore distributed it to another person. After Valenzuela complained, however, the junta awarded the land to him, angering the erstwhile beneficiary.[115]

The above limitations notwithstanding, the fourth-part policies essentially functioned in the interests of land distribution and the expansion of small farming. And with the exception of taxes on rice grown on irrigated lands, the state collected no direct revenues from its irrigation, appropriation, and redistribution of these lands.[116] One official had recommended that those who received irrigated land should begin paying an annual rent and that in the future the government should not appropriate and distribute state-irrigated land but rather simply require payment from the landowners served by the establishment of new canals. Considering the revenue that these changes could have produced, it is notable that the regime chose not to adopt them.[117] Rather the fourth-part law remained a key part of the regime's agrarian reform policies.

Distribution of Private Lands

Even though most of the country's territory remained without clear ownership in the mid-1930s outside of the Eastern sugar region between Santo Domingo and La Romana,[118] privately owned lands represented an important part of the country. And they contributed a not insignificant portion to the distribution campaign. But the terms of these grants differed from state and comunero cessions in ways that made them far less attractive to recipients. Authorities pressured owners to provide peasants with idle terrain for limited, renewable periods, generally around five years. After that time owners with clear property titles had the legal right to evict tenants if the former were ready to utilize their plots, though they had to offer land elsewhere if they possessed other idle areas. Furthermore, tenants were often obligated to return the land sown with artificial pasture or, in other cases, with fruit-bearing trees, receiving no payment for these improvements. Whether contracts were renewed after they expired was a matter of negotiation between owners, tenants, and officials. In land-scarce areas, greater state pressure was applied to maintain tenancies. However, owners with a combination of political power and legal property titles could resist these pressures.[119]

Legally, cessions of private lands had to be voluntary unless they originated from the application of Law no. 758, a 1934 colonization law that prohibited landowners from maintaining large tracts of unused land (over 100 hectares). Although rarely applied, this 1934 law signaled official policy and functioned as a threat to landowners. Department of Agriculture documents indicate various instances of formal notice being given to landowners under this law.[120] Before its application, though, these owners were generally "persuaded" to contribute land to the campaign. In general, large landowners "spontaneously" offered vast areas. For instance, Guillermo Hahn of Puerto Plata delivered 628 hectares in the section of Arroyo Llano; Ramón Martínez, 692 hectares in the commune of Cabrera; and the powerful landowner Oscar Valdez, 922 hectares near Higüey.[121]

In some cases the juntas acted more unilaterally than official procedure dictated, even distributing privately owned land before it had been offered. It was only after 176 hectares belonging to the Amistad sugar company in Imbert, Puerto Plata, had already been handed out by the Bajabonico junta that the company announced it would inform Carretero whether it was "feasible for this enterprise to offer several thousand tareas of montes to be distributed among small agriculturalists." This letter appears to have been a diplomatic protest against the state's action. In this case, the central state retreated and ordered the distributions temporarily suspended. On the other hand, individuals and corporations with less power and autonomy were unable to protest as effectively. When Antonio Núñez complained that two agriculturalists, Gerónimo Gómez and Pedro Aquino, were farming his property, the Bayaguana junta simply informed him that the junta had already given them contracts and that it was obligated to ensure their rights. Núñez could, however, if he wished, add his signature to the contracts as the landowner.[122]

Large landowners were not the only contributors to the land campaign. Outside the East, there were relatively few *latifundistas*. Correspondingly, private lands were often ceded by medium and even small landowners. For instance, Juan Bautista Mercedes recalled that his father had cleared and claimed 50 tareas (3.1 hectares), but as he was able to farm only half the area himself, the other half "was given to another who could [cultivate it]" and it eventually became the latter's legal property.[123]

Although strong pressure was often needed to make owners offer land, it may have sometimes been profitable for them to do so. One function of agrarian reforms in general has been to oblige landowners to be more productive in order to avoid expropriation. In the Dominican Republic, private land distributions under Trujillo offered owners, in principle at least, an especially innocuous and convenient version of this process. Expropriations were, by law, limited to a set number of years. Inefficient private landowners forced to cede their idle terrain could reclaim their property after their contracts with tenants expired, provided that they were then ready to expand production, perhaps with new capital to hire laborers or to graze more cattle. Distributed lands, moreover, often had been monte before, but with a boost from tenants who had cleared the area they might now be used for pasture, for instance, or sold to someone else ready to utilize the land. On the other hand, recipients were not necessarily easy to evict, and the state sometimes pressured owners to renew or continue indefinitely the free tenancies. Furthermore, recipients posed a threat in that they might later be granted property rights to the area by the Tribunal de Tierras if the "owners" did not yet have secure titles.

If tenants were evicted at the end of their contracts (or contract renewals), this system was, in fact, far from a true land distribution. It was also a significant cost for occupants to return the area sown with pasture or, in some cases, with fruit-bearing trees and perennial plants. Yet this was less of a disincentive than sharecropping, which typically required one not only to leave the area cultivated at the end of the allotted period but also to pay the owner one-fifth to one-half of the crop each year of tenancy (except the last). Other traditional forms of tenancy were also more problematic for the peasantry than the contracts guaranteeing free access for at least four or five years. Prior to the spread of commercial agriculture and the scramble to consolidate property rights, putative landowners had frequently permitted tenants to clear a portion of land and harvest crops a couple of times before returning it to the owners sowed with pasture. In other cases, landowners simply "tolerated" squatters who cleared their lands. Often, however, upon seeing the soil bear fruit, the owners quickly sought to evict occupants, generally without compensation for improvements. They were able to do this given that no written agreement prevented peasants' ejection at any time. Jorge Guichardo Reyes of Pretiles, Valverde, complained to Trujillo that ten peasants had been permitted by a local landowning family to clear an area of montes and cultivate it, but then after they had "sweated and put their heart into it" the owners told them to abandon their crops before they ever had the chance to harvest them. Although officials were unable to return the lands to peasants in this case, as there were no junta contracts and the owners presumably held clear titles, in general they did seek to prevent such practices, which were seen as discouraging peasant production. In this instance, the Department of Agriculture required that the owners, Melchor and Perucho González, pay the occupants for their improvements in the amount estimated by a state agricultural instructor.[124]

As tenancy had been insecure and sometimes limited to only one or two years, there was little incentive or opportunity to grow perennial crops and to produce beyond subsistence needs. Furthermore, these periods were too short for trees such as bananas or cacao to bear even their first harvest, and other crops were not considered feasible given sharecropping terms. For example, peasants in Villa Mella had complained to Trujillo that they

would like to work but have nowhere to do so. . . . Where [the owners] do give us land . . . [it is] under the condition that we stay only a year and a half . . . which is not enough time for growing bananas. . . . And with rice . . . they only let us work if we give them half the crop . . . and we must also sell them part of the small bit of rice that we keep at prices set by the owners. . . . Since we wish to work, we are writing to you . . . with the hope that you will offer us your noble assistance.[125]

Thus, at its worst, temporary land "distribution" was a modus vivendi between the free land access that peasants wished to maintain and the sharecropping and tenancy that owners sought to impose.

The existence of ample uncultivated terrain largely without clear property owners was a necessary prerequisite to the Trujillo regime's rural policies and land distributions. In the few places where unused and unowned lands were scarce, as in the Eastern sugar areas around Ramón Santana and La Romana, the government was occasionally forced to buy land to mitigate the grievous problems produced by land monopolization. Notwithstanding the objections of Carretero and numerous other state officials, hundreds of families were ejected in the 1930s by the U.S.-owned Central Romana sugar company (then assignee of the Vicini estate) from the once comunero site of Campiña, with the company reportedly paying some peasants 25 centavos per tarea for their crops, but granting no compensation for collective pasture or woods. To mollify dire conditions, the state distributed land to many of those evicted in, among other places, nearby La Noria, which had belonged to the Vicini family's Compañía de Inversiones Inmobiliarias. Although presumably the land was granted under the rubric of temporary contracts for private lands, it was never returned. Still today, families of those evicted from Campiña grow beans and other food crops on this land. Others, such as Martín Maldonado, temporarily received adjacent lands in, for example, Magarín, Ramón Santana, owned by the Central Romana. Some fifteen years later, however, the company refused to continue lending out its land there (following two renewals of five-year contracts). Subsequently, the state bought some 500 hectares in the area from a wealthy Swiss immigrant family, the Coiscous—lands that the family had reportedly intended to sell to the Angelina sugar mill—and the area was permanently ceded to landless peasants. Maldonado received, and in 1994 still owned, two small plots totaling 2.4 hectares in an area of Ramón Santana known as De Silvain (named after the Coiscou family patriarch, Silvain).[126]

In an interview in 1994, Maldonado stated that "for the poor, Trujillo was the best there ever was." When asked then why Trujillo had permitted the eviction from Campiña, Maldonado articulated attitudes common among elderly Dominican peasants:

Trujillo did not want to do it, to the poor, to the *infeliz* [the humble]. . . . Some say bad things about Trujillo, but I do not agree. Trujillo gave us land, seeds, tools, and food and ten pesos on Saint Rafael's day. . . . Trujillo showed great respect for agriculture. What he wanted was production. He always said his "best friends are the men of work," and those whom he disliked were the vagrants, the thieves, and the politicians. . . . Today people don't thank Trujillo. But Trujillo sent everyone to school . . . even though he didn't want people to deal with politics. In our school, he even got rid of a book on the history of past presidents. One couldn't turn against Trujillo. . . . The bad side of Trujillo was that if one person went against Trujillo, Trujillo might attack other members of the same family even though they had done nothing against Trujillo.[127]

Maldonado's simultaneous appreciation and critique of Trujillo reveals the impact of the regime's agrarian policies. Despite the regime's many pernicious aspects, which were vividly recalled by Maldonado and other elderly peasants, state distribution of lands and agricultural assistance contributed substantially to popular rural acceptance of Trujillo's rule.

The Trujillo state's agrarian reform, an elaborate network of officials regulating access to comunero, state, and private lands, demanding increased peasant production, and providing some agricultural assistance, not only helped secure a social base for the regime. It also structured a sedentarized peasantry dependent on state support for the first time in Dominican history. By offering peasants their own plot of land that they were obliged to farm, the Trujillo state anchored a population accustomed to clearing new plots every few years usually in nearby montes. The government thus eliminated peasants' so-called nomadism, which had frustrated metropolitan rule since the colonial era.[128] The regime's agrarian reform and rural modernization project also established a novel role for national state officials and institutions in peasants' daily lives as the mediators of land access, protectors against eviction, and providers of needed resources. And finally, the state's mediation of peasants' access to land fostered a high level of political control. All individuals who wished to obtain land had to supply a certificate of approval and "good conduct" from the neighborhood authority, the alcalde pedáneo, or from one of various other local state representatives (agricultural district supervisors, colony administrators, or army officials). Certainly, anyone suspected of political disloyalty as well as anyone not considered hard working would be excluded from the regime's provision of land and other benefits. The regime's rural policies thus dramatically increased the national state's power and authority to monitor and control peasant practices. Support for small farming came at the cost of peasants' political autonomy.

Under these new conditions, the Trujillo state was able to impose what past governments, including the U.S. military dictatorship, had been unable to implement for decades: a nationwide system of corvée labor and a rudimentary income tax (in the form of the steeply scaled annual cédula fees).[129] The Trujillo regime thus extracted substantial economic resources from the peasantry without producing either any open opposition or informal resistance widespread enough to significantly hinder state operations.

The regime was effective in realizing these long-standing objectives because, while orchestrating major transformations in rural society and peasant-state relations, it also promised to preserve a core element of peasants' independent economy and identity, the possession of one's own land and means of subsistence. Peasants were generally protected from eviction and could accumulate sufficient time so that when their land was surveyed and later adjudicated, it would be awarded to them by prescription. When property was definitively allocated in the Dominican Republic, it was carried out almost exclusively on the basis of prescription, and outside the sugar areas mostly on the basis of material possession rather than problematic enclosures and private surveys. Most important, peso titles meant very little in the end. Needless to say, the outcome might have been quite different. Had Trujillo structured his political base upon a landed elite, property claims based on peso titles, trochas, and private surveys would have prevailed over squatters' rights and land "distributions." In sum, Trujillo was a dictator whose policies impeded more than they favored the consolidation and expansion of a pre-existing landed elite. These material foundations lent credibility to Trujillo's paternalist and populist claims. Although the regime helped eliminate many of peasants' traditional practices, it also proclaimed an important role for them as small farmers in an incipient commercial economy and modernizing nation. When peasants were approached by the state on these terms, and when they faced alternative prospects of dispossession and nonviable agriculture without state support, they embraced their incorporation by the national state and specifically by the Trujillo regime. The vision of nationalist intellectuals who prior to Trujillo's seizure of power had come to idealize a small farmer mode of modernization began to be realized. Given both the increasing strength of the state under Trujillo and the growing threats to peasants' control over their means of production, a long-sought peasant-state compromise was finally within reach.

4

Negotiating Dictatorship

Landowners, State Officials, and Everyday Contests over Agrarian Reform

The Trujillo regime's agrarian reform was not one that openly expropriated private property from large landowners and redistributed it to the poor, something still almost unprecedented in Latin America in the early 1930s.[1] Rather, it generally gave out lands that had claimants who had not yet consolidated definitive property titles, areas composing the majority of the country at the time. The reform was thus less of an attack on an existing landed elite than an obstacle to its development.[2] Nonetheless, Trujillo's agrarian reforms did eviscerate property claims and at times collide with both a nascent landed elite and foreign agribusiness, when they already had strong property claims or titles. Resistance to land distribution was stiffest and most effective in the case of foreign interests—mainly U.S. sugar companies—who then held some 15 percent of the nation's property, most of it with definitive titles issued in the 1920s by the Tribunal de Tierras or titles awarded then but still under appeal.[3] However, Dominican proprietors also resisted the redistribution of their private property and the discounting of their land claims.

When local officials met resistance to their efforts to redistribute areas claimed as private property, the central state did not always support them. Trujillo's agrarian reforms were represented in the press as populist and nationalist measures to secure land for those ready to till it and to prevent the country's property from becoming monopolized by large landowners and foreign corporations. Yet when officials acted on this discourse, unilaterally distributing lands claimed by others, they were often surprised to discover that the regime was not necessarily willing to discount private property rights to idle lands. Instead what emerged was a pattern of state equivocation and dissimulation. Rather than directly seizing private property, the central state engaged in subtle and often lengthy negotiations, oscillating between harassment and retrenchment, to secure lands from recalcitrant landowners.

The history of the implementation of land distribution in areas of private property or strong legal claims to land highlights the intricate and even delicate operations of state power under Trujillo and the constraints facing what has generally been perceived as a state with virtually unlimited discretion. Rather than a transparent, preconceived, and uniform policy, the regime's land distribution varied substantially in light of the exigencies of local power relations and land tenure in each case. Careful examination of the complex implementation of Trujillo's land distribution reveals how even in highly authoritarian and personalistic regimes such as Trujillo's, power is dispersed and conditional. Squatters, peasants, landowners, foreign corporations, the U.S. legation, local officials, and members of the central state all competed— albeit with highly unequal resources—to shape the contours of Trujillo's rural policies.

Although demonstrating the limits on the regime's power and Trujillo's personal discretion, this history also confirms the Trujillo state's relatively active role in attenuating the negative effects of land and agricultural commercialization on peasants and in mediating peasant-landowner conflicts. This role served both to legitimate the Trujillo dictatorship and to render peasants increasingly dependent on—and thus controllable by—the Dominican state. To some extent this is evident even in the history of the Eastern sugar region, where the massive eviction of peasants by sugar companies in the 1930s might seem to dramatize a supposedly antipeasant and antinationalist impetus of a regime with foreign interests as its only social base. We will see, though, that Trujillo officials had hoped to prevent foreign sugar companies' final consolidation of their holdings and resultant peasant dispossession. But the state proved relatively impotent when faced with giant U.S. sugar corporations possessing freshly minted property titles from the Tribunal de Tierras. This impotence had devastating consequences for thousands of peasants. Ultimately, the Trujillo regime was able only to ameliorate their condition, not to avert their eviction. Although modest compensation at best, even this effort helped sustain political stability and Trujillo's populist image among peasants in the Eastern sugar region.

The Ambiguities of Dictatorship: Contesting the Redistribution of Private Lands

The Trujillo regime's land policies constrained the prospects for land accumulation at a critical juncture in Dominican history. Although when Trujillo came to power most of the country's territory still had no clear titles, the vast majority of the nation's lands had claims of one type or another on them with varying degrees of legitimacy. In general, the state's agrarian reforms and property jurisprudence preempted claims made on the basis of peso titles, enclosures, and land surveys. But in some instances claims were legally well founded and forcefully asserted by influential landowners. These presented the regime with formidable and sometimes inexorable hindrances to its agrarian reform.

Given the out-migration of most of the colonial elite in the era commencing with the Haitian revolution and closing with Dominican independence from Haiti, it is likely that few of those confronting the state with strong legal claims to property were descendants of prominent colonial families. They were instead mostly the descendants of those who had taken advantage of the potential for upward mobility opened up by the elite vacuum created by this out-migration and by the continual wars, revolutions, and political instability of the nineteenth century. They were the caudillos and others who thereby gained local prestige and means sufficient to accumulate cattle and establish claims to the country's still immense undeveloped areas and timber lands. Also, they may have come from the small, relatively elite groups that emerged at the end of the 1800s with the expansion of export crops: agricultural merchants primarily in the Cibao or sugar colonos, mostly in the East, as well as a few who established large farms. Finally, they may have hailed from a number of better-off European families who arrived in the country at the turn of the century.[4] It was doubtless mostly these groups who had taken risks purchasing peso titles—however ambiguous they ultimately were—and staking out property claims by means of enclosures, surveys, and improvements, and, in some cases, by divisions of terrenos comuneros among accionistas through the regular court system.

Some of the landowners the Trujillo state confronted held individual titles from these court rulings. These procedures had awarded full property rights without necessarily considering squatters' claims. Although leading members of the Trujillo regime decried this mode of property acquisition, these adjudications had granted titles that were problematic for the state to ignore. Carretero learned of state resistance to the open violation of legal titles when he objected to court decisions from 1916 and 1917 that had awarded almost all the land in two comunero sites in Sabaneta, Monte Cristi, to Olegario Hernández, despite the fact that Hernández reportedly occupied none of the area and owned only 12 percent of the titles to the sites. On the basis of these decisions, Hernández had pressured residents to stop farming what he had successfully claimed as his property. Contending that the division was made improperly from both a legal and social point of view, Carretero wrote to Trujillo in 1935 that "the existing land division must be declared null and void [and] these lands distributed to poor agriculturalists."[5] However, the local fiscal (state attorney) affirmed the validity of the 1916 and 1917 court decisions and dismissed the possibility of successful legal appeal in favor of squatters.[6] Carretero continued to protest vehemently against Hernández, including to the secretary of the presidency, Moises García Mella, who reasserted that the government would not intervene against an existing court decision. When this provoked an angry response from Carretero, García Mella answered in unequivocal terms: "No one has the right to doubt . . . the Dominican judicial system . . . above all when it is . . . presided over by Generalissimo Rafael L. Trujillo Molina."[7] Carretero's uncompromising position suggests that the Trujillo state was not filled merely with terrorized and corrupt subordinates. At the same time, though, Carretero's open disdain for legal procedures may have hastened his transfer to another department in June 1936.[8]

The Trujillo regime's land policies wavered between the type of legal adherence to private property manifested in the Hernández case and dismissal of any notion of absolute ownership that included the right to leave one's own land idle or to evict squatters at will. There was a contradiction between the regime's affirmation of existing legal constructs of property and its agrarianist objectives. Officials could resolve this contradiction only through dissimulation. Essentially, where titles or strong claims to private property already existed, the state "asked" landowners to cede land for varying numbers of years to landless peasants or squatters. However, these "requests" for "voluntary" cooperation were, in fact, forceful demands for land cessions; indeed, at times a "request" was no more than window dressing for a fait accompli.

This approach gave rise to protests and resistance among landowners as well as to confusion and difficulties for local officials. Some large landowners simply did not respond to official land "requests," leading authorities to write, for instance: "As there was no reply to our first query, we ask you again . . . to give another thousand tareas to be distributed to needy peasants in the name of the Honorable President of the Republic."[9] Frustrated officials frequently complained of owners and claimants refusing to cooperate with requests that they "offer" their lands. The *síndico* (mayor) of Jarabacoa protested, for instance, that "there are numerous persons who wish to work but do not know where they can . . . [while] the landowners neither cultivate . . . nor cede [land]."[10] Under such conditions, the agricultural juntas did at times unilaterally appropriate lands. This occurred particularly in the initial phases of the campaign, when officials were testing the limits of the regime's will and capacity to enact reforms. When owners, or simply claimants, protested these appropriations, local officials were at times upbraided by higher authorities and forced to retrench their distribution plans.

An example from Elías Piña, a central frontier region, illustrates this dynamic. By the mid-1930s, even parts of this peripheral area had seen land accumulation and traditional surveying that left its agricultural junta without unclaimed lands to offer "needy agriculturalists" in some areas, despite a plethora of undeveloped terrain. Faced with owners and claimants refusing to cede those lands, the junta distributed them to peasants without owners' consent. One of these putative owners, Sr. Soto, subsequently denounced to the central state the distribution without his permission of lands he had had "surveyed."[11] The junta explained to Major Carretero that it had authorized peasants to cultivate Soto's lands only "in the belief that as these were uncultivated lands, Sr. Soto would not refuse the noble ideals of our Illustrious Chief, President Trujillo, for the expansion of agriculture in these regions. . . . [Moreover,] if the Junta has the right to authorize contracts only on unsurveyed lands, there are none [to be given] here. . . . The consequences if . . . [Soto is] permitted to keep [his] lands uncultivated are that other landowners will seek to do the same thing, as this is customary here."[12] Despite the junta's prediction that honoring Soto's property rights over even idle lands would jeopardize the land distribution campaign, government officials forced the junta to back down. The central state apparently did not want to violate what was perceived as a strong legal claim to land. This did not mean, though, that the state gave up on distributing Soto's land. Carretero hoped to achieve the junta's original goals by other means.[13] He advised the junta to submit the forms necessary for the state to appropriate private lands in accordance with Law no. 758. "In this way," Carretero wrote to the office of the president, "we will have land to offer the poor in the countryside."[14]

The local junta's actions had been quickly overruled in this case, in part because of Soto's land survey and perhaps because of his political influence. But elsewhere unilateral distributions by juntas of lands with merely private surveys went unnoticed or unimpeded by higher authorities. And in one instance, Carretero explicitly rejected property claims by peso title holders based on private surveys.[15] At the same time, though, the state was often chary of legally problematic actions. For example, an official in Samaná apprised a large sugar corporation, La Agrícola Industrial Dominicana, that he had distributed some of its land. When the company protested, the new chief of the agricultural juntas quashed the distribution, explaining to the official that "there is concern that no protests be made by foreign owners." Acting to respect the property claims and titles of at least influential landowners, the regime nonetheless continued to exhort local functionaries to distribute land. Even though the Samaná official's actions had to be reversed, the junta chief reassured him that the regime was "very satisfied with [his] efforts in the campaign that is being carried out."[16] In the same month, and probably in response to this and similar situations, the secretary of agriculture exhorted all the juntas to "proceed with tact, even when they are within the law

. . . in terms of avoiding tensions and conflicts with national and foreign interests."[17]

The state's reluctance to repudiate legal property norms and to confront
powerful landowners who held strong claims or titles to land led to the
veiled character and cryptic discourse of the distribution campaign, which
the governor of Puerto Plata noted in 1935 was "discreetly socializing the
land."[18] This reluctance produced seemingly deliberate ambiguity in official
directives. When the central state required juntas to obtain "voluntary" cessions of uncultivated areas from landholders, it created a virtually impossible
task for local officials. If owners or claimants were not forthcoming with offers, officials were expected simply to "convince" them to distribute their
lands. The possibility of landholders' opposition was, it seems, intentionally
ignored by the central state, leaving the juntas torn between adherence to the
regime's authoritarian policies and to its legalistic facade. The state appears
to have authorized no guidelines in the case of landholders' resistance. Official "persuasion" was expected to be sufficient to overcome any difficulty.
Carlos Báez, president of the junta of Cabral, complained to higher authorities that there were farms that had been neglected for more than fifteen years,
including those with their own water supply, but their owners refused to
have them distributed to others. Bayoán de Hostos, then Carretero's assistant, responded quickly but unhelpfully: "You can direct yourself in official
capacity to the property owners you refer to and request that their lands be
distributed to poor agriculturalists in the commune."[19] It was clear that Báez
had already attempted this. Thus, in effect, Hostos simply directed Báez to
try again.

Examples abound of the contradictions created by the state's insistence
that officials "convince" owners to distribute their "excess" lands. One landowner from Jarabacoa, R. Robiou, complained to the central state of the
communal junta's unilateral appropriation of his land. Hostos simply ad-
monished the junta president, José Batista Durán, explaining: "This office
would like the Juntas to live in harmony with the landowners in their jurisdiction."[20] On the other hand, two months later, the San Cristóbal junta
leader, Jacinto Pérez, appears to have been penalized for not "requesting"
land more forcefully or persuasively. Most of the land, Pérez had explained,
belonged to large absentee owners living in the capital, and "it will be very
difficult to get many to voluntarily cede part of their land." Three months
later, a new, perhaps more aggressive, junta president reported success in
obtaining lands to distribute and expectations of further contributions by
"constantly contacting landowners." Perhaps Pérez had been dismissed for
his passivity.[21]

Inevitably, the circuitous structure of land distribution and the central state's ambivalence toward private property and landowners left local authorities perplexed. More than a year after the inauguration of the distribution campaign, a circular had to be sent out by the Puerto Plata junta to its sectional subcommittees explaining that land distribution contracts should be issued only with the prior consent of owners. This missive baffled the president of the Villa Isabel subcommittee, Federico Molina, who felt compelled to write to Carretero directly for confirmation. Molina explained to Carretero that for some time he had been distributing plots without owners' permission in order to "eliminate the disorganized waste of idle lands and woods," but would have to suspend this practice until he received further notice from Carretero.[22] Meanwhile, though, other junta presidents continued to act unilaterally. In November 1936, Alcibíades Ogando, president of the Bánica junta, called a meeting of "landowners" to apprise them that all uncultivated, irrigated areas would be distributed at once to needy agriculturalists.[23]

The ambiguous guidelines for implementing land distribution in the minority of lands that were considered private property reflected not only concern for a proper legal facade but also a flexible system of rule conditioned by local power relations and case-by-case negotiation. Sustained efforts at persuasion by state officials were not sufficient in all cases of private land distributions, but they probably were in most, given the potentially high costs of resistance. Pedro Holguín Veras, supervisor of the Agricultural District of San Cristóbal, wrote in 1938 that the land distribution campaign was proceeding slowly. This was because it "has run up against the difficulty of abandoned lands that belong to laggards who struggle to not deliver them to poor agriculturalists. And as they are small plots I cannot apply the laws for colonization [and distribution] of private property [Law no. 758]." Despite these obstacles, however, Holguín reported that "by the method of persuasion," he was "proceeding to overcome these difficulties."[24] Whenever resistance to local officials continued, the secretary of agriculture would generally write directly to landowners, stating, as he did to Antonio Casanovas, that "this Secretary would like you to concede some of your land." At this point an agreement was generally reached. Casanovas had previously refused a request for 3,000 tareas made by the Hato Mayor junta president, Federico Rodríguez, despite the "large number of agriculturalists of the section who have requested that this junta contract land for them to work." But when Secretary of Agriculture Jacobo de Lara wrote to him, he immediately affirmed his willingness to contribute land, pointing out that he had ceded 800 tareas the year before. He preferred now, however, to grant lands other than those requested by the junta because those lands he wished to keep for logging operations and to sell to the sugar mills.[25] Although such haggling occurred frequently with those landowners who had strong claims to private property, few Dominicans outright refused the Trujillo state when requests came from high-level authorities.

One example of this type of state-elite negotiation is the case of Eugenio Santelises of Guayubín, Monte Cristi, who appears to have had strong political connections. Santelises's letters were formatted as if they were intrastate correspondence, suggesting that he himself may have been a functionary at some point. And it was evident that he had had access to intrastate memos concerning his case. Also, he may have been related to the Santelises family, under whose name and operation Trujillo controlled a large lumber business.[26] When the local Guayubín junta distributed lands that Santelises claimed, he protested not the distributions per se, but rather that the land-distribution contracts listed only the junta as the "landowner," suggesting that the lands would never be returned to him: "It is my contrary . . . understanding that [the juntas] can do this only when the legitimate owners do not offer their lands . . . which I did via the Provincial [junta]."[27] Santelises thus acknowledged that it was common for state officials to unilaterally distribute land when owners declined to cooperate. His insistence, though, that he had voluntarily contributed land was contradicted by the president of the Guayubín junta, Tomás Cabrera. Cabrera reported that Santelises had not permitted the distribution of lands from an area he claimed within a comunero site and had demanded instead that squatters purchase their plots from him if they wished to remain.[28] Given this lack of cooperation, the junta defended its unilateral distribution: "An error may have been committed, but if so I do not see what it is, because to make contracts in the name of the Junta when there are no offers from the co-owners is absolutely essential." Without such contracts, Cabrera explained, the "poor agriculturalist" would be left "bereft of the fruits of his labor."[29] In the end, a compromise was reached. Santelises professed that he had always been willing to distribute the 3,000 tareas that he claimed on the basis of 257.50 land pesos he owned in this comunero site. And Cabrera, while remaining unapologetic and even indignant, was compelled to respect Santelises's legal claim to the area: "I will comply with the desire of our friend Santelises and give out land in his name to those that need it. What I will not do is recommend to anyone that they buy it."[30]

It was generally state policy to respect claims to idle lands or areas perceived to be underutilized only if based on property titles that had already been awarded by the Tribunal de Tierras.[31] The area that Santelises claimed had been taken up for consideration by the Tribunal de Tierras but had not yet reached the final step of sentencing. When it did, Santelises's 257.50 land pesos were likely to win him more than 3,000 tareas in any area in which squatters had not already consolidated prescription rights. In a borderline private property case such as this, state caution as well as internal division emerged most clearly. Like other local officials, Cabrera took seriously the regime's populist discourse on property and thus dismissed the legitimacy of Santelises's large land claim. But Santelises was either personally powerful enough, or had a strong enough claim pending a decision in the Tribunal de Tierras, to compel high-level functionaries to oppose Cabrera's actions.

In other instances, however, landowners' protests failed to enlist central state intervention against unilateral distributions by the juntas. This was the case for Tomasina Sosa, who objected to the actions of the same Guayubín junta with which Santelises had battled. Cabrera had distributed to Juan Bautista Peña land that Sosa had already enclosed and partially cultivated. The junta was named as the only "owner" on the distribution contract. Sosa's claim to the property was based on both peso titles and the erection of a fence. But she had reportedly neglected her crops or, at least, not utilized the entire area she had enclosed. When she discovered Peña on "her" lands, Sosa protested this "invasion" of her property to the local juez alcalde. Cabrera reported the matter to Carretero. The latter replied brusquely that if Sosa continued "interrupting the proper functioning of the agricultural campaign," she should be brought to the local district attorney.[32] Sosa's enclosures were evidently not as strong a claim to property as Santelises had held, nor had the Tribunal de Tierras yet taken up her case. In addition, there are no suggestions that Sosa had any political leverage, as Santelises appears to have had. Had she continued to resist, she may well have faced the same fate as the Agramonte family in Los Cerros, Cotuí. Five members of that family were imprisoned after refusing to permit Rafael Liriano to farm 3.8 hectares of uncultivated land that they claimed was theirs.[33]

Most claimants and owners of idle land, though, did not end up incarcerated. Instead, state officials negotiated with and used the threat of Law no. 758 to induce private landowners to cooperate with the land distribution campaign. In 1936, Carretero telegrammed the landowner Ramón Soñé Nolasco: "I would greatly appreciate your spontaneously offering the Agricultural Junta of Seibo around five thousand tareas of your land in the section of San Francisco. In this way, you will avoid for the time being the sanctions of Law no. 758. Please respond immediately."[34] Nolasco never faced this prospect because, as later records show, he contributed land to the distribution campaign.[35] In the final months of 1934 alone, the secretary of agriculture warned 119 landowners that they were in violation of Law no. 758 and had either to cultivate their land or cede it to others.[36]

The state also sought recourse to Law no. 758 in a long, drawn-out case involving the wealthy Swiss-Dominican ranchers, the Coiscous. This case, though, reveals the limits of this tactic in the face of powerful landowners with definitive land titles. It is also an example of how tense, protracted, and theatrical negotiations could be, and the multiplicity of actors—peasants, landowners, employees, local authorities, and central state officials—drawn into property struggles under Trujillo. Silvain Coiscou and his brother Pedro Juan held definitive titles to land in the heart of the Eastern sugar zone around Ramón Santana, precisely the region where peasants were suffering most from landlessness. The Coiscous resisted state efforts to distribute any part of their property. When they refused to cede an area requested by the agricultural junta in 1935, claiming that it was already cultivated and in full use, Carretero issued the following order to the army captain in nearby San Pedro de Macorís: "Tell Silvain's brother that I myself have verified that four thousand tareas of his land remain completely uncultivated; and if he does not cooperate willingly in this patriotic endeavor to expand agriculture . . . that we will use the provisions of law 758 [against him]."[37] However, when Carretero sent "urgent" messages to Secretary of Agriculture Tolentino recommending that Pedro Coiscou "be given notice in accordance with Law no. 758, as this person is completely unwilling to help out the poor," Tolentino replied that such notice had already been given the previous December. Under the law, the family had two years from the date of notification either to put the lands to satisfactory use or to distribute them to others. Carretero thus had to inform the local authorities that "any offering of land [from Coiscou] . . . will have to be voluntary for the time being."[38]

During 1935 and 1936, the state continued to pressure Coiscou, who finally capitulated and "voluntarily" ceded most of the requested land, though only for a limited time.[39] Contracts were issued requiring recipients to return the land after five years, leaving it sown with pasture. Given Coiscou's determination to maintain control over these lands, these five-year contracts represented only a brief postponement of peasants' landless condition. Six years later, peasants, probably numbering in the hundreds, were forcibly evicted from Coiscou's property, as is still bitterly recalled by those who were dispossessed.[40] This outcome contrasted with most cases of private distribution during the Trujillo years, in which owners tended to renew contracts or else provide alternative lands for tenants. In the case of the Coiscou brothers, the state lacked the power and will to impose such conditions in the face of strong opposition backed by definitive property titles.

Pedro Coiscou's rationale for refusing to renew the land contracts was that the land was needed for natural pasture for his expanding herd of cattle.[41] After confirming Coiscou's growing ranching needs, the government abandoned its efforts to obtain cessions of his property. The undersecretary of agriculture nonetheless ordered the Eastern Agricultural Department chief, Francisco Pereyra Frómeta, "to obtain from Sr. Pedro Juan Coiscou agreement to extend [the occupants'] contracts one more year." Coiscou, though, refused even that demand. He complained that the year before he had agreed to prolong occupants' contracts by one year so that they could harvest their crops, but that during that time they had sowed new ones and were now repeating the same request.[42]

Despite Coiscou's initial refusal, Pereyra sought to intimidate him into accepting the extension, albeit in diplomatic and disingenuous fashion. Pereyra indirectly linked any refusal—however much it was permitted by law—with a failure to cooperate with Trujillo and official norms. Such an association could give Coiscou's intransigence the dangerous appearance of political opposition. Pereyra wrote ironically: "Knowing your great spirit of . . . solidarity with the ideas of the Benefactor of the Country and your sharing of his unflagging desire to provide lands where the disinherited may work, for those who lack money to buy their own, it is requested that you . . . grant an extension to the agriculturalists. . . . I thank you in advance, certain of the successful results of my efforts."[43] Yet Coiscou remained unyielding, and repeated his need to use the entire area as pasture. In addition, he protested that peasants had invaded lands and cleared woods beyond the usufructuary rights granted them by the juntas and had been preventing his employees from working in contiguous areas. Land recipients had reportedly threatened those working for Coiscou, calling them "groveling bootlickers [who] are enemies of all of us here." For too long, Coiscou grumbled, he had had to endure "with patience all the harm of the occupation of [his] land by the people of Ramón Santana."[44] In the end, the state failed to compel Coiscou to renew occupants' contracts even for another year.

Coiscou had played a dangerous game, regardless of the fact that he had the law on his side, and it was imperative that his intractable resistance not be construed as political. Notwithstanding his bold refusals to cooperate, he now offered seemingly groveling affirmations of his loyalty to Trujillo. In a missive to Pereyra, he rewrote the history of his defiance as an act of cooperation: "I feel particularly happy and proud to have given . . . my disinterested cooperation, sympathy, and solidarity to the great work of our Illustrious Chief, Generalissimo Rafael Leonidas Trujillo Molina, Benefactor of the New Fatherland. And I harbor the hope of being able to add in the future my small grains of sand to the solid edifice of the Nation that he is building each day in ever more outstanding ways."[45] No matter how transparently false this statement was, Coiscou apparently felt compelled to affirm his commitment to state policies—to policies he had just defied—and to bow deferentially before Trujillo. Despite Coiscou's circumvention of both official goals and state power, his empty affirmations served to reinscribe and perpetuate them. Both state officials and Coiscou had engaged in a disingenuous discourse of harmony throughout this conflict. This theater appears to have provided the space for state-society negotiations inside a highly autocratic system that did not permit any opposition on the surface.

Although the battle had been won by Coiscou, the junta refused to facilitate his victory. It disavowed all responsibility for evicting peasants who remained on the land in violation of the contracts that the juntas had originally drawn up and supervised. The state's counsel asserted that the Department of Agriculture had no legal role in the conflict between Coiscou and his tenants, "since the juridical contract which binds them is a private one and no third party may intervene. If the parties are not able to resolve the dispute by means of friendly, conciliatory efforts, there remains only the judicial road."[46] In other cases too, the department refused landowners' requests for help evicting peasants who remained beyond their contract period.[47]

In the Coiscou case, peasants were ultimately ejected a few years after the contracts had expired. Faced with this eviction, the secretary of agriculture again sought to obtain Coiscou's lands to redistribute them to peasants.[48] The state had exhausted its conventional strategies for land distribution. So on learning that the Coiscous were planning to sell the desired lands to the Vicini family's Ingenio Angelina, it decreed them of "public utility," which allowed the state to acquire them at a price substantially below market value. Nearly 500 hectares were then divided up and granted to peasants in the area. Some of those who received land remained there, farming 2- or 3-hectare plots, when I carried out research in Ramón Santana in the early 1990s.[49]

In cases like those of the Coiscou evictions, events concluded in ways contrary to the state's efforts and goals. The occupants on Coiscou's land had continued to petition the secretary of agriculture to help them gain extensions and ultimately even offered to pay 20 cents per tarea rent each year, a significant sum for them and an indication of the value they assigned to their plots. The government replied that it had already made every effort it could to assist them but had not been successful.[50] This admission of impotence, while probably only half-credible from the perspective of those evicted, reflects the limits and unevenness of the Trujillo state's power and will to assist the peasantry in the face of elite resistance. Despite the appearance of an all-powerful regime under Trujillo's personalistic control, and the implication that any consequences, such as these evictions, were Trujillo's intention, the state was, in fact, unable to simply impose itself on society. Rather, it pressured, negotiated, and in this case ultimately had to purchase land (albeit at a bargain price) in order to attain its desired ends. Land distribution of private lands required halting efforts and constant negotiation with elite landowners.

Tensions over agrarian reform existed not only between state and society but also within the state itself. Many lower-level officials seem to have taken at face value the regime's discourse of agrarian reform. Higher authorities, however, were generally inclined to compromise state policies to reduce conflicts with powerful elites, especially wealthy immigrants and foreign corporations. They feared retaliatory action by foreign governments and capital that could hurt the regime. The case of the wealthy immigrant rancher and sugar colono Nicolás Santoni exemplifies the conflicts among state officials over land distribution and over how much coercion could be deployed against foreign interests.[51] Under strong pressure from Carretero and the local junta, Santoni had agreed to cede for a period of time 5,000 tareas of his property near San Francisco in El Seibo to squatters and other recipients. In addition, he promised to provide wire fencing to protect peasants' crops from his cattle. Yet Santoni evidently had no intention of complying with these offers but instead resisted distribution in informal ways. Shortly after his lands were distributed, he allowed his cattle to ravage the crops of numerous tenants. In addition, he built gates blocking off the main local road where it crossed his (undistributed) land. When occupants bypassed the gate, Santoni demanded that they be evicted for violating and purportedly damaging his property. He also demanded that future contracts be based on sharecropping rather than free tenancy arrangements.

The local junta president, Teófilo Ferrer, was outraged by Santoni's behavior. Ferrer decried the destruction of the peasant's crops and denounced Santoni's demand for the eviction of "the men whom he has destroyed without pity." Ferrer also rejected Santoni's request for sharecropping "[as] violating . . . the Law for the distribution of lands and mocking the noble goals of . . . President Trujillo to secure the happiness of the peasantry." Ferrer declared that he would resign from his position rather than have to accept Santoni's "criminal" actions. But when Hostos investigated the situation, he chose to support Santoni at the expense of peasant interests. He canceled the existing land contracts and directed the secretary of the interior to evict the forty-three land recipients who had been given free use of 3,710 tareas of Santoni's land. (These measures belied the state's claim in the Coiscou and other cases that the junta's leaders could not help evict occupants, an argument made, it seems, only when that was not their objective.) Santoni then altered the terms of the contracts to turn occupants with free tenancy into sharecroppers. He sent the contracts to Hostos after Ferrer refused to approve them.

Ferrer continued to oppose his superior's decision and went over Hostos's head, directly to Carretero, declaring, "The injustices that this man [Santoni] is attempting to commit . . . are so heinous . . . that if I remain quiet I would be in complicity with what I consider to be criminal acts."[52] Residents of the region also protested their plight to the government. One person threatened with eviction, José Javier, excoriated men such as Santoni for having caused "the eviction of countless families . . . [and] the destruction of our Seybana region [El Seibo]. Such arbitrary deeds . . . are harming the fatherland's children, and impoverishing those who, in fact, will be missed tomorrow. . . . [Santoni is seeking] to evict a number of Dominican families. . . . These are the country's children. . . . It would therefore be a great injustice if such an occurrence were permitted without our government's intervention, as only it protects the children of the fatherland."[53] Javier's repeated representation of Dominican peasants as the nation's children and the government as their only protector mirrored the Trujillo state's own discourse of itself as the patron of the men of work and the peasantry as the "true representatives of the nation."[54] Peasants like Javier sought to use official ideology to their own advantage by obliging the state to act on its paternalist discourse.

These protests against Santoni's actions appear to have had some effect. Carretero asked the secretary of agriculture to investigate the matter and, in effect, suspended Hostos's eviction orders. Hostos responded defensively that the only issue in this case was the "attitude" of Teófilo Ferrer: "I suggest that we look for a way to replace Sr. Teófilo Ferrer . . . with someone more disposed to reason and more sensitive to the difficulties that may befall the Dominican Government when foreign interests are involved, as is the case with Sr. Santoni." Carretero was less convinced that foreign policy considerations should prevail in this case. He forwarded Hostos's opinions to the secretary but recommended further investigation under the supervision of the Department of the Interior before any eviction or other new measures be carried out. In the meantime, Carretero argued, Ferrer should not be replaced.[55]

A few months later Santoni ceded new land contracts, apparently without any sharecropping obligations. Although it thus appears that Hostos was overruled, no certain outcome is indicated in governmental records.[56] The case nonetheless highlights the formidable power of some, particularly foreign, elite landowners to resist land distribution efforts, harm peasant interests, and force the state to retreat. More dramatically still, it reveals the surprising fissures and even insubordination that existed within the state. The local junta leader Ferrer defied orders by his superior to favor the rich immigrant landowner Santoni over peasants and squatters, to exempt him, in effect, from the rules of the land distribution campaign. Higher authorities were also divided over the proper course of action. Although Hostos was swayed that Santoni represented foreign interests to which the regime should defer, Carretero was not.

The most dramatic instance of elite-state conflict over land policies involved not a foreign landowner—before whom the state was likely to back down—but rather a prominent Dominican figure, Juan (Juancito) Rodríguez García, who had once been allied with the dictator and became the senator for La Vega province in Trujillo's first government. Although reportedly born in 1890 to "agriculturalists of modest means," between 1910 and 1930 Rodríguez acquired huge numbers of cattle and vast landholdings in the Cibao and quickly became one of the country's largest ranchers.[57] When government officials under Trujillo asked him to distribute some of his land to peasants, he reportedly complied but informally resisted. One elderly peasant recounted how Rodríguez had sought to evict his family and other land recipients by unleashing a horde of pigs at night to ravage their crops. When interrogated by police about the incident, Rodríguez claimed that the pigs had escaped from their sty accidentally.[58] Later, when the government decided to irrigate a large area near La Vega in the Cibao, including around 2,000 hectares of Rodríguez's property, an open conflict developed between Rodríguez and the regime. Not only did the state build a canal in the middle of Rodríguez's immense hacienda, which did not serve the needs of his ranch, but it also required him to cede a fourth of the land irrigated by the unwanted canal, or close to 5,000 tareas. The appropriated land was subsequently distributed to landless peasants as part of a state-organized rice colony.[59] Rodríguez opposed this project, as well as other efforts to carve up, distribute, or forcibly purchase property from him. Ultimately, Rodríguez fled the country and financed various exile invasions to topple the regime. Although various other factors impelled Rodríguez's resistance—including the scaling of the cédula fee into what was for him a huge tax increase and the regime's overall climate of repression—many elderly peasants from La Vega, some former members of the Trujillo state, and one scholar of rural Santo Domingo contend that his resentment over the appropriated land was decisive.[60]

The Rodríguez conflict was an exceptional case of intransigent and ultimately open opposition to the Trujillo regime. In general, the state and the

country's relatively few large landholders from the pre-Trujillo years negotiated and compromised over land distribution. The Trujillo state's agrarian
reform operated in a flexible, tentative, and often disingenuous fashion, allowing the regime to avoid transparent rejection of private property and to
balance distribution objectives with the force of possible resistance to them.
And, by maintaining spaces for individual negotiation, the regime discour-
aged collective opposition to state policies, as might have resulted from a
more absolute and universal attack on landowners and claimants. Finally,
the prospects for only temporary, consensual contracts and, in principle at
least, for still claiming land on the basis of peso titles reduced the incentives
for owners to resist. Combined with fear of state repression, these policies
permitted the regime's agrarian reform to proceed despite the opposition of
those seeking to accumulate or consolidate large estates.

The circuitous character of the regime's agrarian policies not only reflected the limits of state power and autonomy vis-à-vis elites. It also
stemmed from Trujillo's conditional commitment to the peasantry. Most
peasants were able to secure land access throughout the Trujillo dictatorship,
but acquiring property was a distinct, lengthy, and uncertain process. The
form of the land distribution campaign permitted the state to revoke recipients' rights if they did not produce according to official wishes. Via temporary—though generally, in fact, indefinite—tenancy contracts, peasants remained dependent on the state until land rights might be consolidated many
years later. This furthered social and political control in the countryside and
a political culture of dependence and paternalism.

The Limits of Agrarian Reform: Foreign Capital and
Peasant Dispossession in the Eastern Sugar Region

The land distribution campaign was most problematic and constrained
precisely in that area which needed it most, the Eastern sugar region around
San Pedro, Ramón Santana, and La Romana. Although some have suggested
that Trujillo's iron grip was what finally permitted peasants' expropriation by
foreign sugar companies in this region,[61] most land accumulation, awarding
of titles to sugar corporations, and peasant dislocations occurred, in fact,
prior to Trujillo's rise to power in the period from 1900 to 1930.[62] Certainly, a
few of the largest evictions were realized in the 1930s under Trujillo's rule;
and these were especially harmful to peasants given the growing exhaustion
of nearby, available lands. Yet leaders of the Trujillo state sought to prevent
these evictions, and when they seemed inevitable, to provide alternative
lands to displaced occupants. The early Trujillo state acted to mitigate the
destruction of peasant life caused by the sugar companies' land monopoliza-

tion and to prevent similar patterns of land concentration and dispossession from spreading throughout the country. In much of the East, though, and in exceptional cases elsewhere, powerful foreign interests prevailed, highlighting the limits of the regime's agrarian reform and state power vis-à-vis elite forces.

As we have seen, the Trujillo state's affirmation, however half-hearted, of private property compelled the regime to periodically reign in the army of bureaucrats and local officials enacting its professed goals of agrarian reform. Since most of the country in the 1930s lacked definitive property titles, the inconsistencies in official discourse on private property were manageable. In the Eastern sugar zones, however, the widespread consolidation of private property made these contradictions unresolvable. Moreover, conflicts with U.S. sugar companies were especially perilous given the threat of U.S.-government retaliation or even military intervention. In the Eastern sugar region, the regime would have to choose between accepting several large-scale evictions or clearly repudiating the private property rights of U.S. interests. Ultimately the former was chosen. Trujillo bowed to foreign interests, doubtless considering the sparse population of the region—and thus the ability of other areas to absorb its dispossessed—versus the might of U.S. sugar companies.

The regime, though, was far from a servant of foreign capital or the U.S. government.[63] It pressed foreign companies with substantial new taxes and negotiated forcefully with them to distribute unused lands. From the early 1930s to the early 1940s, Trujillo steadily raised taxes on the sugar sector, first circuitously via a doubling of the migration tax, which each company had to pay for the foreign-born workers cutting its cane, and then more directly in the form of taxes on production as well as imported supplies.[64] Still, though a different government might have been far more supportive of their interests and furthered their profits and expansion, foreign sugar companies escaped essentially unscathed from state efforts at land reform. Through taxation, these corporations provided much of the state's income—an estimated 40 percent of government revenues in 1940—and contributed to the economy as well through wages paid to employees.[65] They were also backed by the active support of the U.S. legation in Santo Domingo.[66] Hence, foreign sugar companies wielded leverage with Trujillo that was unique among private institutions. During the first two decades of the regime, U.S. interests within the Dominican Republic remained too strong for Trujillo to dominate as he did other sectors.

The most powerful of these companies, the U.S.-owned Central Romana (part of the transnational South Porto Rico Sugar Company), instigated the gravest land conflict and peasant eviction of the first two decades of Trujillo's rule. The area in dispute comprised some 6,604 hectares in the former comunero site of La Campiña, centered in the sections of Regajo and Magarín of Ramón Santana.[67] Upon Trujillo's seizure of power, Campiña was already on the verge of a large-scale eviction. In 1927 the Tribunal de Tierras had rendered a final verdict granting half of Campiña to the Central Romana (as the assignee of the Vicini Estate Corporation). The other half of the site had been awarded in 1925 to a handful of prominent local figures, most of whom had assigned any property that they received to various foreign sugar corporations, above all the U.S.-owned Ingenio Porvenir.[68] Thus, believing the lands to be theirs now, the sugar companies began to violently evict titleless occupants, even burning their houses and farms.[69] A wide spectrum of labor, nationalist groups, and the press protested the adjudication of land to the sugar companies and their violent eviction of residents, but this apparently had no impact on either then-president Vásquez or the Tribunal de Tierras.[70] During the late 1920s, the Central Romana (or technically, the Vicini Estate Corporation) appealed all adjudications of property in the area to those other than itself both to the Tribunal Superior de Tierras and, when necessary, to the Supreme Court. Final decisions on these lands would remain pending for years, during which time many occupants enjoyed some relief from eviction efforts. But regardless of the outcome of these cases, peasant occupations would be judged illegal and their livelihood jeopardized, given that virtually all of the litigants represented sugar companies.

On April 11, 1931, *La Opinión* printed a letter from Campiña residents to Trujillo's brother Virgilio requesting his help. The writers explained: "All the time we have lived and worked on this land, we believed it to be state property. But if this were not the case, those that claim to be the owners should not have left us here for so many years to the point that today we consider ourselves legal owners. . . . [There are] more than eight thousand souls that subsist in these woods incorrectly called 'Los Vicinis.' By our understanding, these are state lands."[71] As elsewhere, peasants in Campiña considered themselves legitimate landholders on the basis of prescription rights. But, by the court's judgment, an 1893 division of this comunero site and, above all, subsequent private surveys had obviated such claims.[72] In 1935, when efforts to evict squatters in various sections of Campiña intensified, the state's counsel, Luis Henríquez Castillo, reported to Trujillo that most of the occupants of Campiña were now "working on another's soil, with constant threats of expulsion that have become a serious social and political problem and understandably have attracted the Government's attention."[73] That Henríquez deemed the situation a political as well as social problem suggests state concern about the potential for collective resistance and political instability in this area as a result of peasant evictions, landlessness, and the collapse of Trujillo's image as the patron of the men of work.

Public surveyor Miguel Fiallo also expressed his concern about the negative impact of foreign land monopolization on the peasantry and the region overall. To address the situation, Fiallo suggested that the part of Campiña "that had not yet been definitively sentenced by the Tribunal de Tierras . . . offers the promise of . . . colonization."[74] However, Henríquez could find no legal basis for such action. Given the limited possibilities for appeal permitted by earlier court sentences in favor of the sugar companies—in addition to the earlier divisions and surveys of the site—Henríquez reported that no legal opening remained for either the peasantry or the state to claim property in Campiña.

It is problematic now to salvage the legitimate demands of the agriculturalists, despite the new hearing ordered for part of the lands. . . . The companies have unjustly been given an advantageous position whose gravity has been furthered by the passage of time and the sentences given. Therefore the reassertion of peasants' original rights is almost impossible, juridically speaking. Socially and politically, I believe the measure most within the Government's reach is the gradual relocation of these families to other lands belonging to the state.[75]

Fiallo's recommendation to Trujillo to redistribute land to squatters in Campiña would thus be impossible to implement without state appropriation of property to which neither the state nor squatters had, at that time at least, any plausible legal claim.[76]

Ultimately, rather than a radical assault on the sugar companies' legal property in the name of social justice, the Trujillo state permitted multiple, large-scale evictions from Campiña, dislodging several thousand peasants during the second half of the 1930s. The Central Romana and another U.S.-owned company, the Ingenio Santa Fé, forced six hundred families to move, paying them a small amount for their improvements.[77] The alcaldes pedáneos held local meetings at which they instructed occupants to leave the area, offering them other nearby but often less desirable lands to farm for at least five years. Residents suffered as a result of these evictions and were not satisfied with lands elsewhere on a provisional basis as compensation.[78] One peasant from the section of Arroyo Hondo wrote to Trujillo in 1936 questioning the eviction's legitimacy, stating, as others had before him, that peasants had been on these lands for many years, believing the entire site of Campiña to be state land. However, the state was unable or unwilling to intervene against the companies at this point. The evictions proceeded; peasants offered no open resistance to the evictions; and no police or army were used. Peasants brought the animals and what else they could to their state-assigned destinations. Some of their houses were destroyed and others moved with government assistance. After the eviction, many returned surreptitiously for several months to harvest their crops.[79]

Despite the miserable denouement of this conflict, it appears to have stemmed not from state interest or objectives. Rather, the outcome here appears to reflect the state's constrained power as well as its merely conditional and opportunistic support of the peasantry. During the first years of the Trujillo regime, the state appeared to side with peasant occupants in Campiña. Indeed, at first it even encouraged squatters to occupy parts of this area.[80] State officials expressed unanimous interest in preventing the Campiña evictions, strong concern over the "social and political problem" associated with such an outcome, and overall criticism of the adverse impact of the sugar industry's expansion in the East. When peasants finally were evicted from Campiña in the late 1930s, the press and others openly condemned the evictions.[81]

Why then did Trujillo not prevent the Campiña evictions? Despite the state's scrupulous legalistic facade, Trujillo was capable of manipulating or circumventing the legal process whenever he so desired. Conceivably, for instance, through his influence a final Tribunal de Tierras ruling in Campiña might have been indefinitely postponed. In this case, however, extralegal action was nearly impossible because of the power of the U.S. sugar companies. Along with the U.S. legation, the Central Romana was the second most powerful force in the country after Trujillo. The corporation was a veritable juggernaut, given its fantastic relative size, huge contribution to national revenues, and the fact that it was firmly supported by the U.S. legation and State Department. Had Trujillo wished to eviscerate the rights of such an enemy, a redoubtable legal argument would have been necessary to avert its and the U.S. government's wrath. Yet the state's counsel had advised Trujillo that such a legal argument did not exist. If the regime wished to annul Central Romana's private property rights in Campiña, it would have had to blatantly intervene in the judicial process. This would most likely have led to an irreparable conflict with the company and, moreover, with the U.S. government, something that the regime could not sustain for long. Clearly, Trujillo was not willing to pay such a price to help peasant squatters.

However much Trujillo fashioned himself as a nationalist, promoted national self-sufficiency, and bargained vigorously with foreign capital, the regime remained dependent on the United States. Although the U.S. government was now much less ready to intervene to protect U.S. interests abroad than it had been at the time of the occupation, given its turn away from direct intervention during the Good Neighbor policy (1933–45), most Dominicans, including Trujillo, doubtless believed another invasion was still quite possible, which could remove Trujillo from power. The U.S. government could also have paralyzed the regime during the 1930s had it not agreed to suspend amortization on the Dominican foreign debt and to reduce the annual portion of customs revenues—still administered by the U.S. government—that U.S. officials appropriated to meet U.S. bond obligations under the terms of the 1907 treaty.[82] Until the final years of his rule, Trujillo would always deftly retreat before permitting any dramatic rupture with the United States. The regime had sought a means of avoiding the evictions in Campiña, but the state did not have the power, the legal basis, or the will to suppress the rights of U.S. sugar companies. Foreign dependence remained a redoubtable constraint on Trujillo's power within the Dominican Republic.[83]

State officials did, though, work to obtain alternative lands for the dispossessed, including from the sugar companies themselves. Carretero and his successor as chief of the agricultural juntas, Bayoán de Hostos, pressed companies and other powerful landowners to contribute "spontaneously" some of their lands. And they agreed to cede some areas temporarily. That their lands were granted on any terms suggests that while the state's power was limited with respect to the sugar interests, they nonetheless felt obliged to compromise with the regime. It is not possible to know which land grants were distributed to those evicted from Campiña as opposed to other landless peasants. But it is clear that in 1936, one year after the government acknowledged that there was no legal basis for stopping the evictions, tens of thousands of tareas claimed by the sugar interests and large landholders were obtained by the state to mitigate peasant dispossession. Also in areas contiguous to this land-scarce zone, the state similarly provided vast areas for peasant farming both as part of the land distribution campaign and the colonization program.[84] In 1938 one agricultural colony, Pedro Sánchez, reportedly appropriated 59,000 tareas ceded by the Ingenio Santa Fé in return for land that the state agreed to grant elsewhere.[85]

In 1937 the regime passed an unusual law, ostensibly in an effort to bolster the state's limited power to protect squatters from dispossession by sugar corporations. Law no. 1313 authorized new taxes (30 centavos for every 320 pounds of sugar manufactured or in stock) on any sugar company that evicted numerous peasants, including from property to which the company was definitively entitled.[86] Upon proposing the law to the congress, Trujillo justified it in fiscal terms. As evictions would produce masses of dispossessed whom the state was obliged to assist, "the same industrial undertakings as have given rise to such situations should be those which bring to the Government the resources necessary to resolve the problem."[87] The U.S. legation, though, viewed the law as an attack on private property rights. Franklin Atwood, chargé d'affaires in Ciudad Trujillo, immediately reported to the U.S. secretary of state on the ominous implications of the new law for U.S. interests. He feared that this "legislation will give President Trujillo a very dangerous weapon for possible use against American sugar interests in the Dominican Republic. . . . [It] would appear to be unconstitutional in that it will tend to deprive American sugar interests of the free use and control of their property. It will also tend to encourage squatters to encroach further on the private property of American sugar interests in the Republic."[88] The U.S. consul hypothesized that the law was an effort to "mulct" the sugar companies to fund a national "program of social and economic improvement."[89]

On the other hand, the Dominican press depicted the legislation as embodying natural law transcending absolutist conceptions of private property, which now thanks to Trujillo's firm hand would no longer be sacrificed on account of political expediency and state weakness. Evidently, though, the newspapers had already suppressed collective memory of the eviction and nationalist defeat at Campiña, a history which suggested that Trujillo's hand was not always firm, at least not in U.S.-Dominican relations. *La Opinión* published the full text of the legislation for Law no. 1313 in an article entitled "Patriotic Project of the Law for the Prevention of Evictions on the Sugar Estates."[90] On the same day, the editors of *La Opinión* argued that the "patriotic aim of preventing the inhumane eviction of masses of individuals or families from the sugar estates" had been ignored by previous governments "due to fear of confronting powerful capitalist entities."[91] They continued:

Although there are many settlements of squatters on the sugar estates that today legally appear to be without any right to oppose ejection, in reality and honesty these squatters are, before the justice of God, the true and traditional owners of the lands they occupy. The Government, by a sense of elevated legality, cannot declare illegal situations that, formally, operated under the shelter of the law; but it may, by a sense of essential justice and of humanity, avail itself of measures that in fact take on a compensatory character. . . . The people support this Law. They were impatient for a Law of this nature. And their arms are ready to defend it.[92]

Given that *La Opinión* served as a mouthpiece of the regime, this editorial's militant support for Law no. 1313 suggests official interest in fashioning it in populist terms and, more broadly, support for the nationalist-populist project being pushed by certain state leaders.

Dominican congressional deputies also zealously promoted the law. They cast it in a dramatic nationalist light reflecting sentiments hardened by the recent U.S. military occupation and serving to obscure Trujillo's own capitulation, at times, to foreign interests. Deputy Font Bernard condemned the sugar companies for having transformed native Dominicans into "slaves of the intruder." And Deputy Hernández Franco excoriated the "social problems" permitted by pre-Trujillo governments because of "the craven defeatist assumption that our own sovereignty had its limits wherever foreign interests established their wide and always invasive boundaries around their latifundia. . . . Thus, the problem began to emerge of a rural proletariat, wandering and unprepared, uprooted from its own land."[93] Analogously to the way in which peasants invoked official rhetoric of themselves as the "best friends" of President Trujillo to obtain state protección, and to how Carretero, in his missives to him, sought to shape the dictator into a noble and valiant hero who protected the peasantry, congressional deputies encouraged Trujillo to make good on what the eviction law promised.

Yet the conservative Secretary of Justice Julio Ortega Frier pulled Trujillo in the opposite direction and succeeded in countering Law no. 1313's relatively radical potential. Two weeks after the law was passed, Ortega issued a communiqué criticizing those who had interpreted 1313 as "an implicit authorization for the invasion" of private property by squatters. The U.S. legation affirmed the importance of Ortega's intervention into this contest over the meaning of the new law. Atwood reported: "Although [Licenciado] Ortega Frier was unable to prevent the bill from being enacted into law . . . his representations to President Trujillo tended to modify the President's attack on the Dominican sugar industry and saved it, for the moment at least, from the constant threat of heavy fines in case the sugar estates attempt the eviction of squatters from their property."[94]

Pushed in contrary directions by various state actors and interests, the regime's land policies oscillated between a rejection of absolute private property rights, including the right to evict squatters at will, and capitulation to and affirmation of those very rights. Echoing the analogous retraction by then–secretary of agriculture Tolentino from his radical position in support of squatters in 1934, Secretary of Agriculture Rafael Vidal issued a circular elaborating Ortega's communiqué. He criticized local officials for "acts that imply support and even encouragement of new illegal occupations . . . or continued occupation of lands registered to others." The secretary explained that the state must "provide facilities so as not to leave unprotected Dominican peasants . . . [but simultaneously] guarantee the right to private property. . . . The Honorable President of the Republic has perfected a plan to coordinate the system of evictions with the distribution of lands that for some years has been carried out at his initiative. . . . Dominican occupants [threatened with eviction] . . . will be offered the opportunity to establish themselves on lands at the Government's disposal, or they will be sent to agricultural colonies."[95] Responding to the sugar interests and U.S. political influence, the Trujillo regime chose to respect private property rather than act on the more progressive interpretations of "natural law" and agrarian reform being championed by other leading figures.

Yet this disavowal of the full implications of the eviction law did not represent a reversal in policy, but rather a compromise between the state and sugar companies. Most likely, the law was intended from the start as a negotiating tool to scare elite interests. It served, as Atwood put it, as a "weapon" to hang over the heads of sugar companies who refused to make concessions sought by the state—namely, giving sufficient warning time before evictions for squatters to harvest their existing crops and making land contributions for distribution elsewhere. From the start, the law followed Trujillo's typical pattern of threatening elite interests in a blustering manner but then retreating to a flexible stance, and of marshaling a multitude of resources to persuade landowners to "voluntarily" redistribute land.

Indeed, the eviction law may have been employed in only one case—that is, against the Vicini family's Ingenio Cristóbal Colón, notably not a foreign interest. Decree no. 1906 imposed the eviction tax on the Cristóbal Colón almost immediately after Law no. 1313 was issued. Trujillo may have had certain personal motives for targeting this particular ingenio, which was managed by General Luis Felipe Vidal, an enemy of Trujillo's.[96] Yet tensions also existed and were coming to a head between the state and this sugar mill over company efforts to evict squatters from its property in Guayacanes, San Pedro de Macorís. Law no. 1313 and Decree no. 1906 were promulgated precisely as the state intervened in behalf of occupants.

In May of 1937, company manager Vidal informed the government that since 1931 he had been confronting persons without titles or authorization invading the mill's lands. Because these persons had cleared and occupied areas that the mill now needed, he demanded their eviction within fifteen days.[97] This demand quickly mobilized an army of state leaders seeking to resolve the political problems that it evidently created for the state. On May 24, 1937, the provincial governor of San Pedro de Macorís commanded the military to prevent the "violent eviction" planned by the company. Similarly, on June 3, 1937, Secretary of Agriculture Vidal ordered the chief of the Eastern Agricultural Department, Joaquín Garrido Puello, "to interpose his good offices in the sense of ensuring that [the eviction] is not carried out." State leaders insisted that if the company could not allow occupants to remain indefinitely, it at least grant them a delay so that they could harvest their existing crops. Secretary Vidal apprised local officials that if no agreement was reached allowing peasants to stay on the Ingenio Colón's lands, the state would have to provide them with plots elsewhere.[98]

It was the day after the secretary of agriculture instructed Garrido to persuade the managers of the Ingenio Colón not to evict residents from Guayacanes that Trujillo submitted Law no. 1313 to the Chamber of Deputies. And it was immediately following the imposition of the eviction tax on the Colón sugar mill that the company agreed to grant renewable, five-year, rent-free contracts elsewhere on its estate for the occupants it planned to dislodge. (The Ingenio Colón may thus never have been obliged to pay the eviction tax.)[99] No doubt, the timing of these events was not coincidental. Law no. 1313 served its purpose in this case as a negotiating tool, as perhaps it did in other instances in more preemptive fashion. According to the agreement that was reached, occupants could keep their houses where they were indefinitely and would be given a year to harvest their existing crops before being asked to move their farms.[100]

The squatters' responses to the agreement were mixed. Some welcomed the compromise, while others proclaimed to Garrido, in a notable show of defiance, that "they would never leave these lands under any circumstances."[101] Although acting in the name of their interests, Garrido had not included the occupants in the negotiation process, but rather simply informed them of the compromise he had reached with the company. Indeed, such decretory practices structured the regime's paternalistic relations with the peasantry in general. Several occupants, though, sought to go over Garrido's head and appealed directly to Trujillo. José Alonso wrote to the secretary of the presidency to denounce Garrido for demanding that occupants leave within a year. Alonso protested that he had occupied his land continuously for more than thirty years and therefore it had become his "exclusive property."[102] Unfortunately, Alonso's attempt to obtain prescription rights was to no avail, as such right did not apply to lands such as these, for which irrevocable titles had already been awarded by the Tribunal de Tierras.

Yet apparently the state's left hand did not know what its right one was doing. Peasant protests led the undersecretary of the presidency, Pedro Batista, to criticize Garrido's action, informing the secretary of justice that, "On first blush, it seems like an act of disrespect toward the Government's law forbidding collective evictions."[103] A new secretary of agriculture, Manuel Gautier, confronted Garrido, demanding an explanation for why he had ordered peasants to abandon the Ingenio Colón's lands within one year. Garrido defended his actions to the secretary, explaining that he had "intervened in this issue at the behest of the Department of Agriculture," and, by doing so, he had, in fact, prevented rather than caused "mass evictions."[104] This type of confusion within the state was an almost inevitable by-product of Trujillo's system of continually circulating high-level functionaries into different positions almost every year for the purposes of maintaining his control.

The history of the eviction tax law suggests that it was an additional tool with which the state hoped to mediate land conflicts and to pressure sugar companies, if not to accept squatters in areas the companies sought to use, then at least to provide them with some relief in terms of a delay, compensatory lands, and permission to keep their houses. Thus the law sought to maintain some state control over evictions and rural stability. This was expressed in the decree levying the tax on the Ingenio Colón. It condemned the company's planned eviction of "a large number of agriculturalists and families that have their farms and homes established in lands that the Company supposes to be its property" for "creating . . . a serious problem of social disturbance that the Government has the obligation to attend to and remedy."[105] The legislation's deployment against the Ingenio Cristóbal Colón may have increased pressure on other sugar companies to cooperate with state mediation in coterminous and future plans for the eviction of squatters.

These remedies, though, were temporary, and the Eastern sugar region remained a problematic space for state goals of securing peasant land access and increasing food production. Whereas policies toward these ends had succeeded in most of the country by the early 1940s, in the sugar areas peasants were being pushed onto increasingly marginal lands, and many had distribution contracts guaranteeing usufruct rights for only five years. This was a concern to many government officials. In 1938 Bartólome Pujals, chief of the Eastern Agricultural Department, reported that La Romana "confronts the most serious problem any place in the country can face, and that is the absence of small rural property." After observantly lauding Trujillo for having secured land for peasants from large landowners in the region, Pujals nonetheless cautioned that "one has to be concerned that the contracts that regulate the farming of these lands are for five years, during which time the agriculturalists establish their crops, secure their small comforts in life, and organize their properties, so that now they consider them their own, and care for them intensively." Pujals recommended that the state buy additional lands in the region so that peasants could farm without facing possible eviction at the end of their contracts.[106] Similarly in 1940, the head of the Dominican Party, R. Paíno Pichardo, reported, on the one hand, that "agriculture, which once was only a myth in the commune of La Romana, is now acquiring considerable significance due to the important program of land distribution." But he warned the secretary of agriculture that "the contracts that were made with landowners for five years are almost expired and some six hundred families have not procured [their own lands] to continue their agricultural work. It would be desirable for you to take an interest in obtaining another five-year period until it can be determined whether those six hundred families can obtain land in another area since otherwise they would be evicted and suffer the most frightening misery as they had before."[107] Secretary Raúl Carbuccia replied confidently that he had already commissioned the assistant secretary of agriculture, José Seijas, to obtain "a new term that will satisfy the desires of the agriculturalists of La Romana" from the Compañía Anónima de Inversiones Inmobiliarias, the Central Romana, and several individual landowners.[108] However, extensions could not always be secured. After three terms the Central Romana evicted occupants and retook its lands in Magarín, and the state proved unable to provide lands for all of the landless, at least not within the vicinity of Ramón Santana.[109]

In a large swath of the East, peasant existence was suffocated by the expansion of agribusiness and seemingly endless cane fields.[110] Unlike the rest of the country, the Trujillo state was able to offer peasants in this region relatively little protection from the perils of land and agricultural commercialization. Sugar companies and large sugar colonos did make substantial concessions for peasant usufruct rights, particularly during the first half of the regime. But these provided only marginal compensation for the sudden decimation of peasants' erstwhile way of life. Gone were the pasture and woods that they had used for hunting, slash-and-burn agriculture, and crianza libre in the past. Even land recipients lived under the threat of companies refusing to renew their contracts for the small plots that they had depended on the state to secure for them. And many were left with no land at all in the area.

Nonetheless, despite offering only modest recompense for the collapse of peasants' once ample autonomy in the East, Trujillo's land and agricultural policies appear to have successfully projected the image of a paternalistic state. The regime's efforts to assist peasants in the East reflected state interest in preventing rapid growth of a sizable class of permanently dispossessed and disaffected that could threaten political stability. Even among peasants with whom I spoke whose families were evicted from Campiña, the Trujillo state was praised in many ways and rarely blamed for their ejection.[111] Their hostility was directed instead against Central Romana and, to a lesser extent, against local Dominican "speculators" who had acquired land to sell to foreign sugar corporations—"the clever ones in these regions whose actions had rendered all the lands American," as one agriculturalist complained in a letter to Trujillo in 1934.[112] Some peasants contended that Trujillo allowed the eviction only after the sugar companies had agreed to cede other lands in exchange to accommodate at least some of those left landless.[113]

Presumably, Trujillo was not blamed more for the eviction because Campiña was taken over by and benefited the Central Romana, not the regime. Also, the massive dislocations and transformations in the Eastern sugar areas in the period from 1890 to 1940 reportedly did not turn most of the region's peasantry into wage laborers. Much land remained available in nonsugar parts of the East and in neighboring areas to which peasants moved with or without state assistance.[114] Some whose family received new plots expressed gratitude still to Trujillo. Efigenia Montilla, who was evicted as a child from Campiña and is still farming lands the state then gave her family, insisted that Trujillo was indeed "a friend to the poor."[115] Regardless of Trujillo's actual motives, many peasants like Montilla saw a state that often responded to their concerns and sought to offset the negative effects of the forms of capitalist development that they were facing. Like all successful political myths, Trujillo's image as the peasants' protector was based on a measure of truth as well as distortion.

During the 1930s the Trujillo regime adopted public policies in the countryside that led to much peasant acceptance. But these policies were neither transparent nor brazenly imposed. Rather, they were often carried out in a disingenuous and somewhat tentative fashion by a heterogeneous state. Trujillo's agrarian reform was, in fact, a tangled, highly improvisational web of policies that responded to diverse regional concerns, ambiguous property rights, and tense negotiations between the state and elites and sometimes within the state itself. Thus what emerges on close examination of rural polices under Trujillo is a sociology of authoritarian rule in which the dictator no longer monopolizes the analytical stage. Even in such a powerful and personalistic dictatorship, the state did not simply impose itself on a supine society. Rather, state power was exercised daily through negotiation and the balancing of competing forces. In order to maintain that balance, the regime temporized and sometimes reversed course in an intricate dance of dictatorial rule that perpetuated Trujillo's control for thirty-one years.

Recall that when Secretary of Agriculture Rafael Vidal was obliged to retreat from the progressive implications of Law no. 1313, he exhorted local authorities nonetheless to protect "*Dominican* peasants" from landlessness. By emphasizing "Dominican," he had implied that those not considered Dominican should no longer be granted land by the state. Vidal most likely intended to exclude from future state *protección* those identified as

"Haitian"—Haitian immigrants and their descendants—who prior to 1937 had been granted plots in both the land distribution campaign and in agricultural colonies. Similarly in Ramón Santana, when options for providing land to those evicted by the sugar companies were exhausted in 1940, the Eastern Agricultural Department chief unceremoniously canceled land contracts that had been given to "Haitians" as well as to Anglophone Caribbeans and replaced them with ethnic Dominicans. The chief lamented only that "this satisfies merely a small number of those on the list seeking land."[116] These examples highlight that in addition to the leading nationalist-populist voices, such as those of Tolentino, Carretero, and Espaillat, there were also many nationalist-racist elements within the early Trujillo state. And the racism of the Trujillo regime cannot be easily separated out from its populist dimensions. Both were articulated within a nationalist rhetoric. And in a number of cases, it was the same figures advocating both racist and agrarianist projects. The racist dimensions of the Trujillo regime's nationalism, a lurid amplification of long-standing elite discourses it inherited, would be of particular importance in the large frontier regions bordering with Haiti, where Trujillo's most horrific act of state terror—the 1937 Haitian massacre—occurred precisely when the land distribution campaign was cresting. Like that campaign, state actions vis-à-vis the Dominican frontier regions can be seen as part of official efforts to incorporate the countryside into the projects and discourse of the city. It is to the historical plexus of agrarian transformation, racism, and violence in that project of incorporation that we turn in the following chapter.

5

Bordering the Nation

*Race, Colonization, and the 1937 Haitian
Massacre in the Dominican Frontier*

As many intellectuals and functionaries joined the Trujillo
government in the 1930s hoping to realize agrarian policies that had been stymied in the past, so too they hoped, with the unprecedented power of the dictatorship behind them, to mold a broader nationalist agenda. We have already
seen how for various members of Trujillo's cabinet, such as Rafael Espaillat
and César Tolentino, support for small landholding and opposition to massive U.S. sugar companies reflected national as well as popular rural concerns.
Large-scale foreign land ownership was seen as a sacrifice of and threat to national sovereignty. This was precisely the position of the Nationalist Party,
founded in the 1920s, which had attracted a large part of the country's intellectuals and supplied the early Trujillo state with a number of its key figures.[1]

In addition to opposition to U.S. imperialism, there was a second axis to
nationalist discourse from the 1920s that would influence the course of Trujillo's rule and ultimately reshape and harden the geographic and ethnic borders of the nation. This discourse revolved around the history of Haitian immigration to the Dominican Republic. And it reflected the Dominican elite's
long-standing mode of racism that valorized cultural practices associated
with Europe and derided those associated with Africa—the former supposedly representing civilization and modernity, the latter barbarism and backwardness. Specifically, public intellectuals and state officials in the late 1920s
condemned what they termed the "denationalization" of the Dominican
frontier regions. (Bordering with Haiti and known as *la frontera* [the fron-
tier], these extensive areas include some 5,000 square kilometers in the north
and, along with the southern and central frontier areas, comprise roughly
one-fourth of the country's approximately 48,000 square kilometers.)[2] The
frontier lands had been populated largely by ethnic Haitians (Haitian immigrants and their descendants—the latter in theory entitled to Dominican citizenship by virtue of having been born in the country) who lived together with
ethnic Dominicans in a highly integrated and transnational frontier world
extending into Haiti. Much to the chagrin of officials, intellectuals, and other
elite Dominicans, most denizens of this world had remained indifferent or
even hostile to urban visions of Dominican nationality. Dominican intellec-

tuals had sought to define the nation (*la raza*) in monoethnic and Eurocentric terms. Such a vision, however, collided with the country's deep Afro-Dominican cultural heritage as well as the bicultural Haitian-Dominican character and constructs of local and national community pervading the Dominican frontier. As part of their struggle to resolve the tension between local practices and urban and elite visions of the nation, in the early twentieth century leading political figures and writers advanced policies for both the "Dominicanization of the frontier" and European immigration. These policies came together—albeit paradoxically—in official schemes to establish agricultural "colonies," or settlements, composed of European immigrants in the frontier.

Rural colonization in the Dominican Republic originated in the pre-Trujillo years with culturalist and racialist fantasies of spawning a productive Dominican yeomanry by ushering in European immigrant farmers to the country's frontier areas. As had been the case among elites in much of Latin America in the late nineteenth and early twentieth century, national progress was imagined as requiring external—namely, European—forces, ideas, and bodies to help conquer the supposed backwardness and inertia of the local population. Settled in model agricultural colonies, European immigrants would, the lettered class imagined, spread a modern economic and cultural ethos among the popular rural classes. Elite Dominicans envisioned, moreover, that these European settlers would serve as an antidote to the perceived perils presented by decades of Haitian immigration into the frontier. As we will see, these supposed dangers entailed the further influences of cultural practices associated with Africa, as well as possible future demands by the Haitian state for territory in the frontier claimed by the Dominican Republic. Yet almost as soon as a program of "colonization" was actually implemented in the 1920s, its emphasis shifted away from settling immigrants in the frontier to distributing land throughout the country to landless Dominican peasants and resettling them in what were still supposed to be model villages. This transformation, which we will see in the next chapter occurred mainly during the Trujillo years, reflected state efforts to address new problems of landlessness as well as official disillusionment with the poor agricultural performance of immigrant colonists. Here, though, we will first treat the history of colonization as a window into the nationalist, anti-Haitian, and racist discourses that the twentieth century Dominican state and urban intellectuals sought to diffuse throughout the country, particularly in the Dominican frontier, and how these discourses influenced the horrifically violent and tragic incorporation of the frontier population and evolution of the Dominican nation during the Trujillo dictatorship.

Although racialist and anti-Haitian nationalist goals were not ultimately attained through colonization as first envisioned, those goals would to some extent be realized by and serve to legitimate the 1937 Haitian massacre. In this act of state terror, extreme and anomalous even for the Trujillo regime, the Dominican military massacred with machetes some fifteen thousand ethnic Haitians living in the northern frontier regions and contiguous parts of the western Cibao. Also, several months later, the military deported thousands of ethnic Haitians, killing a substantial number, in the southern border provinces. These acts of genocide and terror were followed, but not preceded, by an official campaign of virulent anti-Haitian discourse and ultimately by popular anti-Haitianism in the frontier. This suggests the importance of this bloodbath as a transformative event in the diffusion of anti-Haitian ideology and constructs of a monoethnic nation in the Dominican Republic and, above all, in the subjection of the frontier peasantry and society to metropolitan nationalist norms and central state authority. Although Trujillo's own motives for ordering the massacre are obscure, long-standing anti-Haitian nationalist discourses among Dominican intellectuals and state officials created the possibility of legitimating the slaughter as the realization of a supposedly patriotic project to "Dominicanize the frontier." Indeed, Trujillo quickly marshaled the country's most adroit and strident anti-Haitian thinkers to try to explain and justify the killings both domestically and internationally, figures such as Joaquín Balaguer, whose extreme anti-Haitianism had been obvious prior to the Trujillo years and who came zealously to his defense after the massacre.[3] Far clearer though than the actual causes of the massacre were its devastating and monumental effects: the murder of thousands of people, the decimation of a once vibrantly bicultural and transnational Dominican borderland, and the reconfiguration of local constructs of ethnicity, race, and nation.

The Dominican Frontier and Colonization prior to the Trujillo Regime

In the Dominican frontier regions, particularly the northern frontier areas, a bicultural Haitian-Dominican world evolved over several generations of Haitian immigration and interaction with Dominican residents. This immigration was stimulated during the second half of the nineteenth century by a land surplus and sparse population on the Dominican side of the border amid increasing land and population pressures in Haiti. Because of the region's sparse population, Haitians settling in the Dominican frontier helped constitute what was to a large extent the original society of this part of the country. That society was a bilingual, bicultural, and transnational one, spanning the Haitian and Dominican sides of the border. A status quo boundary between Haiti and the Dominican Republic was accepted by both states at various times during the period from 1900 to 1920 (albeit with continuing disputes in certain sites, above all in the southern Pedernales area).[4] But this border remained entirely porous to travel and held limited meaning for local residents. Although notions of Dominican political sovereignty and nationality impinged on daily life in the Dominican frontier—for instance, in the levying of an immigration tax on those not born on Dominican soil— the territorial as well as cultural boundary between the two countries had little of the significance and strength that was imagined or desired by those living in Santo Domingo and other areas far from the border. In many senses, the border remained an inconsequential political fiction for frontier residents. As one ethnic Haitian who had lived in this region recalled, "Although there were two sides, the people were one, united."[5]

In the early twentieth century, residents of the Dominican frontier often traversed the border repeatedly over the course of a single day, as when ethnic Haitian children went to Haiti to attend school, crossed back to the Dominican Republic for lunch, then returned to school in Haiti in the afternoon, and finally came back home to Dominican territory in the evening.[6] Both ethnic Haitians and ethnic Dominicans generally baptized their children in Haiti.[7] And many grazed their cattle and worked on landholdings comprising both Haitian and Dominican territory.[8] Also, many of the nearest and largest markets were in Haiti, for which reason residents frequently traveled to Haiti or sold goods such as cattle, beans, and other agricultural products to Haitian intermediaries.[9] In addition, the commercial vitality of the Haitian capital drew many Dominicans. Jesús María Ramírez, a man from the southern frontier who became an important local official in the Trujillo years, recalled his excitement on his first trip to Port-au-Prince in 1922: "To go [there] was the dream of all frontier residents. We always heard people talking about its great stores, its markets, distilleries, and sales of liquor . . . [It] was a very vibrant city, with more commercial activity and public life than Santo Domingo."[10] Continual travel to and from Haiti forged communities of friends, relatives, and associates across the border. Bilín, a poor Dominican man from Monte Grande in the northern frontier, recalled: "In those days, we crossed the border without problems. We went over there as much as they came over here. *Papá* had many friends over there. And he would drop us off with his *compadres* and they would take care of me."[11]

Oral histories reveal how ethnic Haitians and ethnic Dominicans living in the northern frontier region had mixed fluidly and often formed families together.[12] Percivio Díaz, one of the richest men in the small Dominican town of Santiago de la Cruz (just east of Dajabón), explained: "This place was made of an amalgam of people, of Haitian men marrying Dominican women and Dominican men marrying Haitian women. Many here are the products of Dominican-Haitian unions. So many that right away there were more Dominican-Haitians than pure Dominicans. ... [T]here never were many pure Dominicans here."[13] Residents of the area had generally understood both Haitian Creole and Spanish, and to some extent the two languages fused forming a new idiom.[14] And no clear economic hierarchy or conflict existed between ethnic Haitians and ethnic Dominicans in the region's rural areas. There was no significant labor competition; in fact, there was relatively little recourse to wage labor at all. The great sugar estates employing Haitian and other West Indian immigrant workers were far removed from this region. Most ethnic Haitians in the area cultivated coffee and subsistence crops on small and medium-size plots with some attention to stock raising, while ethnic Dominican peasants generally placed greater emphasis on hunting and herding livestock on the open range. There was also no notable competition over or shortage of land, as much of the northern frontier remained undeveloped and unsurveyed and property claims vague and inchoate, based on overlapping rights and on titles yet to be adjudicated in most areas. In the *pueblos*, such as Dajabón and Monte Cristi (with populations of more than ten thousand and eight thousand persons, respectively), an ethnic division of labor existed to some extent, with many ethnic Haitians working as artisans (cobblers, tinsmiths, tailors) and domestic workers (launderers and servants).[15] However, no such divisions or class hierarchy prevailed in most of the rural northern frontier.[16]

Much remains to be investigated about the history of the pre-1937 southern frontier world.[17] Here the degree of "transculturation" (the procreative fusion of diverse cultural practices) was reportedly less pronounced than in the north.[18] Some residential ethnic concentration seems to have marked the region, with most ethnic Haitians living together in the hills somewhat apart from the rest of the community. And more Haitians worked as farm laborers for ethnic Dominicans than was the case in the north. Furthermore, in the south, contests over the borderline and state efforts to stop a bustling contraband trade had led to several early-twentieth-century military conflicts and casualties that dovetailed with greater ethnic tension than was evident in the north.[19] But certainly here too ethnic Dominicans associated with Dominicans of Haitian descent, with Haitian immigrants, and with Haitians in Haiti in a fluid social and economic network. There were Haitian influences in the regional dialect and culture. And the commercial integration of the southern border towns with Haiti, in particular Port-au-Prince, was high indeed.[20]

Despite the overall high levels of Haitian-Dominican integration in the frontier, cultural identities as "Dominican" or "Haitian" nonetheless existed. In fact, the porous border and the transnationalism of the region helped preserve Haitian culture and identity. In many border areas, the population was composed mostly of people identified by outsiders as "Haitian."[21] Certain cultural, religious, and linguistic practices, and also various physical features (from darker skin to smaller ears), were coded as Haitian, however much they were shared by both Haitians and Dominicans. And these notions of cultural and physical difference were more hierarchical than egalitarian. Although links were weak between those in the region and the racist and anti-Haitian discourses emanating from the cities, elderly peasants did recall certain forms of differentiation, ethnic stereotypes, and racist constructions of beauty. Frontier Dominicans' understandings of their difference from Haitians drew on invidious cultural stereotypes that imputed, for example, stronger magical, sexual, and healing powers as well as less restraint to Haitians.[22] However, these were ethnic rather than necessarily national distinctions. Ethnic Haitians born in the Dominican Republic were Dominican citizens according to the constitution, and the evidence suggests that they were accepted as part of the Dominican nation by their ethnic Dominican neighbors and by local Dominican officials. Indeed, numerous Haitians recalled that even those born in Haiti could avoid the yearly immigration tax and pass for Dominican citizens once they spoke Spanish well and had lived in the country for a number of years.[23]

In short, ethnic Haitians did not occupy an inferior position in the overall rural economy and society in the frontier. And Dominican frontier denizens had generally viewed Haitians neither as a poorer and subordinate group nor as outsiders. Nor was Haiti seen as being less modern than the Dominican Republic. (The Dominican Republic's relative economic and military superiority developed mostly over the course of the Trujillo regime.) Despite everyday frictions and stereotypes, a high degree of socioeconomic equality and community existed across ethnic difference and also across the national border. Thus forms of prejudice and differentiation between ethnic Haitians and ethnic Dominicans in the region were meshed with and even born of intimacy and integration. They constituted notions of difference but not necessarily otherness or marginality.

When asked how life had been in the frontier before 1937, Doña María, a poor elderly Dominican resident of Dajabón, recounted: "A Haitian was the midwife for my first child. And we lived close to one another. I treated this woman as if she were my mother. If I cooked, I would give her food. And my children really loved her. . . . Haitians and Dominicans had treated each other like brothers and sisters, like sons and daughters."[24] For a humble civilian family such as Doña María's, elite anti-Haitian ideology and constructs of a monoethnic nation had no social or economic basis.

The ways of life and cultural complexity of Dominican frontier society collided with an elite and urban ideal of a Dominican nation excluding and reviling everything Haitian. There was a racial dimension to this ideal, which identified Haitians as "black" in contrast to Dominicans. While Dominican intellectuals recognized African ancestry as a substantial component of Dominican origins, they rarely constructed Dominican national identity in terms of blackness. (Nor have Dominicans, in general, constructed a black identity for themselves, even though, except for a very small elite, most also have not identified themselves as "white.")[25] For the most part, however, Dominican writers sought to define the distinction between *la raza dominicana* and *la raza haitiana* in cultural rather than physical terms (physical distinctions between the two being recognized as problematic even by many virulent anti-Haitian thinkers).[26] The writer, F. E. Moscoso Puello asserted in 1913 that although most Dominicans are "mulattos," they "cannot be confused with Haiti, where men eat people, speak a French patois, and *papalwa* [Vodou priests] abound."[27]

For centuries, the culture of the Dominican peasantry had also been seen by Dominican elites and policy-makers as backward, even African, and the primary obstacle to progress, marked, as one nineteenth-century writer put it, by "religious fanaticism and . . . a peculiar independence rendering it unamenable to enlightened practices . . . of work."[28] And popular Dominican religion, music, and other cultural practices had always exhibited forms traceable to Africa and in common with Afro-Haitians.[29] But in the early twentieth century, "Haitianization" increasingly became the means by which supposedly backward and African dimensions of Dominican culture and society and Haitian-Dominican norms in the Dominican frontier were explained by Dominican intellectuals.[30] This group included figures such as Joaquín Balaguer, Julio Ortega Frier, and Manuel Arturo Peña Batlle, all of whom would go on to hold key posts in the Trujillo regime. These leaders were part of the national bourgeoisie emerging at the turn of the century as the Dominican economy and national infrastructure began to expand.[31] They were university and foreign-educated and, save Balaguer, members of the urban upper class from Santiago and Santo Domingo. They were also all born around the turn of the century—the years when Haitian migration to the frontier and overall West Indian migration to the nascent sugar plantations commenced—and educated at a time when racist scientific discourses were widely diffused in Europe and the Americas.[32] This group of Dominican intellectuals and state leaders demonized popular Haitian culture, and Vodou in particular, as a threat to Dominican nationality,[33] and represented the Haitian presence in the Dominican frontier as a "pacific invasion."[34] This "invasion" was supposedly "Haitianizing" and "Africanizing" the Dominican frontier, rendering popular Dominican culture more savage and backward, and injecting new and undesirable African admixtures into the Dominican social composition. And this was depicted as an obstacle to the goal of rendering the country more modern and "civilized."[35]

The racist opposition of elite Dominicans to the bicultural conditions of the Dominican frontier dovetailed with long-standing state interests in gaining greater political control over the region. With their vast, untamed woods and hills, remoteness from population centers, dispersed peasantry, and scarce infrastructure, these areas had for decades been particularly resistant to subjection to the national state. Since the end of the nineteenth century, state leaders had been struggling to consolidate modern forms of political authority and economic regulation in the region where ethnic Dominicans and ethnic Haitians lived to a large extent apart from the rest of the nation. Also, like most modern states, the Dominican government sought to fix a clear and continuous national border and to regulate the flow of goods and people across it.[36] State officials had attempted for decades to collect customs taxes along the border and eliminate contraband in order to gain revenue, protect Dominican merchants and infant industries, and secure economic autonomy.[37] The borderless frontier also offered an optimal location for revolutionaries, given the ease with which one could flee across the border to Haiti to gather arms and organize forces, and the money that could be made through illegal commerce. Local caudillos who sustained a high level of regional autonomy also derived wealth and power from illicit trade across the border.[38] Thus, establishing and controlling a firm border had long been a matter of official concern. So too had been building markets on the Dominican side of the border, in an effort to reorient the frontier population away from Haiti.[39] And beginning in the 1920s, the government attempted to implement laws requiring official documents (identity cards, passports, visas, or certificates of good conduct) for people to pass through the legal port of entry in Dajabón.[40]

State interest in hardening the border and securing control over the frontier, together with elite prejudices against the Haitian "pacific invasion," gave rise to government efforts to establish agricultural colonies in the region. Initially formulated in the early years of the twentieth century, the first colonization schemes focused on the frontier regions and responded to fears that the growing immigration and presence of ethnic Haitians in that area would support wider territorial claims by the Haitian state, especially as there was no definitive borderline yet drawn between the two countries. In 1907, the year that the nation's first colonization law was passed, one editorial argued: "This spontaneous immigration that flows from the other side of the Massacre [River] [the traditional boundary between Haiti and the Dominican Republic in the north] would have nothing alarming about it if it continued being as it was before, only to occupy, give impetus to agriculture, and supply our cities with food; but there is now the ambition, the egoism or bad faith of . . . [those who assert that] Gran Fond [now Trinitaria near Restauración] has never belonged to the Dominican Republic [but is instead part of Haiti]."[41] Populating these areas with settlers other than Haitians, it was hoped, would consolidate Dominican claims to the territory.

Yet the scattered Dominican peasantry was unlikely to populate this region in sufficient numbers to forestall Haitian immigration and prevail in demographic terms. Overall the country was still sparsely populated, and land remained abundant in regions less remote than the frontier. Furthermore, since most late-nineteenth and early-twentieth-century intellectual and political figures exhibited only contempt for the still highly autarkic Dominican peasantry, they imagined that it would be necessary to populate colonies with European immigrant farmers to "civilize" the countryside, to foster sedentary and commercial agriculture, and thus to settle, claim, and develop frontier lands for the Dominican Republic.[42] State officials spoke of the "moral" and "ethnographic" improvements that would result from European immigration.[43] Similar racist-culturalist discourses had been prevalent throughout late-nineteenth-century Latin America, where European immigration was imagined as a recipe for social and economic progress.[44] But they were particularly invidious, ironic, and problematic in a society like the Dominican Republic, which was predominantly of African descent. In this context, European immigration was represented by elite ideologues as a means of "improving the [Dominican] race" and thus reinforcing the country's lack, in contrast to Haiti, of a black identity as well as privileging of European practices and beliefs. In more concrete terms, these ideologues assumed that European immigrants would bring new agricultural knowledge and habits, simple but heretofore unused tools and techniques, and a work ethic that would help modernize the countryside. Ironic as it may seem, the Dominican state proposed European immigration to consolidate Dominican territorial claims and national identity in the frontier.

This racialist fantasy impelled the country's first colonization law. In 1907 legislation authorized state funds to usher in forty foreign "agriculturalists of the white race" to farm and "colonize" Dominican frontier zones.[45] This legislation, however, was never put into effect, whether because of lack of funds or Secretary of Agriculture Emiliano Tejera's cogent assertion that frontier colonization was doomed to failure given the area's inadequate roads and infrastructure.[46] When colonization plans began again in the mid-1920s, national leaders professed essentially the same goals as those of the 1907 legislation: impeding the so-called pacific invasion of Haitians into the Dominican frontier and developing commercial agriculture through the settlement of European farmers. A 1925 commission on immigrant colonies stated: "The purpose of populating the frontier is connected to the need to cut off or contain the slow but incessant advance . . . [of] the Haitian people . . . toward our territory . . . and to make the frontier lands safe from the usurpation of which it has become the object on the part of the inhabitants of the neighboring Republic." This commission also stressed agricultural development and the admixture of European immigrants as equally important goals.[47]

The first actual colony was established in 1926 under President Vásquez and Secretary of Agriculture Rafael Espaillat. Espaillat, who as we have seen would become secretary of agriculture during the height of Trujillo's land distribution campaign, had participated in the 1925 commission. As had been originally envisioned, this first settlement was developed in the frontier and populated primarily by immigrants. However, the next two colonies established that year, Bonao Arriba and Pedro Sánchez, while also populated by immigrants, were founded far from the frontier. The shift from an exclusive focus on the border regions would be the first example of how colonization was refashioned as the state moved from the realm of discourse into that of actual implementation. The goal of using immigrants to disseminate novel agricultural knowledge and habits, as policy-makers assumed white Europeans would do, was also soon abandoned. In practice, the goal of production proved to be most important to the state. Referring to the colonies established in 1926, Espaillat wrote: "We have sought to exploit to the fullest degree possible all the good that can come from the immigration of men whose race is white and vigorous. To that end we have felt it necessary to use them not only as factors of production but also as teachers for creole agriculturalists."[48] However, in this regard foreign colonization efforts were quickly disappointing. Immigrants were especially vulnerable to disease (malaria), found the work overly exacting, and were reportedly less productive than Dominicans in the same colonies. In terms of agricultural expertise, moreover, Dominicans frequently knew more about the crops for which colony lands were suited.[49]

As a result of disillusionment with foreign colonization, the state shifted its focus to Dominican colonists. Although located in the frontier, five of the subsequent six colonies relied primarily on Dominican peasants. Only a year after his efforts to settle European immigrants in Dominican colonies, Espaillat wrote: "The primary goal pursued by means of frontier colonization is already being realized. Before it began, there was not a single Dominican in the entire region, whereas today, throughout the area [the colonies] encompass, there are scarcely any inhabitants who are not colonists and all of them . . . are Dominicans." At the same time Espaillat held on to racist notions about model colonists, asserting somewhat implausibly that "in the interest of maintaining the race as pure as possible, we have selected families in which the white element is predominant."[50] Espaillat simultaneously envisioned "protecting" the Dominican "race," claiming territory for the Dominican nation, and advancing the economy when he advocated a "network of Frontier Colonies [that] will be able to ensure us in the future of absolute control over our lands, without danger of their being invaded by another race or their remaining unproductive, as has been the case until now."[51] By the end of the 1920s, then, colonization had been refashioned in more nationalist terms as the "Dominicanization of the frontier."[52] The racist "civilizing mission" of the project had not disappeared, though; it had simply been creolized. Espaillat asserted: "We need to educate a large quantity of peasants inhabiting the most remote regions without any contact with civilization. They live like animals and are entirely unproductive for the country."[53] More concretely, the governor of Seibo explained that instructing the peasantry in "modern methods of cultivation" was the "objective that was being pursued" in establishing the colonies.[54]

The colonization project was reconfigured not only because of disillusionment with immigration but also in response to emerging problems of peasant landlessness. Almost immediately after it was implemented in 1926, colonization evolved into a means of distributing land to Dominicans. Securing peasant land access rather than attracting what were supposed to be model immigrant farmers and citizens was a goal already envisioned in the first extensive colonization law, Law no. 670, passed in 1927. This legislation concentrated on the settlement of "poor agriculturalists" and made only a single and indirect reference to immigrants.[55] This agrarianist concern was at the heart of the Jamao colony near Moca in the Cibao. Squatters in Jamao had been pushed onto marginal lands in the hills; even from there, landowners were attempting to evict them. Colonization in this case sought to forestall these evictions and mitigate peasant landlessness. In 1927 the government purchased 14,717 hectares from the Batlle and Ginebra estates in Jamao in order to form the country's largest colony—in fact three-fourths of all colonization lands—and to "distribute" plots there.[56] Jamao's placement outside the frontier reflected how important land access had already become to the colonization program.

These first few colonies faced more failure than success under President Vásquez. The infrastructure they would have needed to thrive required a far greater investment than the state was ready to offer. Officials therefore had to make "titanic" efforts to persuade a number of peasants to join the isolated Pedernales colony close to the Haitian border. Similarly, in Pedro Sánchez in the East, where there was satisfactory soil and some irrigation for rice farming, production was hindered by the absence of decent roads linking colonists to markets.[57] Health conditions—namely, malaria—were also a problem in the colonies, especially in the irrigated ones, such as Villa Vásquez in the northern frontier, where inadequate drainage bred mosquitoes. In the Bonao Arriba colony in the Cibao, not only did malaria spread but, in addition, the land turned out to be unfit for agriculture.[58]

At the end of 1930, there were reportedly 909 families, 3,611 inhabitants, and 19,878 hectares of land within nine colonies.[59] Although a majority of the colonies were located in the border regions, most of the land area was not. Moreover, only approximately 5 percent of the families were immigrants and almost none of them were in the frontier, where the population was supposedly most in need of refinement.[60] And, ironically, the vast majority of the Dominican peasants who were incorporated in the northern frontier colonies were, despite Espaillat's claims, in fact, ethnic Haitians.[61] This situation stemmed from the demographic realities of the sparsely populated border areas. But it also suggests an alternative construction of the Dominican nation that coexisted with official ideals and was embraced by some local functionaries. This view of the nation effectively endowed Haitians born on Dominican soil, and even some born in Haiti, with Dominican citizenship.

Concerns with national sovereignty, race, and culture had initially given rise to colonization as a means of securing and transforming the Dominican borderlands. But once put into practice, colonization was quickly expanded to meet new agrarianist objectives as it responded increasingly to peasant land needs. Nonetheless, the anti-Haitian impetus of the early plans for colonization would continue to play an important role, especially at the ideological level. Furthermore, the same anti-Haitian nationalist discourses driving those early schemes would legitimate the Haitian massacre and have a severe and transformative impact on the Dominican Republic, the frontier world, and visions of the Dominican nation during the Trujillo regime and beyond.

The Dominican Frontier in the Early Trujillo Years

In the 1930s the Haitian-Dominican borderline remained only provisionally drawn, uncertain in several locations, and, most important, still porous to travel and immigration. It thus sustained the transnational character of the Haitian and Dominican frontiers. It was also a clear fault line for the new regime. From Trujillo's viewpoint, the frontier doubtless cried out for increased state presence, a concern heightened by ongoing border disputes with the Haitian government in the early 1930s.[62] Trujillo was also deeply concerned that revolutionary exiles might launch an invasion across the Haitian-Dominican border and that the area would provide easy passage for illegal arms coming into the Dominican Republic.[63] From a military perspective, the border was indeed the regime's Achilles' heel. The long-standing state impulse to police the border and control the region also intensified as Trujillo sought to dominate the national economy, to impose new taxes and fees on external trade, and to promote local industry and import-substitution programs via high tariffs.[64]

Trujillo's efforts at state formation and political control in the frontier converged with continuing cultural and territorial concerns over "Haitianization" in the border areas. This can be seen in the regime's early policies toward frontier colonies. Overall, frontier colonization played only a marginal role in the Trujillo regime from 1930 to 1937. The state did not create any new colonies in the region and significantly expanded only one of the existing ones in this period. Nonetheless, the colonization program served and gave voice to the anti-Haitian nationalism that had originally molded it and that was espoused by key figures who joined the regime, such as Espaillat. Colonization continued to be envisaged as a means of augmenting the frontier's sparse ethnic Dominican population to counteract the so-called pacific invasion of Haitians and to preclude Haitian territorial claims based on the preponderance of ethnic Haitians in the region.[65] In 1935 the editors of *Listín Diario* praised colonization in the frontier for simultaneously meeting official goals for production, "civilization," and "Dominicanization": "[Colonization] in the frontier . . . not only elevates production and re-educates inhabitants who used to wander aimlessly, without God or law, marauding about the region, without work, without producing, and by robbing other people's efforts. It also raises a wall with distinctive features of an authentic Dominicanism in the sites that are closest to the neighboring Haitian state."[66] Reference to an "authentic Dominicanism" with "distinctive features" may have implicitly condemned an "inauthentic Dominicanism" in the Dominican frontier—one that incorporated or shared key features with Haitians. We will see that it was precisely this overlapping of cultural practices between Haitians and Dominicans and the overall biethnic community "in the sites that are closest to the neighboring Haitian state" that made establishing state control over the border seem both particularly necessary and problematic to Trujillo. Cultural homogeneity, long argued for by intellectuals, became a critical concern to the Trujillo state, where it was seen as instrumental to marking political space and consolidating political authority.[67]

Anxieties about the Haitian presence in areas "closest to the neighboring Haitian state" were evident when the Trujillo government founded the agricultural colony of Pedernales in the southern frontier in 1931. In the early years of Trujillo's rule, the regime appears to have been concerned with Haitians primarily in areas where the border was actively disputed by the two countries. Pedernales was the longest and most hotly contested point along the border. Establishing a colony there resulted in the single dramatic action the state took against ethnic Haitians in the pre-1937 period.[68] To make way for the colony, the regime gave ethnic Haitian residents six months to leave the area and offered them a marginal sum for their improvements. The Haitian minister of foreign affairs complained in 1932 to both Dominican and U.S. authorities that reportedly "thousands of Haitians" who had lived there for generations had been forcefully dispossessed by Dominican soldiers.[69]

A small number of ethnic Haitians who were living and working in state agricultural colonies in the northern frontier, where there was no longstanding and heated border dispute, were also dispossessed in the period from 1930 to 1937. But these evictions, though they may have responded to some type of central state directive, were a desultory operation, impelled by individual conflicts and conditioned by local discretion. This operation was also complicated by multiple and contradictory notions of Haitian versus Dominican identity. In 1934 the administrator of the northern border colony of Restauración decided to evict Pierre Damus, a better-off Haitian-born peasant, following a dispute over livestock that had damaged Damus's crops. Damus wrote a letter to Trujillo protesting this arbitrary action. He concluded his letter: "It's true I am Haitian, but I have followed the laws and have a Dominican wife."[70] The chief of colonization, Francisco Read, responded to this complaint with a recommendation that Damus be given one year to harvest his crop before being forced to leave the colony. Read further proposed that because Damus was "hardworking and married to a Dominican woman, he can be offered a plot in the Colonies of Jamao or Pedro Sánchez, which are not border colonies." Read evidently wished to accommodate a productive agriculturalist and understood the goal of evicting Haitians as something relevant only to the frontier region and border concerns.

However, Secretary of Agriculture Tolentino offered a stricter interpretation of state policy. He replied that Damus could be granted a year for his harvest, but that was "the only measure of benevolence possible in this case."[71] Whether this was because Damus was Haitian-born or because, in Tolentino's mind, anyone who was ethnically Haitian was outside of the privileges of Dominican nationality is not clear. The latter interpretation, however, did not prevail in most cases. Still in 1935, Carretero reported that "the population in the [border] Colonies is composed of four Haitian families for each Dominican."[72] And in 1936 an official from the border town of Bánica used a national rather than ethnic criterion for determining who was Haitian. He reported matter-of-factly, "The tenants to whom we have distributed land in the Section are mostly Haitians, but ones born in the country, for which reason they are considered as Dominicans and therefore we resolved to distribute land to them."[73]

Thus the Trujillo state's early policies toward the frontier left room for local interpretation and discretion by individual officials. Indeed, policies may have been left intentionally ambiguous in light of competing interests and ideologies within the state that Trujillo was not ready to resolve. By incorporating the nation's elite statesmen and leading intellectuals into his regime, Trujillo had acquired a number of the most rabidly anti-Haitian nationalists. Imbued with deeply racist and culturalist notions, this cohort of anti-Haitian thinkers and functionaries doubtless imagined expelling rather than assimilating ethnic Haitians as the solution to the racial, cultural, territorial, and political problem they supposedly posed for the Dominican nation. Yet the early Trujillo state appears overall to have accepted a more assimilationist approach to nationalizing the frontier. Although not a central or trumpeted policy, the state took clear steps in the pre-1937 period to integrate ethnic Haitians (as well as ethnic Dominicans) in the frontier into urban Dominican culture and society by the infusion of national symbols, imposition of standard Spanish, and the performance of Dominican nationality. The government changed dozens of Haitian and French names of frontier towns, rivers, and even streams to Spanish ones.[74] The Trujillo regime also built up the then weak Catholic Church in the frontier. In 1935 the archbishop of Santo Domingo entered into an agreement with the Ministry of Interior to send a mission to the border region. In addition to marriages, baptisms, and spreading Christian doctrine, the Frontier Mission of San Ignacio de Loyola founded by the Jesuit priest Felipe Gallego organized celebrations for national holidays, including Trujillo's birthday and the Day of the Benefactor.[75] And between 1932 and 1935 the government significantly expanded the number of public schools in the frontier (both in the south and the north) and established special curricula emphasizing standard Spanish and national symbols and histories.[76] *Listín Diario* reported that their curriculum was designed "to arrest the denationalizing influence of the contiguous country's language" and habits and to inculcate "love of the land, the language, [and] the customs," of the Dominican Republic.[77] A large number of the children served by these new schools were ethnic Haitians. Trujillo, himself of partial Haitian descent,[78] thus backed policies to foster ethnic Haitians' identities as Dominican citizens and subjects of the regime.

Ethnic Haitians who lived in the Dominican frontier themselves recall how Trujillo presented himself to them not as an eliminationist anti-Haitian tyrant but rather as a ruler granting state protection and assistance (namely, free land access) to those offering political loyalty, agricultural production, and taxes to the regime. Isil Nicolas, who was born in Cola Grande near Dajabón, recalled Trujillo's words on one of his early 1930s visits to Dajabón: "He said all people are the same. There are no differences between one another. . . . He told everybody . . . that Dominicans and Haitians have the same blood. . . . And he brought us twenty or thirty trucks of tools, machetes, pickaxes, and rakes. He said these were for us to cultivate the land, and he divided them up. . . . You could use land wherever you found it with one condition, he said. Each citizen must farm productively."[79]

Thus the various anti-Haitian nationalist measures pursued in the early Trujillo years were sporadic and contradictory. Although the Trujillo regime was united ideologically by a discourse of nationalism, how a stronger Dominican nation was to be achieved was not yet uniformly perceived. And more notable than the early Trujillo state's anti-Haitian measures was the extent to which in these years Trujillo publicly silenced and ostensibly ignored the virulently anti-Haitian discourses of many of his advisors and the country's leading intellectuals. It is striking too that prior to the massacre, the state did not enact legislation against Haitian migration. And though the state did repatriate some individuals who failed to pay their immigration tax, and it did dispossess Haitian peasants of lands they were farming in the contested southern Pedernales region, it neither threatened nor carried out any large-scale or systematic deportations of Haitians in the northern frontier.[80]

Trujillo also revealed his independence from anti-Haitian thinkers during the first seven years of his regime by pursuing unprecedented friendly and collaborative relations between Haiti and the Dominican Republic. By cultivating these relations, Trujillo hoped to secure Haiti's political cooperation on an agreement demarcating the highly contested borderline between the two countries. In 1936, following 250 years of conflict, the two states finally resolved the long-disputed border.[81] This brought to a climax endless pronouncements, which had begun in 1934, in the Trujillo-controlled press on the closeness and warmth of Haitian-Dominican political and cultural relations. After the settlement of the border agreement, Haitian president Sténio Vincent renamed Port-au-Prince's main street, La Grand Rue, "Avenue Président Trujillo," while Trujillo christened the northern frontier route between Monte Cristi and Dajabón "Carretera Vincent." Soon thereafter, the editors of the daily newspaper *La Opinión* proclaimed:

The new generation does not remember . . . the old misunderstandings [between Haiti and the Dominican Republic]. The hearts and minds of these youths have been cultivated in a new era, when fortunately the two countries of the island have stopped being rivals, and have become brothers instead. . . . The day should come when, though having distinct personalities, Haiti and the Dominican Republic will become socially speaking, like one country, one home, in which each can pass freely over the entire breadth [of the island].[82]

In these early years of his regime, Trujillo also sought to gain support among the people of Haiti. His efforts included financial support for Haitian artists, intellectuals, political leaders, and newspapers; propaganda concerning successful economic development in the Dominican Republic; and official visits to Haiti in which he handed out gifts and pictures of himself to the crowd, declared his love for the Haitian people, and dramatically kissed the Haitian flag.[83] Even more startling in retrospect, both the Haitian and Dominican press reported that the Dominican president now proudly affirmed his Haitian ancestry.[84] His efforts to establish strong relations with Haiti and to ingratiate himself with elites were, it appears, efforts to gain control over the Haitian state and people. Haitian historian Roger Dorsinville explained: "There was an epoch when Trujillo wanted to have the Haitian elite with him. He made many attempts with the [Haitian] intellectuals . . . to facilitate the visits of businessmen, and of all Haitians of a certain prestige, great writers. . . . At that time, we always thought that Trujillo had the idea to expand his control over the entire island, not with the idea of invading and demolishing everything, but by rendering his power acceptable."[85] Efforts to "render" Trujillo's power "acceptable" to Haitian elites as well as the other ambiguous and contradictory discourses and strategies vis-à-vis Haiti that marked the early Trujillo years would contrast starkly with the widespread official anti-Haitianism that followed Trujillo's ordering of the Haitian massacre in 1937.

Friendly relations with Haiti did not mean that the regime did not simultaneously seek to solidify a well-controlled border between the two countries. To the contrary, there are indications that Trujillo intended the 1936 agreement demarcating the border with Haiti to signal the end of illicit trade and ultimately the unsupervised movements of people across the border.[86] But state efforts to impose a firm border continued to be frustrated by the bicultural, bilingual, and transnational character of the frontier. Popular transnational networks combined with weak national infrastructure on both sides of the border to impede state efforts to pursue rebel groups and exiles as well as cattle smugglers and thieves.[87] Biculturalism and, in particular, the extensive use of Haitian Creole, also hindered the national state's ability to monitor, interpret, and control life in the frontier. Furthermore, frontier residents simply had too much of a personal and economic stake in their transnational world to adhere to official efforts to close the border. State efforts to control and tax trade with Haiti were staunchly resisted by Dominican exporters of livestock and agriculture and by frontier residents in general who depended on Haiti for inexpensive products, such as clothes. And in addition to trade restrictions, new passport fees and regulations requiring Dominicans to obtain permission to travel to Haiti and Haitians to travel to the Dominican Republic produced a barrage of complaints to the government. Both ethnic Dominicans and ethnic Haitians in the Dominican frontier had no interest in curtailing their frequent transit across the border to visit Haitian friends, relatives, and business associates as well as markets. To most denizens of the frontier, state efforts to close the border were contrary to their interests and lacked both sense and legitimacy.[88] It may thus have appeared to government leaders, and ultimately to Trujillo, that to harden the boundary between Haiti and the Dominican Republic in expeditious fashion, a boundary between Haitians and Dominicans also had to be established in the frontier.

The 1937 Massacre

In October 1937, Trujillo commanded his army to kill all "Haitians" living in the Dominican Republic's northwestern frontier and in certain parts of the contiguous Cibao region. Between October 2 and October 8, hundreds of Dominican troops, who came mostly from other areas of the country, poured into the region.[89] With the assistance of alcaldes pedáneos and some civilian reserves, these armed forces rounded up and slaughtered with machete perhaps fifteen thousand ethnic Haitians.[90] Those killed in this operation—still frequently referred to as el corte (the cutting) by Dominicans and as the kout kouto-a (the stabbing) by Haitians—were mostly small farmers, many of whose families had lived in the Dominican Republic for generations.[91] Haitians were slain even as they attempted to escape to Haiti while crossing the fatefully named Massacre River.[92] After the first days of the slaughter, the official checkpoint and bridge between Haiti and the Dominican Republic were closed, thus impeding Haitians' escape.[93] In the following weeks, local priests and officials in Haiti took testimony from refugees and compiled a list that ultimately enumerated 12,168 victims.[94] Subsequently, during the first half of 1938, thousands more Haitians were forcibly deported and hundreds killed in the southern frontier region.[95]

Dominican civilians and local authorities played disparate roles in the massacre. Some assisted the army by identifying and locating Haitians, while others helped Haitians hide and flee. A few were recruited by the army to participate in the killings. Generally, these civilian recruits were prisoners from other areas of the country or local residents already tied to the regime and its repressive apparatus. Above all, local Dominican civilians were compelled by the army to burn and bury the bodies of the victims.[96]

The massacre followed an extensive tour of the frontier region by Trujillo that commenced in August 1937. Trujillo traveled by horse and mule through the entire northern half of the country, both the rich central Cibao region and the northern frontier areas. Touring these provinces, traditionally the most resistant to political centralization, reflected Trujillo's concerns with shoring up control in the region at the time. The Cibao was the locus of elite rivalry with Trujillo in those years. And because the northern frontier had been a traditional area of autonomy and refuge for local caudillos, the U.S. legation in Santo Domingo assumed that the August 1937 tour was intended to "cowe [sic] opposition."[97] Much like earlier frontier tours and his travels in other rural areas, Trujillo shook hands and distributed food and money; attended dances and parties in his honor; and made concerted efforts to secure political loyalty in many heretofore intractable lands.[98] Yet the conclusion of this tour was entirely unexpected. During a dance in Trujillo's honor on Saturday, October 2, 1937, in Dajabón, Trujillo proclaimed:

For some months, I have traveled and traversed the frontier in every sense of the word. I have seen, investigated, and inquired about the needs of the population. To the Dominicans who were complaining of the depredations by Haitians living among them, thefts of cattle, provisions, fruits, etc., and were thus prevented from enjoying in peace the products of their labor, I have responded, "I will fix this." And we have already begun to remedy the situation. Three hundred Haitians are now dead in Bánica. This remedy will continue.[99]

Drawing on the regime's prevailing antivagrancy discourse and support for peasant production, Trujillo explained his ordering of the massacre as a response to alleged cattle rustling and crop raiding by Haitians living in the Dominican Republic. This was the first of a series of shifting rationalizations that misrepresented the massacre as stemming from local conflicts between Dominicans and Haitians in the frontier.

Some Haitians heard Trujillo's words and decided to flee. Others had already left following news of the first killings, which occurred at the end of September.[100] A few recalled clues that something ominous was brewing. Most were incredulous, however, and had too much at stake to abandon their homes, communities, and crops—established over decades or even generations—for what sounded, however horrible, like preposterous rumors. Yet on October 5 these rumors were confirmed when the Dominican Customs Receiver (a U.S. official) in Dajabón filed a grim report. More than two thousand ethnic Haitians had crossed into Haiti from the northern Dominican frontier. They had not been forcibly deported, but rather were escaping bands of Dominican soldiers slaughtering ethnic Haitians. Already some five hundred had been killed in Dajabón alone.[101]

A few Dominicans from the northern frontier recalled that at first Haitians were given twenty-four hours to leave, and that in some cases Haitian corpses were hung in prominent locations, such as at the entrance of towns, as a warning to others. And during the first days of the massacre, Haitians who reached the border were permitted to cross to Haiti over the bridge at the official checkpoint. But the border was closed on October 5. After that, those fleeing had to wade across the Massacre while trying to avoid areas where the military was systematically slaughtering Haitians on the river's eastern bank.[102]

In the towns, victims were generally led away before being assassinated. In the countryside, they were killed in plain view. Few Haitians were shot, except some of those killed while trying to escape. Instead, machetes, bayonets, and clubs were used. This suggests again that Trujillo sought to simulate a popular conflict, or at least to maintain some measure of plausible deniability of the state's perpetration of this genocide. The lack of gunfire was consistent with civilian rather than military violence. It also reduced noise that would have alerted more Haitians and propelled them to flee.

The soldiers who perpetrated this massive slaughter shattered forever the prevailing norms of nation and ethnicity in the premassacre frontier world within which Dominican-born Haitians were more or less accepted as Dominican citizens and as members of a multiethnic national community. Those norms were clear in the testimony of many elderly Dominicans. When asked how Haitians were identified in the slaughter, Lolo, who had been the alcalde pedáneo of Restauración at the time of the massacre, responded by contrasting state practices of identification before and during the massacre: "There were many that they didn't know. But if they had their birth certificate, they presented it. But here they didn't check that. If they checked that, all the Haitians here would have remained because they were all recognized here [as Dominicans citizens]. Only the elderly persons were Haitians. Those that they threw out in 1937 were not Haitians. Most were Dominican nationals."[103] One such Haitian-Dominican, Sus Jonapas, similarly recalled how a baptismal record showing Dominican birth had exempted one from the migration tax, but "when they started killing people, they were no longer interested in whether or not you had a baptismal record."[104] And another Dominican-born Haitian, Emanuel Cour, a schoolteacher living in Ouanaminthe in 1988 who had been fifteen years old at the time of the massacre, remembered: "Those who came over to the Dominican Republic as adults kept their Haitian names. But those who were born there generally got Dominican names. They were Dominican. But when the knife fell, no longer were any distinctions made."[105] Dominican birth (or the appearance thereof), a critical determinant of ethnic Haitians' membership in the Dominican nation prior to the massacre in the frontier, was rendered suddenly meaningless. The outside military units that led the genocidal operation imagined and imposed an absolute distinction between Haitians and Dominicans on a frontier society in which many people had divergent national and ethnic identities as well as multiple and intermixed cultures and ethnicities.

Still, the basis on which Trujillo's genocidal army would draw their imagined absolute distinction between "Haitians" and "Dominicans" was not obvious. Were Haitians whose families had lived in the Dominican Republic for several generations and who spoke Spanish fluently still "Haitian"? And how should children of Haitians and Dominicans be identified? It is often recalled that the Guardia used Spanish pronunciation as a supposed litmus test for deciding who was "Haitian." Many soldiers demanded that those captured utter *perejil* (parsley), *tijera* (scissors), or various other words with the letter *r*. Supposed inability to pronounce the Spanish *r* was then represented as an indicator of Haitian identity. This practice may have been borrowed from local guards who had used it in the past to determine whether ethnic Haitians would be required to pay the annual migration tax (as records of birthplace were not necessarily or easily available). Anyone who pronounced the *r* clearly was presumed to have been born in the country and would not be taxed. Ercilia Guerrier, who lived in Restauración, recalled being stopped prior to the massacre by Dominican soldiers checking to see if immigrants had paid their tax: "You were going to the market or to Loma de Cabrera, you run into the guards, they say to you, 'Stop right there!' And so you do that, you stop. 'Say perejil!' And so you say, '¡Perejil, perejil, perejil!' 'Say *claro*.' ¡Claro, claro, claro!'" Asked if it was ever necessary to produce a

birth certificate or baptismal record to avoid the migration tax, Guerrier replied, "No, no. As soon as you could say that [perejil or claro], you didn't
have any problems with them."[106] Thus when lacking records of Dominican
birth, fluency in Spanish allowed many persons of Haitian descent to pass for
Dominican citizens. Jonapas also recalled: "If you spoke Dominican well,
[Dominicans] said you were not Haitian."[107]

Prior to the massacre, the perejil test was apparently used by local
guardias to distinguish recent Haitian immigrants from assimilated Haitians
presumed to be Dominican nationals. During the massacre, however, this
same test was used by national troops in an effort to distinguish "Haitians"
from "Dominicans," without differentiating between Haitian lineage and
Haitian nationality. In fact, though, ethnic Haitians with deep roots in the
Dominican frontier most likely pronounced perejil fluently and often indis-
tinguishably from ethnic Dominicans in the area.[108] Thus this litmus test was
evidently rigged. It served largely as a pretext, a mock confirmation of the
presumptions and fantasies of an inherent and radical distinction between
ethnic Dominicans and Haitians clung to by outside officials and elites.
Asked whether during the massacre the Guardia demanded that they utter
certain words to determine whether or not they were Haitian, one escapee
from Mont Organizé exclaimed:

"Perejil, perejil, perejil!" They made us say that. Many had to say it, but however well
you said it, there was no way for you to stay. . . . You had to say *tijera colorada, tijera
colorada, tijera colorada* [red scissors]. They were mocking us, trying to trick us. They
told us, "Say that *tú no eres Haitiano* [you're not Haitian]. Say clearly 'tijera.' Say
clearly 'perejil.'" And you said all sorts of things. They told you to say *Generalisimo,
Jefe, Benefactor de la Patria* [Generalissimo, Chief, Benefactor of the Fatherland].
They told you to say it faster to see how well you could speak. They were really
making fun of us.[109]

This refugee's testimony suggested that soldiers' demands to utter words
such as perejil were less a genuine tactic for identifying Haitians than a theater of national linguistic difference separating Haitians and Dominicans. The
perpetrators of the massacre slowed their killing machine for what was
doubtless an often dubious test. Yet, however problematic or false it was, by
acting as if this test was clear and efficacious, the killers imputed to their victims radical cultural difference that served to rationalize the violence and
ethnicize images of the nation. Thus the violence in the Haitian massacre and
the discourse within which it took place were themselves performances that
helped constitute notions of inherent and transhistorical difference between
Haitians and Dominicans.[110]

It appears to have been Dominican frontier residents who frequently determined who was Haitian by pointing out to the Guardia where ethnic Haitians resided and guiding soldiers to their homes.[111] Local officials played this role primarily.[112] Other Dominican frontier residents sought to protect their neighbors from slaughter, helping them hide and escape across the border. An official for the U.S. Military Intelligence Division reported after a trip to the Dominican frontier in December 1937: "In some places, native Dominicans who had sufficient disregard of their own safety are reported to have hidden out Haitian refugees, many of whom had lived among them peacefully for generations."[113] Even local soldiers attempted to help Haitians. Ercilia Guerrier recalled how the local lieutenant, "whom in a small town you know quite well," came to her house on October 2 to warn her family to flee to Haiti immediately.[114] And Emanuel Cour recalled how when he and his mother tried to escape to Haiti, "guardias from our area [who] recognized us" warned them not to take a particular route where an unfamiliar group of soldiers was stationed and were likely to kill them.[115]

Although the U.S. Military Division reported that "no Dominican civilians were involved in the massacre," alcaldes pedáneos and army officials were able to recruit a few civilians, whose loyalty and discretion they trusted, to participate in the killings.[116] But overall, Haitians and Dominicans interviewed, as well as most state documents, rarely mentioned any civilians killing Haitians. To the contrary, most Dominicans were reportedly petrified by a military campaign by the state directed largely against its own citizens. "Local Dominicans were as terrified by the proceedings [of the massacre] as the Haitians themselves," reported a U.S. intelligence official.[117] Unlike other cases of ethnic cleansing in the twentieth century, no prior state policy, local tension, international conflict, official ideology, or escalating attacks had signaled the possibility of such state-directed carnage.[118] To local residents, the genocidal rampage appeared to come out of nowhere, like an act of madness. State-led ethnic violence appeared so inexplicable to most frontier denizens that Doña María did not perceive the massacre, at first, as an attack solely against ethnic Haitians. Reflecting the integration of Haitians and Dominicans, Doña María recalled that at the time, "[e]veryone thought that they were going to kill us, too." The result of the inexplicable violence was suffering and trauma for many ethnic Dominicans in the frontier. Doña María described her husband's condition in the aftermath of the killings: "I had a husband and this man died under the weight and sorrow of witnessing the Haitian massacre, as he had worked with many Haitians. When he went to the Haitian houses and found so many Haitians dead and their houses burned, this man went crazy, and didn't eat anything. He passed all his time thinking with his head lowered, thinking of all the Haitians who had died. He died . . . three months later."[119]

Numerous testimonies of the massacre refer to the horror not just of local residents but of the army as well. The use of military units from outside the region was not always enough to expedite soldiers' killings of Haitians. U.S. legation informants reported that many soldiers "confessed that in order to perform such ghastly slaughter they had to get 'blind' drunk."[120] The U.S. Military Intelligence official reported that "the soldiers who carried out the work are said in many instances to have been sickened by their bloody task. A few are reported to have been summarily executed for refusing to carry out their orders, while many overcame their repugnance to the task by fortifying themselves with rum."[121] And, according to Percivio Díaz of Santiago de la Cruz, "The soldiers who participated in this all went crazy and died because their conscience told them they shouldn't have done it."[122]

On Friday night, October 8, 1937, five days after the massacre began, Trujillo finally halted the slaughter of Haitians in the northern frontier.[123] By that time, the shared frontier world of Haitians and Dominicans had been destroyed. Most of the estimated twenty thousand to fifty thousand ethnic Haitians in the province of Monte Cristi had been killed or had escaped to Haiti. The U.S. legation reported on October 11: "The entire northwest frontier on the Dajabón side is absolutely devoid of Haitians."[124] The devastating impact of this decimation upon the Dajabón parish and its Haitian-Dominican community was clear from a report filed in the log of the École des Frères in Ouanaminthe, where many ethnic Haitians from the Dajabón area had sent their children to school: "Father Gallego of Dajabón has lost two-thirds of his population, at least 20,000. In certain chapels, in Loma and Gouraba, 90 percent of the population has disappeared; instead of 150 to 160 baptisms a month, there is not even one. Some schools, which had 50 students before, now have no more than two or three. It's grievous and heartbreaking what has happened." This report also noted the impact of the killing on the children in the École des Frères: "The number of students with parents disappeared is now 167 [of 267 students]. The poor creatures are all in tears. In the evening one hears nothing but the cries and wails from the houses of the whole town."[125] During the last weeks of October, the relatively few remaining ethnic Haitians in the northern frontier region and contiguous areas would emerge from hiding and flee to Haiti. Many of them would be killed in flight, with the exception of hundreds retrieved by Haitian authorities by truck and ship after the massacre.[126]

A reported six thousand to ten thousand *rescapés* (refugees) arrived in

Haiti bereft of all possessions and without any means of support.[127] Most had lived since birth or for decades on Dominican soil. Some tried to return surreptitiously to their homes in the Dominican Republic to recover some of their lost harvest and livestock. The odds of their surviving such efforts were slim.[128] As Bilín explained: "When they [the Haitians] came back, the Guardia and the civilians killed them, because if a civilian ran into one of them and didn't kill them, the person [the civilian] would be punished. . . . They'd arrest him, because this was a law." Bilín himself participated in this ruthless campaign against "poaching." "They took me to the border [to fight Haitians]. I was just a youth, 18 years old. One had to use a machete."[129] During and immediately following the massacre, many civilian men were recruited to patrol the towns near the border, such as Dajabón. Women and children were temporarily evacuated as Dominican authorities anticipated a military response from Haiti.[130]

However, Haiti did not respond militarily to defend or avenge its compatriots. To the contrary, President Vincent of Haiti acted in every way possible to avoid a military conflict.[131] Under increased domestic pressures because of growing evidence of the extent of the massacre, however, Vincent did eventually seek an investigation of the atrocities and mediation of the conflict by other countries. Unwilling to submit to an inquiry, Trujillo offered instead a sizable indemnity to Haiti, while still refusing any admission of official responsibility. One can only speculate as to why Vincent so readily accepted Trujillo's offer of $750,000 (of which only $525,000 was ever paid) in exchange for an end to international arbitration.[132]

The massacre's diplomatic resolution allowed Trujillo to begin rewriting the slaughter as a nationalist defense against the so-called pacific invasion of Haitians. The indemnity agreement signed in Washington, D.C., on January 31, 1938, unequivocally asserted that the Dominican government "recognizes no responsibility whatsoever [for the killings] on the part of the Dominican State." Furthermore, in a statement made to the governments—Mexico, Cuba, and the United States—that witnessed the accord, Trujillo stressed that the agreement established a new modus operandi to inhibit migration between Haiti and the Dominican Republic. The statement read: "More than an indemnization, a sacrifice to pan-American friendship . . . [this] also represents an acquisition of legal positions that assure the future of the Dominican family, and preclude the single deed capable of altering the peace of the Republic, the only threat that hovers over the future of our children, that constituted by the penetration, pacific but permanent and stubborn, of the worst Haitian element into our territory."[133] In the very signing of the indemnity agreement, the Trujillo regime, in effect, defended the massacre as a response to a mythical illegal immigration by supposedly undesirable Haitians. Trujillo thus turned a moment of international scandal and arbitration that could easily have toppled his regime into the foundational event for the regime's legitimation via an anti-Haitian nationalism. And this nationalism may have garnered some support for Trujillo's rule among some elite Dominicans who had been ambivalent, at best, toward this lower-class, mulatto dictator who was carrying out popular agrarian policies.[134] And it rationalized the massacre and the state's imposition of a well-policed border as necessary to protect a monoethnic national community that the massacre had, in fact, only just established in the frontier.

The accord with Haiti, however, did not signal an end to the madness and terror. In the spring of 1938, Trujillo ordered a new campaign against Haitians, this time in the southern frontier.[135] Here Haitians reportedly received warning and many were able to escape to Haiti before they were attacked. The operation occurred over several months, and thousands were forced to flee. Although known simply as *el desalojo*, or the eviction, hundreds were also reportedly killed in this campaign.[136] And unlike in the northern frontier, some recalled Dominican civilians cooperating in the killing.[137] Most of these attacks, though, appear to have occurred between 1938 and 1940 after el desalojo, when former Haitian residents returned to collect abandoned crops and animals or to steal livestock from the now deserted hills they had recently inhabited. Conflicts ensued with Dominicans who owned or now claimed this property. Trujillo ordered the military to capture and execute those who returned. Soldiers from outside the region sent to carry out the executions soon distributed rifles to "mixed patrols" composed of local officials, military veterans, and trusted civilians, especially those who had recently been involved in conflicts with returning Haitians. Ironically, then, the massacre and eviction of ethnic Haitians produced the very type of local ethnic conflict over poaching that the regime had first claimed was at the root of the killings in the frontier.[138]

As in the north, the southern mountain chain, which was once dense with Haitian coffee growers and laborers, was evacuated. In many sections only the alcalde pedáneo remained.[139] By the end of 1938, long-standing multiethnic communities were only a memory in that large part of the Dominican Republic known as "the frontier."

A World Destroyed, a Nation Imposed

How do we write the history of such seemingly mad state violence? Many have represented the massacre as simply Trujillo's ruthless and tyrannical method for reversing the so-called pacific invasion of Haitian immigrants and supposedly "whitening" the country.[140] And some elite whites may have indeed imagined the massacre as one step toward reducing popular Afro-Caribbean culture and toward at least marginally lightening the overall complexion of the Dominican population. Yet the massacre would not, in fact, significantly alter race or color in the Dominican Republic, which remained overwhelmingly nonwhite. In order to have "whitened" the population, moreover, darker-skinned Dominicans would have had to have been targeted in the massacre as well. That was not the case.

Furthermore, the assumption that the Haitian massacre was a terroristic but logical reaction to Haitian migration collides against several realities. First, most of the "Haitian" families in the frontier were not recent immigrants, but rather had lived in the region for many years, often for several generations. Second, the Trujillo regime never sought, on any systematic basis, to deport Haitians and Haitian-Dominicans living in the frontier, nor did it make Haitian immigration illegal or prohibitively expensive until after the massacre. Instead of the prohibitive immigration fees the regime imposed on certain groups (such as Asians), legislation in 1932 merely raised the entry and annual residence fees required of all other immigrants, including Haitians, from 3 to 6 pesos. (This was a significant but not prohibitive amount of money at the time for a poor immigrant, equal to roughly three weeks of wage labor.)[141] Only in 1939 was new immigration legislation promulgated. Designed by U.S. legal experts, this new law imposed a prohibitive 500-peso immigration fee on all those not "predominantly of caucasian origin" and thereby effectively barred legal Haitian migration for the first time.[142] Finally, after the massacre, Haitians continued to constitute a significant portion of the population in the Dominican Republic outside of the border regions. Neither the massacre itself nor any other official measures ever reduced the population of Haitian sugar workers in the country (unlike Cuba, where tens of thousands of Haitian braceros were expelled by Fulgencio Batista at this same time in the wake of high unemployment during the Depression).[143] There was only one reported instance when the country's plantation workers were attacked during the massacre, in Bajabonico near Puerto Plata (western Cibao), in one of the few sugar plantations close to the northern frontier region.[144] The rest of the country's more than twenty thousand Haitian sugar workers, most of whom resided in the Eastern provinces near La Romana and San Pedro de Macorís, were not targeted.[145] And when Trujillo appropriated the sugar industry in the 1950s, rather than terminate or reduce the importation of Haitian sugar workers, he formalized and expanded the immigration of Haitian braceros (who were exempt from the 500-peso migration tax on non-"caucasian" immigrants).[146]

Thus the massacre followed concerted state efforts neither to stop Haitian immigration nor to "whiten" the nation. Nor did it follow from popular ethnic conflict, in contrast to the Trujillo regime's efforts to portray the slaughter as stemming from local tensions. And we have also seen that relations between the Haitian and Dominican governments were ostensibly on the best of terms in these years. After the massacre, Haitian president Vincent told U.S. officials: "There was no question of any nature whatsoever under discussion between the two governments. Agreement was perfect, relations excellent."[147] It is not possible, it seems, to trace a direct line from the massacre back to an escalation of anti-Haitianism in the Dominican Republic in the early years of the Trujillo regime.

Nonetheless, anti-Haitianism in the Dominican Republic and, at the very least, distinct Haitian and Dominican ethnic identities did play a critical role in this history. They help to explain how the Haitian massacre could be organized and political stability maintained despite such extreme, unprecedented, and unanticipated state terror. For one, Trujillo knew that he would be able to draw on the zealous support of several prominent anti-Haitian intellectuals, such as Acting Secretary of State Joaquín Balaguer, to justify the massacre as a response to the Haitian "pacific invasion." It seems doubtful that the massacre would have occurred had intellectuals like Balaguer not provided the powerful anti-Haitian ideologies of the time, which served to legitimate the slaughter. Also, prejudicial Haitian images doubtless facilitated military compliance with the massacre and rendered plausible Trujillo's violent division of humanity into "Haitians" and "Dominicans." These prejudices similarly may have contributed to Trujillo's decision to kill rather than forcibly evict the Haitian population in the frontier.[148] Moreover, the fact that the group that Trujillo ordered killed was distinguished as "Haitian" meant that most of the population outside the frontier areas was not directly or vitally threatened by state terror. And pretexts casting blame on the Haitian victims, however weak, problematic, and after-the-fact those rationalizations were, seem to have permitted most Dominicans to make some sense of the killings. It is doubtful, in other words, that Trujillo could have ordered the death of fifteen thousand ethnic Dominicans with a similar absence of ideological preparation, clear provocation, or prior justification and nonetheless managed to secure the support of key state figures, the passive acceptance of many others, and the overall participation of the army.

Anti-Haitianism, however, like racism in general, is not in itself an adequate explanation of historical phenomena. Racist ideologies are products, not just causes, of history, ones that vary profoundly in meaning and significance across time and space as a result of different historical conditions that themselves need to be elucidated.[149] What is so striking in the case of the Haitian massacre is that the Trujillo regime's anti-Haitian discourse was the product of rather than the precursor to state terror. Prior to the massacre, the state's primary concern with the "pacific invasion" had not been Haitianization—though this was also a concern, particularly among the elite—but rather that Haitian settlers would support claims by the Haitian state to what was considered Dominican territory. In the period from 1930 to 1937, the dictator's participation in anti-Haitian and racist discourse appears unexceptional within Dominican history. Only following the massacre did the Trujillo regime sponsor virulent anti-Haitian rhetoric decrying supposed Haitian backwardness and savagery; effectively prohibit Haitian migration through the 500-peso immigration fee; and frequently and bitterly condemn the history of a "pacific invasion" by Haitian migrants in culturally racist rather than simply territorial and political terms. The regime took traditional elite prejudices against popular Haitian culture, excoriating its "African"-ness, creolized French, and, above all, the "superstitions" and "fetishism" of Vodou, and circulated them as official ideology.[150] This racist discourse would be spearheaded by prominent anti-Haitian elite intellectuals such as Balaguer, Peña Batlle, and Emilio Rodríguez Demorizi, the regime's foremost historian.[151] And although it varied in intensity in light of Haitian-Dominican relations after the massacre, the Trujillo state continually spread anti-Haitian propaganda throughout the country in speeches (by teachers, officials, and local figures), in the mass media (newspapers, radio, and eventually television), and in new laws, books, and historical texts used in school.[152] Indeed, the relative weakness of popular and official anti-Haitianism before the massacre and the increasing virulence of it afterward suggests how this violence contributed to cultural racism and an ethnicized national identity (including in the frontier) more than vice versa. Violence was a catalyst, not simply a consequence, of racism and identity formation.[153]

Still in the moments immediately following the massacre, the leaders of the regime expressed state interests primarily in eliminating Haitians from the frontier zones and in political concerns over border formation rather than in eliminating Haitians from the entire country. On October 15, 1937, the newly appointed secretary of state ad interim, Julio Ortega Frier, explained to the U.S. legation that he was:

studying a plan whereby Haitians residing in the communes along the Haitian-Dominican frontier would be moved to other parts of the Dominican Republic . . . and [an international accord] to prevent any further infiltration of Haitians into the communes comprised in a zone of 50 to 100 kilometers in width along the Haitian-Dominican frontier. This agreement would not only prevent the entry of Haitians into the Dominican zone but would establish a similar zone on the Haitian side of the frontier from which Dominicans would be excluded. [Licenciado] Ortega Frier was of the opinion that if it were possible to conclude such a reciprocal agreement with the Haitian government, no further incidents would occur along the frontier.[154]

The primary objective of the Dominican government's proposal was not to diminish the overall number of Haitians in the Dominican Republic but rather to eliminate Haitians from the Dominican frontier—and indeed Dominicans from the Haitian border areas as well—where they posed a problem for drawing a clear political, social, and cultural boundary between the two nations.

The overall history and consequences of Trujillo's Haitian and border policies thus suggests the massacre's relationship less to state anti-Haitianism in general, as has understandably often been presumed, but rather to anti-Haitian objectives specifically in connection to the Dominican frontier, and ultimately to state formation and national boundaries. The efforts of the Dominican state to eliminate Haitians were directed essentially at the frontier provinces, not throughout the country. And in terms of its lasting impact on the Dominican Republic, the Haitian massacre materially altered only the frontier, not the nation as a whole. The massacre did not eliminate Haitians from the Dominican Republic, but it did destroy the Dominican frontier's fluidly bicultural and transnational Haitian-Dominican communities.

As a result of the massacre, virtually the entire Haitian population in the Dominican frontier was either killed or forced to flee across the border. In addition to the unspeakable violence that this inflicted upon Haitians, the genocide destroyed the frontier's pre-existing economy, culture, and society. The way of life for the remaining Dominican civilians who had once lived side-by-side with Haitian neighbors and who had frequently married and had children with Haitians was buried and became a haunting memory. Many of these Dominicans were now armed by the state and ordered to kill their former neighbors if they returned. Instead of free and constant movement between Haiti and the Dominican Republic, the state established a well-regulated border between the two countries for the first time, one that was patrolled via a proliferation of new military command posts and that reportedly saw little Haitian immigration beyond that desired for the sugar plantations.[155] For Dominican ranchers who had herded cattle on landholdings that crossed an erstwhile invisible border, the closed border now sealed the demise of their centuries-old cattle trade with (and in) Haiti.[156] From now on, it would be relatively dangerous to traverse the border outside of official checkpoints and without proper authorization. Also, without a large population of ethnic Haitians who lived on more or less equal terms with Dominicans, the influence and certainly normativeness of Haitian cultural practices would be continually reduced over time. Certainly, the boundaries between Dominican and Haitian culture would always remain especially blurry in the frontier. Trade, contraband, and interpersonal and military contact across the border inevitably continued to some extent.[157] Furthermore, despite the mythical attributions of Afro-Dominican practices solely to Haitian influence, their roots in the Dominican Republic were deeper and wider, dating back to the early colonial period in this mostly Afro-Caribbean nation. The state could not simply divest ethnic Dominicans of their culture and worldview overnight. Yet the relative equality and bicultural community of ethnic Dominicans and Haitians, as well as the ease, safety, and frequency of border crossing, terminated with the 1937 genocide.[158] The idea of an ethnically homogenous nation gained plausibility even in the Dominican frontier. The border, once a porous and somewhat artificial division to frontier denizens, had become instead a deep and horrific scar.

This seismic transformation was precisely what elite Dominican figures had fantasized about for decades. Instead of seizing the postmassacre moment to try to eject Trujillo when he was uniquely vulnerable, the country's ministers and state lawyers—many with strong elite roots and anti-Haitian prejudices—rallied behind the dictator and vigorously defended the regime from international scandal and what at first was likely foreign intervention.[159] In some cases, frustrated elite Dominicans were seeing for the first time perhaps the advantages of Trujillo's despotic rule. By eliminating ethnic Haitians and fluid transit across the border, the massacre imposed the traditional elite vision of a Dominican nation constructed in opposition to Haiti even in the once bicultural frontier.

From Trujillo's perspective, though, the benefit of the massacre may have been not only strengthening the border specifically to eliminate Haitians but also eliminating Haitians so as to strengthen the border and state formation in general. The limited impact of the regime's early efforts to police the border and nationalize the frontier prior to 1937 had thrown into relief the impediments to expeditious state formation posed by this bicultural and transnational region and therein reinforced the implicit linkage of political control with the construction of a monoethnic nation. The most obvious means by which the state could justify greater control over the border to the local population was anti-Haitian nationalism and official racism. But in light of the relatively cohesive, multiethnic character of the frontier, official discourse to ethnicize national identity and existing communities fell on deaf ears.

Yet, by means of the Haitian massacre the Trujillo state violently established a new world in the frontier, a world in which a closed border could now be imposed and legitimated. From the state's perspective, the massacre represented the elimination from the frontier of a well-integrated but distinct ethnic group that was linked to and associated with the nation on the opposing side of the country's border. From the perspective of most Dominican residents then living in the frontier, the massacre embodied inexplicable horror. However, by violently excluding Haitian peasants from Dominican frontier communities in which they had been relatively equal members for generations, the Trujillo state imposed, in practice and then in ideology, the elite construction of a monoethnic nation-state on this extensive transnational and bicultural zone. The slaughter—and the memories of this slaughter—established for the first time a profound social division, clear hierarchy, and increasing cultural distance between the populations in the Dominican and Haitian frontiers. And over time this rendered official anti-Haitianism plausible at the popular level, which in turn legitimated as "protection" state control over the frontier and an impermeable border with Haiti.

One elderly Dominican peasant from Loma de Cabrera, Avelino Cruz, expressed decades later a virulent anti-Haitianism, albeit in paradoxical fashion, that appears to embody the transformation in ideology and identity that the massacre brought on for some in the frontier. Cruz had prior connections to the regime's repressive apparatus (he had occasionally been commissioned to carry out local operations), and he was one of few civilians to participate in the killings. In a most extreme and even incoherent interview, Cruz first described in animated fashion his contentment with life prior to the massacre. He explained that he had been married to a Dominican woman when he began another relationship with a Haitian woman, with whom he had two children: "We treated each other well in our relations. My wife and la Haitiana both lived on the same plot of land, in separate houses, but very near. And they cooked together. And also both nursed the children. In other words they got along very, very well, like two sisters." Yet the very relations that Cruz nostalgically recalled as harmonious—and of course the two women may have had memories that differed from his—were destroyed by the massacre in which he took part. When asked about the killings, Cruz transmogrified into a seemingly different person. He recounted in lurid detail the ways in which he had slaughtered Haitians. When asked why he had participated, he explained: "I was roused by an order I had nothing to do with. If it had been necessary to kill my Haitian wife, I would have killed her also. Fortunately she was already in Haiti at the time of the eviction [the massacre]. Because I wasn't going to let them kill me [for disobeying]. But God willed that I didn't have to kill her." His discourse transformed even further when we asked why Trujillo had ordered the massacre. "If Trujillo hadn't done this, the Haitians would have eaten us like meat. Already there would be no Dominicans here."[160]

In the wake of the massacre and the diffusion of anti-Haitian ideologies, some ethnic Dominicans in the frontier, such as Cruz, appear to have embraced the idea that, prior to the "eviction," they had been engulfed by Haitians and were becoming Haitian—a variant on the "pacific invasion" theme (although few went as far as Cruz did by using a cannibalistic metaphor). From this perspective, the massacre may have destroyed their world and, to some extent, their identity, but it had also prevented them from being lost to "Haitianization" and its supposedly retrograde character. This shift in perspective was further illustrated by Percivio Díaz from Santiago de la Cruz, a wealthy self-described Trujillista. Díaz condemned the massacre as "an act of absolute barbarism." "Here," he recalled, "everyone cried after [the massacre]." But while Díaz opposed the killings, he also contended that "we needed to escape from the Haitians, even though in some other way, like arresting and deporting them . . . because by then they were invading us, and we really had to do something about it." Díaz concluded that "el corte was necessary. Because if we didn't do this, we would be Haitians. . . . Already in the frontier we had become Haitians." The massacre, Díaz implied, severed ethnic Dominicans from their immersion and participation in Haitian-Dominican norms and therein constituted them as what he now considered genuine Dominicans. Díaz's comments thus echoed the nation-building project of the Trujillo regime, of turning peasants into "Dominicans," of incorporating them into official norms of the Dominican nation. Díaz also stressed that his view had changed in the decades following the massacre: "But it's only now that I realize . . . [that the massacre] was a necessity . . . now that I am older, and I see what is still happening, that they are invading us in the capital. There are more Haitians there than here [in the frontier]."[161] Thus, in addition to being swayed by the force of official anti-Haitianism, Díaz was reading life in the 1930s frontier through the lens of subsequent and quite different conditions in other regions, where Haitians have played the role of cheap and often illegal laborers.

That much of the anti-Haitian sentiment in the Dominican frontier today is a product of the massacre and subsequent history is further suggested by the greater (and seemingly less contradictory) anti-Haitianism evident among younger Dominicans. A transformation in local anti-Haitianism across the generations was portrayed in the testimony of Evelina Sánchez, an elderly local historian from Monte Cristi. Sánchez replied to our query about whether some Dominicans responded positively to the massacre: "The people did not think this was a good thing. The one who found it so was Trujillo.

They say he wanted to make the Haitians pay for their massacring of children in Moca [during Haitian president Dessaline's unsuccessful attempt to seize control of Santo Domingo in 1805, then under French control]. . . . That's the same reason my son used to say that he wanted to be el Jefe [Trujillo] so that he could get rid of all the Haitians." Simultaneous with her denunciation of the massacre and of her sense that her contemporaries also condemned the killing, Sánchez implied that her son had come to perceive all Haitians in the Dominican Republic as outsiders and anti-Haitian violence as legitimate.[162]

Difference had been transformed into otherness and marginality. After the massacre notions of ethnic difference between Dominicans and Haitians that had existed in a well-integrated frontier community evolved into a widespread and often intense—though also still paradoxical and inconsistent—current of anti-Haitianism. This new mode of racism emerged as a result of state terror and the official anti-Haitianism that followed it and served to rationalize the massacre. Popular anti-Haitianism may have been further amplified by fear of the state and the need to distinguish oneself from the targets of its violence, or by collective interest in justifying the slaughter with which Dominicans were inevitably somewhat associated, even if it had been perpetrated by a brutal dictator. Also, anti-Haitianism may have gained some acceptance because it was propagated by a state that was simultaneously developing substantial popularity in the countryside as a result of its agrarian and rural policies.

The production of Dominican anti-Haitianism would be furthered as well by socioeconomic factors in the postmassacre decades, including a severe new ethnic division of labor. After 1937, Haitians in the Dominican Republic were relegated almost exclusively, and in increasing numbers, to the role of plantation workers at the bottom rung of the labor market.[163] The state and the sugar companies would consistently and flagrantly violate Haitians' human rights, subjecting them to slavelike material conditions with which they became associated. In this new context and in the context of the Dominican Republic's growing economic and military superiority over Haiti after the massacre, Dominican notions of Haitian ethnic and somatic difference would be transformed into a new mode of racism rendering Haitians into inferior and permanent outsiders that prevails still today. This is not to say that these notions completely restructured the sentiments, practices, or even discourse of all Dominicans.[164] It is notable, for instance, that in contrast to the regime's agrarian policies, the massacre and official anti-Haitianism in general were rarely praised during interviews with elderly peasants throughout the Dominican Republic. Among subsequent generations, though, anti-

Haitianism appears to be far more accepted. And overall it became a salient part of everyday discourse in a way that contrasts sharply with the premassacre frontier world.[165]

Although the massacre served to further anti-Haitian nationalism in the Dominican Republic, it was, ironically, economically dysfunctional and had run counter to the Trujillo regime's forceful efforts at rural development and increased agricultural production. The massacre left vast expanses of territory depopulated, crops unharvested, and communities abandoned. Even with scores of prisoners brought in to work the farms abandoned by Haitians, harvests were drastically reduced (and prices increased) for years.[166] One elderly Dominican from Monte Cristi explained: "There was scarcity afterwards because it was the Haitians who had produced most of the food around here. Afterwards, everything was expensive and the town languished. . . . This thing [the massacre] caused a lot of turmoil. And the people became very sad."[167] The state responded to this crisis by continuing its efforts to distribute land and by increasing the number of agricultural colonies along the border. The state also developed new infrastructure in the region (roads, bridges, aqueducts, irrigation, electric plants, postal and telephone service); constructed schools, clinics, and government buildings; and established new municipalities and provinces and, with them, new local governments.[168] These developments multiplied the number of state functionaries in the frontier and the sites from which official discourse emanated. The growing presence of a powerful national state, as well as the expanding infrastructure tying the region to the rest of the country, facilitated the diffusion of anti-Haitianism.

The public works campaigns pursued in the postmassacre frontier were similar to those carried out across the country. But here they were deemed the "Dominicanization of the frontier." Given that virtually all Haitians in the frontier had already been murdered or fled to Haiti, it was now ethnic Dominicans, not ethnic Haitians, who were being "Dominicanized"—that is, integrated into the nation, as elites conceived of it—and subjected to an expansive state. Official discourse conflated modernization and socioeconomic improvements with a new Dominican identity based on anti-Haitianism and in line with traditional urban and elite notions. This discourse was expressed in the national press, where articles reported in laudatory fashion a supposed new mode of national belonging among frontier residents. In 1943, Emilio García Godoy wrote in *La Nación*: "The man of the frontier is learning to turn his back on the savage witchcraft of Haiti that until [1937] had regulated the rhythms of his life without any breath of nationalism and to offer himself, baptized by a new patriotic faith, to the wind and the sun of a land today suffused with ... a regenerating sense of patriotic integration defined by a more knowledgeable concept of Dominican-ness."[169] And an article by a foreign reporter in Monte Cristi that was reprinted in *La Opinión* read:

For these people, the word "nation" had had no meaning. ... All the frontier provinces had become ... "no man's land," as if neither authorities nor boundaries existed. ... Until very recently, the border was but an imaginary line. Today it is definitively drawn. ... They [frontier residents] live [now] in modern "bungalows" and receive newspapers every day. They have at their disposal telephone and radio communication. "Construction" is the word heard most throughout the frontier. ... By building a new national consciousness throughout the frontier, Dominicans have realized something that was once considered impossible.[170]

The massacre was thus implicitly constructed as initiating a process of incorporating the Dominican frontier population into the larger nation as well as modern practices of culture and society. It was written as re-establishing the proper rhythm of the nation in the frontier, imputing a "more knowledgeable concept of Dominican-ness" among ethnic Dominicans in the region, and suturing a deep and conspicuous gap between the urban and rural populations, the capital and the most remote and autonomous areas of the country.

The impact of the 1937 Haitian massacre was ultimately on the character more than the magnitude of the Haitian presence in the Dominican Republic. The main consequence of the bloodbath for Dominicans was the destruction of the Haitian-Dominican frontier world and the transformation of popular meanings of Dominican identity, culture, and nationality. In the immediate aftermath of the massacre, Trujillo reportedly boasted to one of his subordinates: "Now let them say that we have no borders."[171] Through this slaughter, a socially and culturally meaningful border was established and a rigid political border therein facilitated. And the population of the vast frontier areas was subsequently integrated to a greater extent into official and urban constructs of the nation and modernity. What caused Trujillo to order the 1937 massacre will probably remain forever obscure. But what is most striking is how closely its effects realized the pre-1930 anti-Haitian nationalist project of many leading intellectual and political figures, objectives they had first advocated pursuing, above all, through colonization. After the massacre, an ostensibly monoethnic community, bereft of ethnic Haitians, prevailed in the Dominican frontier for the first time. And, over time, this made possible the acceptance—though never complete assimilation—of anti-Haitian nationalism even in these areas. The Trujillo regime thus transformed everyday rural life and peasant subjectivities in the frontier and established the foundations for what the lettered class envisaged as a modern nation. That nation incorporated Haitians and "African" traditions only as marginal elements of a society imagined as monoethnic. As an effort to foment "modern" rather than "primitive" practices, the regime's diffusion of anti-Haitianism can be seen to be ideologically of a piece with Trujillo's overall rural policies, and it would constitute one of the regime's most enduring and infamous legacies. To the extent that a comparatively small number of Haitians would again enter and remain in the Dominican frontier world in subsequent decades, they would be marked as permanent outsiders in ways that they had not been in the past. The massacre had imposed a new national community in the frontier, one imagined for the first time without Haitians, except for the ghosts of Trujillo's victims.

6

Taming the Countryside

Agricultural Colonies as Rural Reform under the Trujillo Regime

Anti-Haitian discourses gained strength and meaning throughout the country during the Trujillo years in the wake of the state's genocidal violence, widespread official anti-Haitianism, and the relegation of ethnic Haitians in the Dominican Republic almost exclusively to work as cane-cutters. But while the Trujillo years produced and consolidated an anti-Haitian mode of racism, other pre-existing racial discourses and policies that lacked mechanisms of nationalist legitimation and were backed by few state interests never shaped policies of major significance. This was the case with schemes for "white" immigration. First formulated in the decades before Trujillo took power, these efforts remained minimal during the dictatorship, which left a legacy of Dominican, not foreign, settlement in agricultural colonies.

As we have already seen, the origins of the colonization program dated back to the pre-Trujillo years and were heavily imbricated with racist and anti-Haitian nationalist discourses and dreams of European immigration among intellectuals and state functionaries. We have also seen, though, that these concerns were to a large extent supplanted by the goals of domestic agrarian reform as soon as the colonization program was actually implemented in the late 1920s. This transformation continued during the Trujillo regime, as agricultural colonies became a key feature of state agrarian policy, especially in the second half of the dictatorship. Rather than reflecting a coherent racial project, as might be expected given the horror of the Haitian massacre and the virulent anti-Haitian rhetoric subsequently sponsored by the regime, agricultural colonies under Trujillo became primarily an instrument of rural reform, regime legitimation, and state formation. Certainly some colonization efforts were linked to immigration schemes under Trujillo, but these were limited measures, and often superficial gestures aimed at improving Trujillo's baleful image overseas. Far more evident is that colonization became a major dimension of the Trujillo regime's project of distributing land to the landless while simultaneously boosting peasant production and subjecting the rural population to the gaze, power, and directives of the national state.[1] Fixed plots, known addresses, surveyed lands, nucleation of

dispersed people, the linkage of settlements to national systems of transportation and communication, and expanding rural services, schools, and bureaucracy all combined to render the countryside increasingly accessible, observable, taxable, and within reach of both state repression and assistance.

Agricultural colonies, one of the most continuous rural programs in the
Dominican Republic in the twentieth century, vastly expanded during the
Trujillo regime from their minimal dimensions prior to the dictatorship.
(And they would continue to expand following Trujillo's assassination under
the term *asentamientos* [settlements].)[2] During the first half of the Trujillo regime the land distribution campaign had been primarily responsible for ensuring peasant access to land. But after the mid-1940s, rapid population
growth, property adjudication, and the expansion of agribusiness began de-
pleting the supply of nearby idle land and unclaimed property. And many
peasants were obliged to turn to government programs of agricultural colonization for help. The degree to which they found adequate support from colonies varied, however, given that the term "colony" would refer over the
course of the regime to diverse agricultural settlements with disparate conditions. With the exception of the Sosúa colony organized in 1940 by Jewish
refugees from Hitler's Third Reich, all were state-supervised, with at least a
nominal state director and set of administrators, and almost all were formed
on property claimed by the state. But within this common legal structure,
colonies ranged from communities that effectively provided settlers with adequate services, infrastructure, and aid (housing, irrigation, clinics, schools,
churches, and an initial stipend) in addition to generally 1 to 6 hectares of
land, to poorly supported settlements that offered colonists the means to eke
out only a marginal existence. Also, a number of colonies were established on
some of the country's most desirable lands, which were acquired by the state
from private owners in return for the development of public irrigation systems. These settlements, though, generally involved only minimal state oversight. Finally, the term "colony" referred to a couple of penal institutions that
were in fact gruesome forced-labor camps for a wide range of criminals and
political prisoners.

Corresponding with their diverse conditions, the agricultural success of
colonies was mixed. While many were characterized by profitable agriculture, others served as a mere safety net for desperate families, and a few simply languished until residents abandoned them after several years.[3] Overall,
though, colonies did offer needed land access and some assistance to many
peasants and generated a substantial portion of the country's produce
(between one-fifth and one-fourth of crops such as rice, coffee, and beans in
1947).[4] In 1953 the colonies under the aegis of the Department of Agriculture

comprised 107,300 hectares of land and 14,220 colonists and their families (69,805 residents).[5] And by the end of 1959 (after a new push to establish colonies), the regime had offered 197,570 hectares of land to 27,109 settlers (some of whom became property owners rather than colonists over time).[6] This represented in 1960 around 9 percent of landed property and 6 percent of rural producers.[7] As most colony lands had previously been woods and pasture, colonization opened up substantial farmland and boosted agricultural production. And together with the land distribution campaign, it constituted a vast state program to provide, mediate, and control peasant land access.

Colonization was represented by state officials as a tutelary process guiding the peasantry to a modern mode of existence, greater agricultural output, and a role in constructing the new Dominican nation. Many peasants, though, embraced colonization and state visions of "progress" only with ambivalence.[8] Except in the case of irrigated lands appropriated from private owners—plots coveted by the rural population in general—colonization required peasants to move often substantial distances and commence new lives in relatively remote regions under frequently difficult conditions, especially at first. Moreover, particularly strict state control was exercised over daily life in most colonies to ensure full cultivation and to limit "unproductive" recreational activities. As a result, colonization held generally less appeal than the land distribution campaign. Furthermore, colonization often embittered those peasants previously living in the isolated and undeveloped areas in which many colonies were established. There most peasants had been surviving satisfactorily until then exploiting los montes. Colonization forcibly transformed their mode of existence; it compelled local residents to resettle within the villages and houses established by the colonies and to become sedentary agriculturalists, ones who then became dependent on the state for land and, over time, aid and inputs. Peasants who had not yet lost their traditional freedoms and land access and now had to renounce their pastoral practices generally resented colonization.

On the other hand, for those coming from areas of land scarcity, state colonies offered welcome aid and a chance to become successful small farmers. In this way, colonization contributed to popular rural support for and legitimation of the Trujillo state. Letters that peasants sent to the state requesting land in colonies reveal how Trujillo's paternalistic and authoritarian discourse permeated rural political culture by the late 1940s. Colonies thus promised land to, and helped legitimate the regime among, the landless while pulling other, reluctant peasants into nucleated villages, sedentarized agriculture, and the watchful gaze of the national state. This history of colonization illuminates disparate peasant perspectives on the Trujillo regime's project of modernity and its mediation of the transition from "nomadic," pastoral practices to sedentary farming and to a greater integration with the cities and the projects of the national state.

Colonization as Rural Reform

When Trujillo incorporated into his regime key figures and functionaries from Vásquez's government, such as Secretary of Agriculture Rafael Espaillat, he provided for much continuity in agricultural policies and specifically in the goals and discourse of colonization. This included colonization's early emphasis on European immigration and frontier settlement. But agrarian reform in the sense of both distributing land and transforming rural practices became increasingly central to colonization as it developed into an important rural policy under the Trujillo dictatorship. This shift began early on, a response in part to numerous complaints from local officials about foreign colonists. For instance in 1933, the administrator of the Eastern colony Pedro Sánchez condemned the fact that prior to Trujillo's rule, "foreign agriculturalists had been invited to the country by the Government as a means of illustrating to Dominicans the development of modern agriculture." But, he complained, "these people have taught us nothing new because they knew nothing. They only serve to corrupt the simple and good customs of our peasant masses."[9] The next year, the regime passed a new colonization law that gave preference to Dominicans over immigrants in frontier colonies and that limited the number of immigrants in these colonies to 25 percent of the total.[10] In 1935, Secretary of Agriculture Andrés Pastoriza wrote: "The initial idea of the colonization program . . . [based on] foreign immigration . . . was discarded by us, viewing it as alien to our true needs and even counterproductive in many cases. . . . Furthermore, it is a primary duty that, before having recourse to foreign immigration, we must grant preference to native workers."[11] Also noteworthy is the fact that none of the new agricultural colonies founded by the Trujillo state in 1936—not coincidentally, just a year after the land distribution campaign was launched—were situated in the frontier, the original venue for colonization as a racialist and nationalist project.[12] The state would continue to sponsor frontier colonization over the course of the regime, both, as the Trujillo press reported, to foment agriculture "even in the most remote zones of the country" and as part of a broader project to "Dominicanize the frontier."[13] But the frontier never became the focus of colonization, representing approximately one-quarter of the program during the Trujillo years.[14]

In 1936, Trujillo ordered the director of the Jamao colony in the Cibao:

"Make Jamao grow. Cultivate it with coffee. No matter what the cost, make sure that this happens."[15] And in 1940 the secretary of agriculture defined colonization's primary objective as "assisting those Dominican agriculturalists who lacked their own lands."[16] These two statements embody the thrust of colonization policy during the regime. It aimed both to provide land to landless peasants and to reorganize and boost peasant production. Officials conceived of agricultural colonies as a model for transforming landless and agro-pastoral peasants into sedentary farmers concentrated in villages and near to roads, selling at least some agricultural surplus, and paying their annual cédula fee.

Toward these ends, the regime vastly expanded the size, number, and resources of the state's agricultural settlements, which eventually included some fifty colonies spread throughout the country.[17] It also developed infrastructure for colonies, such as roads, and variously supplied colonists with tools, pesticides, new seeds, plows, and other forms of assistance in order to facilitate production. Even though these efforts were frequently inadequate, colonization nonetheless contributed to what sociologist Orlando Inoa deemed an economic "revolution" in the Dominican countryside, as farmland was opened up and an increasingly self-sufficient and food-exporting economy developed.[18] The growing importance of colonization to the Trujillo state was evinced in 1946 when the Department of Agriculture was rechristened as the Department of Agriculture, Livestock, and Colonization.

Along with the land distribution campaign, colonization became an integral part of a formidable plexus through which the Trujillo state orchestrated peasants' land access. An example of the complexity of everyday state intervention is the following. Carlos Liriano had title to a 12.4-hectare plot. When in 1947 the state constructed a nearby canal supplying Liriano with irrigation, he was compelled to cede 2.9 hectares to the state. This small area was then offered in equal parts to two landless families. At the same time, two squatters, Luis de la Rosa and Gonzalo de los Santos, had already cleared and cultivated plots on Liriano's land, subsequently asserting that they had viewed the land as terreno comunero, by which they made clear that they meant open-access land. Typically, the state took property ceded for public irrigation first from those areas where squatters or sharecroppers had already settled, in order to cede it to them. But in this case the state apparently had not been aware of de la Rosa and de los Santos. When Liriano complained about their occupation of the area he intended to cede, the state intervened in the conflict. The two squatters agreed to leave only "if it turned out that these lands really did not belong to the state, if they were paid for their improvements, and if they were given land and housing in the [adjacent] agricultural colony Juan de Herrera." The state offered them small plots in another colony and proposed that Liriano pay them for their improvements in an amount agreeable to all parties (no doubt via the forceful mediation of the state).[19] Colonization thus served as one instrument for the Trujillo state's dizzying manipulation of land tenure arrangements and mediation of land conflicts and pressures.

Seeking this sort of state intervention on their behalf, peasants wrote thousands of letters requesting land.[20] Individuals often sought specific irrigated plots in nearby areas when it was known that landowners had to cede them in return for public irrigation. For example, the state approved Cesáreo Cruz Díaz's request for 45 tareas (2.8 hectares) of land in one of the irrigated zones of Baní, which were nominally considered colony lands, though they had almost no administrative structure.[21] In fact, many peasants sought and obtained plots that they were already farming as squatters or sharecroppers.[22] Few expressed readiness to relocate to remote areas, even though the state generally offered transportation to move one's family and belongings to a colony.[23] Those who were desperate, however, requested land in any of the country's far-flung colonies.[24] On December 15, 1952, Miguel Ramírez requested a 60-tarea plot (3.8 hectares) in "whatever State Colony" had lands available. One week later he was offered a "good plot of land in the Agricultural Colony 'Angel Féliz'" in the southern frontier commune of La Descubierta (near Jimaní).[25]

The desperation of a growing number of peasants stemmed from intensifying land pressures in the second half of the trujillato, as the rural population rapidly escalated, the Land Court awarded property rights and titles, and agribusiness expanded. In 1947, Féliz Salvador requested land "in which to work without anyone bothering me, as I was living on lands belonging to the Brugal Company and they asked me for the land, because they needed it." In response, the state offered Salvador land in the Sabaneta de Yásica colony near Puerto Plata.[26] Similarly, in 1952, Porfirio Caraballo of Isabel de Torres, Puerto Plata, was given a plot in the same colony after being threatened by a landowner, José M. Batlle, with eviction.[27] And when the Land Court awarded the land that Manuel Fernández had been farming to another claimant, Fernández petitioned the state for land elsewhere.[28]

In their letters, which were generally addressed directly to Trujillo or to the secretary of agriculture, peasants utilized the Trujillo state's own paternalistic discourse to voice their complaints and to legitimate requests. Echoing official ideology, they typically identified themselves as "hardworking" men or women with families to support who were now in an hour of need, without land or forced to sharecrop. Most letters also expressed loyalty and gratitude to Trujillo, often effusively. In addition, they disingenuously exhibited confidence that Trujillo would help them, given, many wrote, his well-known commitment to the humble (los infelices), sympathy for "the men of work," support for the suffering, and leadership of the first Dominican government supposedly concerned with the poor.[29] The language employed in these letters shows that Trujillo's populist rhetoric had been well assimilated by peasants by the latter half of the regime. When Pablo Bienvenido Medina was offered dry rather than irrigated land by the administrator of the El Llano colony, he denounced this official to the secretary of agriculture: "The norm of our Illustrious Chief, Generalissimo Trujillo, is to attend more to the need of the poor Class than to the landowner; for that reason, I believe, I must be attended to. . . . I am a hard-worker and as the CHIEF says that his best friends are the men of work, this remains my fervent desire."[30] Access to this discourse, though, did not guarantee a successful outcome. The record contains no evidence that Medina was ever granted lands other than those first offered.

The language with which people typically referred to Trujillo in their letters was both personal and deferential, lauding the dictator as "our spiritual father," "our true father" (*nuestro padre único*), or "my beloved and sole leader" (*nuestro amado jefe, mi querido jefe único*).[31] Like the regime's other agricultural policies, land colonization functioned to sustain Trujillo's power and dramatize the importance of his supposed personal intervention. Peasants were not being granted land on the basis of their right to it. Instead, it was a gift bestowed by the great patron, or National Benefactor, as Trujillo was officially called, for which they had to be individually vetted and selected in a process that was insecure at best and humiliating at worst. Although numerous letters eschewed ingratiating language and instead simply requested land, others felt obliged to declare their obedience and filial love to Trujillo and other state leaders. The Tiburcio family from Moca wrote to Trujillo:

For many years, we have been left orphaned without our father and mother . . . who had taught us the proper doctrine of work, as well as obedience and loyalty to your person and your exemplary government. . . . To cover the costs of our deceased parents' sickness and burial, we had to sell almost the entire farm that they left us. This compelled us to work in someone else's land and thus to have to share the products of our sweat and labor with another.

We want to work our own lands. And we beg you to bestow upon us a parcel of land, as you have done for others. As you penetrate ever more deeply inside our hearts, we will try to be worthy children of this land and of this country, exalted and glorified by you, by working with machete, pickax, and hoe.[32]

Three weeks later, the secretary of agriculture offered this family land in any of six agricultural colonies.[33] Fulsome deference and hyperbole also filled Manuel Encarnación's request to Trujillo's brother Héctor when the latter was the nominal president: "If you grant me this miracle [6.3 hectares of land] . . . you can be sure that you will have realized the greatest deed of charity and goodness to satisfy the needs of a poor family, as a result of which I will be, with a father's heart, eternally grateful."[34] However much this effusive deference may have involved strategic dissimulation, it also meant publicly bowing before and reinscribing Trujillo's authority and self-proclaimed identity as the father of the new Dominican nation.

Although appeals were made to the central state to obtain colony land, as with land distribution it was local officials who recommended and approved most awards. Either colony administrators or agricultural district supervisors had to confirm that the prospective colonists were hardworking and committed agriculturalists. The central state (generally the chief of the Colonization Branch) then gave final approval for lands to be ceded.[35] Local officials did at times reject requests sent to them by the secretary of agriculture, because the applicants were not farmers but, for example, tailors or artisans, or because they had land already, or because they were not considered hardworking.[36] For applicants who were judged satisfactory by local officials there was usually land available—though not necessarily houses as well—in one of the country's agricultural colonies. However, the land was not necessarily in the settlement an applicant had desired for its proximity to the applicant's current residence or because of its overall conditions.

After a certain number of years, colonists were granted property rights. The nature of those rights varied over the course of the regime. At times, at least, colonists' plots were considered their inalienable "family property" and therefore could not be sold. Nonetheless, they were allowed to sell their improvements, and thus in effect their land, with state approval.[37] Thus a still-uncharted process of social differentiation sometimes developed, especially in the irrigated, more valuable, and more productive and viable colonies. As early as 1938 the assistant secretary of agriculture warned the official distributing land appropriated from the Compañía Comercial (Villa Isabel, Monte Cristi) to be shrewd, "as many colonists devote themselves to obtaining plots and transferring them to others for commercial purposes."[38] In the fertile and valuable Cibao colonies, such as Jamao and Los Almácigos (near Santiago), several occupants sold their improvements in the late 1940s and early 1950s for 1 to 10 pesos per tarea in plots ranging generally from 10 to 100 tareas. These sales thus often involved substantial sums of money for the Dominican countryside at this time.[39] Colonists also illegally sharecropped and rented their plots, and sometimes sold land without official approval.[40] From early on, the Trujillo state made persistent efforts to control this commerce. When officials became aware of colonists renting or sharecropping their plots, they generally redistributed the land to those actually cultivating it.[41] And in 1952, frustration over the persistence of illegal markets in ceded irrigated lands prompted the secretary of agriculture to recommend their further distribution only when part of a supervised agricultural colony (that is, not when in effect simply a form of land distribution), a policy which was soon adopted. From then on, any areas that the state received as part of the "fourth part" that were not used for such colonies were to be sold.[42]

Although some colonies in well-located and irrigated areas enjoyed periods of success, in other places (and times), colonists abandoned their plots—frequently reapplying for plots elsewhere—because the areas suffered either from poor soil, isolation from markets, or inadequate public services such as schools.[43] Also, the level of state aid varied widely between colonies. For instance, some colonists were responsible for building (or buying) their own homes, while others received free houses as well as a stipend proportional to the size of their household (at least for the first six months of their residence) until their first crops were harvested.[44] Given the value and desirability of irrigated land, stipends were only rarely given to recipients of such land.[45] Aid had to be given to a greater degree in marginal areas, such as the frontier, where farming was not as profitable and few would otherwise be willing to go. However, in light of their distance from markets, the assistance that the state was ready to grant in frontier colonies often proved insufficient. Thus many marginal colonies languished and were even abandoned over the course of the regime.

Despite the uneven performance of its agricultural colonies, the Trujillo state continued to pursue this form of protección of the peasantry, in part, no doubt, because this particular program of agrarian assistance extended the state deeply into rural life. Colonization often occurred in the least-developed areas of the country, where peasants lived scattered across wide and relatively inaccessible areas and outside the efficient reach of the state. In 1943 one official in Barahona complained that residents remaining "dispersed and separated by great expanses" was "impeding officials . . . from exercising strict supervision of their work." He advocated resettling residents to allow for "constant oversight and management" and thus increased production of coffee.[46] Obliging peasants to live in concentrated areas not far from the roads also facilitated the state's ability to monitor and control their leisure activities, to ensure their compliance with vagrancy laws, and to tax them (via the cédula). Efforts to compel residential concentration were tied, moreover, to the centuries-old objective of eliminating the countryside's open-range world of itinerant farming, unenclosed ranching, and forest exploitation. To form and expand colonies, the state would clear the forest, bulldoze away the few existing ranches and even farms that were in the way, and then divide up into agricultural plots what had been primarily woods and pasture. Colonists were generally forbidden to use their plots for livestock. A few exceptions were made to this rule in areas—namely, parts of the frontier—lacking conditions to sustain sedentary agriculture, but animals still had to be enclosed.[47] Officials then ushered in numerous migrants from land-scarce areas and relocated the dispersed local population onto colony plots and into houses in state-created villages. In this way, the colonization program transformed the economy and society of many remote areas.

In the face of growing landlessness, sedentarization and state control were reportedly prices migrant colonists were ready to pay in exchange for free land, houses, and assistance.[48] In general, colonists I spoke with remembered Trujillo's colonization projects with nostalgia, despite their inadequacies. José Adames, who was granted land in the remote northeastern coastal area of Miches, stated: "The colony was one of the best things from Trujillo. And if I had no house, Trujillo gave me one. I did not have fifty tareas and he gave them to me. When we had no money, we [still] had medicine. . . . Trujillo was a Dominican patron, strong and good."[49] Yet there were others who recalled with bitterness the regime's forceful methods of "persuading" peasants in the vicinity of the colonies to join the new settlements. Gregorio Mejía from another colony near Miches recalled:

Before everything had been easy in the hills. When [an official] came to look for me, I told him, "There is no town without country. . . . Here I am and I'm not leaving [the country]." And he said to me that I was not going to leave it, but rather we were going to move over there by the side of the road, "in case either you or someone in your family gets sick. Then it will be easier to get you [medical help]." But I wanted to stay in my hills. But they convinced me [to leave]. . . . Here [in the colony] it was easier because of the road, in case one got sick. . . . But in other ways it was easier [in the hills] because we were near our work and what was there [woods and pasture].[50]

In other ways, too, what the state represented as progress some peasants remembered instead as loss. "The colony made things worse," Antonio Amparo, also in Miches, recalled. Amparo described the effects of colonization on those previously living in the area as a loss of autonomy: "Before we were independent. We made a living and had our means. We had the open range, and we made one conuco here and one there." Colonization meant the end of that way of living: "When the colony was established, then each person had to attend to their own particular property, because then everything was fixed. . . . Before the colony people could use state land. But not afterward. Because it was filled with others, because they put many people [on the land]." Finally, colonization meant the end of a world of mobility and open space: "When the colony [was settled] one could no longer move around. Each one had their plot. . . . After the colony came life became difficult, with people living on top of each other."[51] Although state intervention was welcomed by many peasants who had already lost much of their autonomy and felt that they benefited from the regime's agrarian reforms, those like Amparo, whose independence had not yet been compromised, felt instead the weight of the state's power to impose a new way of life.

One prerogative that the state could exercise in the colonies, but did so only infrequently, was control over the crops grown. Law no. 758, the 1934 colonization law prohibiting landowners from leaving idle large tracts of land, also authorized the state to order colonists to cultivate a particular crop in 90 percent of the area granted to them.[52] And documents show that in certain cases the state did direct peasants to grow particular crops, such as cacao, coffee, or rice, seen as most suited to agricultural conditions and market demand in their area.[53] In some irrigated colonies, for example Jima Abajo, colonists were obligated to grow rice. (However, those I spoke with in Jima stated that they never wished to grow other crops, as the area was best suited for rice.)[54] The Trujillo state had a strong interest in rice production. This crop, which under official commitment to national self-sufficiency had gone from being a heavy import to a major export in the 1930s, was subject to unique taxation in the domestic market.[55] Yet high prices rather than state coercion appear to have been most responsible for making rice a popular crop.[56] And most peasants I spoke with who had been colonists did not recall being compelled to grow particular products. One colonist from Guanito, near San Juan, explained: "Rather you had to grow a certain amount. Because the person called the 'crop overseer' was there to put you to work and make sure you worked. That was the job of the overseer of the colony. But you could grow any crop you wanted. And they brought you seedlings and stumps, for plantains and manioc, for whatever you wanted [to grow]."[57] In 1950 the vast majority of colony land was devoted to food crops. Rice was the main cash crop, constituting about one-fifth of total colony production.[58] The transformation demanded by the Trujillo state—from a pastoral economy to sedentarized farming—was deeper and more primordial than that from subsistence to cash crops, both of which were encouraged by the regime.

Rather than making specific crop demands, the Trujillo state required that all colonists fully cultivate the land they occupied, which, in accordance with the regime's vagrancy law, had to be at least 10 tareas (0.63 hectare). If colonists failed to do so, the state might reassign their idle areas to others. In some cases, it was hardship that prevented colonists from attending to their land, but the state nonetheless repossessed their plots. Mario Campo Pérez received land in the Benefactor colony in the northwestern frontier region. When he fell ill and left his farm unattended until it was overgrown with weeds, it was appropriated by the state. After explaining to the secretary of agriculture, he was eventually able to reclaim his land.[59] Campo's experience, though, highlights the strict demands as well as the insecurity that peasants faced in the agricultural colonies.

A small minority of colonists could be deemed forced laborers. These included a number of prisoners who had their sentences commuted in return for spending their remaining time in one of various agricultural colonies (mostly in the frontier areas). For instance, soon after the Haitian massacre, the state sent a number of prisoners to frontier colonies in an attempt to counter the massacre's detrimental impact on agricultural production in the region. The state generally selected prisoners serving many years, who would thus remain long enough to establish roots and have reason to stay on in the colonies even beyond their sentence. Many such prisoners, along with hundreds of other colonists, received 3-hectare plots in the colonies established in Miches in the late 1950s.[60]

Yet the extent of this form of forced labor should not be overstated. According to official statistics, there were only 52 prisoners among a total of 10,242 colonists in 1947.[61] Furthermore, most prisoner colonists with whom I spoke—granted an exceptional sample of those remaining in the colonies into the 1990s—expressed a certain appreciation for the opportunity to farm and to have their sentences commuted. They generally had been granted as much land as they were ready to use (legally up to 38 hectares) as well as a modest house, tools, animals, medicine, seeds, and also a stipend.[62] They were accompanied by their families and placed under minimal or no guard. Although a few prisoners fled the colonies, most remained, and a number of them became successful ranchers and farmers.[63] For instance, Jesús Santana in the once productive Benefactor Colony in the northern frontier town of Loma de Cabrera held almost 63 hectares, 22 of which were cultivated while the rest were used for livestock.[64] Similarly Lolo Santos recalled that he amassed 1,000 pesos over eight years as a prisoner in the Mariano Cestero colony by growing rice and coffee and raising animals and bees.[65] When I asked one former prisoner colonist still living in the northern frontier colony of Hipólito Billini, Antonio Blanco, what he could tell me about Trujillo, he replied in exceptionally laudatory terms:

Well, I supported him. I can tell you that. I am more grateful to Trujillo than to any other government. Because this [current] government has done nothing for the peasantry [campesinos], nothing. This is a government only for the rich. . . . Not like Trujillo who showed respect for the poor. Trujillo was a difficult government [but one] that helped you with agriculture, above all agriculture. [Now] agriculture has declined and peasants have been forced to migrate to the towns. . . . Many have gone permanently. What I have to tell you is that to Trujillo I must be thankful. If I could give my life for him to return from the dead, I would.[66]

Certainly, the regime exploited prisoners to help develop frontier areas where few Dominicans chose to work. Nonetheless, some prisoner colonists appear to have become supportive clients of Trujillo in exchange for the land they received.

There were, though, some truly nightmarish instances of forced labor under Trujillo in several penal colonies established by the regime. These were not under the aegis of the Department of Agriculture or the Section for Colonization. Rather, they were established by the military and did not involve land distribution or the commuting of sentences. (Thus penal colonies were not included in the statistics for total colonization cited above.) I found scant documentation on the penal colonies. They were, however, recalled in lurid detail by former prisoners, who described how they labored intensively for the state, slept in huge, tightly cramped barracks, remained trapped inside wood and wire fences, were subjected to constant military surveillance and abuse, and were underfed and mistreated. Consequently, many suffered severe illness and death.[67]

The two main penal colonies, located in Azua ("El Sisal") and Nagua ("Julia Molina"), became infamous throughout the country for their baneful conditions. Thousands of prisoners were sent to these colonies, where the state produced sisal and rice, respectively. El Sisal became an institution defined by terror, according to a recent study, when Colonel José Alcántara was appointed as its supervisor in 1952. Alcántara used the colony as a conveniently withdrawn site for the torture and murder of political prisoners as well as for the forced labor of others (some of whom were arrested merely for violation of vagrancy laws).[68] Alcántara is still remembered for his brutal and capricious system of terror, including randomly killing a number of prisoners. Throughout the country I was told that he shot one inmate in the mouth to "cure" him of his toothache, and that he advised prisoners to flee the colony and then shot them in the back as they ran. Disease—such as malaria, tuberculosis, and typhoid—was also rampant in El Sisal. As a result of these horrifying conditions, many attempted to escape despite the formidable obstacles they faced. And some succeeded. Javier Melo, who lives now in Azua near the old colony, managed to escape with the help of a soldier there who had been his friend.[69]

Finally, colonization involved elements of coercion in situations in which the state attempted to transplant the urban poor living in what were deemed marginal areas to agricultural colonies in the countryside. Unemployed workers, recent rural migrants from the countryside, and persons evicted from their homes as a result of state urban renewal plans were "encouraged" by officials to move to agricultural colonies.[70] These actions occurred to some extent throughout the regime as part of an ongoing effort to limit rural-urban migration in the process of economic development. In 1940 one official alluded to this policy: "I have visited various peasants that live in town in the interest of having them prepare themselves to go to reside in the Medina colony where . . . in addition to houses, land, and agricultural implements, each family will receive $6.00 monthly for a period of six months."[71] There is also documentation from the 1950s of struggling artisans, merchants, and poor rural migrants who requested land to become farmers (again) and were then given plots in one of the colonies.[72] In 1958 the secretary of agriculture informed the secretary of labor that anyone requesting employment should instead be settled in the frontier colonies.[73]

In 1958 and 1959, this ruralization drive reached singularly coercive proportions. Planning a vast urban renewal project in the northern and northeastern sections of the capital, the state evicted perhaps thousands of families without notice from their modest dwellings in the marginal neighborhood then known as Faría (now Ensanche Espaillat). Many evicted families were given 10 pesos per person for their homes. They were also offered 3-hectare plots, houses, tools, animals, and a minuscule stipend for twenty months (20 centavos per person) within various agricultural colonies. Nonetheless, moving to a colony did not appeal to the majority of those evicted, who even under the circumstances decided to remain in the capital. Some two hundred of the ejected families, though, did move to the new frontier colony of Carbonera near Dajabón.[74] In addition, 150 houses were prepared for the dislodged urban population in the frontier colonies of Matayaya, Los Jobos, and Sabana Cruz. And some former Faría residents were granted land in the Cotuí colony Sánchez Ramírez. Not surprisingly, the government was proud rather than ashamed of this project. Photographs of Department of Agriculture officials next to overcrowded buses of the dispossessed were printed in the department's annual report, which represented the project as an example of Trujillo's assistance to the poor through urban renewal and agricultural colonization.[75] But as had often been the case in other colonization projects, people were settled in remote areas before adequate infrastructure was in place—namely, irrigation and even potable water. For months, water was transported to the Carbonera colony by truck, while colonists labored on a new aqueduct. Despite their efforts, the soil remained inadequate in many areas. At first there was also no medical clinic in this large settlement with some one thousand persons. Given their recent life in the capital and their limited experience with farming, colonists soon found their marginal rural existence intolerable—not only unproductive but dull and overly regimented as well. Reportedly, most colonists had returned to the capital by 1961.[76]

Thus under Trujillo agricultural colonies embodied a multiplicity of disparate phenomena and purposes, with a mixture of supportive and oppressive valences for residents. In some cases, colonies involved coercive elements. And in numerous instances, colonies suffered from inadequate aid, infrastructure, market access, or general agricultural conditions. But overall, colonization generated a substantial portion of the nation's crops and contributed to a political economy in which the peasantry played an important role in the nation's agricultural self-sufficiency. And although the colonies had uneven results economically, they appear to have been relatively successful in terms of regime legitimation. Máximo Peralta García recalled colonization policy as an effort "to benefit the poor." He said, "It was indeed beneficial because [Trujillo] acted to make sure that whoever didn't have land obtained it. That person then had a plot of land to farm and on which to raise his pig, his goat. That person then possessed land." Although not a colonist himself, Carlos Pujols recalled Trujillo as "a man who concerned himself with the agriculturalists, that is with the hardworking agriculturalist. . . . He paid attention to the poor. . . . When a person was settled in a colony, he helped them. . . . He respected the agriculturalist more than anyone else did."[77] This and similar testimony suggests how colonization helped legitimate the Trujillo state among both land recipients and others who perceived Trujillo as respecting and assisting the peasantry and agricultural and rural development to a greater extent than government leaders before or after him.

At the same time, colonization helped transform even remote rural areas of the Dominican Republic and subject them to government control. By sedentarizing agricultural practices, by concentrating rural denizens in villages, and by authorizing state intervention in the name of modernization and assistance to the poor, the central state gained unprecedented access to and control over the countryside. The efficacy of state intervention flowed in part from the fact that it was not an entirely unwelcome or unilateral imposition of state power. Rather, it represented an exchange, however unequal,

of land access, agricultural assistance, and social services in return for increasing agricultural production and political subjection.

Colonization and Immigration

Although colonization policy under Trujillo served primarily as an instrument of agrarian transformation and establishing state hegemony in the
countryside, it also perpetuated decades-old racist discourses valorizing the
prospects of "white" immigration from Europe. For instance, the same 1934
legislation that limited immigrants to 25 percent of colonists in frontier settlements also stipulated that these colonists must be "white," thus attempting
to ensure that any foreign settlers would be European and not Haitian. (In
1948 this criterion was changed to the more ambiguous "foreigners . . . of desirable assimilation," perhaps reflecting new discursive currents globally that
were moving away from scientific racism after World War II.)[78] But as we
have seen, the Trujillo state's policies toward immigration in its early years
remained ambivalent and were conditioned by officials' disillusionment with
foreign colonists. In this period, the Trujillo state promoted immigration
only if it appeared to be in the fiscal interests of the regime. For instance,
Trujillo proposed grand plans to settle Puerto Ricans in the Dominican Republic in the mid-1930s, which were accompanied by a new wave of editorials
favoring "white" immigration to this "underpopulated" nation. (Puerto Ricans were perceived by Dominican leaders as culturally similar to Dominicans and, on average, lighter in skin color.)[79] But this proposal appears to have
been predicated on Trujillo's anticipation of large amounts of U.S. aid for the
project. When that money did not materialize, the project was abandoned.[80]

Yet in 1938, the regime seemed to shift course when Trujillo made grandi-
ose invitations for European refugees to come to the Dominican Republic.
These measures seemed to be of a piece with the state-sponsored culturally
racist discourse implicitly justifying the Haitian massacre as an effort to halt
the growth of "African" practices in the frontier and to consolidate putatively
Dominican norms derived from European culture.[81] But Trujillo's humanitarian gesture toward European refugees at this time appears to have been
prompted above all by his need to improve his image abroad, following international scandal over the Haitian massacre and in light of growing U.S.
and international enmity toward the rise of dictatorship and state terror in
Europe. In 1938, U.S. president Franklin Roosevelt convened an international
conference in Evian, France, at which U.S. representatives sought to persuade other countries to accept Jewish refugees fleeing from the Third Reich
(even while the United States did not). The Dominican representative at
Evian made the spectacular, and no doubt infeasible, invitation for up to

100,000 European Jewish refugees over time to be placed in agricultural colonies in the Dominican Republic.[82] This and subsequent gestures by Trujillo to assist refugees were effective, notwithstanding how exaggerated as well as hypocritical they proved to be, in distancing Trujillo from European fascism and from Trujillo's own atrocities.[83] Trujillo was roundly applauded in 1940 when several hundred European Jewish refugees were welcomed in the Dominican Republic and, with funding from Jewish charities, established a successful private dairy colony on a 27,000-acre ranch in Sosúa near Puerto Plata.[84] One U.S. scholar commented at the time that Sosúa "has been justly hailed as a humanitarian policy. Of the various Latin American states . . . Santo Domingo alone has taken constructive steps" to aid Jewish refugees from the Third Reich.[85] Indeed, as much press was devoted in the United States to the small Sosúa settlement as had been given three years earlier to the massacre of thousands of Haitians.[86]

Yet belying Trujillo's humanitarian pose were the actual restrictions imposed by the Dominican government on Jewish migrants. The U.S. consul in the Dominican Republic explained that the country wanted immigrants—even white immigrants—only if they were farmers.[87] And in 1939, a 500-peso immigration fee was applied to all "foreigners of the Semitic race" save the five hundred or so Jewish settlers who were part of the Sosúa colony.[88] Some five hundred Central European refugees—mostly middle-class German Jews—who settled in the capital and other urban areas between 1938 and 1940 were forced to pay the enormous fee.[89] The U.S. consul reported that the immigration tax was designed "to put an end to the threatened infiltration of Jews," following the regime's spectacular initial invitation, and noted that "it doubtless is responsible for keeping the numbers to a minimum."[90] Finally, in 1940 the Trujillo state prohibited all Jewish immigration, "no matter how much money they are able to provide," except for the small numbers continuing to be brought into the Sosúa colony.[91] Ultimately, a thousand immigrants would join this colony in the 1940s. Because of emigration (primarily to the United States), however, its total population remained small—a mere 179 persons in 1951 and 100 in 1955. Nonetheless, the colony continued to prosper.[92]

As part of his humanitarian pose, as well as traditional discourses in favor of white agricultural immigrants, Trujillo also welcomed Spanish Republican refugees from Francisco Franco's dictatorship. In 1939 and 1940, several thousand Spanish immigrants arrived, 556 of whom were settled in agricultural colonies. Few however remained for long.[93] Although the state hoped that these refugees would expand agriculture in undeveloped areas, few had experience farming—most were doctors, lawyers, and other urban professionals—

and most were unprepared for the difficult climatic and health conditions, such as malaria, they faced in the colonies.[94] Many also experienced deep political frustrations, having crossed the ocean to escape one oppressive dictatorship only to find themselves living under another. Most Spaniards quickly abandoned the colonies and the Dominican Republic for other parts of Latin America.[95] On June 14, 1940, the Dominican foreign office announced that "the Dominican Government has decided to suspend the immigration to our country of Europeans of whatever race," with the exception of those already contracted for colonization in Sosúa.[96] Several months later, a U.S. military official concluded that "the Generalissimo's publicized scheme of Spanish Colonists on the frontier . . . frankly just does not exist."[97] By 1947 fewer than a hundred of the Spanish refugees remained.[98] Given these poor results, and with the requisite publicity already achieved, immigration efforts were rapidly discarded and would remain on the back burner until the mid-1950s. In 1953 there were only 71 foreign residents out of a total population of 69,895 in the agricultural colonies under the auspices of the Department of Agriculture (which excludes Sosúa).[99]

Although an effusive, refurbished anti-Haitian discourse had combined with international public relations needs to prompt European immigration efforts in the years from 1938 to 1940, the thrust of the regime's rural policies and discourse remained focused on Dominican peasants, on promoting their access to land, and bringing their practices and—particularly in the case of frontier residents—their identities in line with state and urban visions of modernity and the nation. In 1943, Ramón Marrero Aristy, the left-wing Trujillo-era intellectual who would join the government three years later as undersecretary of labor, described Trujillo's project of colonization as "civilizing" the frontier, not by ushering in foreign or white migrants but rather by transforming local Dominicans:

In the face of the desolate panorama of this region, there had been many who prescribed the same old solutions: "We need whites to populate the frontier." "We need Spaniards." "We need Italians." "We need Jews." "We need Puerto Ricans." "We need Dominicans from the Cibao or from the East." But these were bootless cries lost in the desperate silence of that hard land. It was Trujillo who found the answer. The frontier is being populated with the only human element that can guarantee the project of the Government there: with men from the frontier itself. But men with new bodies and spirits. Men that are a product of the countryside and the problems of the frontier . . . but imbued with a new understanding of life and the fatherland. Men born and raised in the Era of Trujillo.[100]

Dominican frontier residents, subject to an intense campaign of Dominicanization in the wake of the 1937 massacre, were represented by Marrero as themselves providing the raw material for the modern nation envisaged by state and urban elites. Even in the frontier, the Dominican peasantry would be "civilized"—that is, "Europeanized," without Europeans.

The Trujillo state did, though, return in earnest to immigrant colonization in the mid-1950s. During a trip to Spain in 1954, Trujillo was reportedly impressed with Valencia's farmers and overall with Generalissimo Franco and the grandeur of Spain.[101] This experience and Trujillo's deepening alliance with Franco, together with intensely pro-Spanish attitudes among some of the leading political figures and intellectuals of the time, led to a new focus on colonization of Spanish immigrants.[102] In 1955, Spanish agents for the Dominican Republic recruited some 3,612 Spaniards, many from Valencia and Burgos, willing to migrate.[103] The Dominican state agreed to pay for their passage (as well as their return if necessary) and offered them cleared plots of land between 3 and 30 hectares. It also promised housing and an $18 per month stipend until the first harvest.[104]

Some immigrants managed to survive and even thrive, and some requested permission to bring their relatives from Spain.[105] The majority of this wave of Spanish migrants, however, abandoned the colonies even more quickly than the last. They were disillusioned by conditions far harsher and plots of land smaller and less fertile than the alluring promises made by Trujillo officials and Spanish intermediaries involved in the business of emigration.[106] Indeed, numerous Spaniards were settled in arid zones where irrigation canals were inadequate or incomplete.[107] They were also frustrated by the sooner than expected cancellation of their stipends.[108] Many immigrants, moreover, had misrepresented themselves as farmers, seeking to migrate to the Dominican Republic simply as a stepping stone to the United States.[109] For those without agricultural experience the conditions were particularly intolerable. The Spanish embassy was soon "deluged with appeals for aid" from "stranded colonists who had refused to settle on the lands provided for them by the Dominican Government."[110] By 1957 half the more than 5,000 Spaniards that ultimately arrived had already left the country.[111] Many others abrogated their immigration contracts to reside in urban areas. By 1959 only 1,069 Spanish colonists remained.[112] Rather than try to rectify the situation, the state quickly aborted its project. Much like earlier efforts, this experiment with "white" immigration failed largely because of the regime's equivocal commitment to it. The one effect that the regime's last experiment with Spanish immigration did have, though, was to arouse anger among the peasantry. Dominican peasants, feeling increasing land pressures themselves, resented resources being expended on foreigners.[113]

Although European immigration remained little more than a series of relatively small and half-hearted failed experiments, it has secured a salient and exaggerated place in common understandings of the Trujillo regime. This is doubtless in part because it embodied racialist and culturalist ideologies openly voiced by elite Dominican figures throughout the twentieth century. Also, some Spanish immigrants themselves espoused these ideologies and represented themselves as carrying out a "civilizing mission" in the Dominican countryside. Jacinta Garachana, a Spanish immigrant, explained immodestly: "What was of interest to Trujillo was for Spaniards to teach Dominicans to be agriculturalists as here there had been no farming. . . . Before Dominicans didn't use tools but rather just burned the fields. . . . The Spanish taught them to prepare the land . . . how to use a plow and oxen . . . how to grow vegetables, onions, potatoes, and so on. . . . Really the Spanish were brought here to teach them . . . to farm." Further reproducing elite Dominican discourse, Garachana added: "That was not the only reason Trujillo brought the Spaniards here. . . . He also wanted to refine the race."[114] Garachana's remarks highlight the dominant racist and culturalist prejudices in the country, which were linked to fantasies of human capital that European immigrants would supposedly contribute to the nation's agricultural development and progress.

Yet even in the late 1950s, the Trujillo state was not deeply conditioned by race, or, more precisely, by the fetishization of physical and genealogical attributes as mythically embodying "superior" or "inferior" cultures. Peoples traditionally maligned as of an "inferior race" could suddenly become associated with industry and other desirable cultural traits and then be welcomed as immigrant colonists. Specifically, a large number of immigrants brought to the Dominican Republic in the 1950s were Japanese. In principle, Asians had been effectively prohibited from migrating to the Dominican Republic by means of the high immigration tax legislated in 1932—legislation that reflected long-standing prejudices among elite Dominicans.[115] But the state evidently exempted Japanese immigrants from the tax after concluding that they were "industrious and disciplined agriculturalists."[116] Between 1956 and 1959, 1,232 Japanese immigrants were settled in Dominican colonies in the northern and southern frontier areas of Neiba, Duvergé, and Dajabón, as well as in Constanza.[117] In terms of agricultural production, the Japanese settlements proved to be relatively successful early on.[118] The large proportion of Japanese immigrants among the 1950s foreign colonists ushered in by Trujillo suggests that rather than an effort to "whiten" the country, colonization's primary goal was to import talented farmers in order to help develop the country.

In sum, support for European migration during the Trujillo regime was equivocal and desultory. The regime sponsored European immigration in the late 1930s primarily to lift the regime's sagging international image through the admission of political refugees, and subsequently in the mid-1950s in response to Trujillo's new-found romance with Spain. But these immigrations never involved large numbers of people. In 1956, including the Japanese who arrived that year and excluding the 1,369 Spaniards who had already returned to Spain, there were 2,902 immigrant colonists in the Dominican Republic.[119] Given limited state assistance, many of them soon abandoned the country. In practice, the colonization program focused overwhelmingly on settling landless Dominican peasants throughout the country, including in the frontier.

"Intensification of Agriculture" and the Perils of Protección

The failed experiments with immigrant settlements in the mid-1950s triggered a new emphasis on Dominican colonization that was part of a broader campaign known as the "intensification of agriculture" in the regime's final years. This campaign responded to intensifying land pressures on the peasantry and the increasing subdivision of plots to marginal levels. The land frontier was finally disappearing as the rural population skyrocketed—having grown almost 75 percent since 1935—and as commercial agriculture expanded.[120] In 1957 the secretary of agriculture ordered officials throughout the country to "intensify" their search for available lands as part of a renewed drive to expand colonization and land distribution.[121] In response, recommendations for colonization came in from local authorities throughout the country.[122] At the same time, these officials reported frankly on the failures of existing colonization efforts in marginal areas without adequate roads, market access, fertile soil, or the requisite state aid and attention, and offered remedies for these problems.[123] The state then commenced a major new initiative between 1957 and 1960, comprising 6,096 additional Dominican colonists, 72,875 hectares of newly colonized land, and numerous areas in which Dominican colonists supplanted immigrants who had abandoned their plots. Dominican colonists who were granted lands forsaken by immigrants, such as those in Guanito, were reportedly eager to obtain these plots.[124] In addition to establishing many new settlements—thirteen in 1958 alone—the government expanded aid to existing Dominican colonies and "rehabilitated" several languishing ones.[125]

Yet even as the regime made a final push at its brand of agrarian reform, distributing plots that some recipients were still successfully farming in the 1990s and addressing inadequacies in existing colonies, it inaugurated new settlements with the same flaws. The colonization program continued to

suffer from rash, expansive plans and poor implementation that reflected the
cavalier character of the regime. Once again, many settlements were established without adequate investigation concerning the area's agricultural conditions, and before the necessary infrastructure and aid were provided or
complete. When the necessary conditions were not established before the
colonists' stipends ran out, many abandoned their plots.[126] Thus, as before,
some colonies survived and even thrived (above all those that were well-
irrigated), while others did not. Limited by the budgetary constraints of a
poor country, hindered by formidable infrastructural needs of remote areas,
and weakened by a ruler who increasingly siphoned off resources to meet the
needs of lavish statecraft as well as personal corruption,[127] colonization had a
checkered history even while playing an important role in the Trujillo state's
agrarian reforms.

Furthermore, near the end of the regime, state officials acted with a
growing recklessness with regard to property laws that would add to the perils faced by peasant beneficiaries of colonization, particularly in the post-
Trujillo period. This is revealed by the history of the Guineal colony near San
Francisco de Macorís in the Cibao. This colony was established in 1958 as a
result of state intervention in a land dispute between Joaquín Gregorio Ortega Fondeur and squatters on a vast area of land (some 6,000 hectares) that
Ortega claimed.[128] It appears that Ortega, an elite Cibao rancher who through
purchases of improvements and land peso titles had been expanding his land
claims for more than a decade, sought in 1954 to have his claims adjudicated
in the Tribunal de Tierras and to evict peasants exploiting the woods and
pasture and growing coffee on lands he believed to be his.[129] After an outcry
from these peasants, the state delayed any court action, in part by imprison-
ing Ortega in 1955, though on what charges is not clear.[130] In 1958, Ortega was
released from prison and again sought to evict peasants. At this time, Horacio Ariza, the state's chief surveyor, suggested establishing an agricultural
colony in the disputed area in order to "avoid legal battles between peasants
[infelices] and powerful landowners. In this way, the existing agriculturalists,
who hold their land in good faith, would become colonists of the Secretary
of Agriculture, . . . [and thus] the working people in one of the Country's
more populated regions may live by their own means." Regarding Ortega's
property claim based, in part, on land peso titles, Ariza announced: "In light
of the progress that has transpired in this Country in this Era of Peace, it is
high time that the legal documents of the Queen of Spain from four hundred
years ago should cease to prevail and that peso titles should be declared null
and expired, so that [lands] which to date have not been cultivated may become the property of the state and of those whose sweat and constant sacri-

fices render them productive."[131] Two days later, the secretary of agriculture requested authorization from then-president Héctor Bienvenido Trujillo (Trujillo's brother) to take over these lands and to distribute them to the "agriculturalists who have cultivated [them] for years, but whose ownership is claimed by Joaquín Gregorio Ortega ... and to distribute the remaining lands to others. Thus, the uncertainty prevailing among these peasants will disappear, concerned that at any moment Sr. Ortega will seek to evict them." Two days after that, the state granted authorization.[132]

When Ortega challenged in court the state's right to appropriate lands that he claimed,[133] Ariza recognized that the government's position was legally problematic: "We have declared ... [the area] state property without our being aware of the existence of any documents in support of the Dominican State's property rights." But, he asserted, "This Department does not claim these lands based on documentary evidence that favors the State, but rather on resolving a social problem."[134] The director of colonization suggested recourse, if necessary, to the state's constitutional right to expropriate land for "public utility and the social good," as had sometimes been used in the past for colonization.[135] Other officials remained concerned, though, that this would be insufficient. The assistant secretary of agriculture suggested buying a number of peso and other titles in the area to support the state's claims to the site.[136]

Nine months later, before the case was settled, Trujillo was gunned down in a failed coup attempt. Two months after that, despite the continuation of the regime without Trujillo, the Tribunal de Tierras awarded lands in the Guineal colony to Ortega and rejected the government's argument that colonists were entitled to their plots. The court decided to favor private property and landowners rather than the dictates of a disintegrating post-Trujillo regime. In fact, colonists should have been aided by legislation passed at the end of 1961 stipulating that landowners whose lands had been wrongfully seized and distributed by the Trujillo state should be indemnified by the government but not granted their property back.[137] Notwithstanding this law, in many cases, including Ortega's, courts ordered property returned to its original owners (or claimants), resulting in decades of legal and violent conflicts over land in the Dominican Republic. The case of the Guineal colony was one of several examples, particularly evident in the regime's final years, of state colonization of lands owned or claimed by individuals whose property rights would be recognized after Trujillo's fall, therein leaving occupants facing eviction. Similar histories unfolded in the Guanito, Miches, and Carbonera (Dajabón) colonies.[138] As we saw in Chapter 4, state functionaries under Trujillo varied greatly in the caution with which they approached

property claims at odds with regime objectives. In general, however, the regime appropriated lands for colonization first and faced the legal and financial ramifications later.[139] In the case of Guineal, colonization officials repudiated the strong legal claims of a large landowner and affirmed instead the
customary meanings and social basis of property based on possession and
use. But the government did not do so in a way that established peasants'
clear legal rights to the land, and it therefore left them in a precarious position. Trujillo's agrarian policies and their problematic legal character thus
rendered peasants dependent on the perpetuation of Trujillo's regime as well
as his putative benevolence and commitment to the "men of work."

In a 1962 hearing on the Ortega case, in which peasants lost the right to
their plots, one squatter stated to the judge, "I consider myself to be the
owner of these lands because what I have cultivated there cannot be taken
from me . . . [and] because I was working in tierras comuneras." The judge
interrupted him, "Which means they were not yours." "Yes sir, they are
mine," this agriculturalist replied, "because you must know that if you plant
cacao nobody else can pull it up." Trying to confront the wide gap between
popular and legal notions of comunero land, the judge then asked him, "And
what do you understand terrenos comuneros to mean?" He answered with
peasants' traditional understanding of what they generally termed tierras
comuneras: "That it has no owners." This man's father similarly asserted his
right to the land he had farmed because "tierra comunera belongs to whoever has cleared it."[140] This exchange reveals the paradoxical impact of the
Trujillo regime's agrarian policies. On the one hand, they helped sustain into
the 1960s peasants' moral economy, endowing them with the right to use any
land they had cleared and cultivated through their and their families' labor
and not recognizing forms of ownership, such as peso titles or enclosures, to
areas that remained monte. On the other hand, in this very hearing in which
this understanding was articulated, peasants would lose their access to land
because this moral economy had not been enshrined into law. Rather it had
been sustained by a paternalistic, authoritarian state that manipulated private
property and other laws more than it restructured them. Many peasants were
thus left in a vulnerable legal position after the fall of Trujillo.

Despite the program's long association with a racist project of European
immigration, colonization during the Trujillo regime functioned, above all,
as an integral part of the regime's agrarian reform, involving both welcome
state assistance and unwanted intervention. Colonization sustained peasant
land access and promoted agricultural production, while also extending the
reach of the state into various remote regions of the country and over rela-

tively autonomous rural lives. It was an important element in the regime's project to represent itself as the embodiment of peasant and national interests, even though it simultaneously increased peasant dependence on the state and enlarged the regime's capacity for effective repression and control in rural areas. Altogether the Trujillo state produced a powerful combination of peasant dependence and support that was effective in underwriting the regime's hegemony in the countryside.

7 Memories of Dictatorship
Rural Culture and Everyday Forms of State Formation under Trujillo

> For me [the era of Trujillo] was good in terms of the respect and order that prevailed, as well as the support [*respaldo*]. . . . There was support in that if you were poor and had no place to work, land had to be given to you to work. . . . And there was support in that no one could abuse you, the poor could not be abused.
>
> Máximo Peralta García[1]

The Trujillo regime may be unique among dictatorships in twentieth-century Latin America for the extent to which elderly peasants have nostalgically recalled its support of the peasantry. Although peasants' recollections of the Trujillo years must be analyzed critically, they provide an invaluable and otherwise unavailable perspective on rural life during the dictatorship. And they suggest that Trujillo's hegemony in the countryside was founded not only on material support during a parlous period of land and agricultural commercialization but also on cultural factors, and specifically on the ways that the regime appeared to fashion state projects to reflect and reinforce peasants' own evolving cultural norms. At the same time, though, peasants evinced substantial ambivalence about the Trujillo era, implicitly lamenting a perceived tradeoff between the support attributed to the state under Trujillo and the expansion of political freedoms attained during subsequent (semi)democratic governments—freedoms, however, also associated with economic decline among the peasantry, widening state corruption, and the disruption of rural values. Nostalgic memories of the Trujillo regime were thus often tinged with fear, mixing desire for and dread of the past.

Peasants' divided sentiments and multiple perspectives regarding the Trujillo years complicate not only monochromatic portrayals of the dictatorship as constituted solely by domination and exploitation but also conventional images of peasant politics as forged in opposition to the intervention of the national state.[2] The Trujillo regime reached deeply into peasants' daily lives and embodied a novel and powerful state presence across the countryside. As with the colonization program, the national state represented its interventions as a type of "civilizing" project (ironically given that peasants' nostalgia for the Trujillo regime today is seen by many other Dominicans as a reflection of rural "barbarism"). The state sought to discipline and shape private as well as public worlds, to transform the peasantry not simply into "productive" laborers but also into "modern" subjects, and to impose various forms of state regulation on rural existence. Yet the state's new presence in rural life and project of modernity appear not to have weakened but rather to have boosted the regime's legitimacy among the peasantry. Even when resented or resisted, state projects were not seen as arbitrary, corrupt, or an instrument of national elites. The state—personified in peasants' memories simply as "Trujillo"—seems to have gained authority much like that of a stern but solicitous father and as a ruler concerned with both maintaining rural values and ushering in progress.

What follows is drawn primarily from recorded discussions with 130 persons, all of whom, unless otherwise noted, were elderly peasants who had lived through all or almost all of the Trujillo years and were still residing in the countryside. I interviewed people in almost every region of the country.[3] The Dominican peasantry can be differentiated, inter alia, by region, economic condition, gender, and generation. Here, though, I seek to illuminate the experiences and analyze the testimony characterizing the peasantry as a whole during the dictatorship.

Memories are, of course, not transparent or ossified reflections of the past but rather selective versions of it that are produced in reaction to subsequent history, as a means of consciously or unconsciously commenting on the present.[4] One cannot know to what degree positive elements of the Trujillo years have been amplified and negative ones effaced in response to current difficult conditions—landlessness, corruption, crime, and poor health care and other public services—and in response to an only incomplete liberal democracy that has failed to provide basic liberal rights, state accountability, or public institutions that assist rather than neglect and humiliate the popular classes.[5] Trujillo would not be remembered as positively if in the decades after his regime the peasantry had fared well economically, if liberal political rights had advanced to a greater degree, if bureaucratic discipline and government probity had appeared to improve rather than decline, and if national pride had not been piqued by a new economy based largely on remittances and export processing in free trade zones. But the fact that peasants' recollections have been conditioned by subsequent realities does not mean that they are false or misrepresentative. Although peasants' general perspective on the Trujillo regime may be continually reshaped over time, their memories of specific conditions and events are unlikely to have been simply invented out of whole cloth. Furthermore, the popular memories analyzed here reflect recollections that were consistent among a large number of peasants and are complemented by documentary evidence. They should be considered seriously, especially given how sharply they challenge conventional understandings of the Trujillo regime.

Memories of Respeto and Order

The most universal and immediate image of the Trujillo years recalled by rural denizens who lived during the regime was of a society governed by respeto. This word conflates a wide gamut of social practices, behaviors, and discourses considered to be respectful, honorable, orderly, decent, and responsible. It variously invokes a world characterized by minimal crime, corruption, and public disorder, by "proper" demeanor and deference in public interactions,[6] and by traditional patriarchal values concerning family, gender, and intergenerational relations. Virtually all the elderly peasants I interviewed, even if otherwise opposed to the regime, lamented a loss of respeto following the Trujillo years.

Yet it is not only in relation to the present that respeto under Trujillo has been valorized. To elderly peasants, Trujillo's rule came to represent a long parenthesis of public order within an overall history of violence, crime, and corruption before as well as after his regime. Peasant perceptions of disorder had intensified in the early twentieth century in the wake of novel social and economic conditions that appear to have reconfigured popular rural understandings of banditry, petty theft, and political violence. In the traditional rural economy, the line between stealing and foraging or sharing had been a blurry one. As sociologist Eugenio de Hostos wrote of the nineteenth-century Dominican peasantry: "Almost all the inhabitants of the countryside . . . go to another's conuco to steal. [To them] neither pilfering nor rustling seems like a crime."[7] But at the beginning of the twentieth century, as land started to be enclosed and the open range gradually waned, particularly in the Cibao and the Eastern sugar areas, and as some peasants thus came to depend more on produce from their small farms for their subsistence, popular notions of property began to harden. Now when even a small portion of a peasant's crops or one animal was taken, it was likely to have been experienced more as theft than inconsequential pilfering or sharing.

It was in these same years that regional caudillos raged with the greatest intensity in the Dominican countryside. And rural banditry spread throughout the East, where peasant land scarcity developed almost overnight following the massive accumulation of land by the sugar companies beginning at the turn of the century. Troops associated with both of these in fact overlapping and not clearly distinguishable types of rebel leaders—caudillos and gavilleros—were conflated in the memories of elderly peasants as los del monte ("those from the woods"). This conflation stemmed in part from the fact that all these forces appropriated crops and animals from peasants, as described by Pedro Zapata (born in 1908) of Ramón Santana, once a center of gavillero activity: "If they came here and you were someone who had a few animals, whether it was a hog, a goat, or whatever, and also a nice *conuquito*, for them it was nothing to just come and grab the pig, kill it, and then grab something to eat from your conuco and cook a meal. You weren't going to say anything to them. The most you could do was to eat your food together with them." Bandits and caudillo forces also confronted peasants at times with threats to their persons, forced recruitment, and sexual exploitation and abuse. Zapata also remembered "[the bad ones who] arrived here and tied you up. You had your woman and they liked her. They tied you to a tree and they went inside to do with her what they pleased. This is what some of the people del monte did. . . . Those del monte did many horrible things."[8] However much the antigovernment, or, more broadly, antistate, politics of caudillos and gavilleros may have been appealing to some peasants, and however much these forces emanated from local rural communities and cultures, their agenda was not agrarianist or peasant-oriented.[9] When the region's gavilleros mobilized against the U.S. occupation, they received high marks for their patriotic opposition to a foreign army still vividly recalled for its brutality. Zapata himself praised some of the rebel leaders as patriots. Nonetheless, almost all the Dominican armed groups were lumped together as los del monte and bitterly resented for their abuses.[10]

In the recollections of elderly peasants, Trujillo was responsible for ending these forms of everyday violence and insecurity of person and property in the countryside. Although there were a few years of mitigated social and political disorder at the end of the U.S. occupation and during at least the first half of Horacio Vásquez's presidency, these did not serve to structure historical memory and mark the arrival of political order for elderly peasants with whom I spoke. The establishment of order and effective government was instead linked to Trujillo's rule.[11] I asked Francisco Soriano of Ramón Santana what the outcome of a free election would have been during Trujillo's first years in office. In reply, Soriano emphasized the suppression of rural banditry and theft as a motive for popular support of the regime: "In the early years, in the old days, people were very pleased with Trujillo, because most of them had experienced the scourge of the gavilleros. Then . . . [people] had no one to turn to for their rights. When Trujillo came, things began to normalize. You had rights, you demanded your rights and you were attended to. . . . [But before Trujillo] there was no order, no respect, nor anything. The early years of Trujillo was when confidence and liberty developed." "Liberty?" I asked with surprise. Soriano replied, "Yes, with the exception of opinions and words that is, not those. . . . But you could go anywhere without qualms or fear. . . . So the people in the early days might have voted for Trujillo. . . . Many were grateful then."[12]

The foundations for popular conservative sentiments regarding order expanded during Trujillo's rule, as most of the rural population came to rely entirely on the cultivation of their small plots of land for subsistence. This transformation also influenced peasant responses to the regime's vividly recalled vagrancy policy, or "10 tarea" law. As the majority of peasants were becoming sedentary "agriculturalists" (as the Trujillo state now identified them), they appear to have grown more resentful toward those who continued to depend on the little remaining open-access land and on other people's produce. These peasants came to be seen as persons who "scrounged," "hustled," or "stole," indeed as "vagrants." Although many believed that Trujillo's antivagrancy policies were implemented too harshly, most nonetheless perceived them as imposing a desirable ethos of production and order that eliminated threats to peasants' property and subsistence and improved the overall rural economy. Specifically, elderly peasants stated that by ensuring that all male agriculturalists cultivated at least 10 tareas, the regime reduced the impetus to appropriate others' crops and animals. As Carlos Pujols stated, "If you were working and producing, you had no need to take anything of mine."[13]

The Trujillo state's campaign to eliminate "vagrants" was recalled by many peasants as a measure supporting the "men of work." Tomo Reyes, a better-off peasant in Sabana Grande de Boyá born around 1912, contrasted the Trujillo years with conditions today: "In terms of agriculture, the man who worked had security then. . . . [He] was supported and he was valued. And the thieves were punished. . . . We should be back in the era of Trujillo. Because what I would like is for the man who works to be supported rather than the vagrants. . . . I am a worker and sometimes I have some bananas or plantains and I go to look for them but they've been taken by vagrants."[14] In the late nineteenth century, such petty appropriation might well have been seen as acting within proper norms. But this was no longer the case during the Trujillo regime. "Yes sir, Trujillo was a dictator," Rafael Esteves, a peasant living in La Noria, recalled, "but food was always available and in abundance . . . and the crime we have today did not exist. . . . When you had your own provisions, your own goat, your hen, you didn't have to come steal them from me."[15] "Trujillo was not a bad man," another person concluded. "You had to produce, but what you produced you kept for yourself."[16] The

Trujillo state had accelerated the transition from subsistence exploitation of el monte to small-scale sedentary agriculture. And this in turn had furthered peasants' desires for order and, it seems, made them more amenable to Trujillo's authoritarian rule.

For Cecilia Rijo of Higüey, her desire for security rationalized a brutal system of repression under Trujillo. "There were many good things then. . . . Everyone had respeto and no one dared put their hands on someone else's things," she said. "Because in the era of Trujillo if you took someone else's belongings, they caught you. Pop! They hung you and the matter was done with." When I inquired how she felt about that policy, she suggested the answer should have been obvious: "That was good! One slept with the door wide open then." This positive memory was accentuated for her by a recent theft of two of her animals. "I just had two pigs stolen from me, from right there. Two pigs when I was sleeping. And do you think in the era of Trujillo, do you think that could happen? That did not happen. Because they caught you. . . . There was respect and no one dared to put one's hands on anyone else or they would be shot."[17] Several people described how thieves were hung by the side of the road so that others "would see what was done to [thieves] and so no one would dare to steal."[18] The political economy of the Trujillo regime helped ensure peasant access to land, but only to a small plot and thus only to a narrow margin beyond subsistence. These conditions intensified, or even created, popular rural attachments to property and fears of crime that served to rationalize Trujillo's authoritarian system.

Why though did peasants not fear the potential for state violence against them of such a brutal, authoritarian regime? To some extent, they did. And several persons I spoke with expressed longing for a government with an "iron hand for those who are evil and a soft hand for those who are good," for a world of "peace" and respeto but without fear.[19] But overall, rural denizens stated that they felt they were not at risk as long as they remained politically acquiescent, hard-working agriculturalists. José del Carmen Paulino of Los Corozos Adentro, La Vega, stated, as many others did, that "Trujillo was bad with thieves and assassins, but not with the men of work."[20] Tavares Blanc said that he did not live with a sense of terror under Trujillo: "No, no. I mean, there would be no reason. I mean why would anyone [from the regime] get involved with us, just working and attending to our families?"[21] Ramón García Peña reflected somewhat self-critically on his own attitudes toward the Trujillo regime: "I still say Trujillo the Great. I don't know why. Perhaps it was because that was the world I was raised in. But we did live very peacefully then."[22]

These testimonies suggest how many peasants seized on the regime's official discourse identifying Trujillo with the "men of work" and affirming peasants and their labor as central to the nation, its economy, and its progress. This novel discourse emanating from the central state offered rural men a new official identity—as the men of work—with which to claim rights to state support and assistance. It is also possible that the Trujillo regime's discourse shaped male peasants own subjective identification as men of work. Numerous men told me that they had supported Trujillo because they were hard-working types and that Trujillo favored and assisted that sort of person.[23] Cruzito Guerrero explained: "For me there was more good than bad [under Trujillo], because I was a man who was dedicated solely to working and raising my family, to working and living peacefully."[24]

Trujillo's ideology of work and the working man could be effective only because it was backed up by concrete policies for promoting peasant agriculture. Manuel de Jesús Belliard, who lived in Monte Cristi during the Trujillo regime, recounted: "[Trujillo] would say that the men of work were his friends and it was true because . . . in local meetings, he gave out . . . grindstones, machetes, hoes, pickaxes, saddles, plows, and oxen for the fields."[25] Most important were policies supporting peasant families' free access to land. Juan Bautista Guerrero contended, "[We] lived better under Trujillo than now . . . as anyone could farm a conuco. Wherever there was state land, Trujillo distributed it."[26] Negrito Viloria similarly recalled: "If you had land and I asked you for ten tareas, you could not refuse me . . . or else I could go and say that you had refused to give them to me. But no one refused to do so as one could lose it all because Trujillo would take it from you then."[27] Santiago Susaña contrasted the Trujillo years with the present: "One lived better [then], a thousand times better. . . . Simply, one had to be dedicated and work. . . . Now we are held back, unable to work, not because we are lazy, but because the lands are in the hands of a few. . . . I know how to farm. . . . But I have no land."[28]

In most rural areas, an overall sense of order and security reportedly prevailed during the Trujillo years despite the perils of noncompliance under the dictatorship.[29] In an era when changing material conditions had given rise to new notions of and dependence on private property among the peasantry, specifically small agricultural plots, the Trujillo regime effectively propagated an ideology linking an authoritarian political system to security of property, control over the fruits of one's labor, and respect for those peasants who worked the land. This linkage contributed to peasants' identification with the regime and Trujillo's hegemony in the countryside.

The Legend of Trujillo's Well-Functioning State

Most literature on the Trujillo regime has focused on the almost surreal corruption and eccentricity of Trujillo and his inner circle. And yet, in terms of everyday rural life under Trujillo, most peasants recall the state overall as having been efficient, responsive, and even relatively honest. The Trujillo state has been remembered, in fact, as a well-functioning machine, one that effectively implemented public policies and that held local authorities accountable to the rule of law.

Certainly the state's bureaucratic machinery could at any time be superseded by the whims and orders of Trujillo, or, in some instances, by members of his inner circle and certain other powerful officials. But the structure of the state itself under Trujillo reportedly established controls over abuses of power by most other state actors—in part through the maintenance of overlapping jurisdictions and competing lines of authority, all radiating out from the dictator. Military officials, leaders of the Dominican Party, and state functionaries at all levels often reported directly to Trujillo's office. This provided Trujillo with information about local conditions from numerous perspectives, including reports by officials on the performance of other functionaries and members of other branches of the state. Such oversight of one official by another contributed to internal surveillance and Trujillo's capacity to control official misconduct.

Most important from the perspective of the peasantry, much power and responsibility for everyday governance devolved upon the large number—some 750 in 1959—of alcaldes pedáneos, the state's lowest-level officials.[30] The alcaldes were central to daily life in the countryside under Trujillo. Their generally close integration in the tiny communities that they oversaw provided the regime with knowledge of and even potential sensitivity to local norms and concerns. This in turn helped endow the regime, or at least that part of it that peasants most frequently encountered, with a face of respeto hardly discernible when one investigates only Trujillo himself and the commanding heights of power.

Although the pedáneos were technically appointed by the síndico, peasants remember having had some voice in their selection. Generally, residents of each section recommended to the síndico candidates for alcalde, often in a local meeting.[31] Alcaldes pedáneos tended to be long-standing members of the community, often slightly better off or connected than other peasants, "a patriarch, an individual considered highly respectable, as well as one who demonstrated adherence to the government," as author Héctor Colombino Perelló put it.[32] In notable contrast to positions at higher levels of the state,

alcaldes tended to remain in office for extensive periods of time under Trujillo. To some extent, traditional local power and the central state grew sym-
biotically, rather than inversely, during the dictatorship.

The alcaldes pedáneos helped execute coercive state policies, such as re-
cruiting prestatarios, approving land distribution requests on the basis of
"good conduct," and at times informing on local residents. Yet they are
rarely recalled for exercising their authority in arbitrary, brutal, or corrupt
fashion. And when certain alcaldes did abuse their positions, peasants acted,
at times, to have those officials removed from office. Local residents protested, for instance, when alcaldes showed favoritism in land distribution or
threatened someone with arrest or denunciation (as an anti-Trujillista) without cause. They conveyed their complaints in letters to Trujillo and to other
authorities and demanded the dismissal of these alcaldes.[33] Elderly peasants
in Sabana Alta, San Juan de la Maguana, recalled forcing its alcalde out of
power by dragging him from his home at four in the morning to the síndico
and demanding his replacement.[34] Peasants complained about misconduct of
other local officials as well. One middle-aged peasant recounted a story that
his father had told him about the Trujillo government responding to complaints that only those who had paid bribes were receiving water from the
state irrigation system by sending a commissioner to their section to investigate the charges. After looking into the matter, the commissioner held a
town meeting in which he publicly castigated the officials in charge of distributing water.[35]

To some extent, peasants' complaints served as a check on the conduct of
alcaldes and other local functionaries, while alcaldes in turn served as a check
on higher-up officials. In a circular issued in 1934, Trujillo instructed all alcaldes pedáneos to write to him directly concerning any "irregularities . . .
[in] the administration of justice." Responding to this circular, the alcalde
pedáneo of Los Botados, Yamasá, reported that his superior, the Yamasá
síndico, had ordered him not to press charges against a cattle thief who was
the síndico's friend. The alcalde wrote to Trujillo that he would rather resign
than comply with the síndico's order, and that he awaited Trujillo's response.[36] Similarly, Amado Susaña, a *segundo alcalde*, or assistant to the alcalde, in Sabana Alta recalled successfully intervening against favoritism by
officials in charge of distributing water from the state irrigation system.[37] In
such cases, the power given to the alcaldes and their assistants seems to have
made the state more accountable to popular needs. Priciliano Mercedes of
Chirino, Monte Plata, who was otherwise highly critical of Trujillo, praised
the responsibility and strict control of functionaries under his rule: "The
good of the Trujillo era was that all officials whatever their position had to be

responsible. . . . If only it were like that again! Whatever your rank . . . as soon as you behaved improperly you were punished. . . . Whether you were a sergeant, a captain, a major, or whatever, [you were] fired. Trujillo would do many bad things. But whoever was not Trujillo had to be very careful about what they did."[38] In their testimony, peasants reconciled the contradiction between the regime's overall bureaucratic legitimacy and Trujillo's own extreme corruption by distinguishing between the dictator and quotidian state operations. Many repeated the cliché, "Trujillo was a tremendous thief, but he was the only one then. Now everyone is."[39] Just as the Trujillo regime fused repression and protección in paradoxical fashion, so too it fused arbitrary rule and bureaucratic legitimation.[40]

State sensitivity to local concerns and maintenance of the rule of law was critical for peasants in the Trujillo era given the new presence and importance of the state in everyday rural life and work. Peasants had come to depend on officials to distribute land, resolve property disputes, and provide agricultural aid and infrastructure. Peasants' complaints to Trujillo about corruption in or inadequate implementation of these policies over the course of the regime suggest both how important the state had become to peasants' survival and that the state sustained an image of accountability among the peasantry.[41]

The benefits for peasants of a well-functioning state were not only more limited everyday corruption. The success of the peasantry's transition from pastoral and slash-and-burn practices to a sedentary agricultural economy depended on new infrastructure and state assistance. The development of roads, for instance, was a crucial prerequisite for peasants to be able to profitably market their surplus crops. Thus many recounted nostalgically how roads and bridges were built and repaired in a timely fashion and how country roads or paths were well maintained.[42] Overall, a large portion of the state budget was devoted to infrastructural and economic development.[43] In 1930 major roads in the Dominican Republic stretched only 171 kilometers, compared with more than 5,000 kilometers in 1960, the bulk of which were completed between 1936 and 1957.[44] The legitimating effects of the regime's attention to public works, including in areas benefiting many peasants, are suggested by popular rural memories. Angel Novoa stated, for instance: "I have never studied. . . . [But I believe that] until Trujillo, there was no development like that which occurred when he ruled. Trujillo ruled . . . for the progress of our country."[45]

For many the most dramatic benefit other than land that the regime provided was irrigation via the state's formidable development of public aqueducts. New irrigation built by the Trujillo state contributed impressively to agricultural development and profitability and has been remembered by residents in places such as Baní and San Juan de la Maguana as constituting the turning point in the life of their region.[46] Positive memories of the development of irrigation were especially pronounced among peasants who received irrigated lands from the Trujillo state, many of whom participated as prestatarios in constructing the canals.[47] Distributed lands were technically part of agricultural colonies, such as the colony organized in Mijo, near San Juan de la Maguana. Some land recipients in Mijo had previously lived by exploiting the area's woodlands for ranching and itinerant farming. According to one recipient, Linor de Los Santos, prior to the state's irrigation project the area around Mijo had been dry, thinly populated, and agriculturally undeveloped. However, some better-off denizens had nonetheless begun to enclose large areas, making Los Santos's and other families' subsistence suddenly problematic. The newly irrigated land that the state redistributed to local residents was thus much needed and appreciated. Los Santos emphasized, though, that the land had been earned, not simply given to him and others, "as it wasn't the government that built this canal, but rather the men from around here." Los Santos was originally granted 1.3 hectares of land, but over time he accumulated sufficient money to acquire another 6.3 hectares. "Trujillo was not bad for us here," he commented. "[He] was good because he made the canals."[48]

In Carretón, Baní, land recipients and other beneficiaries of irrigation also expressed appreciation for the canal built during the Trujillo dictatorship. Reflecting a type of shame evident in a number of peasants' comments when lauding aspects of a regime under which they know that many people suffered, Orgelio Santos commented: "Whether or not I should say this, I have to tell the truth. This canal [built by Trujillo] has been the happiness of the people here. . . . The canal provides us with security which those without it are mad to have."[49] No longer was one dependent on "the grace of Jesus Christ" for rain, as one person explained; rather, one could farm all year long, receiving irrigation every fifteen days.[50] Nilka Martínez recounted the difficulties of life before the canal: "I'm going to tell you. We suffered through hunger and misery. . . . There were times . . . we did not even cook because there was no water. . . . We could not even bathe. . . . After Trujillo made this canal, we lived better. We had water and could farm and cook." Her brother Manuel added, using a cliché common among elderly peasants that developed during Trujillo's rule: "[B]ecause of this canal, we owe our lives to [Trujillo]."[51]

The Trujillo state's extensive construction of canals, bridges, and both main and country roads throughout the Dominican Republic, including in peasant areas, gave substance to the regime's discourse of work and progress. And because many peasants attributed development, the overall efficiency of the state, and its accountability to Trujillo's personal agency, the dictator himself gained legitimacy from this seemingly well-functioning state. Francisco Salazar explained: "[We] liked Trujillo because there were more benefits then . . . Because Trujillo gave an order and within half an hour it was carried out. If you wrote a letter to Trujillo, he answered you. But now you write 60 letters and still you never get anything." Similarly, Máximo Peralta said, "[Trujillo] was a friend of the man of work. He would come to the countryside and provide much support for the man of work. And if someone messed with [you] and did something improper and you could make [Trujillo] aware of it, he would fix it."[52] Although peasants were aware of cruel repression by the regime in some areas, the face of the state that most saw at the everyday level countered the perception that the regime was an arbitrary or terroristic one. "One heard [of bad things] but here he did nothing [bad]," recalled Linor de los Santos. "It was good around here."[53]

Time has doubtless enhanced Trujillo's image. For one, political tyranny has been replaced, in many people's eyes, with another devil: the dictatorship of money and graft, a plutocracy in which justice seems to go to the highest bidder. Nostalgia for a well-disciplined bureaucracy under Trujillo thus serves to excoriate state corruption and lawlessness today. Bartolo Soler, who lives in the Higüey countryside and was born around 1922, averred: "Things are better and worse now than they used to be [under Trujillo]. What I find worse is that there is no longer any respect for the laws. . . . If you have a lot of money . . . because of your money they take away my right to the land and give it to you."[54] Hugo Gunel, a wealthy middle-aged doctor from the town of La Vega, explained the widespread nostalgia for Trujillo in a related fashion: "Trujillo created what had never existed here, the backing of an organized bureaucracy, efficient and disciplined. That never existed before and does not exist now."[55] Gunel also described a telling conflict he had with a peasant whom he had hired: "When I was paying him for his services, he said, 'No, that's not enough,' and he protested, 'The only government in which we were ever worth anything was Trujillo's because under Trujillo one could complain [to him].' . . . [He] said that the only government in which he had rights [was Trujillo's]."[56] It is striking that many peasants felt a greater sense of "worth" and "rights" under Trujillo's autocratic rule, suggesting how effective Trujillo's discourse was at reaching out to and valorizing the "men of work," and how low peasants perceive their current status to be in the nation's legal and political processes. Antonio Hernández in Cotuí denounced the country's putative democracy as shot through with inequity and corruption: "Nowadays they say we are living in a democracy. But this is no democracy. It is democracy for the millionaires but not for the poor."[57] Magdaleno Valdez in Rinón, La Vega, similarly protested: "Now a person without means has no right to live. . . . The ones that have the right to survive are those with means. But we who are laborers, with our arms bare and calloused like this, how can we survive? We must die long before our deaths."[58] It is impossible to discern the degree to which contemporary grievances have amplified or obscured various aspects of the Trujillo dictatorship in popular memories. But it is nonetheless clear that the regime sponsored rural policies and discourses that shaped peasants' experiences and perspectives in powerful ways and that for many legitimated Trujillo's rule despite the regime's brutal and autocratic character.

State Paternalism

The expansion of the state during the Trujillo regime, along with its modes of "order" and "progress," extended into cultural and domestic realms of rural life. The state sought to regulate and transform popular rural practices in the name of modernity, particularly those related to morals, hygiene, health, and education. As well as being "sedentary" and "productive," the new Dominican peasant had to become "sanitary," "decent," "responsible," and literate (at a rudimentary level). The central state infiltrated everyday peasant life not only with vagrancy ordinances, compulsory community labor, political rallies, and local meetings but also with sanitary inspections, "vice" regulations, paternity laws, health clinics, day and night schools, and literacy campaigns. Those with whom I spoke portrayed these measures as establishing a formidable new state presence in their lives, but they generally did not represent them as acts of oppression or an overwhelming barrage by the regime.[59] Peasant acceptance of the state's interventionist project of modernity reflects, in part, the state's simultaneous promotion of pre-existing rural values regarding family, gender, and generational relations.[60] Like its rural policies more broadly, the regime's interventions into peasant life and the private realm negotiated the distance between the city and the countryside and constituted "everyday forms of state formation"[61] in the sense of a deepening nexus between the national state and local rural practices, culture, and identity.

Many of the regime's efforts to transform peasants into modern subjects brought concrete benefits to their lives, such as substantial improvements in public health care. They also, though, entailed onerous obligations and were sometimes harshly enforced and thus inevitably were resisted and resented to some degree. Yet state interventions into rural life appear overall to have added to the state's legitimacy in many eyes. Indeed, they endowed Trujillo with an image as the architect of the modern Dominican Republic, echoing the identity promoted by official discourse of Trujillo as the "Father of the New Fatherland." At the same time, state efforts to promote rural ideals of respeto rendered modernity more culturally continuous with the past and hence more palatable and appealing. In addition, Trujillo's discourse of state patriarchy, of protección in return for loyalty and submission, may have helped legitimate men's own patriarchal authority over women and children and thereby contributed particularly to male peasants' identification with the dictatorship.[62]

Echoing familiar cross-cultural refrains among the elderly in the wake of rapid modernization, elderly Dominican peasants limned with nostalgia a starkly patriarchal society prior to and during the Trujillo regime. When asked simply how things were in the old days, one of the most common, immediate responses of peasants was to lament the loss of children's respect for and deference to adults. Bartolo Soler stated: "Above all, children respected their neighbors. . . . Nowadays it has reached the point that there is no respect for a neighbor, nor a godfather, nor a godmother, nor a father, nor a mother. Then if I went out and saw a man who was older than me, I got down on my knees, and said 'Bless you uncle,' and if I didn't kiss his hand he would give me a beating."[63] Fathers in particular were remembered as exercising control over children's lives. Like many others, Juan Bautista Guerrero recalled how even nineteen-year-old males were not allowed to wear long pants, as they were "not yet men."[64] Francisco Soriano emphasized that children "had to wait for their fathers to find them a fiancé" and to arrange their marriages. Soriano believed that the strict code of intergenerational deference and control stemmed from children's sustained economic dependence on their parents as well as their importance to the family economy.[65] Young people had few opportunities, and limited need, for making their own money. By the 1990s, though, patriarchal and familial control had loosened as women and children gained independent access to capital, higher levels of education, and new prospects for rural-urban and international migration.

But did the Trujillo state help to perpetuate traditional relations of deference and respeto despite rapid economic changes, or did it simply coincide with and mirror rural norms that remained extant during a still early moment in the processes of modernization? In most peasants' recollections, patterns of respeto in social relations were indeed linked to Trujillo's authoritarian rule, however vaguely. Santo Núñez Ramírez, living in Cedro, Miches, described how he and his friends would hide from the patrols of the guardias when they had not paid their annual cédula fee. His words linked the regime's authoritarian rule and its discourse of Trujillo as the nation's father to the extant patriarchal order: "If [the soldiers] saw us, we'd say 'Papá Trujillo,' out of force of habit. And who didn't say 'Papá Trujillo' at that time? He was the 'Father of the Fatherland.' . . . I say 'Papá Trujillo' but out of habit, for he was not my father. But one had to be careful. There was respeto. One had to be respectful in order to be respected. But now there is no respect nor authority, not between civilians [and the military], not between the elderly and the young. Before, when I was growing up, I had to kiss the hands of all those who were older than me. But now not even your own children kiss your hands." But did Trujillo have anything to do with children kissing their elders' hands, I asked in response to Núñez's conflation of authoritarian political order with forms of respeto in society at large? "Yes," he said, respeto existed "because of the dictatorship. . . . Trujillo helped bring respect with a heavy club."[66]

Some peasants gave more specific reasons for crediting Trujillo with a culture of respeto prevailing during his rule. Several persons, particularly ones who lived near to towns, asserted that Trujillo was "good for the family" because of the imposition of "tranquillity," including the limited hours and areas that bars and music were permitted. And one person remarked that the guardia's supervision of those outside late at night made parenting "less of a battle."[67] But above all, peasants stressed the regime's policies and discourses with regard to relations between women and men. On the one hand, the Trujillo state promulgated a number of important laws establishing women's juridical equality, including full property rights and the right to vote (for Trujillo) after 1942.[68] On the other hand, the state sought to promote conventional gender roles and to reinforce existing patriarchal relations. Embodying this contradiction, a 1940 law extending "complete capacity for civil rights to Dominican women" simultaneously proclaimed husbands as the heads of household and legislated patriarchal authority and gendered hierarchy within the family. Men were authorized to choose their family's residence and to prohibit their wives from taking any job they believed conflicted with "the interests of the home or family."[69] With regard to actual conditions for women, Castalia Ortiz remembered with bitterness the constraints on them in the "era of Trujillo." "Without the possibility of outside employment," she said, "women lived like slaves, since one had to take care of the household things, waiting on one's husband, but now no. Now there is more liberty."[70] Men, on the other hand, were more likely to recall these conditions with nostalgia, as did Camilio del Rosario, and to attribute them to Trujillo's rule: "When Trujillo [was in power], women did not use pants, as Trujillo said that pants were only for men. But now women use more pants than we do."[71]

Both women and men, though, approved of what they perceived to be greater protection for women from abusive and illicit male behavior during the Trujillo regime than afterward. Many stated that offensive public conduct toward women was limited under the dictatorship. Francisco Salazar recalled: "Then you could send a girl wherever and no one harassed her."[72] Sanctions against men's disrespectful treatment of women reportedly extended to male responsibility in sexual relations. Male peasants remembered official pressures to "marry" and to support women with whom they had sexual relations.[73] One man recalled: "Trujillo's laws were strict, because you couldn't just run off with a woman. You had to be responsible with her. A man who took a girl had to marry her and make a future with her."[74] It is likely that some young women and men chose to run off together when families objected to their union. But "taking" outside of "marriage" doubtless also encompassed misleading seduction or even coerced sex. Máximo Peralta's recollections suggest that this aspect of respeto—sanctions against "taking" women—was considered a disadvantage by some men, at least those not in the role of father. After describing nostalgically the Trujillo years, Peralta said, "But there were negatives too sometimes because there were demands on you and there was no way around them . . . things like when you couldn't marry but you took a woman. Oh no! You were arrested and had to marry her. . . . By law you had to marry her."[75] Objecting to sexual relations perceived as irresponsible and outside parental and state control, the Trujillo regime promoted patriarchal norms obliging men to create households with and support their sexual partners and children.

Patriarchal norms of respeto stressed that men be "responsible," but not necessarily monogamous. Many men I spoke with stated that they maintained long-term sexual relations with women other than their wives. And although the Trujillo state promoted marriage, it seemed most concerned that men support their children. The government expanded legislation obliging men to support and help care for the offspring of all their sexual relations regardless of marriage, thereby effacing distinctions between "legitimate" and "natural" children that had previously obtained in the Dominican Civil Code.[76] This new law may have played a more limited role in the countryside than in the city, but some agricultural juntas did report securing child support from delinquent fathers.[77] In sum, the Trujillo regime promoted respeto in terms of male "responsibility" to women and children, while also reinscribing male power over them in the private sphere.

In one regard, though, the regime did modify patriarchal inequities in

gender relations. Although not emphasizing monogamy for men, the Trujillo
state revised adultery laws to make them gender neutral. The law had previously excused a husband for the murder of his wife or her lover if the husband caught them in the act of committing adultery. This statute was
amended so that a wife was also excused for killing her husband or his lover
if she caught them engaging in sexual relations.[78] The Trujillo state thus
equalized and modernized, in a sense, but did not eliminate a patriarchal
tradition legitimating violence as a means of resolving affronts to one's
honor.

The Trujillo regime also sought to further a culture of respeto that encompassed elements of both tradition and modernity by regulating public decorum. Such efforts were exemplified in state policies toward prostitution. Following a heated national debate in the 1920s over government efforts to eliminate prostitution, the Trujillo regime chose instead to regulate it (though
only in practice; it remained prohibited by law).[79] This policy reflected both a
modernizing state's concern with public health—namely, the control of venereal disease—and an impulse to organize public conduct along lines traditionally considered orderly and respectful by maintaining a clear geography
of "good" versus "bad" women. Although elderly peasants recalled less prostitution under Trujillo than exists today, the contrast they stressed most was
that prostitution was practiced "with more respeto," in the sense that it was
less obtrusive during the dictatorship.[80] Luisa Montilla, who had lived in Salao
outside Higüey during the Trujillo years (and was now living in the town of
Higüey itself), explained that prostitution had been limited to marginal areas
and establishments, and "no one needed to go there except the men who
wanted to be there. The system was better then because [prostitutes] were
more secluded. . . . But now . . . they leave their zone. . . . In the old days that
was not true because certainly in that Trujillo intervened." The isolation of
prostitutes also served to reinscribe the identity of "honorable" women like
Montilla and presumably their ability to demand respect from men. Montilla
endorsed the benefits of the system wherein "women had to be centered in
the house, those that were house women. And those that were street women
were in the street." She also explained that prostitution was less dangerous to
men's and women's health under Trujillo: "Every week [prostitutes] had to
see the doctor, to see who was good and who was bad, and whoever was sick
would be brought to the hospital and remain there until they were cured."
What happened if a woman chose not to comply with the inspections? "If she
acted independently and infected a man—certainly if it was a minor—she
was headed for jail." Montilla understood this policy to be part of the regime's promotion of work. "Trujillo didn't want people to be sick, no. He

wanted men to be in good shape so that they could be of service. He required healthy men," she explained.[81] The Department of Health organized weekly health examinations and issued health cards to registered prostitutes. Under this system, the police apprehended only "clandestine" prostitutes and those accused of spreading venereal disease to clients.[82]

Octavio Miniel in Ramón Santana also preferred the parameters of sex work during the Trujillo years because it was less obtrusive. "Then there might be a prostitute living right there and if no one told you she was a prostitute there, you would never know it," he explained. "But now they themselves tell you in order to grab your attention." Not only near his home, but also in town Miniel found present-day prostitution offensively conspicuous. "Nowadays if we from the countryside go to town . . . there are times when we are embarrassed, to see young women, naked. . . . Prostitutes were more respectable then . . . .There was more respeto than now." When asked how prostitutes were more respectable, he explained: "More decent, not like now where you go there and a woman just says, 'Hey!' and that's it." When asked if Trujillo was responsible for these conditions, Miniel contended that Trujillo was, but, without explaining, segued directly to the cliché that under Trujillo you could fall asleep outside with a 1,000 pesos in your pocket without anyone robbing you.[83] Generally, Trujillo's regulation of prostitution was recalled as of a piece not only with women's use of "prudent" attire but with children's respect for elders, the relative absence of crime, and an overall "tranquility." The all-encompassing discourse of respeto imputed to the Trujillo regime conflates many aspects of political and cultural order. This discourse has been so hegemonic that the question of the actual extent to which these phenomena were produced by Trujillo's mode of rule apparently does not even arise.

That maintaining forms of order and public decorum in domestic and sexual life was important to the regime is evident in those areas over which the state had the greatest power to shape everyday practices—namely, in the agricultural colonies. There the strictest rules regarding prostitution and adultery appear to have been established. One woman living in the Miches colony in Cedro described how in the Trujillo years the colony supervisor was a man of "respect . . . because if my husband went to see another woman and I went to the head of the colony about it, they evicted [her]."[84] Other women colonists recalled approvingly that men had not been permitted to have two women inside the colonies. María Tavárez explained that "the colony was a place to live tranquilly."[85] Men discovered, for instance, to be cohabiting with someone else's wife were replaced with new colonists, because, as one official then reported, "the intention has been to establish families legally united by matrimony."[86] Envisaged as model communities in which the state could impose its ideal for modern peasant life, prostitutes were also not tolerated within the colonies.[87] "The colony had been beneficial in the sense that there was respeto," Leonardo Núñez said. "There was no corruption. One had to work, honestly. There were no brothels or anything. One had to work hard."[88]

Throughout the country, Trujillo state officials also reached deeply into intimate aspects of peasants' lives with new sanitary regulations designed to produce "modern" subjects and cultural practices in the countryside. Like Progressive Era urban reformers in the United States earlier in the twentieth century, state functionaries envisaged these intrusions as a type of "civilizing mission" to cure the poor of "ignorant" and "unhealthy" habits. This is illustrated in the following 1937 circular to rural officials from the secretary of agriculture: "[You] should not limit your duties to . . . your assigned obligations for your respective jobs. That will not satisfy the goals of developing an intimate relationship with the peasantry [agricultores]. . . . It is necessary to operate in a broader capacity . . . [to] assist them and help them with all problems . . . [c]ounseling them to live better, more hygienically, more comfortably." The circular exhorted rural officials to insist, specifically, that peasants eat more vegetables, change their clothes regularly, and bathe every day. "Hygiene sustains health and nurtures the spirit," the secretary of agriculture preached. But "regrettably, in many houses there is no table [to eat on] . . . and thus we see the children, metal plate and spoon in their hands, on the kitchen floor where many times a pig will come in and share their sancocho [traditional stew]. This . . . is not appropriate for the era of civilization in which we live." Defining modernity in terms of the conventions of urban domestic space, such as a clear and charged division between inside and outside, between a table and the floor, the secretary saw rural conditions as crying out for the paternalistic intervention of the state: "Intervention is necessary; we must direct ourselves to these social problems. They must be taught what is a clean table, what is a bathroom, in short, what is a home."[89]

The state's hygienic discourse led to one of the most salient memories of the Trujillo years, the strict requirement that all families have bathrooms or outhouses.[90] Reportedly, the state provided the poor with the necessary materials—prefabricated latrines—free of charge, while each family was responsible for installing them.[91] Few peasants had previously used outhouses. And at first, many were arrested for failing to build them. One man recounted bitterly how some were punished for not having latrines, "as if they were criminals."[92] Enrique Acevedo Ortiz said, "One never likes being forced to do something even if it is for one's own good."[93] Nonetheless, many others represented the latrine law as a needed improvement preventing the spread of disease (it is possible, though, that some were embarrassed to suggest otherwise). And overall the state seems to have successfully instituted the use of latrines throughout the country.[94]

Many peasants themselves recalled policies such as the "latrine law" in terms that conflated scientific and moral concepts of advancement and thus mimicked the official discourse of "civilization" and "barbarism." Luisa Montilla recounted, for instance, "Before people lived wild. . . . We lived like animals . . . [until Trujillo] emitted that law."[95] Through such interventions into everyday life, the Trujillo state may have projected an image of itself as indeed an instrument of "civilization" while reconfiguring peasants' own ideas about proper modes of existence. "Any house without a latrine is not a home," several persons repeated, doubtless echoing an official cliché.[96] Thus, even when such measures were resented or resisted, they may nonetheless have had ideological effects that gradually bolstered the state's authority.

The government also instituted a similar requirement in 1952 that shoes be worn in Ciudad Trujillo and other municipalities, because, according to a U.S. embassy official, the custom of going barefoot was not seen as in keeping "with the progress of the country."[97] This legislation may have been onerous for some peasants during their infrequent travels to the city. In contrast to the latrine law, however, this order was not prominent in the memories of those with whom I spoke—indeed some did not recall any such regulation at all—and no cases were recalled of persons being jailed for violating this ordinance. Peasants who remembered the shoe ordinance offered few complaints about it. For the relatively few occasions on which they needed but did not have shoes, peasants reportedly constructed their own sandals, purchased inexpensive ones (costing approximately half a peso), or borrowed those of a family member or neighbor.[98] And like the latrine law, most represented the shoe ordinance as a beneficial measure. José Adames explained: "It prevented us from getting diseases and splinters; and no one was arrested for this."[99] Manuel de la Rosa Cedano stated that it was "good so that you became educated to live more hygienically." Yet hygiene, strictly speaking, was not the only concern imputed to the state. De la Rosa stated that people had to be taught "how they should dress." He explained that men were arrested who went outside wearing only underwear or who—making an oblique connection—were openly homosexual ("though they continued to exist in secret").[100] Again, scientific and moral notions of progress were conflated. Defecation in the woods, men in underwear, barefoot peasants, and, for at least one peasant, open homosexuality were recalled as links in a chain of "ignorant" but formerly accepted practices that the state sought to alter for the nation's progress. Trujillo was represented as a stern father raising the population, teaching the peasantry how to behave, dress, and go to the bathroom in "proper" ways.

The Trujillo state rendered these civilizing discourses appealing through major improvements in popular health care, as clearly remembered by elderly peasants and as reported by contemporary observers as well. The regime established public hospitals and clinics offering free medical services throughout the country. According to official figures, the number of hospitals rose from eight to fifty-one and hospital beds from four hundred to seven thousand between 1930 and 1958.[101] The mortality rate declined steadily over the course of the Trujillo regime, and one recent work credits improvements in health care for the doubling of the Dominican population between 1935 and 1960.[102] Manuel Santos Sánchez recalled favorably this aspect of the Trujillo years, even though his brother, an alcalde, had been killed by an army lieutenant in the early years of the regime: "The only good thing [under Trujillo] was the hospitals, because in the hospitals they treated well all those who were sick, and gave them whatever they needed. If an operation was necessary, that was no problem. The doctors were responsible then. Now if you don't have the money, they just let you die."[103] Medical services under Trujillo were also compared favorably with those before the regime. Then ninety-eight-year-old Juan Justo recounted: "During Trujillo, medicine was better than during Horacio Vásquez. Because [Trujillo] was very concerned with medicine and hospitals, and paid attention to disease in the countryside and elsewhere. Before there was a lot of disease . . . and there were no injections. . . . There were no public hospitals and there was perhaps one doctor in town. I was born in El Cerro and when I got sick I had to go to town to buy medicine. . . . The only [government] which gave out medicine was Trujillo's. . . . If you needed it, it was given to you free of charge."[104] Similarly, Máximo Peralta praised the clinic built under Trujillo in the village where he lived as a great improvement over having to travel to town for basic health care. "One cut oneself with a machete while working and one went to the clinic. . . . And it didn't cost a thing."[105]

Peasants also appreciated the regime's promotion of basic education, even though the improvements achieved in education were modest at best. Under Trujillo, elementary schools proliferated—from 526 schools in 1930 to 2,570 in 1953—and mandatory attendance for children was enforced. The U.S. embassy estimated that 43 percent of children attended school in 1954, up from 13 percent in the early Trujillo years, and that two-thirds of these students lived in rural areas. The total number of students rose from 51,000 in 1930 to 260,000 in 1953.[106] Although children's classes were reportedly scheduled so as not to conflict with early-morning work in the fields, tensions did arise at times between work and school. But Francisco Soriano recounted that "if a child said, 'I didn't come to school because my father sent me to work,' the father would be . . . given a warning. And if it happened again, he had to pay a fine of 5.75 pesos."[107]

A system of "emergency schools" was established in 1942 to provide two years of basic education to as many rural youngsters as possible in an effort to combat illiteracy in the countryside. This policy was praised in a publication of the Dominican Party, using the modernizing language of the Trujillo state. "We will succeed in incorporating into the world of citizenship thousands and thousands of individuals," the bulletin read, "who otherwise would remain forever submerged in the darkness of their ignorance and removed from the concert of values that integrate our nationality."[108] Similar attempts to incorporate rural denizens via basic literacy into the national community were made in adult literacy campaigns and a 1952 law making obligatory night classes for anyone fourteen to fifty years old unable to read and write.[109]

Although some people objected to the cruelty of jailing even older men simply for not attending night school (typically because of fatigue), most people praised the regime's mandatory schooling.[110] Manuel de la Rosa Cedano, a peasant from Los Ríos de Higüey born in 1907, argued: "As bad as he may have been, as much of a killer and a totalitarian as he may have been, he had his good part . . . like the literacy campaign for adults."[111] Bernabel Guadalupe Gil explained peasant support for Trujillo's education policies this way: "People never stop having aspirations. A 50-year-old person says, 'Damn! I'm illiterate and I want to learn,' even if it's only to read a sign and to be able to sign one's name. Always, people said, the old people said, 'I'm going to school, even if it's just to learn to sign my name.'"[112] And Carlos Pujols asserted that "an adult is ashamed who doesn't know how to participate like others, and who has to ask everyone to know [what is written]. These were the aspirations of Trujillo, that no one would be illiterate."[113] It is noteworthy that Pujols depicted the state's efforts to eliminate illiteracy as the personal "aspiration" of Trujillo; these measures by the regime to transform traditional life seemed to belie the image of a merely self-aggrandizing and corrupt dictator.

Yet the regime's education efforts were largely ineffective. The state found it difficult to staff rural schools with qualified teachers.[114] Some peasants confirmed that many learned or retained only the most basic skills (to sign their names, read signs, and so forth), whether because some of the teachers were themselves semiliterate or because the regime allocated limited resources to education and chose to emphasize quantity of students over quality of instruction. However, peasant testimony suggests that Trujillo none-theless gained political capital from even these modest educational measures, as they evinced official concern relative to a long history of state neglect of and urban disdain for the peasantry.[115]

Nostalgia Shot Through with Dread

Most rural Dominicans recalled the Trujillo dictatorship with at least as much nostalgia as dread, and more for its "order" and "respeto" than for its terror and abuse. Yet peasants' recollections of the regime were far from simple or one-sided, and encompassed the regime's horrors as well as puta-tive virtues. The facet of everyday life under Trujillo remembered as most oppressive was the harsh and intrusive system of military patrols. The guardia patrolled throughout the country and frequently stopped and inter-rogated civilians. It enforced the state's major regulations governing peasant life and subjected rural areas to the eye and power of the national state as never before. It was the guardia which verified that every family was farming at least 10 tareas, that all houses had latrines, that no one possessed illegal arms, that the road or path by one's house was clear, and that all had paid their cédula fee, voted in the last "election," and, in the case of men, com-pleted their obligatory military service (weekend instruction in marching, ri-fle use, and army discipline lasting for several months). The alcaldes pedáneos acted to some extent as a check on the army's potential for abuse. I was repeatedly told that under Trujillo the guardia rarely patrolled or made arrests in rural areas without the alcalde's permission and that the alcalde could vouch for individuals and prevent soldiers from apprehending people for violations—for example, of the vagrancy law.[116] Nonetheless, many peas-ants spoke of their fear that at any moment the guardia might come and ar-rest them "as if you were a criminal" for mere civil infractions. "You would just be sitting down and a patrol would come," Máximo Peralta recounted, "Right away they were giving orders. One had to live with this repression."[117] And although peasants' represented state violence and repression as rarely arbitrary in its targets under Trujillo, once someone was arrested, the conse-quences were indeed expected to be ruthless and unjust. For instance, some alleged vagrants, particularly repeat offenders, were sent to the infamous pe-nal colonies in Azua and Nagua, where it was widely known that prisoners faced torture as well as horrific sanitary conditions and disease.

Peasants recall with dread as well the state's oppressive control over speech, its elaborate mechanisms of surveillance, and the potentially horrific consequences for even the smallest slip of the tongue. Not only expressions of political opposition but any verbal mishap might have grim consequences.

Most disconcerting perhaps was the knowledge that acquaintances, friends, neighbors, and even (former) spouses might denounce one, perhaps with false information, to gain benefits from the regime or simply out of personal jealousy or animosity. Surveillance was reportedly most intense in the pueblos, reflecting the greater state presence there, the ease with which spies could be planted (for instance, as beggars, shoe shiners, or company employees), and the greater frequency of political rallies and meetings. Only within the towns did I hear stories of people being harassed for their utterances, even absurdly inconsequential ones. After one person came back from a political rally in Higüey, an acquaintance asked him what officials had said at the event. He replied, "And what are they going to say? The same as always." Someone overheard this brief exchange, and the man was arrested.[118] Most peasants recalled living with fear that they might be denounced for "improper" or "disloyal" speech. "Whoever made a mistake and said something was lost," Bartolo Soler explained, "because some bootlicker might make a complaint that you were speaking about the government, even if you really hadn't said anything."[119]

Other oppressive features of discursive control under Trujillo were the virtually obligatory pro-Trujillo plaques, photographs, and buttons that could be found in probably most Dominican households during the regime. Many reported that if a guardia saw that there were no such displays of political loyalty in your home, you would fall under suspicion. Probably most peasants had, if nothing else, a photograph of Trujillo in their house, usually one given to them at a rally or by the alcalde. Many men resented one plaque in particular that appeared symbolically to subvert their own patriarchal authority: "In this house, Trujillo is the boss." This sign was sold privately and cost more than officials could expect most peasants to be able to pay. Still, peasants remembered this particular one bitterly, even when they did not comment on photographs of Trujillo and other more common plaques. Juan Justo recalled: "Here there were men who cried because of this plaque. . . . They didn't dare say anything . . . [but] the people . . . from the pueblo didn't like this. In my house, it was never put up . . . because we were poor and it wasn't distributed to those [who were poor]. . . . There was a man named Nunu. He was one of the ones who finished off the gavilleros [hence, a member of the guardia], a good friend of mine. . . . And he was one of the ones who cried. . . . And I told him, 'Why don't you get rid of it?' and he said to me, 'You get rid of it, tough guy.'"[120] Most people I spoke with stated that they refused to have this sign in their house. One person, though, who did buy and hang it in his home, Ramón Peguero, explained: "In my house, I was the boss. But by means of the *plaquita*, I fulfilled Trujillo's requirements."[121] As perhaps many did, Peguero learned ways to distinguish between public displays of subordination and private sentiments of resistance and dignity.[122]

In the countryside, the regime's control over speech meant a world filled with stark silences, if not the continual declarations of Trujillo's "greatness" required among town and urban dwellers. Although most peasants affirmed that the regime did not touch those who stayed clear of politics and avoided "speaking about the government," the incredibly narrow boundaries of permissible speech, the wide diffusion of government spies, and the possibility of malicious denunciation mined even the average peasant's life. With few exceptions, peasants praised the liberty to speak freely in the post-Trujillo era as a dramatic improvement in their existence.

Finally, many peasants recalled with bitterness taxation in the form of the cédula fee under the Trujillo regime, which was especially vexing since direct monetary exactions on the peasantry had been virtually unprecedented prior to the dictatorship. Peasants often resisted paying this fee, deploying various tricks to simulate compliance or to flee the guardia's patrols. Those caught without their cédula in order composed by far the largest number of arrests in the years after the law's passage. In 1934 an astonishing 1,076 persons were arrested for cédula violations in the province of Monte Cristi, compared with 93 cases for the next most frequent violation, theft. Similar figures were reported throughout the country at the time.[123]

Yet, once the cédula became, in reality, a graduated income and property tax, starting in the 1940s, its burden fell most heavily on the better off. And it thereby gained a certain legitimacy among the peasantry. "The cédula was just," Manuel de la Rosa Cedano said, as "the rich paid more and the poor paid one peso."[124] Some, like the cattle magnate Juancito Rodríguez, chose exile, reportedly after being confronted with this sudden, formidable new tax,[125] while Porfirio Peña of Higüey was said to have poisoned himself after denouncing Trujillo for obliging him to pay a 500-peso fee.[126] "Those who suffered [under Trujillo] were the rich; the poor did not suffer," Francisco Soriano remarked.[127] Notwithstanding dramatic resistance by members of the upper class—or conceivably in part because of it—most peasants recalled the scaled cédula fee as burdensome but fair. Bartolo Soler asked rhetorically, "And how would it not be good? . . . He imposed taxes on those who were able to pay them . . . while he did not attack us, the poor. . . . Don't you think we were going to feel good about that?"[128] Moreover, in the case of Juancito Rodríguez, for instance, most peasants I spoke with hardly sympathized with the plight of this elite landowner (though they did condemn Trujillo's murderous attacks on several others simply for being related to or associated with Rodríguez after he went into exile).[129] Rodríguez had reportedly resisted agrarian programs benefiting the peasantry and was known as a harsh employer and ruthless accumulator of land. Some saw Trujillo's appropriation from the wealthy as a form of distributive justice. Angel Luciano Novoa in Sabana Alta stated: "The good thing that Trujillo did was to take from those who had in this country . . . and then the fat ones [the rich] complained." For Novoa, Trujillo's power to dominate elite individuals made him "like a second god."[130] Taxation, then, although certainly resented and resisted by peasants, also augmented the regime's populist credentials and its image of invincibility.

Peasants certainly remember oppressive aspects of everyday life under the dictatorship. But at the same time, the regime was recalled positively for providing peasants with material benefits, order, and continuity amid change. And Trujillo successfully identified himself with the popular rural classes. Peasants were lauded as the "men of work" and Trujillo's "best friends," their health and education were of sudden concern to the state, and they were incorporated into national political discourse and rituals. The Trujillo state sought simultaneously to transform traditional aspects of everyday peasant life considered "backward," "unhealthy," and "barbaric" and to affirm and promote other rural practices and norms. Because many of the state's demands and interventions were framed in terms of peasants' own values—respeto, patriarchal social relations, customary rights to land—they were widely perceived as legitimate among the popular rural classes. In this way, the Trujillo regime realized what had been seen by many intellectuals and other elite Dominicans for more than a century as an urgently needed mission of peasant domestication and expansion of the national state into rural areas: the transformation of the nation's highly autarkic peasantry into sedentary and productive farmers who assimilated modern practices and yielded an economic surplus, taxes (the cédula fee), and community labor (as prestatarios).

Peasants recalled the dictatorship's predatory and terroristic features. But most stated that these did not characterize their everyday experiences under Trujillo. Sharply contrasting histories differentiated peoples' lives during the Trujillo regime, variations that, in part, broke down by class.[131] Only at the end of the regime, as we will see in the next chapter, did attitudes start to converge across society. In the last years of its rule, the regime would increasingly violate popular norms, peasant land rights, and its own ideology of respeto and protección, alienating growing numbers even of that part of the population, the peasantry, that had been central to its ostensibly smooth hegemony.

8

The Birth of a Dominican Sugar Empire and the Decline of the Trujillo Regime

In 1944, Ellis Briggs, the U.S. ambassador to the Dominican Republic, waxed hyperbolic about what the Trujillo regime had accomplished during its first decade and a half in power. He contended: "The Trujillo dictatorship . . . is the most efficient government the Republic has ever known, and more over-all progress has been achieved during the past fourteen years than during the preceding 438 years since the discovery of the island by Columbus."[1] Two years later, another embassy official, George Scherer, further detailed the achievements of the Trujillo state, reporting that "the Trujillo regime has brought to its highest point the financial standing of the Republic. . . . Its international credit is excellent. The government is extremely well administered, there being little graft. . . . [And] Trujillo has built roads, hospitals and schools, always a dictator's manner of showing improvement in the country, but nevertheless a genuine contribution."[2] Later that year, George Butler, the new U.S. ambassador, even opined that "Trujillo's methods have been so successful that he would triumph in free elections."[3]

The U.S. embassy was not unaware of the terror Dominicans faced under Trujillo. In addition to Briggs's lofty praise of the regime's material accomplishments, he reported, for instance, that "the most representative gesture of a Dominican citizen is looking over his shoulder to see whether he is being overheard."[4] U.S. officials' simultaneously condemned the regime's tyrannical features and praised it for realizing positivist ideals of political order and material progress.[5] And for many years, at least, Trujillo's reign could indeed be represented paradoxically as a type of "terror-and-progress" regime. From the end of World War II until the mid-1950s, the dictatorship was remarkably robust both economically and politically, with abundant signs of material progress and popular acceptance. During these years, the country underwent unprecedented economic expansion, developed a system of national infrastructure and state institutions that were impressive given the country's modest revenues, and paid back its once massive foreign debt. The regime could hardly have appeared stronger or more secure.

Yet from these impressive heights, the regime would suddenly crumble in the late 1950s. Although revolutionary exiles seeking to spark a rural uprising

were easily defeated when they invaded in 1959, they nonetheless helped gal-
vanize an underground opposition movement in the towns and cities. The
opposition was composed primarily of university students, young professionals, and merchants, a new middle class emerging in the wake of the country's
economic expansion. The state responded to this growing opposition with escalating repression, setting in motion a cycle of violence that ultimately broke
the spell of Trujillismo in much of the country. Then, in 1961, as the regime
was spiraling out of control, Trujillo's rule came to an end when he was assassinated by a small group of powerful conspirators, many from within the regime, who were hoping to stage a coup d'etat. Although the coup failed, neither Trujillo's brothers nor sons, nor even his adroit puppet president
Joaquín Balaguer, was able to sustain the regime; rather, they were all forced
to flee the country within eight months of the dictator's demise.

How did the regime fall from its seemingly invulnerable heights in the
early 1950s into an abyss that impelled powerful figures to act against it and to
expect that their conspiracy would not be betrayed?[6] How did widespread resistance to the regime develop in Trujillo's final years, following almost three
decades without any serious opposition to his rule? In this chapter, we will see
how Trujillo altered the country's political economy in the 1950s and adopted
policies that by the end of the decade had alienated erstwhile supporters, undermined the regime's mechanisms of legitimation, and generated a fiscal crisis. These policies can be traced back to Trujillo's sudden "romance" with
sugar.[7] After close to twenty years of promoting his early advisers' vision of a
small farmer model of development in most of the countryside, instead of the
expansion of foreign agribusiness (or of a Dominican landed elite), Trujillo
turned to a very different nationalist project. Rather than simply pressuring
foreign sugar companies to pay higher taxes, as he had successfully done
throughout his regime, he, his personal representatives, and the state began
forcibly purchasing the bulk of foreign interests. Not only did this identify the
Trujillo state with the sugar plantations that had been the object of much
public resentment until then, but, in addition, Trujillo began vastly expanding the industry with large new mills that required the cultivation of immense
new cane fields. The expansion of sugar production meant sacrificing peasant
land access in these areas and interrupting the process of development via
small farming.

The Trujillo regime thus moved from a project of modernity based on
political inclusion and rising productivity of an economically independent
peasantry to one based increasingly on the regime's own large capitalist enterprises. The state thus undermined its earlier popular ideology of development, its rural focus, and its representation of the nation in the figure of the

peasant farmer who was productive, dutiful, and the source of the country's "future wealth." The impetus for change that ultimately led to Trujillo's demise would come predominantly from the small middle class rather than the popular sectors, and as much from within the regime as from without. In many areas of the country, Trujillo reportedly still enjoyed widespread acceptance.[8] But it is unlikely that the emerging opposition would have been so bold or effective had the regime's rural support not been on the wane. Trujillo himself seemed to recognized this when, with his enemies mounting at the end of the 1950s, he attempted to revitalize his peasant base through renewed efforts and promises of land distribution. But this effort would be too little and too late to stop the momentum against his rule. With the regime's escalating repression, irresponsible economic policies, and ultimately intolerable apotheosis of Trujillo, the state lost its legitimacy, support, and climate of order. The regime increasingly fit a model of despotism or "sultanistic" rule defined by the absence of these elements, thus suggesting that such a model points more toward the vulnerabilities or decay of personalistic dictatorships than to their means of endurance. When the Trujillo dictatorship became a despotism without any social foundations and based on little more than terror, it mobilized powerful opposition rather than acquiescence, and its days were numbered.

Authoritarian Heights

In August 1947, amid great nationalist fanfare, the Dominican government delivered a payment of nearly $10 million to U.S. bondholders to liquidate its extant foreign debt, long in advance of bond maturity dates. The once formidable debt had led to direct U.S. government control over Dominican customs revenues and operations between 1904 and 1940 and provided one of the pretexts as well for the U.S. occupation. Trujillo took out a full-page advertisement in the *Washington Post*—in the belly of the beast— entitled "Another Page of History is Written by the Dominican Republic" and vaunting the "liberation of the Dominican Republic's financial burdens" and the recovery of "the scepter of sovereignty that many errors and misfortunes had torn from us."[9]

The elimination of its foreign debt was emblematic of the country's relative affluence in these years. World War II had been a powerful catalyst for Dominican economic growth. Commodity shortages resulting from the war boosted prices for Dominican exports at a time when the country was ready to take advantage of these opportunities. By fostering peasant production and political stability since its early years, the regime had strengthened the nation's agricultural economy and potential. The development of new roads, irrigation, and government credit had opened up the prospects for commercial farming among peasants as well as better-off agriculturalists. Coffee production, in particular, thrived following the war, with exports growing 150 percent between the early 1940s and the mid-1950s.[10] And coffee, like most crops other than sugar, continued to be grown largely by small and medium farmers. Overall, peasants were successfully adapting to the economic and political demands of the regime and the expanding possibilities of production for the market.[11] In addition to agricultural expansion, the country saw the first stages of import-substitution industrialization. Strong state incentives beginning in 1942, primarily tax exemptions granted at the government's discretion to particular companies in what were deemed to be infant industries, spurred manufacturing as well as a new industrial class.[12] And still the Dominican Republic continued to meet most of its own food needs and maintained nearly full employment in this period. The resultant economic growth was dramatic. Between 1942 and 1952, external trade skyrocketed from $32 million to $212 million.[13] National income rose 60 percent between 1946 and 1950 and another 64 percent by 1954. This occurred despite sagging sugar prices thanks to high coffee and cacao earnings, which constituted 53 percent of export revenues in 1954 (compared with sugar's 35 percent and tobacco's 5 percent).[14] The state budget also climbed steeply, from $16 million in 1944 to nearly $100 million by 1954.[15]

Growing state budgets underwrote further public works that made the nation appear increasingly modern and developed. Hospitals, clinics, churches, schools, libraries, markets, highways, aqueducts, irrigation canals, concrete bridges, housing developments, impressive government buildings, new roads in remote areas, and water, power, light, and telephone systems spread across the country.[16] The changes in everyday life were simple and profound. Tap water, for instance, began to be supplied twenty-four hours a day in the capital in 1946.[17] That same year, the state finished construction on the Ciudad Universitaria (University City), a new, modern campus for the Universidad de Santo Domingo, whose enrollment was expanding at a far greater rate than the population at large. Also in the 1940s, the government established the Central Bank, an agricultural bank for financing farm loans and development projects, and the Banco de Reservas (the last via the purchase of National City Bank's local branches).[18] The country's surface prosperity and rising gross national product did not translate into much expanding individual wealth for the majority of the population, which was still rural. But it underwrote new public services and state support that helped ensure peasants' subsistence security and certain basic needs in health care and rudimentary education. And the robust economy until Trujillo's last years—low foreign debt, overall fiscal strength, and expanding financial institutions and national wealth—facilitated continued investment and development.

In 1947 the Trujillo regime also received a diplomatic windfall as a result of the emergence of the Cold War. The struggle against fascism in World War II had given rise to a brief wave of liberal idealism in the U.S. State Department and the U.S. embassy in Ciudad Trujillo. From 1945 to 1947, Washington altered its overall policy of friendly relations with the Trujillo regime and adopted an openly antagonistic stance toward the dictatorship, including an arms embargo against the Dominican Republic. But in 1948 the U.S. government lifted the arms embargo and embraced Trujillo as an ally in the imagined struggle to contain communism. The rapprochement between Trujillo and the United States shored up Trujillo's power above all by discouraging revolutionary exiles and potential internal opponents. Instead of anticipating U.S. recognition of and aid to any anti-Trujillo movement that seized power, they expected instead U.S. intervention, if necessary, to protect the Trujillo regime.

Hence in the late 1940s, the state was running smoothly under Trujillo's command. The economy was booming; the nation was modernizing; foreign debt had been eliminated; and the U.S. government, after a brief moment of liberal repudiation, was again closely allied with the dictator. Moreover, economic development was being achieved without substantial rural dislocation, peasant dispossession, proletarianization, or social and political instability, and without decreasing food production and agricultural self-sufficiency. If Trujillo had died at this time, the country's economic trajectory might have been dramatically different. Sugar might never have become king—nor been nationalized—and a rural economy formed largely by small and medium farmers might actually have been consolidated. But just when the regime and, in some ways, the nation appeared to be thriving, Trujillo moved the country in a new direction at odds with his prior rural policies and ideology. Instead of using the revenues from the economic boom to reinvest in the existing political economy and to further the rural transition from subsistence exploitation to small-scale agriculture, Trujillo set the nation on a new course of expanding sugar production and appropriating foreign interests.

Trujillo's Sugar Empire

Before the end of World War II, the Trujillo regime had made few efforts to promote the sugar industry. State discourse and policy had been at best ambivalent toward this sector, whose expansion ran counter to the regime's nationalist-populist objectives. One U.S. company, the West Indies Sugar Corporation, owned six of the fourteen sugar mills in the country, and another, the South Porto Rico Sugar Company, owned two, including the nation's largest, the Central Romana. Two smaller mills were owned by U.S. citizens. And another, the Ozama plantation, belonged to a Canadian company. The only Dominican-owned mills belonged to the Italian-Dominican Vicini family, and they accounted for only about 10 percent of Dominican sugar production in 1948.[19] The regime radically altered its stance toward the sugar industry, however, over the next decade. Trujillo himself, his associates, or the state developed their own sugar mills and subsequently harassed and forcibly purchased most of the foreign sugar companies. The regime thus vastly expanded and, in a sense, nationalized the industry during the 1950s.

This shift in rural policy appears to have been in response to the expanding potential for export-led development as a result of rising world demand for tropical products in the late 1940s. Sugar, in particular, was in demand because of the decline of the European sugar beet industry caused by the war. In November of 1949, the national newspaper *El Caribe* called on prominent economic observers to analyze the current state of the sugar industry. Many leading figures responded with recommendations to expand sugar production, and some even argued that the industry be nationalized.[20] This staged discussion, a theatrical mechanism the regime often used to gauge and manipulate public opinion regarding new policies, suggested Trujillo's new interest in the business of sugar. The recommendations that were made adumbrated what would become the new policies of the regime, ones that had, in fact, already been quietly initiated. One year earlier, Trujillo had made his first foray into sugar production, purchasing a small sugar mill in Puerto Rico and transporting and reassembling it as the Ingenio Catarey, northwest of the capital. And a few months before *El Caribe*'s solicitation of opinions on the state of the sugar industry, the U.S. embassy relayed reports that Trujillo planned to build "one of the biggest sugar cane mills in the world" on the Haina River, just west of Ciudad Trujillo near San Cristóbal—though this project remained "wrapped in secrecy."[21] The giant Central Río Haina began operations in 1952. That year the country produced a record amount of sugar, 10 percent of it already being cultivated on Trujillo's estates.[22] Three years later, Trujillo developed his last new mill, the Central Esperanza, on lands in the western Cibao.[23]

In addition to establishing new mills, between 1952 and 1957 Trujillo and the Dominican government forcibly purchased the majority of U.S. sugar interests. The project commenced with a campaign to legitimate the appropriations in the press, which in 1952 began a concerted attack on foreign capital and its monopolization of land in certain areas. *El Caribe* called on the president to consider popular desires for expropriating foreign companies "that have forgotten their obligations to the Dominican nation."[24] The campaign was so heated that U.S. embassy observers expressed "grave doubts" about the future of U.S. capital in the Dominican Republic.[25]

The Dominicanization of U.S. capital began modestly in 1952. Trujillo first acquired two of the country's three smallest mills: the Ingenio Monte Llano belonging to the West Indies Sugar Corporation, and the Ingenio Amistad owned by María Luisa Julián, an American citizen. The next year he purchased the U.S.-owned Ingenio Porvenir, and in 1955 he bought out the Canadian-owned Central Ozama. In each case, Trujillo compelled the owners to sell. For instance, the U.S. embassy reported that the Amistad "appears to have been sold against the inclinations of Mrs. Maria Luisa Julian. . . . She is reported to have been told that it would be good policy for her to sell without delay." Similarly, Trujillo biographer Robert Crassweller asserts that Monte Llano was purchased "on a forced basis, for a figure which represented about 40 percent of the actual value."[26] And an accountant at the Ozama reported to the U.S. embassy that the estate had been sold "under considerable duress, and for a sum that was considerably under its replacement value." A staff engineer similarly affirmed that the company had been obliged to sell, "for obviously, that was what Trujillo wanted."[27]

Trujillo now controlled all of the country's mills except those belonging to the Vicini family and to the West Indies and South Porto Rico sugar companies. However, because the latter two enterprises were immense, the majority of sugar production remained in U.S. hands.[28] Further expansion of the regime's sugar empire would require escalating state demands and threats to render production unprofitable and unsustainable for foreign sugar companies. And in keeping with the regime's previous discourse, Trujillo's pressure on the sugar companies was framed in both nationalist and populist terms.

The government raised taxes on sugar production by close to 50 percent in both 1952 and 1953. New taxes on sugar exports and profits were imposed, and a 50 percent down payment was required on estimated taxes in 1954.[29] (Trujillo's holdings were exempted from taxation for twenty years, through legislation granting benefits to new companies that utilized local raw materials.)[30] The government's harassment of foreign sugar companies also took more explicitly populist guises. Despite the protests of both the foreign and the Vicini mills, the state decreed in 1954 a 20 cents per day wage increase for sugar workers (about a 15 percent raise).[31] And the government demanded that sugar companies turn over half of their land to Dominican colonos and also help to finance colono farming. The Dominican press pushed this plan, touted as a measure to favor the Dominican farmer, with bold threats. In December 1953, *La Nación* wrote: "If the sugar mills and great latifundia remain behind and do not support Generalissimo Trujillo in [this plan] . . . they will fall, in a conceivably detrimental manner for them, into a situation in which they may see themselves obliged to accept forcibly . . . their inescapable duty."[32] There was no discussion of payment for the cane already being grown on the lands, of the expenses of dividing the estates into scores of smaller plantations, or the fact that sugar produced by colonos was generally considered more expensive than that harvested on lands owned and cultivated by the mills themselves. The West Indies Sugar Corporation and South Porto Rico Sugar Company protested Trujillo's actions to the U.S. State Department, claiming that the intent was "to eliminate the possibility of profit from the operations of U.S. companies doing business [in the Dominican Republic]. . . . We are faced with nothing less than expropriation through confiscatory measures."[33] Echoing these protests, the U.S. embassy reported to the State Department in 1954: "It is now clear that there can be no long term peace between Trujillo and the large American economic interests until he obtains his objective. This objective appears to be either the cheap acquisition of these properties or their reduction to abject subservience."[34]

Yet despite the pressure the regime was exerting, the major U.S. sugar firms were still not persuaded to sell. The regime then played its final card. In 1954 the Dominican government declared the workers' living quarters provided by the U.S. sugar companies a menace to public health and ordered the construction of satisfactory dwellings with adequate sanitary facilities within sixty days. Believing this to be an impossibly short period for the required renovations, the West Indies offered to spend $5 million over the next four years to build new housing for some twenty thousand workers. The government agreed to consider an extension for only two years. By 1956 the company had spent $3 million for nine hundred new housing units, costs that contributed to company deficits. But on April 10, 1956, the government informed the company that because new housing was still not complete at one of its mills, the Department of Health would suspend its sugar operations and the company would be subject to "judicial action." Whereas previous campaigns had been directed against all the foreign companies (and occasionally against the Vicini mills), this attack was now directed solely against the West Indies.[35] The company's New York office, seeing "the handwriting on the wall," decided to sell its Dominican assets and try to secure a reasonable price.[36] In 1957 the country's largest sugar company, then responsible for 28 percent of the country's sugar production,[37] sold its plantations to

Trujillo's Azucarera Haina for $35,830,000—$10 million up front and the rest in installments to be paid at the end of the 1957, 1958, and 1959 grinding seasons—a price that the U.S. embassy believed was more than $11 million below actual value. The company planned to use the proceeds from the sale to expand its plantations in Cuba (in hindsight an even worse location for foreign investment).[38] The major Dominican newspapers claimed a nationalist victory in the takeover of the West Indies Sugar Corporation by "a genuinely Dominican enterprise." U.S. personnel were quickly replaced with Dominican nationals, as the nation's "Dominicanization" was trumpeted.[39]

Sugar was no longer a foreign enclave in the Dominican Republic. The Trujillo regime had dramatically reversed the historic predominance of U.S. capital in the industry. In 1957, Trujillo's sugar empire, now worth an estimated $80 million, encompassed nearly three-quarters of the country's sugar production. Including the Vicini holdings, Dominican-owned companies produced some 80 percent of the nation's sugar.[40] And the size of the sugar sector had grown immensely. While the area of sugar farming had remained roughly the same between 1935 and 1950, in the 1950s it doubled, while production almost tripled.[41] By 1960 sugar production in the Dominican Republic passed the million-ton mark, up from just over 400,000 in 1948.[42] And sugar accounted for 18 percent of crop land, a jump from 9 percent in 1940.[43]

Trujillo's "Dominicanization" of the sugar industry fit into an overall pattern of harassing and appropriating foreign interests in the 1950s. During these years, numerous U.S. companies lost tax exemptions, suffered severe forms of unfair competition by Trujillo's interests,[44] were obliged to sell large portions of their stock to Dominican investors (and to influential members of the regime),[45] and were forced to invest much of their revenues in the country.[46] Also, the U.S.-owned Compañía Eléctrica de Santo Domingo was compelled to sell all its holdings to the Dominican government at a low price.[47] As with the sugar estates, the Trujillo state applied pressures against the electric company that rendered it unsustainable, unprofitable, and ultimately willing to sell.[48] Most decisive was a 1954 law requiring the president's permission before electricity or water service could be stopped to users who were unable to pay their bills, as "it is the duty of the State to take measures to protect its people . . . including those with the least resources . . . from being deprived of these essentials."[49] Richard Johnson, first secretary of the U.S. embassy, reported that the new law "can only be interpreted as an open invitation on the part of the government for people not to pay their electric bills."[50] And another official summed up well Trujillo's brand of populist nationalism: "This represents a typical Trujillo master-stroke in which he shows his concern for alleviating the condition of the poor at the expense of [others]."[51] This legislation was soon revoked, but it revealed the state's readiness to force its wishes on this large U.S.-owned interest. A few months later, the company was ready to sell for the low price offered by the government.[52]

U.S. embassy officials perceived Trujillo's actions as reflecting both his "rapacious greed" and an ominous shift in his regime toward economic nationalism.[53] Johnson recommended "most strongly that a basic review of our Policy Statement on the Dominican Republic be undertaken," given Trujillo's "frequent abuse ... of American capital."[54] Yet Johnson's recommendation was ignored, and the U.S. government did not alter its policies at this time, nor even after the West Indies Sugar Corporation was forced out of the Dominican Republic four years later. This passivity in the face of Trujillo's expropriations suggests that the Cold War overwhelmed all other considerations in U.S. foreign policy in the post-1947 period. And this helps explain the timing of Trujillo's turn toward sugar and his efforts to Dominicanize foreign interests. Trujillo forcibly purchased U.S. interests when the country's economic boom provided him with sufficient funds to do so,[55] but also only after the monomania of U.S. anticommunism presented him with an opportunity, if handled shrewdly, to act more autonomously vis-à-vis U.S. business interests without jeopardizing U.S.-Dominican relations. Although he bullied and appropriated U.S. capital in the 1950s, he also made himself as useful as possible to the U.S. in its anticommunist campaign. In addition to establishing a U.S. military mission in the Dominican Republic, Washington secured permission for developing an important guided missile tracking station in Sabana de la Mar. As the Department of State reported, Trujillo used "military facilities issues as a bargaining tool for gaining US cooperation in other fields."[56] Also, the Dominican Republic enthusiastically adhered to U.S. positions on nearly every occasion in the United Nations and Organization of the American States, with the exception of its support for Puerto Rican independence.[57] But far from being a passive client state of the United States, the Trujillo regime negotiated a high price for its cooperation.[58]

Yet Trujillo's conquest of the Dominican part of "the American sugar kingdom" came at a high price for the Dominican Republic.[59] Certainly, Trujillo's policies rendered the country impressively autonomous from foreign capital for a small, modernizing nation in the "backyard" of the United States. But Trujillo's romance with sugar reversed the thrust of the regime's pre-1948 rural policies, and this would be problematic for the regime in both political and economic terms. It cost Trujillo popular rural support. And the regime's new political economy made the country more vulnerable to the vicissitudes of external trade, particularly to sugar prices and markets, than it had been in the pre–World War II period.

Ironically, Trujillo increased Dominican dependency on sugar at a time when the world market for sugar was contracting. The rising sugar prices that had presumably caught Trujillo's eye in the late 1940s were a momentary boom, as had been apparent to many Dominican and U.S. officials at the time. In 1949 the governor of the Central Bank, Jesús María Troncoso, cautioned that there was no clear market for any increased Dominican sugar production.[60] U.S. embassy officials expressed the same doubts, pointing out that "sugar will probably be in serious world over-supply within the next few years, with continued high production in the Western hemisphere, with full recovery of the European beet sugar industry, and with increases in war-damaged areas like Java and the Philippines." These observers also stressed the constraints imposed by the lack of a bona fide world market for sugar. Some 90 percent of sugar exports were sold on the basis of special trade agreements at set ("preferential") prices determined largely by political factors.[61] "Since the Dominican Republic is virtually excluded from the protected United States market by the present American sugar quota policy," the embassy concluded, "serious problems of selling additional sugar on the world market may arise."[62] In the late 1940s, the United States granted the Dominican Republic a minuscule 8,133-ton quota, an inconsequential portion of the over 400,000 tons the country then produced. As the Dominican Republic became increasingly important to its anticommunist campaign, the U.S. government did raise the Dominican sugar quota. By 1958 it reached 58,000 tons. Still, this was only about 7 percent of Dominican sugar exports (and tiny compared with the roughly 3 million tons allocated to Cuba).[63] Barring a large and unexpected increase in the U.S. sugar quota, the prospects for expanding sugar exports would remain dim, as they had appeared from the start. The country would have to sell its sugar on the open market, in effect a residual market where sugar was dumped and prices were often below the cost of production.

To pay for this unpromising sugar empire, Trujillo would drain the state's formerly strong economic resources. Ostensibly, the new Dominican sugar industry began as Trujillo's personal investment. For instance, the Central Río Haina was developed by a private company whose major shareholders were close associates of Trujillo.[64] However, Trujillo relied on the state's unprecedented revenues and reserves to expand his holdings. In early 1954, the Dominican government purchased from Trujillo his sugar plantations for the inflated price of $43 million (or, according to one report, $53 million).

This was a fantastic sum for the Dominican government, equivalent to approximately half the annual budget.[65] The funds from the sale helped provide Trujillo with the capital he needed to then purchase the West Indies and other foreign sugar holdings. A few years later, though, the state would sell back to Trujillo on easy credit terms the same companies it had bought from him.[66] The back-and-forth shuffling of companies between private and public ownership at the dictator's discretion—maneuvers that added immensely to Trujillo's income in those years—illustrated the ways in which the state and Trujillo, the national treasury and Trujillo's personal account, had become one and the same.[67] Overall, moreover, these moves indicated a major change in the regime's previously conservative fiscal policies, which were no longer protected from Trujillo's excesses and corruption.

State funds were expended not only to purchase the sugar plantations but also to provide infrastructure for the new sugar companies. The state spent $8 million to develop the port of Haina serving the Río Haina and Catarey mills,[68] and additional funds to construct roads and rail lines to transport cane to the Río Haina mill—located on the coast to facilitate shipping— from the sugar plantations, situated inland where the soil was suitable for sugar production. The new sugar companies continued, moreover, to be exempt from taxation imposed on the rest of the industry. As a result the state lost enormous possible tax revenues, and foreign companies no longer shouldered most of the risk of volatile sugar prices. When sugar prices were high, the regime garnered huge profits that were funneled back into the Dominican economy more than ever before. But when prices fell, the negative impact on the economy was also unprecedented.

In addition to the fiscal perils of Trujillo's 1950s romance with sugar, the state's new political economy curtailed its politics of supporting free access to land among the peasantry. To the contrary, in the 1950s the regime was responsible for much peasant dispossession. Above all, in order to grow sugar for the regime's Central Río Haina, the state forced reportedly thousands of peasants and ranchers from land throughout the province of Monte Plata and in areas near Cotuí, as well as by the Haina River around San Cristóbal. In the southwestern quadrant of Monte Plata province, the lives of the many sedentary farmers were destroyed by the eviction. In these areas, Trujillo reportedly paid landholders for their farms and houses, but generally at minimal prices, perhaps a quarter or a half of what they were worth. Pedro Cordones, an elderly land surveyor from the area, recalled how, "in [the towns of] San Francisco . . . and Chirino, for example, there had been lots of coffee, cacao . . . and rice . . . because these places are highly fertile. . . . But Trujillo's boundless ambition led to the razing of these lands. . . . All of these [areas]

Trujillo occupied to grow cane. . . . Monte Plata, in particular, fell victim of the jaws of Trujillo."[69]

The northern part of Monte Plata around Sabana Grande de Boyá was, on the other hand, mostly open range used for hunting and pasture. There residents lost vast areas that they had collectively exploited and which they believed belonged "to the virgin"—that is, the Church—though a large tract had been claimed by the powerful landowner José Antonio Jiménez. They received no compensation for the loss of pasture and woods and only a small amount for their individual improvements (cultivated lands and houses). The better-off ranchers hired help to move their cattle to other locations, but most peasants were able only to sell the few animals that they could quickly round up. Because these evictions occurred precisely at the time when the country's land frontier was disappearing, few could find unclaimed lands nearby to exploit. Thus, reportedly around half of the residents stayed in the area to work for the sugar companies, though some left for the cities, and others resettled in agricultural colonies.[70] One person who remained, Cleyto Aybar, told me: "The worst thing that [Trujillo] did around here was take away our means of work. All of us were left in the air, with nothing at all."[71]

The final decade of the Trujillato saw several other collective evictions as the dictator brazenly expanded his sugar as well as ranching and rice interests. The U.S. embassy heard reports that at the end of 1953, the army pushed close to twenty-five hundred persons off some 50,000 acres of lands to the west of Cabrera. Most were squatters and evacuated their areas without incident. But when a few who claimed legal title to their property refused to leave, they were reportedly killed. That same year, others were dispossessed from lands in the Bonao–San Francisco area.[72] The following year soldiers also ejected some five hundred families from arid lands in Valverde that Trujillo claimed and planned to develop with irrigation.[73] And peasants recounted how in 1957 and 1958 Trujillo ordered the eviction of thousands from a zone north of the capital (Villa Mella, La Victoria, Dajao) and stretching into the province of Monte Plata. The state gave residents virtually no notice. A few occupants reportedly refused the small compensation offered, so as not to condone the appropriation. A number of the former occupants found work on Trujillo's cattle ranch "Hacienda Estrella." Others were hired by the now Trujillo-owned Ozama plantation. Some who had family with land elsewhere moved there to farm. The rest went to the capital or to one of the state's agricultural colonies.[74] Given that the amount of cultivated sugar lands grew from 91,894 to 183,213 hectares between 1948 and 1960, it is possible that peasants lost access to as much as 90,000 hectares that were taken over by new sugar fields, mostly plantations developed by the Trujillo regime.[75]

In the areas of large-scale dispossession, the regime lost the measure of legitimacy and support it had previously secured among the peasantry. Priciliano Mercedes was one of those evicted in 1958 from lands near La Victoria north of the capital. Until that time, he stated, he had "lived under an illusion. . . . Before there were all the speeches and posters on the corner that [Trujillo's] best friends were the men of work. And one lived completely with that sentiment, believing it. But when I saw how he repaid us in 1957 and 1958 with that eviction, that is not how one treats someone one cares about. It was when the eviction occurred . . . [that] I became convinced that Trujillo was not just, that he was not truly loyal. I was stripped of the illusion that Trujillo was truly loyal."[76] The perils of dependence on Trujillo's paternalistic authoritarianism had become painfully clear. Peasants hurt by the expansion of Trujillo's own latifundia lost their faith that this ruler would represent their interests in return for loyalty and "work" (agricultural production), as Trujillo had promised since the early 1930s.

Bitterness over Trujillo's evictions as well as his sudden identification with the sugar companies coincided with rare and dramatic manifestations of opposition in the Eastern sugar areas. In April of 1957, shortly after Trujillo purchased the West Indies company and canceled an existing contract with local stevedores, most of the monuments dedicated to Trujillo in the major sugar town, San Pedro de Macorís, were smeared with manure. By one of the statues, someone wrote with manure, "This is what you are."[77] This extraordinary resistance suggests that Trujillo's expansion of and identification with the sugar plantations was creating politically volatile workers rather than loyal small farmers, as his earlier policies had.

Why did a dictator who had so successfully negotiated the social and economic changes of rapid modernization for the popular rural classes suddenly become an agent of their dispossession, dislocation, and disillusionment?[78] And why did Trujillo become enamored with conventional and superficial symbols of modernity, such as gigantic sugar mills, ones long ago repudiated by the nation's leading intellectuals, and turn his back on the alternative path to modern agriculture extolled by most of his advisers?[79] After World War II, Trujillo may have felt that the state's alliance with the peasantry was of declining importance to the regime. Certainly, Trujillo had a more secure political hold on the country than he had had in the mid-1930s when that alliance was forged. And, as we have seen, peasant production no longer appeared to be the only feasible means of economic development and augmenting state wealth, as it had when Trujillo came to power amid a global depression. The rise in international commodity prices following World War II, the expanding revenues of the Dominican state (and Trujillo personally), and the Cold War together allowed Trujillo to pursue export-led development and to appropriate the most glaring symbol of foreign power in the country—that is, the sugar industry.

Trujillo may have believed that he could realize this nationalist coup (and imperial mimicry) without producing any major or unresolvable rural problems resulting from dispossession and the exhaustion of the land frontier. During the same period when the state was displacing thousands of peasants from lands in Monte Plata to grow cane for the Central Río Haina and thereby increasing land pressures across the country, the government ran a full-page announcement in the press inviting landless agriculturalists either to request state land or "where there are no State lands available . . . [to] identify lands with owners or occupants who are not working them, so that the Government may make agreements with them to donate the lands to the applicants."[80] Also at that time, the state exhorted local alcaldes to secure land for all who were landless and "to thus make them veritable owners of their land, their labors and their fruits."[81] Trujillo thus looked to old policies and populist rhetoric to try to forestall rural instability and grievances. But these measures were too modest to alter the overall direction of the regime, a direction that was diametrically opposed to its earlier political economy and peasant politics.

The expansion of sugar thus reflected a 1950s regime characterized by growing arrogance, miscalculations, and illusions. In addition to trampling on peasant interests in the new sugar areas, Trujillo brazenly ignored the lack of existing demand for Dominican sugar as well as the perils of expending huge state and personal funds to purchase foreign corporations. Part of the explanation for Trujillo's errors and recklessness in the 1950s, in addition to hubris, is that the dictator was surrounding himself more and more with yes-men. Trujillo's functionaries and advisers became less independent and informative over time, as occurs with probably most powerful leaders. His subordinates grew increasingly fearful of controverting el Jefe's opinions, admitting failure, or being the bearers of bad news.[82] They sought to win the fierce competition for the dictator's favor and avoid the harsh punishments meted out to some who had the courage to be forthright and critical.[83] Long gone were the days when, as with the land distribution campaign in 1935, key advisers would redirect the Generalísimo's plan of action and foster a quite different policy. Local U.S. officials, attempting to explain Dominican efforts to expand sugar production despite its dim prospects, stated that "apparently the plan has been carried forward only at the Generalissimo's insistence" and referred to it as "a project of Generalísimo Trujillo himself."[84] Respected, long-time advisers, such as the Puerto Rican agronomist Carlos Chardón, who steadfastly opposed the move toward sugar felt obliged to abandon their posts and, in Chardón's case at least, the country. After Chardón voiced criticism of Trujillo's new policies in 1949, he informed the U.S. embassy that he would leave to work for the Venezuelan government.[85] All the members of Trujillo's cabinet except for Balaguer were deemed "worthless" by a retiring Spanish ambassador in 1957, who told his U.S. counterpart that "the only man with enough courage to stand up to Trujillo," Arturo Despradel, had lost his position because of it.[86] And finally, the reports from local officials that Trujillo relied on to apprise him of local conditions became less informative and accurate. Trujillo passed through San Pedro de Macorís in 1958 and asked about the general welfare there (one year after his statues had been smeared with manure by local residents). Officials reported that the situation was completely satisfactory, only to be contradicted by a local priest who stated that, in fact, poverty and hunger were becoming endemic in several urban areas.[87] All of these developments reflected Trujillo's declining capacity as a leader. He no longer surrounded himself with or followed the recommendations of sound or independent-minded policy makers and forthright officials.

Unchecked by prudent advisers, Trujillo had increased Dominican dependence on an oversupplied, erratic, and politically determined world sugar market and brutally dislocated thousands of peasants. Instead of expanding peasant production and promoting the important coffee and cacao crops, grown on relatively small farms, the regime turned another large swath of the country over to plantation agriculture worked by a Haitian and Dominican proletariat. Rather than leading to nationalist glory, Trujillo's sugar policies would help push the state into an inexorable decline.[88] Between 1958 and 1961, both local and international conditions would generate powerful forces for political change in the Dominican Republic that would ultimately sweep the Trujillo regime from power.

Despotic Twilight

In 1955, Trujillo hosted a spectacular "International Fair for the Peace and Brotherhood of the Free World" in Ciudad Trujillo. The fair was intended to promote the Dominican Republic as a modern site for tourism, trade, and investment, and to laud the Era of Trujillo, now in its twenty-fifth year. Forty-two other countries participated, many building pavilions along the avenues of the fair grounds. However, the event was designed primarily to showcase Dominican modernization and growth in recent decades.[89] The fair's exhibits on the country's commercial development and putative economic and social achievements evoked positive comments in a *New York*

Times editorial. And U.S. embassy observers described the fair as "excellent and highly impressive,"[90] while the governments of France, Japan, and other countries sent letters of praise for the "miraculous" progress and "splendor" characterizing the Dominican Republic under Trujillo.[91] Trujillo's speech accepting the fair's dedication in his honor reflected the prevailing nationalist ideology of the Trujillo regime and its claims that over the past twenty-five years Trujillo himself had managed to constitute an autonomous and modern Dominican nation:

I received in 1930 a Republic which lacked some of its essential attributes as a sovereign entity; today I present it to history as a nation without the ties which limit its actions, with full financial autonomy and standing on a basis of equality with the freest nations of the world.

There was delivered to me a people with a weak sense of identity, with their territory still undefined, and today I offer to my fellow citizens a country the demarcation of whose frontiers has been completed. . . .

There was entrusted to me a nation pauperized, mortgaged to foreign capital and without resources to cover its own necessities and satisfy its commitments to international order, and today I show it transformed into an independent economic entity.[92]

Financial independence and international prestige, along with definitive borders and a stronger sense of national identity and pride, had taken center stage in the regime's ideology and claims to legitimation, displacing the early, more populist discourse valorizing peasant citizens and agriculture as the agents of the country's progress.

The International Fair marked the height of the regime's strength. But it also represented the beginning of the end for the dictatorship and dramatized Trujillo's growing excesses and arrogance. The government spent at least $15 million on the fair—including exorbitant items such as a $5,000 crown for the fair's queen, Trujillo's daughter Angelita. (Some even calculated that the fair cost as much as $30 million, nearly a third of the government budget, if one included related projects such as new hotels.)[93] The cost was extreme for a nation and economy the size of the Dominican Republic, and the country never fully recovered. The fair, like Trujillo's takeover and expansion of the sugar industry, demonstrated the regime's unprecedented economic might and the country's participation in the world of modern capital. But, in retrospect, they were both signs that Trujillo had lost all sense of the regime's limits and it was beginning to spin out of control.

Huge government expenditures in the 1950s for Trujillo's sugar empire as well as for spectacular boondoggles such as the International Fair rendered the state highly vulnerable to an economic downturn that came in the late

1950s. Considerable government arrearage began after the fair.[94] Then in 1959 prices fell for all of the country's principal exports (sugar, coffee, cacao, and tobacco), sending the economy into an unprecedented tailspin. The price of sugar fell below the cost of production. The West Indies Sugar Corporation, whose purchase by Trujillo's Central Haina seemed like a coup in 1957, now appeared to be "a white elephant."[95] Central Haina required $30 million in foreign loans to meet its obligations that year, including a final $8.6 million still due to the West Indies. With neither great profits nor taxes being generated by sugar nor strong coffee or cacao earnings to counteract the loss, foreign exchange reserves and state revenues dropped dramatically. Arrearage then reached crisis proportions, estimated at $44 million. And for the first time the peso began selling at a discount to the dollar. The Central Bank was obliged to solicit more than $35 million in foreign loans, a radical departure for the Trujillo state, which for years had been unwilling to sacrifice its image of a nation without foreign debt.[96]

The final straw leading the state into fiscal crisis was the staggering expenditures for defense in 1959. The government spent an estimated $25 million on weapons in addition to the record $39 million already budgeted for the armed forces that year.[97] This military buildup was part of Trujillo's aggressive response to the regime's multiplying external enemies at the time. Liberal and left-wing movements had overturned dictatorial regimes in Colombia, Venezuela, and Cuba, in 1957, 1958, and 1959, respectively, and the latter two brought to power long-time opponents of Trujillo, Rómulo Betancourt and Fidel Castro. Cuba quickly provided Dominican exiles and other anti-Trujillo forces (including several military leaders from the Cuban Revolution) a strategic site for organizing and launching an attack on Trujillo. Trujillo responded with a huge military expansion that would have been a difficult drain on the economy under the best conditions and was devastating in the context of an economic downturn.

Excessive government spending and a state fiscal crisis required new taxes that fell heavily on a rising class of professionals and merchants, exacerbating the already growing disaffection of these groups.[98] With the economic growth and urban development of the Trujillo years had also come expanding access to higher education. Enrollment at the Universidad de Santo Domingo, which had only 169 students in 1920 and 328 in 1936, reached 2,449 by 1951 and continued to grow until the end of the Trujillo regime.[99] As a result, thousands of young lawyers, doctors, professors, students, technical workers, and merchants had swelled the ranks of the middle classes. In 1935 there had been only 5,559 technical workers and professionals in the country. By 1950 the number had risen to 12,168 and to 23,190 by 1960.[100] Unlike the new entrepreneurial class, which had developed via state incentives granted to companies at the discretion of the president, these professional groups proved less controllable through the regime's system of rewards and punishments.[101] Many among them believed that their careers were hurt by the Trujillo state's widening control over the economy as well as its system of patronage, which favored members of an earlier, often less-educated, generation.[102] Many also felt stymied by their lack of political rights and freedoms. The state's failure to establish any substance behind the facade of constitutionalism was now coupled with fiscal mismanagement and economic crisis. Together, these rendered the regime's legitimating discourse as an agent—indeed a necessary agent—of progress untenable for the new professional classes. Economic development and modernization had been central to the regime's ideology, social acceptance, and state control. But ultimately they helped hasten the regime's demise by fostering groups that opposed the dictatorship and by producing an increasingly complex society that outgrew Trujillo's capacity to rule effectively. Within the new professionals' political imaginary of modernity, the Trujillo regime no longer had a role.

In the late 1950s, members of the new professional classes began secretly meeting to oppose the regime. U.S. ambassador Joseph Farland reported at the close of 1958 that there was now evidence of "a very self-conscious professional group centering around the University and that they are reportedly trying to change the government via a 'liaison . . . with disgruntled or ambitious military elements.'"[103] In 1958 anti-Trujillo slogans were found written on blackboards in classrooms at the university, their authors inspired perhaps by the recent fall of the dictators Gustavo Rojas Pinilla in Colombia and Marcos Pérez Jiménez in Venezuela.[104] Farland also heard unprecedented criticism of the regime from high officials within the government itself.[105] The U.S. consulate general believed that "80 to 90 per cent of literate Dominicans are anti-Trujillo and would like to have a representative form of government oriented toward the west."[106] By January of 1959, the embassy reported that the situation in the Dominican Republic had moved suddenly "from one in which a serious revolutionary attempt was considered almost impossible to one in which it is possible. . . . Given a continuation of . . . [current conditions] a serious insurrectionary attempt [seems] inevitable."[107]

In response to growing opposition, Trujillo ceded more power to some of his most brutal subordinates, choosing to repress the growing resistance rather than develop reforms that might have, at least, mitigated the crisis. One prominent state figure complained to a U.S. official that Trujillo's inner circle was being filled with "savage animals."[108] This development can be traced back to 1957 with the formation of the Military Intelligence Service

(S.I.M.), the notorious secret police soon led by Johnny Abbes García, a man infamous for his cruelty even among Trujillo's henchmen. This organization expanded the country's espionage system, carried out much of the dictatorship's dirty work, and made Abbes a redoubtable figure in the regime. His hard-line positions encouraged the deployment of forms of repression beyond traditional normative limits, which, in turn, only mobilized more opposition. The S.I.M. grew rapidly in the regime's final years as it responded to new forms of resistance that its own repressive actions helped produce.[109]

On June 14 and 20, 1959, approximately two hundred Dominican exiles and Cuban and other Latin American revolutionaries launched an invasion of the Dominican Republic from Cuba with the hope of igniting the country's already explosive conditions and overthrowing the Trujillo regime.[110] Some forces landed by plane in the mountainous central region of Constanza, and others invaded by ship on the northern shore west of Puerto Plata, also in the Cibao. The insurgents, many of whom came from prominent Dominican families (including Juancito Rodríguez's son, José Horacio Rodríguez), were well equipped and trained, and even had some initial successes against the Dominican army.[111] But they had expected and needed peasant support to carry out guerrilla warfare and to spark a popular uprising. In contrast to the late 1940s, when exiles had also sought to invade the country and overthrow Trujillo, the revolutionaries had landed when the Dominican economy was in crisis and domestic opposition was gathering strength. Nonetheless, there were no indications of collaboration with the insurgents among local civilians. To the contrary, many peasants assisted the army and, by some accounts, were responsible for apprehending most of the expeditionaries.[112] As a result, all the insurgents were defeated within a couple of weeks.

Continuing loyalty to the state among much of the peasantry helps explain why these insurgents were quickly captured while, for instance, Fidel Castro's minuscule exile invasion of Cuba fostered peasant revolution in Oriente and while the Sandinista guerrillas were able to survive for more than a decade in the Nicaraguan countryside before overthrowing the Somoza dynasty. Memoirs of the Dominican exiles recall their own discussions during the invasion of the stark and decisive difference between the responses of Cuban and Dominican peasants to the landing of rebel troops, a difference exiles explained as being a product of Dominican peasants' "indoctrination" by the Trujillo state.[113] It seems, however, that Trujillo opponents would have been well served by a more precise understanding of the regime's elements of support and opposition. Had the exiles headed to areas where peasants had recently suffered from dispossession, such as the province of Monte Plata, they might have received a more welcoming reception. Instead they landed in the Cibao where small farming and relative prosperity still prevailed.[114] The exiles' ignorance of their enemy, of the regime's strengths and weaknesses, thus contributed to their failure. Certainly peasants feared reprisal for collaboration and may have been spurred by the promise of material rewards for attacking the revolutionaries.[115] And nationalist and possibly antisocialist sentiments may have been piqued by the insurgents' association with the Cuban revolutionaries. An embassy official reported at the time of the invasion: "Every campesino . . . from eight to eighty appears to be armed with a newly sharpened machete. . . . Conversation with any and everyone begins and ends with talk of invasion: 'Send us the "barbudos" [Cuban revolutionaries]; we want to shave them.' . . . In all the roadside bars and restaurants the small merengue bands or juke box blare day and night with a catchy . . . tune. . . . The translated title is 'Fidel Castro will pay for it.'"[116] But had the Cibao peasantry vehemently opposed the regime, neither these concerns nor Trujillo's brutal system of rewards and punishments would have effectively mobilized the peasantry to quash the insurgents.

Most of the expeditionaries did not die in combat but were captured and then executed by the Dominican military. Only six soldiers were spared. "As a result," Farland reported, "a surprisingly large number of influential Dominican families are embittered and are in mourning."[117] After the invasion, the state made numerous arrests of those it suspected of being connected with the opposition, including members of distinguished families.[118] And several highly respected state figures were assassinated at this time, presumably at Trujillo's orders.[119] But this increased state terror did not put an end to resistance against the regime. Instead it galvanized it. The underground opposition now spread across the country's major towns and gave rise to what became known as the 14th of June Movement, in honor of the date on which the revolutionaries landed. This movement was formed mainly by the students, merchants, seminarians, and other middle- and upper-middle-class Dominicans who had been most clearly opposed to Trujillo in recent years.[120] Thus although the exiles' dreams of revolution were naive and quickly shattered, their quixotic gesture was nonetheless effective. It inspired the urban resistance and fueled the cycle of intensifying state terror and growing opposition that would create fertile terrain for a coup and lead to the collapse of the regime.

As the dictatorship attempted to crush the nascent opposition movement, it also sought to rebuild support among the popular rural classes. Notwithstanding the seeming impossibility of the plan, following the 1959 invasion Trujillo ordered that a letter be sent to "all the campesinos, thanking them for the collaboration they offered to the Government in the annihilation of the invading forces last month" and affirming the regime's commitment to "providing social and economic benefits to those without the necessary means to provide for the sustenance of their families."[121] At Trujillo's insistence, the assistant secretary of the presidency, Virgilio Díaz Grullón, sent out a circular to each of the 750 alcaldes pedáneos requesting a list of all inhabitants in their sections. He then made copies of the letter and had one addressed to each rural resident. With difficulty, he convinced Trujillo to use a stamp of his signature rather than personally signing each one.[122] Through these myriad letters, Trujillo sought to reassert the peasant-state alliance upon which, early on, he had consolidated his regime:

Dear Ally and Friend,

Since the year 1930 . . . until the present date . . . the Dominican government has maintained a policy of support for the peasant class and of constantly improving its living and working conditions . . . as once I summed up in the phrase, recorded by history, that "My best friends are the men of work." Recently, during the ceaseless effort to disturb our peace to which international communism has subjected us, the Dominican peasantry offered its heroic and decisive assistance to the national armed forces and effectively contributed to the immediate and complete annihilation of communist mercenaries. There is no greater proof than this of the absolute support and unwavering loyalty of our peasantry for the government and no better moment than the present to reaffirm the strong bonds of friendship and solidarity that unite the men of the countryside with their political leaders. With a keen understanding of these deep sentiments of friendship and solidarity . . . I address myself personally to you to reiterate the absolute disposition of the government to adopt as many measures as may be necessary for the collective betterment of the section in which you reside, for which I have already asked your alcalde pedáneo for a report.

I take this occasion to express to you my personal trust and friendship,

[signed] Rafael Leonidas Trujillo[123]

Two days before this letter was distributed, the secretary of agriculture had, in fact, asked all the mayors (síndicos) to form lists of landless peasants in their areas and to indicate whether or not they would be willing to move to existing colonies.[124] Trujillo also offered indemnification to peasants for losses incurred during the invasion, sponsored an exhibit in the National Museum enshrining the machetes used by peasants against the insurgents, and gave medals to those now lauded as the "immortal machateros." Farland reported that Trujillo's actions "appear to have been made with an eye to the future . . . [and] constitute strong inducement for campesinos to support the regime in any forthcoming invasion."[125]

Meanwhile, on their own, peasants and local authorities had already begun to request broader state initiatives and assistance, thus anticipating and creating pressures for Trujillo's renewed "politics of peasant support." In the latter half of 1959, alcaldes pedáneos, mayors, leaders of the Dominican Party, and members of the army decried landlessness and potential evictions and proposed that idle and squatter lands be secured for the landless.[126] One mayor emphasized explicitly the political advantages that would accrue from such state action.[127] Peasants also flooded the state—both before and after Trujillo's personal letter to them—with a constant stream of land requests, many for private lands irrigated by newly built state canals and thus subject to partial appropriation and distribution.[128]

Peasants' letters to Trujillo suggest that they had become emboldened to demand increased compensation for their backing of the regime. Requests were now for larger amounts of land—that is, 3 to 12 rather than 1 to 3 hectares. Some even asked for money to buy or rent land if the state could no longer provide plots.[129] These growing demands reflected peasants' calculation of what they were owed for political loyalty in this moment of regime vulnerability. Land requests now explicitly stressed the writer's personal adherence to Trujillo. One peasant cited, for example, his having immediately joined "Trujillo's national army" to fight the "mercenary invasion."[130]

As we saw in Chapter 6, the state did distribute a substantial amount of land to thousands of peasants in its final years. And in 1960, it promised a "vast program" to grant land to the landless and eliminate latifundia through the government purchase of private estates.[131] All this was doubtless an effort to shore up support in the countryside. But the regime's traditional political economy, providing generally free access to land and a significant measure of state assistance for small farming, was already entering into crisis in many areas, in large part because of Trujillo's own policy of expanding sugar production. In general, the state could now offer plots only in colonies distant from where the recipient lived and in other undesirable areas. Yet the regime in no way reversed its sugar policies of expanding cane fields at the expense of peasant farming and ranching. Hence despite the regime's final push for expanding land distribution, the twilight of Trujillo's rule was marked by growing land pressures and official concerns over a new wave of rural-urban migration, which had until then been steady but comparatively modest during the dictatorship.[132] To satisfy peasant needs at this point, a more profound land reform and investment in small farming would have been necessary, a deeper and more radical commitment than the regime—or any future Dominican government—would be willing and able to undertake.

The unprecedented scale of repression against largely middle-class opponents in the nation's towns and cities further undermined the regime's efforts to consolidate support among the peasantry, when this brutal crackdown provoked a dramatic and completely unexpected battle between Trujillo and the Catholic Church. If Trujillo had sought deliberately to destroy his own regime, including peasant support, he could hardly have been more effective than by attacking the Church. The close and supportive alliance between Trujillo and the Church that had existed since the early years of the dictatorship had been strengthened in the 1950s when the state poured millions of dollars into constructing churches, establishing monasteries, aiding poor parishes, subsidizing religious missions, and funding seminaries and Catholic scholarships. Trujillo himself donated much personal money to the Church and attended Mass frequently.[133] In return for state support, the Church glorified Trujillo's rule. The clergy celebrated countless Masses for the Generalissimo's health, awarded him various honors, and praised his reign from the pulpit and at public events and mass demonstrations.[134] The Church's actions gave the dictatorship an appearance of normalcy and even moral virtue and of great power and authority that helped maintain Trujillo's control.

However, the Church turned suddenly and dramatically against Trujillo in January 1960, after the regime ordered a brutal and unprecedented crackdown against hundreds of perceived opponents. After an extensive assassination plot against Trujillo was discovered, the regime arrested an estimated thousand or more persons associated with the 14th of June Movement, principally from "the country's best trained (in many cases U.S.-educated) professional and commercial" classes. Many of those rounded up were quickly released, but dozens were killed. And nearly three hundred were tried for the assassination attempt. Some of these defendants were later slain by the regime.[135] The Church responded forcefully to the regime's vicious repression, issuing two pastoral letters in 1960 that were read in Masses throughout the country. The letters demanded respect for human rights, offered solidarity to those who had suffered political repression, and called for the release of political prisoners by Easter.[136]

"This must be taken calmly. You can't fight the Church," was reportedly Trujillo's initial reaction to this unprecedented act of public defiance by what had been one of the regime's strongest allies and instruments of legitimation.[137] Yet this canny response quickly gave way to a reckless one that would profoundly undermine Trujillo's rule. Throughout the following year, the regime's repressive forces brutally attacked, kidnapped, imprisoned, and expelled from the country numerous priests, nuns, bishops, and seminarians. Church leaders were slandered in the press and on the radio, called "agents of the Vatican dictatorship," and accused of being communists, agents of Castro, and "terrorist" conspirators. Religious missions and schools were also deprived of state support and closed down. At the same time, in an effort to cover up the conflict, Trujillo relentlessly demanded that local ecclesiastic authorities declare him "Benefactor of the Church," which they categorically refused to do.[138]

Following the regime's attacks and harassment, the Church renounced the strong position it had adopted in the pastoral letters. It issued a conciliatory letter to Trujillo on January 10, 1961, disavowing "misinterpretations" and "inaccuracies" inferred from its pastoral letters. It regretted the recent deterioration in Church-state relations and offered renewed cooperation with the government. But it still made no offer to name Trujillo as its "benefactor," as the dictator continued to demand.[139] Trujillo responded to this act of conciliation as if he were determined not to resolve the conflict, suggesting again that he had at this point lost his political instincts or will to survive, surrounded himself with inadequate advisers, or simply could no longer restrain his megalomania and rage. The anticlerical campaign and attacks on individual priests accelerated in the final months of the regime, reaching a fever pitch by the time of Trujillo's assassination. Foolishly, Trujillo presented the population with a stark choice between himself and the Catholic Church, and that was a contest he was bound to lose.[140]

Although peasants had displayed solidarity with neither the exiles' attempts to topple the regime nor the underground opposition, the regime's conflict with the Church did mobilize peasant resistance. The dictator's attacks on the Catholic Church and on esteemed local bishops brazenly crossed the line of tolerable behavior applied to even the most powerful of leaders, as Trujillo had rarely done before in most peasants' eyes. The pastoral letters, moreover, opened up a stunning breach in Trujillo's armor. They presented an open repudiation of official discourse by an alternative source of authority, thus exposing the limitations of the regime's hegemony. The conflict manifested the decline of Trujillo's capacity to rule and the emerging prospects for resistance and change. Under these conditions, for the first time on record, some peasants openly opposed the state.

Nicolás Genao y Genao was from a family of tenant farmers and also worked at the neighborhood *colmado* (store) near the town of La Vega in the Cibao. In the wake of the regime's conflict with the Church, the police sought to prevent residents from attending Mass in La Vega, where the local bishop, the Spanish-born Francisco Panal Ramírez, had become a relatively outspoken critic of the regime.[141] Genao defied these efforts, attending Mass and asking the police rhetorically by what authority they sought to stop him. Genao subsequently heard from a friend in the guardia that the state was organizing a "spontaneous" rally for April 18, 1961, against Panal, and plans had been made to burn down the church (which ironically had been built three years before with $65,000 of Trujillo's "personal" funds).[142] In an interview with Genao in 1992, he recounted how he marched off to the governor's house and warned him: "Prepare yourself. You better have a lot of men, because I certainly do." When the protestors gathered the next day to denounce the bishop and destroy the church, carrying rocks and sticks, Genao and others were waiting for them with similar ammunition. They stopped the protestors from entering the building and eventually forced them and the police to retreat. Afterward, Genao and his correligionaries were imprisoned for attacking demonstrators, and Genao was fired from his job.[143] The church was subsequently desecrated, as elderly residents of La Vega recalled, when regime officials rounded up a number of putative prostitutes, transvestites, and "vagabonds" to dance in the church—some supposedly naked, others dressed like priests—to a pro-Trujillo merengue, "Pidiendo Limosna," with accordion and drums.[144] More surprising still, rather than covering up the sacrilegious invasion, the national press broadcast that some fifty women, "who presumably are prostitutes," had spontaneously disrupted "Mass with merengues and protests," bearing placards that read: "In the church and wherever, we say, 'Viva Trujillo.'"[145] A more graphic abandonment of the politics of respeto could hardly be imagined.

A campaign similar to that unleashed against Panal had been directed against the Boston-born bishop Thomas Reilly in San Juan de la Maguana who, like Panal, valiantly continued to criticize the regime even when the Church hierarchy began backing down. Reilly was slandered in the press, physically harassed, demonstrated against, and threatened with deportation. As in La Vega, Mass was prohibited. And ultimately his church residence and private home were attacked by a crowd led by the infamous Colonel José María Alcántara. Reilly's valuable library was destroyed and his furniture ruined and plundered, as were the church's cars. He and the parish's priests and nuns fled to the capital, where Reilly was later violently apprehended by the military.[146] According to several elderly residents from Mijo (near San Juan de la Maguana) who later spoke with Reilly, a guardia ordered to execute Reilly refused upon seeing that his intended victim was a bishop whom the soldier knew personally. Both Reilly and this soldier were saved from state violence by the fact that Trujillo was assassinated the night of Reilly's arrest and that president Joaquín Balaguer subsequently commanded that Reilly not be harmed.[147] Balaguer had the bishop released and extended apologies to him for his imprisonment.[148] Balaguer's actions suggest that even the erstwhile puppet president and close advisor to Trujillo had strongly opposed the dictator's anti-Church campaign, indicating again that by the time of his assassination, Trujillo was listening only to his more reckless and hard-line advisers.

Trujillo's actions against the Church violated the incredibly wide boundaries within which the regime had been able to operate without generating open opposition, eviscerated the regime's own ideology linking it with the Catholic Church, and ruptured the state's discourse of respeto upon which it had justified its rule as promoting traditional social values. Prior to the Church conflict, though, Genao contended that most peasants in the area had been pleased with Trujillo because he had compelled owners to "lend out" their land and had protected workers from abuse. However, when I asked Genao why he and others had been willing to oppose the regime, he explained: "Simply that [the problem with the Church]. As soon as Trujillo turned against the Church, one could be the biggest supporter of Trujillo, but Dominicans . . . would not accept it. If we live with faith from the beginning of our lives and are baptized Christians, we have to defend our church, its bishops and priests. . . . We defended the bishop against Trujillo and we are still here. And where are Trujillo and his followers?"[149] Although the brave actions of Genao and others in La Vega appear to have been unique, peasants throughout the country expressed to me universal outrage concerning Trujillo's anti-Church actions. After praising just about every aspect of life under Trujillo, Linor de los Santos, an elderly peasant who had received irrigated land from the Trujillo state in Mijo near San Juan de la Maguana, condemned Trujillo's attack on the Church: "The people felt awful, completely awful, about this. It really shocked many people. It was the only conflict that Trujillo had here in San Juan."[150] Similarly Vicente López, from a village in Cotuí, stated: "We believed that Trujillo's government was bad when it conspired against the Church. Not before when all persons had to comply with the rule of law. But at the end, Trujillo was doing things capriciously and that's why he fell in 1961."[151] Like many others, Negrito Viloria from La Vega believed that in the end Trujillo became excessively arrogant "and wished to be more than the Pope. That's when his disgrace came." Another peasant from the La Vega countryside, Elvira Antonia, recounted: "He wanted to be the head of the Church too. All who were Christians felt bad [then] when they said, 'God in the heavens and Trujillo on earth.' People began to say that this man had gone crazy."[152]

When recounting both Trujillo's conflict with the Church and the regime's sweeping peasant evictions, peasants had recourse to a new language of illegitimacy to describe the state. They remembered Trujillo in his final years as "crazy" and megalomaniacal, and his rule as predatory and arbitrary, in a manner echoing academic discourse on the regime as "sultanistic." Particularly in the regions most affected by peasant dispossession or Church-state conflict, such as Monte Plata and La Vega, peasants became, as Priciliano Mercedes put it, "disillusioned" with Trujillo. In his final years, Trujillo's actions undermined the state's propeasant discourse and thus the perceived legitimacy of his regime.

In addition to the Church, Trujillo lost a second major ally in his final years, the U.S. government. And a sudden breakdown in U.S.-Dominican relations exacerbated the regime's moribund image and provided an important impetus for Trujillo's assassins. Unlike in the immediate post–World War II period, U.S. government opposition to Trujillo at this time did not stem from an upsurge in liberal sentiments. Rather, just as the Cold War had linked the two governments for years, it—and specifically the Cuban Revolution—was now driving them apart. As soon as Trujillo's demise began to appear likely because of the escalating crisis faced by his regime—one that appeared akin to that of Fulgencio Batista in Cuba before his fall—the U.S. government sought a role in the transition process to ensure that when change did come, it would not hurt U.S. strategic and business interests nor move in a socialist direction.[153] The U.S. government also needed to distance itself from a dictatorship it had supported for decades to reduce anti-American sentiments after the regime crumbled. And finally, the U.S. State Department was compelled to oppose Trujillo to secure hemispheric backing against Fidel Castro's increasingly socialist and authoritarian regime, which was then its primary foreign policy concern in Latin America. Liberal governments such as Rómulo Betancourt's in Venezuela demanded that dictatorships of the right as well as the left be opposed as a precondition of their alliance with the United States against Castro.[154] Hence in early 1959, despite "the importance of the Island of Hispaniola in the framework of [U.S.] hemispheric defense plans,"[155] the U.S. government again prohibited arms sales to the Dominican Republic and withdrew all its military missions.[156] U.S. officials in Santo Domingo also began cultivating relations with "a moderate group of internal dissidents who appear to meet U.S. requirements," in U.S. officials' imperious words. The loss of U.S. support for Trujillo decreased Trujillo's aura of invulnerability. Specifically, U.S. officials emboldened Trujillo's assassins by making clear that they would immediately recognize and support, rather than resist, a "moderate" force overthrowing the dictator.[157]

By 1960 the Trujillo regime had lost its traditional alliances with the Church, the U.S. government, and even a portion of the peasantry. Also, the formerly solid economic foundations of the Trujillo state were crumbling and, with it, the legitimating discourse of Trujillo as a powerful instrument of national progress. Finally, Trujillo was attacking his enemies counterproductively. The regime's infamous murder in 1960 of Minerva Mirabal, one of the leaders of the 14th of June Movement, and her sisters María Teresa and Patria, also members of the underground resistance, created martyrs of these young women and thus hurt the regime probably more than they would have if they had remained alive.[158] The unprecedented levels of imprisonment, torture, and assassination of the regime's perceived opponents, along with the rupture with the Church, only intensified the resistance to the regime in its final years, as its excesses reached a point at which people "lost their fear" of repression, in the words of historian Roberto Cassá.[159] In the context of declining overall legitimacy and support, state violence mobilized more opposition than it immobilized. Trujillo could not maintain his rule by force alone.

Indeed, under these deteriorating conditions, former supporters of Trujillo and elements within the regime joined the conspiracy against the dictator. And the plotters secured powerful allies in the army, according to one of those involved in the assassination plan, by playing on the "fear that Trujillo's mistakes and appearance of insanity would plunge the country into chaos."[160] The calculus of risks and potential rewards for collaborating with the regime or its opponents was shifting increasingly in favor of the latter. As the Church and the U.S. government had already done, members of the Trujillo state now sought to distance themselves from a crumbling dictatorship.

On May 30, 1961, following months of planning and steady contact with the U.S. consulate and C.I.A., a group of at least fourteen conspirators, including high-ranking officials from within the regime, attempted an assassination and coup d'état against Trujillo.[161] That evening at 10:00 P.M., a reported eight assailants in three cars ambushed Trujillo's unescorted Chevrolet on a quiet stretch of the Malecón between the capital and el Jefe's home in San Cristóbal. Firing dozens of rounds, they killed the sixty-nine-year-old dictator in a dramatic gun battle with Trujillo and his chauffeur. They then stuffed Trujillo's body into the trunk of one of their cars to bring to General José Román Fernández, secretary of the Armed Forces and one of the principal conspirators. Román had demanded hard evidence of Trujillo's death before he would proceed with the planned coup against the Trujillo family. By chance, however, the ambush had been witnessed by General Arturo Espaillat, a powerful figure in the regime's inner circle. Not knowing of Román's involvement in the conspiracy, Espaillat went straight to Román's home to inform him of Trujillo's assassination. Román might have succeeded in carrying out the coup nonetheless, if necessary by shooting

Espaillat. But instead he feigned ignorance of the conspiracy, and this allowed all but two of the plotters to be quickly captured and later killed.[162]

Figurehead president Joaquín Balaguer, along with the dictator's eldest son, Ramfis (then commander of the Air Force), tried to maintain the regime after Trujillo's death through partial liberalization, populist promises, and ultimately the turning over of Trujillo's properties to the state, the nonsugar parts of which were supposed to be redistributed to peasants.[163] But it was too late for the regime's political heirs to pick up the pieces. Its foundations had already crumbled by the time the dictator was gunned down. Without any redoubtable allies, the regime would be toppled with relative ease. In November the Trujillo family was forced to flee the country, and Balaguer soon thereafter, in the face of pressure from a wide spectrum of business and urban groups, dissident elements within the armed forces, and U.S. officials who feared the development of a "Castro-like" opposition.[164] Trujillo's myriad statues were torn down, the formerly official Dominican Party was dissolved, and the name with which Christopher Columbus had christened the capital, Santo Domingo de Guzmán, was restored. A council of state that included the two surviving conspirators of Trujillo's assassination headed a new provisional government. And in December 1962, democratic elections were held. Longtime Trujillo opponent and former exile leader Juan Bosch was elected president on the populist platform of the Dominican Revolutionary Party, which Bosch had founded in 1939 while in Cuba.[165]

But Trujillo's authoritarian legacy was not so easily overcome. In 1963, just seven months into his term, Bosch was ousted by a military coup backed by members of the industrial class and other business groups.[166] The coup would usher in a long period of authoritarianism and quasi-democracy in the Dominican Republic persisting into the late 1990s—corrupt elections, widespread violations of civil rights, and extensive state terror in certain periods, which resulted in the death of some two thousand Dominicans between 1966 and 1972. Joaquín Balaguer, who returned from exile in 1965, again became the country's president in 1966 and ruled the country for most of the following three decades (1966–1978, 1986–1996).[167]

Balaguer's domination of Dominican politics represented, in certain senses, a continuation of Trujillo's regime. Both leaders maintained an authoritarian system, albeit a gradually liberalizing one under Balaguer, while presiding over much infrastructural and economic development —economic modernity (growth) without political modernity (liberal democracy).[168] Balaguer also continued certain facets of Trujillo's agrarian reform—namely, the colonization program. Many new colonies, now known as asentamientos (settlements), were established on lands confiscated from the estates of Trujillo and his inner circle. And this program continued to be a major public policy, encompassing a substantial portion of the peasantry, of the country's farm land, and of its agricultural production.[169]

Yet Balaguer intervened in a profoundly different moment in the nation's history, and hence his rule differed sharply from Trujillo's. When Trujillo captured power, most peasants had not been sedentary agriculturalists. Most land lacked definitive property titles. Much of the countryside remained untamed and sparsely populated. The rural population was still highly dispersed, and the nation—the city and the countryside—appeared to both peasants and elites to be deeply divided, politically and culturally. And the state's reach into rural areas, where the vast majority of the country lived, remained limited and often ineffective. This included the nation's border with Haiti and the frontier regions, where ethnic Dominicans and ethnic Haitians lived far from the vision of a homogenous nation and of firm national boundaries extolled by elites in the capital. As we have seen, all this changed radically during the Trujillo regime through comprehensive agrarian reform, the development of infrastructure, the expansion of state bureaucracy, and an overall project of rural modernization. Dominican society was also radically altered by the unspeakable atrocities of 1937 and 1938 against tens of thousands of ethnic Haitians, the resultant transfiguration of life in the frontier provinces, and official efforts to diffuse a concept of the Dominican nation in opposition to Haitian-ness. Under Balaguer, the state would not play the same role that it had during the Trujillo regime of orchestrating deep structural transformations in the countryside. The nation's centuries-old, relatively autarkic and "nomadic" independent peasantry had already been conquered and, in a sense, seduced by the national state— integrated in and subjected to the state's economic, political, and cultural projects—by the time Balaguer came to power.

Furthermore, while Balaguer perpetuated Trujillo's rural populist discourse, his commitment to small-scale agriculture, and indeed to agriculture in general (including sugar), would wane over time and would be too weak to sustain the country's peasantry—a neglect of the peasantry that, as we have seen, had roots in the late Trujillo years. This weak state commitment was evident in inadequate colonization and land distribution efforts, disregard of roads and irrigation in peasant areas, discriminatory pricing policies that hurt agriculturalists, and minimal credit for small farmers. As a result, by 1980 only 36 percent of occupied land was held by small and medium farmers, compared with 70 percent in 1960 (even after the sugar expansion of the 1950s). Given the dearth of state assistance, even a large portion of the asentamientos have been left idle or underutilized, and more than a third of agrarian reform beneficiaries have been obliged to turn to wage labor for complementary income. By the early 1980s, a country that had been nearly self-sufficient in agriculture under Trujillo was importing an estimated one-fourth of its food.[170] In these same years, foreign investment, tourism, free trade zones (for export processing), and remittances from Dominican emigrants became central to the Dominican economy, further weakening the state's concern with supporting the peasantry and, to some extent, with agriculture in general.[171] At the same time, peasants' growing contact with the city and international currents gave rise to new needs and desires for education and consumer goods, while rural schools and public services suffered gravely from state neglect. In light of these conditions, large numbers of rural denizens have migrated to the cities. In 1981, for the first time in Dominican history, the nation's population was primarily urban.[172] In a vicious circle for the peasantry, this migration has made the popular rural classes a smaller and weaker constituency, hence more neglected by the Dominican state.[173] By the 1980s the Dominican Republic was no longer a peasant nation.

The controlled modernization pursued by the Trujillo regime and its discourse valorizing the peasantry and rural values both eased and coerced peasants into the country's processes of modernity in the twentieth century. Faced with mounting threats to their traditional freedoms by new commercial and state forces, no longer able to head to the monte that had once offered their ancestors refuge from plantation slavery and a racist colonial state, and promised inclusion in the nation's "progress," the peasantry embraced the projects of the Trujillo regime. Yet Balaguer and other post Trujillo governments would gradually shift to a new economic model.[174] They would move the country away from the more self-sufficient, protected, and somewhat isolated nation of the Trujillo years, in which the peasantry and the agricultural sector played key roles in development, and toward an increasingly neoliberal version of modernity. By the 1990s, the Dominican Republic was synchronized with the rhythms of expanding global capital to an extent not seen since the late-sixteenth-century colonial plantation society. And at the end of the 1900s, as at the end of the 1500s, the rural population would find themselves on the move, searching for opportunities and a better life on the margins of modernity. This time, though, they would not head to los montes, but rather to the city, to Santo Domingo, to New York, and beyond.

Notes

The following abbreviations are used in the Notes and Bibliography:

AGI   Archivo General de Indias (Seville)
AGN   Archivo General de la Nación (Santo Domingo)
Exp.   Expediente
FRUS Foreign Relations of the United States
Leg.   Legajo
RG   Record Group from the United States National Archives and Records
         Administration (Washington, D.C., and College Park, Maryland)
SA   Secretaría de Agricultura
SSJA   Secretaría de Agricultura, Sección del Supervisor de Juntas Agrícolas
TST   Tribunal Superior de Tierras (Santo Domingo)

Introduction: The Paradoxes of Despotism

1. Quoted in Ramón Marrero Aristy, *La República Dominicana: Origen y destino del pueblo cristiano más antiguo de América*, vol. 3 (Ciudad Trujillo: Editora del Caribe, 1958), 181.

2. I use the term "peasantry" broadly for all rural inhabitants who rely for their living primarily on their own labor and that of their family (and community) rather than on working as, or hiring, wage laborers. Because probably most rural Dominicans into the twentieth century were as pastoral as they were agricultural, and engaged in itinerant more than sedentary farming, neither "small farmers" nor "smallholders" seems apt for this population. This broad use of the term "peasants" is not meant to disavow the important economic, social, and ideological differences that have existed within this population. Cf. Deborah Bryceson, "Peasant Theories and Smallholder Policies: Past and Present," in *Disappearing Peasantries? Rural Labour in Africa, Asia and Latin America,* ed. Deborah Bryceson, Cristóbal Kay, and Jos Mooij (London: Intermediate Technology Productions, 2000), 2. See also Eric Wolf, "Types of Latin American Peasantry: A Preliminary Discussion," *American Anthropologist* 57 (1955), 452–71; Sidney Mintz, "A Note on the Definition of Peasantries," *Journal of Peasant Studies* 1 (1973), 91–106.

3. In 1935, 82 percent of the population was rural. In 1960, 70 percent of the population remained rural, still one of the highest in Latin America and the Caribbean. Pablo Maríñez, *Agroindustria, estado y clases sociales en la era de Trujillo (1935–1960)* (Santo Domingo: Fundación Cultural Dominicana, 1993), 58; Pedro L. San Miguel, *Los campesinos del Cibao: Economía de mercado y transformación agraria en la República Dominicana, 1880–1960* (San Juan: Editorial de la Universidad de Puerto Rico, 1997), 7.

4. Charles Curtis to Sec. of State, no. 25, 7 Mar. 1930, RG59, 839.00/3357; W. A. Bickers to Sec. of State, no. 587, 21 Apr. 1930, 839.00/3395; cf. Memo. of a conversation with Col. Richard Cutts, 7 May 1930, 839.00/3389; Joseph Cotton to Curtis, 19 Mar.

1930, 839.00/3355; Eric Roorda, *The Dictator Next Door: The Good Neighbor Policy and the Trujillo Regime in the Dominican Republic, 1930–1945* (Durham: Duke University Press, 1998), 27–62.

5. "¿Dónde están los intelectuales?" *Unión Cívica*, 22 Aug. 1962. On the Vásquez period, the rise of Trujillo, and the role of the intellectuals, see Andrés Mateo, *Mito y cultura en la era de Trujillo* (Santo Domingo: Librería La Trinitaria, 1993), 21–63; Arístides Incháustegui, "El ideario de Rodó en el trujillismo," *Estudios Sociales* 18, no. 60 (1985), 51–63; Diógenes Céspedes, "El efecto Rodó, nacionalismo idealista vs. nacionalismo práctico: Los intelectuales antes de y bajo Trujillo," *Cuadernos de poética* 6, no. 17 (1989), 7–56; Francisco Antonio Avelino, *Las ideas políticas en Santo Domingo* (Santo Domingo: Editorial Arte y Cine, 1966); Raymundo González, "Notas sobre el pensamiento socio-político dominicano," *Estudios Sociales* 20, no. 76 (1987), 14–15.

6. Many of those killed were from the Moca and Puerto Plata areas of the Cibao. Félix Mejía, *Viacrucis de un pueblo: Relato sinóptico de la tragedia dominicana bajo la férula de Trujillo* (Santo Domingo: Sociedad Dominicana de Bibliofilos, 1995), 54, passim.

7. Juan Bosch, "Visión de la Era de Trujillo," paper presented at the Museo Nacional de Historia y Geografía, 2 Apr. 1991. See also Joseph Farland to Sec. of State, 14 July 1959, RG59, 739.00; 26 Apr. 1960, no. 86.2–60, Central Intelligence Agency (released to author under the Freedom of Information Act); U.S. embassy to Sec. of State, 13 July 1960, no. 7, RG59, 839.00/7–1360. Historian Theodore Draper stated that when he was in the Dominican Republic during the Trujillo years, he "discovered that . . . the peasants worshiped [Trujillo], and that he could have won honest elections as overwhelmingly as his fixed elections, and that the only ones who seemed disturbed were a few intellectuals and other dubious middle-class characters." Theodore Draper, *Castro's Revolution: Myths and Realities* (New York: Praeger, 1962), 29.

8. I conducted interviews with 130 rural denizens from twenty of the country's thirty provinces between 1992 and 1994. Unless otherwise stated, those interviewed were peasants between the ages of 55 and 110. The great majority of those I spoke with were friends and family of friends and acquaintances of mine from Santo Domingo who introduced them to me directly or indirectly, and thus most interviews began with some degree of trust already established. The small number of those interviewed who were not introduced to me by friends or acquaintances I met in central gathering places, such as local colmados. Most of the interviews were conducted in conjunction with Ciprián Soler, a professor of history at the Universidad Autónoma de Santo Domingo, whose interviewing skills were invaluable in fostering fruitful discussions. Although our interview style varied, we generally began with open-ended questions to allow people to frame their own narratives of the "old days." In response to what was stated, we then became more specific—for example, requesting further information and, as the interview proceeded, sometimes asking about contradictions in their accounts or plausible alternative interpretations. We never pressed people to speak about a subject if they showed any reluctance to do so. I am also drawing on testimony collected in collaboration with historian Lauren Derby in 1987 and 1988 in the Dominican frontier regions.

9. Castillo's comment, "You are only children," referred to me and Ciprián Soler.

Interview with Castillo, Catorce de Cumayasa, La Romana, 30 Dec. 1992. Throughout the book, quotations from oral testimony are my translations. Interview locations are listed by *sección* followed by the nearest municipality.

10. "False consciousness" is Catherine LeGrand's characterization of the mindset imputed in much of the literature to peasants under Trujillo. She controverts this school of thought in "Informal Resistance on a Dominican Sugar Plantation during the Trujillo Dictatorship," *Hispanic American Historical Review* 75, no. 4 (1995), 594–95, passim. For traditional assumptions about peasant adherence to the regime, see, e.g., Roberto Cassá, *Movimiento obrero y lucha socialista en la República Dominicana (desde los orígenes hasta 1960)* (Santo Domingo: Fundación Cultural Dominicana, 1990), 597; Jan Lundius and Mats Lundahl, *Peasants and Religion: A Socioeconomic Study of Dios Olivorio and the Palma Sola Movement in the Dominican Republic* (New York: Routledge, 2000), 162, 522. See also Orlando Inoa, *Estado y campesinos al inicio de la era de Trujillo* (Santo Domingo: Librería La Trinitaria, 1994); Mujeres en Desarrollo (MUDE), *La era de Trujillo: Décimas, relatos y testimonios campesinos* (Santo Domingo: Taller, 1989), esp. 86. On Trujillo's overall capacity to rule for three decades, see Jonathan Hartlyn, *The Struggle for Democratic Politics in the Dominican Republic* (Chapel Hill: University of North Carolina Press, 1998), 45–52; Howard Wiarda, *Dictatorship and Development: The Methods of Control in Trujillo's Dominican Republic* (Gainesville: University of Florida Press, 1968). Two exceptional works treating forms of popular support and ideology under Trujillo are San Miguel, *Los campesinos* and Rosario Espinal, *Autoritarismo y democracia en la política dominicana* (San José, Costa Rica: CAPEL, 1987). See also Lauren Derby's exploration of urban space, political ritual, and state ceremony during the Trujillo regime, "The Magic of Modernity: Dictatorship and Civic Culture in the Dominican Republic, 1916–1962" (Ph.D. diss., University of Chicago, 1998). Other important works on the regime include Frank Moya Pons's study of the formation of a Dominican industrial elite via state concessions under Trujillo, "Import-Substitution Industrialization Policies in the Dominican Republic, 1925–61," *Hispanic American Historical Review* 70, no. 4 (1990), 539–77; Roberto Cassá's history of the economy under Trujillo, *Capitalismo y dictadura* (Santo Domingo: Editora de la Universidad Autónoma de Santo Domingo, 1982), and his study of the working class in the pre-Trujillo and Trujillo periods, *Movimiento obrero*; and Eric Roorda's exploration of U.S.-Dominican relations during the first half of the Trujillo regime, *The Dictator Next Door*. See also the historical-sociological studies of Pablo Maríñez, *Agroindustria*, an overview of commercial agriculture and rural society under Trujillo, and *Resistencia campesina: Imperialismo y reforma agraria en República Dominica (1899–1978)* (Santo Domingo: Centro de Planificación y Acción Ecuménica, 1984), 73–94, an early treatment of the Trujillo regime's rural policies.

11. E.g., Timothy Wickham-Crowley, *Guerrillas and Revolution in Latin America: A Comparative Study of Insurgents and Regimes since 1956* (Princeton: Princeton University Press, 1992), 9; Alain Rouquié, *The Military and the State in Latin America* (Berkeley: University of California Press, 1987), esp. 167.

12. Juan Linz, "Totalitarian and Authoritarian Regimes," in *Handbook of Political Science*, vol. 3, ed. Fred Greenstein and Nelson Polsby (Reading, Mass.: Addison-Wesley, 1975). More recently Linz and Houchang Chehabi have written: "The social

bases of a sultanistic regime are restricted to its clients: family members and their cronies." H. E. Chehabi and Juan J. Linz, "A Theory of Sultanism 1," in *Sultanistic Regimes*, ed. Chehabi and Linz (Baltimore: Johns Hopkins University Press, 1998), 20. Max Weber first formulated the ideal type of "sultanism," which was defined as an extreme version of a personalistic or "patrimonial" state. Max Weber, *Economy and Society: An Outline of Interpretive Sociology*, ed. Guenther Roth and Claus Wittich (Berkeley: University of California Press, 1978), 231–32, 260.

13. See, e.g., Guillermo O'Donnell, *Bureaucratic Authoritarianism: Argentina, 1966–1973, in Comparative Perspective* (Berkeley: University of California Press, 1988), 39–69, passim; Pamela Constable and Arturo Valenzuela, *A Nation of Enemies: Chile under Pinochet* (New York: Norton, 1991); Linz, "Totalitarian and Authoritarian Regimes."

14. Antonio Gramsci, *Selections from the Prison Notebooks of Antonio Gramsci*, ed. Quintin Hoare and Geoffrey Nowell Smith (New York: International Publishers, 1980), 104–6, 161, 170, 244, 326–28; Alain Grosrichard, *The Sultan's Court: European Fantasies of the East* (New York: Verso, 1998), x, 32, passim.

15. Linz, "Totalitarian and Authoritarian Regimes," 259–63; Chehabi and Linz, "A Theory of Sultanism 1," and "A Theory of Sultanism 2: Genesis and Demise of Sultanistic Regimes"; and Jonathan Hartlyn, "The Trujillo Regime in the Dominican Republic," in *Sultanistic Regimes*, ed. Chehabi and Linz; Wickham-Crowley, *Guerrillas*, 9; Rouquié, *The Military*, esp. 167; Robert Fatton, Jr., *Haiti's Predatory Republic: The Unending Transition to Democracy* (Boulder: Lynne Rienner, 2002). An example of the hegemony of the sultanistic model in representations of Trujillo's rule is Alan Knight, "Latin America," in *The Oxford History of the Twentieth Century*, ed. Michael Howard and Wm. Roger Louis (New York: Oxford University Press, 1998), 286.

16. Grosrichard, *The Sultan's Court*, x, 32, passim.

17. Dean Rusk to John Kennedy, 15 Feb. 1961, in *FRUS, 1961–1963*, 617; Cassá, *Capitalismo*, 509. For a midregime breakdown of Trujillo's income sources and mechanisms of enrichment, see J. F. McGurk to Sec. of State, no. 334, 17 Sept. 1945, RG59, 839.001.

18. Frank Moya Pons, *The Dominican Republic: A National History* (Princeton: Markus Wiener, 1998), 365.

19. By one estimate, a third of these properties belonged to the Trujillo sugar industry; another third was farm land cultivated with various crops; and the rest were ranches. Also, the Trujillo family owned extensive pine forests and marginal land, particularly in the San Juan Valley. Ana Gutiérrez-San Martín, *Agrarian Reform Policy in the Dominican Republic: Local Organization and Beneficiary Investment Strategies* (New York: University Press of America, 1988), 46; Marlin Clausner, *Rural Santo Domingo: Settled, Unsettled, and Resettled* (Philadelphia: Temple University Press, 1973), 102–5; *Quinto censo nacional agropecuario, 1960* (Santo Domingo: Dirección General de Estadística y Censos, 1962), x; Lundius and Lundahl, *Peasants and Religion*, 511.

20. Roorda, *The Dictator Next Door*, 97.

21. George Butler to Sec. of State, no. 455, 10 Feb. 1947, RG59, 839.00. The main newspapers when Trujillo stole the presidency, *Listín Diario* and *La Opinión*, were forced out of business in 1940 and 1947, respectively. Trujillo then established new na-

tional papers (*La Nación* and *El Caribe*) in which he personally owned a major share and placed close allies in editorial positions.

22. Jesús de Galíndez, *Un reportaje sobre Santo Domingo* (Santo Domingo: Editora Cole, 1999), 16.

23. Wiarda, *Dictatorship*, 135.

24. Charles Hauch to George Scherer, 19 Mar. 1946, RG59, 839.00; Paul Carr to Richard Johnson, 14 Oct. 1953, RG59, 739.00; William Phciffer to Sec. of State, no. 18, 11 July 1955, RG59, 739.00(w); Ramón Font Bernard, "Trujillo: Treinta años de su muerte," paper presented at the Museo Nacional de Historia y Geografía, 4 Apr. 1991; anonymous interview with one of Trujillo's long-term lovers, Santiago Rodríguez, 1992.

25. Jesús de Galíndez, *La era de Trujillo: Un estudio casuístico de dictadura hispano-americana* (Buenos Aires: Editorial Americana, 1958), 129. In 1946 the journalist Albert Hicks listed 134 victims of political assassination by the Trujillo regime. Albert Hicks, *Blood in the Streets: The Life and Rule of Trujillo* (New York: Creative Age, 1946), 228–30. A probably greater number died from malaria and other diseases while incarcerated, given horrendous prison conditions. See Robert Crassweller, *Trujillo: The Life and Times of a Caribbean Dictator* (New York: Macmillan, 1966), 103. And a still greater number died in the penal colonies described in chap. 6. On repression during the Trujillo regime, see also Mejía, *Viacrucis*, 54, passim; Bernardo Vega, *Control y represión en la dictadura Trujillista* (Santo Domingo: Fundación Cultural Dominicana, 1986), *Unos desafectos y otros en desgracia: Sufrimientos bajo la dictadura trujillista* (Santo Domingo: Fundación Cultural Dominicana, 1985), and *La vida cotidiana dominicana a través del Archivo Particular del Generalísimo* (Santo Domingo: Fundación Cultural Dominicana, 1986).

26. See Crassweller, *Trujillo*, 311–28; Bernardo Vega, *Almoina, Galíndez y otros crímenes de Trujillo en el extranjero* (Santo Domingo: Fundación Cultural Dominicana, 2001). Ironically, Galíndez had himself argued in his thesis that "the Trujillo dictatorship is not so bloody as the exiles assert." *La era de Trujillo*, 129. Galíndez's thesis was published shortly after his death in 1956.

27. Emilio Cordero Michel, "Las expediciones de junio de 1959," *Estudios Sociales* 25, no. 88 (1992), 59.

28. See Crassweller, *Trujillo*, passim; Joseph Farland to Sec. of State, no. 67, 7 Aug. 1959, RG59, 739.00(w).

29. Galíndez, *La era de Trujillo*, 110–22; Crassweller, *Trujillo*, 76–77, 100.

30. Scherer to Sec. of State, no. 11065, 19 July 1946, RG59, 839.00.

31. The book's jacket cover announces that the work contains "events of near incredible grotesquerie, with characters seemingly straight from the pages of penny thrillers." Crassweller, *Trujillo*. Galíndez's *La era de Trujillo* also focuses on the commanding heights of the state rather than society at large. The largest component of Dominican society, the peasantry, scarcely appears in the pages of either book. The absence of citations in both also limits their usefulness to scholars.

32. Several recent studies of particular social groups in the twentieth-century Dominican Republic have already carried out this type of research with illuminating results. See San Miguel, *Los campesinos*; Cassá, *Movimiento obrero*; Moya Pons, *Empresa-*

rios en conflicto: Políticas de industrialización y sustitución de importaciones en la República Dominicana (Santo Domingo: Fondo para el Avance de las Ciencias Sociales); LeGrand, "Informal Resistance"; and Inoa, *Estado y campesinos*, which offers an alternative perspective to my own. See also Jeffrey Gould, *To Lead as Equals: Rural Protest and Political Consciousness in Chinandega, Nicaragua, 1912–1979* (Chapel Hill: University of North Carolina Press, 1990), which analyzes social acceptance of the early Somoza regime among the popular rural classes. For comparative perspective on how deeper analyses of the peasantry can transform our understanding of historical processes, see David Newbury and Catharine Newbury, "Bringing the Peasants Back In: Agrarian Themes in the Construction and Corrosion of Statist Historiography in Rwanda," *American Historical Review* 105, no. 3 (2000), 832–77.

33. Drawing on Gramsci's evocative formulations, I use the term "hegemony" to refer to acceptance of a system that is secured by means other than merely force and the threat of repression, means that range from material benefits to strategic constraints to cultural and subjective forces—e.g., perceptions of the possible and likely alternatives to an existing system. See Gramsci, *Selections*, 104–6, 161, 170, 244, 326–28; Goran Therborn, *The Ideology of Power and the Power of Ideology* (London: New Left, 1980); Adam Przeworski, *Capitalism and Social Democracy* (New York: Cambridge University Press, 1988), 133–204. Noteworthy in the Dominican case is Juan Bosch's statement in the mid-1940s that Trujillo had "succeeded in forming an ideological foundation that already feels natural in the Dominican air and that will be very difficult to overcome, if indeed it ever will be able to be overcome." Incháustegui, "El ideario de Rodó," 54.

34. A clear break with the conventional historiography in this respect is San Miguel, *Los campesinos*, esp. 315–16. Lowell Gudmundson argues that, while generally viewed as an urban and working-class phenomenon in Latin America (as in Argentina and Chile), populist state projects held much appeal among peasant farmers during transitions to intensive agricultural production in a number of cases between 1850 and 1950—Costa Rica, Puerto Rico, *ranchero* Mexico, and Andean Colombia and Venezuela—as I have found in the Dominican Republic. Lowell Gudmundson, *Costa Rica before Coffee: Society and Economy on the Eve of the Export Boom* (Baton Rouge: Louisiana State University Press, 1986), 153–60. A related argument is made in Catherine LeGrand, *Frontier Expansion and Peasant Protest in Colombia, 1830–1936* (Albuquerque: University of New Mexico Press, 1986), 122–23.

35. For similar interpretations, see Pedro L. San Miguel, "La ciudadanía de Calibán: Poder y discursiva campesinista en la Era de Trujillo," in *Política, identidad y pensamiento social en la República Dominicana (Siglos XIX y XX)*, ed. Raymundo González, Michiel Baud, Pedro L. San Miguel, and Roberto Cassá (Madrid: Doce Calles, 1999), 269–89, and *Los campesinos*, 300–322. For other perspectives on land distribution and colonization under Trujillo, see Inoa, *Estado y campesinos*, 86–101; Maríñez, *Resistencia*, 87–88, and *Agroindustria*, 106–9; and Cassá, *Capitalismo*, 129–31.

36. By "moral economy," I am referring to popular notions of economic rights, customary obligations, and limits on what even the powerful may do. See E. P. Thompson, *Customs in Common* (New York: Free Press, 1991), esp. 343, 345; James C.

Scott, *The Moral Economy of the Peasant: Subsistence and Rebellion in Southeast Asia* (New Haven: Yale University Press, 1976).

37. H. Hoetink, "The Dominican Republic in the Twentieth Century: Notes on Mobility and Stratification," *New West Indian Guide* 74, nos. 3 & 4 (2000), 214. On rural mobilization by caudillos, see Bruce Calder, *The Impact of Intervention: The Dominican Republic during the U.S. Occupation of 1916–1924* (Austin: University of Texas Press, 1984), 116–19; María González Canalda, "Desiderio Arias y el caudillismo," *Estudios Sociales* 18, no. 61 (1985), 34; and Mats Lundahl and Jan Lundius, "Socioeconomic Foundations of a Messianic Cult: Olivorismo in the Dominican Republic," in *Agrarian Society in History: Essays in Honour of Magnus Mörner*, ed. Mats Lundahl and Thommy Svensson (New York: Routledge, 1990), 214–15; and Lundius and Lundahl, *Peasants and Religion*, 431–32, 469–92.

38. Emelio Betances, *State and Society in the Dominican Republic* (Boulder: Westview, 1995), 100. Reflecting the growth in bureaucracy, state records increased at an astonishing rate. Whereas there are only two or three packets of annual records of the secretary of agriculture at the beginning of the regime, for the final years there are perhaps sixty or seventy.

39. The history of the Trujillo regime's rural policies is consistent with political scientist James Scott's thesis that official interventions in the name of development and progress function to shore up state power and social control (even if they do not lead to economic advancement). James Scott, *Seeing Like a State: How Certain Schemes to Improve the Human Condition Have Failed* (New Haven: Yale University Press, 1998), passim. Similarly, political scientist Merilee Grindle writes about agrarian reform in Latin America: "The sources and effects of reforms differed throughout the region . . . but a consistent outcome in all countries was the increased influence of the state on economic and political conditions in rural areas. In large part, then, a major beneficiary of agrarian reform initiatives was the state itself." Merilee Grindle, *State and Countryside: Development Policy and Agrarian Politics in Latin America* (Baltimore: Johns Hopkins University Press, 1986), 8.

40. These statistics from 1958 include "land distribution" and "colonization" efforts, the former representing most of the land (308,144 hectares out of 496,079) and the vast majority of recipients (115,829 out of 140,717). To calculate the percentages, I used 1960 figures for total farm land and landholders. The colonization figures include landholdings in the twenty-six colonies in which occupants were officially granted their land as private property in 1953 (and thus at that point these areas stopped being listed as colonies). Manuel Ramos, "La ciudad y el campo: Medidas para contrarrestar la emigración rural," *Renovación* 7, no. 26 (July–Aug. 1960), 55–58; *Quinto censo nacional agropecuario*, x. Certainly, given the biases of statistics produced under a dictatorial government, aggregate figures provided by the regime cannot be relied on completely. Also, they lump together and oversimplify what were complex, varied, and sometimes ambiguous phenomena. What are more certain than official figures are the myriad, specific records of the campaign in the Department of Agriculture files upon which I have relied. Those sources, moreover, are corroborated by the fieldwork I conducted with elderly peasants, including interviews with a number of land recipi-

ents reported in the department's records. Together, these sources illuminate a major, nationwide distribution of land to squatters and landless peasants and suggest a history similar to that represented by official statistics.

41. For comparative perspective on "reconstituted peasantries" throughout the Caribbean, see Sidney Mintz, *Caribbean Transformations* (Baltimore: Johns Hopkins University Press, 1984), 131–56.

42. Michiel Baud has used the term "controlled modernization" for the Trujillo regime in reference to its "constant drive to modernize and transform the Dominican economy and society, without accepting foreign influence and cultural change." Michiel Baud, "'Un permanente guerrillero': El pensamiento social de Ramón Marrero Aristy (1913–1959)," in *Política*, ed. González et al., 191, 210.

43. For a related argument about the development of a clientelist relationship between peasants and the state in the post-Trujillo period, see San Miguel, *El pasado relegado*, 177–82.

44. I have been influenced here by Sheldon Garon's perspective on a similar dialectic in Japanese history. See Garon, *Molding Japanese Minds: The State in Everyday Life* (Princeton: Princeton University Press, 1997), esp. 3–7.

45. Mateo, *Mito y cultura*, 75–78. Thus, in 1908 the prominent intellectual Santiago Guzmán Espaillat titled one of his presentations: "Does the Dominican Republic Constitute a Nation?" Julio Jaime Julia, *Guzmán Espaillat, el civilista* (Santo Domingo: Taller, 1977), 20.

46. An example of this political platform is "Lo que ha hecho 'La Opinión' en dos años de intensa lucha por el prestigio, el engrandecimiento y el porvenir de la República," *La Opinión*, 10 Jan. 1929. This project was also supported by the Nationalist Party, which was formed in 1924 at the end of the U.S. occupation. See Francisco Antonio Avelino, *Reflexiones sobre algunos cumbres del pasado ideológico dominicano* (Santo Domingo: n.p., 1995), 198–201; González, "Notas sobre el pensamiento socio-político dominicano," 14–15.

47. This was the case even in much of the Cibao, the region, along with the sugar zones, where agriculture was most developed. Michiel Baud, *Peasants and Tobacco in the Dominican Republic, 1870–1930* (Knoxville: University of Tennessee Press, 1995), 165.

48. Hoetink, "The Dominican Republic," 220.

49. Calder, *The Impact of Intervention*, 42–43.

50. Juan Bosch, *Composición social dominicana: Historia e interpretación* (Santo Domingo: Alfa y Omega, 1991), 377.

51. Under the 1907 accord, 55 percent of the duties paid went to service the debt and 45 percent was turned over to the Dominican government. Roorda, *The Dictator Next Door*, 14.

52. Hoetink, "The Dominican Republic," 214.

53. Eugen Weber, *Peasants into Frenchmen: The Modernization of Rural France, 1870–1914* (Stanford: Stanford University Press, 1976), 5.

54. Farland to Sec. of State, no. 299, 31 Dec. 1958, RG59, 839.00; Stanley Slavens to Sec. of State, no. 289, 30 Sept. 1953, RG59, 839.12.

55. On the establishment in the period from 1918 to 1950 of the Wilsonian principle that political, ethnic, and linguistic frontiers should coincide, and how this led to

multiple mass expulsions and exterminations of minorities in many countries, see E. J. Hobsbawm, *Nations and Nationalism since 1780: Programme, Myth, Reality* (Cambridge: Cambridge University Press, 1990), esp. 131–34. On anti-Haitianism throughout Europe and the Americas in the early twentieth century, see Laënnec Hurbon, *Le barbare imaginaire* (Port-au-Prince: H. Deschamps, 1987), esp. 88–107.

56. See Nicolás Rizik, *Trujillo y la estadística* (Ciudad Trujillo: Editora Montalvo, 1945), 91–94; Maríñez, *Agroindustria*, 50, 58, passim; Inoa, *Estado y campesinos*, 1/5, 180–85; Pedro L. San Miguel, "The Dominican Peasantry and the Market Economy: The Peasants of Cibao, 1880–1960" (Ph.D. diss., Columbia University, 1987), 101–5, 296–98; Félix Olivares Morillo, *Trujillo y la política del Cacao y del Café* (Santo Domingo: Taller, 1995), esp. 150–52. Overall, economic growth was strong during the Trujillo years, reaching 8 percent per year in real terms in the 1950s. This compares favorably, for example, with Cuba and Haiti during this period, which remained more or less stagnant, and finds analogy with Puerto Rico during its rapid industrial growth under Operation Bootstrap. Arthur Mann, "Public Expenditure Patterns in the Dominican Republic and Puerto Rico, 1930–1970," *Social and Economic Studies* 24, no. 1 (1975), 50, 54; Institut Haitien de Statistique, *Comptes-Nationaux 1954–55 à 1971–72* (Port-au-Prince, 1974); Susan Schroeder, *Cuba: A Handbook of Historical Statistics* (Boston: G. K. Hall, 1982), 568. A revisionist portrayal of the Trujillo regime's counter-developmental effects based mostly on the 1950s state sugar industry is Claudio Vedovato, *Politics, Foreign Trade and Economic Development in the Dominican Republic* (London: Studentlitteratur, 1984). The most comprehensive account of the economic dimensions of the Trujillo regime is Cassá, *Capitalismo*.

57. Ronald Grele, *Envelopes of Sound: The Art of Oral History* (Westport, Conn.: Precedent, 1990), 248.

58. On the problematic character of political liberalism throughout Latin America today, see Guillermo O'Donnell, "Polyarchies and the (Un)rule of Law in Latin America," in *The (Un)rule of Law and the Underprivileged in Latin America*, ed. Juan Méndez et al. (Notre Dame: University of Notre Dame Press, 1998).

59. See Virginia Yans-McLaughlin, "Metaphors of Self in History: Subjectivity, Oral Narrative, and Immigration Studies," in *Immigration Reconsidered: History, Sociology, and Politics*, ed. Yans-McLaughlin (New York: Oxford University Press, 1990), 257.

60. See R. Michael Malek, "Rafael Leonidas Trujillo: *A Revisionist Critique of his Rise to Power*," *Revista Interamericana* 7, no. 3 (1977), 444.

61. On populism in Fulgencio Batista's Cuba at this time, see Robert Whitney, *State and Revolution in Cuba: Mass Mobilization and Political Change, 1920–1940* (Chapel Hill: University of North Carolina Press, 2001), chap. 7; and in Puerto Rico, Ramón Grosfoguel, "The Divorce of Nationalist Discourses from the Puerto Rican People: A Sociohistorical Perspective," in *Puerto Rican Jam: Rethinking Colonialism and Nationalism*, ed. Frances Negrón-Muntaner and Ramón Grosfoguel (Minneapolis: University of Minnesota Press, 1997), 64.

62. Aldo Lauria-Santiago, *An Agrarian Republic: Commercial Agriculture and the Politics of Peasant Communities in El Salvador, 1823–1914* (Pittsburgh: University of Pittsburgh Press, 1999), 235; Jan Suter, "Transformaciones políticas y sociales en El Sal-

vador, 1910–1945: Apuntes para una reinterpretación," presentation at the Tenth Congress of the AHILA, Leipzig, 20–25 Sept. 1993; Victor Bulmer-Thomas, *The Political Economy of Central America since 1920* (New York: Cambridge University Press, 1987), 61–67; David McCreery, "Wage Labor, Free Labor, and Vagrancy Laws: The Transition to Capitalism in Guatemala, 1920–1945," in *Coffee, Society, and Power in Latin America*, ed. William Roseberry, Lowell Gudmundson, and Mario Samper Kutschbach (Baltimore: Johns Hopkins University Press, 1995).

63. Joanna Swanger, "Lands of Rebellion: Oriente and Escambray Encountering Cuban State Formation, 1934–1974" (Ph.D. diss., University of Texas at Austin, 1999), 149–223.

64. Some peasants did receive state land during these years (Swanger, "Lands of Rebellion," 149–223). And a number of sugar *colonos* secured rights of permanent occupancy to the land they farmed, provided they continued to pay their rent and supply the sugar mills with the agreed-to amounts of sugar cane (Whitney, *State and Revolution*, 160). Still, not only did the Cuban government not live up to its land reform promises, but its measures in behalf of squatters were inherently limited in scope, given that they applied only to state land, not to the large areas of haciendas comuneras (jointly owned property similar to the Dominican Republic's terrenos comuneros) then in the process of litigation. In the Dominican Republic, on the other hand, both terrenos comuneros and state lands were distributed to peasants and awarded mostly on the basis of squatters' rights. Duvon Corbitt, "*Mercedes* and *Realengos*: A Survey of the Public Land System in Cuba," *Hispanic American Historical Review* 19, no. 3 (1939), 283.

65. Bert Useem, "Peasant Involvement in the Cuban Revolution," *Journal of Peasant Studies* 5, no. 1 (1977).

66. Michel Gobat, "Soldiers into Capitalists: The Rise of a Military Bourgeoisie in Pre-Revolutionary Nicaragua (1956–1967)" (unpublished paper, 1991); Gould, *To Lead as Equals.*

67. Laura Enríquez, *Agrarian Reform and Class Consciousness in Nicaragua* (Gainesville: University Press of Florida, 1997); Luis Serra, *Movimiento cooperativo campesino: Su participación política durante la revolución sandinista, 1979–1989* (Managua: UCA, 1991), 32–34.

68. Gould, *To Lead as Equals*; Cristóbal Rugama Núñez, *La reforma agraria de Nicaragua* (Managua: Instituto Agraria de Nicaragua, n.d. [c. 1976]).

69. Agrarian reforms then have provided a potent means—though certainly not a guarantee—of avoiding political instability and popular resistance by ensuring land access and rendering the population increasingly dependent on, subject to, and identified with the national state. In the case of El Salvador, one suspects that its agrarian reform in the 1980s was not more successful because the vast majority of the economically active population in 1991 (more than 71 percent) remained landless (at least 52 percent) or tenants (19 percent). See Mitchell Seligson, "Thirty Years of Transformation in the Agrarian Structure of El Salvador, 1961–1991," *Latin American Research Review* 30, no. 3 (1995); Martin Diskin, "Distilled Conclusions: The Disappearance of the Agrarian Question in El Salvador," *Latin American Research Review* 31, no. 2 (1996). In the Dominican Republic, though, only around 6 percent of the rural population were

tenants, and 15 to 25 percent (depending on the time of year) were engaged in wage labor. *Cuarto censo nacional agropecuario, 1950* (Ciudad Trujillo: Dirección Nacional de Estadística, Oficina Nacional del Censo, 1950), vii–xiv, xvii; *Quinto censo nacional agropecuario*, part 1, x–xii, 44–52, 56, 116, 138; part 2, x, xiv. For comparative purposes, see J. Mark Ruhl, "Agrarian Structure and Political Stability in Honduras," *Journal of Interamerican Studies and World Affairs* 26, no. 1 (1984), 33–68; Rachel Sieder, "Honduras: The Politics of Exception and Military Reformism (1972–78)," in *Authoritarianism in Latin America since Independence*, ed. Will Fowler (Westport, Conn.: Greenwood Press, 1996).

70. *Quinto censo nacional agropecuario*, 9.

Chapter 1: Freedom in el Monte

1. Columbus named the island Española, though it was often referred to as Santo Domingo, the name of its capital. Today, "Hispaniola" generally refers to the entire island.

2. Justo del Río Moreno and Lorenzo López y Sebastián, "El comercio azucarero de La Española en el siglo XVI: Presión monopolística y alternativas locales," *Revista Complutense de Historia de América* 17 (1991); Mervyn Ratekin, "The Early Sugar Industry in Española," *Hispanic American Historical Review* 34, no. 1 (1954).

3. Sidney Mintz, "The Localization of Anthropological Practice: From Area Studies to Transnationalism," presentation at the University of Chicago, 6 Nov. 1995. The early emergence of large-scale export agriculture and the rapid elimination of aboriginal societies rendered Caribbean nations "modern" soon after European colonization.

4. See Noble David Cook, "Disease and the Depopulation of Hispaniola, 1492–1518," *Colonial Latin American Review* 2, nos. 1–2 (1993), 214–20. See also Lynne Guitar, "Cultural Genesis: Relationships among Indians, Africans and Spaniards in Rural Hispaniola, First Half of the Sixteenth Century" (Ph.D. diss., Vanderbilt University, 1998), who stresses that although the Taíno peoples were rapidly decimated, some persons of aboriginal descent survived and mixed with other groups, and Indian cultural and linguistic traces remained.

5. Pedro Bonó, *Papeles de Pedro F. Bonó*, ed. Emilio Rodríguez Demorizi (Barcelona: Gráficas M. Pareja, 1980), 192. On the transition from slaves to peasants in Brazil, see Michiel Baud and Kees Koonings, "A lavoura dos pobres: Tobacco Farming and the Development of Commercial Agriculture in Bahia, 1870–1930," *Journal of Latin American Studies* 31, no. 2 (1999), 328–29.

6. For suggestive parallels in the development of the Puerto Rican peasantry, see Angel Quintero Rivera, "The Rural-Urban Dichotomy in the Formation of Puerto Rico's Cultural Identity," *New West Indian Guide* 61, nos. 3–4 (1987); Genaro Rodríguez Morel, "Esclavitud y plantación azucarera en Puerto Rico: S. XVI," in *Esclavos com e sem açucar* (Funchal, 1996), cap. 205.

7. On Caribbean peasantries, see Mintz, *Caribbean Transformations*, 131–56, and "From Plantations to Peasantries in the Caribbean," in *Caribbean Contours*, ed. Sidney Mintz and Sally Price (Baltimore: Johns Hopkins University Press, 1985), 127–54.

8. Michel-Rolph Trouillot, *Peasants and Capital: Dominica in the World Economy* (Baltimore: Johns Hopkins University Press, 1988), 21.

9. Pierre Chaunu, *Sevilla y América, siglos XVI y XVII* (Seville: Universidad de Sevilla, 1983), 73–75.

10. Juan de Echagoian, "Relación de la isla Española enviada al Rey D. Felipe II por el Lic. Echagoian, oidor de la Audiencia de Santo Domingo," *Boletín del Archivo General de la Nación* 4, no. 19 (1941), 446; Roberto Cassá and Genaro Rodríguez, "Consideraciones alternativas acerca de las rebeliones de esclavos en Santo Domingo," *Ecos* 2, no. 3 (1994), 162.

11. Lorenzo López y Sebastián and Justo del Río Moreno, "Comercio y transporte en la economía del azúcar antillano durante el siglo XVI," *Anuario de Estudios Americanos* 49 (1992), 84.

12. Genaro Rodríguez Morel, "Esclavitud y vida rural en las plantaciones azucareras de Santo Domingo. Siglo XVI," *Anuario de Estudios Americanos* 49 (1992), 94, 99–100.

13. "Relación de la isla Española enviada al Rey D. Felipe II por el Lic. Echagoian," 446; Chaunu, *Sevilla y América*, 77; Cassá and Rodríguez, "Consideraciones alternativas," 162. Other estimates of the slave population made in the mid-1500s by Church and state officials range from 12,000 to 30,000, with most around 25,000 (Cassá and Rodríguez, "Consideraciones alternativas," 162n; Carlos Esteban Deive, *La esclavitud del negro en Santo Domingo (1492–1844)* (Santo Domingo: Museo del Hombre Dominicano, 1980), vol. 2, 602–5. Unfortunately, there is no precise figure on which we can rely for the number of slaves. The first official census was not until 1606, after the decline of the sugar industry and the economy overall. It reported a mere 800 slaves working as sugar workers, 6,790 slaves cultivating other crops—mostly ginger—550 slaves laboring on ranches, and 1,556 domestic slaves (including on the sugar plantations) (Deive, *La esclavitud del negro*, 604–5).

14. Cassá and Rodríguez, "Consideraciones alternativas," 165. However, because some slaves were resold and sent to Panama (and other slaves were imported to Santo Domingo as contraband and thus not recorded), one cannot calculate the slave population solely from official records of slave arrivals. In the early sixteenth century, the sugar plantations also used enslaved Indians brought from other islands in the region. Rodríguez Morel, "Esclavitud y vida rural," 92.

15. Quoted in Benjamin Keen's introduction to Alonso de Zorita, *The Lords of New Spain: The Brief and Summary Relation of the Lords of New Spain* (London: Phoenix House, 1963), 23.

16. The mining of precious metals in colonies with large Indian populations also required less extensive credit than sugar plantations, which depended on expensive equipment and enslaved Africans. See Kenneth Andrews, *The Spanish Caribbean: Trade and Plunder 1530–1630* (New Haven: Yale University Press, 1978), 13, 54–80; Rodríguez Morel, "Esclavitud y vida rural," 100–107; López y Sebastián and Río Moreno, "Comercio y transporte"; Río Moreno and López y Sebastián, "El comercio azucarero," 57. Puerto Rico's smaller sugar industry similarly declined at this time. Cuba, though, actually developed a modest sugar industry then, doubtless reflecting Havana's privileged position as the fleet's port of call and Spain's most important military outpost in the Caribbean. See Fernando Picó, *Historia general de Puerto Rico* (Río Piedras: Ediciones Huracán, 2000), 60; Alejandro de la Fuente, César García del Pino, and

Bernardo Iglesias Delgado, "Havana and the Fleet System: Trade and Growth in the Periphery of the Spanish Empire, 1550–1610," *Colonial Latin American Review* 5, no. 1 (1996).

17. Eric Williams, *Capitalism and Slavery* (London: André Deutsch, 1964). In the early 1700s, slaves sold in Cuba for two to three times their price in Jamaica. David Eltis, *Economic Growth and the Ending of the Transatlantic Slave Trade* (New York: Oxford University Press, 1987), 35–36. Nor was contraband a viable option for large-scale sugar production and commerce. See Robin Blackburn, *The Making of New World Slavery: From the Baroque to the Modern, 1492–1800* (New York: Verso, 1997), 138–39.

18. This was also the case in Puerto Rico. Quintero Rivera, "The Rural-Urban Dichotomy"; Michiel Baud, "A Colonial Counter Economy: Tobacco Production on Española, 1500–1870," *New West Indian Guide* 65, nos. 1–2 (1991), 27.

19. E.g., Chaunu, *Sevilla y América*, 68–80; Frank Peña Pérez, "Despoblación y miseria en Santo Domingo en el siglo diecisiete," *Investigación y Ciencia* 1, no. 1 (1986), 83–92.

20. Bosch, *Composición social dominicana*, 117.

21. Similarly, Kimberly Hanger argues that in colonial New Orleans, Spanish neglect was appreciated by the "majority of settlers, slaves, and native inhabitants." Hanger, *Bounded Lives, Bounded Places: Free Black Society in Colonial New Orleans, 1769–1803* (Durham: Duke University Press, 1997), 9.

22. The most complete treatment of slavery in Santo Domingo is Deive, *La esclavitud del negro*.

23. See Antonio Sánchez Valverde, *Idea del valor de la isla española, y utilidades, que de ella puede sacar su monarquía* (1785; repr. as *Idea del valor de la isla española*, Santo Domingo: Editora Nacional, 1971), 169–71.

24. Deive, *La esclavitud del negro*, 157–90, 253–302, 401–500.

25. In 1785, Antonio Sánchez Valverde referred to 12,000 to 14,000 slaves out of a total population of roughly 125,000 persons. Sánchez Valverde, *Idea del valor*, 169. One dubious population estimate published in 1822 indicated that as much as 29 percent of the population was enslaved in 1794. This figure is based on an estimate of 30,000 for the slave population, which would be 16,000 more— more than double—the estimate for the slave population in 1783, 14,000 (which is a more plausible figure). Yet it is doubtful that more than a few thousand slaves entered Santo Domingo during that eleven-year period. See Carlos Larrazábal Blanco, *Los negros y la esclavitud en Santo Domingo* (Santo Domingo: Julio D. Postigo e Hijos, 1975), 184.

26. Larrazábal Blanco, *Los negros y la esclavitud*, 183–84.

27. Ira Berlin, *Many Thousands Gone: The First Two Centuries of Slavery in North America* (Cambridge: Belknap Press of Harvard University Press, 1998), 52–53, 124, 186–87, 212; Frank Tannenbaum, *Slave and Citizen* (Boston: Beacon Press, 1992), 69–71.

28. Information in this paragraph on manumission in Santo Domingo draws on my survey of records in AGN, Archivo Real de Higüey and Archivo Real de Bayaguana, as well as the sources cited below, particularly the work of, and my conversations with, Raymundo González.

29. Raymundo González, "Esclavos reclamaron su libertad en los tribunales de

justicia," *El Caribe*, 14 Dec. 1991. In addition to the notarial records used by González, the proposal made to the Santo Domingo *audiencia* in 1784 to prohibit slaves from buying their liberty "without the consent of their masters" also suggests that this was indeed considered possible. Javier Malagón Barcelo, *Código Negro Carolino (1784)* (Santo Domingo: Taller, 1974), 88. See also the work of Kimberly Hanger on Spanish New Orleans in this period, who found that one out of every seven compensated manumissions was contested by slave owners. Hanger, *Bounded Lives*, 19, 25–27, 49–51, 70–71, 186. The norms governing the cost of freedom for slaves appear to have varied across time and space within Latin America and to have been established largely by custom and legal precedent. Spanish colonial norms for manumission were rooted to some extent in Spain's overall legal codification in the thirteenth century, the *Siete Partidas*, which enabled slaves to purchase their freedom and, in certain circumstances, to gain it automatically. Tannenbaum, *Slave and Citizen*, 50–54; Blackburn, *The Making of New World Slavery*, 50–51; David Brion Davis, *The Problem of Slavery in Western Culture* (New York: Oxford University Press, 1988), 242–43, 265–70. See also Richard Graham, "Free African Brazilians and the State in Slavery Times," in *Racial Politics in Contemporary Brazil*, ed. Michael Hanchard (Durham: Duke University Press, 1999), 31; Rebecca Scott, *Slave Emancipation in Cuba: The Transition to Free Labor, 1860–1899* (Princeton: Princeton University Press, 1985), 13–14, 105–7.

30. Raymundo González, "Campesinos y sociedad colonial en el siglo dieciocho dominicano," paper presented at the Quinto Congreso Dominicano de Historia, Santo Domingo, 24–27 Oct. 1991; Dorvo Soulastre, *Voyage par terre de Santo-Domingo, Capitale de la Partie Espagnole de Saint-Domingue, au Cap-François, Capitale de la Partie Française de la même isle* (Paris: Chaumerot, 1809), reprinted in *La era de Francia en Santo Domingo: Contribución a su estudio*, ed. Emilio Rodríguez Demorizi (Ciudad Trujillo: Editora del Caribe, 1955), 58.

31. Alejandra Liriano, *El papel de la mujer de origen africano en el Santo Domingo colonial, siglos XVI–XVII* (Santo Domingo: Centro de Investigación para la Acción Femenina, 1992), 53–55. A preliminary survey of records in AGN, Archivo Real de Higüey and Archivo Real de Bayaguana, indicated that more than a third of manumissions in these records were freely granted.

32. See, e.g., AGN, Archivo Real de Higüey, leg. 27, exp. 137.

33. Malagón, *Código Negro*, 46; Sánchez Valverde, *Idea del valor*, 170–72; Deive, *La esclavitud del negro*, vol. 2, 405; Larrazábal Blanco, *Los negros y la esclavitud*, 180. For comparative purposes, see Hanger, *Bounded Lives*, 19, 35–37; Kathleen Higgins, *"Licentious Liberty" in a Brazilian Gold-Mining Region: Slavery, Gender, and Social Control in Eighteenth-Century Sabará, Minas Gerais* (University Park: Pennsylvania State University Press, 1999), 44–46.

34. Raymundo González, "Vida de los esclavos en siglo XVIII," *El Caribe*, 3 Apr. 1993. See also Frank Moya Pons, "Dominican National Identity: A Historical Perspective," *Punto 7 Review* 3, no. 1 (1996), 15. Cf. Larrazábal Blanco, *Los negros y la esclavitud*, 177–82.

35. Carlos Esteban Deive, *Los guerrilleros negros: Esclavos fugitivos y cimarrones en Santo Domingo* (Santo Domingo: Fundación Cultural Dominicana, 1997), esp. 72–73;

Frank Moya Pons, *Historia colonial de Santo Domingo* (Santiago de los Caballeros: Universidad Católica Madre y Maestra, 1974), 80–85; Guitar, "Cultural Genesis," 273–75.

36. Deive, *Los guerrilleros negros*, 251.

37. Raymundo González, "Esclavos 'ocultos' fueron fuente de conflicto durante la colonia," *El Caribe*, 1 May 1993.

38. On analogous developments in Puerto Rico, see Quintero Rivera, "The Rural-Urban Dichotomy," esp. 130–31.

39. Raymundo González, "Autonomía de la vida rural fue una característica de evolución de sociedad dominicana en siglo XVIII," *El Caribe*, 10 Aug. 1991, and "Frontera ganadera y dispersión rural caracterizan siglo XVIII dominicano," *El Caribe*, 24 Aug. 1991.

40. Maroons from Saint Domingue founded the village of El Naranjo, for instance, in the southern border areas around 1787. Rafael Leonidas Pérez y Pérez, "La libertad de los esclavos africanos en el Valle de Neyba (siglo XVIII)," *Investigación para el Desarrollo* 2, no. 4 (1998), 37–42. See also Deive, *Los guerrilleros negros*, 91–190; Raymundo González, "Principal motivo de los esclavos franceses para huir a la parte española de la isla era lograr su libertad," *El Caribe*, 8 May 1993; Larrazábal Blanco, *Los negros y la esclavitud*, 165–68.

41. González, "Autonomía de la vida rural."

42. Malagón, *Código Negro*, passim; H. Hoetink, *The Dominican People, 1850–1900: Notes for a Historical Sociology* (Baltimore: Johns Hopkins University Press, 1982), 188–92; Carlos Deive, "El prejuicio racial en el folklore dominicano," *Boletín del Museo del Hombre Dominicano* 4, no. 8 (1977).

43. Larrazábal Blanco, *Los negros y la esclavitud*, 184; Frank Moya Pons, *El pasado dominicano* (Santo Domingo: Fundación J. A. Caro Alvarez, 1986), 102–3; Roberto Cassá, *Historia social y económica de la República Dominicana*, vol. 1 (Santo Domingo: Alfa y Omega, 1992), 109; C. Lyonnet, "Estadística de la Parte Española de Santo Domingo, 1800," in *La era de Francia*, ed. Rodríguez Demorizi, 191. See also Lundius and Lundahl, *Peasants and Religion*, 405.

44. Sociologist Harry Hoetink has portrayed Dominican society from early on as an infinite continuum of racial distinctions based on "shade" and other physical features whose polarities were associated with either European colonists or enslaved Africans, rather than as a predominantly two- or three-tier (black-mulatto-white) racial system. We have evidence of such a continuum beginning in the nineteenth century, at least at the elite level (see below), and it clearly exists today in the Dominican Republic. It is possible that popular prejudices differentiated peasants along an infinite continuum of skin shades and physical features. But we do not have evidence of such prejudices having any salient social or political impact on everyday peasant life. See Harry Hoetink, *Caribbean Race Relations. A Study of Two Variants* (New York: Oxford University Press, 1971); Harry Hoetink, "'Race' and Color in the Caribbean," in *Caribbean Contours*, ed. Sidney Mintz and Sally Price (Baltimore: Johns Hopkins University Press, 1985).

45. Hoetink, *The Dominican People*, 102–3; Moya Pons, "Dominican National

Identity," 15; Deive, *La esclavitud del negro*, vol. 2, 553–98; Silvio Torres-Saillant, "Creoleness or Blackness: A Dominican Dilemma," *Plantation Society of the Americas* 5, no. 1 (1998), 31; Hanger, *Bounded Lives*, 110.

46. Raymundo González, "Libertos en la sociedad esclavista," *El Caribe*, 30 Nov. 1991; personal communication with González, 23 June 1999.

47. Located in the north-central Cibao region, Santiago became an important city during the 1700s following the expansion of trade with Saint Domingue.

48. María Rosario Sevilla Soler, *Santo Domingo, tierra de frontera* (Seville: EEHA, 1981), 89–130; Antonio Gutiérrez, *Población y economía en Santo Domingo, 1700–1746* (Seville: Diputación Provincial, 1985), 99–123, 157–58; Baud, "A Colonial Counter Economy."

49. His Majesty Charles III, Madrid, to Real Audiencia de la Ysla Española, Santo Domingo, 12 Apr. 1786, AGI, Santo Domingo, leg. 969. I am indebted to Raymundo González for lending me this document.

50. Charles III to Real Audiencia, 12 Apr. 1786, AGI, Santo Domingo, leg. 969. For similar developments in Puerto Rico at this time, see Francisco Scarano, "Congregate and Control: The Peasantry and Labor Coercion in Puerto Rico before the Age of Sugar, 1750–1820," *New West Indian Guide* 63, nos. 1–2 (1989), 35–36.

51. Governor Joseph Solano, "Conclusiones de la Junta de Fomento de Santo Domingo," 16 Oct. 1772, AGI, Santo Domingo, leg. 969. Cited in González, "Campesinos y sociedad colonial."

52. See Raymundo González, "Ideología del progreso y campesinado en el siglo diecinueve," *Ecos* 1, no. 2 (1993).

53. Cited in Raymundo González, "La visión del mundo rural dominicano cambió mucho a través del siglo XVIII," *El Caribe*, 31 Aug. 1991. See also Sevilla Soler, *Santo Domingo*, 87.

54. Pedro Catani to D. Pedro Porlier, 15 Nov. 1788, AGI, Santo Domingo, leg. 968. Cited in González, "Campesinos y sociedad colonial."

55. Pedro Catani to His Majesty, "Informe sobre la comisión para capturar el negro incógnito," Santo Domingo, 25 May 1793, AGI, Santo Domingo, leg. 998. Copy courtesy of Raymundo González.

56. Malagón, *Código Negro*, xvii–xix, xlvi; Liliana Obregón, "Black Codes in Latin America," in *Africana: The Encyclopedia of the African and African American Experience*, ed. Kwame Anthony Appiah and Henry Louis Gates, Jr. (Redmond, Wash.: Basic Civitas, 1999). See also Louis Sala-Molins, *L'Afrique aux Amériques: Le Code Noir espagnol* (Paris: Presses Universitaires de France, 1992).

57. Malagón, *Código Negro*, 94, 98, passim.

58. Malagón, *Código Negro*, 162, 164, 171–73, 175–76, 180, 184, 187–88, 192.

59. Malagón, *Código Negro*, lix–lx, passim; Manuel Lucena Salmoral, *Los códigos negros de la América Española* (Alcalá de Henares: UNESCO, 1996), 108–23.

60. Catani, "Informe."

61. See Sevilla Soler, *Santo Domingo*, 75–87, 125–30; Sánchez Valverde, *Idea del valor*, 146n.

62. Baud, "A Colonial Counter Economy."

63. Charles III to Real Audiencia, 12 Apr. 1786, AGI, Santo Domingo, leg. 969; AGN, Archivo Real de Higüey, leg. 10, exp. 88, 24 Apr. 1786; Hanger, *Bounded Lives*, 77. See also estimates of the slave population in Larrazábal Blanco, *Los negros y la esclavitud*, 184, and my discussion of their accuracy in note 25 above.

64. In 1809, with the help of British forces, Dominicans ejected the French and returned to Spanish rule. In 1821, Dominicans declared independence from Spain; in 1822, Haiti occupied and annexed what was then called "Spanish Haiti." In 1844, Dominicans fought for and obtained independence from Haiti. Subsequently Haiti repeatedly invaded the Dominican Republic until 1856, but remained unsuccessful in its efforts to regain control of the entire island. In 1861 the Dominican Republic was annexed to Spain at the initiative of the Dominican government. Almost immediately afterward, however, a "war of restoration" erupted, and permanent Dominican independence was finally achieved in 1865 (save the U.S. military dictatorship from 1916 to 1924 and also the 1965 U.S. occupation).

65. *Secretaría de Estado de Agricultura é Inmigración, Memoria, 1908* (Santo Domingo: n.p., 1909), 10–11.

66. H. Hoetink, "El Cibao 1844–1900: Su aportación a la formación social de la República," *Eme Eme: Estudios Dominicanos* 8, no. 48 (1980), 12.

67. Scarano, "Congregate and Control," 32–33; Ramiro Guerra y Sánchez, *Azúcar y población en las Antillas* (La Habana: Cultural S.A., 1935), 59–60; Violeta Serrano, "La hacienda comunera," *Economía y Desarrollo*, no. 39 (1977).

68. See Robert Ellickson, "Property in Land," *Yale Law Journal* 102, no. 1315 (1993). Ellickson offers a useful typology of land-property regimes distinguishing between private, group, "horde," and open-access property (the last three considered forms of "public property") that range from ownership by a "small number of persons" ("private property") to universal entry privileges (open-access regimes). I am indebted to Rebecca Scott for directing me to this essay.

69. San Miguel, *Los campesinos*, 198.

70. In 1716, e.g., Gregorio Pascual acquired 22 pesos of land in Baiguá. AGN, Archivo Real de Higüey, leg. 16, exp. 61. In the late eighteenth century, Sánchez Valverde referred to accionistas with rights varying from 2.5 to 25 or 30 pesos (Sánchez Valverde, *Idea del valor*, 148–49). See also Antonio Gutiérrez Escudero, "Diferencias entre agricultores y ganaderos en Santo Domingo: Siglo dieciocho," in *Noveno Congreso Internacional de Historia de América* (Seville: Asociación de Historiadores Latinoamericanistas Europeos, 1992), 287–91; Raymundo González, "De la reforma de la propiedad a la reforma rural," *Ecos* 3, no. 4 (1995). In a 1934 compilation of notary records from the early twentieth century, mainly from the Cibao and the Eastern sugar zone, the number of owners in each site varied from 5 to 149, its size from 226 to 6,396 hectares, and the total land pesos of the coproprietors from several hundred to 80,000. "Informes suministrados por los notarios de la República Dominicana sobre el estado de las mensuras y particiones de los terrenos comuneros según la ley del año 1911," Biblioteca Nacional de la República Dominicana, Colección Julio Ortega Frier.

71. AGN, Archivo Real de Bayaguana and Archivo Real de Higüey. Because the number of land pesos in a site was set at the outset while the monetary value of a site

changed over time, the monetary value of land pesos also had to change over time. Land pesos thus became an independent unit with meaning only in relation to the total number of land pesos in a site.

72. Raymundo González, personal communication, 1 Nov. 1992.

73. E.g., land sale of Miguel Agüero and Diego Pérez to Gerónimo Tatabera (spelling not clear), 2 Dec. 1788, AGN, Protocolos Notariales de Avelino Vicioso (notary) and Felipe Sánchez Recio (surveyor), 1893, 1911–12. This document was generously lent to me by Julie Franks.

74. Alfonso Sosa Alburquerque, *Apuntes históricos sobre la propiedad territorial de Santo Domingo* (Santo Domingo: Imprenta Montalvo, 1926), 12–13; Alcibíades Alburquerque, *Títulos de los terrenos comuneros de la República Dominicana* (Ciudad Trujillo: Impresora Dominicana, 1961), 14. Note also Decree no. 4772, 22 June 1907, *Gacetas Oficiales*, nos. 1800–1801, 29 June 1907 and 3 July 1907.

75. For the earliest records I have seen of this form of joint ownership, see AGN, Archivo Real de Higüey, leg. 16, no. 61, 23 Aug. 1716, and leg. 13, no. 23, 16 Sept. 1716. See also Samuel Hazard, *Santo Domingo, Past and Present; with a glance at Hayti*, 3d ed. (Dominican Republic: n.p., n.d.) (originally printed in 1873), 482.

76. AGN, Archivo Real de Higüey leg. 13, exp. 66.

77. Sánchez Valverde, *Idea del valor*, 148–49.

78. The prevalence of squatters caused legal historian José Antonio Bonilla Atiles to conclude that owners almost universally accepted squatting on their lands; otherwise, he argued, there might have been clandestine occupations here and there but never would property rights have been "violated in such an extensive manner." José Antonio Bonilla Atiles, *Legislación de tierras dominicanas: El sistema Torrens* (Santo Domingo: Librería Dominicana, 1974), 172. See also *Secretaría de Estado de Agricultura é Inmigración, Memoria, 1908*, 42. The language of "tolerance" of squatters can be found throughout the records of litigation in the Tribunal Superior de Tierras (Land Court) from 1920 to 1961.

79. See, e.g., Juan Bosch, *La Guerra de la Restauración* (Santo Domingo: Editora Corripio, 1987).

80. In the interviews I conducted, "tierras comuneras" was almost always the term used by elderly peasants to refer to all lands that had had no clear signs of occupation. This understanding of property among peasants is evident as well in court records of land conflicts. See, e.g., "Notas estenográficas de la audiencia celebrada el día 25 de enero de 1962," TST, d.c. 7, San Fco. de Macorís, parcela nos. 91-Bis, 91-Bis–2a, and 91–1. See also Baud, *Peasants and Tobacco*, 62.

81. Pedro Mir, *Cuando amaban las tierras comuneras* (Santo Domingo: Siglo Veintiuno, 1978), 184.

82. Interview with Francisco Eduardo Salazar (born 1902), Nizao, Baní, 28 Aug. 1992.

83. Interview with "Miguel," Batey Lechuga, Ramón Santana, 15 Dec. 1992.

84. Slave rebellions, banditry, and small uprisings also marked this period, particularly the 1790s. See AGN, Archivo de la Nación de la República Dominicana Cortesía del Archivo Nacional de Cuba, leg. 4, signatura 43, 1793–94; Deive, *Los guerrilleros negros*, 216–34; Raymundo González, "El 'Comegente' atacaba personas y pro-

piedades cerca de las poblaciones" and "Para capturar al 'Comegente' comisionó la Real Audiencia a uno de sus oidores," *El Caribe*, 5 and 12 Oct. 1991.

85. Frank Moya Pons, *Manual de historia dominicana*, 8th ed. (Santo Domingo: UCMM, 1984), esp. 219–23. See also Alejandro Angulo Guridi, "Examen crítico de la anexión de Santo Domingo a España," in *Antecedentes de la anexión a España*, ed. Emilio Rodríguez Demorizi (Ciudad Trujillo: Montalvo, 1955), 402–3. On the other hand, free persons of color had not necessarily identified with slaves, as they had not in Saint Domingue either prior to the revolution and emancipation. See Torres-Saillant, "Creoleness or Blackness," 33; Carolyn Fick, *The Making of Haiti: The Saint Domingue Revolution from Below* (Knoxville: University of Tennessee Press, 1990).

86. San Miguel, "The Dominican Peasantry," 30, 32. See also Jorge Machín, "Orígenes del campesinado dominicano durante la ocupación haitiana," *Eme Eme: Estudios Dominicanos* 1, no. 4 (1973).

87. Eltis, *Economic Growth*, 35–36; San Miguel, "The Dominican Peasantry," 16; Hanger, *Bounded Lives*, 9, 11; Herbert Klein, *African Slavery in Latin America and the Caribbean* (New York: Oxford University Press, 1986), 89–112. In Cuba, sugar plantations expanded when taxes were lowered and slave prices fell after the ten-month English occupation of Havana in 1762. But these developments were modest compared with the fantastic growth of slave plantations following the permanent elimination of slave taxes in 1789 and the Haitian Revolution. Louis Pérez, *Cuba: Between Reform and Revolution* (New York: Oxford University Press, 1988), 57–85.

88. See above. Given the substantial emigrations and demographic changes of the early nineteenth century, it is unfortunate that the last slave population estimates are from the late 1700s.

89. Jacqueline Boin and José Serulle Ramia, *El proceso de desarrollo del capitalismo en la República Dominicana (1844–1930)*, vol. 2 (Santo Domingo: Ediciones Gramil, 1985), 129–30.

90. San Miguel, "The Dominican Peasantry," 28–29; Frank Moya Pons, "The Land Question in Haiti and Santo Domingo," in *Between Slavery and Free Labor: The Spanish-Speaking Caribbean in the Nineteenth Century*, ed. Manuel Moreno Fraginals, Frank Moya Pons, and Stanley L. Engerman (Baltimore: Johns Hopkins University Press, 1985), 189. Much remains unknown about this agrarian reform, such as the number of beneficiaries, who the recipients were, and the extent of resistance to it by property owners (or claimants).

91. Machín, "Orígenes del campesinado dominicano," 24, 28.

92. Franklin J. Franco Pichardo, "La sociedad dominicana de los tiempos de la independencia," in *Duarte y la independencia nacional*, ed. Franklin Franco et al. (Santo Domingo: Instituto Tecnológico de Santo Domingo, 1976), 27–34; Moya Pons, "The Land Question," 193.

93. On the other hand, new agricultural taxes were levied that might have been a disincentive to agricultural production. Moya Pons, "The Land Question," 192–93, 197–98; Frank Moya Pons, *La dominación haitiana, 1822–1844* (Santiago de los Caballeros: Universidad Católica Madre y Maestra, 1978), 87–89.

94. Moya Pons, "The Land Question," 203–4.

95. Moya Pons, "The Land Question," 206; Guillermo Moreno, "De la propiedad

comunera a la propiedad privada moderna, 1844–1924," *Eme Eme: Estudios Dominicanos* 9, no. 51 (1980), 52–53.

96. The manifesto represented the struggle for independence more as a revolution against "despotism," "tyranny," and a particular "series of injustices" than as an expression of Dominican nationalism per se. "Manifestación de los pueblos de la parte del Este de la Isla antes Española ó de Santo Domingo, sobre las causas de su Separación de la República Haitiana," Decree no. 1, 16 Jan. 1844, *Colección de leyes, decretos y resoluciones: 1844–1847,* vol. 1 (Santo Domingo: Listín Diario, 1927), 9. There were, though, also grievances rooted in culture and identity, at least for certain (more elite) groups. See Moya Pons, *La dominación haitiana,* 87, passim.

97. Moya Pons, "The Land Question," 193–94, 203–6; San Miguel, "The Dominican Peasantry," 29–30; José Antonio Martínez Bonilla, "Origen de la propiedad agraria en la República Dominicana" (Doctoral thesis in law, no. 125, Universidad de Santo Domingo, 1945), 30–31.

98. Franco, "La sociedad dominicana de los tiempos de la independencia," 27–34.

99. Moya Pons, *La dominación haitiana,* 88.

100. For comparative purposes, see Marshall Sahlins's discussion of the "original affluent society" in *Stone Age Economics* (Chicago: Aldine, 1978), 1–39.

101. Alburquerque, *Títulos de los terrenos comuneros,* 31, supra.

102. Baud, "A Colonial Counter Economy," 39, 40. See also Moya Pons, *La dominación haitiana,* 89–90; Moya Pons, "The Land Question," 198.

103. Cf. Baud, *Peasants and Tobacco,* 37, 41–42, passim.

104. See Verena Martínez-Alier, *Marriage, Class and Colour in Nineteenth-Century Cuba: A Study of Racial Attitudes and Sexual Values in a Slave Society* (Ann Arbor: University of Michigan Press, 1974).

105. See Hoetink, *The Dominican People,* 188; Moya Pons, *El pasado dominicano,* 200.

106. See Franklin J. Franco Pichardo, *Sobre racismo y antihaitianismo (y otros ensayos)* (Santo Domingo: Impresora Vidal, 1997); Silvio Torres-Saillant, "Introduction to Dominican Blackness," Dominican Studies Working Papers Series 1 (1999), 14.

107. Moya Pons, *The Dominican Republic,* 213.

108. Deive, "El prejuicio racial," 90, passim; Hoetink, *The Dominican People,* 189.

109. Rodolphe Garczynski, "Life in Santo Domingo City," *Appletons' Journal* 9, no. 223 (28 June 1873), 839–42. I am indebted to Aldo Lauria-Santiago for sharing a copy of this article with me. On aesthetic racism in the Dominican Republic, see also Deive, "El prejuicio racial," 80–84.

110. Hoetink, *The Dominican People,* 189–92.

111. Cited and analyzed in Pedro L. San Miguel, *La isla imaginada: Historia, identidad y utopía en La Española* (Santo Domingo: Isla Negra and La Trinitaria, 1997), 177, passim.

112. The exceptions to this were the small, heavily populated islands with large sugar industries, such as Barbados, St. Kitts, and Antigua, where there were few opportunities for peasant land acquisition.

113. For comparative purposes, see Sidney Mintz, "Slavery and the Rise of Peas-

antries," in *Roots and Branches: Current Directions in Slave Studies*, ed. Michael Craton (New York: Pergamon, 1979); Mintz, *Caribbean Transformations*, 146–56.

114. Hoetink, *Caribbean Race Relations*, and "'Race' and Color in the Caribbean."

115. See also Silvio Torres-Saillant, "Tribulations of Blackness: Stages in Dominican Racial Identity," *Latin American Perspectives* 25, no. 3 (1998), 126–46; Moya Pons, "Dominican National Identity," 14–25.

116. Raymundo González, "Ideología y mundo rural: 'Civilización y Barbarie,' revistados," *Estudios Sociales* 29, no. 106 (1996), 45.

Chapter 2: Imagining Modernity

1. Avelino, *Las ideas políticas en Santo Domingo*, 68, passim; Avelino, *Reflexiones*, 198–201; González, "Notas sobre el pensamiento socio-político dominicano," 14–15.

2. On the transformation of the elite, see Moya Pons, *El pasado dominicano*, 199–206; Hoetink, *The Dominican People*, 167–69.

3. Antonio Peláez Campomanes, "Memoria sobre el estado actual de la parte española de la Isla de Santo Domingo," 8 Nov. 1860, cited in Machín, "Orígenes del campesinado dominicano," 29.

4. This contrasts sharply with the high person-land ratio in Puerto Rico at the time of 169 inhabitants per square mile. Luis Martínez-Fernández, *Torn between Empires: Economy, Society, and Patterns of Political Thought in the Hispanic Caribbean, 1840–1878* (Athens: University of Georgia Press, 1994), 88–95.

5. Baud, "A Colonial Counter Economy," 41–43.

6. See, e.g., Soulastre, *Voyage par terre de Santo-Domingo*, 59; Angulo Guridi, "Examen crítico de la anexión de Santo Domingo a España."

7. See art. 26, "Ley sobre policía urbana y rural," 2 July 1855, *Gaceta Oficial*, no. 2170, 1 Mar. 1911. Alcaldes pedáneos should not be confused with jueces alcaldes (who generally are also called simply "alcaldes"). The latter are justices of the peace functioning at the municipal level of the court system, or the *alcaldía*, and deciding on local and petty crimes.

8. Regulation for the commune of Santo Domingo, no. 95, 19 Oct. 1846, and Regulation for the communes of Seibo and Higüey, no. 98, 21 Jan. 1847, *Colección de leyes, decretos y resoluciones*, vol. 1 (Santo Domingo: Imprenta de García Hermanos, 1880); Law no. 147, 23 June 1848, *Colección de leyes, decretos y resoluciones*, vol. 2 (Santo Domingo: Listín Diario, 1927); "Ley sobre policía urbana y rural," 2 July 1855, and "Ley sobre la represión del ocio i la vagancia," 11 June 1855, *El Porvenir*, 14 Mar. 1875; Wenceslao Vega, "El régimen laboral y de tierras en la Primera República," *Eme Eme: Estudios Dominicanos* 5, no. 30 (1977), 18–22; Clausner, *Rural Santo Domingo*, 96–97.

9. "Ley sobre la represión del ocio i la vagancia"; Regulations no. 95 and no. 98; Law no. 147.

10. See, e.g., McCreery, "Wage Labor," 206–31.

11. See "Ley sobre policía urbana y rural," 1855; Baud, *Peasants and Tobacco*, 166–67.

12. See, e.g., arts. 11–13, Law no. 147.

13. See Law no. 147. On state incentives promised to farmers to grow cash crops

that were, most likely, never implemented, see Félix Olivares Morillo, *Caficultura y legislación agrícola en el siglo diecinueve* (Santo Domingo: San Rafael, 1980), 90–91.

14. Law no. 147; "Ley sobre policía urbana y rural"; Bonilla Atiles, *Legislación de tierras dominicanas*, 171.

15. Bonó, *Papeles*, 82n; José Ramón Abad, *La República Dominicana: Reseña general geográfico-estadística* (Santo Domingo: Imprenta de García Hermanos, 1888), 264–65.

16. Martínez-Fernández, *Torn between Empires*, 92–93.

17. Hoetink, *The Dominican People*, 96, 100.

18. James Scott and B. J. Kerkvliet, "How Traditional Rural Patrons Lose Legitimacy," *Cultures et développement: Revue internacionale des sciences du développement* 5, no. 3 (1973), 525.

19. Hoetink, *The Dominican People*, 51–52.

20. Bonilla Atiles, *Legislación de tierras dominicanas*, 172; *Secretaría de Estado de Agricultura é Inmigración, Memoria, 1908*, 42; "Los terrenos comuneros y los productos para la exportación," *Listín Diario*, 24 July 1895; "Terrenos comuneros: Notable é importante resolución," *Listín Diario*, 25 Nov. 1895; "Mensura de terrenos comuneros en Los Llanos," *El Eco de la Opinión*, 5 Jan. 1895. In a few sites, owners purportedly did manage to curb squatters in accordance with the new laws and even to require a minimum number of land pesos for full use rights in the area. W. S. Courtney, "Los campos de oro de Santo Domingo," in *Riqueza mineral y agrícola de Santo Domingo*, ed. Emilio Rodríguez Demorizi (Santo Domingo: Editora del Caribe, 1965), 106; U.S. Commission of Inquiry, *Report of the Commissioner of Inquiry to Santo Domingo* (Washington, D.C.: Government Printing Office, 1871), 276, 278; Moya Pons, "The Land Question," 188, 193; Hazard, *Santo Domingo, Past and Present*, 36.

21. Fernando Ravelo de la Fuente, *Jurisprudencia del Tribunal de Tierras: Sentencias del Tribunal Superior de Tierras, y de Jurisdicción Original en materia posesoria, correspondientes a los años 1939, 1940, 1941, 1942 y 1943* (Ciudad Trujillo: Luis Sánchez Andujar, 1947), 495–501; José Ramón López, "La caña de azúcar en San Pedro de Macorís, desde del bosque virgen hasta el mercado," *Ciencia* 2, no. 3 (1975).

22. "Illegible" is James Scott's term. See Scott, *Seeing Like a State*, passim.

23. See, e.g., Regulation no. 95. See also Jaime de Jesús Domínguez, *La dictadura de Heureaux* (Santo Domingo: Editora Universitaria, 1986), 208; "D. Emiliano Tejera: Su notable carta al interventor de aduana: La crianza libre," *Listín Diario*, 24 and 26 Nov. 1894.

24. "D. Emiliano Tejera: Su notable carta"; Emiliano Tejera, "Párrafos de las memorias presentadas por D. Emiliano Tejera en su calidad de ministro de Relaciones Exteriores, al presidente de la República en los años 1906–1907 i 1908," *Clio*, no. 51 (1942), 14–15. See also José Ramón Abad, "La crisis agrícola-comercial, I" and "La crisis agrícola-comercial, IV," *Listín Diario*, 26 and 31 Jan. 1895; Bonó, *Papeles*, 225.

25. Abad, "La crisis agrícola-comercial, III," *Listín Diario*, 29 Jan. 1895.

26. Sahlins, *Stone Age Economics*, 1–39; Abad, *La República Dominicana*, 297–98.

27. Interview with Juan Justo, Higüey, 31 July 1992. The nostalgic sentiments expressed today by peasants echo attitudes reportedly prevailing when the pastoral

economy still existed. See Tejera, "Párrafos de las memorias presentadas por D. Emiliano Tejera," 15.

28. Interview with Antonio (Papito) Amparo, Cedro, Miches, 2 Aug. 1992.

29. Interview with Negro Castillo, Bonao, Higüey, 18 July 1992.

30. Interview with Francisco Soriano, Ramón Santana, 23 Dec. 1992.

31. Interview with José Mota Rivera, Ramón Santana, 17 Dec. 1992.

32. Interview with Mariano d'Oleo Mesa, El Cercado, San Juan de la Maguana, 3 Oct. 1992.

33. The term "imagined community" is appropriated from Benedict Anderson, *Imagined Communities* (London: Verso, 1994).

34. Interview with Juan Bautista Mercedes, El Regajo, Ramón Santana, 18 Dec. 1992.

35. Interviews with Negro Castillo, Bonao, Higüey, 18 July 1992, and Reyes García Rodríguez, Carril de Haina, San Cristóbal, 27 Jan. 1993.

36. Interview with Francisco Soriano, Ramón Santana, 23 Dec. 1992.

37. *Secretaría de Estado de Agricultura é Inmigración, Memoria, 1908*, 33.

38. Sec. de E. de Fomento y Obras Públicas, *Ley sobre crianza de animales domésticos de pasto* (Santo Domingo: Imprenta de García Hermanos, 1895), 9–10.

39. Resolution no. 3957, 23 Feb. 1900, and Decree no. 4043, 21 June 1900, *Colección de leyes, decretos y resoluciones*, vol. 16 (Santo Domingo: Listín Diario, 1929); Emiliano Tejera to Heureaux, 19 Oct. 1895 in *Clío* 9, nos. 49–50 (1941), 194–95; García Rodríguez, "De la ley sobre crianza"; Domínguez, *La dictadura de Heureaux*, 208–9; Miguel Pichardo to Ulises Heureaux, 30 Aug. 1895, *Presidencia de la República, copiadores de Ulises Heureaux*, vol. 47, 578. A transcription of Pichardo's letter was generously loaned to me by Cyrus Veeser.

40. See this and reports by other inspectors in *Documentos anexos a la memoria que presenta el Secretario de Estado de Agricultura é Inmigración, 1908* (Santo Domingo: n.p., 1909). See also "Una voz de aliento," *Revista de Agricultura* 1, no. 13 (1906), 214; *Gaceta Oficial* 25, no. 1879 (1 Apr. 1908).

41. *Revista de Agricultura* 7, no. 2 (1911), 38–42.

42. Quoted in Bryan, "La producción campesina," 54. Closure of the open range would be carried out on a community-by-community basis mostly during the Trujillo regime. See Dominican Republic, *Censo agro-pecuario, 1940: Resumen nacional* (Ciudad Trujillo: Dirección General de Estadística Nacional, 1940), 2; Héctor B. Goico, *Guía Policial* (Ciudad Trujillo: Editora Montalvo, 1949), 76–77; Ernest Charles Palmer, "Land Use and Landscape Change along the Dominican-Haitian Borderlands" (Ph.D. diss., University of Florida, 1976), 108.

43. García, "La ley sobre crianza"; Domínguez, *La dictadura de Heureaux*, 208–9. On the formation of new Dominican elites, see Hoetink, *The Dominican People*, 165–77; Moya Pons, *El pasado dominicano*, 199–206; Baud, *Peasants and Tobacco*, esp. 109–14; Julie Franks, "Transforming Property: Strategies of Political Power and Land Accumulation in the Dominican Sugar Region, 1880–1930" (Ph.D. diss., State University of New York at Stony Brook, 1997), chap. 3. Sugar colonos were planters, either landowners or tenants, contracted to sell their crops to the mills.

44. Baud, *Peasants and Tobacco*, 162; Domínguez, *La dictadura de Heureaux*, 208–9. On the transformation of the San Juan de la Maguana area from cattle ranching to agriculture by the late 1920s, see Lundius and Lundahl, *Peasants and Religion*, 461–502, 514. This transformation did not give rise to a concentration of land in the hands of a few large landowners. Instead, small and medium farmers continued to prevail through the Trujillo years.

45. Hoetink, *The Dominican People*, 177.

46. Olivares, *Caficultura*, 115–21; Michiel Baud, "Transformación capitalista y regionalización en la República Dominicana, 1875–1920," *Investigación y Ciencia* 1, no. 1 (1986), 22–24; Baud, "The Origins of Capitalist Agriculture," 136–39; San Miguel, "The Dominican Peasantry," 40–42; Moya Pons, *Manual de historia dominicana*, 363–64, 405.

47. Baud, *Peasants and Tobacco*, 63–64, 71–72, 109, 164, passim; Hoetink, *The Dominican People*, 172–73.

48. On attitudes toward foreign capital, see Olivares, *Caficultura*, 80–120; Baud, "The Origins of Capitalist Agriculture," 141–42; Moya Pons, *Manual de historia dominicana*, 407–8; "En la elaboración del azúcar está la salvación del país," *Gacetas Oficiales*, nos. 177, 178, 180, 181 (25 June 1877, 1 July 1877, 16 July 1877, 2 Aug. 1877). On the Dominican sugar industry and land accumulation, see José del Castillo, "The Formation of the Dominican Sugar Industry: From Competition to Monopoly, from National Semiproletariat to Foreign Proletarian," in *Between Slavery and Free Labor*, ed. Moreno Fraginals et al.; Humberto García-Muñiz, "The South Porto Rico Sugar Company: The History of a United States Multinational Corporation in Puerto Rico and the Dominican Republic, 1900–1921" (Ph.D. diss., Columbia University, 1997), esp. 262–67, 411; Franks, "Transforming Property," chap. 3.

49. On peasants' relationship to the market in the nineteenth- and twentieth-century Cibao, see Baud, *Peasants and Tobacco*; San Miguel, *Los campesinos*.

50. See Doug Yarrington, *A Coffee Frontier: Land, Society, and Politics in Duaca, Venezuela, 1830–1936* (Pittsburgh: University of Pittsburgh Press, 1997), esp. 201–8. For comparative purposes, see also LeGrand, *Frontier Expansion*; Gudmundson, *Costa Rica before Coffee*; Laird Bergad, *Coffee and the Growth of Agrarian Capitalism in Nineteenth-Century Puerto Rico* (Princeton: Princeton University Press, 1983); Fernando Picó, *Libertad y servidumbre en el Puerto Rico del siglo xix (los jornaleros utuadeños en vísperas del auge del café)* (Río Piedras: Ediciones Huracán, 1979), and *Amargo café (los pequeños caficultores de Utuado en la segunda mitad del siglo xix)* (Río Piedras: Ediciones Huracán, 1981); William Roseberry, *Coffee and Capitalism in the Venezuelan Andes* (Austin: University of Texas Press, 1983); Mario Samper, *Generations of Settlers: Rural Households and Markets on the Costa Rican Frontier, 1850–1935* (Boulder: Westview, 1990); Florencia E. Mallon, *The Defense of Community in Peru's Central Highlands: Peasant Struggle and Capitalist Transition, 1860–1940* (Princeton: Princeton University Press, 1983); Brooke Larson, *Colonialism and Agrarian Transformation in Bolivia: Cochabamba, 1550–1900* (Princeton: Princeton University Press, 1988).

51. Cf. Bonó, *Papeles*, 223, 263.

52. "Crísis," *Eco de la Opinión*, 25 July 1884; "D. Emiliano Tejera: Su notable carta"; Abad, *La República Dominicana*, 263; Hoetink, *The Dominican People*, 12–13.

53. Bernardo Vega, *Trujillo y Haití*, vol. I *(1930–1937)* (Santo Domingo: Fundación Cultural Dominicana, 1988), 20.

54. Antonio Lluberes, "La larga crisis azucarera, 1884–1902," *Estudios Sociales* 23, no. 81 (1990); Bonham Richardson, *Economy and Environment in the Caribbean: Barbados and the Windwards in the late 1800s* (Gainesville: University Press of Florida, 1998).

55. Interview with Tavares Blanc, Loma de Cabrera, 16 Jan. 1993.

56. Interview with Bernabel (Guadalupe) Gil, Paso de El Medio, El Seibo, 17 Dec. 1992.

57. Bonó, *Papeles*, 327, 281.

58. Baud writes: "The groups of men traveling through the countryside, drinking and waiting for work in the *ventorillas* (the roadside shops), were objects of disgust and fear" ("The Origins of Capitalist Agriculture," 146–48; cf. Hoetink, *The Dominican People*, 14–17).

59. "De actualidad (colaboración)," *El Eco de la Opinión*, 5 Mar. 1892.

60. Eugenio María de Hostos, "Falsa alarma, crisis agrícola," in *Hostos en Santo Domingo*, ed. Emilio Rodríguez Demorizi, vol. 1 (Ciudad Trujillo: Imp. J. R. Vda. García, 1939), 162–63, 172; Lundius and Lundahl, *Peasants and Religion*, 450, 462–63.

61. E.g., Rafael Abreu Licairac, "La agricultura en el Cibao," *Eco de la Opinión*, 2 Sept. 1893.

62. Roorda, *The Dictator Next Door*, 13–15.

63. Rafael Abreu Licairac, *La cuestión palpitante* (Santo Domingo: Listín Diario, 1906), 27–32. Another example counterposing the Cibao and the East is Enrique Jiménez, *Sobre economía social americana* (Santo Domingo: n.p., 1932).

64. López, "La caña de azúcar," 133.

65. See, e.g., *Secretaría de Estado de Agricultura é Inmigración, Memoria, 1908*; José Ramón López, *Censo y catastro de la común de Santo Domingo: Informe que al honorable ayuntamiento presenta el director del censo y catastro de 1919* (Santo Domingo: El Progreso, 1919), 50. See also the entire run of *Revista de Agricultura* commencing in 1905.

66. Law no. 4577, 9 June 1905, *Gaceta Oficial*, no. 1598, 17 June 1905; Ley sobre franquicias agrícolas, 26 June 1911, *Gaceta Oficial*, no. 2207, 8 July 1911. Ironically, the 1911 law was repealed by the U.S. military government (Exec. Order no. 286, 3 May 1919, *Gaceta Oficial*, no. 3010, 10 May 1919). See also Baud, *Peasants and Tobacco*, 150–52.

67. Moya Pons, *Manual de historia dominicana*, 427–73; Julio Campillo Pérez, *Elecciones dominicanas (contribución a su estudio)*, 2d ed. (Santo Domingo: Academia Dominicana de la Historia, 1978), 433–36.

68. *Boletín del Congreso*, no. 17, 8 June 1911; José Ramón López, "La especulación de las tierras," *El Tiempo*, 18 and 22 Oct. 1910; José Ramón López, "La tierra," *El Nacional*, 16 Nov. 1911 (republished in José Ramón López, *Ensayos y artículos*, ed. Manuel Rueda (Santo Domingo: Fundación Corripio, 1991), 215–17). See also, e.g., "El problema de la tierra," *Listín Diario*, 14 July 1927. On the development of sugar in the Barahona area, see Lundius and Lundahl, *Peasants and Religion*, 448–50.

69. Mateo, *Mito y cultura*, 58–78n; Incháustegui, "El ideario de Rodó"; Céspedes, "El efecto Rodó."

70. Throughout the Hispanic Caribbean and Haiti, the creole farmer became, in

varying ways, a nationalist symbol during the 1920s. Arcadio Díaz-Quiñones, "The Hispanic-Caribbean National Discourse: Antonio S. Pedreira and Ramiro Guerra y Sánchez," in *Intellectuals in the Twentieth-Century Caribbean*, ed. Alistair Hennessy, vol. 2 (New York: Macmillan, 1992); Silvia Alvarez Curbelo, "La mirada en la tierra (imaginario de los propietarios antillanos en la década de los '20), *Revista Interamericana* 18, no. 2 (1988); Hans Schmidt, *The United States Occupation of Haiti, 1915–1934* (New Brunswick: Rutgers University Press, 1971, 1995), 150–51.

71. The ambiguity of land ownership in the Dominican Republic was not unique among the open-range economies that prevailed into the nineteenth century in certain parts of Latin America. In Costa Rica, e.g., historian Lowell Gudmundson found that in ranching areas "land tenure, even for the precoffee wealthy, was not fundamentally a system of private, exclusively held property. . . . The wealthy saw no need for, nor practical possibility of, denying ready access to annual planting lands" and pasture. Lowell Gudmundson, "Peasant, Farmer, Proletarian: Class Formation in a Smallholder Coffee Economy, 1850–1950," *Hispanic American Historical Review* 69, no. 2 (1989), 228–29.

72. Franks, "Transforming Property," 105.

73. Raymundo González, "De la reforma de la propiedad a la reforma rural"; Gutiérrez Escudero, "Diferencias entre agricultores y ganaderos."

74. San Miguel, "The Dominican Peasantry," 227.

75. See Francisco Moscoso Puello's critical portrait of the sugar industry in his novel, *Cañas y bueyes* (Santo Domingo: Amigo del Hogar, 1975), first published in 1936 during Trujillo's rule.

76. The legal procedures used for these divisions came from parts of the country's Civil Code pertaining to the division of estates bequeathed to multiple heirs. Sosa Alburquerque, *La propiedad territorial*, 13–15; Ruíz Tejada, *La propiedad inmobiliaria*, 27, 74–75; Bonilla Atiles, *Legislación de tierras dominicanas*, 355; Juan Sánchez, *La caña en Santo Domingo* (Santo Domingo: Taller, 1972), 60; "Mensura de terrenos comuneros en Los Llanos," *El Eco de la Opinión*, 5 Jan. 1895; Vetilio Alfau Durán, "La agricultura en Higüey," *Listín Diario*, 12 Nov. 1938; San Miguel, "The Dominican Peasantry," 220–25; Adolf Berle, "Memorandum on Comunero Land System," circa 1918, 31–34, in possession of Roberto Cassá. I am indebted to Professor Cassá for lending me this document.

77. Francisco J. Peynado, "Deslinde, mensura y partición de terrenos," *Revista Jurídica*, no. 4 (1919); Octavio A. Acevedo, *Tópicos técnicos*, vol. 2 (Santo Domingo: n.p., 1919), 67–79; Central Romana et al., "¡Escandaloso! Protesta de los Hacendados sobre las particiones de terrenos," *Listín Diario*, 27 Feb. 1915; Alburquerque, *Los terrenos comuneros*, esp. 81–83, 147–60; M. de J. Camarena Perdomo, "Los motivos de la Ley de Registro de Tierras," *Anales de la Universidad de Santo Domingo* (Ciudad Trujillo: Listín Diario, Apr. 1938), 130–41.

78. Very few of the more than one hundred elderly peasants I spoke with from throughout the country had ever possessed titles.

79. For examples, see Ravelo, *Jurisprudencia*, 44, 341–51, 538–39; and Freddy Prestol Castillo, *Jurisprudencia de tierras en la era de Trujillo: El litigio catastral en la Suprema Corte de Justicia, años desde 1930 hasta 1956* (Ciudad Trujillo: Del Caribe, 1957), 298.

80. Jorge Valdez, *Un siglo de agrimensura en la República Dominicana* (Santo Domingo: Ediciones Tres, 1981), 25.

81. Lands surveyed to Nicanor Pérez in 1914 reportedly had been previously surveyed to Miguel Febles in 1893. See TST, d.c. 2, part 8, *parcela* (plot) no. 367. On private surveys in the San Juan region, see Lundius and Lundahl, *Peasants and Religion*, 513.

82. Emiliano Castillo Sosa, "Situación actual de la mensura y partición de los terrenos comuneros" (Doctoral thesis in law, no. 21, Universidad de Santo Domingo, 1942), 35. According to Castillo, 162 sites had been submitted to land divisions under the 1911 law. (For notary accounts of these proceedings, see "Informes suministrados por los notarios.") However, only a modest portion of these divisions were ever completed due, among other things, to inadequate private funds, competing claims, and subsequent legislation that interrupted and superseded the 1911 procedures, as described below.

83. Ravelo, *Jurisprudencia*, 498.

84. Law no. 5089, 25 May 1912, *Gaceta Oficial*, no. 2031, 1 June 1912.

85. The concept of prescription, while extant in Greece, was first elaborated in Roman law, and later assimilated into Spanish jurisprudence, developed in the *Siete Partidas* of Alfonso X in the thirteenth century. Although the laws promulgated for the Spanish colonies contained no specific doctrine concerning prescription, it was affirmed in relationship to royal lands from early on. In 1566, e.g., Philip II ordered that "possession from time immemorial, being proven according to the conditions of the Law of Foro . . . is sufficient to acquire [property] from Us and our successors." Martínez Bonilla, "Origen de la propiedad agraria en la República Dominicana," 19. See also Ots Capdequí, *El régimen de la tierra*, 155–63.

86. Manuel Ramón Ruíz Tejada, *Estudio sobre la propiedad inmobiliaria en la República Dominicana* (Santo Domingo: Taller, 1990), 25; *Código Civil de la República Dominicana*, ed. Fabio T. Rodríguez (Ciudad Trujillo: Editora Montalvo, 1950), 376–82.

87. Until 1912 most writers implicitly rejected the applicability of prescription rights in terrenos comuneros and condemned their use by those without sufficient peso titles. E.g., "Los terrenos comuneros y los productos para la exportación," *Listín Diario*, 24 July 1895; "Terrenos comuneros: Notable e importante resolución," *Listín Diario*, 25 Nov. 1895; Francisco M. García Rodríguez, "Mensura jeneral," *El Eco de la Opinión*, 14 Oct. 1893 and 25 Nov. 1893. Similarly, the authors of Cuba's 1902 Law no. 62 to dismantle that nation's analogous system of haciendas comuneras rejected a proposal to permit occupants to prescribe against co-owners as an "attempt upon sacred rights" and condemned the "occupation of vast areas by tenants in *comuneros* without titles . . . [as an] anti-juridical and violent condition . . . which can never be sanctioned by the State." Leopoldo Cancio, Rafael Cruz Pérez, and Octavio Giberga, "No. 62," *Gaceta de la Habana* 64, no. 55 (5 Mar. 1902). See also Antero Regalado, *Las luchas campesinas en Cuba* (Havana: Departamento de Orientación Revolucionario del Comité Central del Partido Comunista de Cuba, 1974), 44–58.

88. "Un asunto grave," *Listín Diario*, 19 June 1915. For another example, see Felipe A. Cartagena hijo, Public Notary, 10 Oct. 1934, "Informe sobre los terrenos comuneros."

89. Since the turn of the century the term "gavilleros" had been used by the press and government, at least, to refer to bandits, some of whom others considered revolutionaries. See María Filomena González Canalda, "Gavilleros, 1904–1924," paper presented at the Quinto Congreso Dominicano de Historia, 24–27 Oct. 1991; and, e.g., "De nuevo los rumores políticos," *Listín Diario*, 7 July 1915. On the gavilleros, see also Calder, *The Impact of Intervention*, chaps. 5–7, esp. 120; Peynado, "Deslinde, mensura y partición de terrenos," 3; Julie Franks, "The Gavilleros of the East: Social Banditry as Political Practice in the Dominican Sugar Region, 1900–1924," *Journal of Historical Sociology* 8, no. 2 (1995); María Filomena de Silié, untitled paper delivered at the conference "Trujillo: Treinta años de su muerte," Santo Domingo, 9 Apr. 1991; García-Muñiz, "The South Porto Rico Sugar Company," 414–28; Roberto Cassá, "Gavillerismo, delito común y sector azucarero en el Este," *Isla Abierta* (supplement to *Hoy*), 2 Dec. 1994, and "Emergencia del gavillerismo frente a la ocupación militar," *Isla Abierta* (supplement to *Hoy*) 3 Mar. 1995; Lundius and Lundahl, *Peasants and Religion*, esp. 477–79. "Information Delivered Verbally by Messenger at the Request of A. T. Bass and H. W. Turner, Respectively Manager and Assistant Manager of the Consuelo Sugar Company, San Pedro de Macorís, Dominican Republic," 26 Oct. 1918, RG59, M626, roll 69; and, e.g., "Horroroso incendio en Neyba" and "Noticias de la revolución," *Listín Diario*, 14 July 1914, and "Ataques gavilleros en campos de Puerto Plata," *Listín Diario*, 16 Aug. 1915. On peasant attitudes toward gavilleros, see chap. 7.

90. See Lars Schoultz, *Beneath the United States: A History of U.S. Policy toward Latin America* (Cambridge: Harvard University Press, 1998).

91. William Russell to Sec. of State, no. 2W, 12 Sept. 1917, RG59, 839.041. See also James Sullivan to Sec. of State, no. 93, 1 May 1914, RG59, 839.52.

92. Miguel Fiallo, "La 'Ley de Registro de Tierras': La adquisición de nuestras tierras," *Listín Diario*, 12 Sept. 1926.

93. The U.S. military dictatorship imposed an important land and improvements tax that immediately generated protests and effective resistance, beginning with the sugar interests and other large landowners who were the ones most affected by it. See Calder, *The Impact of Intervention*, 110–13. On resistance to the tax, see also San Miguel, *El pasado relegado*, 217–27. Given most peasants' tiny plots, their lack of titles, and low land values—around 5 pesos per hectare in most areas in the 1930s—the 0.5 percent tax would generally have been inconsequential even if applied to them (which is doubtful, because of the high transaction costs). For land prices, see José Fernández to Sec. of Agric., no. 704, AGN, SA, leg. 40, 1937.

94. See Calder, *The Impact of Intervention*, esp. 99–102. Calder demonstrates that the U.S. military government in the Dominican Republic had a "surprisingly negative attitude toward foreign investors" and adopted measures "meant to control and limit outside economic penetration, especially in sugar agriculture." See 239–40, 110–13.

95. See Derby, "The Magic of Modernity," chap. 2.

96. Cited in Calder, *The Impact of Intervention*, 99.

97. Rufus Lane to Mil. Gov., 1 May 1919, RG38, B1; Knapp to Chief of Naval Operations, 29 May 1917, cited in Clausner, *Rural Santo Domingo*, 194.

98. Calder, *The Impact of Intervention*, esp. 99–102; Clausner, *Rural Santo Domingo*, 194.

99. Exec. Order no. 363, 6 Dec. 1919, *Colección de Ordenes Ejecutivas* (Santo Domingo: Listín Diario, 1929).

100. *Gaceta Oficial*, no. 3138, 31 July 1920.

101. Invented by Robert Torrens, the Torrens system was first legislated in 1858 in South Australia and then spread widely throughout the world, including parts of the United States. The most distinctive feature of this system is that every land transaction is mediated by the state—i.e., technically the seller sells a piece of land to the state and the buyer then buys it from the state. This allows every purchase to be secure and irrevocable. Also, titles are registered by site rather than by owner, so they can be easily reviewed. For more on the Torrens system, see Ruíz Tejada, *La propiedad inmobiliaria;* and Bonilla Atiles, *Legislación de tierras dominicanas*.

102. The mensura catastral is distinct from *mensuras ordinarias* (traditional surveys authorized by the regular, or "ordinary," judicial system), from *mensuras generales* (surveys only of the perimeter of a comunero site), and from *mensuras particulares* (private surveys of individual land claims that involved no judicial oversight), which were prohibited within terrenos comuneros after the 1920 law. Mensuras particulares were not part of a judicial process of title adjudication; they referred only to surveying, a technical procedure of drawing property maps without any binding legal authority in and of themselves. *Mensuras catastrales* and even *ordinarias*, on the other hand, denoted surveys that were the first step in a long judicial process—sometimes with long hiatuses between steps and taking decades to complete—in which titles would ultimately be awarded by the courts (the Land Court in the case of *mensuras catastrales* and the ordinary court system for the *mensuras ordinarias*). As a result, reference to these "surveys" is often a synecdoche for the entire judicial process including titling. Yet it is vital to distinguish between the drawing of a survey, simply a map that is supposed to represent status quo conditions, and the process of awarding titles.

103. Thomas Snowden, "Proclama," 30 Mar. 1920, *Gaceta Oficial*, no. 3105, 7 Apr. 1920.

104. Evan Young to Sec. of State, 31 May 1929, RG59, 839.52.

105. Patricia Seed, *Ceremonies of Possession in Europe's Conquest of the New World, 1492–1640* (Cambridge: Cambridge University Press, 1995), 16–40.

106. Antonio Gutiérrez Escudero, "La propiedad de la tierra en Santo Domingo: Del latifundio al terreno comunero," *Temas Americanistas* 4 (1993), esp. 22; Raymundo González, "Comisión del siglo XVIII fue origen 'amparos reales' sobre tierras," *El Caribe*, 13 June 1998, and "De la reforma de la propiedad a la reforma rural."

107. Clausner, *Rural Santo Domingo*, 199n; Calder, *The Impact of Intervention*, 107–8; memo no. 1069, 23 Oct. 1928, RG59, 839.52.

108. Bonilla Atiles, *Legislación de tierras dominicanas*, 453–55; Felipe Zaglul Criado, "Evolución histórica de los fallos y violaciones de los mecanismos de publicidad en el saneamiento inmobiliario de la legislación de principios de siglo: Sus efectos en el despojo de tierras al campesinado" (Doctoral thesis in law, no. 1529, Universidad Autónoma de Santo Domingo, 1989), 49–52.

109. The sugar companies probably acquired most of their territory through prescription claims. See, e.g., TST, d.c. 2, part 8, San Pedro de Macorís, parcela no. 367; *Boletín Judicial* 25, no. 297 (1935).

110. "El Central Romana pega fuego al poblado de Caimoní," *Listín Diario*, 6 Aug. 1921; Emilio Morel, "El crimen está consumado," and "Sobre la destrucción del Higüeral," *Listín Diario*, 13 and 19 Aug. 1921; "R. L. Waddell, incendario del Higüeral en la cárcel," *Listín Diario*, 25 Aug. 1921; "XXXI carta de Fco. Aug. Cordero," *Patria*, 10 Dec. 1927; García-Muñiz, "The South Porto Rico Sugar Company," 396–406; Luis de Padilla D'Onis, *Alrededor de la crisis* (Santo Domingo: La Provincia, 1924), 46–49; Germán Sosa et al., "Se denuncian publicamente serios atropellos apacíficos propietarios del Este," *La Opinión*, 13 Sept. 1927; "Otra vez se convierte el Ingenio Quisqueya en escenario de tragedia," *La Opinión*, 4 Mar. 1927; "Notas llaneras," *Listín Diario*, 7 Sept. 1926; Roberto Cassá, "Campiña: Un caso aislado de lucha agraria," *Isla Abierta* (supplement to *Hoy*), 14 July 1990.

111. Alvarez, *Estudio de la Ley de Tierras*, 166.

112. Roberto Cassá, *Historia social y económica de la República Dominicana*, vol. 2 (Santo Domingo: Editora Alfa y Omega, 1986), 136.

113. Dominican Republic, *Censo agro-pecuario, 1940*, 4–5.

114. "El catastro nacional y un nuevo impuesto," *La Opinión*, 29 Jan. 1929; García-Muñiz, "The South Porto Rico Sugar Company," 386.

115. *Secretaría de Estado de Agricultura é Inmigración, Memoria, 1926* (Santo Domingo: n.p., 1927), 7–9, 21.

116. Rafael Vidal, "Las hiperboles de 'Patria,'" *Listín Diario*, 2 and 3 Sept. 1926.

117. "El Congreso Nacional debe votar leyes que nos pongan en guardia contra el latifundismo azucarero: Es necesario que se nacionalicen la tierra, el subsuelo y aquellas industrias que existen en el país," *Listín Diario*, 6 Aug. 1927; "Notas editoriales: Otro aspecto de la industria azucarera," *La Opinión*, 5 June 1928.

118. "La alarmante amenaza de las factorías azucareras: La República Dominicana y Haití, antes dos estados soberanos, conviértense en dos colonias yankis," *La Información*, 6 July 1927; "El ejemplo de Cuba," *La Opinión*, 6 July 1927; "Los colonos del Central Romana," *La Información*, 7 July 1927; "El Licdo: Troncoso de la Concha contra el monopolio azucarero," *La Información*, 14 July 1927; "El problema de la tierra," *Listín Diario*, 14 July 1927; "El latifundio extrangero," *La Información*, 17 July 1927; "Silencio criminal," *La Información*, 27 July 1927; "El Congreso Nacional debe votar leyes que nos pongan en guardia contra el latifundismo azucarero"; "El obrerismo contra la expansión del latifundio extrangero," *La Información*, 5 July 1927; Cassá, "Campiña," 9.

119. Cited in Díaz-Quiñones, "The Hispanic-Caribbean National Discourse," 111.

120. "El ejemplo de Cuba," *La Opinión*, 6 July 1927.

121. Franklin Frost to Sec. of State, no. 566, 6 Aug. 1927, RG59, 839.52.

122. Cited in R. Emilio Jiménez, *Trujillo y la paz* (Ciudad Trujillo: Impresora Dominicana, 1952), 10–11; *Enciclopedia dominicana* (Barcelona: Publicaciones Reunidas, 1976), 138.

Chapter 3: Peasant-State Compromise and Rural Transformation

1. Valentina Peguero, "Trujillo and the Military: Organization, Modernization and Control of the Dominican Armed Forces, 1916–1961" (Ph.D. diss., Columbia University, 1993), chap. 2; Hoetink, *The Dominican People*, chap. 5.

2. Calder, *The Impact of Intervention*; Crassweller, *Trujillo*, chap. 5. In 1921, the

Guardia Nacional Dominicana changed its name to the Policía Nacional Dominicana (Dominican National Police), and in 1928 to the Ejército Nacional (National Army), the latter partly a nationalist effort to distance the force from the body created by the United States. But in everyday conversation the force continued to be referred to as "the Guardia," and a soldier as "a guardia." Peguero, "Trujillo and the Military," 71, 122.

3. Roorda, *The Dictator Next Door*, 34.

4. John Cabot to Sec. of State, 10 Jan. 1930, no. 1560, RG59, 839.00/3343; Charles Curtis to Sec. of State, no. 64, 14 Apr. 1930, RG59, 839.00/3378; "El natalicio del Presidente," *La Opinión*, 22 Oct. 1929; Efraín Naranjos, "Tras las lentes de la verdad," *La Opinión*, 24 Oct. 1929; Incháustegui, "El ideario de Rodó," esp. 52; Mateo, *Mito y cultura*, 21–48; R. Michael Malek, "Rafael Leonidas Trujillo Molina: The Rise of a Caribbean Dictator" (Ph.D. diss., University of California, Santa Barbara, 1971), 150.

5. Curtis to Sec. of State, no. 25, 7 Mar. 1930, RG59, 839.00/3357; W. A. Bickers to Sec. of State, no. 587, 21 Apr. 1930, RG59, 839.00/3395.

6. Joseph Cotton, Dept. of State, to Curtis, U.S. legation, 19 Mar. 1930, RG59, 839.00/3355; Roorda, *The Dictator Next Door*, 27–62.

7. Mateo, *Mito y cultura*, 21–48, 80–81; Incháustegui, "El ideario de Rodó," 52–53; Céspedes, "El efecto Rodó"; Ramón Font Bernard, "El enigma Trujillo," *Hoy*, 6 Mar. 1999; Belarminio Ramírez Morillo, "Balaguer en el reloj de la historia," *Hoy*, 2 June 1999; González, "Notas sobre el pensamiento socio-político dominicano," 14–15; Baud, "Un permanente guerrillero," 191, 210; interview with writer Héctor Colombino, Baní, July 1992. Céspedes estimates that under Trujillo's rule, 149 "intellectuals" were incorporated into the regime, 56 of them in high positions, 80 as midlevel bureaucrats, and 13 as low-level functionaries. Céspedes, "El efecto Rodó," 27.

8. W. A. Bickers, U.S. consul, "Political and Economic Conditions," 24 May 1930, RG59, 839.00/3415, and other documents in this set (839.00/34); "El General Desiderio Arias," *Renovación*, no. 232, 16 Oct. 1973; Lundius and Lundahl, *Peasants and Religion*, 149–52.

9. On the effort to sedentarize the population, see, e.g., Juan Núñez, "Campaña agrícola en el Seybo," *Listín Diario*, 22 July 1935.

10. Scott, *Seeing Like a State*.

11. The most dramatic success, in this sense, was rice, which would change from a major import to an export during the 1930s. Inoa, *Estado y campesinos*, 175–208. See also Rizik, *Trujillo*, 91–94, 113; Maríñez, *Agroindustria*, esp. 50, 58; San Miguel, "The Dominican Peasantry," 101–5, 296–98.

12. Pedro San Miguel argues this with regard to the Cibao region in *Los campesinos*, esp. 341.

13. Interviews conducted in the years 1992 to 1994 in all provinces of the Dominican Republic except Santiago, Valverde, Puerto Plata, and Samaná.

14. Inoa, *Estado y campesinos*, 78.

15. Even during the brief periods when there had been universal male suffrage prior to Trujillo's rule, peasants were generally not courted by presidential candidates visiting their area, but rather they were mobilized by local leaders. See Jesús María Ramírez hijo, *Mis 43 anos en la Descubierta* (Santo Domingo: Editora Centenario, 2000), 31.

16. *Listín Diario*, 7 Apr. 1931. Cited in Inoa, *Estado y campesinos*, 77.

17. Inoa, *Estado y campesinos*, 80. "Protection to the working man" was also the second tenet of the platform of the Confederation of Parties that ran Trujillo as president in 1930. enc. to Curtis to Sec. of State, no. 58, 7 Apr. 1930, RG59, 839.00/3369.

18. Rafael L. Trujillo, *Discursos, mensajes y proclamas*, vol. 1 (Santiago: Editorial El Diario, 1946), 239.

19. "El mensaje presidencial," *La Opinión*, 2 Mar. 1933.

20. Marrero, *La República Dominicana*, 172–74, 181.

21. Inoa, *Estado y campesinos*, 79.

22. E.g., Guerrero, síndico, to Sec. of Agric., 23 July 1934, AGN, SA, leg. 181, 1934.

23. J. M. González, "Resumen de los trabajos de más relieve realizados durante el año 1934," 19 Dec. 1934, AGN, SA, leg. 19, 1937.

24. "Lo que representan las revistas cívicas para la política del país," *La Opinión*, 23 Jan. 1933.

25. "En sin igual revista que no admite paralelo y que fue más bien una epopeya cívica, 38,000 Capitaleños pidieron la reelección de Gen. Trujillo," *La Opinión*, 13 Mar. 1933. See also "La gran revista cívica y la mujer dominicana," *La Opinión*, 6 Mar. 1933.

26. Law no. 390, 10 Dec. 1940, *Gaceta Oficial*, no. 5535, 18 Dec. 1940; Law no. 391, 17 Dec. 1940, *Gaceta Oficial*, no. 5537, 21 Dec. 1940; Galíndez, *La era de Trujillo*, 176–77. For a summary of legal measures promulgated by the Trujillo state in favor of women and these laws' patriarchal limitations, see Olga María Veras and Rosina de Alvarado, "La mujer en el derecho dominicano," *Eme Eme: Estudios Dominicanos* 10, no. 58 (1982).

27. Interview with Leonardo Núñez et al., Cedro, Miches, 1 Aug. 1992. Núñez had lived near Santiago when he was young. Later he moved to a state agricultural colony in Miches.

28. Law no. 247, 29 Dec. 1931 and Law no. 911, 23 May 1935, *Gaceta Oficial*, no. 4796, 29 May 1935; Law no. 372, 14 Nov. 1940, *Gaceta Oficial*, no. 5524, 21 Nov. 1940; Law no. 990, 7 Sept. 1945, *Gaceta Oficial*, no. 6325, 13 Sept. 1945; Law no. 2565, 30 Nov. 1950, *Gaceta Oficial*, no. 7218, 9 Dec. 1950; Wendell Woodbury to Sec. of State, no. 469, 1 Dec. 1953, RG59, 839.112; Dirección General de la Cédula Personal de Identidad, *Evolución e importancia de la cédula en la era de Trujillo* (Ciudad Trujillo: Arte y Cine, 1948).

29. *Secretaría de Estado de lo Interior, Policía, Guerra y Marina, Memoria, 1933* (Santo Domingo: n.p., 1934), 84–85.

30. *Enciclopedia Dominicana* (1976).

31. H. F. Arthur Schoenfeld to Sec. of State, no. 1473, 2 Mar. 1934, and enc., "Occupation of Private Lands by Squatters," a memorandum of a conversation with Judge Robert C. Round, legal counsel for Central Romana, Inc., RG59, 839.52/89.

32. Schoenfeld to Sec. of State, no. 1473, 2 Mar. 1934, and enclosed circular from Tolentino, RG59, 839.52/89.

33. E.g., Pancho Retituyo et al. to Gov., La Vega, 3 Dec. 1935, AGN, SA, SSJA, leg. 4, 1936; José Pichardo to Trujillo, 7 Aug. 1959, AGN, SA, leg. 1132, 1959.

34. Trinidad to Trujillo, 27 Nov. 1934, AGN, SA, leg. 182, n.d.

35. Tolentino to Sec. of the Pres., no. 5541, 3 Dec. 1934, AGN, SA, leg. 182, n.d.

36. James Scott, *Weapons of the Weak: Everyday Forms of Peasant Resistance* (New Haven: Yale University Press, 1985), 309, 338–40.

37. Carretero to Tolentino, 28 Jan. 1935, AGN, SA, SSJA, leg. 4, 1936.

38. Carretero to Tolentino, 14 Feb. 1935, AGN, SA, SSJA, leg. 3, 1936; Carretero to Tolentino, 5 Feb. 1935, AGN, SA, SSJA, leg. 3, 1936.

39. Paulino to Carretero, 18 Oct. 1935, AGN, SA, SSJA, leg. 6, 1936; Enrique Curiel, report no. 454, 18 Apr. 1934, AGN, SA, leg. 200, 1934.

40. Tolentino to Trujillo, no. 5144, 8 Nov. 1934, AGN, SA, leg. 181, 1934.

41. Memo no. 45, 4 Sept. 1939, AGN, SA, leg. 179, 1939.

42. "Campaña agrícola: Socialización de la tierra, Ley no. 762," *Listín Diario*, 3 Jan. 1935; Memo. to the Bajabonico Junta, 30 Nov. 1935, AGN, SA, SSJA, leg. 1a, 1936.

43. "Sobre el reparto de tierras," *Listín Diario*, 27 May 1935.

44. Law no. 623, 23 May 1944, *Gaceta Oficial*, no. 6090, 7 June 1944; and, e.g., Juez Alcalde, Tubano, to Sec. of Agric., n.d., n.n., AGN, SA, leg. 6, 1936.

45. Exec. Order no. 404, 16 Feb. 1920, *Gaceta Oficial*, no. 3094, 28 Feb. 1920. The 10-tarea requirement was implicit in the mid-nineteenth-century police laws, previously stipulated in local ordinances, and proposed as early as 1793 by Spanish colonial authorities. The unprecedented enforcement of the law under Trujillo was responsible for the mistaken belief held by most elderly peasants with whom I spoke that the legislation was established during his regime.

46. "Memoria de la Gobernación Provincial de Samaná," *Secretaría de Estado de lo Interior y Policía, Memoria, 1938* (Ciudad Trujillo, 1939), 384.

47. "Ley sobre policía urbana y rural," 2 July 1855, *Gaceta Oficial*, no. 2170, 1 Mar. 1911.

48. "El reparto de la tierra y el éxodo campesino," *Listín Diario*, 26 June 1935.

49. Víctor Garrido, Sec. of Trans. and Public Works, A. Rogers, Advisory Engineer to the Exec., and Tolentino to Trujillo, 3 Jan. 1935, AGN, SA, leg. 207, 1935.

50. Tejera, "Párrafos," 15; Bonó, "Apuntes," 225; Francisco Peynado, *Por la inmigración: Estudio de las reformas que es necesario emprender para atraer inmigrantes á la República Dominicana* (Santo Domingo: Imp. La Cuna de América, 1913), 51, and "Deslinde, mensura y partición de terrenos," 3. U.S. occupation officials came to a similar conclusion about the origins of Dominican rebels. Calder, *The Impact of Intervention*, 120.

51. "El reparto de las tierras," *La Opinión*, 24 Jan. 1936.

52. "Sobre el reparto de tierras," *Listín Diario*, 27 May 1935.

53. Peynado, "Deslinde, mensura y partición de terrenos," 3.

54. "Discurso del Sr. Manuel M. Morillo, oficial mayor de la Secretaría de Agricultura en el mitin agrícola," *Listín Diario*, 30 Oct. 1935.

55. Cabot to Sec. of State, no. 1570, 10 Jan. 1930, RG59, 839.00/3314; Curtis to Sec. of State, no. 23, 6 Mar. 1930, RG59, 839.00/3356.

56. *Secretaría de Estado de Agricultura y Trabajo, Memoria, 1935* (Ciudad Trujillo, 1936), 268–69, 275–76; *Secretaría de Agricultura é Inmigración, Memoria, 1926* (Santo Domingo: n.p., 1927), 7–9, 20–22; Curtis to Sec. of State, no. 23, 6 Mar. 1930, RG59, 839.00/3356.

57. Garrido, Rogers, and Tolentino to Trujillo, 3 Jan. 1935, AGN, SA, leg. 207, 1935.

58. Telegrams from Carretero to Trujillo, no. 37290, 16 Dec. 1934, AGN, SA, leg. 182, n.d.; 28 Jan. 1935, AGN, SA, SSJA, leg. 6, 1936; and n.d., 16 Oct. 1935, 29 Jan. 1935, and 5 Feb. 1935, AGN, SA, SSJA, leg. 3, 1936.

59. Franklin Atwood to Sec. of State, no. 3123, 13 Feb. 1936, RG59, 839.52/103; Dominican Republic, Junta Nacional de Alimentación y Agricultura, *Algunos aspectos sobre la situación agrícola y alimenticia de la República Dominicana, 1941–1945* (Ciudad Trujillo: n.p., 1946), 2; Valentín Junta to Bayoán de Hostos, nos. 18 and 305, 2 Sept. 1936 and 2 Dec. 1936. Most elderly peasants I spoke with said that even ten tareas provided subsistence during the Trujillo years. This is plausible given the limited extent of commerce, taxes, and other monetary needs, and given land fertility and the minimal agricultural inputs necessary at the time.

60. Junta Nacional de Alimentación y Agricultura, *Algunos aspectos sobre la situación agrícola*. For a breakdown of the yearly distributions between 1934 and 1947, see Maríñez, *Agroindustria*, 44.

61. Rafael Trujillo Molina, *Evolución de la democracia en Santo Domingo*, 2d ed. (Ciudad Trujillo: Editora del Caribe, 1955), 38; rural producers are interpolated from Dominican Republic, *Cuarto censo nacional agropecuario, 1950*, viii–ix, and Dominican Republic, *Quinto censo nacional agropecuario, 1960*, x. It is possible that distribution figures double-count recipients who received land more than once.

62. Junta Nacional de Alimentación y Agricultura, *Algunos aspectos sobre la situación agrícola*, 2.

63. In 1950 only 4.5 percent of all rural producers were sharecroppers and 1.7 percent were renters, while 60.2 percent owned their own land, 13 percent were "free beneficiaries," 6.3 percent held the land by (state) grants, and 1.6 percent were colonists. Moreover, fewer than one-fourth of men over fourteen working in the countryside were engaged in paid labor. The statistics for 1960 are similar, except that paid laborers actually decreased to 15 percent of total rural workers (probably a reflection of the time of year the census was taken). See *Cuarto censo nacional*, vii–xiv, xvii; Dominican Republic, *Censo agro-pecuario, 1940*, 3; *Quinto censo nacional*, part 1, x–xii, 44–52, 56, 116, 138; part 2, x, xiv.

64. Decree no. 4772, 22 June 1907, *Gaceta Oficial*, nos. 1800–1801, 29 June 1907 and 3 July 1907; "El catastro nacional y un nuevo impuesto," *La Opinión*, 29 Jan. 1929.

65. Unfortunately, the categories of comunero, state, and private land were not disaggregated in state statistics on land distribution.

66. Ramírez, *Mis 43 años*, 58–60.

67. Rocha to Hostos, AGN, SA, SSJA, leg. 5, 1936; Jacinto Pérez to Hostos, no. 5, 21 May 1936 and Pérez to Carretero, no. 6, 22 May 1936, AGN, SA, SSJA, leg. 1a, 1936.

68. Carretero would again appear in the historical record when he was assigned to the Northern frontier after the 1937 Haitian massacre, where he deployed the regime's postmassacre anti-Haitian discourse to bolster his requests for state assistance to the region. José Luis Sáez, S.J., *Los Jesuitas en la República Dominicana*, vol. 1 *(1936–1961)* (Santo Domingo: Museo Nacional de Historia y Geografía, 1988), 87. On the massacre and anti-Haitianism, see chap. 5.

69. José Pichardo to Hostos, 17 Aug. 1936; Pichardo to Hostos, nos. 6 and 57, 6 Nov. 1936, AGN, SA, SSJA, leg. 6, 1936.

70. Tenares Junta to Juntas General Supervisor, 6 Nov. 1936, AGN, SA, SSJA, leg. 6, 1936.

71. AGN, SA, SSJA, leg. 2, exps. 15–23, 1936.

72. See, e.g., Neiba Junta report, 15 Apr. 1936, AGN, SA, SSJA, leg. 1a, 1936; Alcibíades Ogando to Colonization Service Agronomist, no. 44, 31 Dec. 1940, AGN, SA, leg. 1, 1941.

73. Santiago Rodríguez to Sec. of Agric., 30 Nov. 1936, AGN, SA, SSJA, leg. 5, 1936.

74. Carretero to Trujillo, 14 Feb. 1935, AGN, SA, SSJA, leg. 3, 1936. Also see Miguel Rivera to Sec. of Colonization, no. 12, 18 Jan. 1951, AGN, SA, leg. 175, 1951.

75. Félix Tomás del Monte i Andújar to Carretero, 13 Mar. 1935; and Carretero to Asst. Sec. of Agric., no. 231, AGN, SA, SSJA, leg. 4, 1936; Carretero, n.d., AGN, SA, SSJA, leg. 4, 1936; Carretero to Sec. of Agric., no. 225, 6 Mar. 1935, AGN, SA, SSJA, leg. 1, 1936.

76. Decree no. 83, 20 Aug. 1923; Law no. 670, 19 Apr. 1934, *Gaceta Oficial*, no. 4672, 21 Apr. 1934. See also Law no. 766, 16 Oct. 1934, *Gaceta Oficial*, no. 4727, 20 Oct. 1934.

77. "El catastro nacional y un nuevo impuesto," *La Opinión*, 29 Jan. 1929; Salvador Fernández Moscoso, "Consideraciones sobre la mensura en la República Dominicana," *Revista Jurídica Dominicana* 3, no. 2 (1941), 317.

78. For a fuller treatment of the Trujillo regime's reform and manipulation of the nation's land laws, see Richard Lee Turits, "The Foundations of Despotism: Peasants, Property, and the Trujillo Regime (1930–1961)" (Ph.D. diss., University of Chicago, 1997), 229–53.

79. By 30 Sept. 1955, 64.06 percent of the country had been submitted to the *mensura catastral* (Manuel Ramón Ruíz Tejada, "El éxito del sistema Torrens en la República Dominicana, bajo el régimen instituido por el Generalísimo Trujillo," *Revista Jurídica Dominicana* 17, nos. 54–55 (1955). By 1966, all but 10 percent of the country had been surveyed (Clausner, *Rural Santo Domingo*, 199).

80. Law no. 585, 24 Oct. 1941, *Gaceta Oficial*, no. 5661, 28 Oct. 1941. The ten-year prescription period instituted by Executive Order no. 511 had been temporary, applying only to those who had possessed the land at the time of the law's passage. To reduce rights based on fencing and traditional surveys rather than land use, legislation also required cultivation of at least half an occupied area in order to obtain prescription in state lands. Law no. 890, 4 May 1945, *Gaceta Oficial*, no. 6250, 7 May 1945.

81. Interview with Enrique Acevedo Ortiz, Las Charcas, Azua, 30 Aug. 1992.

82. Interview with Cecilia Rijo, Juan Pablo Duarte, Higüey, 17 July 1992. During the Trujillo years, Rijo lived in Caña Honda, Higüey.

83. Law no. 3705, 19 Dec. 1953, *Colección de Leyes, Resoluciones, Decretos y Reglamentos* (Ciudad Trujillo: Imprenta J. R. Vda. García, 1956), vol. 1, 800–801; Law no. 1231, 16 Dec. 1929, *Colección de Leyes, Decretos y Resoluciones* (Santo Domingo: J. R. Vda. García, 1930); J. Enrique Hernández, "El derecho de propiedad del predio rural en Santo Domingo," *El Caribe*, 23 Jan. 1953.

84. E.g., anonymous interview in Loma de Cabrera, 16 Jan. 1993.

85. Interview with Cecilia Rijo, Juan Pablo Duarte, Higüey, 17 July 1992.

86. Interview with Novoa, Sabana Alta, San Juan de la Maguana, Oct. 1992.

87. "El fin de la Ley de Tierras," *La Opinión*, 28 June 1933. See also "El Ejecutivo ha propuesto al Congreso hoy la total definitiva supresión del Tribunal de Tierras," *La Opinión*, 27 June 1933.

88. Law no. 5478, 2 Feb. 1961, *Gaceta Oficial*, no. 8547, 4 Feb. 1961; "Terrenos comuneros pasarán al Estado conforme nueva ley," *El Caribe*, 25 Nov. 1960. The formal abolition of peso title rights was soon revoked. Seven months after Trujillo was assassinated that same year, new legislation reinstated peso titles' prior juridical status. Law no. 5773, 26 Dec. 1961, *Gaceta Oficial*, no. 8637, 11 Jan. 1962.

89. Neiba Junta report, 15 Feb. 1936, AGN, SA, SSJA, leg. 1a, 1936.

90. Juan Herrera to Hostos, telegram no. 225, 28 June 1936, AGN, SA, SSJA, leg. 6, 1936; Higüey Junta reports, 15 Feb. and 15 Mar. 1936, AGN, SA, SSJA, leg. 6, 1936; La Vega Junta reports, 29 Feb. 1936 and 14 Mar. 1936, AGN, SA, SSJA, leg. 4, 1936; interview with Antonio Taveras, La Romana, Jima Abajo, 21 Nov. 1994.

91. Memorandum of 22 Dec. 1934, AGN, SA, SSJA, leg. 4, 1936.

92. Tolentino to Pagán, 22 May 1934 and letter from Pagán, 23 Apr. 1934, AGN, SA, SSJA, leg. 4, 1936; Agricultural Instructor Manuel Reyes Mota to Supervisor, Agric. Dist. of Trujillo, Monte Plata, 6 June 1940, and report of Pedro C. Renvill, AGN, SA, leg. 174, 1940.

93. La Vega Junta report, 29 Feb. 1936, AGN, SA, SSJA, leg. 4, 1936.

94. Interview with Antonio Taveras, La Romana, Jima Abajo, 21 Nov. 1994.

95. Law no. 961, 23 May 1928, *Gaceta Oficial*, no. 3979, 9 June 1928.

96. Félix Olivares, "La fundación de las primeras colonias agrícolas" (unpublished manuscript, 1992). I am indebted to Mr. Olivares for sharing this manuscript with me.

97. See, e.g., memo no. 2121, 5 Sept. 1931, AGN, SA, leg. 111, 1935 and Law no. 124, 10 Nov. 1942, *Gaceta Oficial*, no. 5826, 17 Nov. 1942; cf. Olivares, "La fundación de las primeras colonias."

98. Norris B. Lyle and Richard A. Calman, eds., *Statistical Abstract of Latin America, 1965*, 9th ed. (Los Angeles: University of California Press, 1965).

99. Trujillo, *Evolución de la democracia*, 37–38. On the one hand, these figures may underestimate the amount of distributed irrigated land because some irrigated areas were state property and thus could be distributed in their entirety. On the other hand, these figures may overestimate the amount of land the state acquired through the fourth-part law from private owners, because the 1942 law permitted owners to pay in cash rather than land. Also, at various moments after 1952, the state considered selling rather than distributing irrigated lands that were not under the supervision of an agricultural colony, reportedly in response to speculation. It seems though that most irrigated terrain was ceded under the rubric of "colonization," even when the colony apparatus was only nominal. "Plan para la venta de las tierras irrigables propiedad del Estado," 18 Jan. 1952; Sec. of Agric. to Juan Andújar, no. 26913, 3 Oct. 1952, AGN, SA, leg. 194, 1952.

100. The 1907 law stipulated that all men between the ages of eighteen and sixty had to pay 1 peso or work on public labor three days a year. Later, the tax was raised to 2

pesos or four days a year. Then it was lowered to 1 peso, but the option to work in lieu of taxation was dropped, to the chagrin of the rural poor. As a result, some areas, at least, reported increased resistance to it. Under Trujillo, the option of corvée labor was re-established, along with the alternative of paying 25 centavos for each day of public work. Ley de Caminos, 23 Mar. 1907, *Gaceta Oficial*, no. 1775, 27 Mar. 1907; Reglamento para la Apertura i Conservación de los Caminos Públicos, 27 Nov. 1908, *Colección de Leyes, Decretos y Resoluciones*, vol. 19 (Santo Domingo: Listín Diario, 1929); Exec. Order no. 212, 18 Sept. 1918, *Colección de Leyes, Decretos y Resoluciones*, vol. 20 (Santo Domingo: Listín Diario, 1929); Law no. 1308, 23 Apr. 1930, *Colección de Leyes, Decretos y Resoluciones* (Santo Domingo: J. R. Vda. García, 1931), 115; *Secretaría de Estado de lo Interior y Policía, Memoria, 1927* (Santo Domingo: n.p., 1928); San Miguel, *Los campesinos*, 265–88; Inoa, *Estado y campesinos*, 105–52.

101. San Miguel, *Los campesinos*, esp. 277–81; Inoa, *Estado y campesinos*, esp. 147.

102. Joaquín Cocco to Gov., Prov. Trujillo, no. 3955, 17 Apr. 1939, AGN, SA, leg. 179, 1939; San Miguel, *Los campesinos*, 280–88; Inoa, *Estado y campesinos*, 121–52.

103. San Miguel, *Los campesinos*, 270–74.

104. Interview, e.g., with Angel Luciano Novoa, Linor de los Santos, and other peasant recipients of irrigated land, Las Zanjas, San Juan de la Maguana, 4 Oct. 1992.

105. Rodríguez to Hostos, no. 143, 21 Nov. 1936, AGN, SA, SSJA, leg. 5, 1936.

106. See San Miguel, *Los campesinos*, 306–7; Inoa, *Estado y campesinos*, 101.

107. Aquilino Martínez to Sec. of Agric., 10 Nov. 1947, and Nemesis Martínez to Chief of the Colonization Branch, 29 Nov. 1947, no. 55, AGN, SA, leg. 46, 1947.

108. See José Pimentel to Marino Cáceres, Sec. of Agric., 20 Dec. 1947; Cáceres to Pimentel, no. 25799, 22 Dec. 1947, AGN, SA, leg. 51b, 1947; Hernández Franco to Huberto Bogaert, Sec. of Agric., 6 Sept. 1944, and Bogaert to Hernández Franco, 9 Sept. 1944, no. 20741, AGN, SA, leg. 2, 1942; Pimentel to Sec. of Agric., 8 Sept. 1952; Francisco Pereyra, Sec. of Agric., no. 6752, 10 Dec. 1952, AGN, SA, leg. 194, 1952.

109. See AGN, SA, leg. 46, 1947.

110. Manuel Aguiles Comas to Asst. Sec. of Agric., 19 Dec. 1936, and José Fernández to Sec. of Agric., no. 154, 3 Mar. 1937, AGN, SA, leg. 40, 1937.

111. See, e.g., César Gómez Portes to Sec. of Agric., 7 Nov. 1937; Sec. of Agric. to Gómez, 6 Dec. 1937, AGN, SA, leg. 40, 1937. However, lands smaller than a certain size were not ultimately appropriated, as one-fourth of an already tiny plot would serve no one.

112. Interview with Francisco Eduardo Salazar, Nizao, Baní, 29 Aug. 1992.

113. For analogous processes of hegemony under François Duvalier's dictatorship, see Michel-Rolph Trouillot, *Haiti: State against Nation* (New York: Monthly Review, 1990), 152–56.

114. Genaro Brito to Sec. of Agric., no. 495, 20 Sept. 1944, AGN, SA, leg. 10b, 1944.

115. Valenzuela to Humberto Bogaert, 10 Sept. 1944; Brito to Sec. of Agric., no. 533, 2 Oct. 1944 and no. 694, AGN, SA, leg. 10b, 1944.

116. Rice even for the domestic market was taxed significantly (1 or 2 centavos a pound). In general, however, prices were high enough (8 to 16 centavos a pound in the 1940s) to keep peasant production relatively profitable, especially in irrigated areas.

This was affirmed in interviews I conducted (see chap. 6) and suggested by the formidable increases in rice cultivation. Decree no. 4703, 8 Nov. 1947, *Gaceta Oficial*, no. 6709, 12 Nov. 1947; Inoa, *Estado y campesinos*, 180–208.

117. Leonidas Grullón to Sec. of Treasury and Commerce, 26 Nov. 1938, AGN, SA, leg. 326, 1938; Juan Román to Sec. of Treasury and Commerce, no. 9415, 14 Dec. 1938, AGN, SA, leg. 326, 1938.

118. "Lo que ha hecho 'La Opinión' en dos años de intensa lucha por el prestigio, el engrandecimiento y el porvenir de la República," *La Opinión*, 10 Jan. 1929; García-Muñiz, "The South Porto Rico Sugar Company," 386.

119. Interviews with Juan Bautista Mercedes, El Regajo, Ramón Santana, 18 Dec. 1992; Esperanza Salazar (a member of the Gaspar Hernández junta under Trujillo), El Cruce de Naranjo, Nagua, Nov. 1994; and Narciso Núñez, Mata Bonita, Nagua, Nov. 1994. On renewal negotiations, see chap. 4.

120. Law no. 758, 10 Oct. 1934, *Gaceta Oficial*, no. 4725, 13 Oct. 1934. See the Silvain Coiscou case, described in chap. 4; see also the notice given to 266 persons between 21 Dec. 1934 and 26 Apr. 1935, requiring them to immediately cultivate or distribute their lands in Jovero, Monte Plata, and La Romana. Hostos to Carretero, no. 669, 28 Oct. 1935, AGN, SA, SSJA, leg. 4, 1936.

121. J. Joaquín Cocco to Trujillo, no. 455, 27 May 1935, AGN, SA, SSJA, leg. 3, 1936; Francisco Alemany to Hostos, n.d., AGN, SA, SSJA, leg. 5, 1936; Carretero, n.d., AGN, SA, SSJA, leg. 4, 1936.

122. Carretero to Cornelio Julian, 30 Nov. 1935; and Julian to Carretero, 30 Nov. 1935, AGN, SA, SSJA, leg. 1a, 1936; Rafael Saldaña to Juan Bautista Mejía, no. 24, 4 Dec. 1936, AGN, SA, SSJA, leg. 1a, 1936.

123. Interviews with Juan Bautista Mercedes, El Regajo, Ramón Santana, 18 Dec. 1992; Santiago Susaña, Las Zanjas, San Juan de la Maguana, 4 Oct. 1992; Angel Pérez, síndico of Guayubín, n.d., SA, SSJA, leg. 2, exps. 15–23, 1936.

124. Reyes to Trujillo, 19 Mar. 1935, AGN, SA, leg. 207, 1935; Agustín Hernández to Modesto Díaz, 12 May 1935, AGN, SA, leg. 207, 1935.

125. Letter to Trujillo, Yagüaza, 12 Feb. 1935, AGN, SA, SSJA, leg. 4, 1936. Carretero asked local authorities to find them land without these obligations. Carretero to síndico, Villa Mella, no. 86, 18 Feb. 1935, AGN, SA, SSJA, leg. 4, 1936.

126. Reinaldo Roa, Ramón Santana Junta report, 16 May 1936, AGN, SA, SSJA, leg. 5, 1936; interview with Maldonado, De Silvain, Ramón Santana, 26 Nov. 1994. On the Campiña evictions, see chap. 4.

127. Interview with Maldonado, De Silvain, Ramón Santana, 26 Nov. 1994. For an analysis of similar comments by other elderly peasants, see chap. 7.

128. For comparative purposes, see Scott, *Seeing Like a State*, 1, passim.

129. See also San Miguel, *El pasado relegado*, 142–46, 211–12, and "La ciudadanía de Calibán."

Chapter 4: Negotiating Dictatorship

1. Major programs for agrarian reform in Latin America, as in Asia, would generally develop between 1940 and 1970. See Peter Dorner, *Latin American Land Reforms in*

Theory and Practice: A Retrospective Analysis (Madison: University of Wisconsin Press, 1992). Mexico is the clearest exception to this pattern.

2. In this regard, the Trujillo dictatorship finds analogies with the early Somoza regime, but contrasts sharply with other parts of Central America. Gould, *To Lead as Equals*; Lauria-Santiago, *An Agrarian Republic*, 234–37; McCreery, "Wage Labor."

3. Dominican Republic, *Censo agro-pecuario, 1940*, 1, 4–5. The country's major sugar estates were all owned by U.S. citizens, with the exception of the Canadian-owned Ozama Sugar Company and the Italian-Dominican Vicini family's Compañía Anónima de Explotaciones Industriales (CAEI).

4. On the Dominican elite, see Hoetink, *The Dominican People*, 165–77; Moya Pons, *El pasado dominicano*, 199–206; Baud, *Peasants and Tobacco*, 109–14, passim; Franks, "Transforming Property," chap. 3.

5. Carretero to Trujillo, 23 Oct. 1935, AGN, SA, SSJA, leg. 4, 1936.

6. Ramón Estepan to Appellate Court of Santiago, no. 1642, 14 Nov. 1935, AGN, SA, SSJA, leg. 4, 1936.

7. Carretero to García Mella, 8 Jan. 1936; García Mella to Carretero, no. 803, 9 Jan. 1936, AGN, SA, SSJA, leg. 4, 1936.

8. Hostos to Eduardo Guerrero, no. 1959, 6 July 1936, AGN, SA, SSJA, leg. 3, 1936. Another hypothesis is that Trujillo reassigned Carretero because he felt threatened by his subordinate's growing popularity and power, evinced by the fact that peasant requests for land were now frequently being directed to Carretero rather than Trujillo. E.g., Pedro Franco to Carretero, 13 June 1936, AGN, SA, SSJA, leg. 2, exps. 15–23, 1936.

9. Castillo to P. García Salloso, no. 3, 23 Sept. 1936, AGN, SA, SSJA, leg. 2, exps. 15–23, 1936.

10. José Batista to Supervisor of Agricultural Juntas, no. 166, 31 July 1935, AGN, SA, SSJA, leg. 4, 1936.

11. It is safe to presume that property in marginal regions such as Elías Piña had not yet been adjudicated by the Tribunal de Tierras, and thus that "surveyed" here referred to a privately commissioned survey. Although such a survey implied a strong property claim, as it could be used to document symbolic "possession" and thus to consolidate property via prescription, it was in no way a definitive title.

12. Mulio A. Pérez to Carretero, 10 Jan. 1935, AGN, SA, SSJA, leg. 3, 1936.

13. Carretero to Pres., Elías Piña Junta, 3 Jan. 1935, AGN, SA, SSJA, leg. 3, 1936.

14. Carretero to Asst. Sec. of the Pres., 12 Jan. 1935, AGN, SA, SSJA, leg. 3, 1936.

15. See the case of Dulce Echevarría, discussed in chap. 3.

16. Adriano Horton, Pres. of Samaná Junta, to Hostos, 3 July 1936 and 12 July 1936; Hostos to Horton, no. 2009, 15 July 1936; Hostos to Horton, no. 1857, 30 June 1936, AGN, SA, SSJA, leg. 2, exps. 15–23, 1936. See also Horton to Carretero, 30 May 1936, and Horton to Hostos, 3 July 1936, AGN, SA, SSJA, leg. 2, exps. 15–23, 1936.

17. Manuel A. Lora to Supervisor of the Agricultural Juntas, no. 2522, 30 June 1936, AGN, SA, SSJA, leg. 2, exps. 15–23, 1936.

18. Report no. 2–36, 2 Jan. 1936, in *Secretario de Estado de lo Interior, Policía, Guerra y Marina, Memoria, 1935* (Ciudad Trujillo, 1936).

19. Báez to Carretero, 14 May 1936, and Hostos to Báez, no. 1383, 18 May 1936, AGN, SA, SSJA, leg. 6, 1936.

20. Hostos to Durán, no. 638, and Durán to Hostos, 24 Mar. 1936, AGN, SA, SSJA, leg. 1a, 1936.

21. Report of José Ojeda and José Báez, vice presidents, San Cristóbal Junta, 30 Sept. 1936; Jacinto Pérez to Hostos, no. 5, 21 May 1936; Pérez to Carretero, no. 6, 22 May 1936; Pérez to Hostos, no. 96, 18 June 1936, AGN, SA, SSJA, leg. 1a, 1936.

22. Molina to Carretero, 22 Dec. 1935, AGN, SA, SSJA, leg. 3, 1936.

23. Ogando to Supervisor of the Agricultural Juntas, no. 163, 28 Nov. 1936, AGN, SA, SSJA, leg. 2, exps. 15–23, 1936.

24. Holguín to Sec. of Agric., "Report of the Agricultural District of San Cristóbal," 30 Nov. 1938, AGN, SA, leg. 149, exp. 402, 1938.

25. The final outcome of this case was not indicated in the records. Rodríguez to Sec. of Agric., no. 82, 22 June 1936; Lara to Casanovas, no. 2564, 2 July 1936; Casanovas to Lara, 16 July 1936, AGN, SA, SSJA, leg. 6, 1936.

26. Franklin Franco, *La era de Trujillo* (Santo Domingo: Fundación Cultural Dominicano, 1992), 96–97; Juan Bosch, *La fortuna de Trujillo* (Santo Domingo: Alfa y Omega, 1989), 101.

27. Santelises to Carretero, 8 June 1936, AGN, SA, SSJA, leg. 2, exps. 15–23, 1936.

28. Santelises to Monte Cristi Junta, 14 Mar. 1936; Ml. F. Tavárez to Santelises, no. 2484, 23 Dec. 1919; Cabrera to Pres., Monte Cristi Provincial Junta, no. 55, 9 Apr. 1936; Cabrera to Carretero, no. 56, 9 Apr. 1936; and Santelises to Carretero, 8 June 1936, AGN, SA, SSJA, leg. 2, exps. 15–23, 1936.

29. Cabrera to Carretero, no. 56, 9 Apr. 1936; Cabrera to Pres., Monte Cristi Provincial Junta, no. 55, 9 Apr. 1936, AGN, SA, SSJA, leg. 2, exps. 15–23, 1936.

30. Cabrera to Carretero, no. 56, 9 Apr. 1936, AGN, SA, SSJA, leg. 2, exps. 15–23, 1936.

31. "Underutilized" areas referred not only to incomplete cultivation but sometimes also to pasture. Some ranchers claimed more land for their cattle than the state believed was necessary.

32. Cabrera to Carretero, no. 81, 1 June 1936, and Carretero to Cabrera, no. 1693, 9 June 1936, AGN, SA, SSJA, leg. 2, exps. 15–23, 1936.

33. Moya, Pres., Cotuí Junta, to Carretero, AGN, SA, SSJA, leg. 5 (formerly leg. 1), 1936.

34. Carretero to Nolasco, n.d., AGN, SA, SSJA, leg. 6, 1936.

35. Ramón Beras, Pres., Santa Cruz del Seibo Junta, biweekly report, n.d., AGN, SA, SSJA, leg. 3, 1936.

36. "Resumen de las actividades desplegadas por la Secretaría de Estado de Trabajo, Agricultura, Industria y Comercio durante el periodo comprendido de 1930 a 1935," AGN, SA, leg. 207, 1935.

37. Carretero to Captain Hermida, 23 May 1935, AGN, SA, SSJA, leg. 6, 1936.

38. Carretero to Tolentino, n.d., AGN, SA, SSJA, leg. 3, 1936; Carretero to Tolentino, 23 May 1935; Carretero to Quiterio Berroa, Commissioner for the Exec. Branch in the East, AGN, SA, SSJA, leg. 4, 1936.

39. Andrés Pastoriza, Sec. of Agric., to Commissioner of the Exec. Branch in the East, 21 Oct. 1935, AGN, SA, SSJA, leg. 4, 1936.

40. Interviews conducted in 1992 in Ramón Santana.

41. Coiscou to San Pedro de Macorís Junta, 13 Dec. 1940, AGN, SA, leg. 449 (formerly 173), 1940. Cf. Rafael Durán (Jarabacoa) to Sec. of Agric., 23 July 1936, AGN, SA, SSJA, leg. 4, 1936.

42. Pereyra Frómeta to Sec. of Agric., no. 1476, 28 June 1940; Raúl A. Carbuccia to Chief of the Eastern Agricultural Dept., no. 12782, 23 Oct. 1940, and no. 88, 5 Nov. 1940; and Coiscou to Pereyra Frómeta, 11 Jan. 1941, AGN, SA, leg. 449 (formerly 173), 1940. José A. Fernández, Asst. Sec. of Agric., to Pereyra, no. 15354, 7 Dec. 1940; Coiscou to San Pedro Junta, 13 Dec. 1940; Aquilo Núñez, Pres., Ramón Santana Junta, to Sec. of Agric., 11 Oct. 1940; and Frómeta to Sec. of Agric., no. 2678, AGN, SA, leg. 214, 1941.

43. Pereyra to Coiscou, no. 2883, 20 Dec. 1940, AGN, SA, leg. 214, 1941.

44. Coiscou to Pereyra, 11 Jan. 1941, and Pereyra to Asst. Sec. of Agric., no. 135, AGN, SA, leg. 214, 1941.

45. Coiscou to Pereyra, 11 Jan. 1941, AGN, SA, leg. 214, 1941.

46. Alfonso Mieses to Asst. Sec. of Agric., no. 12, 18 Mar. 1941, AGN, SA, leg. 214, 1941.

47. Mieses to Sec. of Agric., no. 39, 18 Nov. 1941, AGN, SA, leg. 214, 1941.

48. Humberto Bogaert to Sec. of the Pres., no. 10610, 18 May 1944, AGN, SA, leg. 10b, 1944.

49. Jaime Guerrero Avila to Sec. of Agric., no. 196, 7 Jan. 1952, and other documents in AGN, SA, leg. 191, 1952; interview with Martín Maldonado, 26 Nov. 1994, de Silvain, Ramón Santana.

50. Raymundo Silvestre et al. to Sec. of Agric., 13 Mar. 1941; Emilio Espinola, Sec. of Agric., to Pres., Ramón Santana Junta, no. 5119, 14 June 1941, SA, leg. 214, 1941.

51. On this case, see Gen. Antonio Ramírez, Prov. Gov., El Seibo, to Sec. of the Interior, Police, Army and Marines, no. 585, 26 May 1937, AGN, SA, leg. 25, exps. 9–37, 1937; Teófilo Ferrer, Pres., El Seibo Junta, to Hostos, 1 Oct. 1935; Ferrer to Hostos, 9 Oct. 1935; Ferrer to Carretero, 14 Oct. 1935; Hostos to Sec. of the Interior, Police, War and Marines, no. 629, 14 Oct. 1935; Ferrer to Carretero, n.d.; and a copy of Santoni's sharecropping contract, AGN, SA, SSJA, leg. 1, 1936.

52. Ferrer to Carretero, 22 Oct. 1935, AGN, SA, SSJA, leg. 1, 1936.

53. Letter of José Javier, annexed to "Nómina de las atribuciones sobre lite de propiedades en los sitios denominados, 'La Gerónima y Cañada Mala,'" AGN, SA, SSJA, leg. 1, 1936.

54. "Ponderado discurso del agrónomo Señor de Hostos en la reunión de agricultores en 'Paso del Cibao,'" Listín Diario, 17 July 1935.

55. Carretero to Pastoriza, 23 Oct. 1935; Hostos to Carretero, no. 671, 28 Oct. 1935; Carretero to Pastoriza, no. 319, 30 Oct. 1935, AGN, SA, SSJA, leg. 1, 1936.

56. However, various problems continued between Santoni and tenants for several years, as did official investigations. Melchor Contín Alfau, press commissioner, 7 Feb. 1936, AGN, SA, SSJA, leg. 1a, 1936; Raúl A. Carbuccia, Asst. Sec. of Agric., to Chief of the Eastern Agricultural Dept., no. 6828, 13 Oct. 1938, AGN, SA, leg. 358, 1938.

57. Enciclopedia dominicana (1976), vol. 6, 143–44; Secretario de Estado de Agricultura é Inmigración, Memoria, 1926, 119–25; Clausner, Rural Santo Domingo, 226.

58. Interview with Nicolás Genao y Genao, La Vega, 4 Apr. 1992.

59. Rodríguez owed 4,989.18 tareas in Jima Abajo and Jima Arriba in return for state irrigation. Humberto Bogaert, Sec. of Public Works and Irrigation, to Sec. of Agric., no. 14870, 29 July 1947, AGN, SA, leg. 46, 1947; interview with colonist Ramón Abreu, Jima Abajo, La Vega, 21 Nov. 1994.

60. Tensions also reportedly arose when Rodríguez resisted pressure to sell to Trujillo a thousand head of his cattle. Interviews with peasants in La Vega province, including Ramón Abreu, Jima Abajo, 21 Nov. 1994, and Marcelino Cepeda and Domingo Severino Hernández, Jima Abajo, 2 Mar. 1992; and with members of the Trujillo state—namely, a former assistant secretary of agriculture, Domingo Hasbún, Santo Domingo, 5 Aug. 1992, and Braulio Alvarez Sánchez, Jarabacoa, Mar. 1992. Also see Clausner, *Rural Santo Domingo*, 226–28; and Francisco de Moya Franco to the Pres., 2 Feb. 1944, AGN, SA, leg. 10b, 1944. Despite criticism of Rodríguez remembered by many peasants, overall in the Dominican Republic, he is generally recalled as a hero for having devoted his fortune, life-in-exile, and family to trying to overthrow the Trujillo dictatorship. See *Enciclopedia Dominicana* (1976), vol. 6, 143–44; Leida G. de León, "Hay en La Vega dos calles," *Listín Diario*, 14 July 1992; and José Diego Grullón, *Cayo Confites: La revolución traicionada* (Santo Domingo: Alfa y Omega, 1989).

61. See, e.g., Cassá, "Campiña," 9.

62. Wilfredo Lozano, *La dominación imperialista en la República Dominicana, 1900–1930* (Santo Domingo: Taller, 1976), 158.

63. See Roorda, *The Dictator Next Door*.

64. Vega, *Trujillo y Haití*, vol. I, esp. 133–44; A. M. Warren, U.S. embassy, to Sec. of State, no. 1119, 14 Sept. 1943, RG59, 839.61351/245; Warren to Sec. of State, no. 1479, 13 Jan. 1944, RG59, 839.61351/280; Michael Hall, *Sugar and Power in the Dominican Republic: Eisenhower, Kennedy, and the Trujillos* (Westport: Greenwood, 2000), 20. The migration tax entailed both entry and annual residence fees.

65. R. M. Scotten, U.S. legation, to Sec. of State, no. 27, 5 July 1940, RG59, 839.613.

66. Vega, *Trujillo y Haití*, vol. I, passim.

67. Luis Henríquez Castillo to Sec. of the Pres., no. 35-D-7, 30 May 1935, AGN, SA, SSJA, leg. 4, 1936.

68. Miguel Fiallo to Sec. of the Pres., 4 June 1935, AGN, SA, SSJA, leg. 4, 1936.

69. "XXXI carta de Fco. Aug. Cordero," *Patria*, 10 Dec. 1927; "Un grave caso en el cual debe terciar la justicia," *La Opinión*, 31 Oct. 1929.

70. See, e.g., "La Federación del Trabajo de La Romana y el caso de 'La Campiña,'" *La Opinión*, 21 July 1927; and Franklin Frost, U.S. legation, to Sec. of State, no. 566, 6 Aug. 1927, RG59, 839.52, 1910–29.

71. *La Opinión*, 11 Apr. 1931.

72. Surveys commissioned in the 1890s by the Italian-born magnate Juan Bautista Vicini documented "occupation" from far enough back for property rights to be awarded to him on the basis of prescription alone. Vicini had acquired his peso titles to the site around 1890 in a purportedly illicit deal with Dominican dictator Ulises Heureaux. Turits, "Peasants, Property, and the Trujillo Regime," 379–87.

73. Henríquez to Sec. of the Pres., 35-D-7, 30 May 1935, AGN, SA, SSJA, leg. 4, 1936.

74. Fiallo to Sec. of the Pres., 4 June 1935, AGN, SA, SSJA, leg. 4, 1936.

75. Henríquez to Sec. of the Pres., 35-D-7, 30 May 1935, AGN, SA, SSJA, leg. 4, 1936.

76. For a more extensive treatment of this case, see Turits, "Peasants, Property, and the Trujillo Regime," 379–96.

77. R. Paíno Pichardo to Sec. of Agric., 19 Mar. 1940, AGN, SA, leg. 449 (formerly 173), 1940.

78. Máximo González to Trujillo, 3 June 1935, AGN, SA, SSJA, leg. 3, 1936.

79. Interviews with Victoria Soriana, La Romana, 8 Jan. 1993; Efigenia Montilla and Jorge Castillo, Catorce de Cumayasa, La Romana, 30 Dec. 1993; Juan Maruca, Regajo Plumita, Ramón Santana, 18 Dec. 1992; and Augustina Torres, Las Flores, Higüeral, 10 Jan. 1993. Soriana, Montilla, and Torres had all been evicted from Campiña. Maruca had been *segundo*, or assistant, alcalde in the area at the time.

80. H. F. Arthur Schoenfeld to Sec. of State, no. 1473, 2 Mar. 1934, and enclosure, "Occupation of Private Lands by Squatters," RG59, 839.52/89; Enrique Curiel to Sec. of Agric., no. 454, 18 Apr. 1934, AGN, SA, leg. 200, 1934.

81. Vetilio Alfau Durán, "La cuestión de las tierras del Este," *La Nación*, 22 Apr. 1940; Bonilla Atiles, *El sistema Torrens*, 161–62. Bonilla's book is based on lectures given as professor and vice rector of the Universidad de Santo Domingo in 1946.

82. Roorda, *The Dictator Next Door*, esp. 68–72; Bernardo Vega, *Trujillo y el control financiero norteamericano* (Santo Domingo: Fundación Cultural Dominicana, 1990), 92–106, 592–94, passim; Crassweller, *Trujillo*, 181–82. Throughout the Trujillo period, however, U.S. and international aid remained minimal. U.S. Agency for International Development, *U.S. Overseas Loans, Grants and Assistance from International Organizations* (Washington, D.C.: Agency for International Development, 1978), 45, 50, 183–84, passim.

83. It was not only in the Eastern sugar region that foreign interests thwarted land distribution efforts, as several large sugar companies created similar problems in the southwest. See, e.g., Carretero to Trujillo, 6 Feb. 1935, AGN, SA, SSJA, leg. 3, 1936; C. Armando Rodríguez to Sec. of the Pres., 29 June 1935, AGN, SA, SSJA, leg. 4, 1936.

84. This included 24,680 tareas in the neighboring province of Hato Mayor that were ceded by approximately twenty-five landowners in 1935. Melchor Contín Alfau, press commissioner, 7 Feb. 1936, AGN, SA, SSJA, leg. 1a, 1936.

85. Servio Peguero to Tolentino, no. 19, 19 Mar. 1938, AGN, SA, leg. 351.

86. Law no. 1313, 11 June 1937, *Gaceta Oficial*, no. 5033, 11 June 1937.

87. Cited in translation in Franklin Atwood to Sec. of State, no. 3896, 9 June 1937, RG59, 839.52.

88. Atwood to Sec. of State, no. 3896, 9 June 1937, RG59, 839.52.

89. Walter Reineck to Sec. of State, no. 747, 9 June 1937, and no. 749, 12 June 1937, RG59, 839.52.

90. *La Opinión*, 8 June 1937.

91. "Otra ley trascendental," *La Opinión*, 8 June 1937.

92. Translation of "Otra ley trascendental," *La Opinión*, 8 June 1937, appended to Atwood to Sec. of State, no. 3896, 9 June 1937, RG59, 839.52.

93. "Votos de los Señores Diputados," *La Opinión*, 14 June 1937.

94. Atwood to Sec. of State, no. 3912, 25 June 1937, RG59, 839.61351/75.

95. Emphasis in original. Rafael Vidal to Chiefs of the Agricultural Departments, no. 27, 26 June 1937, AGN, SA, n.d., n.n.

96. Atwood to Sec. of State, no. 3900, 12 June 1937, RG59, 839.61351/72.

97. L. F. Vidal to Joaquín Garrido Puello, Chief of the Eastern Agricultural Dept., and Garrido to Sec. of Agric., no. 333, 9 June 1937; and Garrido to Sec. of Agric., no. 411, 15 June 1937, AGN, SA, leg. 25, 1937.

98. Francisco Augusto Cordero to Sec. of the Interior, no. 585–5/37, 24 May 1937, AGN, SA, leg. 25, 1937. See also Gen. José del Carmen Ramírez to L. F. Vidal, no. 1012, 17 May 1937; Rafael Vidal to Garrido, no. 3984, 3 June 1937, AGN, SA, leg. 25, 1937.

99. Since the company produced 13,000 short tons, or 81,250,320 pound bags of sugar per year, its annual tax would have been about $25,000. Furthermore, as it held in stock 25,000 bags, an immediate payment of $7,500 would have been owed. Reineck to Sec. of State, no. 749, 12 June 1937, RG59, 839.52/109.

100. L. F. Vidal to Garrido, and Garrido to Sec. of Agric., no. 333, 9 June 1937; Garrido to Sec. of Agric., no. 411, 15 June 1937, AGN, SA, leg. 25, 1937.

101. Garrido to Sec. of Agric., no. 411, 15 June 1937, AGN, SA, leg. 25, 1937.

102. José Alonso to Sec. of the Pres., 9 Sept. 1937, AGN, SA, leg. 19, 1937.

103. Batista to Julio Ortega Frier, no. 22152, 17 Sept. 1937, AGN, SA, leg. 19, 1937.

104. Gautier to Garrido, no. 7745, 14 Oct. 1937, and Garrido to Gautier, no. 1501, 18 Oct. 1937, AGN, SA, leg. 19, 1937.

105. Decree no. 1906, 11 June 1937, *Gaceta Oficial*, no. 5033, 11 June 1937.

106. Pujals to Sec. of Agric., no. 1279, 12 May 1938, AGN, SA, leg. 358, 1938.

107. Paíno to Sec. of Agric., 19 Mar. 1940, AGN, SA, leg. 449 (formerly 173), 1940.

108. Carbuccia to Paíno, no. 3465, 25 Mar. 1940, AGN, SA, leg. 449 (formerly 173), 1940.

109. Interview with Martín Maldonado, de Silvain, Ramón Santana, 26 Nov. 1994.

110. Sugar expansion did though also create new commercial opportunities for a small part of the peasantry that was able to secure land in contiguous areas or in the few small farms that even today interrupt the vast stretches of territory owned by sugar companies. The influx of sugar workers expanded the domestic market and thus stimulated peasant commercial production, as crops were sold both to company stores and directly to those living on the plantations. In some places, this even resulted in migration to areas near the sugar companies where peasants could farm and sell to the plantations. See LeGrand, "Informal Resistance," 582–83. On the other hand, peasants were sometimes restricted from selling produce within the plantations. Carretero complained in 1935 that peasant produce was not being purchased by company stores, while workers were compelled to buy from these stores because they were often paid with vouchers (Carretero to Trujillo, 10 June 1935, AGN, SA, SSJA, leg. 3, 1936).

111. Interview with Victoria Soriana, La Romana, 8 Jan. 1993.

112. Antonio Traviezo to Trujillo, 27 Nov. 1934, AGN, SA, leg. 181, 1934. Cf. Cassá, "Campiña."

113. Interview with Efigenia Montilla, Catorce de Cumayasa, La Romana, 30 Dec. 1992.

114. Interviews in the East, 1992.

115. Interview with Efigenia Montilla, Catorce de Cumayasa, La Romana, 30 Dec. 1992.

116. Pereyra to Sec. of Agric., no. 1899, 28 Aug. 1940, AGN, SA, leg. 449 (formerly 173), 1940.

Chapter 5: Bordering the Nation

1. Avelino, *Reflexiones*, 198–201; González, "Notas sobre el pensamiento socio-político dominicano," 14–15.

2. I am including in the northern frontier the present-day provinces of Monte Cristi, Dajabón, Santiago Rodríguez, and the northern tip of Elías Pina. The provinces of Pedernales, Barahona, Independencia, and most of Baoruco, San Juan, and Elías Piña compose the southern and central frontier. Dominicans use the term *la frontera* to refer to all of these areas.

3. See, e.g., Joaquín Balaguer, "El imperialismo haitiano," *El Imparcial*, 13 Dec. 1927; José Israel Cuello, ed., *Documentos del conflicto domínico-haitiano de 1937* (Santo Domingo: Taller, 1985), 51–140; and, for Balaguer's explicit defense of the massacre as preventing the disappearance of "a nation of Hispanic origin and lineage," "El ministro dominicano expone las razones que a su juicio justifican el Gobierno del Presidente Trujillo," *El Tiempo* (Bogotá), 15 Oct. 1945.

4. Report of the U.S. military government, 23 Feb. 1923, RG38, Misc. Recs., box 6, esp. 88, 91.

5. Anonymous interview in Ouanaminthe, 1988. In 1987–88, historian Lauren Derby and I conducted interviews with elderly Dominican and Haitian peasants who had lived in the Dominican frontier during the 1930s. Interviews were carried out in the Dominican and Haitian frontiers and around agricultural settlements established in Haiti for refugees of the Haitian massacre (in Terrier Rouge, Grand Bassin, Savane Zonbi, Thiote, and Dosmond). Some of those interviewed asked that we not use their names. All interviews hereafter cited from 1987 and 1988 were conducted jointly with Lauren Derby.

6. In Dajabón, for instance, many children attended a school run by French Jesuits in Ouanaminthe, Haiti. See the Oct. 1937 entry in the log book kept by (and in 1988 still in the possession of) L'École des Frères, Ouanaminthe. Given the complexity of identities in the Dominican frontier, naming the region's residents is inevitably problematic. Those I am imperfectly calling "ethnic Haitians" were, in fact, more or less Haitian, and more or less Dominican, depending on the political or cultural context in which they found themselves and on the aspects of their identities they chose to, or were obliged to, draw upon at any given time. As we will see, though, in the moment of the massacre, all such fluidity, simultaneity, and ambiguity of identity dissolved. (I am indebted to William Chester Jordan, Susan Naquin, and Stephanie Smallwood for their insights on this point.)

7. Dominican Republic, Comisión para el Establecimiento de Colonias de Inmigrantes, *Informe que presenta al Poder Ejecutivo la Comisión creada por la Ley Núm. 77 para estudiar las tierras de la Frontera y señalar los sitios en que se han de establecer las Colonias de Inmigrantes* (Santo Domingo: J. R. Vda. García, 1925), 19; *Secretaría del Estado de lo Interior, Policía, Guerra y Marina, Memoria, 1933*, xviii.

8. Interviews in the Dominican frontier, 1987–88; Harold Utley, major, Gendarmerie d'Haiti and Glenn Miller, major, Guardia Nacional Dominicana, "Agreement Respecting Border Troubles," 12 May 1920, RG38, Misc. Recs., box 6.

9. See *Secretaría de Estado de lo Interior, Policía, Guerra y Marina, Memoria, 1935*; Amado Gómez to Trujillo, 26 June 1935 and Gómez to Sec. of Agric., no. 1640, 4 Sept. 1935, AGN, SA, leg. 207, 1935; Michiel Baud, "Una frontera-refugio: Dominicanos y haitianos contra el Estado," *Estudios Sociales* 26, no. 92 (1993), and "Una frontera para cruzar: La sociedad rural a través de la frontera domínico-haitiana (1870–1930)," *Estudios Sociales* 26, no. 94 (1993).

10. Ramírez, *Mis 43 años*, 22–23.

11. Interview with Bilín, Monte Grande, May 1988.

12. This is also affirmed in Freddy Prestol Castillo, "Delito y delincuentes en la frontera," *La Nación*, 4 Apr. 1959.

13. Interview with Percivio Díaz, Santiago de la Cruz, Apr. 1988. In other areas of the frontier, however, Haitians and Dominicans were said to have engaged more in concubinage than marriage, in the sense that Haitian women were treated as mistresses or second wives by Dominican men. Interviews in Haiti and the Dominican Republic, 1987–88.

14. Héctor Incháustegui Cabral, "La poesía de tema negro en Santo Domingo," *Eme Eme: Estudios Dominicanos* 1, no. 5 (1973), 16–19.

15. Dominican Republic, Gobierno Provisional de la República Dominicana, *Primer Censo Nacional de la República Dominicana 1920* (Santo Domingo: Editora de la Universidad Autónoma de Santo Domingo, 1975), 149.

16. Interviews in northern Dominican frontier, 1987–88. See also Freddy Prestol Castillo, *Paisajes y meditaciones de una frontera* (Ciudad Trujillo: Cosmopolita, 1943), 33–40; Baud, "Una frontera-refugio," 42.

17. Interviews conducted by Lauren Derby and me included some southern frontier areas but focused on the northern frontier, because it was there that most ethnic Haitians were killed during the Haitian massacre.

18. A racist and anti-Haitian expression of this perspective is Prestol Castillo, "Delito y delincuentes en la Frontera." The concept of "transculturation" was developed by Fernando Ortiz, *Cuban Counterpoint: Tobacco and Sugar* (Durham: Duke University Press, 1995), 97–103.

19. Ramírez, *Mis 43 años*, 77–80, passim. See also Pedro Troncoso Sánchez, *Ramón Cáceres* (Santo Domingo: Editorial Stella, 1964), 343–46, 352; *Secretario de Estado de Relaciones Exteriores, Memoria, 1910* (Santo Domingo: Imp. La Cuna de América, 1911); *Mensaje que el Presidente de la República presenta al Congreso Nacional* (Santo Domingo: Imp. La Cuna de América, 1912), 7, 124–28; Vega, *Trujillo y Haití*, vol. I, 122–33; Dana Munro to Sec. of State, no. 323, 10 Feb. 1932, RG59.

20. See Ramírez, *Mis 43 años*, 13–75; Lundius and Lundahl, *Peasants and Religion*, 453–60.

21. In the Dajabón parish comprising the area between Dajabón and Restauración, a Jesuit missionary estimated thirty thousand residents of Haitian descent (raza haitiana) out of a population of thirty-five thousand. Sáez, *Los Jesuitas en la República Dominicana*, 60, 71. The U.S. legation in Santo Domingo reported a more conservative

estimate of seventeen thousand (Atwood to Sec. of State, no. 39, 25 Oct. 1937, RG84, 800-D). In 1937 a Dominican colonel offered a high estimate of fifty thousand persons in Monte Cristi province (Manuel Emilio Castillo to Trujillo, 18 Oct. 1937, AGN, cited in Bernardo Vega, *Trujillo y Haití*, vol. II, *[1937–1938]* [Santo Domingo: Fundación Cultural Dominicana, 1995], 77). Census data did not provide information on the number of ethnic Haitians in the Dominican Republic, but only of documented Haitian migrants, a mere 3,816 out of a total population of 87,022 in Monte Cristi province in 1935 (Vega, *Trujillo y Haití*, vol. II, 345).

22. Lauren Derby, "Haitians, Magic, and Money: *Raza* and Society in the Haitian-Dominican Borderlands, 1900–1937," *Comparative Studies in Society and History* 36, no. 3 (1994); interviews in the Dominican frontier, 1987–88.

23. Interview, e.g., with Ercilia Guerrier, Mont Organizé, Haiti, 1988.

24. Interview with Doña María, Dajabón, Apr. 1988.

25. Official statistics continued in the Trujillo era to identify a majority of Dominicans as "mixed." A 1935 census recorded 13 percent of the population as "white," 19 percent "black," and 68 percent "mestizo" (Jean Price-Mars, *La República de Haití y la República Dominicana: Diversos aspectos de un problema histórico, geográfico y etnológico* [Madrid: Industrias Gráficas España, 1958], 181). But in fact, it seems that a two- or three-tier racial schema was still far less significant for most Dominicans than was color. In 1932 when the cédula was first issued, one author surveyed how people in the Cibao identified their own *color* for their identity cards. Echoing nineteenth-century observations (see chap. 1), she concluded: "Here we distinguish ourselves by the following classification of colors: White, *Indio*, light *Indio*, dark *Indio*, Mulatto, red Mulatto, and *Moreno* (dark). . . . Very few identify themselves as black, except for those who are Haitians or from the English colonies [in the Caribbean]; ours call themselves *moreno*" (M. Ubaldo Gómez, "El color de los dominicanos," *Bahoruco* 3, no. 106 [20 Aug. 1932], 18–20). Much has been made of these color identities in the Dominican Republic, particularly the intermediate category of indio, which, over time, became inflated on the cédula to include even the darkest-skinned Dominicans. Some scholars have pointed to this as evidence of a false racial or ethnic identification with Indians and a denial of African racial heritage among Dominicans that became a legal institution during the Trujillo regime (see, e.g., Ernesto Sagás, *Race and Politics in the Dominican Republic* [Gainesville: University Press of Florida, 2000], 67, 76). And yet, the term "indio" has generally been used in everyday conversation as an adjective with virtually no indigenous genealogical referent in mind (beyond the metaphorical) for a somatic and skin color range within a continuum of racial appearances—namely, somewhat lighter-skinned than the mean but still clearly nonwhite. And it has not served as a substitute for "black." To this day the term "moreno" is used to describe the color of darker-skinned Dominicans in everyday conversation and "black" is used as a racial category in official statistics (but not for "color" on the cédula). Few Dominicans of color have disavowed being of partial African descent. Nonetheless, the absence of a black identity, and indeed the absence of any collective identity or notion of community based on color among nonwhites in the Dominican Republic, requires further study. As suggested in chap. 1, this mode of race and racism doubtless evolved in light of the intense but short-lived character of plantation slavery; the early, pre-

emancipation development of a mostly Afro-Dominican peasantry comprising most of the country's population; the multiple independence wars and caudillo rebellions that required mass mobilization across color lines; and the country's comparatively limited history of both de jure and de facto racial segregation, including in marriage. Also note that the term "indio" was common among Dominicans and Dominican officials already in the pre-Trujillo period. See Walter Cordero, "El tema negro y la discriminación en la República Dominicana," *Ciencia* 2, no. 2 (1975), 155; Secretaría de Estado de lo Interior y Policía, Dirección del Primer Censo Nacional, *Instrucciones generales para los inspectores, sub-inspectores, enumeradores y relativas al uso de cada planilla* (Santo Domingo: n.p., 1920), 23; and a 1918 identification card, a photograph of which appears in Calder, *The Impact of Intervention*, following 96. See also Torres-Saillant, "Tribulations of Blackness," 126–46; Moya Pons, "Dominican National Identity," 14–25; Hoetink, "'Race' and Color in the Caribbean," 55–84; San Miguel, *La isla imaginada*, 59–100; Michiel Baud, "'Constitutionally White': The Forging of a National Identity in the Dominican Republic," in *Ethnicity in the Caribbean: Essays in Honor of Harry Hoetink*, ed. Gert Oostindie (London: Macmillan Caribbean, 1996); Derby, "Haitians, Magic, and Money"; and Ninna Nyberg Sorensen, "There Are No Indians in the Dominican Republic: The Cultural Construction of Dominican Identities," in *Siting Culture: The Shifting Anthropological Object*, ed. Karen Fog Olwig and Kirsten Hastrup (New York: Routledge, 1997), 292–310.

26. Although culture and biology were often conflated, most twentieth-century Dominican intellectuals espoused an essentially culturalist rather than biological racism and construction of race. See, e.g., José Ramón López, "Colonización de la frontera occidental," in *José Ramón López, ensayos y artículos*, ed. Manuel Rueda (Santo Domingo: Fundación Corripio, 1991); Federico Alvarez, "Nuestro primer siglo de vida independiente," *Renovación* (Jan.–Mar. 1953), 12. The clearest exception to this rule is Balaguer. (See, e.g., Joaquín Balaguer, *La realidad dominicana: Semblanza de un país y de un régimen* [Buenos Aires: Imprenta Ferrari Hermanos, 1947], 104, 115–16.)

27. Cited in Vega, *Trujillo y Haití*, vol. I, 31.

28. Rafael Abreu Licairac, "Dominicanos y haitianos," *El Eco de la Opinión*, 12 Nov. 1892. See also González, "Notas sobre el pensamiento socio-político dominicano," 13–14; Américo Lugo, *A punto largo* (Santo Domingo: La Cuna de América, 1901), 211.

29. Carlos Andújar Persinal, *La presencia negra en Santo Domingo: Un enfoque etnohistórico* (Santo Domingo: Búho, 1997); Carlos Esteban Deive, "La herencia africana en la cultura dominicana actual," in *Ensayos sobre cultura dominicana*, ed. Bernardo Vega et al. (Santo Domingo: Museo del Hombre Dominicano, 1988). See also Martha Ellen Davis, *La otra ciencia: El vodú dominicano como religión y medicina populares* (Santo Domingo: Editora Universitaria, 1987); Carlos Esteban Deive, *Vodú y magia en Santo Domingo* (Santo Domingo: Taller, 1996), esp. 170–78.

30. For example, at the turn of the twentieth century, the famous Dominican intellectual Américo Lugo defended Julián Reyes before the Dominican Supreme Court against charges of practicing superstition: "It is not enough," he argued, "that you say that these are the laws and they are obligatory, because these people [from the frontier] are generally incapable of understanding what law is; nor can one establish even

that they are Dominicans, for they have become completely Haitianized, and not even Haitianized but Africanized." Lil Despradel, "Las etapas del antihaitianismo en la República Dominicana: El papel de los historiadores," in *Política y sociología en Haití y la República Dominicana*, ed. Suzy Castor et al. (Mexico City: Universidad Nacional Autónoma de Mexico, 1974), 102.

31. Hoetink, *The Dominican People*, 177.

32. See Nancy Leys Stepan, *"The Hour of Eugenics": Race, Gender, and Nation in Latin America* (New York: Cornell University Press, 1991); Matthew Frye Jacobson, *Barbarian Virtues: The United States Encounters Foreign Peoples at Home and Abroad, 1876–1917* (New York: Hill and Wang, 2000); Mark Mazower, *Dark Continent: Europe's Twentieth Century* (New York: Knopf, 1999), chap. 3.

33. These prejudices were local variants of elite intellectual discourses circulating throughout the Americas in this period (including in Haiti). These discourses excoriated African and Afro-American religious practices, including what was termed "voodoo," "hoodoo," conjuration, and so on, as a form of "fetishism" supposedly reflecting the earliest stage of religion and civilization, and in some cases, as with images of Haiti, mythically linked to child sacrifice and cannibalism. See, e.g., Robert Hamill Nassau, *Fetishism in West Africa: Forty Years' Observation of Native Customs and Superstitions* (New York: Negro Universities Press, 1969 [1904]); Hesketh Prichard, *Where Black Rules White: A Journey across and about Hayti* (Shannon: Irish University Press, 1900), 74–101. See also Michael Gómez, *Exchanging Our Country Marks: The Transformation of African Identities in the Colonial and Antebellum South* (Chapel Hill: University of North Carolina Press, 1998), 283; Hurbon, *Le barbare imaginaire*, 88–107, 141–43; Trouillot, *Haiti: State against Nation*, 117, 133; Horacio Pérez Licairac, "La cuestión racial en Santo Domingo," *Cuadernos Dominicanos de Cultura*, no. 14 (1944), 78.

34. See, e.g., Balaguer, "El imperialismo haitiano."

35. On twentieth-century anti-Haitian Dominican intellectuals, see San Miguel, *La isla imaginada*, 61–100; Baud, "Constitutionally White"; Sagás, *Race and Politics*, 46–55; Raymundo González, "Peña Batlle y su concepto histórico de la nación dominicana," *Anuario de Estudios Americanos* 48 (1991), 585–631; Mateo, *Mito y cultura*, esp. 127–83. See also [Rafael] Abreu Licairac, "El objetivo político de los haitianos," *El Eco de la Opinión*, 9 July 1892; "Contábamos con la réplica," *El Eco de la Opinión*, 27 Aug. 1892; and "Contestación al periódico 'Le Droit,'" *El Teléfono*, 28 Aug. 1892.

36. On the importance of firm borders to Dominican constructs of sovereignty, see *Boletín del Congreso* 2, no. 17 (3 June 1911), 2. For comparative perspective, see Peter Sahlins, *Boundaries: The Making of France and Spain in the Pyrenees* (Berkeley: University of California Press, 1989), esp. 3–7; José Antonio Maravall, *Estado moderno y mentalidad social*, vol. 1 (Madrid: Revista de Occidente, 1972), 88–149; Anderson, *Imagined Communities*, 170–78; Malcolm Anderson, *Frontiers: Territories and State Formation in the Modern World* (Oxford: Polity, 1997).

37. See Ramírez, *Mis 43 años*, 8, 23, 25; Law no. 3733, 26 June 1897 and Law no. 3788, 10 Feb. 1898, *Colección de Leyes, Decretos y Resoluciones*, vols. 14 and 15 (Santo Domingo: J. R. Vda. García, 1924); *Boletín del Congreso* 2, no. 17 (8 June 1911), 2–3; "Editorial," *El Teléfono*, 1 Nov. 1891; Baud, "Una frontera-refugio," 48–49; Baud, "Una frontera para cruzar," 16–17.

38. Baud, "Una frontera-refugio," 54–55.

39. Law no. 3733, *Colección de Leyes, Decretos y Resoluciones*, vol. 14.

40. Derby, "Haitians, Magic, and Money," 502.

41. "Los haitianos siguen invadiéndonos," *El Diario*, 21 Feb. 1907.

42. See chap. 2 and González, "Notas sobre el pensamiento socio-político domini-cano," 6–7.

43. Report of P. M. Rubirosa hijo, Gov. of San Pedro de Macorís, in *Documentos anexos a la memoria que presenta el Secretario de Estado de Agricultura é Inmigración, 1908* (Santo Domingo: n.p., 1909).

44. See, e.g., Aline Helg, "Race in Argentina and Cuba, 1880–1930: Theory, Policies, and Popular Reaction," in *The Idea of Race in Latin America*, ed. Richard Graham (Austin: University of Texas Press, 1990); Thomas Skidmore, *Black into White: Race and Nationality in Brazilian Thought* (Durham: Duke University Press, 1993), 124–44.

45. Law no. 4747, 20 Apr. 1907, *Gaceta Oficial*, no. 1782, 22 Apr. 1907.

46. *Secretaría de Estado de Agricultura é Inmigración, Memoria, 1908*, 70–75.

47. Dominican Republic, Comisión para el Establecimiento de Colonias de Inmi-grantes, *Informe para estudiar las tierras de la Frontera*, 5–7.

48. *Secretario de Estado de Agricultura é Inmigración, Memoria, 1926*, 29.

49. Olivares, "Fundación de las primeras colonias."

50. *Secretario de Estado de Agricultura é Inmigración, Memoria, 1927* (Santo Do-mingo: n.p., 1928), 45.

51. *Secretario de Estado de Agricultura é Inmigración, Memoria, 1928* (Santo Do-mingo: n.p., 1929), 59.

52. See, e.g., L. E. Henríquez Castillo, "El caso domínico-haitiano," *La Opinión*, 19 Jan. 1929.

53. *Secretario de Estado de Agricultura é Inmigración, Memoria, 1927*, 40.

54. *Secretaría de Estado de lo Interior, Policía, Guerra y Marina, Memoria, 1927* (Santo Domingo: n.p., 1928).

55. Secretaría de Estado de Agricultura é Inmigración, *Ley no. 670 sobre coloni-zación* (Santo Domingo: J. R. Vda. García, 1927).

56. Olivares, "Fundación de las primeras colonias"; *Secretario de Estado de Agri-cultura é Inmigración, Memoria, 1927*, 42.

57. Olivares, "Fundación de las primeras colonias."

58. *Secretario de Estado de Agricultura, Memoria, 1937* (Ciudad Trujillo, 1938).

59. Tomás Pastoriza, *La colonización agrícola en la era de Trujillo* (Ciudad Trujillo: Secretaría de Estado de Agricultura, Pecuaria y Colonización, 1946), 3–4.

60. *Secretaría de Estado de Agricultura y Comercio, Memoria, 1930* (Santo Domingo: n.p., 1931), 38–48; Olivares, "Fundación de las primeras colonias"; *Secretaría de Estado de lo Interior, Policía, Guerra y Marina, Memoria, 1927* (Santo Domingo: n.p., 1928); P. M. Vargas Santana to Special Commissioner of the Pres. from the Eastern Provinces, no. 305, 24 Nov. 1935, AGN, SA, leg. 351, 1938; "Editorial: Sobre las colonias agrícolas," *Listín Diario*, 30 Dec. 1935.

61. Carretero and Francisco Read to Sec. of Agric., no. 721, 3 May 1935, AGN, SA, leg. 209, 1935.

62. Dana Munro to Sec. of State, no. 346, 15 Mar. 1932, RG59, M1272, roll 32; To-

lentino, no. 2304, 18 Dec. 1930, AGN, SA, leg. 111, 1935; Vega, *Trujillo y Haití*, vol. I, 122–33.

63. Vega, *Trujillo y Haití*, vol. I, 54–59, 105–21, 148–57, 196–97. In 1946, Dominican exiles sought access to Haiti from President Lescot (Orme Wilson to Sec. of State, no. 1369, 22 Mar. 1946, RG59, 839.00), but he refused the request (U.S. embassy, Port-au-Prince, to Sec. of State, 21 Mar. 1946, RG59, 839.00).

64. E. M. H., "Memorandum," 9 Sept. 1938, RG84, 710–800 2; Law no. 391, 2 Nov. 1932, *Colección de Leyes, Decretos y Resoluciones*. See also Cassá, *Capitalismo*. Nationalist and statist goals were also evident in February 1937 when the government announced a new currency that would replace all foreign monies over the next ten years. Until then, the U.S. dollar (legal currency since 1899), the Haitian Gourde (pegged to the dollar), and even the Mexican peso had circulated widely along side a small number of Dominican coins dating back to 1881. New Dominican coins were put into circulation to replace foreign coins in 1938, but it was not until 1946 that bills were printed to replace the dollar. These were the first Dominican bills since the nineteenth century. Victor Vargas Aquino, "Consideraciones acerca de la evolución histórica de la moneda en la República Dominicana" (Doctoral thesis in law, Universidad de Santo Domingo, 1952), 43–48. See also Ignacio Agramonte, "El trazado fronterizo y la creación de la moneda nacional: Las dos obras cumbres de Trujillo," *La Nación*, 22 Mar. 1948, which lauds the establishment of national currency overall, without which it was "impossible to consider a State modern."

65. Reynaldo Valdez to Sec. of the Interior, no. 1221, 4 June 1937, AGN, SA, leg. 40, 1937; Moisés García Mella, *Alrededor de los tratados de 1929 y 1935 con la República de Haití* (Ciudad Trujillo: Imprenta Listín Diario, 1938), 6; Félix M. Nolasco, *Listín Diario*, 11 Feb. 1932 (reproduced in Vega, *Trujillo y Haití*, vol. I, 132–33).

66. "Editorial: Sobre las colonias agrícolas," *Listín Diario*, 30 Dec. 1935. See also "La frontera dominicana comienza a ser lo que debe ser: Dominicanizante," *La Opinión*, 9 Mar. 1932.

67. In general, the drive to "protect" strong borders may lead modern states to oppose cultural mixture in frontier regions, even when they accept it elsewhere. See, e.g., Timothy Snyder, "'To Resolve the Ukrainian Problem Once and for All': The Ethnic Cleansing of Ukrainians in Poland, 1943–1947," *Journal of Cold War Studies* 1, no. 2 (1999), 86–120.

68. *Mensaje que el Presidente de la República presenta*, 7, 124–28; Vega, *Trujillo y Haití*, vol. I, 122–33.

69. Vega, *Trujillo y Haití*, vol. I, 131. See also Luis Ortiz Matos to Sec. of Agric., 25 Oct. 1962, AGN, SA, leg. 1820, 1963.

70. Pierre Larrochel Damus to Trujillo, 9 Sept. 1934; Damus to Sec. of Agric., 25 Sept. 1934, AGN, SA, leg. 182, n.d.

71. Read to Sec. of Agric., no. 753, 5 Oct. 1934; Tolentino to Read, 9 Oct. 1934, AGN, SA, leg. 181, 1934.

72. Carretero and Read to Sec. of Agric., no. 721, 3 May 1935, AGN, SA, leg. 209, 1935.

73. Alcibíades Ogando to Supervisor of the Agric. Juntas, no. 25, 17 Apr. 1936, AGN, SA, leg. 2, 1936.

74. "Los nombres de poblaciones y ríos o arroyos fronterizos son cambiados por Dominicanos," *La Opinión*, 3 Sept. 1931; "Nombres de ciudades y aldeas que han sido substituidos por otros nombres," *Revista de Educación* 7, no. 25 (1935), 68–69.

75. Sáez, *Los Jesuitas en la República Dominicana*, 53–55.

76. "La política escolar del Honorable Presidente Trujillo," *Revista de Educación* 7, no. 28 (1935), 21.

77. "Notable plan de estudios para las escuelas fronterizas," *Listín Diario*, 30 Jan. 1935; "Editorial: Plan de estudios para las escuelas fronterizas," *Listín Diario*, 31 Jan. 1935.

78. Trujillo's maternal grandmother, Luisa Erciná Chevalier, was Haitian. Crassweller, *Trujillo*, 26–27.

79. Interview with Isil Nicolas, Ouanaminthe, 1988.

80. Interviews in the Dominican frontier, 1987–88; Balaguer to Quentin Reynolds, coeditor, *Collier's Weekly*, no. 27826, 9 Dec. 1937, RG84, 800-D.

81. Jean Ghasmann Bissainthe, *Perfil de dos naciones en La Española* (Santo Domingo: n.p., 1998); Vega, *Trujillo y Haití*, vol. I, 224–32.

82. *La Opinión*, 14 Apr. 1937.

83. "Chronique," *Le Temps* (Port-au-Prince), 14 Mar. 1936; Crassweller, *Trujillo*, 153–63.

84. *La Croisade*, 14 Mar. 1936. Reproduced in "Los Presidentes Vincent y Trujillo: Dos soldados de la Paz Americana," *Listín Diario*, 28 Mar. 1936.

85. Interview with Roger Dorsinville, Port-au-Prince, 1988.

86. A cartoon in the Santiago newspaper, *La Tribuna* (26 May 1937), e.g., depicted two peasants discussing Trujillo's orders that under the border agreement of 1936, all goods (and people) would now have to pass through the proper entry points.

87. Baud, "Una frontera para cruzar," 20–21; on smuggling often covered up as "theft," see Utley and Miller, "Agreement Respecting Border Troubles."

88. Rafael Merens Montes to Sec. of Agric., 16 Jan. 1934, SA, leg. 181, 1934; Paulino Vásquez to Sec. of Agric., no. 84, 6 May 1935; Emilio Ramírez to Trujillo, 14 May 1935; Miguel Lama to Sec. of Agric., 17 May 1935; Vicente Tolentino to Sec. of Pres., no. 2478, 18 May 1935; Amado Gómez to Trujillo, 26 June 1935, AGN, SA, leg. 207, 1935. See also Utley and Miller, "Agreement Respecting Border Troubles"; Freddy Prestol Castillo, *El Masacre se pasa a pie* (Santo Domingo: Taller, 1973), 92; Baud, "Una frontera para cruzar," 17; Baud, "Una frontera-refugio," 51–52; Lundius and Lundahl, *Peasants and Religion*, 157, 453–60, 511–12; Manuel de Jesús Rodríguez, "Nuestras fronteras," *La Voz del Sur*, 1 Oct. 1910.

89. Ercilia Guerrier remembered hearing that fifty new troops had arrived while only one local soldier remained in her area. "When we were running, [the guardias] were people we had never seen before," she said. Interview with Ercilia Guerrier, Mont Organizé, 1988.

90. The conventional figure of Haitian deaths given in the Dominican Republic is 17,000, which was reiterated by Joaquín Balaguer, acting foreign minister at the time of the massacre (Balaguer, *La palabra encadenada* [Santo Domingo: Taller, 1985], 300). A higher estimate of 20,000 is reached by subtracting the 10,000 ethnic Haitians who reportedly crossed over into Haiti during and after the massacre from the 30,000 ethnic

Haitians who a Catholic missionary estimated in 1936 were resident in the parish of Dajabón alone (only part of the northern frontier area, what was then Monte Cristi province). There were almost no ethnic Haitians left in this parish after the massacre, suggesting that 20,000 were killed just in this region (Sáez, *Los Jesuitas en la República Dominicana*, 60, 71). In the month after the massacre, Father Émile Robert in Ouanaminthe, Haiti (across the river from Dajabón) and another priest collected from refugees the names of 2,130 persons killed. However, they were able to interview only a small portion of those who escaped (J. M. Jan, *Collecta IV: Diocese du Cap-Haitien documents 1929–1960* [Rennes: Simon, 1967], 82; Melville Monk to Rex Pixley, 3 Nov. 1937, RG84, 800-D). When Lauren Derby and I spoke with Father Robert in Guadeloupe in 1988, he estimated that at least 15,000 persons must have been killed.

91. Those interviewed in 1987–88 in the Dominican frontier and in Haiti described substantial Haitian settlement in the frontier dating back to the 1870s. Of the Haitians interviewed, the vast majority had lived in the Dominican Republic for at least fifteen years prior to the massacre and a large portion had been born there. Also, in 1934 a government official confirmed the Dominican birth and citizenship of much of the ethnic Haitian population in the frontier (Julián Díaz Valdepares, "Alrededor de la cuestión haitiana," *Listín Diario*, 10 Dec. 1937).

92. The river was rechristened Río Massacre in the eighteenth century, purportedly after a battle between Spanish soldiers and French buccaneers.

93. Interviews in the Dominican frontier and Haiti, 1987–88. See also R. Henry Norweb to Sec. of State, no. 16, 11 Oct. 1937, RG84, 800-D; Vega, *Trujillo y Haití*, vol. I, 348, 355.

94. "Roosevelt Praises Dominican Stand," *New York Times*, 21 Dec. 1937. Cf. Cuello, *Documentos*, 512. Some of these affidavits are available in U.S. legation records. See enc. to Ferdinand Mayer to Sec. of State, no. 19, 17 Dec. 1937, RG84, 800-D. The exactitude of this figure gives it plausibility as a list of specific individuals known to have been killed.

95. On the history of the Haitian massacre, see Juan Manuel García, *La matanza de los haitianos: Genocidio de Trujillo, 1937* (Santo Domingo: Alfa y Omega, 1983), esp. 59, 69–71; Cuello, *Documentos*, 60–85; Vega, *Trujillo y Haití*, vol. I, 325–412; Vega, *Trujillo y Haití*, vol. II; Roorda, *The Dictator Next Door*, chap. 5; and Thomas Fiehrer, "Political Violence in the Periphery: The Haitian Massacre of 1937," *Race and Class* 32, no. 2 (1990), 1–20; Edward Paulino Díaz, "Birth of a Boundary: Blood, Cement, and Prejudice and the Making of the Dominican-Haitian Border, 1937–1961" (Ph.D. diss., Michigan State University, 2001). See also the testimonial novel by Castillo, *El Masacre*, 49.

96. E.g., interview with Miguel Otilio Savé (Guelo), Monte Cristi, 1988; testimony of Cime Jean, Ouanaminthe, 3 Oct. 1937, RG84, 800-D; García, *La matanza de los haitianos*, 59, 67–71; Cuello, *Documentos*, 60–85; and Prestol Castillo, *El Masacre*, 49.

97. Atwood to Sec. of State, no. 4021, 15 Sept. 1937, RG84, 800-801.2.

98. Interviews with Erciiia Guerrier, Mont Organizé; Percivio Díaz, Santiago de la Cruz, 1988. Virtually every elderly frontier resident we interviewed recalled Trujillo's multiple visits to the region in the early 1930s.

99. Jan, *Collecta IV*, 82–83.

100. Cuello, *Documentos*, 61; testimony by Parchide Pierre and Cime Jean, Oua-naminthe, 3 Oct. 1937, RG84, 800-D.

101. Isidro Medina to Thomas Norris, 5 Oct. 1937, RG84, 800-D.

102. Unless otherwise stated, the description of the massacre is drawn from inter-views in Haiti and the Dominican Republic, 1987–88. For a more detailed exploration of the Haitian massacre, see Turits, "A World Destroyed, A Nation Imposed: The 1937 Haitian Massacre in the Dominican Republic," *Hispanic American Historical Review* 82, no. 3 (2002).

103. Interview with Lolo, Restauración, 1988.

104. Interview with Sus Jonapas, Dosmond, Haiti, 1988.

105. Interview with Emanuel Cour, Ouanaminthe, 1988.

106. Interview with Ercilia Guerrier, Mont Organizé, 1988.

107. Interview with Sus Jonapas, Dosmond, 1988.

108. This is also suggested in Edwidge Danticat, *The Farming of Bones: A Novel* (New York: Soho, 1998), 195, 265. The Spanish *r*, moreover, has tended to be barely rolled even by ethnic Dominicans in the frontier and much of the country, when placed at the end or in the middle of words. See Max Jiménez Sabater, *Más datos sobre el español de la República Dominicana* (Santo Domingo: Editora del Sol, 1975).

109. Anonymous interview, Mont Organizé, 1988.

110. The idea that pronunciation of *perejil* did indeed serve to distinguish Haitians and Dominicans would become one of the most common features of even brief treat-ments of the massacre. See, e.g., Alan Cambeira, *Quisqueya La Bella: The Dominican Republic in Historical and Cultural Perspective* (Armonk, N.Y.: M. E. Sharpe, 1997), 182–83. See also Rita Dove's poem on the massacre in Dove, *Selected Poems* (New York: Vintage, 1993), 133–35.

111. Testimony of Cime Jean, Ouanaminthe, 3 Oct. 1937, RG84, 800-D; García, *La matanza*, 69–71.

112. Interview with Lolo, Restauración, 1988.

113. Howard Eager, Bureau of Insular Affairs, "Memorandum for the Chief, Mili-tary Intelligence Division, G-2; Subject: Haitian-Dominican Incident," n.d., RG165, Reg. Files. This was confirmed in interviews with refugees from the massacre living in Haiti, 1987–88.

114. Interview with Ercilia Guerrier, Mont Organizé, 1988.

115. Interview with Emanuel Cour, Ouanaminthe, 1988.

116. Eager, "Memorandum," RG165, Reg. Files; anonymous interview, Mariano Cestero (a colony in Restauración), 1988; interviews with Ezequiel Hernández, Mari-ano Cestero, and Avelino Cruz, Loma de Cabrera, Apr. 1988.

117. Eager, "Memorandum," RG165, Reg. Files.

118. For comparative purposes, see Eagle Glassheim, "National Mythologies and Ethnic Cleansing: The Expulsion of Czechoslovak Germans in 1945," *Central European History* 33, no. 4 (2000).

119. Interview with Doña María, Dajabón, 1988.

120. Atwood to Sec. of State, no. 39, 25 Oct. 1937, RG84, 800-D.

121. Eager, "Memorandum," RG165, Reg. Files. See also Prestol, *El Masacre*, 24. On sol-diers' resistance, see also *Washington Post*, 10 Nov. 1937; Hicks, *Blood in the Streets*, 107.

122. Interview with Díaz, Santiago de la Cruz, 1988. For similar testimony, see García, *La matanza*, 56.

123. Nonetheless, some killings reportedly continued in the region for the next couple of days and erupted in various points across the Cibao, such as Puerto Plata, Santiago, and Moca, until around Oct. 20. Norweb to Sec. of State, no. 16, 11 Oct. 1937, RG84, 800-D; Eager, "Memorandum," RG165, Reg. Files; Cuello, *Documentos*, 60–85.

124. Norweb to Sec. of State, no. 16, 11 Oct. 1937, RG84, 800-D.

125. Log book, Oct. 1937, L'École des Frères, Ouanaminthe. Gallego himself reported that "Of the 34,000 inhabitants who had been in the Mission, only some 4,000 remain, the Dominicans no one else." Sáez, *Los Jesuitas en la República Dominicana*, 71.

126. "Le massacre continue," *Le Mouvement*, 29 Nov. 1937 and 6 Dec. 1937; Vega, *Trujillo y Haití*, vol. II, 344; Norweb to Sec. of State, no. 107, n.d., RG84, 800-D.

127. Vega, *Trujillo y Haití*, vol. II, 344–45.

128. Orlando Inoa, "Cacería de haitianos: La matanza después de la Matanza," *El Siglo*, 25 June 1993.

129. Interview with Bilín, Monte Grande, May 1988.

130. Log book, Oct. 1937, L'École des Frères, Ouanaminthe.

131. "Memoire confidentiel sur les difficultés entre Haiti et la Republique Dominicaine remis a la Legation des États Unis D'Amerique, par le Président d'Haiti," RG84, 800-D; Mayer to Sec. of State, no. 120, 22 Nov. 1937, RG84, 800-D.

132. Interview with Father Émile Robert, Guadeloupe, 1988; Cuello, *Documentos*, 51–78.

133. Cuello, *Documentos*, 456, 466.

134. See Crassweller, *Trujillo*, passim.

135. See Vega, *Trujillo y Haití*, vol. II, 366; Mayer to Sec. of State, no. 95, 12 Mar. 1938, and Eugene Hinkle to Sec. of State, 10 Sept. 1938, no. 441, RG84, 800-D.

136. Interview with Danés Merisier, Savane Zonbi, Haiti 1988.

137. Anonymous interview, Aguas Negras, June, 1988.

138. Ramírez, *Mis 43 años*, 63n, 66–75.

139. Ramírez, *Mis 43 años*, 73.

140. E.g., Vega, *Trujillo y Haití*, vol. I, 392, 304–9; Cambeira, *Quisqueya La Bella*, 183–85.

141. Law no. 279, 29 Jan. 1932, *Colección de Leyes, Decretos y Resoluciones*; cf. Law no. 250, 19 Oct. 1925, *Gaceta Oficial* no. 3693, 24 Oct. 1925. This law also ended exemptions from all migration fees and obligations for those of the "caucasian race," which had been in place since 1912 (Law no. 5074, 7 May 1912, *Gaceta Oficial*, no. 2295, 11 May 1912). In 1928, Secretary Espaillat had condemned the "clandestine" and "undesirable" immigration of Asians and demanded "restrictive measures that would absolutely impede the immigration of those of the yellow race" (*Secretario de Estado de Agricultura é Inmigración, Memoria, 1928* [Santo Domingo: n.p., 1929], 55).

142. Law no. 95, 11 Apr. 1939, *Gaceta Oficial*, no. 5299, 17 Apr. 1939; Edward Anderson, U.S. consul, Ciudad Trujillo, "An Analysis of the Dominican Immigration Laws and Regulations," 26 June 1939, RG59, 839.55/108.

143. Marc C. McLeod, "Undesirable Aliens: Race, Ethnicity, and Nationalism in

the Comparison of Haitian and British West Indian Immigrant Workers in Cuba, 1912–1939," *Journal of Social History* 31, no. 3 (1998).

144. Melville Monk, Cap-Haitien customs, to Rex Pixley, 21 Oct. 1937, RG84, 800-D.

145. Balaguer to Reynolds, no. 27826, 9 Dec. 1937, RG84, 800-D. Outside the targeted region, Haitians who were not braceros were also not attacked during the massacre.

146. Suzy Castor, *Migración y relaciones internacionales (el caso haitiano-dominicano)* (Santo Domingo: Editora Universitaria, 1987); José Israel Cuello, *Contración de mano de obra haitiana destinada a la industria azucarera dominicana, 1952–1986* (Santo Domingo: Taller, 1997), esp. 36–42; Andrew Wardlaw, "End of Year Report: 1945," 14 Mar. 1946, RG59, 839.00; Phelps Phelps to Sec. of State, no. 636, 13 Feb. 1953, 739.00(w).

147. Enc. to Mayer to Sec. of State, no. 13, 9 Dec. 1937, RG84, 800-D.

148. For official U.S. and Haitian views that it would have been feasible to expel Haitians from the Dominican frontier, see Eager, "Memorandum," RG165, Reg. Files; enc. to Mayer to Sec. of State, no. 13, 9 Dec. 1937, RG84, 800-D. See also Balaguer, *La palabra encadenada*, 300.

149. Thomas Holt, "An 'Empire over the Mind': Emancipation, Race, and Ideology in the British West Indies and the American South"; and Barbara Fields, "Ideology and Race in American History," in *Region, Race, and Reconstruction: Essays in Honor of C. Vann Woodward*, ed. J. Morgan Kousser and James McPherson (New York: Oxford University Press, 1982).

150. See, e.g., V. Díaz Ordóñez, *El más antiguo y grave problema antillano* (Ciudad Trujillo: La Opinión, 1938); Ana Richardson Batista, "Dominicanización fronteriza," *La Nación*, 24 May 1943; J. R. Johnson Mejía, "Contenido racional de la política de dominicanización fronteriza," *Boletín del Partido Dominicano*, 30 July 1943; Manuel Peña Batlle, *El sentido de una política* (Ciudad Trujillo: La Nación, 1943).

151. See San Miguel, *La isla imaginada*, 82–95; Baud, "Constitutionally White," 132–39; Lauren Derby, "Histories of Power and the Power of History in the Dominican Republic" (unpublished manuscript, 1989).

152. Frank Moya Pons, "La frontera política," *Rumbo* 5, no. 271 (12 Apr. 1999); Bernardo Vega, "Variaciones en el uso del anti-haitianismo en la era de Trujillo," presentation at the Latin American Studies Association, Washington, D.C., 28–30 Sept. 1995; Derby, "Histories of Power."

153. Lauren Derby and Richard Turits, "Historias de terror y terrores de la historia: la masacre haitiana de 1937 en la República Dominicana," *Estudios Sociales* 26, no. 92 (1993), 65, 75.

154. Atwood to Sec. of State, no. 25, 15 Oct. 1937, RG84, 800-D.

155. Hinkle to Sec. of State, no. 373, 7 July 1938, RG84, 710-Haiti; Ellis Briggs to Sec. of State, no. 232, 19 Aug. 1944, RG84, 710–30; Julio Ibarra to Sec. of the Interior, no. 480, 15 May 1957, and related documents in AGN, SA, leg. 903, 1957; Francis Spalding to Sec. of State, no. 44, 29 July 1957, RG59, 739.00.

156. Palmer, "Land Use and Landscape Change," 89, 103.

157. For an interpretation that emphasizes this continuity, see Paulino Díaz, "Birth of a Boundary," chaps. 4–6.

158. See, e.g., F. Ducoudray h., "Los secretos del vodú," *¡Ahora!* 7 Apr. 1980, and "Los conucos de Yesí Elá," *¡Ahora!* 14 Apr. 1980.

159. Atwood to Sec. of State, no. 54, 5 Nov. 1937, RG84, 800-D; Roorda, *The Dictator Next Door*, 135; Cuello, *Documentos*, passim; H. C. R., "Memorandum: Conversation with Emilio Rodríguez Demorizi, Director of the National Archives," 26 May 1943, RG84, 702–711.

160. Interview with Avelino Cruz, Loma de Cabrera, Apr. 1988.

161. Interview with Percivio Díaz, Santiago de la Cruz, Apr. 1988.

162. Interview with Evelina Sánchez, Monte Cristi, 1988.

163. See note 146.

164. On the paradoxes of Dominican anti-Haitianism, see Baud, "Constitutionally White," 140–41.

165. Anti-Haitianism today, as in the early twentieth century, is clearest among elite Dominicans. See, e.g., José Gautier's essay in *El Nacional*, 19 Nov. 1987; Luis Homero Lajara Burgos, "Dimensión," *Hoy*, 23 July 1991; Luis Julián Pérez, *Santo Domingo frente al destino* (Santo Domingo: Editora Taller, 1990).

166. Juan Valerio to Sec. of Agric., no. 19, 19 Nov. 1941, AGN, SA, leg. 203, 1941; Emilio Espinola to Supervisor of Frontier Colonies, no. 4887, 7 June 1941, AGN, SA, leg. 203, 1941; Andrés Monclús to Chief of the Mil. Advisers to the Pres., 10 May 1943, AGN, SA, leg. 3, 1942.

167. Anonymous interview, Monte Cristi, 1987.

168. Andrew Wardlaw, annual report, 14 Mar. 1946; monthly economic reports, 21 Mar. and 24 Apr. 1950, RG59, 839.00; Spalding to Sec. of State, no. 44, 29 July 1957, RG59, 739.00; and Ramírez, *Mis 43 años*, 76–90.

169. Emilio García Godoy, "Hoy y mañana," *La Nación*, 4 July 1943.

170. R. J. Urruela, "Las escuelas y los alimentos han resuelto el viejo problema fronterizo en la isla española," *La Opinión*, 18 Apr. 1945.

171. The pronoun "them" is ambiguous. It may refer to Haitian leaders, Dominican critics, or frontier denizens. Robert Crassweller, letter to author, 19 Jan. 1988.

Chapter 6: Taming the Countryside

1. For multiple perspectives on the history of agricultural colonization under Trujillo, see Lundius and Lundahl, *Peasants and Religion*, 515–16; Inoa, *Estado y campesinos*, 157–80; San Miguel, *Los campesinos*, 307–12; Frank Rodríguez, "Trujillo y la colonización agrícola," *Hoy*, 4 May 1992.

2. Louk Box and Barbara de la Rive Box-Lasocki, "¿Sociedad fronteriza o frontera social? Transformaciones sociales en la zona fronteriza de la República Dominicana (1907–1984)," *Boletín de estudios latinoamericanos y del Caribe* (Amsterdam), no. 46 (1989), 58–61.

3. See also San Miguel, *Los campesinos*, 308–9; Palmer, "Land Use and Landscape Change," 105, 108.

4. Mariñez, *Agroindustria*, 42.

5. *Secretaría de Estado de Agricultura, Memoria, 1953* (San Cristóbal, 1954), 37. These statistics do not include various colonies outside the aegis of the Department of Agriculture, such as the Sosúa colony. They also exclude areas that had once been but were officially no longer colonies—namely, areas of state land that had, technically at least, become colonists' private property, as was supposed to occur automatically following occupation for a period varying between one and ten years (generally the latter), depending on circumstances and legal reforms. See., e.g., *Secretaría de Estado de Agricultura, Memoria, 1957* (Ciudad Trujillo, 1958), 80–81. Finally, they did not include the small number of "colonies" that were not state owned but rather forms of private land distribution from large landowners secured under the promise of state oversight. See *Secretaría de Agricultura, Industria y Trabajo, Memoria, 1941* (Ciudad Trujillo, 1942). Some of these colonies nonetheless became, in effect, peasant property, such as the 252 hectares in La Noria that had belonged to the Vicini family's Compañía de Inversiones Inmobiliarias.

6. These figures differ slightly from those used to compile the aggregate statistics for colonization and land distribution presented in the introduction, because those aggregate figures cover only through 1958 (statistics for distribution comparable to those for colonization for 1959 are not available). *Secretaría de Estado de Agricultura, Memoria, 1959* (Ciudad Trujillo, 1960), 72; Ramos, "La ciudad y el campo," 55–58. A small number of these colonies, however, had already been abandoned because of poor agricultural conditions. See *Secretaría de Estado de Agricultura, Memoria, 1958* (Ciudad Trujillo, 1959), 21. Other estimates of colonization place the total land distributed at between 125,000 and 145,000 hectares and the number of recipients at only approximately 12,000. In light of the information I cite above, however, these estimates appear to be incomplete. Furthermore, given that there were already 10,242 colonists in 1947 and, by all accounts, the bulk of colonization occurred after that year, the low estimates are implausible. *Secretaría de Estado de Agricultura, Pecuaria y Colonización, Memoria, 1947* (Ciudad Trujillo, 1948), 188; cf. Frank Rodríguez and Otto Fernández, "Notas sobre las políticas agrarias en la República Dominicana," *Ciencia* 3, no. 1 (1976), 45; Gifford E. Rogers, "Régimen de la tenencia de tierras en la República Dominicana" (Santo Domingo: International Development Services, Dec. 1962).

7. Dominican Republic, *Quinto censo nacional agropecuario*, x; Mariñez, *Resistencia*, 87.

8. See Ramón Marrero Aristy, "La posición del trabajador," *La Opinión*, 18 Sept. 1945.

9. Servio Peguero to Tolentino, no. 19, 19 Mar. 1933, AGN, SA, leg. 351, 1938. See also Olivares, "Fundación de las primeras colonias."

10. Law no. 758 of 9 Oct. 1934, *Gaceta Oficial*, no. 4725, 13 Oct. 1934.

11. "Resumen de las actividades desplegadas por la Secretaría de Estado de Trabajo," 4–5.

12. *Secretaría de Estado de Agricultura y Trabajo, Memoria, 1935*, 3–5. Sabaneta de Yásica was in the commune of Puerto Plata; Pedro García in Santiago; and San Rafael in Sabana de la Mar (Samaná). *Secretario de Estado de Agricultura, Memoria, 1937*. However, three small military and penal colonies were established in southern border

areas. See *Secretaría de Estado de lo Interior, Policía, Guerra y Marina, Memoria, 1934* (Santo Domingo: n.p., 1935), 460–63; Inoa, *Estado y campesinos*, 164–65.

13. "La política de colonización fronteriza del Excelentísimo Presidente Trujillo Molina," *La Nación*, 5 Mar. 1945.

14. In 1950 fourteen of the forty-two agricultural colonies were considered "frontier colonies," and they comprised 18,565 hectares out of 78,052 hectares and 2,935 of 12,949 colonists. *Secretaría de Estado de Agricultura, Pecuaria y Colonización, Memoria, 1950* (San Cristóbal, 1951) 115, 117, 137.

15. César A. Caamaño to Read, no. 151, 9 Aug. 1935, AGN, SA, leg. 2–1, 1935.

16. *Secretaría de Estado de Agricultura, Industria y Trabajo, Memoria, 1939* (Ciudad Trujillo, 1940), 136, 118.

17. See colony figures above. Numerous documentary constraints hinder analysis of colonization in the Dominican Republic. For instance, no complete and accurate listing of all colonies, their correct date of establishment, precise location, and number of beneficiaries and residents exists. (Cf. Rogers, "Régimen de la tenencia de tierras en la República Dominicana"; Rodríguez and Fernández, "Notas sobre las políticas agrarias," 45, 49; Box and de la Rive Box-Lasocki, "¿Sociedad fronteriza o frontera social?" 56–61.) Colonization records were not centralized or well organized. My information comes primarily from a myriad of individual reports within the Department of Agriculture files, mostly communication between colony administrators and the secretary of agriculture. Often, the entire history of any particular colony or case is unknown. Nonetheless, these documents reveal the overall outlines of Trujillo's colonization program.

18. Inoa, *Estado y campesinos*, 174, 208. See also Mariñez, *Resistencia*, 87. For an example of plow shortages in the colonies, see Joaquín Garrido to Sec. of Agric., no. 435, 1 Mar. 1938, AGN, SA, leg. 358, 1938. The state obtained the property it distributed for colonization from multiple sources, probably the largest being areas legally designated as comunero sites with strong though still unsettled claims by individual landowners.

19. S. Cabral Romero to Sec. of Agric., no. 1226, 7 Nov. 1947; Carlos Liriano to State Lawyer, 17 Oct. 1947; and Cabral Romero to Chief of the Colonization Branch, 19 Nov. 1947, AGN, SA, leg. 51b, 1947.

20. See AGN, SA, legs. 46, 37, and 51b, 1947, and leg. 194, 1952.

21. Cesáreo Cruz Díaz to Sec. of Agric., 25 Apr. 1947, and Francisco Pereyra Frómeta to Baní Agricultural Supervisor, no. 3841, 2 Sept. 1947, AGN, SA, leg. 46, 1947.

22. Cf. Miguel A. Báez Díaz to Sec. of Public Works and Irrigation, no. 1625, 25 Sept. 1947, and other documents in AGN, SA, leg. 55, 1947.

23. See, e.g., Francisco de Moya Franco to Gregorio Mercado, no. 3445, 8 Feb. 1952, AGN, SA, leg. 194, 1952. An example of an applicant who was unwilling to move is Manuel Cabrera to Sec. of Agric., 19 May 1952, AGN, SA, leg. 194, 1952.

24. E.g., Ramón Emilio Cepeda to Trujillo, 16 Sept. 1947, AGN, SA, leg. 37, 1947.

25. Miguel Ramírez to Sec. of Agric., 15 Dec. 1952, and Andrés Eurípides Díaz to Miguel Ramírez, no. 36542, 22 Dec. 1952, AGN, SA, leg. 37, 1947.

26. Féliz Salvador to Pres., 6 May 1947, and Pereyra Frómeta to Salvador, no. 1913, 28 May 1947, AGN, SA, leg. 46, 1947.

27. Alberto Bogaert to Sec. of the Pres., no. 23718, 3 Sept. 1952, and Caraballo to Trujillo, 5 July 1952, AGN, SA, leg. 194, 1952.

28. Manuel (Toribio) Fernández to Héctor Trujillo, 10 Oct. 1952, AGN, SA, leg. 194, 1952.

29. See examples in AGN, SA, leg. 194, 1952; AGN, SA, leg. 46, 1947; AGN, SA, leg. 37, 1947; and AGN, SA, leg. 51b, 1947.

30. Pablo Bienvenido Medina to Sec. of Agric., 15 Mar. 1952, and Pereyra Frómeta, chief of the Colonization Branch, no. 2582, 29 May 1952, AGN, SA, leg. 194, 1952. One finds the same official populist discourse being used by local officials to push Trujillo to advance policies favoring the peasantry. Luis Tomás Saillant, special inspector of irrigation, wrote to Trujillo in 1944: "It escapes no one that the poor agriculturalist does not obtain a just benefit, and as you have made clear at all times the noble sentiments of support for the peasantry that motivate you, I consider that the solution to the problem lies in your hands" (Saillant to Trujillo, 19 Jan. 1944, AGN, SA, leg. 10b, 1944).

31. See, e.g., Miguel Ramírez to Sec. of Agric., 15 Dec. 1952, AGN, SA, leg. 37, 1947; Cesáreo Cruz Díaz to Sec. of Agric., 25 Apr. 1947, AGN, SA, leg. 46, 1947; José M. Ramos to Trujillo, 20 Oct. 1952, AGN, SA, leg. 194, 1952; and other documents in these same *legajos*.

32. Miguel Tiburcio Peña, José Jorge Peña, et al. to Trujillo, 29 Feb. 1952, AGN, SA, leg. 194, 1952.

33. Moya Franco to Miguel Tiburcio Peña et al., no. 7566, 20 Mar. 1952, AGN, SA, leg. 194, 1952.

34. Manuel Encarnación to Héctor Trujillo, 12 Dec. 1952, AGN, SA, leg. 194, 1952. See also Prudencio Morales Mañán to Trujillo, 14 June 1952, AGN, SA, leg. 194, 1952.

35. See, e.g., S. Deño (?) to Chief of the Colonization Branch, no. 79, 6 Dec. 1952, and Pereyra Frómeta to Sec. of Agric., no. 6919, 17 Dec. 1952, AGN, SA, leg. 37, 1947 (misfiled).

36. See AGN, SA, legs. 46, 37, and 51b, 1947.

37. See Pereyra Frómeta, to Sec. of Agric., no. 1513, 29 Apr. 1947, and other similar documents in AGN, SA, leg. 39, 1947.

38. Raúl Carbuccia to Dir. of National Irrigation Service, no. 4283, 7 July 1938, AGN, SA, leg. 351, 1938.

39. See AGN, SA, leg. 175, 1951; AGN, SA, leg. 51b, 1947; and AGN, SA, leg. 37, 1947.

40. Law no. 1783, 5 Aug. 1948, *Gaceta Oficial*, no. 6829, 25 Aug. 1948.

41. For examples, see AGN, SA, leg. 176, 1951. Also see R. A. Martínez Gallardo to Sec. of Agric., 28 Apr. 1958, AGN, SA, leg. 1051, 1958.

42. Moya Franco to Pres., no. 2582, 1 Feb. 1952, AGN, SA, leg. 37, 1947 (misfiled).

43. See Pedro María Almonte to Sec. of Agric., 22 Sept. 1952, AGN, SA, leg. 197, 1952.

44. In 1954 the roughly fifty agricultural colonies included 13,200 state-built houses, 403 schools, and 52 churches or *ermitas* ("Reparten más de 3 millones de tareas fértiles entre 102 mil agricultores," *El Caribe*, 2 Mar. 1954). Most colonists' stipend at this time was 60 centavos per day for each member of the family, then a substantial contribution to one's subsistence. Interview with Frank Vidal, Santo Nuñez Ramírez, Emilio Mota, Leonardo Nuñez, and Hipólito Nuñez, Cedro, Miches, 1 Aug. 1992.

45. Stipends were given at first to colonists in the irrigated colonies of Villa Vásquez (Olivares, "Fundación de las primeras colonias") and Jima Abajo (interview with Ramón Abreu, Jima Abajo, La Vega, 21 Nov. 1994).

46. Andrés Monclús to Chief of the Mil. Assts. to the Pres., 10 May 1943, AGN, SA, leg. 3, 1942.

47. See, e.g., Carretero and Read to Sec. of Agric., no. 721, 3 May 1935, AGN, SA, leg. 209, 1935. Some colonists continued using their land for raising animals much to the chagrin of administrators who threatened to reappropriate their plots. See, e.g., Manuel Matos to Chief of the Colonization Branch, no. 23, 20 Feb. 1952, AGN, SA, leg. 37, 1947.

48. Interviews in Miches, Aug. 1992, and in other colonies during 1992. Peasant attitudes toward state intervention into personal and cultural life within the colonies is discussed in chap. 7.

49. Interview with José Adames, Guineo, Miches, 1 Aug. 1992.

50. Interview with Gregorio Mejía and Felicia Ciprián, Cedro, Miches, 1 Aug. 1992. Peasants liked to live near their work, as Mejía stated—which was most possible in the hills and monte—in part because women and children played a major role in cultivating a family's food crops. Michiel Baud, "Patriarchy and Changing Family Strategies: Class and Gender in the Dominican Republic," *History of the Family* 2, no. 4 (1997), 358.

51. Interview with Antonio (Papito) Amparo, Cedro, Miches, 2 Aug. 1992.

52. See Law no. 758, 18 Sept. 1934, *Gaceta Oficial*, no. 4725, 13 Oct. 1934.

53. See, e.g., P. M. Vargas Santana to Special Commissioner of the Pres. from the Eastern Provinces, no. 305, 24 Nov. 1935, AGN, SA, leg. 351, 1938. See also various documents in AGN, SA, legs. 1022 and 1027, 1958.

54. Interview with colonist Ramón Abreu, Jima Abajo, La Vega, 21 Nov. 1994.

55. Inoa, *Estado y campesinos*, 175–208.

56. Several elderly peasants I spoke with recalled that despite taxes, strong market demand made rice prices generally high enough to stimulate production. Interview, e.g., with Aurelio Mercedes Disla, Caballero Abajo, Cotuí, 5 Apr. 1992. Cf. Inoa, *Estado y campesinos*, 180–208, esp. 194.

57. Interview with anonymous colonist, Sabana Alta, San Juan de la Maguana, Oct. 1992.

58. *Secretaría de Estado de Agricultura, Pecuaria y Colonización, Memoria, 1950* (San Cristóbal, 1951), 123.

59. Mario E. Campo Pérez to Sec. of Agric., 30 Apr. 1941; and Emilio Espinola to Campo, 20 May 1941, AGN, SA, leg. 203, 1941.

60. Andrés Monclús to Chief of the Mil. Assts. to the Pres., 10 May 1943, and Humberto Bogaert to Chief of the Mil. Assts. to the Pres., no. 8102, 21 May 1943, AGN, SA, leg. 3, 1942; Interviews in Miches, Aug. 1992.

61. *Secretaría de Estado de Agricultura, Pecuaria y Colonización, Memoria, 1947*, 188. It is possible that numerous prisoner colonists were not identified as such because their sentences had already expired. Also, the above figures do not include the prisoners sent to several penal colonies under military rather than Department of Agriculture jurisdiction, which are described below.

62. Interview with Domingo Henríquez, Mariano Cestero, Restauración, 17 Jan. 1993. See also Jesús Santana to Trujillo, 18 Mar. 1947, AGN, SA, leg. 51b, 1947.

63. The number that reportedly escaped was surprisingly small. See Tulio H. Collado to Sec. of Agric., no. 44, 17 May 1938, AGN, SA, leg. 43, exp. 399, 1938.

64. Jesús Santana to Trujillo, 18 Mar. 1947, AGN, SA, leg. 51b, 1947. See also John Butler, attaché's report, 15 May 1940, RG59, 839.52.

65. Interview with Lolo Santos Sánchez, Carretón, 16 Aug. 1992.

66. Interview with Antonio Blanco, Hipólito Billini, Loma de Cabrera, 19 Jan. 1993. Blanco had been imprisoned for killing a man in a fight.

67. Orlando Inoa provides grim details of hunger, death, and disease in penal colonies established in the early years of the Trujillo regime. See Inoa, *Estado y campesinos*, 164–66.

68. Rafael Cuello, *El Sisal: Esclavitud y muerte en la era de Trujillo* (Santo Domingo: Susaeta, 1998); Spalding to Sec. of State, no. 4, 2 July 1957, RG59, 839.00.

69. Interviews with Javier Melo, Azua, 30 Aug. 1992; Francisco de Jesús Concha, Villa Juana, Santo Domingo, 27 Dec. 1992; Confesor Gúzman, Baní, 23 Aug. 1992; Manuel Santos Sánchez (Cheo), Carretón, Baní, 15 Aug. 1992; Carlos and Jesús Pujols, Estebanía, Azua, 30 Aug. 1992.

70. Interview with Domingo Hasbún, former assistant secretary of state for agriculture under Trujillo, Gazcue, Santo Domingo, 5 Aug. 1992.

71. Pedro Renvill, Santo Domingo agricultural supervisor, "Informe durante el mes de septiembre de 1940," AGN, SA, leg. 174, 1940.

72. E.g., Gregorio Mercado to Trujillo, 30 Jan. 1952, and Moya Franco to Mercado, no. 3445, 8 Feb. 1952, AGN, SA, leg. 194, 1952; Prudencio Morales Mañán to Trujillo, 14 June 1952, and A. Bogaert to Sec. of the Pres., no. 17110, 30 June 1952, AGN, SA, leg. 194, 1952; and José Arias to Sec. of Agric., 17 July 1944, AGN, SA, leg. 10b, 1944.

73. Miguel Dájer to Ramón Marrero Aristy, no. 1964, 30 Jan. 1958, AGN, SA, leg. 1016, 1958.

74. See AGN, SA, leg. 1027, 1958.

75. *Secretaría de Estado de Agricultura, Memoria, 1958*, 31.

76. This information comes from various documents in AGN, SA, leg. 1027, 1958, including reports made after the fall of the regime concerning complaints from those who were evicted and moved to these colonies. Other sources include interviews with Emiliano Vargas García, Ana María Vargas, Estela Cruz, and Eriberto Antonio, Carbonera, Dajabón, 19 Jan. 1993, and with Rhadamés Bolívar Maldonado Pinal, Santo Domingo, 8 Jan. 1993.

77. Interviews with Máximo Peralta García, Bonao, Higüey, 19 July 1992; and Carlos Pujols, Estebanía, Azua, 30 Aug. 1992.

78. Also, colonists and others recognized by the state as farmers who were deemed to be of the "caucasian race" were exempted from immigration fees. Law no. 758, 10 Oct. 1934, *Gaceta Oficial*, no. 4725, 13 Oct. 1934; Law no. 1783, 12 Aug. 1948, *Gaceta Oficial*, no. 6829, 25 Aug. 1948.

79. E.g., "Problemas fundamentales," *La Opinión*, 26 and 27 Mar. 1936; "Sobre la proyectada inmigración borinqueña a los campos del Este," *Listín Diario*, 16 Mar. 1934.

The U.S. legation reported: "The Dominican Government would welcome only Puerto Ricans it would consider 'white'" (James W. Gantenbein, "Memorandum on Possible Increased Immigration of Puerto Ricans into the Dominican Republic," 10 Apr. 1936, RG59, 1930–39, M1272, roll 32).

80. This project became serious only after Franklin Roosevelt's government formulated its plan to "rehabilitate" Puerto Rico. See Trujillo to Roosevelt, 3 Feb. 1936; Sumner Welles to H. F. Arthur Schoenfeld, no. 409, 19 Mar. 1936 (stamped not dated); Schoenfeld to Sec. of State, no. 3240, 10 Apr. 1936, RG59, 839.52; Department of State, Division of the American Republics, to Mr. Duggan, 19 Apr. 1938, RG59, 839.55/75; and Gantenbein, "Memorandum," 10 Apr. 1936.

81. Emilio García Godoy referred specifically to "an ethnically improved population" following the "incidents of the year 1937." "Hoy y mañana," *La Nación*, 4 July 1943. See also J. R. Johnson Mejía, "Contenido racional de la política de dominicanización fronteriza," *Boletín del Partido Dominicano*, 30 July 1943.

82. Trujillo had reportedly contemplated Jewish immigration to Dominican agricultural colonies since Apr. 1936, thus before the Haitian massacre. Yet in this early plan for German Jewish immigration, each immigrant family was obliged to have at least $1,000 in its possession (far above the usual $50 requirement); and the project appears never to have been realized. See Gantenbein, "Memorandum," 10 Apr. 1936. Similarly, in January 1937, Trujillo responded with apparent interest to overtures made by the American Jewish Congress to settle an unspecified number of European Jews as agriculturalists in the Dominican Republic (Trujillo to Stephen Wise, 9 Jan. 1937, RG59, 839.52). Actual Jewish immigration, however, proceeded only in the aftermath of the regime's 1938 offer at the Evian Conference. Anderson, "An Analysis of the Dominican Immigration Laws." Cf. Bernardo Vega, *Nazismo, Fascismo y Falangismo en la República Dominicana* (Santo Domingo: Fundación Cultural Dominicana, 1985), 180. The U.S. opposed Haiti's invitation at the same time to usher in fifty thousand Jewish refugees. Roorda, *The Dictator Next Door*, 144.

83. Roorda, *The Dictator Next Door*, 143–48.

84. Law no. 221, 24 Feb. 1940, *Gaceta Oficial*, no. 5420, 28 Feb. 1940; William Pheiffer to Sec. of State, no. 454, 5 Feb. 1957, RG59, 839.000. The colony was operated independently by the Dominican Republic Settlement Association of the American Jewish Joint Agricultural Corporation. This private corporation contributed an initial sum of $200,000 and then an additional $60–70,000 per year. Trujillo donated the land for the colony (26,685 acres)—after he purchased it from the United Fruit Company—in return for $100,000 worth of shares in the association.

85. Mark Wischnitzer, "The Historical Background of the Settlement of Jewish Refugees in Santo Domingo," *Jewish Social Studies* 4, no. 1 (1942), 45.

86. Roorda, *The Dictator Next Door*, 146.

87. Edward Anderson, "Restrictions Imposed upon the Admission of Refugee Immigrants into the Dominican Republic," no. 848, 17 Feb. 1939, RG59, 839.55/108.

88. Law no. 85, 9 Mar. 1939, *Gaceta Oficial*, no. 5286, 11 Mar. 1938. The fees for the Sosúa settlers may have been waived under the standard exemption of all agricultural colonists of "the caucasian race" from immigration and residence fees (Law no. 758, 10

Oct. 1934, *Gaceta Oficial*, no. 4725, 13 Oct. 1934). See also Law no. 48, 23 Dec. 1938, *Gaceta Oficial*, no. 5258, 28 Dec. 1938; Anderson, "An Analysis of the Dominican Immigration Laws"; Law no. 95, 11 Apr. 1939, *Gaceta Oficial*, no. 5299, 17 Apr. 1939.

89. Anderson, "Restrictions Imposed upon the Admission of Refugee Immigrants"; John Butler, Intelligence Report, 22 Jan. 1942, RG59, 839.5540/1.

90. Anderson, "An Analysis of the Dominican Immigration Laws."

91. James Rosenberg, founder of the Dominican Republic Settlement Association, quoted in Roorda, *The Dictator Next Door*, 146.

92. Richard Lankenau to Sec. of State, no. 194, 20 Sept. 1950, RG59, 839.02; Belton to Sec. of State, no. 795, 27 June 1952, RG59, 839.411; Affeld to Sec. of State, no. 463, 4 Feb. 1955, 839.411; Pheiffer to Sec. of State, no. 454, 5 Feb. 1957, RG59, 839.00.

93. Charles Burrows to Sec. of State, no. 1159, 17 Sept. 1947, RG59, 839.00; C. Harvey Gardiner, *La política de inmigración del dictador Trujillo: Estudio sobre la creación de una imagen humanitaria* (Santo Domingo: UNPHU, 1979).

94. *Secretaría de Estado de Agricultura, Industria y Trabajo, Memoria, 1940*, 80.

95. Gardiner, *La política de inmigración*, esp. 35–40, 80; Jimenes-Grullón, *La propaganda de Trujillo*, 21–22; David Curiel to northern agricultural supervisor, no. 9, 7 Jan. 1941, AGN, SA, leg. 1, 1941; Egon Tausch, memorandum for Mr. Reed, 28 May 1943, RG84, 1943 (vol. 13), correspondence, 800B–811.1; Eduardo Capó Bonnafous, *Medina del mar Caribe: Seminovela*, 2d ed. (Santo Domingo: Sociedad Dominicana de Bibliofilos, 1986); Bernardo Vega, *La migración española de 1939 y los inicios del Marxismo-Leninismo en la República Dominicana* (Santo Domingo: Fundación Cultural Dominicana, 1984).

96. A. Despradel to Chargé d'Affaires, 14 June 1940, enc. to Hinkle to Sec. of State, no. 1269, 15 June 1940, RG59, 839.55/119.

97. Jonathan Butler, capt., U.S. Marine Corps, 19 Nov. 1940, RG165, Reg. File 6010–9185.

98. Charles Burrows to Sec. of State, no. 1159, 17 Sept. 1947, RG59, 839.00.

99. *Secretaría de Estado de Agricultura, Memoria, 1953* (San Cristóbal, 1954), 37.

100. Ramón Marrero Aristy, "Un problema vital de la frontera," *La Nación*, 12 Dec. 1943. On Marrero, see Baud, "Un permanente guerrillero."

101. Pheiffer to Sec. of State, no. 152, 27 Sept. 1954, RG59, 739.00(w); Pheiffer to Sec. of State, no. 166, 11 Oct. 1955, RG59, 839.16162.

102. San Miguel, *La isla imaginada*, 82–95; Baud, "Constitutionally White," 132–39; Affeld to Sec. of State, no. 324, 13 Feb. 1956, RG59, 739.00(w). According to one member of Trujillo's inner circle, "the idea to bring Spanish immigrants was more the idea of Peña Batlle and Ortega Frier and backed also by Doña María [Trujillo's third wife] who was of Spanish origin, even though Trujillo was himself quite taken with things Spanish and a close associate of Generalissimo Franco." Interview with Braulio Alvarez Sánchez, Jarabacoa, Mar. 1992.

103. *Secretaría de Estado de Agricultura, Memoria, 1955* (Ciudad Trujillo, 1956), 89; Gardiner, *La política de inmigración*, 181. The several immigrants with whom I spoke stated that they came out of a spirit of adventure and desire to know more of the world, because of enticing depictions of the country offered by intermediaries, or because they preferred the Caribbean climate (interview with Angel Luciano Novoa,

Jacinta Garachana, and Victoriano Espinal, Sabana Alta, San Juan de la Maguana, Oct. 1992).

104. Interview with Jacinta Garachana (Spanish immigrant), Sabana Alta, San Juan de la Maguana, Oct. 1992. The stipend was generally considered barely enough for subsistence. Interview with Camilo del Rosario, Milciade Oscar Moquete Susaña, Amado Susaña, Angel Luciano Novoa, Jacinta Garachana, Victoriano Espinal, Sabana Alta, San Juan de la Maguana, Oct. 1992. See also Pheiffer to Sec. of State, no. 49, 25 July 1955, RG59 739.00(w).

105. See lists of the crop values among Spanish immigrants in AGN, SA, leg. 902, 1957, and requests concerning family members in AGN, SA, leg. 904, 1957.

106. Interview with Jacinta Garachana, Sabana Alta, San Juan de la Maguana, Oct. 1992; Pheiffer to Sec. of State, no. 166, 11 Oct. 1955, RG59, 839.16162; Desmond to Sec. of State, no. 397, 12 Jan. 1955, and no. 381, 20 Mar. 1956, RG59, 839.00.

107. Interview with Camilo del Rosario, Milciade Oscar Moquete Susaña, Amado Susaña, Angel Luciano Novoa, Jacinta Garachana, and Victoriano Espinal, Sabana Alta, San Juan de la Maguana, Oct. 1992; Affeld to Sec. of State, no. 463, 4 Feb. 1955, RG59, 839.411.

108. Víctor Aliño Bigne to Sr. Montás, 30 Oct. 1956, AGN, SA, leg. 902, 1957.

109. Pheiffer to Sec. of State, no. 49, 25 July 1955, RG59, 739.00(w).

110. Pheiffer to Sec. of State, no. 166, 11 Oct. 1955, RG59, 839.16162.

111. Henry Hammond to Sec. of State, no. 336, 3 Jan. 1958, RG59, 839.06.

112. Similarly, while 582 Hungarian refugees arrived in 1957 (following the 1956 Soviet invasion), only six colonists remained by 1959. Pheiffer to Sec. of State, no. 679, 7 May 1957, RG59, 839.00; *Secretaría de Estado de Agricultura y Comercio, Memoria, 1959* (Ciudad Trujillo, 1960), 50; Gardiner, *La política de inmigración*, 193–205.

113. Pheiffer to Sec. of State, no. 49, 25 July 1955; Phelps to Sec. of State, no. 955, 22 May 1953; Pheiffer to Sec. of State, no. 76, 7 Aug. 1956, RG59, 739.00(w). See also William Affeld to Sec. of State, no. 97, 17 Aug. 1956, RG59, 839.00. This resentment was also expressed spontaneously in some interviews.

114. Interview with Jacinta Garachana, Sabana Alta, San Juan de la Maguana, Oct. 1992.

115. Law no. 279, 29 Jan. 1932, *Colección de Leyes, Decretos y Resoluciones*. Indeed as early as 1846, Dominican men of letters promoted immigration from Spain while opposing the entry of *asiáticos* and *cocolos* (black West Indian immigrants). See Sócrates Nolasco, *Obras completas: Ensayos históricos*, vol. 2 (Santo Domingo: Corripio, 1994), 241. Also noteworthy in this respect is the acceptance of some two hundred refugees from Shanghai in 1950. Williman Belton to Sec. of State, no. 780, 20 June 1952, RG59, 839.411.

116. *Secretaría de Estado de Agricultura y Comercio, Memoria, 1957* (Ciudad Trujillo, 1958), 78.

117. *Secretaría de Estado de Agricultura y Comercio, Memoria, 1959*, 50; Gardiner, *La política de inmigración*, 206–27; Juan Tomás Montás, supervisor for the settlement of immigrant agriculturalists, 28 Dec. 1956, AGN, SA, leg. 901, 1957.

118. José Almonte to Sec. of Agric., no. 105, 5 Aug. 1957, AGN, SA, leg. 905, 1957; AGN, SA, leg. 1051, 1958; Amado Hernández, Sec. of the Pres., no. 820, 14 Jan. 1957,

AGN, SA, leg. 901, 1957. Stephens to Sec. of State, no. 173, 16 Oct. 1956, RG59, 839.49; Stephens to Sec. of State, no. 187, 22 Oct. 1956; Farland to Sec. of State, no. 221, 5 Nov. 1957 and no. 492, 9 Apr. 1958, RG59, 839.00.

119. *Secretaría de Estado de Agricultura, Memoria, 1956* (Ciudad Trujillo, 1957), 142, 165.

120. Mariñez, *Agroindustria*, 58. On regime policies that contributed to land pressures at the end of the regime, see chap. 8.

121. Luis R. Mercado to Juan Tomás Ramírez, no. 7726, 14 June 1957, AGN, SA, leg. 903, 1957.

122. Various documents in AGN, leg. 903, 1957 and leg. 1027, 1958.

123. Genaro A. Brito to Sec. of Agric., no. 764, 27 Jan. 1958, and numerous other documents in AGN, SA, leg. 1027, 1958; Francisco Prats-Ramírez to Sec. of Agric., no. 2160, 28 May 1957, AGN, SA, leg. 903, 1957.

124. Interviews with colony residents Camilo del Rosario, Milciade Oscar Moquete Susaña, Amado Susaña, Angel Luciano Novoa, Jacinta Garachana, and Victoriano Espinal, Sabana Alta, San Juan de la Maguana, Oct. 1992. Dominicans were given on average smaller plots, and only a portion of them received a stipend. Thus the state could provide land for a greater number of Dominicans than immigrants in the abandoned plots. See lists of colonists, their plots, and stipends in AGN, SA, leg. 1051, 1958. For a list of 502 "poor Dominican agriculturalists" who were given some 11,000 tareas, presumably abandoned by Spanish immigrants, in the colonies of Vallejuelo and Guanito (respectively in El Cercado and Sabana Alta, San Juan), see AGN, SA, leg. 903, 1957. Also see report by Juan Tomás Ramírez, chief of agric. dev. for Dominican Colonies, 13 Sept. 1957, and other documents, AGN, SA, leg. 903, 1957.

125. *Secretaría de Estado de Agricultura, Memoria, 1957*, 68–81; *Secretaría de Estado de Agricultura, Memoria, 1958*, iv–vi, 9–14; *Secretaría de Estado de Agricultura y Comercio, Memoria, 1959*, 72–73; and *Secretaría de Agricultura y Comercio, Memoria, 1960* (Ciudad Trujillo, 1961), 147, 151.

126. "Agricultores amenazan dejar abandonada colonia de Miches," *Unión Cívica*, 28 July 1962.

127. See chap. 8.

128. Miguel Dájer, Sec. of Agric., to Héctor Trujillo, no. 012446, 14 June 1958; Luis Ruiz Trujillo to Dájer, no. 12071, 16 June 1958; Horacio Ariza to Gen. Dir. of Agric., no. 568, 30 Dec. 1959, AGN, SA, leg. 1133, 1959.

129. In 1924, one Joaquín Ortega was governor of the province of Pacificador (now Duarte) in which the city of San Francisco is located. This was, I am presuming, either the same Joaquín Ortega or his father.

130. After Trujillo's assassination, Freddy Prestol Castillo would represent Ortega and claim in court that "certain political figures in the town . . . [had] provoked the yearning of the infelices to occupy lands that were not theirs" for unspecified political purposes, and that peasants had therein entered Ortega's lands only after his arrest. It is unlikely, however, that such a huge area of pasture and woods had not been exploited already by hundreds of peasants. "Notas estenográficas de la audiencia celebrada el día 25 de enero de 1962."

131. Horacio A. Ariza, "Memorandum," 12 June 1958, AGN, SA, leg. 1133, 1959.

132. Dájer to Héctor Trujillo, no. 012446, 14 June 1958, and Luis Ruiz Trujillo to Dájer, no. 12071, 16 June 1958, AGN, SA, leg. 1133, 1959.

133. José F. Tapia to Sec. of Agric., 12 Aug. 1960, AGN, SA, leg. 1133, 1959.

134. Ariza to Manuel de Js. Viñas, Gen. Dir. of Agric., no. 568, 30 Dec. 1959, AGN, SA, leg. 1133, 1959. This bold assertion was supported by both Viñas and the head of legal affairs for the Department of Agriculture (Viñas to Sec. of Agric., no. 1443, n.d., and Manuel A. Valdez to Sec. of Agric., no. 23, 23 Feb. 1960, AGN, SA, leg. 1133, 1959).

135. Dennis Stamers to Sec. of Agric., no. 7431, 13 Sept. 1960, AGN, SA, leg. 1133, 1959. See also the Coiscou case recounted in chap. 4; Decree no. 4484, 15 July 1947, *Gaceta Oficial*, no. 6666, 25 July 1947; Decree no. 7600, 3 Sept. 1951, *Gaceta Oficial*, no. 7325, 8 Sept. 1951; Decree no. 7665, 30 Sept. 1951, *Gaceta Oficial*, no. 7340, 2 Oct. 1951; and Decree no. 7752. 10 Nov. 1951, *Gaceta Oficial*, no. 7353, 21 Nov. 1951.

136. Silvestre Alba de Moya to Dir. of Colonization et al., no. 18251, 30 Sept. 1960, AGN, SA, leg. 1133, 1959.

137. Article 2, Law no. 5719, 20 Dec. 1961 (*Gaceta Oficial*, no. 8634, 8 Jan. 1962) and Article 40, Law no. 5879, 27 Apr. 1962 (*Gaceta Oficial*, no. 8671, 14 July 1962).

138. Dájer to Private Secretary to Trujillo, no. 1412, 23 Jan. 1958, AGN, SA, leg. 1027, 1958; Turits, "Peasants, Property, and the Trujillo Regime," 623n, 683n.

139. Note Horacio Ariza's comment in response to complaints that reached his office regarding the Sánchez Ramírez colony. "It is true that we have occupied these lands without going through the legal work of paying for them" (Ariza to Gen. Dir. of Irrig., no. 129, 14 Oct. 1959, and other documents, AGN, SA, leg. 1133, 1959).

140. "Notas estenográficas de la audiencia celebrada el día 25 de enero de 1962."

Chapter 7: Memories of Dictatorship

1. Interview, Bonao, Higüey, 19 July 1992.

2. E.g., Eric Wolf, "On Peasant Rebellions," *International Social Science Journal* 21 (1969), 292.

3. The only regions in which I did not conduct interviews during the 1990s were Samaná, parts of the Cibao around Santiago and Puerto Plata, and the southern frontier.

4. See Raymond Williams, *Marxism and Literature* (Oxford: Oxford University Press, 1977), 115; Daniel James, "Meatpackers, Peronists, and Collective Memory: A View from the South," *American Historical Review* 102, no. 5 (1997), esp. 1410–12.

5. Avishai Margalit, *The Decent Society* (Cambridge: Harvard University Press, 1996), 1, cited in O'Donnell, "Polyarchies and the (Un)rule of Law." On the negative economic and political conditions of the post-Trujillo period, and particularly the 1980s and 1990s, see Rosario Espinal and Jonathan Hartlyn, "The Dominican Republic: The Long and Difficult Struggle for Democracy," in *Democracy in Developing Countries*, ed. Larry Diamond et al., 2d ed. (Boulder: Lynne Rienner, 1999), 469–517. On dictatorial nostalgia during difficult posttransition moments elsewhere, see Juan J. Linz and Alfred Stepan, *Problems of Democratic Transition and Consolidation: Southern Europe, South American and Post-Communist Europe* (Baltimore: Johns Hopkins University Press, 1996), 451.

6. On a similar concept of respeto in Puerto Rico, see Anthony Lauria, Jr., "'Re-

speto,' 'Relajo' and Inter-Personal Relations in Puerto Rico," *Anthropological Quarterly* 32, no. 2 (1964), 55–57.

7. Eugenio de Hostos, "Quisqueya, su sociedad y algunos de sus hijos," in *Hostos en Santo Domingo*, ed. Rodríguez Demorizi, vol. 1, 287. This article was first published in 1892.

8. Interview with Pedro Zapata, La Curvita, Ramón Santana. 23 Dec. 1992. Francisco Eduardo Salazar related an account of three brothers' retaliation against gavilleros who had abducted their sisters (interview in Nizao, Baní, 29 Aug. 1992). Both women and men reported that rape by gavilleros and other rebellious forces was not uncommon. See also González Canalda, "Gavilleros, 1904–1924," and, on forced recruitment, interview with Enrique Mercedes Duarte, Caballero Abajo, Cotuí, 5 Apr. 1992; "Lo matan por negarse al reclutamiento militar (un acto de barbarie único)," *Listín Diario*, 21 Dec. 1915.

9. Franks, "The Gavilleros of the East." For a similar depiction of the difficulties faced by peasants between 1900 and 1916, see Rafael Morel, "De tiempos de Concho: Marrullería campesina," *Patria*, 23 July 1927. Pedro San Miguel points out that caudillo rebellions and their requisitions and forced recruitment were especially burdensome to peasants in the Cibao since the nineteenth century, because significant parts of the population there were already agrarianized. See San Miguel, *El pasado relegado*, 134, 138. See also Lundius and Lundahl, *Peasants and Religion*, 470, 473.

10. On U.S. military abuses, see Calder, *The Impact of Intervention*, 123–32.

11. Interview, e.g., with Antonio Polanco (born in 1908), Hipólito Billini, Loma de Cabrera, 19 Jan. 1993.

12. Interview in Ramón Santana, 23 Dec. 1992.

13. Interview with Carlos Pujols, Estebanía, Azua, 30 Aug. 1992. Also see Arturo E. Mejía, "Campaña agrícola: Socialización de la tierra—vagancia," *Listín Diario*, 5 Jan. 1935; and report of Sec. Rafael Espaillat, 31 Jan. 1926, *Secretaría de Agricultura é Inmigración, Memoria, 1925* (Santo Domingo: n.p., 1926).

14. Interview with Tomo Reyes, Sabana Grande de Boyá, 24 Jan. 1993.

15. Interview with Rafael Esteves, La Noria, La Romana, 22 Dec. 1992.

16. Interview with Leonardo Núñez, Frank Vidal, Santo Núñez Ramírez, Emilio Mota, Hipólito Núñez, Eleuterio Jesús Pérez, and Ramón Peguero, Cedro, Miches, 1 Aug. 1992. A similar point is made in Aristy, "La posición del trabajador."

17. Interview with Cecilia Rijo, Juan Pablo Duarte, Higüey, 17 July 1992.

18. Interview with Cruzito Guerrero, Bonao, Higüey, 19 July 1992.

19. See, e.g., interview with Juana Taveras (Doña Nena), Pontón, La Vega, 8 Feb. 1992.

20. Interview with José del Carmen Paulino, Los Corozos Adentro, La Vega, 2 May 1992.

21. Interview with Tavares Blanc, Loma de Cabrera, 16 Jan. 1993.

22. Interview in Pontón, La Vega, 9 Feb. 1992.

23. Interview, e.g., with Antonio Hernández, El Rincón, La Vega, Apr. 1992.

24. Interview with Cruzito Guerrero, Bonao, Higüey, 19 July 1992.

25. Interview in Villa Duarte, Santo Domingo, Jan. 1993. In 1957, for instance, the regime reportedly distributed, inter alia, 5,000 grindstones, 2,432 machetes, 1,491 hoes,

442 axes, 389 shovels, 268 rakes, 144 sprinklers, and 133 plows, as well as some 19,000 pounds of pesticide (*Secretaría de Estado de Agricultura, Memoria, 1957, 27*). For earlier distributions, see, e.g., *Secretaría de Estado de Agricultura, Industria y Trabajo, Memoria, 1942* (Ciudad Trujillo, 1943), 31.

26. Interview with Juan Bautista Guerrero and Negro Castillo, La Otra Banda, Higüey, 18 July 1992.

27. Interview with Negrito Viloria, Pontón, La Vega, 2 May 1992.

28. Interview with Santiago Susaña, Las Zanjas, San Juan de la Maguana, 4 Oct. 1992.

29. See also Peggy Levitt, *The Transnational Villagers* (Berkeley: University of California Press, 2001), 113.

30. Virgilio Díaz Grullón, *Antinostalgia de una era* (Santo Domingo: Fundación Cultural Dominicana: 1990), 132.

31. Interviews, e.g., with Bernabel Guadalupe Gil (born 1913), Paso del Medio, El Seibo, 17 Dec. 1992; Juan Maruca, Regajo Plumita, Ramón Santana, 18 Dec. 1992; Eufelio Gómez Hernández, Monte Grande, Loma de Cabrera, 18 Jan. 1993.

32. Interview with Héctor Colombino Perelló, Baní, July 1992.

33. E.g., Teófilo Jiménez to Trujillo, 26 July 1937; Juan Ogando to Sec. of Agric., 11 Jan. 1937; José Rosendo to Sec. of Agric., 22 Jan. 1937, AGN, SA, leg. 25, 1937. See also San Miguel, *Los campesinos*, 115.

34. Interview with Victoriano Espinal (Piculín), Camilo del Rosario, Milciade Oscar Moquete Susaña (Chicho), Angel Novoa, and Jacinta Garachana, Sabana Alta, San Juan de la Maguana, Oct. 1992.

35. Interview with Milciade Oscar Moquete Susaña, Sabana Alta, San Juan de la Maguana, Oct. 1992.

36. Nicolás de la Rosa to Trujillo, Yamasá, 20 Dec. 1934, AGN, Gob. de Santo Domingo, unnumbered leg., 1925–34.

37. Interview with Amado Susaña (born in 1919), Sabana Alta, San Juan de la Maguana, Oct. 1992.

38. Interview with Priciliano Mercedes, Chirino, Monte Plata, 31 Jan. 1993.

39. Similarly in 1938, the U.S. legation in Ciudad Trujillo reported that despite Trujillo's extensive personal enrichment via graft and corrupt monopolies, his regime was "condoned by business men on the ground that it is more efficient . . . to pay a fixed graft to one person than as in the past to pay graft to each petty official with the inevitable delay and loss in efficiency [it causes]." E. M. H., "Memorandum," 9 Sept. 1938, RG84, 710–800.2.

40. I am grateful to Michiel Baud for stressing this point.

41. See, e.g., Eliseo Melo to Trujillo, 23 June 1947, AGN, SA, leg. 51b.

42. Interviews with Máximo Peralta García, Bonao, Higüey, 19 July 1992; and Angel Vólquez, Ramón Santana, 17 Dec. 1992.

43. Mann, "Public Expenditure Patterns," 57–60.

44. Gómez, *Relaciones de producción*, 125. See also Moya Pons, *El pasado dominicano*, 202–3; Ramos, "La ciudad y el campo," 54.

45. Interview with Angel Luciano Novoa (born in 1916), Sabana Alta, San Juan de la Maguana, Oct. 1992.

46. Interviews with Carlos Américo Peguero Matos, San Juan de la Maguana, 3 Oct. 1992; Héctor Colombino Perelló, Baní, July 1992; Mario Díaz, Baní, 21 Aug. 1992.

47. See chap. 3.

48. Interviews with Linor de los Santos, Las Zanjas, San Juan de la Maguana, 4 Oct. 1992; and Amado Susaña, Sabana Alta, Oct. 1992.

49. Interview with Orgelio Santos, Carretón, Baní, 15 Aug. 1992.

50. Interview with Angel Valdez, Nizao, Baní, 29 Aug. 1992.

51. Interview with Nilka and Manuel Martínez, Carretón, Baní, 15 Aug. 1992.

52. Interview with Francisco Eduardo Salazar, Nizao, Baní, 29 Aug. 1992; and Máximo Peralta García, Bonao, Higüey, 19 July 1992.

53. Interview with Linor de los Santos, Las Zanjas, San Juan de la Maguana, 4 Oct. 1992.

54. Interview in La Ceiba, Higüey, 18 July 1992.

55. Interview with Hugo Gunel, Pontón, La Vega, 1 Mar. 1992.

56. Interview with Hugo Gunel, Pontón, La Vega, 1 Mar. 1992.

57. Interview in El Rincón, La Vega, Apr. 1992.

58. Interview with Magdaleno Valdez and Antonio Hernández, El Rincón, La Vega, Apr. 1992.

59. Cf. José Oviedo, "La tradición autoritaria" (unpublished ms., 1986).

60. On traditional patriarchal ideologies and practices, see Baud, *Peasants and Tobacco*, 67–68, 117–22; Baud, "Patriarchy and Changing Family Strategies," 355–77.

61. The phrase is taken from Gilbert Joseph and Daniel Nugent, eds. *Everyday Forms of State Formation: Revolution and the Negotiation of Rule in Modern Mexico* (Durham: Duke University Press, 1994).

62. For an analogous point, see Baud, "Patriarchy and Changing Family Strategies," 371.

63. Interview in La Ceiba, Higüey, 18 July 1992.

64. Interview with Juan Bautista Guerrero, La Otra Banda, Higüey, 18 July 1992. Similarly, Baud writes: "Children were kept under close control until an advanced age. Older men and women tell that they '*no pertenecían,*' that they had no control over their own lives" when they were young ("Patriarchy and Changing Family Strategies," 360). Although the elderly appear nostalgic for the deference children once showed, Baud's comments suggest that as children, they may have experienced their subordination as oppressive.

65. Interview with Francisco Soriano, Ramón Santana, 23 Dec. 1992. See also Sherri Grasmuck and Patricia Pessar, *Between Two Islands: Dominican International Migration* (Berkeley: University of California Press, 1991), 140.

66. Interview with Santo (Gallito) Núñez Ramírez, Cedro, Miches, 1 Aug. 1992.

67. Interview with Ramón García Peña, La Vega, 9 Feb. 1992.

68. Galíndez, *La era de Trujillo,* 176–77.

69. Law no. 390, 10 Dec. 1940, *Gaceta Oficial,* no. 5535, 18 Dec. 1940. See also Veras and Alvarado, "La mujer en el derecho dominicano," 51–70.

70. Interview with Castalia and Ramón Ortiz, Los Tumbao, Baní, 24 Sept. 1992.

71. Interview with Camilo del Rosario, Sabana Alta, San Juan de la Maguana, Oct. 1992.

72. Interview with Francisco Eduardo Salazar, Nizao, Baní, 29 Aug. 1992. Similar remarks were made by Nilka Martínez, interview in Carretón, Baní, 15 Aug. 1992.

73. In popular discourse, "to marry" generally referred to both legal marriage and cohabitation. Formal marriage was not a common practice in the countryside, and men and women who formed families together were recognized as husband and wife without recording their union with the state. Under Trujillo the state did promote marriage as a legal institution through, e.g., periods of free civil marriages, but these measures may have pertained more to urban than rural dwellers. See, e.g., Law no. 492, 20 Jan. 1944, *Gaceta Oficial*, no. 6026, 29 Jan. 1944; B. Gimbernard, cartoon, *La Tribuna* (Ciudad Trujillo), 8 June 1937; R. Emilio Jiménez, "El niño y la mujer en la política de Trujillo," *La Nación*, 4 July 1952.

74. Interview with Leonardo Núñez, Frank Vidal, Santo Núñez Ramírez, Emilio Mota, Hipólito Núñez, and Eleuterio Jesús Pérez, Cedro, Miches, 1 Aug. 1992.

75. Interview with Máximo Peralta García and Cruzito Guerrero, Bonao, Higüey, 17 July 1992.

76. Baud, "Patriarchy and Changing Family Strategies," 361; Baud, *Peasants and Tobacco*, 122; interview with Rhadamés Bolívar Maldonado Pinal (a lawyer during the Trujillo period and later fiscal), Santo Domingo, 8 Jan. 1993; Law no. 2402, 7 June 1950, *Gaceta Oficial*, no. 7132, 13 June 1950; and Gabriel Hernández Mota, "Estudio acerca de la Ley 2402 del 13 de junio del 1950" (Doctoral thesis in law, no. 271, Universidad de Santo Domingo, 1956), 4–6, 46, passim.

77. José Antonio Batista and Guarín Soñe Genao to Bayoán de Hostos, 13 Apr. 1936, AGN, SA, SSJA, leg. 1a, 1936.

78. Altagracia Martínez García, "Consideraciones acerca de la supresión del delito de adulterio" (Doctoral thesis in law, Universidad de Santo Domingo, 1950), 27–34.

79. Luis Peguero Moscoso, "Estudio jurídico-sociológico de la prostitución en la República Dominicana" (Doctoral thesis in law, no. 124, Universidad de Santo Domingo, 1945), 42.

80. Interview with Camilo del Rosario, Sabana Alta, San Juan de la Maguana, Oct. 1992.

81. Interview with Luisa Montilla, Higüey, 17 July 1992.

82. See Bienvenido Velez Toribio, "La prostitución en Santo Domingo: Necesidad de su legalización" (Doctoral thesis in law, no. 147, Universidad de Santo Domingo, 1950), 108–11, 126–28, passim.

83. Interview with Octavio Miniel, Batey Campiña, Ramón Santana, 13 Dec. 1992; interview with Máximo Peralta García, Bonao, Higüey, 19 July 1992.

84. Anonymous interview, Cedro, Miches, 1 Aug. 1992.

85. Interview with María Adolfina Tavárez, Mariano Cestero, Restauración, 17 Jan. 1993; Marino Madepa to Sec. of Agric., no. 564, 27 Dec. 1950, and Domingo Hasbún to Sec. of Agric., no. 213, 17 Jan. 1951, AGN, SA, leg. 176, 1951.

86. Olegario Helena Guzman to Sec. of Agric., no. 316, 28 Feb. 1958, AGN, SA, leg. 1027, 1958.

87. Interview, e.g., with María Adolfina Tavárez and Carlos María Mercedes, Mariano Cestero, Restauración, 17 Jan. 1993.

88. Interview with Leonardo Núñez, Cedro, Miches, 1 Aug. 1992.

89. Departmental Order no. 3, 12 June 1937, AGN, SA, leg. 46, 1937.

90. Goico, *Guía Policial*, 192–93. Department of Agriculture documents show that efforts to legally require latrines (or be subject to arrest) were implemented at least in the agricultural colonies as early as 1931 (Sec. of Health to Tolentino, 20 Sept. 1931, and Tolentino to Sec. of Health, 25 Sept. 1931, AGN, SA, leg. 20, n.d.). According to one author, the latrine requirements were formally implemented in the country as a whole in 1935. The policy was anticipated by the U.S. military dictatorship, which constructed and required latrines in certain rural areas. Pedro Encarnación Jiménez, *Los negros esclavos en la historia de Bayona, Manoguayabo y otros poblados* (Santo Domingo: Alfa y Omega, 1993), 138–39, 160.

91. Interviews with Bartolo Soler, La Ceiba, Higüey, 18 July 1992, and Antonio Hernández, El Rincón, La Vega, Apr. 1992. Some persons reported, however, that those with certain means had to pay a small amount for their latrines. Interview, e.g., with Manolo Pimentel, Paya, Baní, 29 Sept. 1992.

92. Interview with Juan de la Paz Herrera, whose father was arrested for not having a latrine, Bacuí al Medio, La Vega, 29 May 1992. De la Paz nonetheless stated that the law was a positive one.

93. Interview with Enrique Acevedo Ortiz, Las Charcas, Azua, 30 Aug. 1992.

94. Pedro Zapata, e.g., stated that as soon as the law was promulgated, it was enforced; and that though now one could find houses without latrines, in the past all houses had them (interview in La Curvita, Ramón Santana, 23 Dec. 1992).

95. Interview with Luisa Montilla, Higüey, 17 July 1992. The fact that Montilla had moved into the town of Higüey from the surrounding countryside after the end of the Trujillo regime may have furthered her adoption of dominant constructs of "civilization" and "barbarism."

96. Interview with Leonardo Núñez, Frank Vidal Area, Santo Núñez Ramírez Area, Emilio Mota, Hipólito Núñez, and Eleuterio Jesús Pérez, Cedro, Miches, 1 Aug. 1992.

97. Johnson to Sec. of State, no. 141, 29 Aug. 1952, RG59, 739.00(w); Johnson to Sec. of State, no. 578, 27 Jan. 1953, RG84, box 36. Several elite Dominicans with whom I spoke argued that Trujillo passed this law to benefit his own interests in shoe manufacturing (interview, e.g., with Hugo Gunel, Pontón, La Vega, 1 Mar. 1992). In the 1930s, small newspapers such as *La Tribuna* had printed almost daily articles demanding that the state impose sanitary regulations, including that shoes be worn in urban areas (Catón, "Canela fina," *La Tribuna*, 17 June 1937).

98. Interviews with Eufelio Gómez Hernández, Loma de Cabrera, 18 Jan. 1993; José Adames, Guineo, Miches, 1 Aug. 1992; Luisa Montilla, Higüey, 17 July 1992; and Bartolo Soler, La Ceiba del Salado, Higüey, 18 July 1992.

99. Interview with José Adames, Guineo, Miches, 1 Aug. 1992. Similar views were expressed by Nilka Martínez (interview in Carretón, Baní, 15 Aug. 1992).

100. Interview with Manuel de la Rosa Cedano, Higüey, July 19, 1992. In the late 1940s, Trujillo ordered that a number of putatively homosexual men be sent to the Julio Molina penal colony in Nagua to cut rice for six months. This reportedly occurred in response to accounts of a series of rapes of boys. Interviews with Rhadamés Bolívar Maldonado Pinal, Santo Domingo, 8 Jan. 1993; Francisco de Jesús Concha

(who had been imprisoned for nine months in this colony, Julia Molina), Villa Juana, Santo Domingo, 27 Dec. 1992; and Manuel de la Rosa Cedano, Higüey, 19 July 1992.

101. The Brookings Institution, *Refugee Settlement in the Dominican Republic: A Survey Conducted under the Auspices of the Brookings Institution* (Washington, D.C.: Brookings Institution, 1944), 91–93; George Greco to Sec. of State, 19 Feb. 1953, RG59, 839.00-TA; Henry Hammond to Sec. of State, no. 438, 5 Mar. 1958, RG59, 839.55; Farland to Sec. of State, no. 492 and 227, 9 Apr. and 21 Nov. 1958, RG59, 839.00. Seventeen of the fifty-one hospitals in 1958 were run by the Dominican social security agency, which was separate from the system of public hospitals.

102. Nelson Ramírez, "Análisis de la situación demográfica en la República Dominicana," in *Seminario sobre problemas de población en la República Dominicana* (Santo Domingo: Editora de la Universidad Autónoma de Santo Domingo, 1975), 65; Rosemary Vargas-Lundius, *Peasants in Distress: Poverty and Unemployment in the Dominican Republic* (Boulder: Westview, 1991), 99.

103. Interview with Manuel (Cheo) Santos Sánchez, Carretón, Baní, 15 Aug. 1992.

104. Interview with Juan Justo, Higüey, 31 July 1992.

105. Interview with Máximo Peralta García, Bonao, Higüey, 19 July 1992.

106. Johnson to Sec. of State, no. 920, 6 Apr. 1954, RG59, 739.00; Calder, *Impact of Intervention,* 39–40; Clausner, *Rural Santo Domingo,* 220–21.

107. Those who could not pay the fine were forced to spend five days in jail. Interview with Francisco Soriano, Ramón Santana, 23 Dec. 1992. Parents of a few of those with whom I spoke were, in fact, punished when they told their children to weed rather than go to school (interview, e.g., with Ramón García Peña, La Vega, 9 Feb 1992). See also Levitt, *The Transnational Villagers,* 113.

108. O. Báez Soler, "Cultura y cultivo en la Era de Trujillo," *Boletín del Partido Dominicano,* no. 111 (30 Oct. 1942); Clausner, *Rural Santo Domingo,* 220–21. See also Sec. of Educ. and Fine Arts, *Ley de alfabetización obligatoria para adultos* (Ciudad Trujillo, 1955); "La muerte del analfabetismo es la creación de un nuevo ciudadano," *Juventud,* 12 Sept. 1941.

109. Richard Barr to Sec. of State, no. 180, 15 Sept. 1952, RG59, 839.43; Barr to Sec. of State, 8 Oct. 1952, RG59, 839.43.

110. The U.S. embassy similarly asserted that literacy and basic education had advanced in the Dominican Republic and served as one of the ways the regime secured support among the population. U.S. embassy to Sec. of State, no. 7, 13 July 1960, RG59, 839.00.

111. Interview with Manuel de la Rosa Cedano, Higüey, 19 July 1992.

112. Interview with Bernabel Gil, 17 Dec. 1992, Paso del Medio, El Seibo.

113. Interview with Carlos Pujols, Estebanía, Azua, 30 Aug. 1992.

114. Clausner, *Rural Santo Domingo,* 222–23.

115. On the neglect of public education in the early twentieth century, see Calder, *Impact of Intervention,* 34–40.

116. Interviews, e.g., with Francisco Soriano, Ramón Santana, 23 Dec. 1992; Manuel Santos Sánchez (Cheo), Carretón, Baní, 15 Aug. 1992; Juan Maruca, Regajo Plumita, 18 Dec. 1992; and Ramón Peña de la Rosa (Momo), an alcalde for more than twenty years under Trujillo, Pontón, La Vega, 29 Feb. 1992.

117. Interview in Bonao, Higüey, 19 July 1992.

118. Interview with Celestino Montilla, Higüey, 17 July 1992.

119. Interview with Bartolo Soler, La Ceiba del Salado, Higüey, 18 July 1992.

120. Interview with Juan Justo, Higüey, 31 July 1992.

121. Interview with Ramón Peguero et al., Cedro, Miches, 1 Aug. 1992.

122. Scott, *Weapons of the Weak*, esp. 284–89.

123. *Secretaría de Estado de lo Interior, Policía, Guerra y Marina, Memoria, 1934* (Santo Domingo: n.p., 1935), 438–50.

124. Interview in Higüey, 19 July 1992.

125. The 1945 reform of the cédula fee obligated Rodríguez to pay 500 pesos per year rather than the 50 pesos he had owed the year before or the 1 peso he had owed prior to 1940. Many elderly peasants from La Vega province averred that the cédula demand was one of the triggers for Rodríguez's political opposition and exile. Interviews, e.g., with Ramón Abreu, Jima Abajo, 21 Nov. 1994; also Marcelino Cepeda and Domingo Severino Hernández, Jima Abajo, 2 Mar. 1992.

126. Interviews with Máximo Peralta García, Bonao, Higüey, 19 July 1992; and Antonio (last name not given), El Salado, Higüey, 18 July 1992.

127. Interview in Ramón Santana, 23 Dec. 1992.

128. Interview with Bartolo Soler, La Ceiba del Salado, Higüey, 18 July 1992.

129. Interview, e.g., with Martín Maldonado, de Silvain, Ramón Santana, 26 Nov. 1994. The regime's frightening policy of attacking all members of a family when one of them opposed the regime was exemplified by Trujillo's repression of those who had been close to Rodríguez, including his former employees, former lovers, and, above all, his children with the latter. They were variously monitored, harassed, imprisoned, and even killed, as in the case of Rafael de Jesús Taveras, the eldest son of Juana Taveras (Doña Nena) and Juancito Rodríguez. Interview with Juana Taveras, Pontón, La Vega, 8 Feb. 1992.

130. Interview with Angel Luciano Novoa, Sabana Alta, San Juan de la Maguana, Oct. 1992.

131. An inverse correlation between support for Trujillo and socioeconomic status is suggested by survey data. See Bernardo Vega, "Menos de la mitad de los Dominicanos cree que Trujillo fue un mal gobernante," *Listín Diario*, 29 June 1984.

Chapter 8: The Birth of a Dominican Sugar Empire

1. Ellis Briggs to Sec. of State, no. 609, 3 Jan. 1945, RG59, 839.00.

2. George Scherer to Sec. of State, no. 1034, 3 July 1946, RG59, 839.00.

3. George Butler to Sec. of State, no. 306, 24 Dec. 1946, RG59, 839.00.

4. Briggs to Sec. of State, no. 609, 3 Jan. 1945, RG59, 839.00.

5. Ralph Ackerman to Sec. of State, no. 342, 25 Oct. 1949, RG59, 839.00. See also E. M. H., "Memorandum," 9 Sept. 1938, RG84, 710–800.2; Richard Johnson to Sec. of State, no. 920, 6 Apr. 1954, RG59, 739.00.

6. See Eduardo García Vásquez, "Notas sobre el 30 de mayo de 1961," *Ecos* 6, no. 7 (1999).

7. Crassweller titles one of his chapters "Sugar: Not a Business but a Romance," *Trujillo*, 251–59.

8. The U.S. embassy reported in 1959 that peasants "are either apolitical or support Trujillo." Farland to Sec. of State, 14 July 1959, RG59, 739.00. Similarly, the U.S. Central Intelligence Agency concluded in 1960 that while there was growing dissatisfaction with Trujillo from the Dominican upper and middle classes, the Church, and even within the military, the peasantry "still regard Trujillo as the Benefactor." "The Outlook for the Dominican Republic," 26 Apr. 1960, no. 86.2–60, Central Intelligence Agency (released to author under the Freedom of Information Act). See also U.S. embassy to Sec. of State, 13 July 1960, no. 7, RG59, 839.00.

9. *Washington Post*, 11 Aug. 1947. See also "Exposición del Sec. Balaguer ante Cámaras Legislativas," *El Caribe*, 18 Sept. 1953.

10. Production crested in 1956 after the regime established monopoly control over the coffee industry and raised taxes on export crops, hurting especially better-off peasants. Morillo, *Trujillo*, 136, 147, 152, passim.

11. Walter Cordero, *Tendencias de la economía cafetalera dominicana, 1955–1972* (Santo Domingo: Editora de la Universidad Autónoma de Santo Domingo, 1975), 19, 73–109; San Miguel, *Los campesinos*, 305–41; Inoa, *Estado y campesinos*, 204.

12. Rafael Francisco de Moya Pons, "Industrial Incentives in the Dominican Republic, 1880–1983" (Ph.D. diss., Columbia University, 1987), 70, passim; Hoetink, "The Dominican Republic," 215.

13. Luis Gómez, *Relaciones de producción dominantes en la sociedad dominicana, 1875/1975* (Santo Domingo: Alfa y Omega, 1984), 115–17.

14. Allen Lester to Sec. of State, no. 781, 25 June 1952, RG59, 839.10; Richard Desmond to Sec. of State, no. 35, 18 July 1955, RG59, 739.00(w); Gómez, *Relaciones de producción*, 117.

15. Andrew Wardlaw, end-of-year report, 14 Mar. 1946, RG59, 839.00; Johnson to Sec. of State, no. 620, 8 Jan. 1954, RG59, 739.00(w).

16. See, e.g., Richard Lankenau to Sec. of State, no. 497, 7 Feb. 1951, RG59, 839.00.

17. Butler to Sec. of State, no. A-570, 22 Oct. 1946, RG59, 839.50.

18. Galíndez, *La era de Trujillo*, 224. On the agricultural bank (Banco Agrícola e Industrial, first called the Banco Agrícola e Hipotecario), see San Miguel, *Los campesinos*, 150–88.

19. Gómez, *Relaciones de producción*, 107; Cassá, *Capitalismo*, 261.

20. Ackerman to Sec. of State, no. 406, 11 Nov. 1949, RG59, 839.00(w).

21. Ackerman to Sec. of State, no. A-419, 18 Aug. 1949, RG59, 839.00(w).

22. Hall, *Sugar and Power*, 22, 24; Ackerman to Sec. of State, no. 850, 29 June 1951, RG59, 739.00(w).

23. Pheiffer to Sec. of State, no. 18, 11 July 1955, RG59, 739.00(w).

24. Johnson to Sec. of State, no. 376, 14 Nov. 1952, RG59, 739.00(w).

25. Johnson to Sec. of State, no. 375, 14 Nov. 1952, RG59, 739.00(w).

26. Lester to Sec. of State, no. 97, 8 Aug. 1952, RG59, 739.00(w); Crassweller, *Trujillo*, 254.

27. John Montel to Sec. of State, no. 644, 5 May 1955, RG59, 839.2351.

28. Hall, *Sugar and Power*, 22. For a breakdown of production and sales by mill in 1952, see "Estado general consolidado de producción, exportación, consumo local y existencias de azúcar," AGN, SA, leg. 194, 1952.

29. Slavens to Sec. of State, no. 524, 9 Jan. 1953, RG59, 839.11; Pheiffer to Sec. of State, no. 461, 27 Nov. 1953, RG59, 739.00(w); Montel to Sec. of State, no. 251, 15 Nov. 1954, RG59, 839.20. The tax rate rose with the price for sugar exports. At 3.615 cents per pound, e.g., the tax came to 0.767 cent a pound. A. Kirstein, Jr., Pres., West Indies Sugar Corp., and Frank Lowry, Vice Chair, South Porto Rico Sugar Co., "Memorandum to the Department of State of the United States of America," 21 Jan. 1954, RG59, 839.235.

30. Belton to Sec. of State, no. 393, 22 Dec. 1950, RG59, 739.00(w); Ackerman to Sec. of State, no. 850, 29 June 1951, RG59, 739.00(w). See also Crassweller, *Trujillo*, 257; Hall, *Sugar and Power*, 22.

31. Wendell Woodbury to Sec. of State, no. 933, 9 Apr. 1954, RG59, 839.00.

32. "Dos triunfos más del Generalísimo Trujillo," *La Nación*, 19 Dec. 1953.

33. Kirstein and Lowry, "Memorandum," 21 Jan. 1954, RG59, 839.235.

34. "Annual Economic Report: 1953," no. 957, 27 Apr. 1954, RG59, 839.00.

35. E. I. Kilbourne, Pres., West Indies Corp., "Memorandum to the Department of State of the United States of America," 23 Apr. 1956, RG59, 839.235.

36. Spalding to Sec. of State, no. 647, 25 Apr. 1957, RG59, 839.2351.

37. Trujillo then controlled 43 percent of the sugar industry; the South Porto Rico Sugar Co. controlled 22 percent, and the Vicini estate 9 percent. Richard Stephens to Sec. of State, no. 289, 6 Dec. 1956, RG59, 839.2351.

38. Stephens to Sec. of State, no. 426, 29 Jan. 1957, RG59, 839.2351; Pheiffer to Sec. of State, no. 429, 27 Jan. 1957, RG59, 839.000; Spalding to Sec. of State, no. 647, 25 Apr. 1957, RG59, 839.2351.

39. Stephens to Sec. of State, no. 426, 29 Jan. 1957, RG59, 839.2351; Spalding to Sec. of State, no. 713, 20 May 1957, RG59, 839.00.

40. Hall, *Sugar and Power*, 22, 24, 102; Spalding to Sec. of State, no. 774, 18 June 1957, RG59, 839.00.

41. San Miguel, "The Dominican Peasantry," 101–2; Dominican Republic, *Cuarto censo nacional agropecuario, 1950*, xix; Dominican Republic, *Quinto censo nacional agropecuario*, 156.

42. Hall, *Sugar and Power*, 24, 102. Some of this expansion was due to the South Porto Rico Sugar Company's agreeing to a request from the regime to invest $8–10 million to expand its Central Romana plantation and milling capacity to 350,000 tons by 1960, the largest in the world (Robert Allen to Sec. of State, no. 336, 21 Dec. 1956; Stephens to Sec. of State, no. 426, 29 Jan. 1957, RG59, 839.2351). This agreement may explain why the South Porto Rico, unlike the West Indies, was able to keep most of its holdings, selling only its old Santa Fé mill to the regime.

43. "Crop land" includes fallow areas but not pasture or woods. There were 3 million tareas of sugar in 1960. The other main crops then—rice, corn, manioc, cacao, coffee, and plantains—accounted for approximately a million or more tareas each. Dominican Republic, *Quinto censo nacional agropecuario*, 156; Dominican Republic, *Censo agro-pecuario, 1940*, 4–5.

44. See, e.g., Ackerman to Sec. of State, no. 423, 2 June 1950, RG50, 839.112. When the U.S.-owned Presidente Brewery outcompeted Trujillo's beer, Dominicana, despite

his efforts to restrict their market, the former was obliged to buy the latter, including its virtually unsellable stocks of beer, for the grossly inflated price of $1.5 million. Slavens to Sec. of State, no. 452, 11 Dec. 1952, RG59, 839.316. See also Ackerman to Sec. of State, no. 803 and no. 850, 8 and 29 June 1951, RG59, 739.00(w).

45. Hammond to Sec. of State, no. 447, 10 Mar. 1958, RG59, 839.00.

46. The U.S.-owned telephone company was obliged to monitor phone calls for the regime and, in 1958, to sell 40 percent of its stock to Dominicans. "Annual Economic Report: 1953," no. 957, 27 Apr. 1954; Spalding to Sec. of State, no. 91, 20 Aug. 1958, RG59, 839.00.

47. The U.S. embassy reported that the sale price was $5 million (28 percent) below its $18 million book value. William Affeld to Sec. of State, no. 35, 18 July 1955, RG59, 739.00(w); Johnson to Sec. of State, no. 481, 2 Dec. 1953, RG59, 839.2614.

48. "Annual Economic Report: 1953," no. 957, 27 Apr. 1954, RG59, 839.00.

49. "Ley regulariza servicio agua y energía eléctrica," El Caribe, 30 Dec. 1953.

50. Johnson to Sec. of State, no. 598, 31 Dec. 1953, RG59, 739.00(w).

51. Woodbury to Sec. of State, no. 596, 31 Dec. 1953, 839.2614.

52. Pheiffer to Sec. of State, no. 800, 26 Feb. 1954, RG59, 739.00(w).

53. See "Annual Economic Report: 1953," no. 957, 27 Apr. 1954, RG59, 839.00; Johnson to Sec. of State, no. 920, 6 Apr. 1954, RG59, 739.00.

54. Johnson to Sec. of State, no. 977, 5 May 1954, RG59, 739.00.

55. Crassweller, Trujillo, 251–59.

56. Dept. of State, "Special National Intelligence Estimate," 10 Mar. 1959, in FRUS, 1958–1960, vol. 5 (Washington: U.S. Government Printing Office, 1991), 367–68.

57. On Puerto Rican independence, see, e.g., the 7 Dec. 1949 editorial of La Opinión. See also Hall, Sugar and Power, 53–54.

58. Trujillo was far from an instrument of U.S. interests in the period from 1930 to 1945 as well, as demonstrated in Roorda, The Dictator Next Door.

59. Eric Williams, From Columbus to Castro: The History of the Caribbean (New York: Vintage, 1984), 428–42.

60. William Belton to Sec. of State, no. 438, 25 Nov. 1949, RG59, 839.00.

61. Hall, Sugar and Power, 80.

62. Lankenau to Sec. of State, no. 319, 28 Apr. 1950, RG59, 839.20.

63. Hall, Sugar and Power, 73–97.

64. Harry Zerbel to Sec. of State, 2 Apr. 1951, RG59, 839.318.

65. Woodbury to Sec. of State, no. 696 and 751, 29 Jan. and 12 Feb. 1954, RG59, 839.10; "Annual Economic Report: 1953," no. 957, 27 Apr. 1954, RG59, 839.00.

66. Crassweller, Trujillo, 255–56.

67. Slavens to Sec. of State, no. 289, 30 Sept. 1953, RG59, 839.12.

68. Slavens to Sec. of State, no. 354, 19 Nov. 1952, RG59, 839.25.

69. Interview with Pedro Cordones, Monte Plata, 31 Jan. 1993. For documentation of numerous purchases by the Azucarera Haina of large and small plots, generally at 5 to 10 pesos per tarea, see AGN, SA, leg. 776, 1957.

70. Interviews with Rhadamés Bolívar Maldonado Pinal, Santo Domingo, 8 Jan. 1993; and Emilio Jiménez, Sabana Grande de Boyá, 24 Jan. 1993.

71. Interview with Cleyto Aybar, Sabana Grande de Boyá, 24 Jan. 1993. Interviews also with Manuel María Pérez, El Carril de Haina, 23 Jan. 1993; Ciprián Marín Durán, Tomo Reyes, and Emilio Jiménez, Sabana Grande de Boyá, 24 Jan. 1993; and Rhadamés Bolívar Maldonado Pinal, Santo Domingo, 8 Jan. 1993. See also Jiménez, *Los negros esclavos*, 176–77. According to Crassweller, José Antonio Jiménez offered Trujillo a large part of his estate to belay Trujillo's order to assassinate him following a political conflict between the two (*Trujillo*, 253). The prices Trujillo paid to those dispossessed varied widely. Manuel Pérez received 17 pesos per tarea for his 75 tareas in Carril (near Haina), which had already been surveyed at the time. But in the more withdrawn regions that had not yet been submitted to the mensura catastral, such as Sabana Grande de Boyá, residents informed me that they received only a few pesos per tarea of cultivated land. One of the only persons who had a commercial farm in the Sabana Grande area, Tomo Reyes, received a mere 400 pesos for his 200 tareas of coffee and cacao. Cleyto Aybar received 70 pesos for his house.

72. Johnson to Sec. of State, no. 616, 7 Jan. 1954, RG59, 839.16.

73. Woodbury to Sec. of State, no. 260, 16 Nov. 1954, RG59, 839.16.

74. Compensation was given for existing crops (reportedly 3 pesos for each mature coconut tree, e.g.). Interview with Priciliano Mercedes, Chirino, Monte Plata, 31 Jan. 1993. In 1958 there was also an eviction of a hundred or so pastoral peasants in Matanzas near the Southern town of Baní. For a novel based on this event, see Héctor Colombino Perelló, *La jaula* (Santo Domingo: Impresora Cacique, 1978).

75. Cassá, *Capitalismo*, 263.

76. Interview in Chirino, Monte Plata, 31 Jan. 1993.

77. Pheiffer to Sec. of State, no. 679, 7 May 1957, RG59, 739.00(w).

78. I am grateful to Alejandro de la Fuente for suggesting this formulation to me.

79. Economic explanations for the shift toward sugar are problematic. Some scholars have argued that even if sugar was unprofitable—at least without state subsidies— it provided foreign exchange that Trujillo desperately desired. But the irony is that Trujillo altered the nation's economy at a time when it was robust, running smoothly, and yielding ample foreign exchange (largely via the foreign sugar industry). See Vedovato, *Politics*, 38–53; Hall, *Sugar and Power*, 21–22.

80. "Aviso," *El Caribe*, 24 Nov. 1953. Also, the state reportedly appropriated some 16,000 acres in Barahona (on the legal grounds of being of "public utility" and "social interest") in order to protect peasant squatters there from being dispossessed by the legal owners. Pheiffer to Sec. of State, no. 218, 4 Sept. 1953, RG59, 739.00(w).

81. "Secretaría del Trabajo, Economía y Comercio hace recomendaciones a pedáneos sobre éxodo campesinos," *El Caribe*, 25 Dec. 1953.

82. Especially in the second half of the regime, Trujillo was often called Jefe, meaning "boss" or "chief," by his subordinates. Crassweller, *Trujillo*, 162.

83. See Crassweller, *Trujillo*, passim.

84. Desmond to Sec. of State, no. 13, 7 July 1955, RG59, 839.00.

85. Ackerman to Sec. of State, no. 486, 9 Dec. 1949, RG59, 839.00.

86. Stephens to Sec. of State, no. 385, 15 Jan. 1957, RG59, 739.00.

87. Hammond to Sec. of State, no. 491, 8 Apr. 1958, RG59, 839.00.

88. Vedovato, *Politics*, 55–56.

89. Crassweller, *Trujillo*, 293–99; Derby, "The Magic of Modernity," 405–18.

90. *New York Times*, 21 Dec. 1955. Cited in Affeld to Sec. of State, no. 264, 23 Dec. 1955, RG59, 739.00(w).

91. Derby, "The Magic of Modernity," 410.

92. Repr. in Crassweller, *Trujillo*, 295.

93. Desmond to Sec. of State, no. 381, 20 Mar. 1956, RG59, 839.00; Affeld to Sec. of State, no. 650 and 272, 9 May and 30 Dec. 1955, RG59, 739.00(w).

94. Pheiffer to Sec. of State, no. 635, 16 Apr. 1957; Hammond to Sec. of State, no. 491, 10 Oct. 1958, RG59, 839.00.

95. Hammond to Sec. of State, no. 349, 8 Jan. 1958; Farland to Sec. of State, no. 33, 17 July 1959, RG59, 839.00.

96. Ronald Webb to Sec. of State, no. 460, 6 May 1959, RG59, 839.00; Charles Hodge to Sec. of State, no. 140, 5 Oct. 1959, RG59, 839.10; Farland to Sec. of State, no. 228, 16 Dec. 1959, RG59, 739.00. The government quietly began seeking foreign loans in 1956 (Pheiffer to Sec. of State, no. 250, 20 Nov. 1956, RG59, 739.00; Pheiffer to Sec. of State, no. 635, 16 Apr. 1957, RG59, 839.00). But the government turned to this strategy too late. By then the economic crisis had rendered the regime's stability so precarious that foreign banks refused to extend funds (Farland to Sec. of State, no. 33, 17 July 1959, RG59, 839.00; Hodge to Sec. of State, no. 154, 16 Oct. 1959, RG59, 839.2612). It was the International Monetary Fund that saved the country from financial peril, providing the country with $11,250,000 in standby credit at the end of 1959 (Farland to Sec. of State, no. 238, 31 Dec. 1959, RG59, 739.00[w]).

97. Other estimates for arms purchases ranged from $7 million (for the first three months of 1959) to $50 million or more. Farland to Sec. of State, no. 504, 33, and 221, 5 June, 17 July, and 11 Dec. 1959; Dearborn to Sec. of State, no. 152, 16 Oct. 1959, RG59, 739.00(w); Hodge to Sec. of State, no. 154, 16 Oct. 1959, RG59, 839.2612.

98. See, e.g., Spalding to Sec. of State, no. 179, 6 Oct. 1958, RG59, 839.432. New taxes implemented in 1959, the U.S. embassy reported, "most adversely affected . . . those who constitute the backbone of the opposition—the middle class." Dearborn to Sec. of State, no. 152, 11 Oct. 1959, RG59, 739.00(w).

99. Hoetink, "The Dominican Republic," 220; Galíndez, *La era de Trujillo*, 224.

100. Gómez, *Relaciones de producción dominantes en la sociedad dominicana*, 130.

101. Moya Pons, "Industrial Incentives in the Dominican Republic," 70; Spalding to Sec. of State, no. 179, 6 Oct. 1958, RG59, 839.432.

102. Farland to Sec. of State, no. 512, 22 June 1959; Farland to R. R. Rubottom, Asst. Sec. of State for Inter-American Affairs, 14 July 1959, RG59, 739.00.

103. Farland to Sec. of State, no. 225, 10 Nov. 1958, RG59, 739.00.

104. Spalding to Sec. of State, no. 424, 20 Feb. 1958, RG59, 839.432.

105. Farland to Sec. of State, no. 225, 10 Nov. 1958, RG59, 739.00.

106. Dearborn to Sec. of State, 22 Mar. 1961, in *FRUS, 1961–1963*, vol. 12, 621.

107. Robert Cox to Sec. of State, no. 624, 27 Jan. 1959, RG59, 739.00.

108. Farland to Sec. of State, no. 225, 10 Nov. 1958, RG59, 739.00. See also Crassweller, *Trujillo*, 329–407.

109. Crassweller, *Trujillo*, 329–41, 384, 390; Dearborn to Sec. of State, no. 218, 10 Dec. 1959, RG59, 739.00; Bernard, "Trujillo: Treinta años de su muerte."

110. Farland to Sec. of State, no. G-11, 28 July 1959, RG59, 739.00; Michel, "Las expediciones," 59.

111. Farland to Rubottom, 14 July 1959; Farland to Sec. of State, no. 529, 26 June 1959, RG59, 739.00.

112. Farland to Sec. of State, no. 529, 6, and 228, 26 June, 3 July, and 16 Dec. 1959; Lofton to Sec. of State, no. 16 and 66, 9 July and 6 Aug. 1959; Dearborn to Sec. of State, no. 219, 10 Dec. 1959, RG59, 739.00. See also Cassá, *Movimiento obrero*, 597.

113. Mayobanex Vargas, *Testimonio histórico junio 1959* (Santo Domingo: Editora Cosmos, 1981), 39–43.

114. On conditions in 1959 where the exiles landed, see Lofton to Sec. of State, no. 66, 6 Aug. 1959, RG59, 739.00; San Miguel, *Los campesinos*. Presumably, the Cibao was selected by the exiles because it was a center of opposition among the emerging middle classes and old powerful landowners. And it was the former home of many exile leaders, such as Juancito Rodríguez.

115. Farland to Sec. of State, no. 58, 31 July 1959, RG59, 739.00(w).

116. Lofton to Sec. of State, no. 17, 9 July 1959, RG59, 739.00. Antonio Hernández, a peasant from El Rincón, Cotuí, also recalled searching "the hills of Constanza . . . with our knives, in our boots . . . [for] the *barbudos* [the bearded ones]." Interview with Hernández, El Rincón, Apr. 1992.

117. Farland to Rubottom, 14 July 1959, RG59, 739.00. See also Cordero, "Las expediciones de junio de 1959," 59; Farland to Sec. of State, no. G-11, 28 July 1959, RG59, 739.00.

118. Farland to Sec. of State, no. 484, 15 June 1959, RG59, 739.00; Farland to Sec. of State, no. 22, 10 July 1959, and Dearborn to Sec. of State, no. 123, 18 Sept. 1959, RG59, 739.00(w).

119. Farland to Sec. of State, no. 46, 24 July 1959, RG59, 739.00(w); Dearborn to Sec. of State, no. 218, 10 Dec. 1959, and Farland to Sec. of State, no. 228, 16 Dec. 1959, RG59, 739.00.

120. See Roberto Cassá's detailed treatment of opposition to the Trujillo regime in the late 1950s and of the rise of the 14th of June Movement, *Los orígenes del Movimiento 14 de junio: La izquierda dominicana I* (Santo Domingo: Editora Universitaria—UASD, 1999). On the composition of the resistance, see also "Country Economic Program, Dominican Republic," 1 Aug. 1960, RG84; Piero Gleijeses, *The Dominican Crisis: The 1965 Constitutionalist Revolt and American Intervention* (Baltimore: Johns Hopkins University Press, 1978), 27–29; Crassweller, *Trujillo*, 357–94; and José Israel Cuello, *¿Qué era la resistencia antitrujillista interna a la hora de la invasión de Constanza, Maimón y Estero Hondo, el 14 de junio de 1959?* (Santo Domingo: Taller, 1983).

121. Díaz Grullón, *Antinostalgia de una era*, 131–34; Alberto Genao to Trujillo, 5 Oct. 1959, AGN, SA, leg. 1133, 1959.

122. Díaz Grullón, *Antinostalgia de una era*, 131–34.

123. Trujillo to Ramón Antonio Marte Sedeño, Pontón, La Vega, 19 Oct. 1959. This letter was in the possession of Negrito Viloria of Pontón, La Vega, who kindly showed it to me on 2 May 1992.

124. Sec. of Agric. and Pres. of the Commission of Rural Improvement to Munici-

pal Síndicos and the Subcommissioners of Rural Improvement, circular MR-4, 17 Oct. 1959, AGN, SA, leg. 1133, 1959.

125. Farland to Sec. of State, no. 58, 31 July 1959, RG59, 739.00(w).

126. See e.g., V. Alvarez Piña to Sec. of Agric., no. 16452, 1 Sept. 1959, and other documents in AGN, SA, leg. 1132 as well as 1133, 1959. See also Ludovino Fernández to Trujillo, 8 Jan. 1958, AGN, SA, leg. 1027, 1958.

127. Carlos Alberto Alvarez to Provincial Deputy, Puerto Plata, 10 Aug. 1959, AGN, SA, leg. 1132, 1959.

128. Some denounced particular landowners with idle land. E.g., Antonio Germán to General Dir. of Internal Revenue, 18 Aug. 1959, and other docs., AGN, SA, leg. 1132, 1959. See AGN, SA, leg. 1133, 1959 for numerous peasant land requests, including for plots in newly irrigated areas in Cotuí, Esperanza, Jarabacoa, Guayacanes, Pedro Santana, and Pedernales.

129. Arturo Padilla, e.g., asked for 300 pesos under such circumstances. Padilla to Trujillo, 7 Nov. 1959, AGN, SA, leg. 1133, 1959.

130. Marcelino Sosa to Trujillo, 28 Nov. 1959, AGN, SA, leg. 1133, 1959. The file containing these land requests docs not include reports of state action taken in response.

131. San Miguel, *El pasado*, 172. See also "Agricultores Julia Molina agradecen Plan de Tierras," *El Caribe*, 24 Mar. 1960.

132. See, e.g., Ramos, "La ciudad y el campo." In 1953, during the expansion of Trujillo's sugar empire, new legislation prohibited peasants from migrating to the city, but this measure was not widely enforced. Lester to Sec. of State, no. 504, 7 Dec. 1953, RG59, 839.16; Lester to Sec. of State, no. 718, 5 Feb. 1954, RG59, 839.20. The state did take action, though, as we have seen, to move some urban dwellers to agricultural colonies in its last few years.

133. See Frank Moya Pons, "Notas para una historia de la iglesia en Santo Domingo," *Eme Eme: Estudios Dominicanos* 1, no. 6 (1973), 3–37; Karl Leveque, "La Iglesia en tres crisis dominicanas," *Ahora*, no. 471 (20 Nov. 1972), 4–5; Esteban Rosario, *Iglesia católica y oligarquía* (Santiago de los Caballeros: Editora Búho, 1991); Julio Rodríguez Grullón, *Trujillo y la Iglesia* (Santo Domingo: Panamericana, 1991); Johnson to Sec. of State, no. 920, 6 Apr. 1954, RG59, 739.00.

134. Johnson to Sec. of State, no. 920, 6 Apr. 1954, RG59, 739.00; "La ominosa dictadura de Trujillo," *El Tiempo* (Bogotá), 31 Mar. 1945; various articles in *El Caribe*, 5 Nov. 1958; "Agricultores Julia Molina Agradecen Plan de Tierras," *El Caribe*, 24 Mar. 1960.

135. "Country Economic Program, Dominican Republic," 1 Aug. 1960, RG84.

136. John Barfield to Sec. of State, no. 61, 15 Aug. 1960, RG84. Besides the increase in repression and the widening number of middle-class opponents of the regime, the Church's about-face may have been impelled by the new papal nuncio, Archbishop Lino Zanini, who was reportedly an exceptionally liberal and strong-willed figure (Balaguer, *La palabra encadenada*, 312–13). Moreover, the Catholic Church, in general, was moving forcefully with the antidictatorial tide of the late 1950s, as shown by its role in the downfall of Juan Perón in Argentina, Marcos Pérez Jiménez in Venezuela, and Gustavo Rojas Pinilla in Colombia.

137. Balaguer, *La palabra encadenada*, 310.

138. Zenón Castillo de Aza, *Trujillo, Benefactor de la Iglesia* (Ciudad Trujillo: Editora del Caribe, 1955); Zenón Castillo de Aza, "Trujillo, Benefactor de la Iglesia Católica en la República," *El Caribe*, 14 Mar. 1960; Augusto Ortega, "Trujillo, Benefactor de la Iglesia Católica Dominicana," *El Caribe*, 24 Mar. 1960; "Claustro USD apoya título Benefactor Iglesia," *El Caribe*, 24 Mar. 1960; and Farland, memo no. 323, 18 Mar. 1960, RG84, box 1. See also Sáez, *Los Jesuitas en la República Dominicana*, 183–203; Balaguer, *La palabra encadenada*, 309–13; Pérez Memén, "Iglesia y Estado," 168–86, 213; Karl Leveque, "La Iglesia en tres crisis dominicanas," 2–9; and Crassweller, *Trujillo*, 381–94.

139. Pérez Memén, "Iglesia y Estado," 181; Sáez, *Los Jesuitas en la República Dominicana*, 200–201; Crassweller, *Trujillo*, 388–92; Cassá, *Los Orígenes del movimiento 14 de junio*, 267–270.

140. See *Una carta histórica al obispo de San Juan de la Maguana* (Ciudad Trujillo: La Nación, 1961); Pérez Memén, "Iglesia y Estado," 184; Leveque, "La Iglesia en tres crisis dominicanas," 8; Rafael Augusto Sánchez, "El Concordato sería una fuente de complicaciones," *El Caribe*, 1 Apr. 1960; Rafael Ravelo Miquís, "En torno al Concordato," *El Caribe*, 12 Nov. 1960; and Rafael Andújar Susaña, "En torno al Concordato," 12 Dec. 1960.

141. Interview with Nicolás Genao y Genao, La Vega, 4 Apr. 1992; Sáez, *Los Jesuitas en la República Dominicana*, 202–3; Leveque, "La Iglesia en tres crisis dominicanas," 8.

142. Farland to Sec. of State, no. 332, 2 Jan. 1958, RG59, 739.00(w).

143. Interview with Nicolás Genao y Genao, La Vega, 4 Apr. 1992. According to the press, both the "enraged crowd" and those defending the church were arrested. On this and other staged popular attacks on the Church, see J. Rafael Khouri and Ml. R. Martínez Quiñones, "Turba ataca casa de Panal: Quema la del Padre Henríquez," "Los Veganos protestan maquinaciones de Panal," "30,000 protestan en SF Macorís trama de prelados," and "En todo el país repudian maquinaciones terroristas de obispos Reilly y Panal," all in *El Caribe*, 19 Apr. 1961.

144. Interviews with Juana Taveras (Doña Nena), Pontón, La Vega, 8 Feb. 1992; Elvira Antonia, Bacuí al Medio, La Vega, 3 May 1992; and Negrito Viloria, Pontón, La Vega, 2 May 1992.

145. *El Caribe*, 24 Apr. 1961, cited in Bernardo Vega, *Kennedy y los Trujillo* (Santo Domingo: Fundación Cultural Dominicana, 1991), 10.

146. Interview with Carlos Peguero Matos, San Juan de la Maguana, 3 Oct. 1992; "Monseñor Tomás Reilly y la muerte de Trujillo," *Listín Diario*, 1 Aug. 1992; P. Antonio Camilo G., "Gratitud nacional para monseñor Tomás F. Reilly," *Listín Diario*, 28 July 1992; Crassweller, *Trujillo*, 385–86, 392–93.

147. Interview with Linor de los Santos and Carlos (last name not given), Mijo, San Juan de la Maguana, 4 Oct. 1992.

148. Interview with Carlos Peguero Matos, San Juan de la Maguana, 3 Oct. 1992. See also "Monseñor Tomás Reilly y la muerte de Trujillo," *Listín Diario*, 1 Aug. 1992; Crassweller, *Trujillo*, 385–86, 392–93; Vega, *Kennedy y los Trujillo*, 7–11; Bernardo Vega, *Los Estados Unidos y Trujillo. Los días finales: 1960–1961* (Santo Domingo: Fundación Cultural Dominicana, 1999), 660–61, passim. After his death in Boston in 1992, Reilly's

body was brought back to the San Juan church to be entombed. Many articles appeared in the national press in honor of his courage and service to the Dominican Republic (e.g., P. Antonio Camilo G., "Gratitud nacional para monseñor Tomás F. Reilly," *Listín Diario*, 28 July 1992).

149. Interview in La Vega, 4 Apr. 1992.

150. Interview in Las Zanjas, San Juan de la Maguana, 4 Oct. 1992. See chap. 7 for Linor de los Santos's expression of positive sentiments toward Trujillo.

151. Interview in Caballero Abajo, Cotuí, 5 Apr. 1992.

152. Interviews with Negrito Viloria, Pontón, La Vega, 2 May 1992; and Elvira Antonia, Bacuí al Medio, La Vega, 3 May 1992.

153. See Farland to Rubottom, 14 July 1959; Farland to Sec. of State, no. 228, 16 Dec. 1959, RG59, 739.00; Robert Woodward to Pres. John Kennedy, 10 July 1961, *FRUS, 1961–1963*, 646; Bernardo Vega, *Eisenhower y Trujillo* (Santo Domingo: Fundación Cultural Dominicana, 1991), esp. 211–12.

154. Dean Rusk to Kennedy, 15 Feb. 1961; Dearborn to Sec. of State, 24 Feb. 1961 in *FRUS, 1961–1963*, 617, 620.

155. Rubottom to Farland, 13 Mar. 1959, RG59, 739.00.

156. Farland to Sec. of State, no. 228, 16 Dec. 1959, RG59, 739.00.

157. "Memorandum from the Cuban Task Force of the National Security Council to the President's Special Assistant for National Security Affairs," 15 May 1961, *FRUS, 1961–1963*, vol. 12, 629. See also Dean Rusk to Kennedy, 15 Feb. 1961; "Memorandum by the Under Secretary of State (Bowles)," 3 June 1961, *FRUS, 1961–1963*, vol. 12, 617–18, 629, 638.

158. On Minerva Mirabal's leadership role, see Cassá, *Los Orígenes del movimiento 14 de junio*, passim. A historical novel exploring the history and radicalization of the Mirabal sisters is Julia Alvarez, *In the Time of the Butterflies* (Chapel Hill: Algonquin Book of Chapel Hill, 1994).

159. Cassá, *Los orígenes del movimiento 14 de junio*, 274.

160. García, "Notas," 72.

161. García, "Notas," 303. Recently published testimonies indicate that there were more conspirators than earlier stated. "Presentación," *Ecos* 6, no. 7 (1999), 9–10.

162. Espaillat later stated: "He should have shot me. When he walked out of the house [with me that night] he doomed his coup and himself." Arturo Espaillat, *Trujillo: The Last Caesar* (Chicago: Henry Regnery, 1963), 20. See also "Editorial Note," *FRUS, 1961–1963*, 634; Miguel Angel Bissié, "Mis memorias sobre el ajusticiamiento de Trujillo el 30 de mayo de 1961," *Ecos* 6, no. 7 (1999); Crassweller, *Trujillo*, 436–43; Bernard Diederich, *Trujillo: The Death of a Dictator* (Princeton: Markus Wiener, 2000 [1978]), esp. 137–38; interview by historian Robert Alexander with Rafael de la Maza (brother of one of Trujillo's assassins, Antonio de la Maza), Washington, D.C., 22 June 1961, personal archive of Robert Alexander, Rutgers University, New Brunswick, New Jersey. I am indebted to Professor Alexander for sharing his materials with me.

163. The properties of the Trujillo family and their close associates that were confiscated in the next couple of years comprised approximately 200,000 hectares, almost half of which were allocated for redistribution to peasants. Clausner, *Rural Santo Domingo*, 232–36; Gómez, *Relaciones de producción*, 102–5.

164. "Telegram from the Consulate General in the Dominican Republic to the Department of State," 17 Nov. 1961, *FRUS, 1961–1963*, 677.

165. Hartlyn, *The Struggle*, 68, 76. Bosch made agrarian reform a major campaign issue, calling for the distribution of Trujillo's properties to peasants. But his short presidency accomplished little in that regard. Clausner, *Rural Santo Domingo*, 236–37, 251.

166. They were impelled, political scientist Jonathan Hartlyn suggests, by concerns that they would lose the industrial incentives and state protection that they had enjoyed under Trujillo's rule. Many feared, moreover, state expropriation of their interests, given that there was no "clear line between Trujillo's 'expropriable' investments and their private investments." Hartlyn, *The Struggle*, 78–87 (quotation on 79).

167. On the post-Trujillo period, see Espinal and Hartlyn, "The Dominican Republic," 469–517; Moya Pons, *The Dominican Republic*, 381–444.

168. Moya Pons, *The Dominican Republic*, esp. 381–85; Espinal and Hartlyn, "The Dominican Republic"; Michiel Baud, "The Changing Face of Dominican Modernity," paper presented at the meeting of the Latin American Studies Association, Miami, Fla., 18 Mar. 2000.

169. Gutiérrez-San Martín, *Agrarian Reform Policy*, esp. 1, 62.

170. Gutiérrez-San Martín, *Agrarian Reform Policy*, 1, 49, 64–65, passim; Vargas-Lundius, *Peasants in Distress*, 170, passim; Carlos Dore y Cabral, *Reforma agraria y luchas sociales en la República Dominicana, 1966–1978* (Santo Domingo: Taller, 1981), 23; Vedovato, *Politics*, chaps. 5 and 6; Luis Crouch, "La búsqueda de la autosuficiencia: Alimentaria y política" (unpublished paper, 1983).

171. Espinal and Hartlyn, "The Dominican Republic," 499; San Miguel, *El pasado relegado*, 152–57; Levitt, *Transnational Villagers*, 45–46.

172. In 1981 the urban population constituted 52 percent of the nation (compared with 30 percent in 1960 and 18 percent in 1935). Edilberto Loaiza, "Tamaño y composición de la población en la República Dominicana, 1950–2000," in *Población y sociedad: Seminario Nacional, 1983*, ed. Consejo Nacional de Población y Familia (Santo Domingo: CONAPOFA, 1985), 19–59. On rural-urban migration, see Vargas-Lundius, *Peasants in Distress*, 317–27.

173. For instance, the declining terms of trade for the peasantry may reflect the government's interests in keeping food prices down to permit low wages and stability among the expanding working class. Moya Pons, "Industrial Incentives," 571–72.

174. Baud, "The Changing Face of Dominican Modernity."

Select Bibliography

This bibliography lists sources on the Dominican Republic consulted for this book. It does not include comparative and theoretical works cited in the endnotes.

Archival Sources

ARCHIVO GENERAL DE LA NACIÓN (SANTO DOMINGO)
    Archivo de la Nación de la República Dominicana Cortesía del Archivo Nacional de Cuba
    Colección de Leyes, Decretos y Resoluciones, 1880–1956
    Gaceta Oficial, 1877–1962
    Memoria, Secretaría de Estado de Agricultura, 1908–61
    Memoria, Secretaría de Estado de lo Interior, 1927–40
    Memoria, Secretario de Estado de Relaciones Exteriores, 1910
    Records of the Gobernación de Santo Domingo
    Records of the Gobierno Militar
    Records of the Secretaría de Agricultura
NATIONAL ARCHIVES AND RECORDS ADMINISTRATION (WASHINGTON, D.C., AND COLLEGE PARK, MARYLAND)
    Record Group 38, Records of the Office of the Chief of Naval Operations, Military Government of Santo Domingo
    Record Group 59, General Records of the Department of State
    Record Group 84, Records of the Foreign Service Posts of the Department of State
    Record Group 139, Records of the Dominican Customs Receivership
    Record Group 165, Records of the War Department General and Special Staffs, Military Intelligence Division
PERSONAL ARCHIVE OF ROBERT JACKSON ALEXANDER (RUTGERS UNIV., NEW BRUNSWICK)
    Records of conversations and correspondence with Dominican leaders
TRIBUNAL SUPERIOR DE TIERRAS (SANTO DOMINGO)
    Expedientes Catastrales

Newspapers

El Caribe	*La Información*	*La Opinión*	*La Tribuna*
El Diario	*Juventud*	*Patria*	*Unión Cívica*
Eco de la Opinión	*Listín Diario*	*El Porvenir*	
Hoy	*La Nación*	*El Siglo*	
El Imparcial	*El Nacional*	*El Teléfono*	

Printed Sources

Abad, José Ramón. *La República Dominicana: Reseña general geográfico-estadística.* Santo Domingo: Imprenta de García Hermanos, 1888.

Abreu Licairac, Rafael. *La cuestión palpitante.* Santo Domingo: Imp. Listín Diario, 1906.

Acevedo, Octavio A. *Tópicos técnicos.* Santo Domingo: El Progreso, 1919.

Alburquerque, Alcibíades. *Títulos de los terrenos comuneros de la República Dominicana.* Ciudad Trujillo: Impresora Dominicana, 1961.

Alburquerque Contreras, Rafael. "La parcela catastral." *Revista Jurídica Dominicana* 9, no. 29 (Jan.–Mar. 1948): 27–29.

———. "La prescripción del artículo 2,262 del Código Civil." *Revista Jurídica Dominicana* 9, nos. 25–26 (Jan.–June 1947): 40–41.

———. "El problema de los terrenos comuneros." *Revista Jurídica Dominicana* 17, nos. 54–55 (1955): 100–105.

Alvarez, Federico. "Nuestro primer siglo de vida independiente." *Renovación* (Jan.–Mar. 1953): 11–18.

Alvarez, José de Js. "Studies on the A-B-O, M-N, and Rh-Hr Blood Factors in the Dominican Republic with Special Reference to the Problem of Admixture." *American Journal of Physical Anthropology* 9, no. 2 (June 1951).

Alvarez, Julia. *In the Time of the Butterflies.* Chapel Hill: Algonquin Books of Chapel Hill, 1994.

Alvarez Sánchez, Aristides. *Estudio de la Ley de Tierras.* Santo Domingo: Editorial Tiempo, 1986.

Andrews, Kenneth. *The Spanish Caribbean: Trade and Plunder 1530–1630.* New Haven: Yale University Press, 1978.

Andújar Persinal, Carlos. *La presencia negra en Santo Domingo: Un enfoque etnohistórico.* Santo Domingo: Búho, 1997.

Angulo Guridi, Alejandro. "Examen crítico de la anexión de Santo Domingo a España." In *Antecedentes de la anexión a España,* ed. Emilio Rodríguez Demorizi. Ciudad Trujillo: Editora Montalvo, 1955.

———. *La fantasma de Higüey.* Santo Domingo: Imprenta de A. M. Dávila, 1857.

Augelli, John P. "Nationalization of the Dominican Borderlands." *Geographical Review* 70, no. 1 (Jan. 1980): 15–27.

Avelino, Francisco Antonio. *Las ideas políticas en Santo Domingo.* Santo Domingo: Editorial Arte y Cine, 1966.

Ayala, César. *American Sugar Kingdom: The Plantation Economy of the Spanish Caribbean, 1898–1934.* Chapel Hill: University of North Carolina Press, 1999.

Baez Evertsz, Franc. *Azúcar y dependencia en la República Dominicana.* Santo Domingo: Editora de la Universidad Autónoma de Santo Domingo, 1978.

Balaguer, Joaquín. *La isla al revés: Haití y el destino dominicano.* Santo Domingo: Librería Dominicana, 1984.

———. *La palabra encadenada.* Santo Domingo: Taller, 1985.

———. *La realidad dominicana: Semblanza de un país y de un régimen.* Buenos Aires: Imprenta Ferrari Hermanos, 1947.

———, ed. *El pensamiento vivo de Trujillo (antología).* Ciudad Trujillo: Impresora Dominicana, 1955.

Baud, Michiel. "A Colonial Counter Economy: Tobacco Production on Española, 1500–1870." *New West Indian Guide* 65, nos. 1–2 (1991): 27–49.

———. "'Constitutionally White': The Forging of a National Identity in the Dominican Republic," in *Ethnicity in the Caribbean: Essays in Honor of Harry Hoetink,* ed. Gert Oostindie (London: Macmillan Caribbean, 1996).

———. "Una frontera para cruzar: La sociedad rural a través de la frontera domínico-haitiana (1870–1930)." *Estudios Sociales* 26, no. 94 (1993): 5–28.

———. "Una frontera-refugio: Dominicanos y haitianos contra el estado." *Estudios Sociales* 26, no. 92 (1993): 39–64.

———. "Ideología y campesinado: El pensamiento de José Ramón López." *Estudios Sociales* 19, no. 64 (Apr.–June 1986): 63–81.

———. "The Origins of Capitalist Agriculture in the Dominican Republic." *Latin American Research Review* 22, no. 2 (1987): 135–53.

———. "Patriarchy and Changing Family Strategies: Class and Gender in the Dominican Republic." *History of the Family* 2, no. 4 (1997): 355–77.

———. *Peasants and Tobacco in the Dominican Republic, 1870–1930.* Knoxville: University of Tennessee Press, 1995.

———. "'Un permanente guerrillero': El pensamiento social de Ramón Marrero Aristy (1913–1959)." In *Política, identidad y pensamiento social en la República Dominicana (Siglos XIX y XX),* ed. Raymundo González, Michiel Baud, Pedro L. San Miguel, and Roberto Cassá. Madrid: Doce Calles, 1999.

———. "The Quest for Modernity: Latin American Technocratic Ideas in Historical Perspective." In *The Politics of Expertise in Latin America,* ed. Miguel Centeno and Patricio Silva. New York: St. Martin's, 1998.

———. "Realidades e ideologías de la modernidad en la República Dominicana del siglo veinte." *Estudios Sociales* 34, no. 124 (Apr.–June 2001): 9–50.

———. "Transformación capitalista y regionalización en la República Dominicana, 1875–1920." *Investigación y Ciencia* 1, no. 1 (Jan.–Apr. 1986): 17–45.

Betances, Emelio. *State and Society in the Dominican Republic.* San Francisco: Westview, 1995.

Bissié, Miguel Angel. "Mis memorias sobre el ajusticiamiento de Trujillo el 30 de mayo de 1961." *Ecos* 6, no. 7 (1999): 99–128.

Boin, Jacqueline, and José Serulle Ramia. *El proceso de desarrollo del capitalismo en la República Dominicana (1844–1930).* Santo Domingo: Ediciones Gramil, 1985.

Bonilla Antiles, José Antonio. *Legislación de tierras dominicanas: El sistema Torrens.* Santo Domingo: Librería Dominicana, 1974.

Bonó, Pedro F. *El Montero: Novela de costumbres.* Prefacio de E. Rodríguez Demorizi. 1856. Reprint, San Francisco de Macorís: Comisión Organizadora Permanente de la Feria Nacional del Libro, 1989.

Bosch, Juan. *Composición social dominicana: Historia e interpretación.* 13th ed. Santo Domingo: Alfa y Omega, 1983.

———. *La fortuna de Trujillo.* 3d ed. Santo Domingo: Alfa y Omega, 1989.

———. *La Guerra de la Restauración.* Santo Domingo: Editora Corripio, 1987.

———. *La mañosa.* Santo Domingo: Alfa y Omega, 1990.

———. *Trujillo: Causas de una tiranía sin ejemplo.* Caracas: Librería Las Novedades, 1959.

———. "Visión de la Era de Trujillo." Paper presented at the Museo Nacional de Historia y Geografía, 2 Apr. 1991.

Box, Louk, and Barbara de la Rive Box-Lasocki. "¿Sociedad fronteriza o frontera social? Transformaciones sociales en la zona fronteriza de la República Dominicana (1907–1984)." *Boletín de estudios latinoamericanos y del Caribe* (Amsterdam), no. 46 (June 1989): 49–69.

Brea, Ramonina. *Ensayo sobre la formación del estado capitalista en la República Dominicana y Haití.* Santo Domingo: Taller, 1983.

Brookings Institution. *Refugee Settlement in the Dominican Republic: A Survey Conducted under the Auspices of the Brookings Institution.* Washington, D.C.: Brookings Institution, 1944.

Bryan, Patrick E. "La producción campesina en la República Dominicana a principio del siglo veinte." *Eme Eme: Estudios Dominicanos* 7, no. 42 (May–June 1979): 29–62.

Cabral, Marcos A. *Memoria que presenta el Inspector General de Agricultura de la Provincia Capital al Señor Ministro de Fomento y Obras Públicas.* Santo Domingo: Imprenta de la Lucha, 1900.

Calder, Bruce. *The Impact of Intervention: The Dominican Republic during the U.S. Occupation of 1916–1924.* Austin: University of Texas Press, 1984.

Camarena Perdomo, M. de J. "Los motivos de la Ley de Registro de Tierras." In *Anales de la Universidad de Santo Domingo.* Ciudad Trujillo: Listín Diario, Apr. 1938.

Cambeira, Alan. *Quisqueya La Bella: The Dominican Republic in Historical and Cultural Perspective.* Armonk, N.Y.: M. E. Sharpe, 1997.

Campillo Pérez, Julio. *Elecciones dominicanas (contribución a su estudio).* Santo Domingo: Academia Dominicana de la Historia, 1978.

Capó Bonnafaus, Eduardo. *Medina del mar Caribe: Seminovela.* 2d ed. Santo Domingo: Sociedad Dominicana de Bibliofilos, 1986.

Carta histórica al obispo de San Juan de la Maguana. Ciudad Trujillo: La Nación, 1961.

Cassá, Roberto. "Antecedentes inmediatos del gavillerismo en el Este." *Isla Abierta* (supplement to *Hoy*). 4 Nov. 1994.

———. "Campiña: Un caso aislado de lucha agraria." *Isla Abierta* (supplement to *Hoy*). 14 July 1990.

———. *Capitalismo y dictadura.* Santo Domingo: Editora de la Universidad Autónoma de Santo Domingo, 1982.

———. "Emergencia del gavillerismo frente a la ocupación militar." *Isla Abierta* (supplement to *Hoy*). 3 Mar. 1995.

———. "Gavillerismo, delito común y sector azucarero en el Este." *Isla Abierta* (supplement to *Hoy*). 2 Dec. 1994.

———. *Historia social y económica de la República Dominicana.* Vol. 1. Santo Domingo: Alfa y Omega, 1992.

———. *Historia social y económica de la República Dominicana.* Vol. 2. Santo Domingo: Alfa y Omega, 1986.

———. *Movimiento obrero y lucha socialista en la República Dominicana (desde los orígenes hasta 1960).* Santo Domingo: Fundación Cultural Dominicana, 1990.

———. *Los orígenes del Movimiento 14 de Junio: La izquierda dominicana I.* Santo Domingo: Editora Universitaria–UASD, 1999.

———. "Orígenes remotos del gavillerismo." Unpublished manuscript, 1995.

Cassá, Roberto, and Franklin Franco. "La sociedad dominicana durante la ocupación haitiana." In *Duarte y la independencia nacional*. Santo Domingo: Instituto Tecnológica de Santo Domingo, 1976.

Cassá, Roberto, and Genaro Rodríguez. "Consideraciones alternativas acerca de las rebeliones de esclavos en Santo Domingo." *Ecos* 2, no. 3 (1994): 155–91.

Castillo de Aza, Zenón. *Trujillo, benefactor de la Iglesia*. Ciudad Trujillo: Editora del Caribe, 1955.

Castillo Sosa, Emiliano. "Situación actual de mensura y partición de los terrenos comuneros." Doctoral thesis in law, no. 21, Universidad de Santo Domingo, 1942.

Castor, Suzy. *Migración y relaciones internacionales (el caso haitiano-dominicano)*. Santo Domingo: Editora Universitaria, 1987.

Céspedes, Diógenes. "El efecto Rodó, nacionalismo idealista vs. nacionalismo práctico: Los intelectuales antes de y bajo Trujillo." *Cuadernos de poética* 6, no. 17 (Jan.–Apr. 1989): 7–56.

Cestero, Tulio. *El problema dominicano*. New York: n.p., 1919.

Chardón, Carlos E. "The Caribbean Island Economy." *Scientific Monthly* 69, no. 3 (Sept. 1949): 169–72.

Chaunu, Pierre. *Sevilla y América, siglos dieciseis y diecisiete*. Seville: Universidad de Sevilla, 1983.

Chez Checo, José, and Rafael Peralta Brito. *Azúcar, encomiendas y otros ensayos históricos*. Santo Domingo: Taller, 1979.

Clausner, Marlin. *Rural Santo Domingo: Settled, Unsettled, Resettled*. Philadelphia: Temple University Press, 1973.

Colombino Perelló, Héctor. *La jaula*. Santo Domingo: Impresora Cacique, 1978.

Cook, Noble David. "Disease and the Depopulation of Hispaniola, 1492–1518." *Colonial Latin American Review* 2, nos. 1–2 (1993): 213–45.

Cordero, Walter. "El tema negro y la discriminación en la República Dominicana." *Ciencia* 2, no. 2 (Jan.–Mar. 1975): 151–62.

———. *Tendencias de la economía cafetalera dominicana, 1955–1972*. Santo Domingo: Editora de la Universidad Autónoma de Santo Domingo, 1975.

Cordero Michel, Emilio. "Las expediciones de junio de 1959." *Estudios Sociales* 25, no. 88 (Apr.–June 1992): 35–60.

Courtney, W. S. "Los campos de oro en Santo Domingo." In *Riqueza mineral y agrícola de Santo Domingo*, ed. Emilio Rodríguez Demorizi. Santo Domingo: Editora del Caribe, 1965.

Crassweller, Robert D. *Trujillo: The Life and Times of a Caribbean Dictator*. New York: Macmillan, 1966.

Crouch, Luis. "La búsqueda de la autosuficiencia: Alimentaria y política." Unpublished manuscript, 1983.

Cruz Infante, José. *El 30 de mayo: Una fecha sin padrino*. n.p., n.d.

Cuello, José Israel. *Contración de mano de obra haitiana destinada a la industria azucarera dominicana, 1952–1986*. Santo Domingo: Taller, 1997.

———. *¿Qué era la resistencia antitrujillista interna a la hora de la invasión de Constanza, Maimón y Estero Hondo, el 14 de junio de 1959?* Santo Domingo: Taller, 1983.

————, ed. *Documentos del conflicto dominico-haitiano de 1937*. Santo Domingo: Taller, 1985.

Cuello, Rafael. *El Sisal: Esclavitud y muerte en la Era de Trujillo*. Santo Domingo: Susaeta, 1998.

Danticat, Edwidge. *The Farming of Bones*. New York: Soho, 1998.

Davis, Martha Ellen. *La otra ciencia: El vodú dominicano como religión y medicina populares*. Santo Domingo: Editora Universitaria, 1987.

Deive, Carlos Esteban. *La esclavitud del negro en Santo Domingo (1492–1844)*. 2 vols. Santo Domingo: Museo del Hombre Dominicano, 1980.

————. *La Española y la esclavitud del indio*. Santo Domingo: Fundación García Arevalo, 1995.

————. *Los guerrilleros negros: Esclavos fugitivos y cimarrones en Santo Domingo*. Santo Domingo: Fundación Cultural Dominicana, 1997.

————. "La herencia africana en la cultura dominicana actual." In *Ensayos sobre cultura dominicana*, ed. Bernardo Vega et al. Santo Domingo: Museo del Hombre Dominicano, 1988.

.————. "El prejuicio racial en el folklore dominicano." *Boletín del Museo del Hombre Dominicano* 4, no. 8 (Jan.–Mar. 1977): 75–96.

————. *Vodú y magia en Santo Domingo*. Santo Domingo: Taller, 1996.

de la Rosa, Gilberto. *Petán: Un cacique en la era de Trujillo*. Santiago de los Caballeros: Universidad Católica Madre y Maestra, n.d.

del Castillo, José. "The Formation of the Dominican Sugar Industry: From Competition to Monopoly, from National Semiproletariat to Foreign Proletarian." In *Between Slavery and Free Labor: The Spanish-Speaking Caribbean in the Nineteenth Century*, ed. Manuel Moreno Fraginals, Frank Moya Pons, and Stanley L. Engerman. Baltimore: Johns Hopkins University Press, 1985.

del Castillo, Luis. *Prolegómenos de enseñanza cívica*, 3d ed. Santiago: Imp. de Manuel Tavares, 1927.

del Monte y Tejada, Antonio. *Historia de Santo Domingo*. Vol. 3. Ciudad Trujillo: Impresora Dominicana, 1953.

Derby, Lauren. "Haitians, Magic, and Money: *Raza* and Society in the Haitian-Dominican Borderlands, 1900–1937." *Comparative Studies in Society and History* 36, no. 3 (July 1994): 488–526.

————. "Histories of Power and the Power of History in the Dominican Republic." Unpublished manuscript, 1989.

————. "The Magic of Modernity: Dictatorship and Civic Culture in the Dominican Republic, 1916–1962." Ph.D. diss., University of Chicago, 1998.

————. "*Tigueraje*: Race, Class and Self-Fashioning in the Dominican Republic." Paper presented at the Africa in the Americas Conference, Harvard University, 2 Oct. 1998.

Derby, Lauren, and Richard Turits. "Historias de terror y terrores de la historia: La masacre haitiana de 1937 en la República Dominicana." *Estudios Sociales* (Santo Domingo) 26, no. 92 (Apr.–June 1993): 65–76.

Despradel, Lil. "Las etapas del antihaitianismo en la República Dominicana: El papel de los historiadores." In *Política y sociología en Haití y la República Dominicana*, ed. Suzy Castor et al. Mexico City: Universidad Nacional Autónoma de México, 1974.

Díaz, Xiroibma. "Notas sobre la vida política de Horacio Vásquez." *Eme Eme: Estudios Dominicanos* 2, no. 2 (Mar.–Apr. 1974): 111–23.

Díaz Grullón, Virgilio. *Antinostalgia de una Era*. Santo Domingo: Editora Corripio, 1989.

Díaz Ordóñez, V. *El más antiguo y grave problema antillano*. Ciudad Trujillo: La Opinión, 1938.

Diederich, Bernard. *Trujillo: The Death of a Dictator*. Princeton: Markus Wiener, 2000.

Domínguez, Jaime de Jesús. *La dictadura de Heureaux*. Santo Domingo: Editora Universitaria, 1986.

———. *La sociedad dominicana a principios del siglo veinte*. Santo Domingo: Taller, 1994.

Dominican Republic. *Censo agro-pecuario, 1940: Resumen nacional*. Ciudad Trujillo: Dirección General de Estadística Nacional, 1940.

———. *Código Civil de la República Dominicana*. Ed. Fabio T. Rodríguez. Ciudad Trujillo: Editora Montalvo, 1950.

———. *Colección de Ordenes Ejecutivas*. Santo Domingo: Listín Diario, 1929.

———. Comisión para el Establecimiento de Colonias de Inmigrantes. *Informe que presenta al Poder Ejecutivo la Comisión creada por la Ley Núm. 77 para estudiar las tierras de la Frontera y señalar los sitios en que se han de establecer las colonias de inmigrantes*. Santo Domingo: Imprenta de J. R. Vda. García, 1925.

———. *Cuarto censo nacional agropecuario, 1950*. Ciudad Trujillo: Dirección Nacional de Estadística, Oficina Nacional del Censo, 1950.

———. Dirección General de la Cédula Personal de Identidad. *Evolución e importancia de la cédula en la era de Trujillo*. Ciudad Trujillo: Arte y Cine, 1948.

———. Gobierno Provisional de la República Dominicana. *Primer censo nacional de República Dominicana, 1920*. Santo Domingo: Editora de la Universidad Autónoma de Santo Domingo, 1975.

———. Junta Nacional de Alimentación y Agricultura. *Algunos aspectos sobre la situación agrícola y alimenticia de la República Dominicana, 1941–45*. Ciudad Trujillo, 1946.

———. *Mensaje que el Presidente de la República presenta al Congreso Nacional*. Santo Domingo: Imp. La Cuna de América, 1912.

———. *Quinto censo nacional agropecuario, 1960*. Santo Domingo: Dirección General de Estadística y Censos, 1962.

———. Secretaría de Estado de Educación y Bellas Artes. *Ley de alfabetización obligatoria para adultos*. Ciudad Trujillo, 1955.

———. Secretaría de Estado de Fomento y Obras Públicas. *Ley sobre crianza de animales domésticos de pasto*. Santo Domingo: Imprenta de García Hermanos, 1895.

Dore y Cabral, Carlos. *Reforma agraria y luchas sociales en la República Dominicana, 1966–1978*. Santo Domingo: Taller, 1981.

Ducoudray, Félix Servio. *Los "gavilleros" del Este: Una epopeya calumniada*. Santo Domingo: Editora de la Universidad Autónoma de Santo Domingo, 1976.

Escoto Gómez, Luis. "Origen y evolución de la propiedad rural en Santo Domingo—los terrenos comuneros." Doctoral thesis in law, no. 213, Universidad de Santo Domingo, 1953–54.

Espaillat, Arturo. *Trujillo: The Last Caesar.* Chicago: Henry Regnery, 1963.

Espinal, Rosario. *Autoritarismo y democracia en la política dominicana.* San José, Costa Rica: Centro Interamericano de Asesoría Electoral, 1987.

———. "Indagaciones sobre el discurso trujillista y su incidencia en la política dominicana." *Ciencia y Sociedad* 12, no. 4 (Oct.–Dec. 1987): 629–46.

Espinal, Rosario, and Jonathan Hartlyn. "The Dominican Republic: The Long and Difficult Struggle for Democracy." In *Democracy in Developing Countries,* ed. Larry Diamond et al., pp. 469–517. Boulder: Lynne Rienner, 1999.

Fernández Moscoso, Salvador A. "Consideraciones sobre la mensura en la República Dominicana." *Revista Jurídica Dominicana* 3, no. 2 (Apr. 1941): 315–19.

Fernández Rodríguez, Aura Celeste. "Origen y evolución de la propiedad y de los terrenos comuneros en la República Dominicana." *Eme Eme: Estudios Dominicanos* 9, no. 51 (Nov.–Dec. 1980): 5–45.

Fiehrer, Thomas. "Political Violence in the Periphery: The Haitian Massacre of 1937." *Race and Class* 32, no. 2 (Oct.–Dec. 1990): 1–20.

Font Bernard, Ramón. "Trujillo: Treinta años de su muerte." Paper presented at the Museo Nacional de Historia y Geografía, 4 Apr. 1991.

Foreign Relations of the United States, 1958–1960. Washington, D.C.: U.S. Government Printing Office, 1991.

Foreign Relations of the United States, 1961–1963. Washington, D.C.: U.S. Government Printing Office, 1996.

Franco Pichardo, Franklin J. *La era de Trujillo.* Santo Domingo: Fundación Cultural Dominicano, 1992.

———. *Los negros, los mulatos y la nación dominicana.* Santo Domingo: Alfa y Omega, 1984.

———. *Sobre racismo y antihaitianismo (y otros ensayos).* Santo Domingo: Impresora Vidal, 1997.

———. "La sociedad dominicana de los tiempos de la independencia." In *Duarte y la independencia nacional,* ed. Franklin Franco et al. Santo Domingo: Instituto Tecnológico de Santo Domingo, 1976.

Franklin, James. *The Present State of Hayti (Santo Domingo) with Remarks on Its Agriculture, Commerce, Laws, Religion, Finances, and Population, etc. etc.* London: John Murray, 1828.

Franks, Julie. "The *Gavilleros* of the East: Social Banditry as Political Practice in the Dominican Sugar Region, 1900–1924." *Journal of Historical Sociology* 8, no. 2 (June 1995): 158–81.

———. "Property Rights and the Commercialization of Land in the Dominican Sugar Zone, 1880–1924." *Latin American Perspectives* 26, no. 1 (Jan. 1999): 106–28.

———. "Transforming Property: Strategies of Political Power and Land Accumulation in the Dominican Sugar Region, 1880–1930." Ph.D. diss., State University of New York at Stony Brook, 1997.

Galíndez, Jesús de. *La era de Trujillo: Un estudio casuístico de dictadura hispanoamericana.* Buenos Aires: Editorial Americana, 1958.

———. *Un reportaje sobre Santo Domingo.* Santo Domingo: Editora Cole, 1999 (1955).

Gallegos, Gerardo. *Trujillo: Cara y cruz de su dictadura.* n.p., n.d.

García, José Gabriel. *Compendio de la historia de Santo Domingo*. Santo Domingo: Talleres de Publicaciones Ahora, 1968.

García, Juan Manuel. *La matanza de los haitianos: Genocidio de Trujillo, 1937*. Santo Domingo: Alfa y Omega, 1983.

García Mella, Moisés. *Alrededor de los tratados de 1929 y 1935 con la República de Haití*. Ciudad Trujillo: Imprenta Listín Diario, 1938.

García Vásquez, Eduardo. "Notas sobre el 30 de mayo de 1961." *Ecos* 6, no. 7 (1999): 57–98.

García-Muñiz, Humberto. "The South Porto Rico Sugar Company: The History of a United States Multinational Corporation in Puerto Rico and the Dominican Republic, 1900–1921." Ph.D. diss., Columbia University, 1997.

Gardiner, C. Harvey. *La política de inmigración del dictador Trujillo: Estudio sobre la creación de una imagen humanitaria*. Santo Domingo: Talleres de la Universidad Nacional Pedro Henríquez Ureña, 1979.

Gautreau, Julio. *Vicentico: Héroe y mártir dos veces*. Santo Domingo: Biblioteca Nacional, 1986.

Ghasmann Bissainthe, Jean. *Perfil de dos naciones en La Española*. Santo Domingo: n.p., 1998.

Gimbernard Pellerano, Jacinto. *Trujillo: Un estudio de su dictadura*. 2d ed. Santo Domingo: Publicaciones América, 1985.

Gleijeses, Piero. *The Dominican Crisis: The 1965 Constitutionalist Revolt and American Intervention*. Baltimore: Johns Hopkins University Press, 1978.

Goico, Héctor B. *Guía Policial*. Ciudad Trujillo: Editora Montalvo, 1949.

Golfi, Luis J. "Memoria general sobre la bahía y península de Samaná." In *Samaná: Pasado y porvenir*, ed. Emilio Rodríguez Demorizi. Santo Domingo: Editora del Caribe, 1973.

Gómez, Luis. "Algunos cambios en la comunidad campesina dominicana (1920–1970)." *Cuadernos del CENDIA* 289, no. 9 (1980).

———. *Relaciones de producción dominantes en la sociedad dominicana, 1875/1975*. Santo Domingo: Alfa y Omega, 1984.

Gómez, M. Ubaldo. "El color de los dominicanos." *Bahoruco* 3, no. 106 (20 Aug. 1932): 18–20.

González, Nancie. "Desiderio Arias, caudillo y héroe cultural." *Pequeño Universo de la Facultad de Humanidades* (Santo Domingo) 1, no. 1 (July–Sept. 1971): 3–9.

González, Raymundo. "Autonomía de la vida rural fue una característica de evolución de sociedad dominicana en siglo XVIII." *El Caribe*. 10 Aug. 1991.

———. *Bonó, un intelectual de los pobres*. Santo Domingo: Editora Búho, 1994.

———. "Campesinos y sociedad colonial en el siglo dieciocho dominicano." Paper presented at the Quinto Congreso Dominicano de Historia, Santo Domingo, 24–27 Oct. 1991.

———. "El 'Comegente' atacaba personas y propiedades cerca de las poblaciones." *El Caribe*. 5 Oct. 1991.

———. "De la reforma de la propiedad a la reforma rural." *Ecos* 3, no. 4 (1995): 179–92.

———. "Esclavos 'ocultos' fueron fuente de conflicto durante la colonia." *El Caribe*. 1 May 1993.

———. "Esclavos reclamaron su libertad en los tribunales de justicia." *El Caribe*. 14 Dec. 1991.

———. "Frontera ganadera y dispersión rural caracterizan siglo XVIII dominicano." *El Caribe*. 24 Aug. 1991.

———. "Ideología del progreso y campesinado en el siglo diecinueve." *Ecos* 1, no. 2 (1993): 25–44.

———. "Ideología y mundo rural: 'Civilización y Barbarie,' revistados." *Estudios Sociales* 29, no. 106 (Oct.–Dec. 1996): 39–47.

———. "Libertos en la sociedad esclavista." *El Caribe*. 30 Nov. 1991.

———. "Notas sobre el pensamiento socio-político dominicano." *Estudios Sociales* 20, no. 76 (Jan.–Mar. 1987): 1–22.

———. "Para capturar al 'Comegente' comisionó la Real Audiencia a uno de sus oidores." *El Caribe*. 12 Oct. 1991.

———. "Peña Batlle y su concepto histórico de la nación dominicana." *Anuario de Estudios Americanos* 48 (1991): 585–631.

———. "Principal motivo de los esclavos franceses para huir a la parte española de la isla era lograr su libertad." *El Caribe*. 8 May 1993.

———. "Vida de los esclavos en siglo XVIII." *El Caribe*. 3 Apr. 1993.

———. "La visión del mundo rural dominicano cambió mucho a través del siglo XVIII." *El Caribe*. 31 Aug. 1991.

González Canalda, María Filomena. "Desiderio Arias y el caudillismo." *Estudios Sociales* 18, no. 61 (July–Sept. 1985): 29–50.

———. "Gavilleros, 1904–1924." Paper presented at the Quinto Congreso Dominicano de Historia, Oct. 24–27, 1991.

Grullón, José. *Cayo Confites: La revolución traicionada*. Santo Domingo: Alfa y Omega, 1989.

Grullón, M. C. *Sobre nuestro tabaco*. Santo Domingo: Imprenta Montalvo Hno., 1919.

Guitar, Lynne. "Cultural Genesis: Relationships among Indians, Africans and Spaniards in Rural Hispaniola, First Half of the Sixteenth Century." Ph.D. diss., Vanderbilt University, 1998.

Gutiérrez Escudero, Antonio. "Diferencias entre agricultores y ganaderos en Santo Domingo: Siglo dieciocho." In *Noveno Congreso Internacional de Historia de América*. Seville: Asociación de Historiadores Latinoamericanistas Europeos, 1992.

———. *Población y economía en Santo Domingo (1700–1746)*. Seville: Diputación Provincial, 1985.

———. "La propiedad de la tierra en Santo Domingo: Del latifundio al terreno comunero." *Temas Americanistas* 4 (1983): 21–26.

Gutiérrez-San Martín, Ana. *Agrarian Reform Policy in the Dominican Republic: Local Organization and Beneficiary Investment Strategies*. New York: University Press of America, 1988.

Hall, Michael. *Sugar and Power in the Dominican Republic: Eisenhower, Kennedy, and the Trujillos*. Westport, Conn.: Greenwood, 2000.

Hartlyn, Jonathan. *The Struggle for Democratic Politics in the Dominican Republic*. Chapel Hill: University of North Carolina Press, 1998.

————. "The Trujillo Regime in the Dominican Republic." In *Sultanistic Regimes*, ed. H. E. Chehabi and Juan J. Linz. Baltimore: Johns Hopkins University Press, 1998.

Hazard, Samuel. *Santo Domingo, Past and Present: With a Glance at Hayti*. 3d ed. Dominican Republic: n.p., n.d.

Henríquez Ureña, Pedro. *La cultura y las letras coloniales en Santo Domingo*. Buenos Aires: Imprenta de la Universidad de Buenos Aires, 1936.

Henríquez y Carvajal, Francisco. *Cayacoa y cotubanama*. Santo Domingo: ONAP, 1985.

Hicks, Albert. *Blood in the Streets: The Life and Rule of Trujillo*. New York: Creative Age, 1946.

Hoetink, Harry. *Caribbean Race Relations: A Study of Two Variants*. New York: Oxford University Press, 1971.

————. "El Cibao 1844–1900: Su aportación a la formación social de la República." *Eme Eme: Estudios Dominicanos* 8, no. 48 (May–June 1980): 3–19.

————. *The Dominican People, 1850–1900: Notes for a Historical Sociology*. Translated by Stephen K. Ault. Baltimore: Johns Hopkins University Press, 1982.

————. "The Dominican Republic, c. 1870–1930." In *The Cambridge History of Latin America*, ed. Leslie Bethell, vol. 5. Cambridge: Cambridge University Press, 1986.

————. "The Dominican Republic in the Twentieth Century: Notes on Mobility and Stratification." *New West Indian Guide* 74, nos. 3 and 4 (2000). 209–33.

————. "'Race' and Color in the Caribbean." In *Caribbean Contours*, ed. Sidney Mintz and Sally Price, pp. 55–84. Baltimore: Johns Hopkins University Press, 1985.

————. *Santo Domingo y el Caribe: Ensayos sobre cultura y sociedad*. Santo Domingo: Fundación Cultural Dominicana, 1994.

Incháustegui, Arístides. "El ideario de Rodó en el trujillismo." *Estudios Sociales* 18, no. 60 (Apr.–June 1985): 51–63.

Incháustegui Cabral, Héctor. "La poesía de tema negro en Santo Domingo." *Eme Eme: Estudios Dominicanos* 1, no. 5 (Mar.–Apr. 1973).

Inoa, Orlando. *Estado y campesinos al inicio de la era de Trujillo*. Santo Domingo: Librería La Trinitaria, 1994.

Jan, J. M. *Collecta: Diocese du Cap-Haïtien, Documents, 1929–1960*. Vol. 4. Rennes: Simon, 1967.

Jimenes-Grullón, Juan I. *La propaganda de Trujillo al desnudo*. Havana: Unión Democrática Antinazista Dominicana, 1944.

Jiménez, Enrique. *Sobre economía social americana*. Santo Domingo: n.p., 1932.

Jiménez, Pedro Encarnación. *Los negros esclavos en la historia de Bayona, Manoguayabo y otros poblados*. Santo Domingo: Alfa y Omega, 1993.

Jiménez, Ramón Emilio. *Al amor del bohío*. Santo Domingo: n.p., 1975 (1927).

————. *Trujillo y la paz*. Ciudad Trujillo: Impresora Dominicana, 1952.

Jiménez Sabater, Max. *Más datos sobre el español de la República Dominicana*. Santo Domingo: Editora del Sol, 1975.

Julia, Julio Jaime. *Guzmán Espaillat, el civilista*. Santo Domingo: Taller, 1977.

Larrazábal Blanco, Carlos. *Los negros y la esclavitud en Santo Domingo*. Santo Domingo: Julio D. Postigo e Hijos, 1975.

Las Casas, Bartolomé de. *Historia de las Indias escrita por Fray Bartolomé de Las Casas Obispo de Chiapa.* Madrid: Ginesta, 1875–76.

LeGrand, Catherine. "Informal Resistance on a Dominican Sugar Plantation during the Trujillo Dictatorship." *Hispanic American Historical Review* 75, no. 4 (1995): 555–96.

Levitt, Peggy. *The Transnational Villagers.* Berkeley: University of California Press, 2001.

Liriano, Alejandra. *El papel de la mujer de origen africano en el Santo Domingo colonial, siglos XVI–XVII.* Santo Domingo: Centro de Investigación para la Acción Femenina, 1992.

Lluberes Navarro, Antonio. "El enclave azucarero, 1902–1930." *Historia y Geografía* 2 (1983): 7–59.

———. "La economía del tabaco en el Cibao en la segunda mitad del siglo diecinueve." *Eme Eme: Estudios Dominicanos* 1, no. 4 (Jan.–Feb. 1973): 35–60.

———. "La larga crisis azucarera, 1884–1902." *Estudios Sociales* 23, no. 81 (July–Sept. 1990): 21–65.

Loaiza, Edilberto. "Tamaño y composición de la población en la República Dominicana, 1950–2000." In *Población y sociedad: Seminario nacional, 1983,* ed. Consejo Nacional de Población y Familia, pp. 19–59. Santo Domingo: CONAPOFA, 1985.

López, José Ramón. "La caña de azúcar en San Pedro de Macorís, desde el bosque virgen hasta el mercado." *Ciencia* (Santo Domingo) 2, no. 3 (June–Sept. 1975): 125–41.

———. *Censo y catastro de la común de Santo Domingo: Informe que al honorable ayuntamiento presenta el director del censo y catastro de 1919.* Santo Domingo: El Progreso, 1919.

———. *Ensayos y artículos.* Edited by Manuel Rueda. Santo Domingo: Fundación Corripio, 1991.

———. *El gran pesimismo dominicano.* Santiago de los Caballeros: Universidad Católica Madre y Maestra, 1975.

———. *Manual de agricultura para los maestros de escuelas rudimentarias.* Santo Domingo: J. R. Vda. García, 1920.

López y Sebastián, Lorenzo, and Justo del Río Moreno. "Comercio y transporte en la economía del azúcar antillano durante el siglo XVI." *Anuario de Estudios Americanos* 49 (1992): 55–87.

Lozano, Wilfredo. *La dominación imperialista en la República Dominicana, 1900–1930.* Santo Domingo: Taller, 1976.

Lucena Salmoral, Manuel. *Los códigos negros de la América Española.* Alcalá de Henares: UNESCO, 1996.

Lugo, Américo. *A punto largo.* Santo Domingo: La Cuna de América, 1901.

Lundahl, Mats, and Jan Lundius. "Socioeconomic Foundations of a Messianic Cult: Olivorismo in the Dominican Republic." In *Agrarian Society in History: Essays in Honour of Magnus Mörner,* ed. Mats Lundahl and Thommy Svensson. New York: Routledge, 1990.

Lundius, Jan, and Mats Lundahl. *Peasants and Religion: A Socioeconomic Study of Dios Olivorio and the Palma Sola Movement in the Dominican Republic.* New York: Routledge, 2000.

Lyonnet, Pierre. "C. Lyonnet: Estadística de la parte española de Santo Domingo, 1800." In *La era de Francia en Santo Domingo: Contribución a su estudio*, ed. Emilio Rodríguez Demorizi. Ciudad Trujillo: Editora del Caribe, 1955.

Machín, Jorge. "Orígenes del campesinado dominicano durante la ocupación haitiana." *Eme Eme: Estudios Dominicanos* 1, no. 4 (Jan.–Feb. 1973): 19–34.

MacMichael, David. "The United States and the Dominican Republic." Ph.D. diss., University of Oregon, 1964.

Malagón Barcelo, Javier. *Código Negro Carolino (1784)*. Santo Domingo: Taller, 1974.

Malck, R. Michael. "Rafael Leonidas Trujillo: A Revisionist Critique of His Rise to Power." *Revista Interamericana* 7, no. 3 (fall 1977): 436–45.

———. "Rafael Leonidas Trujillo Molina: The Rise of a Caribbean Dictator." Ph.D. diss., University of California, Santa Barbara, 1971.

Mann, Arthur. "Public Expenditure Patterns in the Dominican Republic and Puerto Rico, 1930–1970." *Social and Economic Studies* 24, no. 1 (Mar. 1975): 47–83.

Maríñez, Pablo. *Agroindustria, estado y clases sociales en la era de Trujillo (1935–1960)*. Santo Domingo: Fundación Cultural Dominicana, 1993.

———. *Resistencia campesina: Imperialismo y reforma agraria en República Dominicana (1899–1978)*. Santo Domingo: Centro de Planificación y Acción Ecuménica, 1984.

Marrero Aristy, Ramón. *La República Dominicana. Origen y destino del pueblo cristiano más antiguo de América*. Vol. 3. Ciudad Trujillo: Editora del Caribe, 1958.

Marte, Roberto. *Cuba y la República Dominicana: Transición económica en el Caribe del siglo diecinueve*. Santo Domingo: CENAPEC, 1988.

Martínez, Samuel. "From Hidden Hand to Heavy Hand: Sugar, the State, and Migrant Labor in Haiti and the Dominican Republic." *Latin American Research Review* 34, no. 1 (1999): 57–84.

Martínez Bonilla, José Antonio. "Origen de la propiedad agraria en la República Dominicana." Doctoral thesis in law, no. 125, Universidad de Santo Domingo, 1945.

Martínez-Fernández, Luis. *Torn between Empires: Economy, Society, and Patterns of Political Thought in the Hispanic Caribbean, 1840–1878*. Athens: University of Georgia Press, 1994.

Mateo, Andrés. *Mito y cultura en la era de Trujillo*. Santo Domingo: Editora de Colores, 1993.

Medina Benet, Víctor M. *Los responsables: Fracaso de la tercera república*. 2d ed. Santo Domingo: Amigo del Hogar, 1976.

Mejía, Félix. *Viacrucis de un pueblo: Relato sinóptico de la tragedia dominicana bajo la férula de Trujillo*, 3d ed. Santo Domingo: Sociedad Dominicana de Bibliofilos, 1995.

Mejía, Luis F. *De Lilís a Trujillo*. Santo Domingo: Editora de Santo Domingo, 1976.

"Memorial de Araujo y Rivero." *Boletín del Archivo General de la Nación* 5, no. 22 (June 1942): 212.

Mir, Pedro. *Cuando amaban las tierras comuneras*. Santo Domingo: Siglo Veintiuno, 1978.

Monclús, Miguel A. *Calidoscopia de Haití*. Buenos Aires: Editorial Américalee, 1953.

Moreau de Saint-Méry, M. L. E. *Descripción de la parte española de Santo Domingo*. 1796. Reprint. Ciudad Trujillo: Editora Montalvo, 1944.

————. *Description topographique, physique, civile, politique et historique de la partie française de l'isle Saint Domingue.* Philadelphia: Chez Auteur, 1797–98.

Moreno, Guillermo. "De la propiedad comunera a la propiedad privada moderna, 1844–1924." *Eme Eme: Estudios Dominicanos* 9, no. 51 (Nov.–Dec. 1980): 47–129.

Moscoso Puello, Francisco. *Cañas y bueyes.* Santo Domingo: Amigo del Hogar, 1975.

Moya Pons, Frank. *La dominación haitiana, 1822–1844.* 3d ed. Santiago de los Caballeros: Universidad Católica Madre y Maestra, 1978.

————. "Dominican National Identity: A Historical Perspective." *Punto 7 Review* 3, no. 1 (fall 1996): 14–25.

————. *The Dominican Republic: A National History.* Princeton: Markus Wiener, 1995.

————. "The Dominican Republic since 1930." In *The Cambridge History of Latin America,* ed. Leslie Bethell, Vol. 7. New York: Cambridge University Press, 1984.

————. "La economía dominicana y el partido azul." *Eme Eme: Estudios Dominicanos* 5, no. 28 (1977): 3–11.

————. *Empresarios en conflicto: Políticas de industrialización y sustitución de importaciones en la República Dominicana.* Santo Domingo: Fondo para el Avance de las Ciencias Sociales, 1992.

————. "La frontera política." *Rumbo* 5, no. 271 (12 Apr. 1999): 4.

————. "Haiti and Santo Domingo, 1790–c. 1870." In *The Cambridge History of Latin America,* ed. Leslie Bethell, Vol. 3. Cambridge: Cambridge University Press, 1985.

————. *Historia colonial de Santo Domingo.* Santiago de los Caballeros: Universidad Católica Madre y Maestra, 1974.

————. "Import-Substitution Industrialization Policies in the Dominican Republic, 1925–61." *Hispanic American Historical Review* 70, no. 4 (1990): 539–77.

————. "Industrial Incentives in the Dominican Republic, 1880–1983." Ph.D. diss., Columbia University, 1987.

————. "The Land Question in Haiti and Santo Domingo." In *Between Slavery and Free Labor: The Spanish-Speaking Caribbean in the Nineteenth Century,* ed. Manuel Moreno Fraginals, Frank Moya Pons, and Stanley L. Engerman. Baltimore: Johns Hopkins University Press, 1985.

————. *Manual de historia dominicana.* 8th ed. Santiago de los Caballeros: Universidad Católica Madre y Maestra, 1984.

————. "Notas para una historia de la Iglesia en Santo Domingo." *Eme Eme: Estudios Dominicanos* 1, no. 6 (May–June 1973): 3–37.

————. *El pasado dominicano.* Santo Domingo: Fundación J. A. Caro Alvarez, 1986.

Mujeres en Desarrollo (MUDE). *La era de Trujillo: Décimas, relatos y testimonios campesinos.* Santo Domingo: Taller, 1989.

Muñoz Regalado, Regino. *Preámbulo de la religión trujilloniana.* Ciudad Trujillo: Pol. Hermanos, 1954.

Nolasco, Sócrates. *Obras completas: Ensayos históricos.* Vol. 2. Santo Domingo: Fundación Corripio, 1994.

————. *Viejas memorias.* Santo Domingo: Editorial El Diario, 1941.

Olivares Morillo, Félix Ramón. *Apuntes históricos.* Santo Domingo: Secretaría de Estado de Agricultura, 1985.

————. *Caficultura y legislación agrícola en el siglo diecinueve.* Santo Domingo: San Rafael, 1980.

————. "La fundación de las primeras colonias agrícolas." Unpublished manuscript, 1992.

————. *Trujillo y la política del cacao y del café.* Santo Domingo: Taller, 1995.

Ortiz Tilles, Helen. "The Era of Lilís: Political Stability and Economic Change in the Dominican Republic." Ph.D. diss., Georgetown University, 1975.

Otero Nolasco, Salvador. "Sobre terrenos comuneros." *Revista Judicial* 2, no. 9 (Sept. 1907): 145–46.

Ots Capdequí, José M. *El régimen de la tierra en la América Española durante el periodo colonial.* Ciudad Trujillo: Editora Montalvo, 1946.

Oviedo, José. "La tradición autoritaria." Unpublished manuscript, 1986.

Padilla d'Onis, Luis. *Alrededor de la crisis.* Santo Domingo: La Provincia, 1924.

Palmer, Ernest Charles. "Land Use and Landscape Change along the Dominican-Haitian Borderlands." Ph.D. diss., University of Florida, 1976.

Pastoriza, Tomás C. *La colonización agrícola en la era de Trujillo.* Ciudad Trujillo: Secretario de Estado de Agricultura, Pecuaria y Colonización, 1946.

Paulino Díaz, Edward. "Birth of a Boundary: Blood, Cement, and Prejudice and the Making of the Dominican-Haitian Border, 1937–1961." Ph.D. diss., Michigan State University, 2001.

Peguero, Valentina. "Trujillo and the Military: Organization, Modernization and Control of the Dominican Armed Forces, 1916–1961." Ph.D. diss., Columbia University, 1993.

Peña Batlle, Manuel Arturo. *Ensayos históricos.* Santo Domingo: Taller, 1989 (1954).

————. *El sentido de una política.* Ciudad Trujillo: La Nación, 1943.

Peña Pérez, Frank. "Despoblación y miseria en Santo Domingo en el siglo diecisiete." *Investigación y Ciencia* 1, no. 1 (Jan.–Apr. 1986): 83–92.

Peralta, Freddy. "La sociedad dominicana del siglo diecinueve vista por Pedro Francisco Bonó." *Eme Eme: Estudios Dominicanos* 5, no. 29 (Mar.–Apr. 1977): 13–54.

Pérez, Luis Julián. *Santo Domingo frente al destino.* Santo Domingo: Editora Taller, 1990.

Pérez Cabral, Pedro Andrés. *La comunidad mulata: El caso sociopolítico de la República Dominicana.* Caracas: Gráficas Americanas, 1967.

Pérez Maracallo, Ramón María. "La función social del derecho de propiedad." Doctoral thesis in law, no. 9, Universidad de Santo Domingo, 1944.

Pérez Memén, Fernando. *El Arzobispo Fernando Carvajal y Rivera: Un crítico de la política colonial (y otros ensayos históricos).* Santo Domingo: Talleres de la Universidad Nacional Pedro Henríquez Ureña, 1987.

Pérez Oviedo, J. Ismael. *Anhelos.* San Pedro de Macorís: Cámara de Agricultura del Este, 1925.

Pérez y Pérez, Rafael Leonidas. "La libertad de los esclavos africanos en el Valle de Neyba (siglo XVIII)." *Investigación para el Desarrollo* 2, no. 4 (July 1998): 37–42.

Peynado, Francisco J. "Deslinde, mensura y partición de terrenos." *Revista Jurídica* 4 (1919): 1–19.

————. *Por la inmigración: Estudio de las reformas que es necesario emprender para atraer inmigrantes a la República Dominicana*. Santo Domingo: Imp. y Librería de J. R. Vda. García, 1909.

"La política escolar del Honorable Presidente Trujillo." *Revista de Educación* 7, no. 28 (July–Aug. 1935): 8–23.

Prestol Castillo, Freddy. *El Masacre se pasa a pie*. Santo Domingo, Taller, 1973.

————. *Paisajes y meditaciones de una frontera*. Ciudad Trujillo: Cosmopolita, 1943.

Price-Mars, Jean. *La República de Haití y la República Dominicana: Diversos aspectos de un problema histórico, geográfico y etnológico*. Madrid: Industrias Gráficas España, 1958.

Prichard, Hesketh. *Where Black Rules White: A Journey across and about Hayti*. Shannon: Irish University Press, 1900.

Ramírez, Jesús María, hijo. *Mis 43 años en la Descubierta*. Santo Domingo: Editora Centenario, 2000.

Ramos, Manuel. "La ciudad y el campo: Medidas para contrarrestar la emigración rural." *Renovación* 7, no. 26 (July–Aug. 1960): 52–63.

Ratekin, Mervyn. "The Early Sugar Industry in Española." *Hispanic American Historical Review* 34, no. 1 (Feb. 1954): 1–19.

Ravelo de la Fuente, Fernando E. *Jurisprudencia del Tribunal de Tierras: Sentencias del Tribunal Superior de Tierras, y de Jurisdicción Original en materia posesoria, correspondientes a los años 1939, 1940, 1941, 1942 y 1943*. Ciudad Trujillo: Luis Sánchez Andujar, 1947.

"Relación de la isla Española enviada al Rey D. Felipe II por el Lic. Echagoian, oidor de la Audiencia de Santo Domingo." *Boletín del Archivo General de la Nación* 4, no. 19 (Dec. 1941): 441–63.

Río Moreno, Justo del, and Lorenzo López y Sebastián. "El comercio azucarero de La Española en el siglo XVI: Presión monopolística y alternativas locales." *Revista Complutense de Historia de América* 17 (1991): 39–78.

Rizik, Nicolás. *Trujillo y la estadística*. Ciudad Trujillo: Editora Montalvo, 1945.

Rodríguez, Frank, and Otto Fernández. "Notas sobre las políticas agrarias en la República Dominicana." *Ciencia* 3, no. 1 (Jan.–Mar. 1976): 43–57.

Rodríguez Demorizi, Emilio, ed. *Antecedentes de la anexión a España*. Ciudad Trujillo: Editora Montalvo, 1955.

————. *La era de Francia en Santo Domingo: Contribución a su estudio*. Ciudad Trujillo: Editora del Caribe, 1955.

————. *Hostos en Santo Domingo*. Ciudad Trujillo: Imp. J. R. Vda. García, 1939.

————. *La imprenta y los primeros periódicos de Santo Domingo*. Ciudad Trujillo: Imprenta San Francisco, 1944.

————. *Papeles de Pedro F. Bonó*. 2d ed. Barcelona: Gráficas M. Pareja, 1980.

————. *Samaná: Pasado y porvenir*. Santo Domingo: Editora del Caribe, 1973.

————. *Viajeros de Francia en Santo Domingo*. Santo Domingo: Editora del Caribe, 1979.

Rodríguez Grullón, Julio. *Trujillo y la Iglesia*. Santo Domingo: Panamericana, 1991.

Rodríguez Morel, Genaro. "Esclavitud y plantación azucarera en Puerto Rico: S. XVI." In *Escravos com e sem açúcar: Actas do seminário internacional, Funchal, 17 a 21 de junho de 1996*. Funchal: Centro de Estudos de História do Atlântico, Secretaria Regional do Turismo e Cultura, 1996.

———. "Esclavitud y vida rural en las plantaciones azucareras de Santo Domingo: Siglo XVI." *Anuario de Estudios Americanos* 49 (1992): 89–117.

Rogers, Gifford. *Régimen de la tenencia de tierras en la República Dominicana*. Santo Domingo: International Development Services, 1962.

Roorda, Eric. *The Dictator Next Door: The Good Neighbor Policy and the Trujillo Regime in the Dominican Republic, 1930–1945*. Durham: Duke University Press, 1998.

Rosario, Esteban. *Iglesia católica y oligarquía*. Santiago de los Caballeros: Editora Búho, 1991.

Ross, Eduardo. *La obra cristiana del Benefactor de la Patria*. Ciudad Trujillo: Editora del Caribe, 1959.

Ruíz Tejada, Manuel Ramón. *Estudio sobre la propiedad inmobilaria en la República Dominicana*. 2d ed. Santo Domingo: Taller, 1990.

———. "El éxito del sistema Torrens en la República Dominicana, bajo el régimen instituido por el Generalísimo Trujillo." *Revista Jurídica Dominicana* 17, nos. 54–55 (1955): 94–98.

Sáez, José Luis. *Los Jesuitas en la República Dominicana*. Santo Domingo: Museo Nacional de Historia y Geografía, 1988.

Sagás, Ernesto. *Race and Politics in the Dominican Republic*. Gainesville: University Press of Florida, 2000.

Sala-Molins, Louis. *L'Afrique aux Amériques: Le Code Noir espagnol*. Paris: Presses Universitaires de France, 1992.

San Miguel, Pedro Luis. *Los campesinos del Cibao: Economía de mercado y transformación agraria en la República Dominicana, 1880–1960*. San Juan: Editorial de la Universidad de Puerto Rico, 1997.

———. "La ciudadanía de Calibán: Poder y discursiva campesinista en la era de Trujillo." In *Política, identidad y pensamiento social en la República Dominicana (Siglos XIX y XX)*, ed. Raymundo González, Michiel Baud, Pedro L. San Miguel, and Roberto Cassá, pp. 269–89. Madrid: Doce Calles, 1999.

———. "Crisis económica e intervención estatal: El plan de valorización del tabaco en la República Dominicana." *Ecos* 2, no. 3 (1994): 55–77.

———. "The Dominican Peasantry and the Market Economy: The Peasants of Cibao, 1880–1960." Ph.D. diss., Columbia University, 1987.

———. "Entre el agrarismo oficial y el agrarismo campesino: La lucha por la tierra en Santo Domingo (1968–1978)." Paper presented at the Latin American Studies Association, Twentieth International Congress, Guadalajara, Mexico, 17–19 Apr. 1997.

———. "Exacción estatal y resistencias campesinas en el Cibao durante la ocupación norteamericana de 1916–1924." *Ecos* 1, no. 2 (1993): 77–100.

———. *La isla imaginada: Historia, identidad y utopía en La Española*. Santo Domingo: La Trinitaria, 1997.

———. *El pasado relegado*. Santo Domingo: La Trinitaria, 1999.

Sánchez, Eladio. *Proyecto de ley sobre partición de terrenos comuneros*. Santo Domingo: La Cuna de América, 1912.

Sánchez, Juan J. *La caña en Santo Domingo*. Santo Domingo: Taller, 1972.

Sánchez Báez, Hipólito. *Legislación sanitaria dominicana y legislación sobre seguridad social*. Ciudad Trujillo: Secretaría de Estado de Salud Pública, 1953.

Sánchez i Sánchez, Carlos. *El caso-domínico-haitiano*. Ciudad Trujillo: Montalvo, 1958.

Sánchez Valverde, Antonio. *Idea del valor de la isla española, y utilidades, que de ella puede sacar la monarquía*. 1785. Reprint, *Idea del valor de la isla española*. Santo Domingo: Editora Nacional, 1971.

Schoenrich, Otto. *Santo Domingo: A Country with a Future*. New York: Macmillan, 1918.

Sevilla Soler, María Rosario. *Santo Domingo, tierra de frontera*. Seville: Escuela de Estudios Hispano-Americanos, 1981.

Silié, María Filomena de. Untitled paper presented at the conference "Trujillo: Treinta años de su muerte." Santo Domingo, 9 Apr. 1991.

Silié, Rubén. *Economía, esclavitud y población: Ensayos de interpretación histórica del Santo Domingo español en el siglo dieciocho*. Santo Domingo: Editora de la Universidad Autónoma de Santo Domingo, 1976.

———. "El hato y el conuco: Contexto para el surgimiento de la cultura criolla." In *Ensayos sobre cultura dominicana*, ed. Bernardo Vega et al., pp. 143–69. Santo Domingo: Museo del Hombre Dominicano, 1988.

———. "La trata de negros en Santo Domingo: Siglo dieciocho." *Ciencia* 2, no. 3 (July–Sept. 1975): 99–109.

Sommer, Doris. *One Master for Another: Populism as Patriarchal Rhetoric in Dominican Novels*. London: University Press of America, 1983.

Sorensen, Ninna Nyberg. "There are no Indians in the Dominican Republic: The Cultural Construction of Dominican Identities." In *Siting Culture: The Shifting Anthropological Object*, ed. Karen Fog Olwig and Kirsten Hastrup, pp. 292–310. New York: Routledge, 1997.

Sosa Alburquerque, Alfonso. *Apuntes históricos sobre la propiedad territorial de Santo Domingo*. Santo Domingo: Imprenta Montalvo, 1926.

Soulastre, Dorvo. "Viaje por tierra de Santo Domingo, capital de la parte española de Santo Domingo, al Cabo Francés, capital de la parte francesa de la misma isla." In *La era de Francia en Santo Domingo: Contribución a su estudio*, ed. Emilio Rodríguez Demorizi. Ciudad Trujillo: Editora del Caribe, 1955.

Tejada Olivares, Luis Fernando. "La matanza de haitanos y la política de dominicanización de la frontera: Un proceso de acumulación originaria." *Realidad Contemporánea* 2, nos. 8–9 (1979): 37–102.

Tejera, Emiliano. "Párrafos de las memorias presentadas por D. Emiliano Tejera en su calidad de ministro de Relaciones Exteriores, al presidente de la República en los años 1906–1907 i 1908." *Clio* 51 (1942): 15.

Torres-Saillant, Silvio. "Creoleness or Blackness: A Dominican Dilemma." *Plantation Society of the Americas* 5, no. 1 (spring 1998): 29–40.

———. "Hacia una identidad racial alternativa en la sociedad dominicana." *Op. Cit.* no. 9 (1997): 235–51.

———. "Introduction to Dominican Blackness." Dominican Studies Working Papers Series 1 (1999).

———. "Tribulations of Blackness: Stages in Dominican Racial Identity." *Latin American Perspectives* 25, no. 3 (May 1998): 126–46.

Troncoso Sánchez, Pedro. *Ramón Cáceres*. Santo Domingo: Editorial Stella, 1964.

Trujillo Martínez, Rafael. *Un discurso del General y Doctor Rafael L. Trujillo Hijo y seis comentarios acerca del mismo*. Ciudad Trujillo: Editora del Caribe, 1960.

Trujillo Molina, Rafael L. *Discursos, mensajes y proclamas*. Vol. 1. Santiago de los Caballeros: Editorial El Diario, 1946.

——— *Evolución de la democracia en Santo Domingo*. 2d ed. Ciudad Trujillo: Editora del Caribe, 1955.

Turits, Richard Lee. "Dominican-Haitian Relations." In *Africana: The Encyclopedia of the African and African American Experience*, ed. Kwame Anthony Appiah and Henry Louis Gates, Jr. Redmond, Wash.: Basic Civitas, 1999.

———. "The Foundations of Despotism: Peasants, Property, and the Trujillo Regime (1930–1961)." Ph.D. diss., University of Chicago, 1997.

———. "A World Destroyed, A Nation Imposed: The 1937 Haitian Massacre in the Dominican Republic." *Hispanic American Historical Review* 82, no. 3 (Aug. 2002): 589–635.

Urbano Gilbert, Gregorio. *Mi lucha contra el invasor yanqui de 1916*. Santo Domingo: Editora de la Universidad Autónoma de Santo Domingo, 1975.

U.S. Commission of Inquiry. *Report of the Commissioner of Inquiry to Santo Domingo*. Washington, D.C.: Government Printing Office, 1871.

Valdez, Jorge. *Un siglo de agrimensura en la República Dominicana*. Santo Domingo: Ediciones Tres, 1981.

Vargas, Mayobanex. *Testimonio histórico junio 1959*. Santo Domingo: Editora Cosmos, 1981.

Vargas-Lundius, Rosemary. *Peasants in Distress: Poverty and Unemployment in the Dominican Republic*. Boulder: Westview, 1991.

Vedovato, Claudio. *Politics, Foreign Trade and Economic Development: A Study of the Dominican Republic*. New York: St. Martin's, 1986.

Veeser, Cyrus. "Remapping the Caribbean: Private Investment and United States Intervention in the Dominican Republic, 1890–1908." Ph.D. diss., Columbia University, 1997.

Vega, Bernardo. *Almoina, Galíndez y otros crímenes de Trujillo en el extranjero*. Santo Domingo: Fundación Cultural Dominicana, 2001.

———. *Control y represión en la dictadura trujillista*. Santo Domingo: Fundación Cultural Dominicana, 1986.

———. *Eisenhower y Trujillo*. Santo Domingo: Fundación Cultural Dominicana, 1991.

———. *Los Estados Unidos y Trujillo. Los días finales: 1960–1961*. Santo Domingo: Fundación Cultural Dominicana, 1999.

———. *Kennedy y los Trujillo*. Santo Domingo: Fundación Cultural Dominicana, 1991.

——— . *La migración española de 1939 y los inicios del Marxismo-Leninismo en la República Dominicana*. Santo Domingo: Fundación Cultural Dominicana, 1984.

———. *Nazismo, Fascismo y Falangismo en la República Dominicana*. Santo Domingo: Fundación Cultural Dominicana, 1985.

———. *Trujillo y el control financiero norteamericano*. Santo Domingo: Fundación Cultural Dominicana, 1990.

———. *Trujillo y Haití.* Vol. 1 *(1930–37).* Santo Domingo: Fundación Cultural Dominicana, 1988.

———. *Trujillo y Haití.* Vol. 2 *(1937–38).* Santo Domingo: Fundación Cultural Dominicana, 1995.

———. *Unos desafectos y otros en desgracia: Sufrimientos bajo la dictadura trujillista.* Santo Domingo: Fundación Cultural Dominicana, 1986.

———. "Variaciones en el uso del anti-haitianismo en la era de Trujillo." Paper presented at the Latin American Studies Association, Nineteenth International Congress, Washington, D.C., 28–30 Sept. 1995.

———. *La vida cotidiana dominicana a través del Archivo Particular del Generalísimo.* Santo Domingo: Fundación Cultural Dominicana, 1986.

Vega, Wenceslao. "El régimen laboral y de tierras en la Primera República." *Eme Eme: Estudios Dominicanos* 5, no. 30 (May–June 1977): 16–26.

Veras, Olga María, and Rosina de Alvarado. "La mujer en el derecho dominicano." *Eme Eme: Estudios Dominicanos* 10, no. 58 (Jan.–Feb. 1982): 51–70.

Villalba, Domingo. "Ante el concepto socialista de la propiedad." *Revista Jurídica Dominicana* 2, no. 2 (Apr. 1940): 74–75.

Viñas, Manuel de Jesús, hijo. "Condición jurídica de las tierras en la República Dominicana, al cumplir ésta el primer centenario de vida independiente." *Revista Jurídica Dominicana* 6, no. 1 (Feb. 1944): 761–64.

Wiarda, Howard. *Dictatorship and Development: The Methods of Control in Trujillo's Dominican Republic.* Gainesville: University of Florida Press, 1968.

Wischnitzer, Mark. "The Historical Background of the Settlement of Jewish Refugees in Santo Domingo." *Jewish Social Studies* 4, no. 1 (1942): 45–58.

Wucker, Michele. *Why the Cocks Fight: Dominicans, Haitians, and the Struggle for Hispaniola.* New York: Hill and Wang, 1999.

Zaglul Criado, Felipe. "Evolución histórica de los fallos y violaciones de los mecanismos de publicidad en el saneamiento inmobilaria de la legislación de principios de siglo: Sus efectos en el despojo de tierras al campesinado." Doctoral thesis in law, no. 1529, Universidad Autónoma de Santo Domingo, 1989.

Index